AF572772

The Nineteenth Century Paintings in the Walters Art Gallery

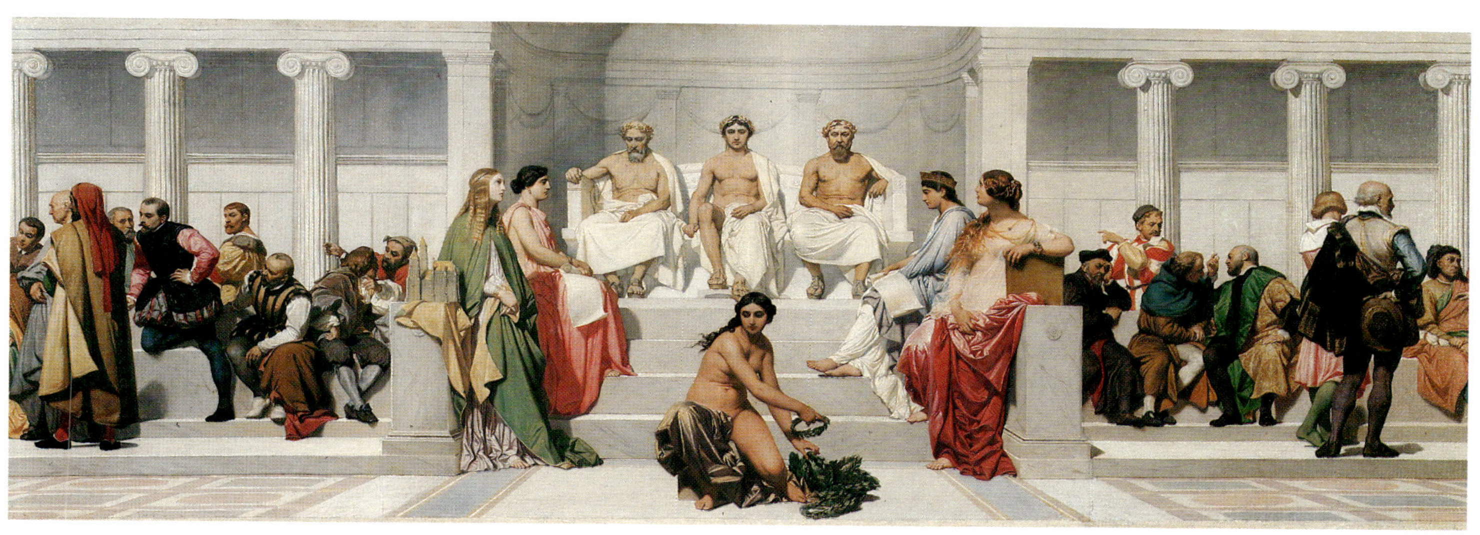

William R. Johnston

Published by the Trustees of the Walters Art Gallery
Baltimore, Maryland
U.S.A.

Title page:
Delaroche *The Hemicycle* (detail), no. 23

L.C. 82–050988

ISBN 0–911886–25–7
Printed in the United States of America

Colophon

Type set in Baskerville
by Service Composition, Baltimore, Maryland
Color Separations by Capper, Inc.,
Knoxville, Tennessee

Printed by Schneidereith & Sons, Baltimore, Maryland

Photography by Harry J. Connolly, Jr.

Design and Production by Anne Garside

Jacket Design and Headings: C. R. MacLellan and Associates/Baltimore

The catalogue has been made possible by a grant
from the National Endowment for the Arts, a Federal Agency.

Contents

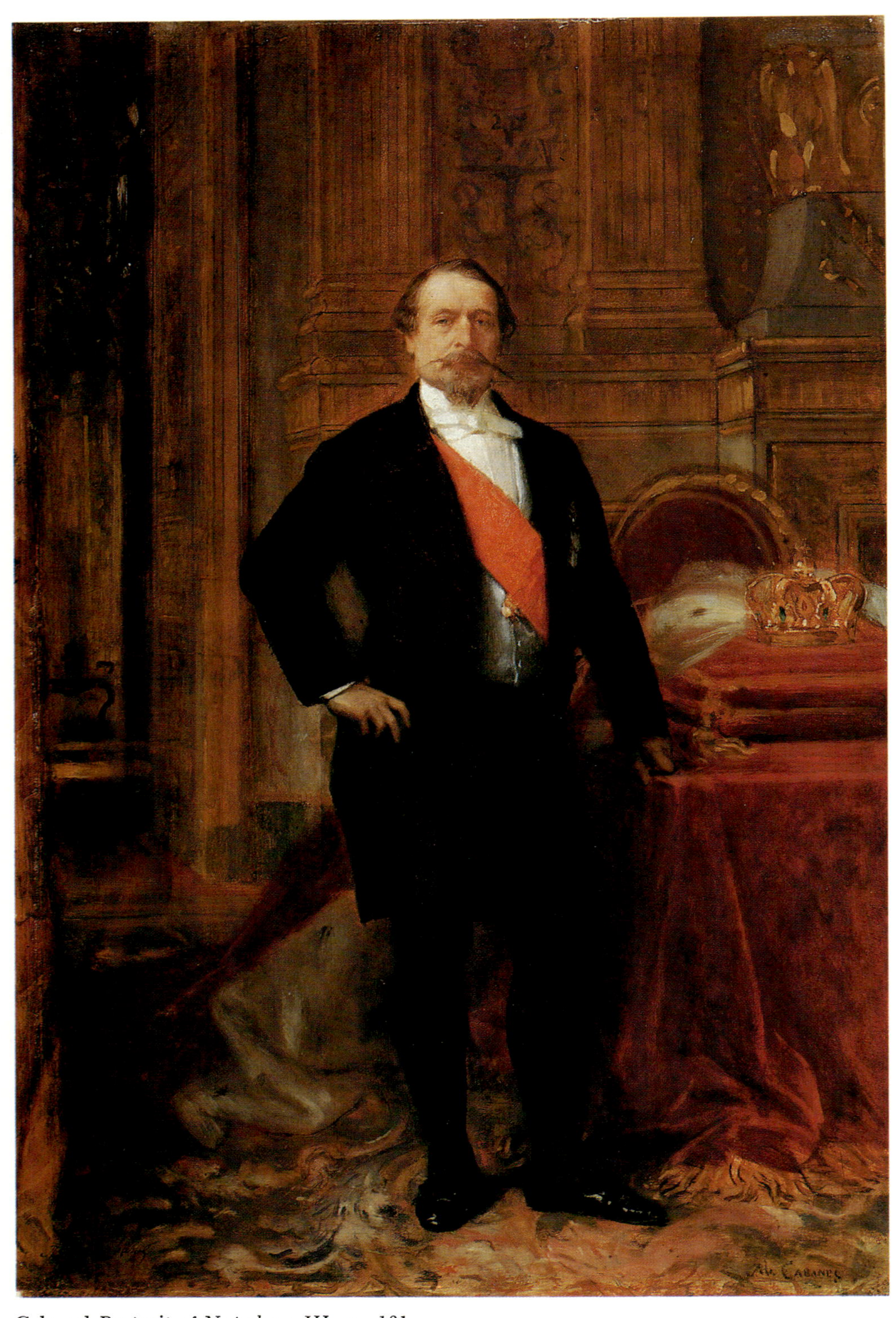

Cabanel *Portrait of Napoleon III,* no. 131

Acknowledgements

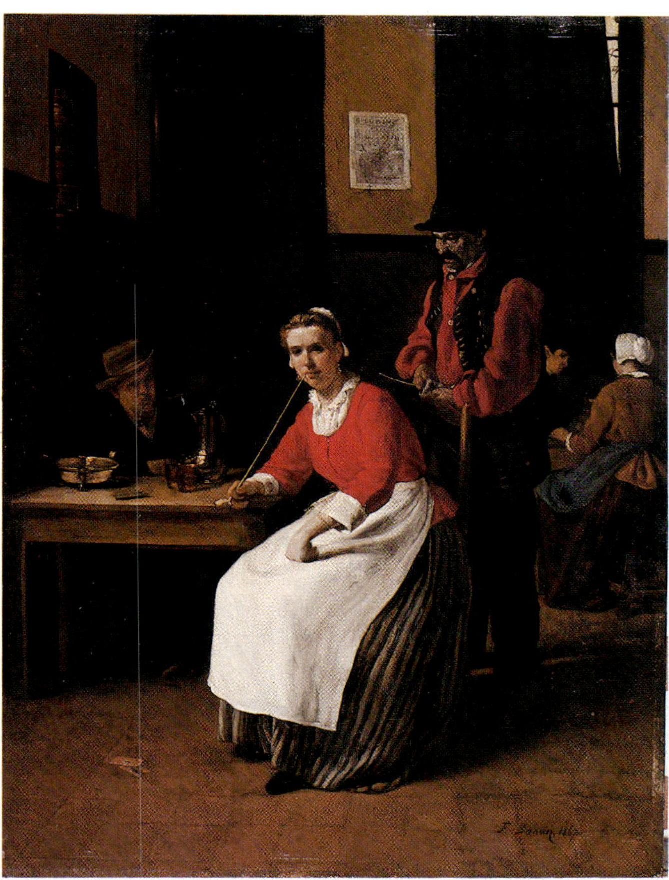

Bonvin *Interior of a Tavern,* no. 82

A collections catalogue is by its nature a collaborative publication drawing upon the contributions of colleagues past and present. I wish to thank Richard H. Randall, Jr., director of the Gallery from 1966 to 1981 and Robert P. Bergman, the present director, for their encouragement in this undertaking. Anne Garside, editor for the Gallery from 1978 to 1980, directed each phase in the production of this publication and Muriel Toppan undertook the arduous task of proofreading the manuscript and overseeing the work through its various stages. Harry J. Connolly, Jr., who remained undaunted by all requests regardless of their magnitude, photographed the pictures in both color and black and white. To his predecessor, Sherley B. Hobbs and his department members, Ruth E. Silk and Jean Carroon, is extended my gratitude. Without the diligence of Winifred Kennedy, registrar of the Gallery from 1934 to 1972 and her successor, Leopoldine H. Arz and her associates, this catalogue would not have been possible. Elisabeth C. G. Packard and the Conservation Department's present painting section led by Sian B. Jones and E. Melanie Gifford labored to prepare the pictures for photography and charitably answered innumerable questions regarding the conditions of the works. That the catalogue has been completed is testimony to the dedication of the curatorial secretaries, Lucy R. Eldridge, Pamela M. Himmelrich, and Catalina E. Davis.

In preparing the entries I have drawn upon the expertise of many individuals far and near. I am deeply indebted to Gerald Ackerman, Eva J. Allen, Marjorie Allthorpe-Guyton, Harry Berry, Katharine Baetjer, Miss S. H. Berresford, Albert Boime, Daniel Buscarlet, William A. Coles, Malcolm Cormack, the late Jos de Gruyter, Simon Dickinson, Lorenz Eitner, Jean-Jacques Fernier, Christopher Forbes, Jacques Foucart, Kenneth J. Garlick, Jorg Garms, Robert L. Herbert, Jean Humbert, C. C. Hungerford, Richard Hunnewell, Lee Johnson, Evelyn Joll, A. Lang, Derek Lawson, Kurt T. Luckner, Charles Mann, Pierre Miquel, André A. Moerman, Edward Morris, Dewey F. Mosby, Priscilla E. Muller, Glen Peck, Gabor O. Pogany, Harley Preston, Claudie Ressort, Mme. Claude Rico-Robert, Joseph Rishel, Sigrid Russ, Robert Schmit, Timothy Stevens, Charles Stuckey, Vern G. Swanson, Robert Tschoudoujney, Gabriel Weisberg, Henry Wyndham, and Norman Ziff.

Lilian M. C. Randall and Madeleine F. Beaufort generously shared with me their enthusiasm for the collection as well as information pertaining to histories of the paintings that they discovered in the course of preparing for publication the diaries of G. A. Lucas and S. P. Avery, respectively. Jean C. Wilson, Eleanor Clark, Janet Headley and Margaret Cooke deserve special notice for their assistance in preparing individual entries for this work.

The assistance and patience of my wife Sona and my son Frederic proved essential for the completion of this catalogue.

Without grants from the National Enlowment for the Arts the research involved in preparing the catalogue could not have been undertaken and the completed work would not have been published. I wish to thank the Trustees of the Walters Art Gallery for supporting me in this venture.

William R. Johnston

Alphabetical Index of Artists

Numbers refer to catalogue entries.

A Guide to the Catalogue

Biographies precede the entries for each artist. An attempt has been made to condense the information on well-published figures and to expand the discussion for lesser known ones.

Titles of paintings traditionally employed at the Gallery appear at the beginning of each entry unless otherwise stated, and alternative titles are listed below.

Supports for pictures in this publication are either fabric or panel. Measurements are given in both meters and inches, with height preceding width.

Signatures, dates, and their location are listed, and colormen's stencils and various labels have been transcribed. Since many frames are contemporaneous with the pictures, marks on their reverses are also provided.

Condition entries list information abridged from the records of the Gallery's Department of Conservation.

Provenances of Walters pictures are often problematic. Many records are believed to have been lost in the fire that destroyed downtown Baltimore, including the Walters' offices, in 1904. Records of Henry Walters' acquisitions are incomplete in Baltimore. Many invoices may never have reached the Gallery and others were mutilated by the collector in the interests of privacy. In such instances, the writer has listed the earliest reference to a work in William's and Henry's catalogues.

Numbers on Walters objects are assigned according to media. In the instance of a painting numbered "37. 392" the first two digits "37" refer to pictures, and the numbers "392", to the sequence in which the work was catalogued in 1934.

A list of abbreviations of frequently used bibliographic references appears on page 208.

PAGE GUIDE TO COLOR ILLUSTRATIONS

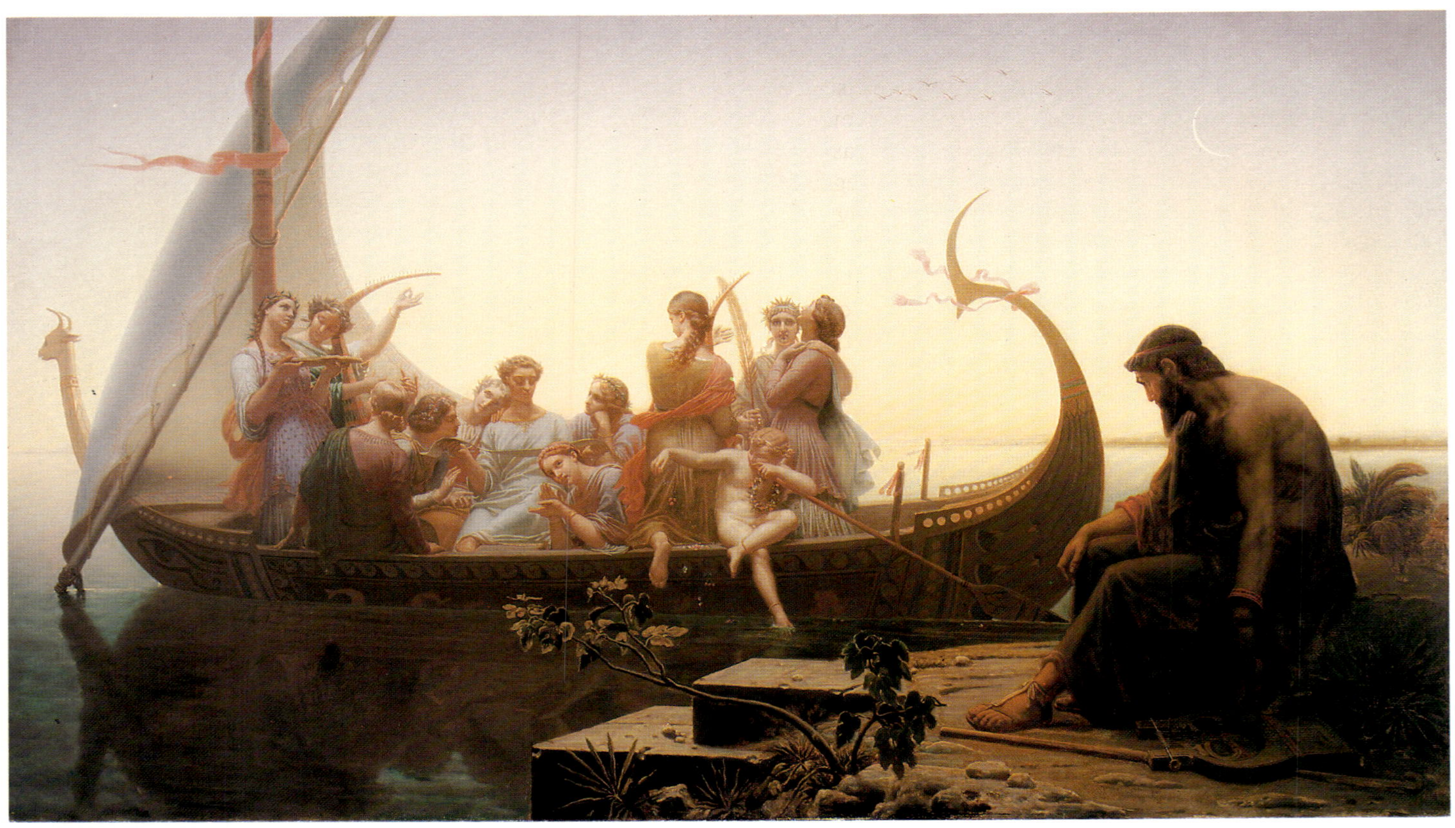

Gleyre *Lost Illusions,* no. 100

Preface

Nineteenth-century critics were unanimous in their praise of William T. Walters' collection of "contemporary" art and its educational value. Wishing to share with fellow citizens the pleasures of viewing contemporary European art, Walters, as early as the mid-1870s, began to open his Gallery at regular intervals and to publish catalogues informing his visitors of the various artists, their training and their accomplishments. This same proselytizing spirit may even have determined the growth of the collection, influencing the selection of such then illustrious compositions as Delaroche's *Hemicycle* and *Christian Martyr* and Gleyre's *Lost Illusions,* albeit in replica form.

After William's death in 1894, Henry Walters, sharing in so many of his father's interests, continued to enrich the collection with works that had been unavailable to the senior Walters or had escaped the latter's attentions. His bequest to Baltimore in 1931 of the Gallery and its wide-ranging holdings contained as its kernel a superb collection of nineteenth-century paintings.

To pursue the Herculean task of adapting the Gallery to a public museum, an advisory committee of distinguished scholars and museum personnel was selected and a small staff, including five young curators, hired. The preliminary identification and cataloguing of the nineteenth-century pictures was assigned to George Heard Hamilton, who, working with the registrar, Winifred Kennedy, completed the task by 1936. He resigned in that year in order to join the faculty of his alma mater, Yale University.

In the refitting of the building only a portion of one Gallery was allotted to nineteenth-century art. The advisory committee divided the pictures into two categories: exhibitable works, which were reserved for rotation or for special exhibitions, and "discards." The latter, including such pictures as Puvis de Chavannes' *Hope* and Gleyre's *Lost Illusions,* were separated from their frames and assigned to storage bins. In the following years, limitations in space prevented the full utilization of the nineteenth-century holdings in Baltimore, although a number of the Walters pictures, most notably the romantic and Impressionist works, were featured in such major exhibitions as "French Painting from David to Toulouse Lautrec," Metropolitan Museum of Art, 1941; "The Spirit of Modern France," Toledo Museum of Art, 1946–47, and "From Ingres to Gauguin," Baltimore Museum of Art, 1951.

Although the demands of his position prevented him from specializing in nineteenth–century art, the associate curator for European Painting and Oriental Art and later director of the institution, Edward S. King, undertook research in the field, writing two significant articles on Walters pictures: "Delacroix's Paintings in the Walters Art Gallery, *Journal of the Walters Art Gallery,* 1938, pp. 85–112, and "Ingres as a Classicist," *Journal of the Walters Art Gallery,* 1943, pp. 69–113.

Few paintings were added in the course of these years, but more importantly the process of "deaccessioning" that wreaked havoc with so many museums was practiced only to a very limited extent. As a result, the integrity of the collection begun by William T. Walters was preserved, whereas the private collections of so many of his contemporaries—August Belmont, John Taylor Johnston, Mary J. Morgan and A. T. Stewart, to cite a few—were either dispersed at auction or, as in the case of Catharine Lorillard Wolfe's collection, absorbed in large institutions.

The completion of a modern addition to the Walters Art Gallery in 1974 permitted the first installation of a significant portion of the nineteenth-century holdings. Two years later, a grant from the National Endowment for the Arts enabled the assistant director, William R. Johnston, to travel, pursuing studies of the collection in the Bureau de documentation at the Louvre Museum, the Witt Library, University of London, and in the Art Reference Room of the New York Public Library. Actual writing of the catalogue had to be postponed because of the exigencies of exhibition schedules. Sufficient progress, however, had been made by 1979 to apply for and to receive a grant from the National Endowment for the Arts to support the publication of this catalogue. This comprehensive and informative volume, the fruit cultivated during many years of Bill Johnston's toil in the vineyard, proudly introduces to the public the fascinating nineteenth-century paintings collection of the Walters Art Gallery.

Robert P. Bergman
Director

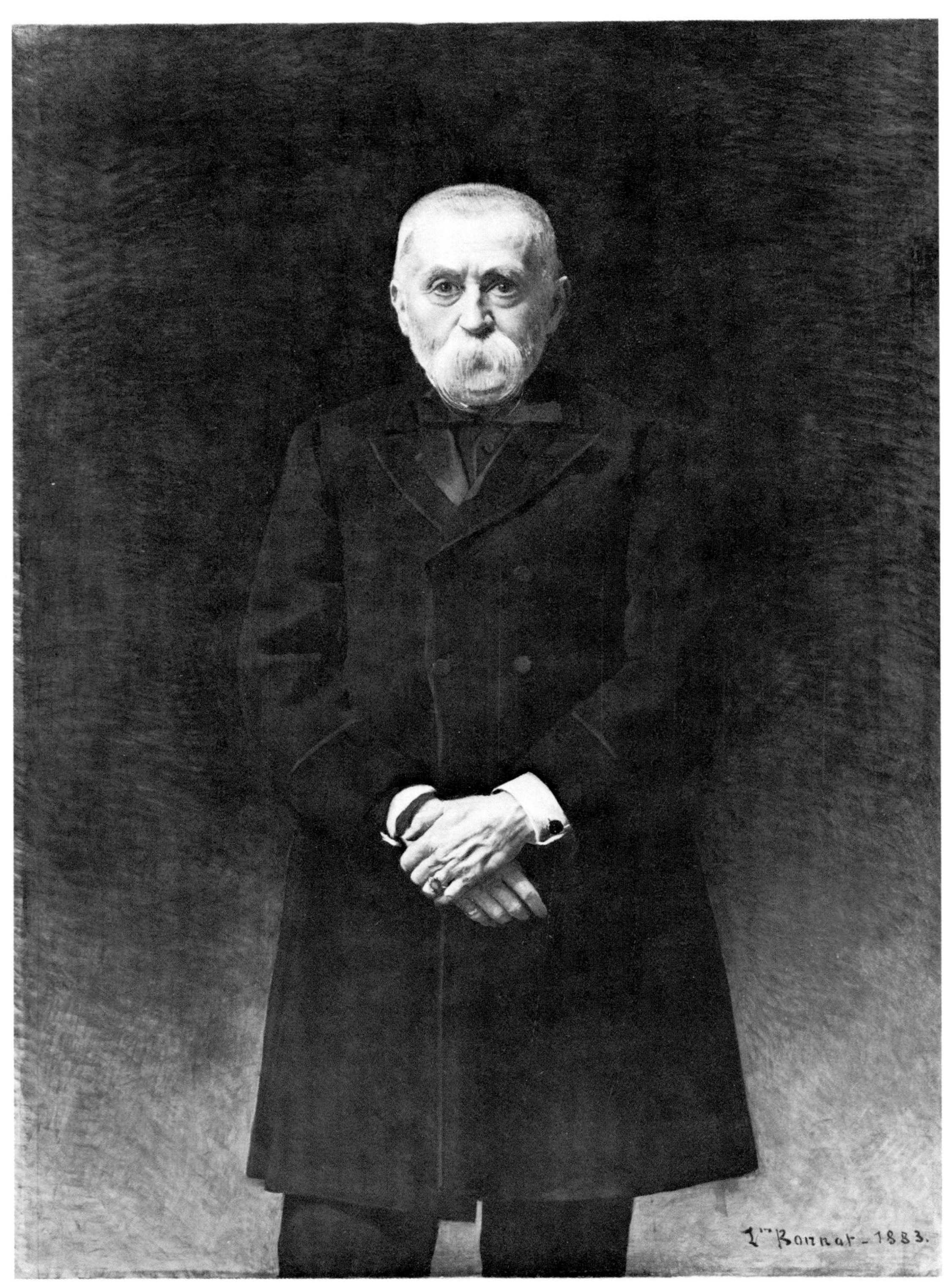

Bonnat *Portrait of William T. Walters,* no. 137

The History of the Collection

The collection of nineteenth-century paintings in the Walters Art Gallery is the achievement of two generations of the Walters family, of William Thompson Walters (1819–1894) and his son Henry (1848–1931). The former endeavored to compile a collection broadly representative of the art of his time whereas the latter, benefiting from historical perspective, sought significantly to enrich the holdings with works that fell outside the range of his father's interests. Between them, they succeeded in assembling a collection acclaimed by their contemporaries as among the richest in this country. That these holdings have remained almost completely intact renders the Walters Art Gallery a unique repository for the study of art and taste in the nineteenth century.

William Walters answered equivocally to inquiries regarding his origins and youth. His death certificate, however, records that he was born in 1819, in Liverpool, a town flanking the west shore of the Susquehanna River, north of Harrisburg, Pennsylvania.[1] His father Henry served as the local banker and postmaster, whereas his mother Jane was a daughter of the prominent Thompson family of Thompsontown on the Juniata River. After training as a civil engineer at the University of Pennsylvania, Walters worked briefly in Ferrandsville and Pottsville in the coal and iron industries before leaving central Pennsylvania in 1841 for Baltimore. In that city, he entered a commission merchant house, and by 1850 had emerged as the senior partner of W. T. Walters and Company, a prosperous business dealing in domestic and imported liquors, which was said to enjoy "credit without limit."

In addition, Walters' interests extended to the new methods of transportation, both the shipping lines running between Baltimore and Savannah, and to railroads, notably the Northern Central Railroad of which he became a controlling director. In 1845 William married Ellen Harper of Philadelphia. The marriage resulted in three children, two of whom survived, Henry and Jennie.

William Walters' passion for collecting may have been sparked by his mother. To her is ascribed the statement:

> *The busy portions of a young man's life . . . are taken up full enough to keep him out of mischief or contamination. It is his leisure time and surplus money that must be provided for and a young man can employ his time and money in no better way than by devoting them to accumulating and appreciating the noble works of literature and of art.*[2]

Her son later echoed similar sentiments concerning the ameliorating effects of art in a letter to a friend, Frank Newcomer, in which he pronounced:

> *To surround your family with forms of material beauty and loveliness—with illustrations of virtue and noble deeds—with admonitions of duty and affection, is to impress them that there is a literature of art by no means second to that of letters in importance of its teachings.*[3]

Walters' interest in art must have been long-standing: he consistently maintained that the first five dollars he earned he spent buying a painting by the Swiss artist E. A. Odier, *Napoleon Crossing the Alps*.[4] His early collecting remains otherwise undocumented. After a move in 1857 to a town house in fashionable Mount Vernon Place, William Walters emerged as a major patron of American artists, enjoying cordial relations with such local talents as the sculptor, William Henry Rinehart, and the painter of Western subjects, Alfred Jacob Miller, as well as with a number of New York artists, among them John Kensett, Asher B. Durand and Charles Loring Elliott. Consistent in his American purchases were preferences for realistically rendered detail and for works small in scale. The latter trait, in particular, was to extend to his European holdings, which remained relatively less cumbered with the monumental salon paintings prized by many contemporaries.[5]

The indirect though pervasive influence of the Belgian dealer Ernest Gambart can be detected in William Walters' early purchases of European paintings. Featured in the autumn of 1859 at the National Academy of Design's second exhibition, "Collection of English and French Paintings," was a painting from Gambart's London Gallery, Jean-Léon Gérôme's *Duel After the Masquerade* (no. 105). This work, according to *The New York Times*, had "excited more admiration than any work of a French artist since the appearance of Couture's *Decadence*."[6] No doubt attracted by the melodramatic subject, the carefully contrived composition and its smooth surface, Walters paid $2,500 for this work, a variant of a composition executed for the Duc d'Aumale in 1857.

On the same occasion, Walters bought nine additional paintings by artists whom Gambart had promoted internationally. Two of the works, small sentimental domestic scenes (nos. 89 and 90?), were by Pierre-Edouard Frère, leader of the artists' colony

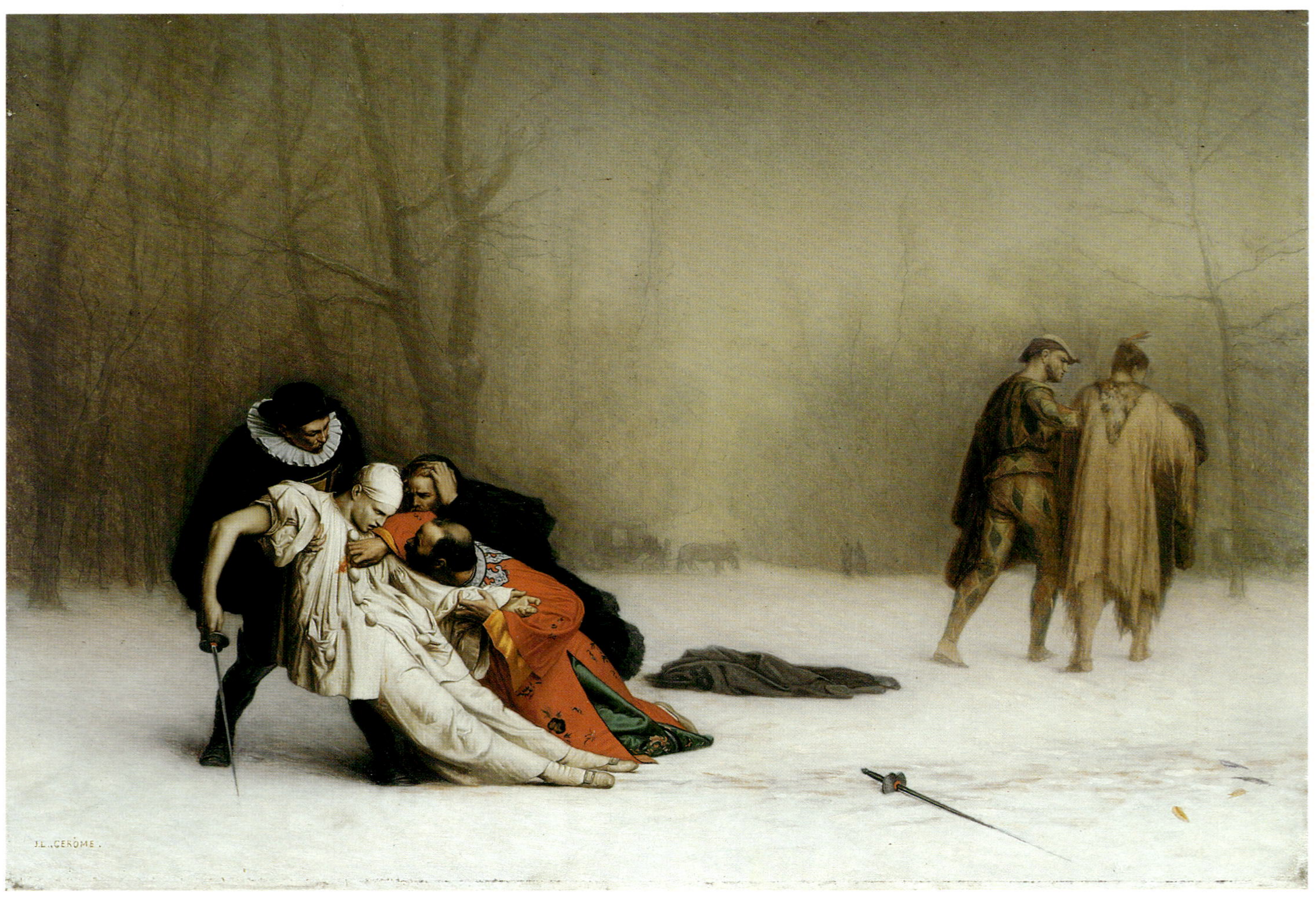

Gérôme *Duel After the Masquerade,* no. 105

at Ecouen outside Paris. Frère then enjoyed an extraordinary following as a result of Gambart's efforts and of the unbridled admiration of the critic John Ruskin.[7]

Deciding to commission works from French artists as he had from their American counterparts, Walters wrote to George A. Lucas, a Baltimorean residing in Paris, asking him to order a picture from Hugues Merle. How he came to choose the young artist who was yet to make his reputation as a rival to William Bouguereau in figure painting remains unknown. The subject, however, from Nathaniel Hawthorne's *The Scarlet Letter* (no. 112), was appropriately American.

With the outbreak of the Civil War in the United States, Walters departed for Europe with his family. After being detained briefly in New York on charges of bearing messages for Jefferson Davis,[8] he sailed, reaching Paris by August 1861, and immediately sought help from George Lucas in settling his family in Paris. Lucas' subsequent role in the formation of the Walters collection proved invaluable, as can readily be ascertained in the diaries the expatriate maintained in the course of fifty-two years' residence in Paris.[9] Lucas' perseverance in following the art market was essential for such endeavors as the compilations of the A.-L. Barye bronze collection and of the albums of watercolors by Léon Bonvin.[10] In the painting collection, however, Lucas' role was more that of an agent who acted as an intermediary between the collector and the artist and who dealt with the myriad of transactions involving dealers, brokers, framers and packers.

Serving in a similar capacity for other Americans, notably Robert Garrett of Baltimore and Samuel P. Avery, John Taylor Johnston, and William H. Vanderbilt of New York, Lucas supplemented his income with commissions.

The Walters' sojourn in Paris lasted four years, interrupted by frequent trips outside France. In 1862 the entire family toured Italy in the spring and Switzerland in the summer. A visit to London that autumn ended tragically when Mrs. Walters, catching a chill during a visit to the Crystal Palace, succumbed to pneumonia. Though grief-stricken by his sudden

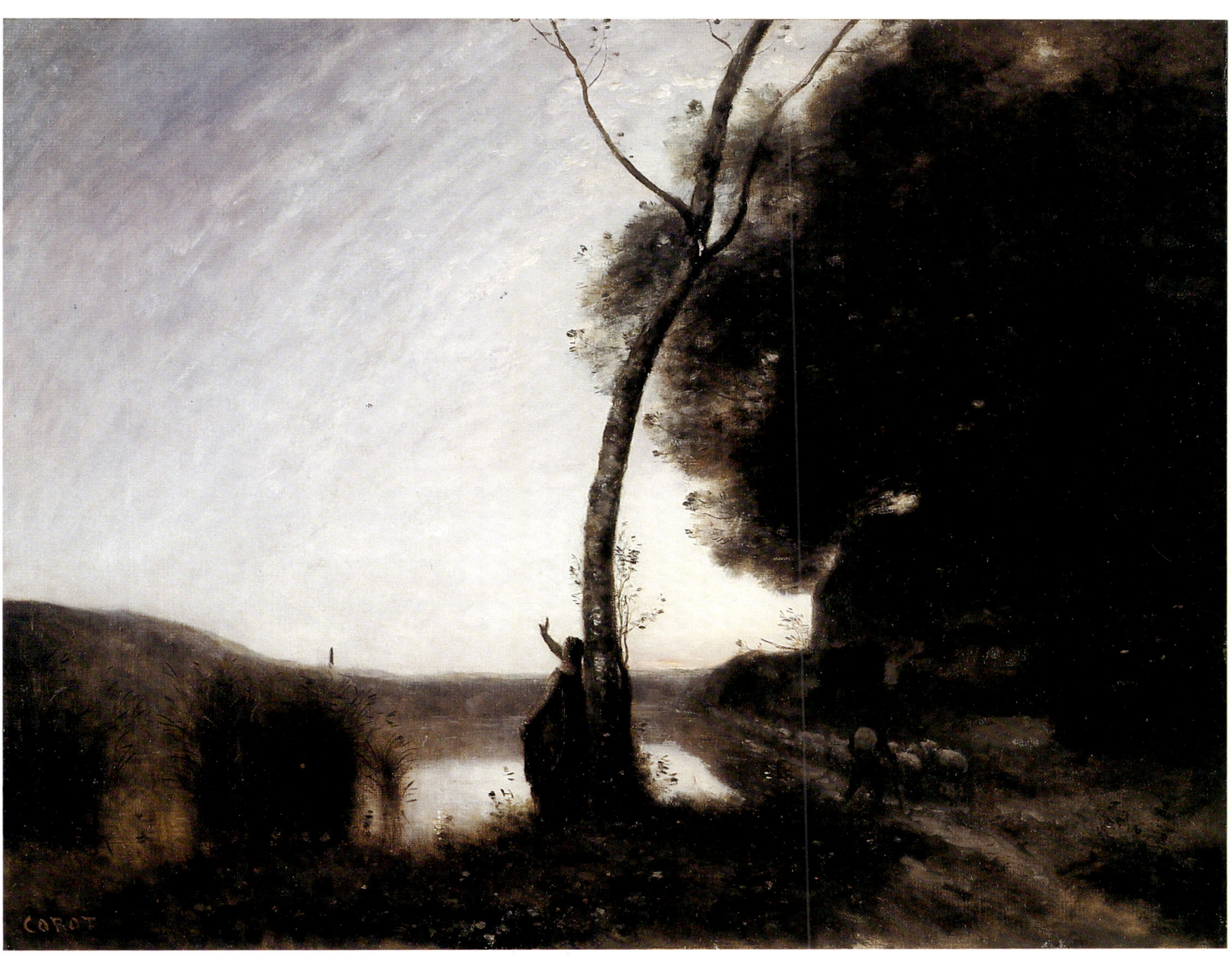

Corot *The Evening Star,* no. 37

loss, Mr. Walters was not deterred from travel. Later trips were to The Netherlands, Düsseldorf, Vienna, Italy, and to London on several occasions.

In Paris, with Lucas as his mentor, Walters frequented the art dealers and studios. Apparently he remained oblivious to the various controversies in styles, techniques and hierarchies of subjects that wracked the art community of the Second Empire. There is no evidence, for example, that he visited the controversial Salon des Refusés which opened in May 1863. Instead, he sought out those artists whose works were already familiar to him, Merle, Plassan, Lambinet, and the members of the Ecouen colony, especially Frère, T. Duverger and A. Schenck. In the course of these forays he made a number of relatively modest purchases, few of which remained in the collection.

However, it was a visit in November 1861 to examine the *Young Christian Martyr,*[11] described by Paul Delaroche as "the saddest and holiest" of his compositions,[12] followed the same day by a meeting with Jean-Léon Gérôme, that may have engendered the commission for the latter's *The Christian Martyrs' Last Prayer* (no. 108). Not until more than twenty years had passed did Gérôme complete the assignment.

Another important purchase, which anticipated the emphasis on landscape painting that would emerge in the collection, was Corot's *The Evening Star* (no. 37). Though Lucas and Robaut differ slightly in their recollections of the transaction, Walters, visiting the artist in February 1864, evidently failed to persuade Corot to part with *L'Etoile du Berger,* then in progress, and accepted in its stead a smaller replica.

Likewise, *Lost Illustions* (no. 100), a reduction of Charles Gleyre's celebrated composition *Le Soir,* was prepared as an ébauche by Léon Dussart and finished by the master. This repetition of a composition, said to have recorded a vision experienced by the artist on the banks of the Nile in 1835, may have been commissioned in Paris through the dealer Goupil, although it was not completed until after Walters had returned to Baltimore.

One outgrowth of Mr. Walters' European sojourn was his decision to launch the career of S. P. Avery as a dealer in New York.[13] The move may have been promoted by the highly successful auction at the Old Dusseldorf Gallery in New York in February 1864, in which Mr. Walters disposed of a number of paintings said to have been acquired over a span of ten years.[14] Though many of the works were by the French artists Plassan, Chavet, Duverger, Baugniet and Trayer, then in fashion, it was the strength of the American holdings, which included paintings commissioned from Eastman Johnson, W. T. Richards, Asher B. Durand, and John Kensett among others, that distinguished the Walters sale from other recent sales in New York, notably from that of John Wolfe, which had excelled in salon pictures purchased from Gambart, as well as in paintings of the Düsseldorf School.[15] The following month, Walters and Avery formed a partnership in which the former supplied funds and stock from Europe, and the profits were shared. Equally successful was a second auction of pictures consigned by Walters to Avery, held in New York that April, and although a third sale, late in 1866, proved less satisfactory, Avery's career was by then assured.

William Walters returned to Baltimore in the summer of 1865 to immerse himself in business. He turned his attention from the liquor house to railroads, and together with several fellow Baltimoreans began to buy and consolidate lines in the South that had become bankrupt in the course of the War. Eventually, the Atlantic Coast Line Railroad emerged. He also served as a finance commissioner for the city and participated in the local banking community. Apparently indefatigable, Walters avidly pursued other interests, especially husbandry and horticulture, drawing upon Lucas' services to supply livestock and seeds from Europe.

Periodically Mr. Walters visited Europe, renewing his knowledge of the foreign art markets. He was in London and Paris in 1867, attending the Exposition Universelle. Appointed a United States commissioner to the Vienna International Exhibition in 1873, he embarked that year with his family on an extended tour, visiting Paris, Berlin, Dresden, Vienna, London, Brussels, Switzerland, and Italy. On his itinerary in 1878 were a visit to Paris for the Exposition Universelle and stops at Amsterdam, Frankfurt, Dresden, Munich, Vienna, London and Dublin. His last journey in 1883 included a prolonged stay in London in March, followed by a hurried tour of the Continent. Collapsing on his return to London, partially paralysed by an arthritic condition, Walters had to cable his friend Lucas for assistance. He did not venture abroad again, sending his son Henry in his place to the 1889 Exposition Universelle.

The study of Oriental art rather than the search for European paintings may have been the primary motive for these travels. Ever since admiring the Oriental collection lent by Sir Rutherford Alcock to the International Exhibition in London in 1862, Walters had developed a consuming interest in the arts of China and Japan, which may have outranked his interest in painting in his later years.[16]

Nevertheless the painting collection continued to grow, augmented with pictures found abroad and with purchases made at the now burgeoning New York auctions. Foremost among the former was Delaroche's widely acclaimed *Hemicycle* (no. 23) extricated from France during the upheavals of the Commune. In this work, Delaroche's vast composition for the amphitheater of the Ecole des Beaux-Arts was reduced to the scale usually associated with the artist. One of the most ambitious works of Louis-Philippe's reign, the original mural introduced eminent artists of the past into the awards proceedings that marked the apogee in the training of France's most promising talents. Presiding on a central dais were the "Immortals of Antiquity," Ictinus, Apelles and Phidias, flanked by personifications of Greek, Gothic, Roman, and Renaissance Art, and extending beyond, the Renaissance masters were appropriately grouped so as to display the artist's historical eruditon. This illusionary realm of the past was linked to the present through the semi-nude figure of Fame in the central foreground, who leaned forward to dispense laurel wreaths to the recipients of the Ecole's awards.

Delaroche's mural drew a remarkable following, particularly among English and American tourists (Figure 1). One admirer in 1847, Charles Dickens, went so far as to extol the mural as "the greatest work of art in the world."[17] The impact of the composition was far-reaching, as is reflected in numerous monuments: in England, for example, in Henry Armstead's and John Philip's friezes for the Albert Memorial, and in Daniel Maclise's fresco *The Spirit of Chivalry* for the House of Lords, and in America, in Frank Furness' reliefs for the facade of the Pennsylvania Academy of the Fine Arts. The mural's fame, however, was in part attributable to Henriquel-Dupont's reproductive engraving, shown in the Salon of 1853 and at the 1855 Exposition Universelle. It was in preparation for the production of this engraving that the Walters replica is believed to have been executed by Delaroche and his pupils. Its acquisition by

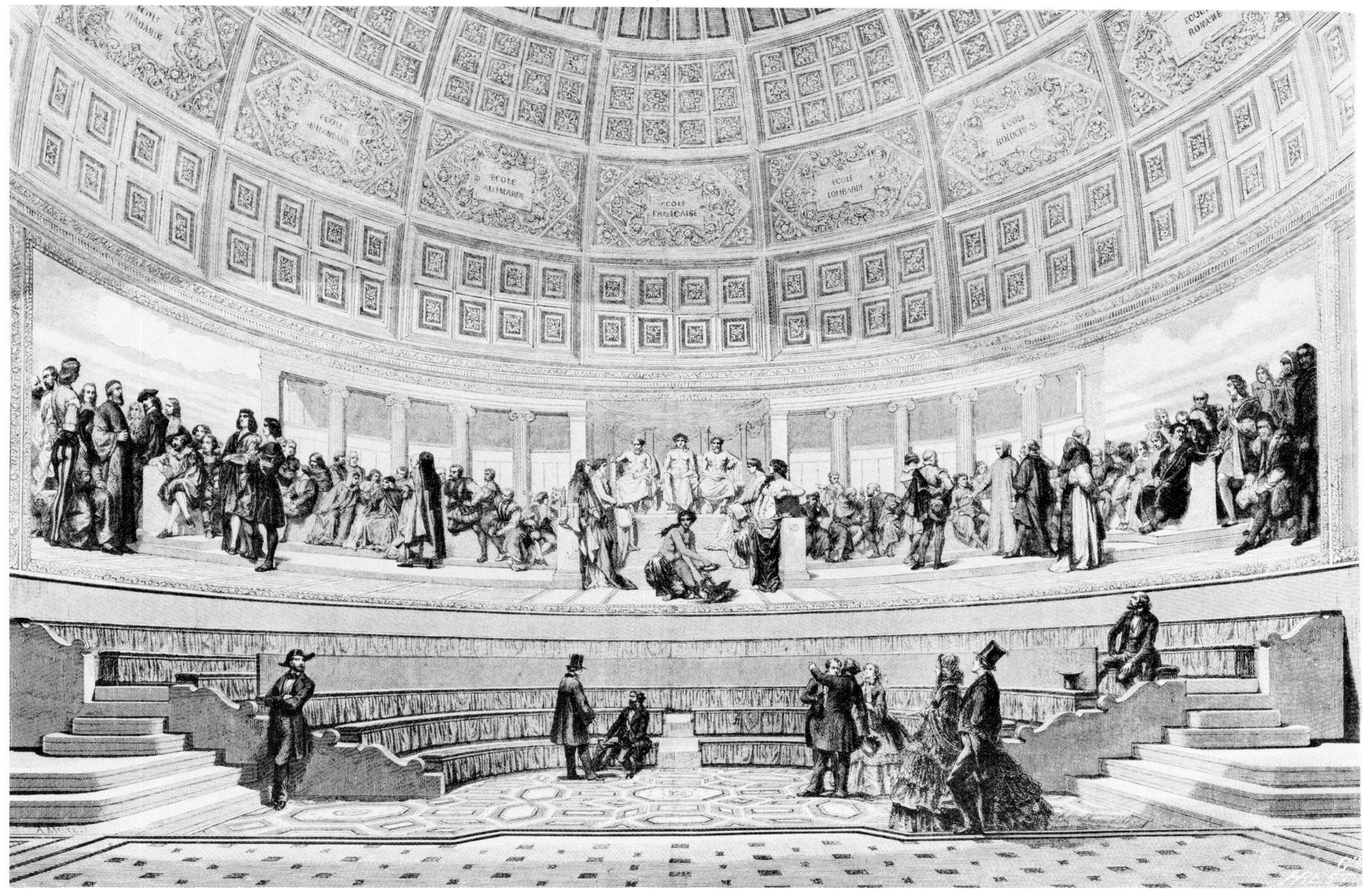

Figure 1: Delaroche's *Hemicycle* in The Ecole des Beaux-Arts, Paris, from an engraving by A. Moore.

William Walters led the critic Edward Strahan to rhapsodize:

> *I have seen nothing in America which seems so perfectly to bridge the two continents, and place the connoisseurship of the new world in connection with that of the old, the subject dedicated to the history of art, and treated with unexampled distinction of style, seems in effect to transport whole Vaticans and Louvres to these shores.*[18]

Another foreign purchase, of which Walters was equally proud, was Corot's *The Martyrdom of Saint Sebastian* (no. 35) first shown at the 1853 Salon and again at the 1867 Exposition Universelle. After substantially reworking it on several occasions, Corot, with characteristic generosity, donated the painting to a lottery held for the benefit of orphans of the 1870–71 War. Eventually it entered an English private collection and was bought by Walters in the course of his 1883 travels. The idyllic nature of the landscape, reworked with successive layers of translucent paint, the range of values and the religious overtones as well as its sheer size contributed to the admiration accorded this painting by nineteenth-century viewers.

In the late 1870s and early 1880s, William Walters began to collect farther afield. In Vienna, in November 1878, Lucas, acting on behalf of his Baltimore client, bought Rotta's *Hopeless Case* (no. 230), Pettenkofen's *The Market at Szolnok* (no. 205) and Knaus' *Mud Pies* (no. 199). These purchases may have been prompted by a visit to the Austrian capital undertaken earlier in the year by Walters in the company of Lucas and S. P. Avery. Similarly, William Walters' protracted stay in London in 1883, preceded by the visit of his son Henry in the spring of 1881, resulted in a spate of purchases through Gambart's nephew, Charles Deschamps. Millais' *News from Home* (no. 261), a number of Alma-Tadema's reconstructions of life in ancient Rome (nos. 264–267) and *The Edict of Charles V* (no. 170) by the latter's Belgian master, Baron Leys, were among the additions to the collection at that time.

Art collecting in New York in decades following the Civil War "came into vogue with a virulence of an epidemic" as was observed by Wesley Towner.[19] The full scope of this phenomenon can be gleaned

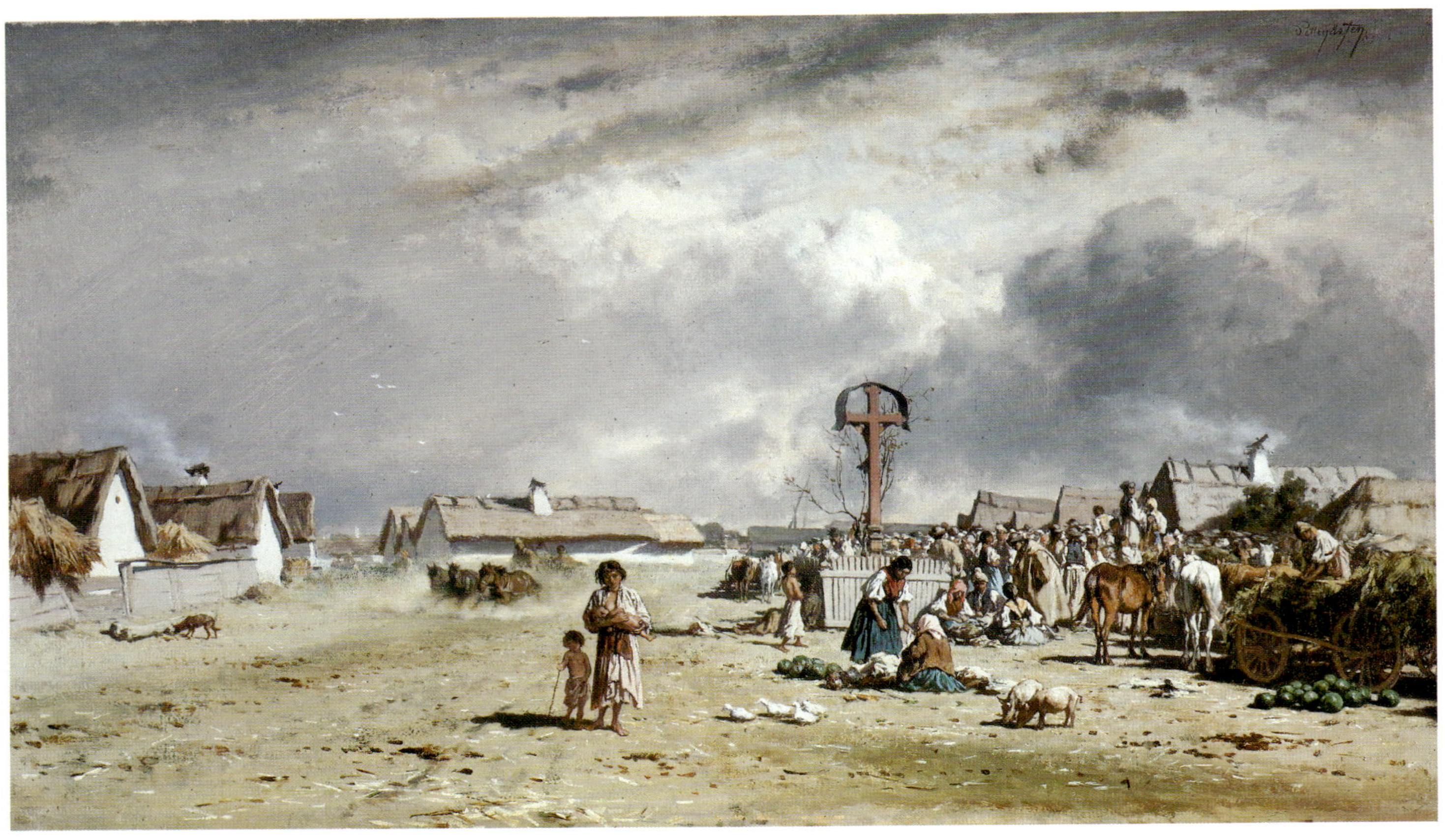

Pettenkofen, *The Market at Szolnok,* no. 205

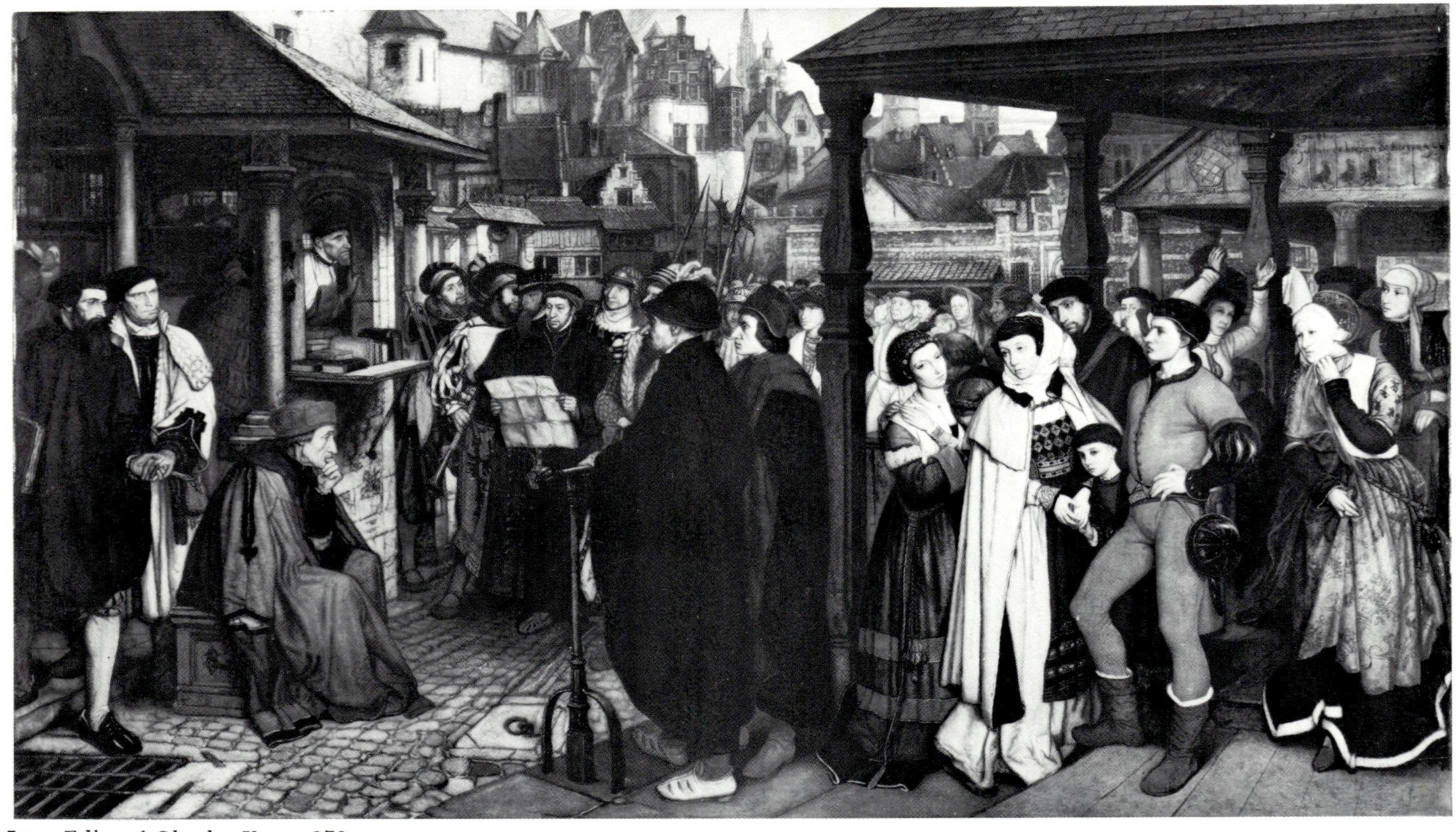

Leys *Edict of Charles V,* no. 170

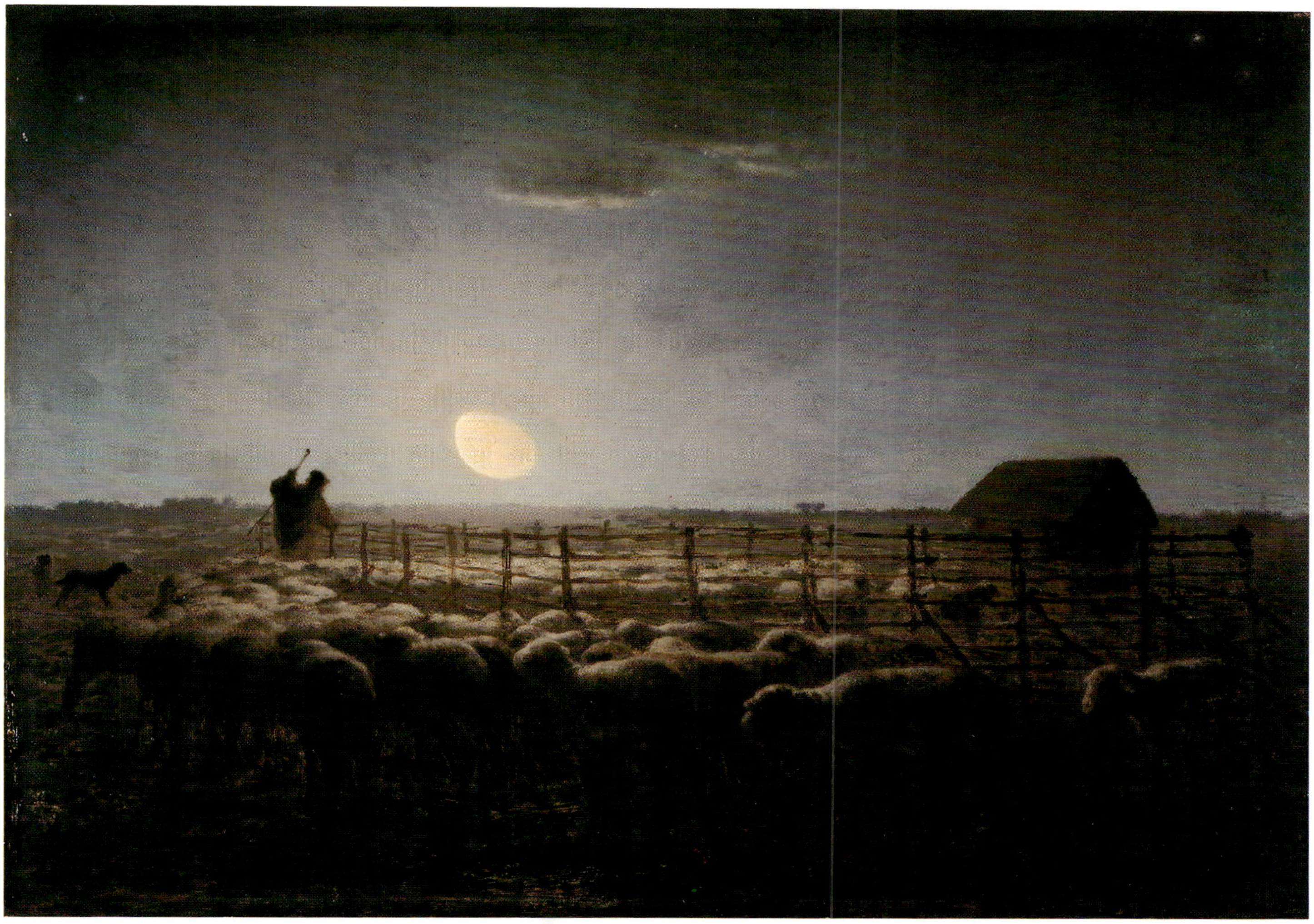

Millet *Sheepfold, Moonlight,* no. 62

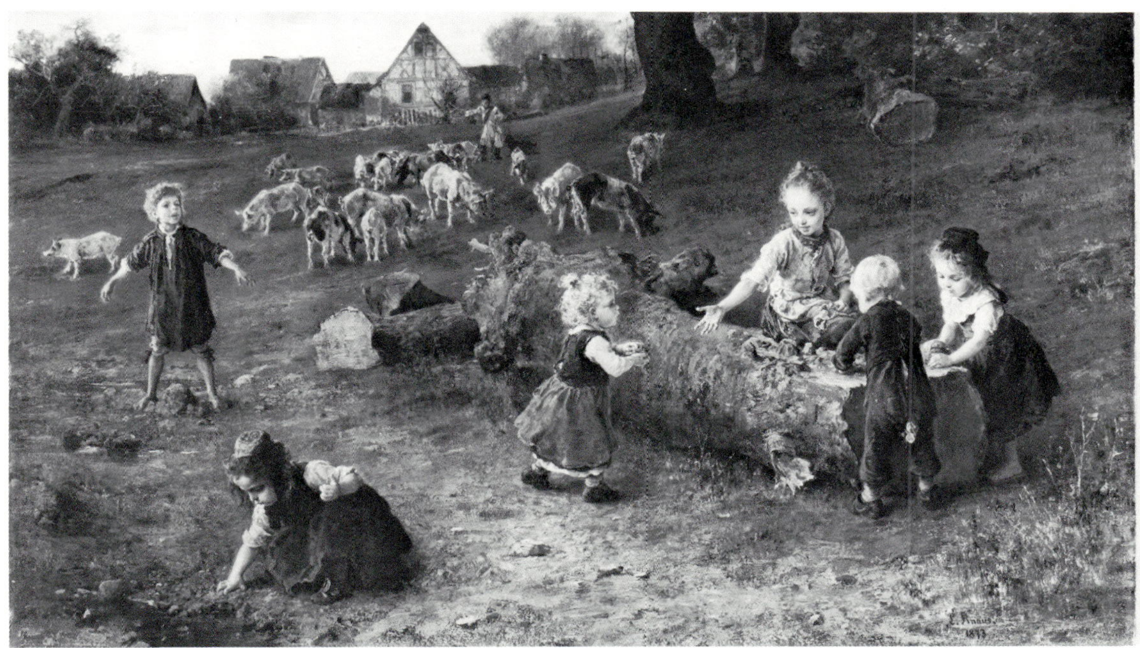

Knaus *Mud Pies,* no. 199

from the deluxe three volumes of Edward Strahan's *The Art Treasures of America*.[20] Inevitably many of these collections were dispersed at auctions, providing Walters with opportunities to enhance his holdings. At the August Belmont sale in 1872 be bought J.-L. Gérôme's *Diogenes* (no. 107). The liquidation of the holdings of John Taylor Johnston, a fellow railroad financier and client of Lucas and S. P. Avery, led to the purchase of Vernet's *Italian Brigands Surprised by Papal Troops* (no. 8), Daubigny's *Twilight* (no. 67) and an early work of Decamps, *The Suicide* (no. 18). Other sales figuring either directly or indirectly in the formation of the Walters collection included that of John Wolfe in 1882 (nos. 133, 196), Mary J. Morgan in 1886 (nos. 143, 30) and of H. Probasco. From the Probasco sale, a Cincinnati collection, Walters acquired Couture's allegory of vanity, *Soap Bubbles* (no. 103), Rousseau's *Early Summer Afternoon* (no. 56) and Schreyer's *Arabs in Egypt, Sunrise* (no. 195).

The direction of William Walters' buying was altered in 1883 by the "Cent Chefs-d'Oeuvre" exhibition held in Paris that summer at the Galerie Georges Petit. Though ostensibly organized to raise funds for free schools, the exhibition did much to augment the prestige associated with collecting. Eighty-seven nineteenth-century pictures interspersed with thirteen Old Masters were lent by a roster of distinguished owners, among them the Princesse de Sagan, Baroness Nathaniel Rothschild, Baron Gustave de Rothschild, Prince A. de Broglie and M. F. Bischoffsheim. A significant portion of the pictures came from the Defoer and Viot collections, which fortuitously were to be dispersed at Petit's within several years. Assembled were works by Géricault, Delacroix, Decamps, Marilhat, Isabey and Scheffer, together with landscapes by Corot, Rousseau, Millet, Troyon, Diaz, and Fromentin as well as several by the Spaniard, Fortuny, and the Belgian, Leys. Though he lay crippled in London, unable to attend the exhibition, William Walters subscribed to the deluxe commemorative folio published by Ludovic Baschet with etched illustrations and a text by Albert Wolff, a journalist for *Figaro*.[21] Subsequently, Walters took special pride in the fact that four additions to his collection, Delacroix's *Christ on the Cross* (no. 14) and *Christ on the Sea of Galilee* (no. 16), Millet's *Sheepfold, Moonlight* (no. 627) and Troyon's *Cattle Drinking* (no. 47), had been numbered among the "Cent Chefs-d'Oeuvre." Late in 1886 he commissioned from the Art Age Press of Gilliss Brothers and Turnure a reprinting of Wolff's text with one alteration, the substitution of an essay on the sculptor Barye by Gustave Planche for the original Géricault entry.[22]

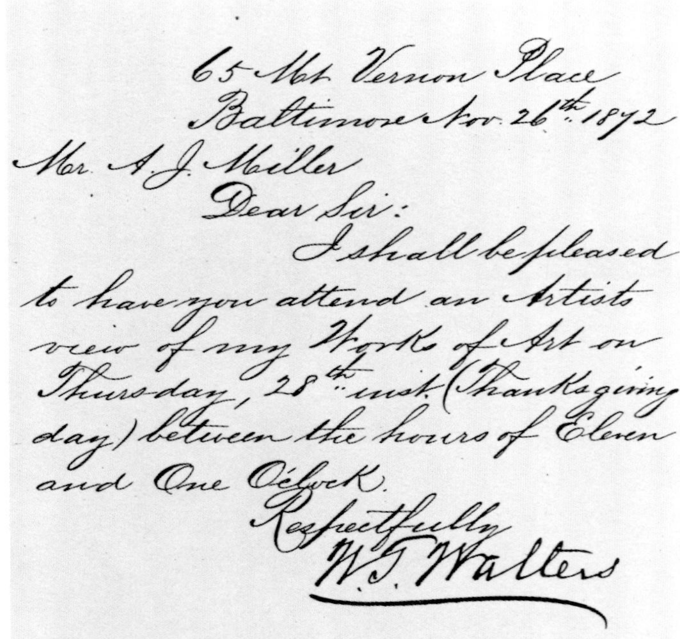
65 Mt. Vernon Place
Baltimore Nov. 26th 1872
Mr. A. J. Miller
Dear Sir:
I shall be pleased to have you attend an Artists view of my Works of Art on Thursday, 28th inst. (Thanksgiving day) between the hours of Eleven and One O'clock.
Respectfully
W. T. Walters

Figure 2: Invitation from W. T. Walters to the Baltimore painter, Alfred Jacob Miller, to an artist's viewing of his collection on November 28, 1872. *Collection of the L. Vernon Miller family.*

At the American Art Association in New York, between November 15, 1889, and January 15, 1890, an exhibition was held to raise funds for the benefit of the Barye Monument Association.[23] William Walters headed the venture, with the collectors Cyrus J. Lawrence, Henry C. Marquand and James C. Welling serving as vice-presidents. In addition to exhibiting the works of the animalier, one hundred paintings by contemporaries and friends of Barye, described as members of "the phalanx of 1830," were included. Represented were Géricault,[24] Delacroix, Corot, Daubigny, Decamps, Dupré, Millet, Rousseau, and Troyon, all either the sculptor's associates at Barbizon or friends of his youth. The parallels between the Barye Monument Association project and the "Cent Chefs-d'Oeuvre" exhibition held six years earlier were obvious to all.[25]

In reviewing William Walters' collection the nineteenth-century critics concurred regarding its magnificence and its educational value. Edward Strahan, in 1878, alluded to the collection as "an educator of taste not to be excelled in the New World"[26] whereas Alfred Mathews, ten years later, emphasized the Baltimorean's "regard for the sentiment, the pathos, the poetry that is the informing spirit of every true incarnation of the beautiful."[27] Likewise, a writer for the *Philadelphia Ledger* in 1893 noted how Mr. Walters sought to promote home talent "by assembling specimens of the best works by modern masters as objects of study and instruction."[28]

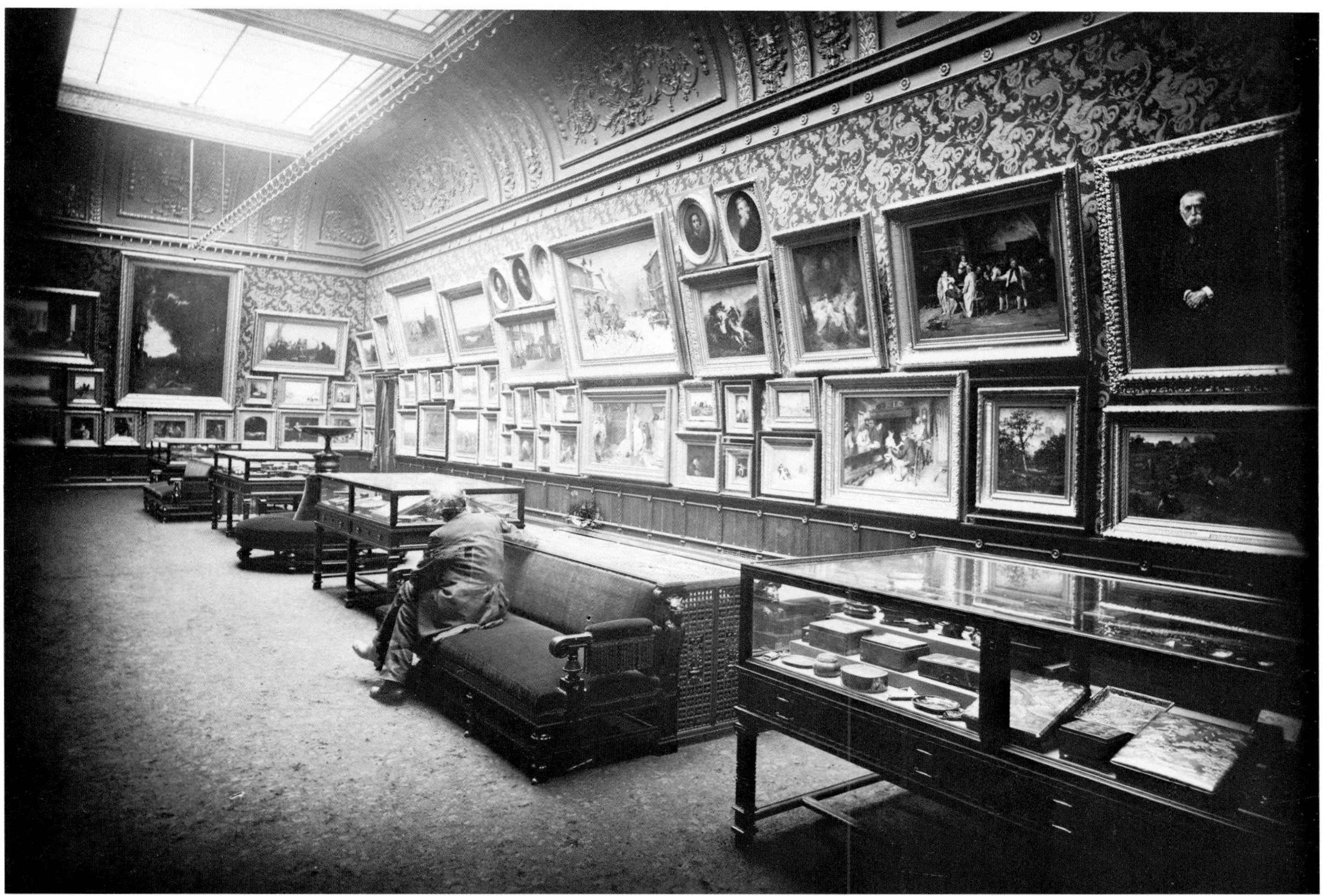

Figure 3: An unidentified guest in W. T. Walters' picture gallery in about 1884. The center of the gallery is occupied by sofas and cabinets containing oriental artifacts.

William Walters was a proselytizer who wished to share the benefits of owning art, as he saw them, with fellow Americans. To accomplish this objective he installed his collections in special galleries which he opened not only to artists and writers but also, on occasion to the public (Figure 2). Though invitations to private viewings were not generally publicized, sufficient examples were recorded to suggest that Mr. Walters frequently served as host on such occasions. He is known to have held a special viewing for artists as early as Thanksgiving Day, 1872.[29] About 1876, he adopted a program of openings for the benefit of the Association for the Improvement of the Condition of the Poor (later the Family and Children's Society) which became a local tradition, lasting fifty-five years. On Wednesdays of February, March and April, Saturdays of April, February 22, and Easter Monday, the public was welcomed, with a fee of fifty cents a visitor being levied for the benefit of the charity.[30] Preceding these annual events were private viewings to which were invited prominent members of the Baltimore and Washington communities.

The installations in the late 1870s have been described by Edward Strahan.[31] Two rooms on the ground floor were allotted to pictures, the smaller for watercolors and the larger for oil paintings. The latter, however, overflowed into the living quarters, where they were interspersed with oriental and western bric-a-brac in several rooms, including a "Marie-Antoinette boudoir" and a Dutch seventeenth-century style bedroom. In contrast to the more palatial residences of his contemporaries in New York, William Walters' house on Mount Vernon Place presented a surprisingly modest facade, belying the wealth within.

To alleviate overcrowding, an enlarged gallery was erected behind the house in time for the 1884 opening[32] (Figure 3). The front parlors were limited to western decorative arts and the upstairs was allotted to the works of Antoine-Louis Barye. The former picture galleries and the bridge-room between the house and galleries were lined with cases for the oriental collections, by then consisting of over 4,000 items. Drawing aside heavy portieres, the visitor entered a spacious gallery with walls and carpet of

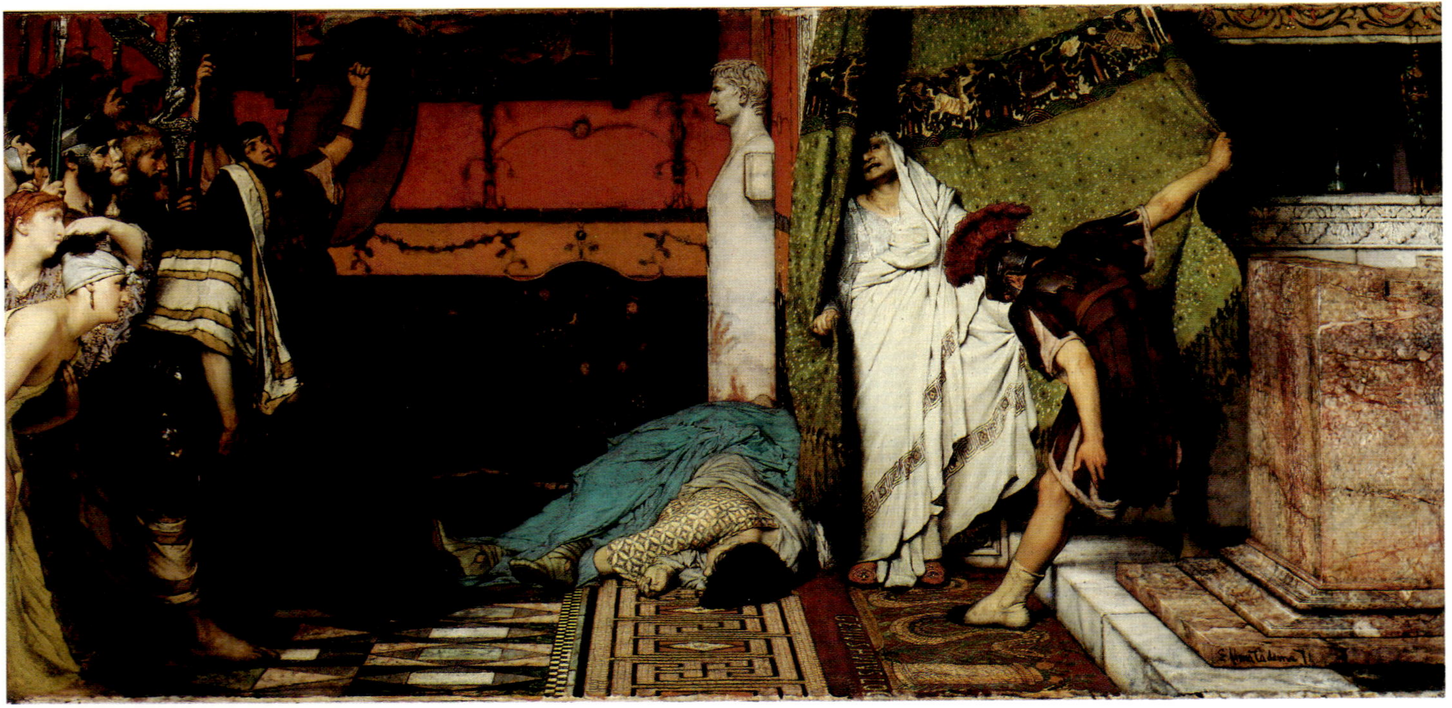

Alma Tadema *A Roman Emperor,* no. 264

"dark rich, warm tint; the half-arched ceiling fretted with reliefs finished in bronze, harmonizing with the carved gilt picture frames." Extending the length of the gallery was a row of ebony cases containing oriental lacquers and curios alternating with sofas upholstered in dark green velvet. Dominating the gallery at the 1884 opening were the recently acquired Alma-Tademas (nos. 264, 265, 266) and Corot's *Saint Sebastian.* (no. 35)

In conjunction with the openings for the benefit of the Poor Association, William Walters published a series of catalogues of his painting collection. The first, appearing about 1878, was a modest guide listing the pictures for the visitor in counter-clockwise sequence.[33] The titles and the artists' names were followed by brief, usually rather inconsequential comments. For the 1884 opening, however, a more ambitious format was adopted, closely modeled after the catalogues of W. H. Vanderbilt's collection. The artist's name, his place of birth, and the picture's title were printed in red to separate them from the listings of the artist's teachers and medals as well as the work's dimensions and provenance which appeared in black. The entry numbers coincided with those appearing on brass tags pinned to the picture frames. Catalogues adhering to this format were published in succeeding years by William and his son Henry, enabling readers to follow the growth of the collection.[34]

William Walters did not live to see the completion of a more aesthetically rewarding publication, *Notes Critical and Biographical: Collection of W. T. Walters,* issued in 1895 by J. M. Bowles from the press of Carlon and Hollenbeck, Indianapolis (Figure 4). It contained a series of biographical essays and interpretive comments for each artist by Richard B. Gruelle, a landscape painter from Indiana who had first visited the Walters Gallery in the spring of 1892. The handsome typography with an ornamental title page, and chapter headbands and decorative initials in intertwined vines, was the work of the distinguished American book designer, Bruce Rogers, who drew for this youthful venture from William Morris' *Poems by the Way* issued by the Kelmscott Press in 1891.[35]

Less out of filial duty than of shared interests, Henry Walters pursued endeavors in both commerce and art that were analogous to those of the senior Walters. To prepare for a business career he took degrees at Georgetown University and the Lawrence Scientific School (Harvard University) and sought practical experience working for the Valley Railroad of Virginia and the Pittsburgh and Connellsville Railroad. In 1889, he joined his father at the Atlantic Coast Line Railroad, eventually attaining the position of Chairman of the Board. In addition, Henry Walters followed his father's banking interests, also becoming chairman of the board in 1915 of the Baltimore bank, the Safe Deposit and Trust Company. So successful was he in these pursuits that by the 1920s he bore the reputation of being "the richest man in the South." As befitted his wealth, he contributed to a wide range of philanthropic and cultural institutions although the full scope of his generosity

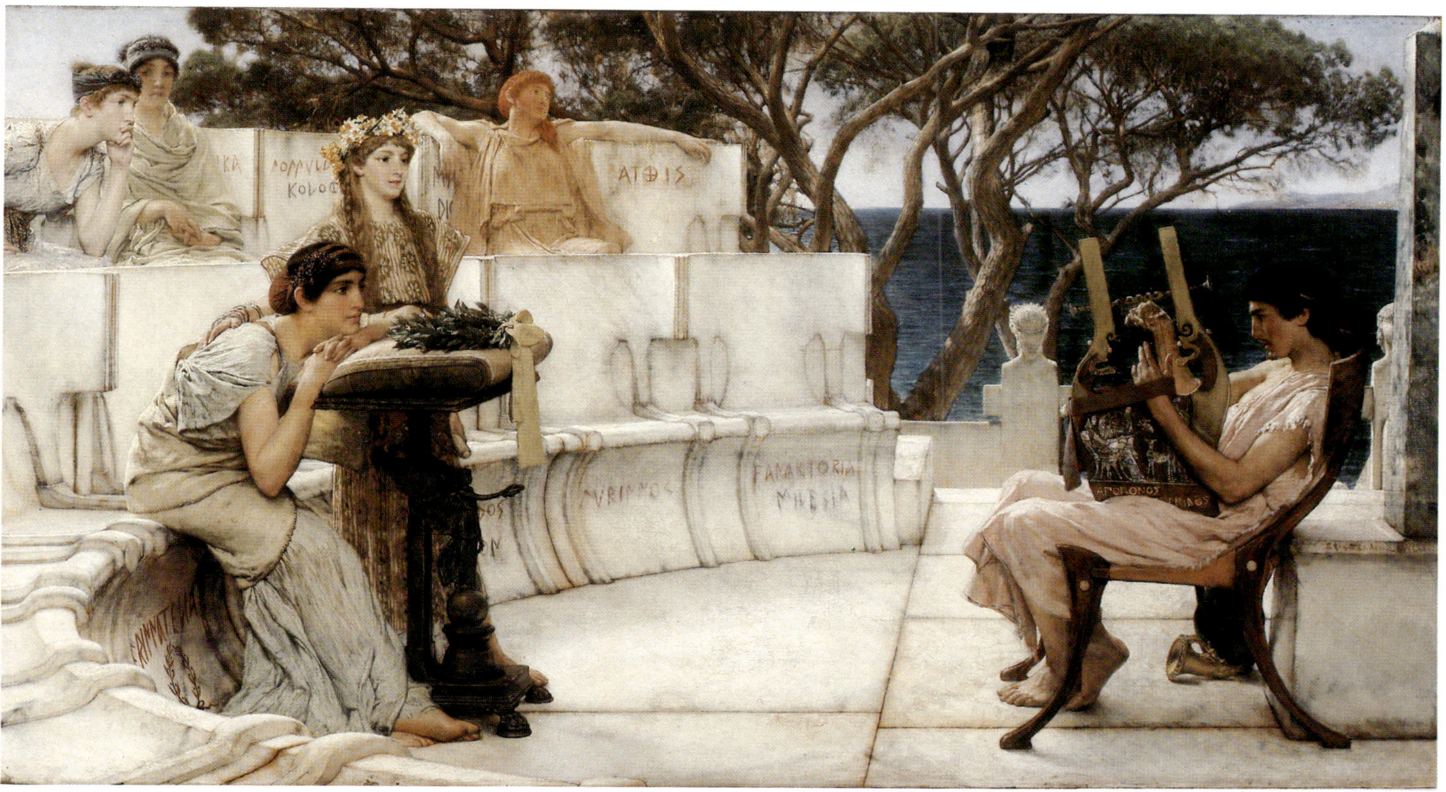

Alma Tadema *Sappho,* no. 266

remains unascertained as a result of his extreme adversion to publicity and of the anonymous character of many of his gifts[36] (Figure 5).

Henry Walters had been introduced to the art market in his youth when he accompanied his father and G. A. Lucas on their rounds of museums, dealers and studios. While attending lycée in Paris he is said to have befriended a scion of the Durand-Ruel family noted for their promotion of Impressionism. Later he accompanied his father on European journeys and participated in various activities associated with the collection, serving for example, as an "auditor" for the Barye Monument Association.

Though his purchases reflected an abiding interest in nineteenth-century painting and Oriental art, Henry was not willing to limit himself to the fields dear to his father, but sought from the outset to collect works of art illustrating the range of human achievement. As early as 1893, at the World's Columbian Exposition, he began to patronize the dealer Dikran Kelekian, buying Mesopotamian cylinder seals, and by 1899 he was collecting classical antiquities. Perhaps it is with the art of the book that Henry Walters was most closely associated. He bought the Lefferts collection from George Richmond in 1902 and within two years he was a customer of Léon Gruel of Paris and Leo S. Olschki of Florence.

The purchase that most drastically transformed the scope of his collection occured in April 1902, when he acquired the contents of the Palazzo Accoramboni in Rome from Don Marcello Massarenti. To house this extraordinary assemblage of Old Masters, mostly Italian paintings, and Greek and Roman antiquities, he was compelled to replace the 1884 gallery with a much larger structure, modeled in its interior after the Palazzo dell'Università, Genoa.[37] The nineteenth-century art, however, was reinstalled in much the same arrangement as before (Figure 6), and, to stress the continuity in the collection, a bust of the senior Walters by Rinehart was mounted in a cartouche above the doorway of the new building.

Given Henry Walters' reluctance to record his thoughts, one must surmise that in his purchases of nineteenth-century painting he was motivated less by preferences for individual schools of painting than by the desire to fortify the historical breadth of the collection. Though he visited Europe almost annually, Henry Walters continued to draw upon the assistance of his friend since youth, the aging George Lucas, in negotiations with artists, dealers and auction houses. In New York, where he resided following his father's death, Henry Walters attended major auctions and patronized dealers, principally Durand-Ruel, Knoedler, and eventually Wildenstein.

To redress the collection's shortcomings in early nineteenth-century painting, Henry Walters bought in 1899 from Durand-Ruel in New York Delacroix's

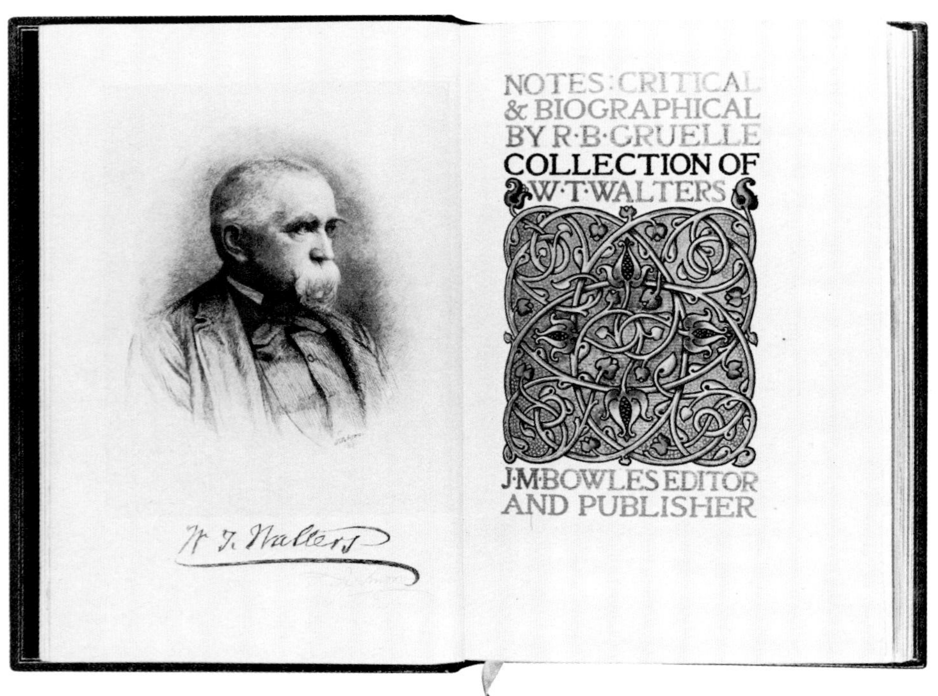

Figure 4: *Notes: Critical and Biographical by R. B. Gruelle,* Collection of W. T. Walters—J. M. Bowles Editor and Publisher 1895, one of six copies rubricated on Whatman paper with etching of W. T. Walters by Thomas Johnson as frontispiece.

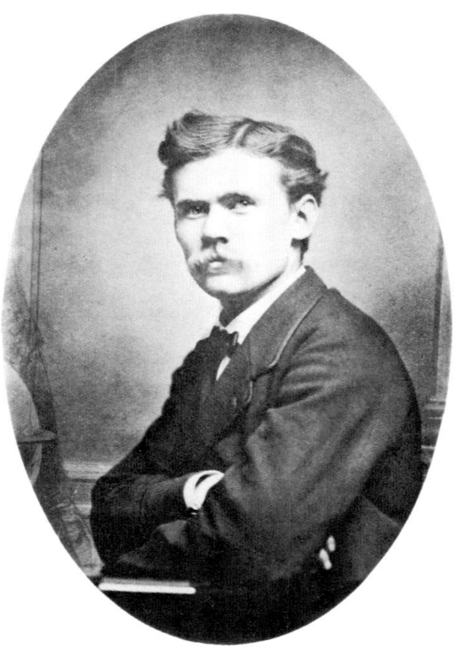

Figure 5: Henry Walters (1848-1931) as a young man. Said to be after a portrait by George Baker.

early sketch for *The Battle of Poitiers* (no. 12) and at the P.-A. Chéramy sale in Paris, in 1908, he included among his purchases the *Portrait of Mme. Tangry* (?) attributed to J.-L. David (no. 1). Ingres was one of the major painters entirely to elude the grasp of the senior Walters. Rectifying this gap, Henry Walters acquired *The Betrothal of Raphael* (no. 4) at the Mrs. S. D. Warren Sale in 1903; the *Oedipus and the Sphinx* (no. 7), another work from the Chéramy Sale in 1908; the version of the *Odalisque* (no. 6) executed for William I, King of Württemberg, at Wildenstein in 1925, and the *Reclining Venus* (no. 5) after Titian from an unknown source, shortly before his death.

At the opposite extreme, Henry Walters added to the collection pictures by later nineteenth-century artists associated with Impressionism. Though he had obviously been familiar with their works for some time, visiting, for example, the joint exhibition of Monet and Rodin conceived by Georges Petit in the summer of 1889,[38] he did not attempt to represent them in the collection until 1903. Accompanying Lucas to Mary Cassatt's studio that April, he purchased from the American artist for a combined fee of 25,000 francs Monet's captivating work of about 1872, *Springtime* (no. 155) and Degas' haunting portrait of his cousin, Estelle Musson Balfour (no. 151). Nine years later, he further augmented his holdings in this direction at the Cyrus J. Lawrence auction. Lawrence, also a banker and railroad financier, had been a client of Lucas, especially for Barye bronzes, and had served with the two Walters in the Barye Monument Association. In the course of his first trip abroad in 1874, the New York collector had also developed a taste for the Impressionists and had subsequently acquired a number of their works through Durand-Ruel. At the Lawrence sale, Henry Walters bought Degas' *Before the Race* (no. 152), two coastal scenes by Boudin (nos. 148 and 149) and Lépine's *Bassin de la Villette* (no. 159).[39] Other purchases of this nature included Sisley's *View of Saint-Mammès* (no. 157) and Manet's incomparable *At the Cafe* (no. 153), both bought at Durand-Ruel in 1909–10.

Despite these avant-garde additions, Henry Walters did not neglect the more conservative painters esteemed by his father. At the 1898 sale of the collection of the American expatriate William H. Stewart, he successfully bid for Mariano Fortuny's *Arab Fantasia* (no. 215) and Meissonier's *End of a Game of Cards* (no. 119) and as late as 1917 at the James B. Haggin et al. sale he bought no less than three paintings by J.-L. Gérôme (nos. 106, 110, 111) whose reputation with the public was by then sinking to its nadir.

There was little growth in the nineteenth-century collection following Henry Walters' bequest of the Gallery to Baltimore in 1931. Given severe limitations in space and overcrowding in the storerooms, the curators were reluctant to purchase works or to solicit gifts. Exceptions to the rule included Prince Serge Belosselsky's donation of a portrait of his great-grandmother by Winterhalter (no. 190) and Mrs.

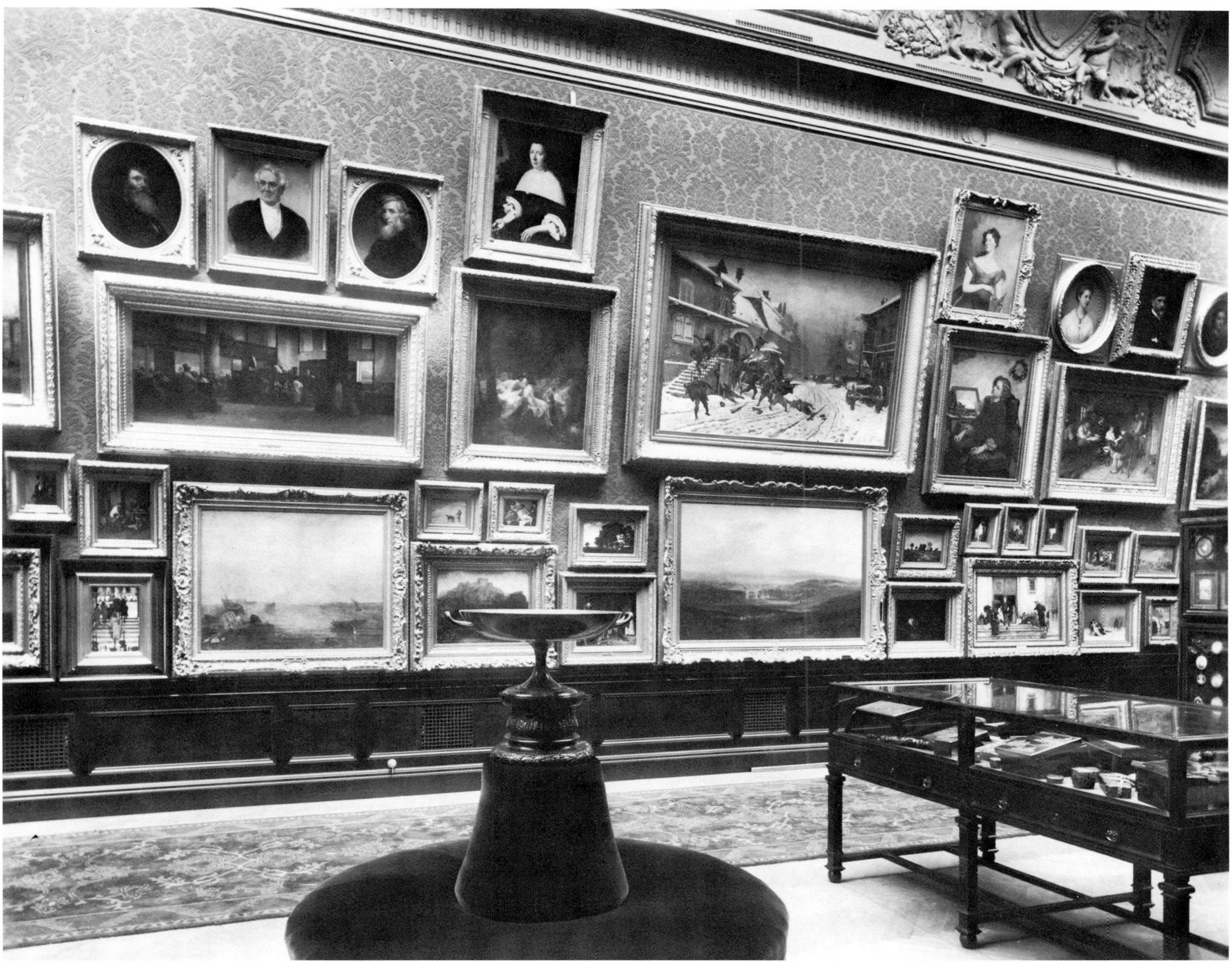

Figure 6: The installation of the nineteenth-century painting gallery in Henry Walters' building of 1905. In the top center is the only pre-nineteenth century picture acquired by W. T. Walters, a portrait of an elderly woman by Pieter Nason which was thought to be Bartholomeus Van der Helst's portrait of Anna Maria Schurmann.

Margaret McCauley Turk's gift of a pair of witty domestic scenes by De Braekeleer (nos. 163–164).

The completion in 1974 of an addition to the building, alleviating the lack of space, coincided with the public's renewed interest in nineteenth-century art. Since the expansion the Gallery has benefited from the generosity of a number of donors. To cite several, the relatively weak holdings of eastern European painting have been strengthened by the additions of a scene of Tartar horsemen by the Polish-born Munich painter Josef Brandt (no. 207) and of a miniature landscape by the Russian Ivan Pochitonoff (no. 209), gifts of Mr. and Mrs. L. Whiting Farenholt and Miss Laura Delano, respectively. L. J. B. Perrault's salon painting *Maternity* (no. 145) presented by Mrs. R. Dennison Frick and J. J. Veyrassat's *Harvest Scene* (no. 74) given by Mrs. William S. Hilles, in contrast reinforce aspects of French painting for which the Gallery is justifiably noted.

Of the two hundred and sixty-eight pictures listed in this catalogue one hundred and sixty-two belonged to William T. Walters, ninety-one to his son Henry and only seventeen were added following the Gallery's opening as a public museum. Though representing but one facet of their collections, the nineteenth-century section bears testimony to the tastes and determination of two remarkable individuals who sought to share with their fellow citizens their appreciation of the fine arts.

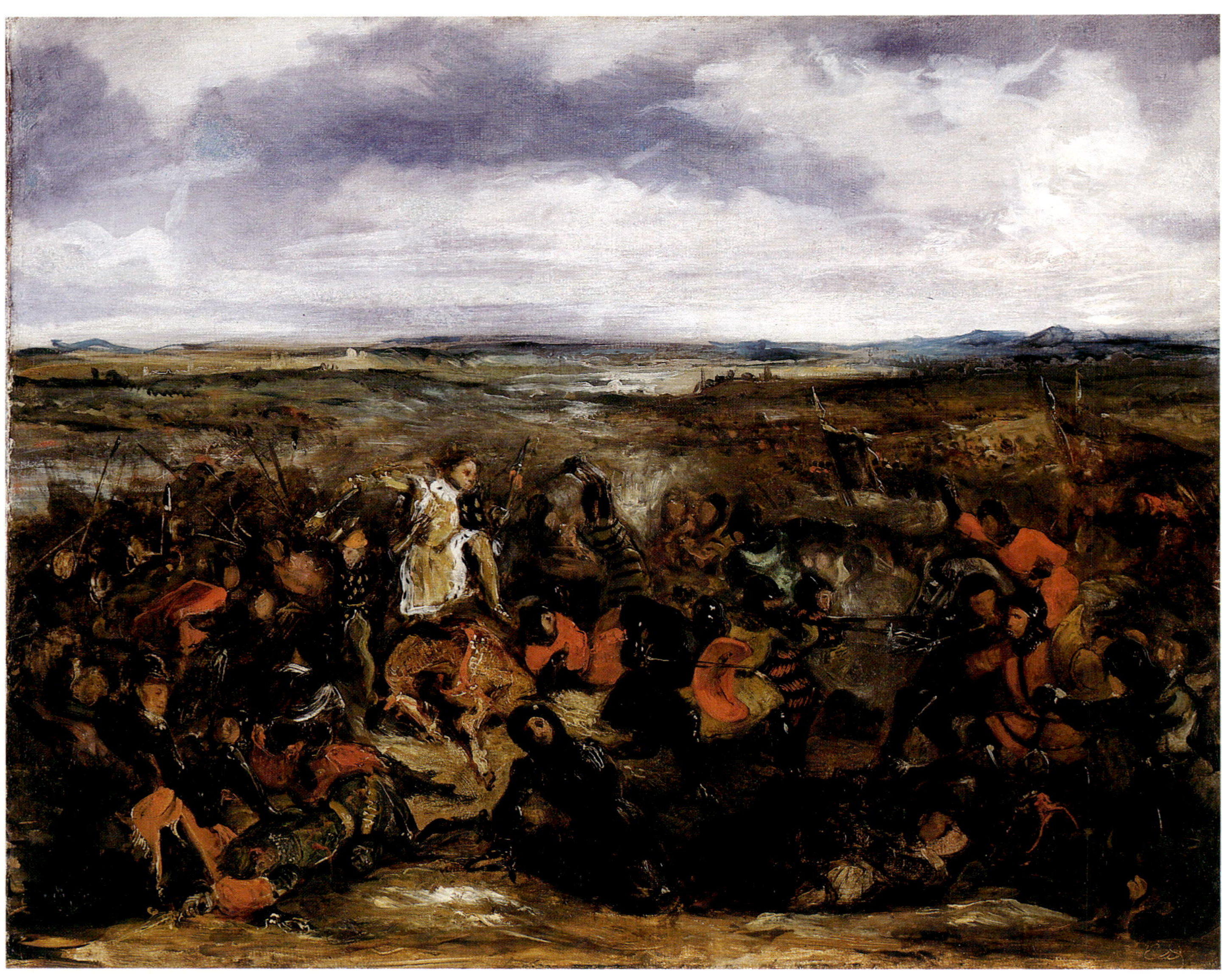

Delacroix *Sketch for the Battle of Poitiers,* no. 12

FOOTNOTES

1. The death certificate no. A 7180 C, Office of the Registrar of Vital Statistics, Health Department, City of Baltimore, lists William Walters' birthplace as Liverpool and his age at his death as seventy-five years and six months. In a number of publications he is said to have been born in 1820 rather than 1819 and his birthplace is listed variously as Harrisburg, Liverpool or Thompsontown, Pennsylvania.
2. Milton Reizenstein, "The Walters Art Gallery," *New England Magazine* new series 12 (July 1895): 558.
3. Typescript of a letter from W. T. Walters to Frank Newcomer written from Paris, March 15, 1864.
4. This work was inadvertently sold at the auction of the furnishings of the residence of the late William T. Walters, held at the Alcazar, Baltimore, November 30–December 1, 1942, no. 153.
5. For discussions of the American collection see Edward S. King and Marvin C. Ross, *Catalogue of The American Works of Art,* Baltimore, 1956 and William R. Johnston, "American Paintings in the Walters Art Gallery," *Antiques* 106 (1974): 853–61.
6. *New York Times,* September 10, 1859, p. 4. Couture's *Decadence* refers to Thomas Couture's controversial *Les Romains de la Décadence* of 1847, in the Louvre.
7. Jeremy Maas, *Gambart, Prince of the Victorian Art World,* London, Barrie and Jenkins, 1975, p. 93.
8. Unidentified newspaper clipping in the Ritter family Bible.
9. Lilian M. C. Randall, ed., *The Diary of George A. Lucas: An American Art Agent in Paris, 1857–1909,* Princeton, Princeton University Press, 1979.
10. William R. Johnston, "The Barye Collection," *Apollo* 100 (1974): 56–63 and William R. Johnston, "The Léon Bonvin Collection of the Walters Art Gallery," *The Drawings and Watercolors of Léon Bonvin,* Cleveland, The Cleveland Museum of Art, 1980, pp. 15–19.
11. Lilian M. C. Randall, op. cit., 2:124.
12. Louis Ulbach, "Paul Delaroche," *Revue de Paris* 26 (1857): 368. This composition is represented in the Walters collection by a replica (no. 24).
13. Madeleine Fidell Beaufort, Herbert L. Kleinfield and Jeanne K. Welcher, *The Diaries 1871–1882 of Samuel P. Avery, Art Dealer,* New York, Arno Press, 1979, pp. xv–xx, and Lilian Randall, op. cit., 1:12.

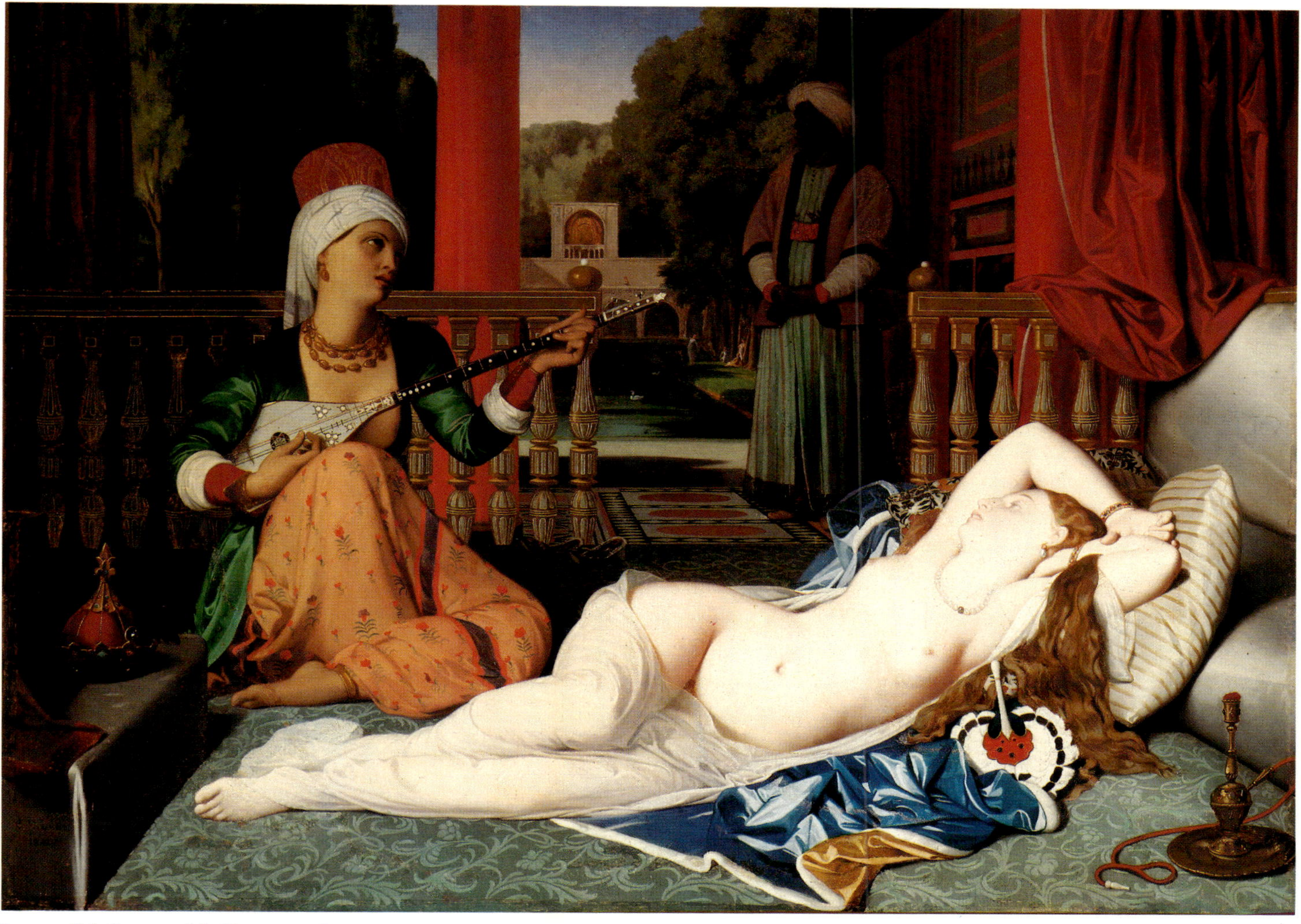

Ingres *Odalisque with Slave,* no. 6

14. *Catalogue of a Most Valuable Collection of Pictures of the American, French and German Schools,* Henry H. Leeds & Co., New York, February 12–13, 1864.
15. *New York Daily Tribune,* February 13, 1864.
16. *Oriental Collection of W. T. Walters, 65 Mt. Vernon Place,* Baltimore, 1884, p. ix.
17. Charles Dickens, letter to W. Harrison Ainsworth, 18 March 1847, in *The Pilgrim Edition, The Letters of Charles Dickens,* Graham Storey and K. J. Fielding, eds., Oxford, Clarendon Press, 1981, 5:37.
18. Edward Strahan (Earl Shinn), *The Art Treasures of America, being the choicest works of art in the public and private collections of North America,* Philadelphia, Gebbie and Barrie, c. 1878, p. 82.
19. Wesley Towner, *The Elegant Auctioneers,* New York, Hill and Wang, 1970, p. 29.
20. Edward Strahan (Earl Shinn), *The Art Treasures of America,* 3 vols. Philadelphia, Gebbie and Barrie, 1880.
21. Albert Wolff, *Cent Chefs-d'Oeuvre, The Choice of the French Private Galleries,* New York, Knoedler & Co., n.d.
22. Albert Wolff et. al, *Notes Upon Certain Masters of the XIX century,* New York, Gilliss Brothers & Turnure, The Art Age Press, 1886.
23. *Catalogue of the Works of Antoine-Louis Barye exhibited at the American Art Galleries . . . for the Benefit of the Barye Monument Fund,* New York, J. J. Little & Co., 1889.
24. The Géricault, no. 576 *Lion Couchant,* lent by Cottier & Co., might well have been *Lion in Repose* now in the Walters Art Gallery, no. 10.
25. Dorothy Miner, "The Publishing Ventures of a Victorian Connoisseur, A sidelight on William T. Walters." *The Papers of the Bibliographical Society of America* 57 (1963): 294.
26. Edward Strahan (Earl Shinn), *The Art Treasures of America . . .* c. 1878, p. 94.
27. Alfred Mathews, "The Walters Art Collection at Baltimore," *Magazine of Western History* 10, no. 1 (May 1889): 3–4.
28. *Philadelphia Ledger,* January 31, 1893, p. 3.
29. A letter from W. T. Walters to Alfred Jacob Miller dated November 26, 1872, inviting the artist to a special viewing on Thanksgiving Day, November 28, is in the possession of the L. Vernon Miller family.
30. The Poor Association's annual report for October 1875 to October 1876 provides the earliest listing of a Walters benefit. The proceeds were $734.00. Between 1884 and 1931 they totalled $125,521.95. Precedents for the Walters benefit openings were set by August Belmont and John Taylor Johnston, who opened their picture galleries for the U.S. Sanitary Commission in the course of the Civil War.
31. Edward Strahan, op. cit., pp. 81–82.

32. *The Art Collections of Mr. William T. Walters, Catalogue and Descriptive and Critical Articles, Published by Permission of Mr. Walters,* Baltimore, The Baltimore American, 1884.
33. For a discussion of the exhibition catalogues and William T. Walters' other publications see Dorothy Miner, op. cit. pp. 271–311.
34. Catalogues appeared in 1878, 1884, 1887, 1888, 1893, 1895, 1897, 1899, 1901, 1903, 1909 and 1929.
35. Dorothy Miner, op. cit., p. 299.
36. Among his philanthropic and cultural interests were a public bath system in Baltimore City; the Department of Art as Applied to Medicine, The Johns Hopkins University; the American Academy in Rome; a Military hospital at Passy, France; the Wadsworth Atheneum, Hartford, Connecticut, and the Metropolitan Museum of Art, New York. It was characteristic of Henry Walters that in donating the main building to Georgetown Preparatory School, Garrett Park, he should request that it be listed as a "Gift of the Class of 1869."
37. The architect was William Adams Delano of Delano and Aldrich.
38. Lilian M. C. Randall, op. cit., 2: 695.
39. In addition, Henry Walters purchased at this sale two drawings by Daumier, a painting by J. L. Brown, a portrait of a boy by Ribot and a Raffaelli. The paintings did not enter the Baltimore collection.

APPENDIX A

Forgeries Excluded from the Catalogue

The following paintings acquired by William and Henry Walters are not included in this catalogue since they have long been rejected as not being by the artists to whom they were attributed.

37.219 Richard Parkes Bonington, *Beach Scene with Figures,* canvas, .381 x .514 (15″ x 20¼″)

37.15 John Constable, *The Old Mill,* canvas, 1.09 x .998 (43″ x 39¼″)

37.213 John Constable, *Landscape with Anglers,* canvas, .638 x .762 (25⅛″ x 30″)

37.235 John Constable, *The Lock,* canvas, .578 x .724 22¾″ x 28½″)

37.180 John Constable, (perhaps William Müller), *Landscape with Windmill,* panel, .222 x .287 (8¾″ x 11¼″)

37.200 John Crome, *Landscape,* canvas, .214 x .273 (8⅜″ x 10¾″)

37.212 John Crome, *Landscape with Figures,* canvas, .482 x .4 (19″ x 15¾″)

37.2407 J. Freeman, *Landscape with Figures,* signed and dated: 1806, panel, .265 x .345 (10⅜″ x 13⅝″)

37.32 Joseph Mallord William Turner, R. A., *St. Michael's Mount,* canvas, 1.023 x 1.278 (40¼″ x 50 5/16″)

37.36 Joseph Mallord William Turner, R. A., *Ehrenbreitstein,* canvas, .595 x .738 (23⅜″ x 29″)

37.132 Joseph Mallord William Turner, R. A., *Grand Canal, Venice,* canvas, .61 x .916 (24″ x 36″)

APPENDIX B

Paintings Withdrawn from the Collection

Listed below are works recorded as having been exhibited in the Walters collection in Baltimore. Excluded are pictures bought expressly for resale. Dates in parentheses refer to the sale of works.

Alma-Tadema, Laura Theresa, *A Landscape* (before 1884)

Alma-Tadema, Lawrence, *The Roman Mother* (before 1884)

Alma-Tadema, Lawrence, *Catullus at Lesbia's* (before 1887)

Appiani, Andrea, *Prudence* (1950)
ex. coll. Massarenti, canvas, .473 x .362 (18$\frac{5}{8}$″ x 14$\frac{3}{8}$″)

Appiani, Andrea, *Charity* (1950)
ex. coll. Massarenti, canvas, .473 x .362 (18$\frac{5}{8}$″ x 14$\frac{3}{8}$″)

Appiani, Andrea, *Force* (1950)
ex. coll. Massarenti, canvas, .473 x .362 (18$\frac{5}{8}$″ x 14$\frac{3}{8}$″)

Appiani, Andrea, *Justice* (1950)
ex. coll. Massarenti, canvas, .473 x .362 (18$\frac{5}{8}$″ x 14$\frac{3}{8}$″)

Bischoff, Théophile, *The Dropped Stitch* (before 1884)

Bochmann, Gregor von, *Farm Scene*, 1879 (1942)
panel, .27 x .435 (10$\frac{5}{8}$″ x 17$\frac{1}{8}$″)

Boks, E.-J., *Corpus Deliciti* (before 1884)

Boldini, G., *My Garden* (before 1884)

Chaplin, Charles, *At the Shrine* (before 1884)

Clays, P. J., *The Approach to Antwerp* (before 1884)

Couture, Thomas, *A Zouave* (before 1884)

Couture, Thomas, *Liberty in Chains* (before 1887)

Dunoury, Le Comte, *Scene on the Nile* (1942)
after J. L. Gérôme, canvas, .445 x .75 (17$\frac{1}{2}$″ x 29$\frac{1}{2}$″)

Fortuny y Marsal, M., *Interior of a Slaughter House* (1950)
canvas, .733 x 1.317 (28$\frac{7}{8}$″ x 51$\frac{7}{8}$″)

Guillemin, T. A. (probably A.-M Guillemin), *The Print Vendor* (before 1884)

Hamon, J. L., *Feeding the Pets* (before 1884)

Heilbuth, Ferdinand, *A Promenade* (before 1884)

Hiddeman, F. P., *The Philosophy of the Ball* (before 1884)

Hubner, Carl W., *The Emigrant's Adieu* (before 1884)

Jacovacci, Francesco, *The Borghese Palace* (before 1884)

Jacque, Charles E., *Sheep Drinking* (before 1887)

Jacque, Charles E., *Village Poor* (before 1887)

Koller, G., *Charity* (before 1884)

Lagye, Victor, *Flemish Costume* (before 1884)

Lambinet, E.-C., *Still Life* (before 1884)

Landelle, L., *An Italian Shepherd Boy* (before 1884)

Millet, F., *A Summer Landscape* (before 1884)

Muller, L. K., *Head of a Young Woman, Two Views of Houses* (1951)
3 panels mountel together, .26 x .16 (10$\frac{1}{4}$″ x 6$\frac{5}{16}$″)

Odier, E. A., *Napoleon's Retreat from Moscow* (1942)
.451 x .59 (17$\frac{3}{4}$″ x 23$\frac{1}{4}$″)

Pasini, A., *Constantinople* (before 1884)

Plassan, A. E., *The Baby's Bath* (before 1884)

Plassan, A. E., *The Return of the Nurse* (before 1884)

Plassan, A. E., *Contemplation* (before 1884)

Plassan, A. E., *The Model* (before 1909)

Ribot, Théodule, *Mignone* (1951)
ex. coll. Cyrus J. Lawrence, canvas, .56 x .465 (22$\frac{1}{16}$″ x 18$\frac{5}{16}$″)

Robert-Henry, J. H., *Leda and the Swan* (1942)
panel, .297 x .12 (11$\frac{3}{4}$″ x 4$\frac{3}{4}$″)

Roehn, Alphonse, *Views of Margate Lighthouse* (1951)
ex. coll. Massarenti, .471 x .66 (18″ x 26″)

Rudder, Jan de, *Eight Decorative Panels of Water Fowl* (1942)
Lengths: 13′7$\frac{3}{4}$″; 12′5$\frac{1}{2}$″; (4 panels) 5′1$\frac{3}{4}$″; (2 panels) 3′11″

Schenck, August, *Putti and Goats around Maypole* (1942)
canvas, .423 x .737 (16$\frac{5}{8}$″ x 29″)

Schott, G., *Goose Girl* (1942)
canvas (?) .581 x .466 (22$\frac{7}{8}$″ x 18$\frac{3}{8}$″)

Thaulow, Fritz, *The Ocean* (1951)
canvas, .817 x 1 (32$\frac{1}{4}$″ x 39$\frac{3}{8}$″)

Tissot, James, *Marguerite at the Well* (before 1884)

Turner, J. M. W. (attributed to), *The Wreck* (1951)
ex. coll. J. D. Ichenhauser, canvas, .71 x .915 (28″ x 36″)

Van Marcke, Emile, *Cow, Bright Sunlight* (1951)
ex. coll. John Wolfe, canvas, .493 x .76 (19$\frac{3}{8}$″ x 27$\frac{7}{8}$″)

Van Marcke, Emile, *Study from Nature* (1951)
canvas, .58 x .677 (22$\frac{7}{8}$″ x 26$\frac{5}{8}$″)

Vibert, J. G., *Gulliver Bound* (before 1884)

Vidal, V., *Portrait of . . .* (1950)

Vollon, A., *Landscape* (1950)
canvas, .71 x 1.05 (28″ x 41$\frac{3}{8}$″)

Weber, Otto, *Hay Gathering* (before 1884)

Ziem, F. F. G. P., *Sunset, South of France* (1950)
ex. coll. J. Stricker Jenkins, canvas, .898 x 1.173 (35$\frac{3}{8}$″ x 46$\frac{1}{4}$″)

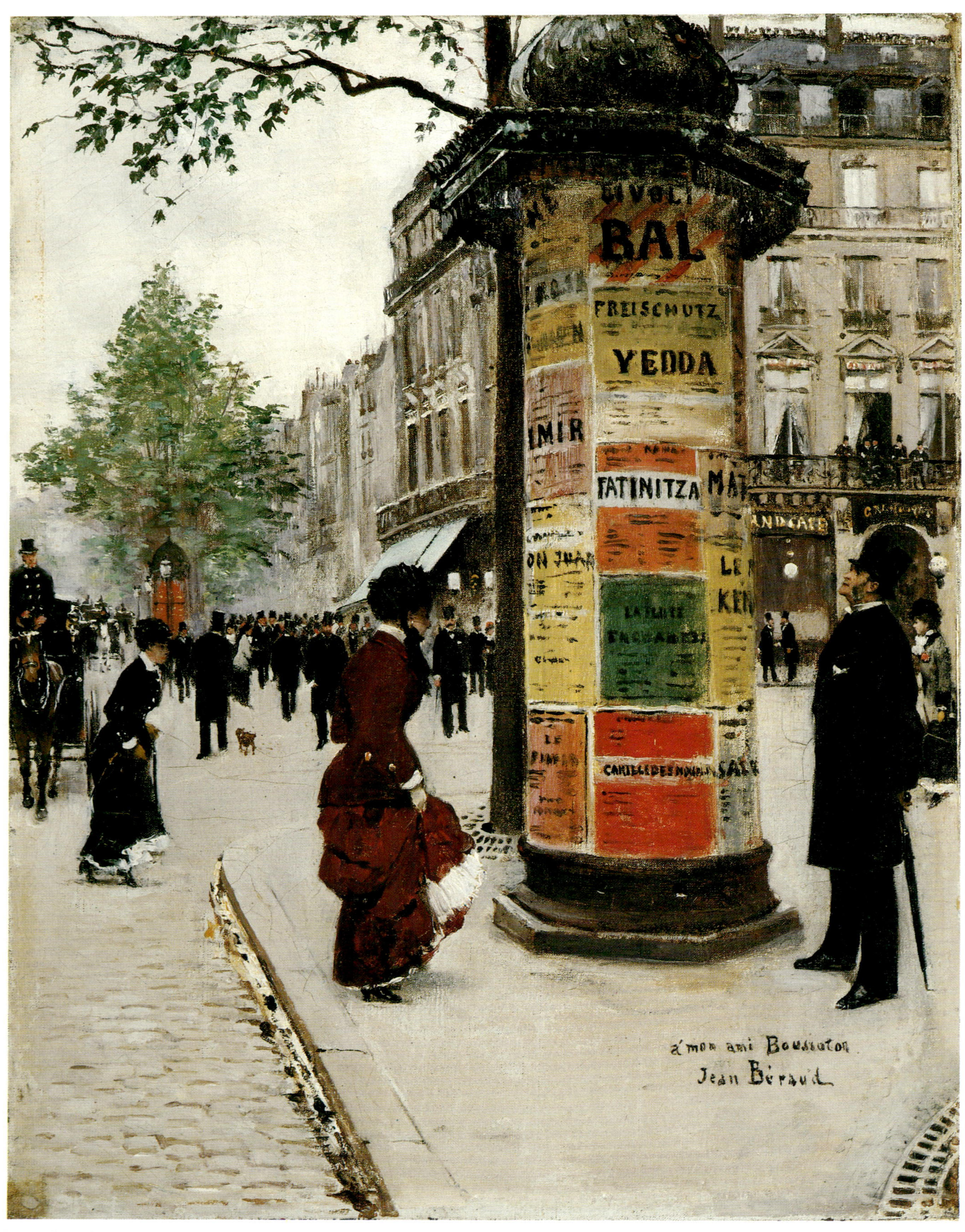

Béraud *Paris Kiosk,* no. 146

French Paintings

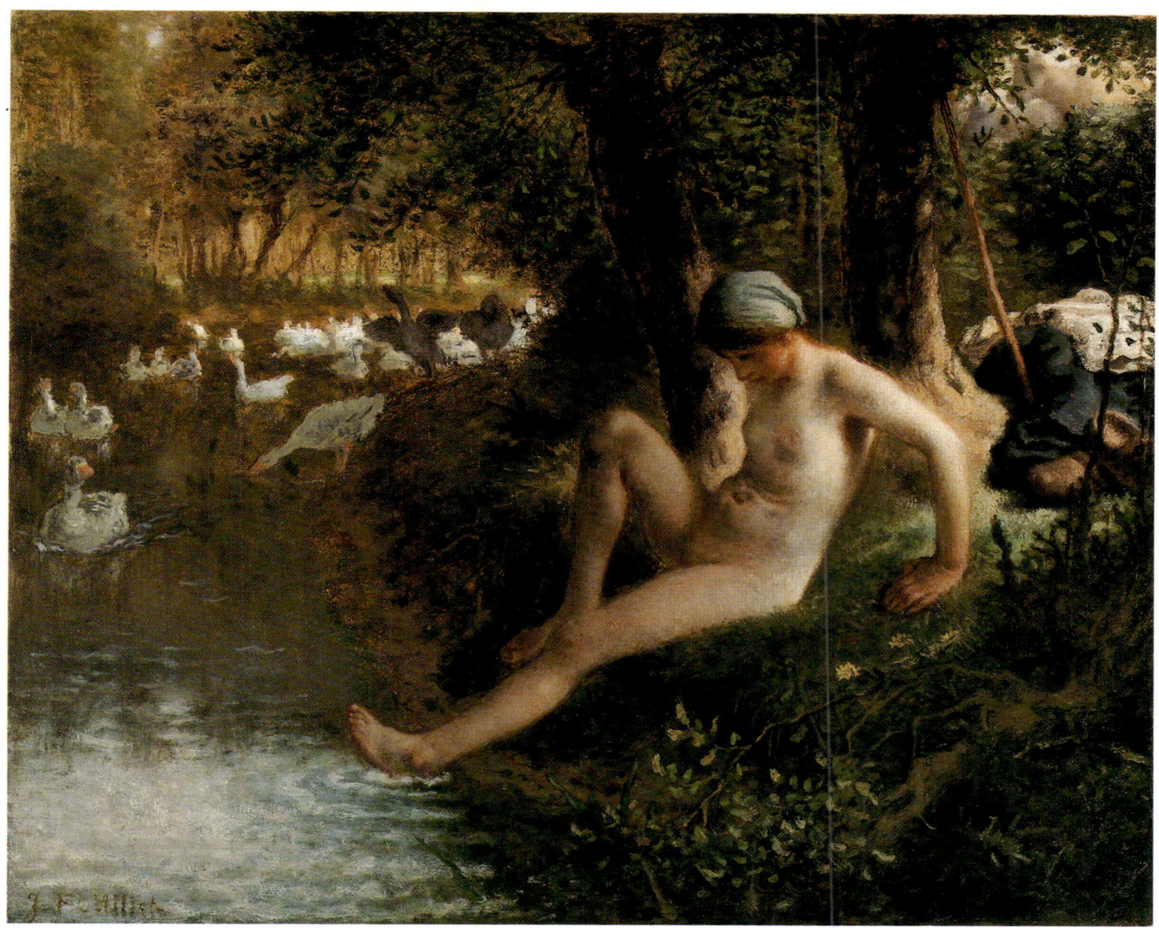

Millet *The Goose Girl,* no. 63

Jacques-Louis David

French: Paris, 1748 - Brussels, 1825

David embodied the late eighteenth-century revolutionary fervor in such austere, moralizing neoclassical works as *The Oath of the Horatii* (1784–85), *Brutus* (1789) and the *Death of Socrates* (1787). His theatrical, realistic paintings, recording the "martyrdoms" of Lepeletier de Saint-Fargeau, Marat, and Joseph Bara, served as virtual manifestos of the Revolution. After the fall of Robespierre, and a brief period of imprisonment during which he conceived what he regarded as his masterpiece in the "Greek" vein, *The Sabine Women* (1799), David turned his allegiance to the Empire. In the role of *premier peintre de l'Empereur* he executed the colossal *Coronation of the Emperor and Josephine* (1806–07) and the *Distribution of Eagles* (1810). His contributions to the subsequent development of French art proved enduring. Among the more than three hundred pupils to enter his studio between 1780 and 1816 were many of the future leaders of the romantic and neoclassical movements. Included in their number were the painters Drölling, Gérard, Girodet, Gros, Ingres and Isabey and the sculptors Bartolini, David d'Angers and Rude, to name but a few.

With the restoration of the Bourbon monarchy in 1816, David, as a former associate of Robespierre and a member of the National Convention which had condemned Louis XVI, fled to Brussels where he resided in exile until his death nine years later. There he was received by William I of the Low Countries, and welcomed by his enthusiastic Belgian followers. He continued to derive an income from the exhibition of his pictures, notably a replica of the *Coronation of the Emperor* and the *Mars and Venus* (1824), and to receive pupils, founding a school of Belgian neoclassical painting rivaling that of the Bruges painter, Joseph-Benoît Suvée. Among David's pupils were François-Joseph Navez (1787–1869) of Charleroi, as well as a number of less noted painters including J. D. Odevaere, J. Paelinch, J. A. Senave, M. G. Stapleaux, H. A. V. van der Haert and P. van Hanselaere. Navez had studied with the master in Paris from 1813 to 1816 and then had accompanied him in his exile to Brussels, although he was absent from Brussels from late 1817 to 1822. David's own production, in his last years, included a number of portraits that show no diminution in prowess, as well as several mythological subjects, a *Love and Psyche* (1817) and a *Mars Disarmed by Venus* (1821–24) painted in a more sensuous, languid, decorative style that marked a sharp departure from his earlier work.

Attributed To David

1. Portrait of Mme. Morel de Tangry?

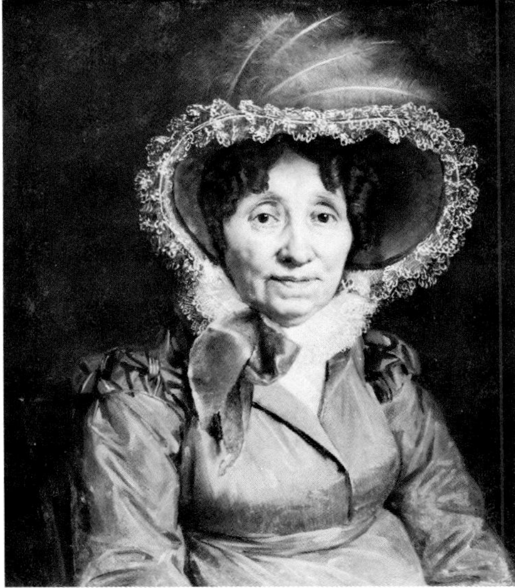

37.392 c.1820

The artist has portrayed a strong featured, vital looking old lady with unrestrained candor. She appears half-length and seated, staring directly outwards. Her dress includes a lace-trimmed bonnet decorated with plumes and tied beneath her chin with a blue ribbon, and a high-waisted, puce-colored redingote or outer garment. Except for a corner of the brown chair-back, the background is painted a neutral slate color.

This portrait has shared the vicissitudes in attribution and identification of the Louvre Museum's celebrated *The Three Women of Ghent* (R.F.902). When the latter painting, which received its name from an inscription on the envelope held by the central figure, was acquired by the Louvre in 1894, the subjects were identified by a descendant as Mme. Morel de Tangry and her two daughters. Mme. de Tangry, née Isabelle Rose van Tieghem (Chateau de Vichte: 1784 — Brussels: 1833) was the second wife of Anselme Louis Joseph Morel de Tangry (1727–1795), magistrate of Courtrai and president of a society, the Gard 'Olphe. *The Three Women of Ghent* has variously been described as one of the masterpieces in virile realism of the artist's years in exile, as a collaborative work of David and one of his pupils, and as a product of one of his Belgian pupils, most probably Navez.

The Baltimore painting is very similar stylistically to the group portrait and its subject has likewise been identified, by tradition and on the basis of similarities in physiognomy, as Mme. Morel de Tangry. It should be observed, however, that the lady in the Baltimore picture is shown with fuller lips and with fewer frown lines than her counterpart in the Louvre picture. Unfortunately, the burgomaster, Adolphe Max, made no mention of the single-figure portrait in his 1894 correspondence with the Louvre curator in which he identified his grandmother in the Paris painting, provided the picture's full history, and alluded to an earlier pastel showing her at the age of thirty. The artist's use of a canvas sold in Paris rather than in Brussels is also noteworthy and raises the possibility that the Baltimore painting was executed by a French rather than Belgian pupil.

Support: Fabric, .655 x .55 (25⅞" x 21⅝")

Marks: Stencil on canvas: *BELOT/Rue de L'Arbre Sec No 3/A Paris.* Labels on stretcher: *164/A Dumas,* in oval: *Massé* in oval: *2319* in rectangle: *Rue de Laval, 37/P Hombert Fils/Doreur Encadreur/Paris* in rectangle.

Label on frame: a clipping from the P.-A. Chéramy sale catalogue of 1908 identifying the subject as Mme. Morel de Tangry.

Condition: Cleaned 1936. Revarnished 1951. Lined and cleaned 1955. The paint in the lady's garments has become somewhat transluscent with age.

Provenance: Alexandre Dumas fils; P.-A. Chéramy Sale, Paris, May 7, 1908, no. 47.

Exhibitions: "Themes and Variations in Painting and Sculpture," Baltimore Museum of Art, 1948, no. 6; "From Ingres to Gauguin," Baltimore Museum of Art, 1951, no. 4; "Man and his Years," Baltimore Museum of Art, 1954, no. 52. "Problem Paintings: paintings without Authors," Vassar College Art Gallery, Poughkeepsie, N.Y., 1965, no. 23.

References:

Louis Rouart, "La collection de M. Chéramy," *Les Arts* 6, no. 64 (April 1907): 12 (illus.), 17; Walters cat., 1929, p. 87, no. 392; Aline B. Louchheim, "Do People or Portraits Change?" *Art News* 44, no. 5 (April 15, 1945): 11, illus.; Louis Hautecoeur, *Louis David.* Paris, La table ronde, 1954, p. 266.

Artist unknown, French School

2. Nude Boy

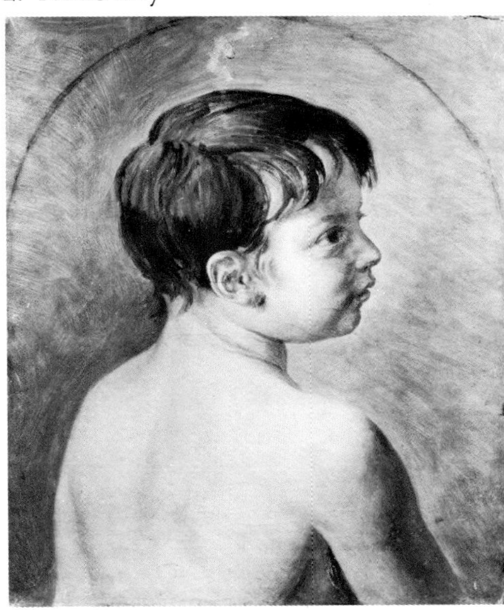

37.2005 French School, early 19th century

A nude, fair-haired boy is shown three-quarters length from the back. His head, turned to the right, is seen in profile. The background is rendered in thinly applied strokes of neutral beige and grey.

Support: Fabric, .458 x .378 (18" x 14⅞")

Marks: Stencil on reverse of original canvas: *BELOT/rue de l'Arbre Sec/No 5.*

Condition: Discolored varnishes were removed in 1948 and the surface was given a film of mastic varnish. A lining was applied with a wax adhesive in 1957.

Provenance: Gift of the Estate of Mrs. Frances Eaton Weld, 1947.

Pierre Nicolas Legrand

French-Swiss, Pont-L'Evêque, 1758 - Berne, 1829

The career of Legrand, a little-known painter of mythological subjects and portraits, bridged the transition in French painting from neoclassicism to romanticism. Legrand, who is known in France as Legrand (Sicot) and in Switzerland as Legrand de Sérant, trained at the Free School of Drawing in Rouen under J. B. Decamps, a pupil of Largillière, showing promise in drawing after the antique and after the nude. His first exhibition was in Lille in 1784. Though he had settled in Berne in 1794, Legrand exhibited in the Paris Salon of 1796, winning notice with his portrait of Joseph Cange, a prison guard remembered for his generosity during the Terror, and again, with less success, in the Salon of 1799. He next appeared at the Salon in 1814 with an allegorical sketch glorifying Louis XVIII's entry into Paris, and also figured prominently in exhibitions in Berne in 1818 and 1827.

In French public collections Legrand is represented by only one painting, a portrait of a man in the Musée F. Mandet, Riom, whereas in the museum in Berne there are eight of his paintings, including a highly neoclassical *Priam and his family weeping over Hector* and the more romantic *Cain killing Abel* and *The Fall of the Titans.*

Legrand also worked briefly as an illustrator.

3. The Apotheosis of Nelson

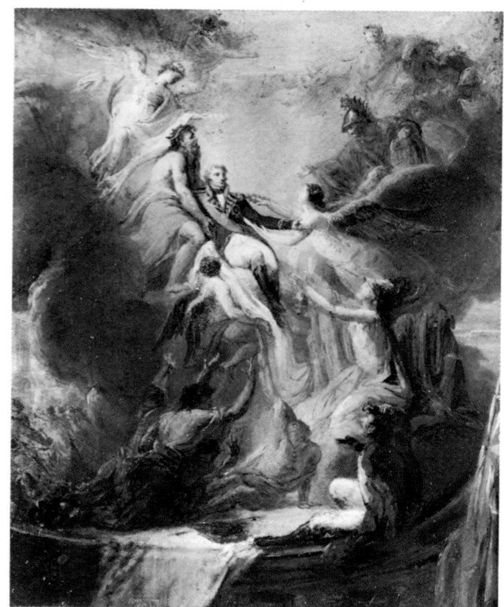

37.205 c.1816

This sketch preceded a project for an *Apotheosis of Nelson* that was exhibited by Legrand in Berne in 1818 and is now preserved in the Ferens Art Gallery, Hull (canvas, .604 x .495). The figures in the Walters sketch can be identified by following the 1818 Berne catalogue entry no. 51, transcribed by Michael Compton in a bulletin of the Ferens Art Gallery, Summer 1964, p. 6. Admiral Nelson, shown in the center, ascends to Olympus assisted by the crowned, bearded figure of Poseidon, Fame, the winged female who offers the hero a crown of laurel, and a winged male, not cited in the 1818 entry. Nelson is being received by the helmeted Mars and by other Olympians in the background. Above, the Goddess of Glory extends a crown of stars, symbolic of immortality, and the genius of negotiation, in the guise of Mercury, announces the hero's arrival. Seated behind Great Britain, who raises her arms in farewell, is the shrouded figure of one of the Fates. On the ship's bridge in the foreground, several crew members appear prostrated by grief while the battle still rages.

The final version differs from the Baltimore sketch principally in that Great Britain turns her head away in sorrow and Fame blows her trumpet while proffering the laurel wreath.

An earlier version of the subject in the Maritime Museum, Greenwich (canvas, .622 x .521) shows the composition reversed with Nelson erroneously lacking his left arm. An English private collection preserves a preliminary drawing (red and black chalk, white paper, .265 x .38) of the fallen marine in the right foreground, which is most closely related to the figure in the Greenwich picture. It was on the basis of the inscription, *Le Grand faciebat,* appearing at the bottom of the Greenwich painting that the Hull and Walters versions were attributed to Legrand. Formerly the Walters picture was attributed to Samuel Drummond (1765-1844).

Support: Paper mounted on canvas, .561 x .442 (22" x 17⅜")

Provenance: Unknown.

References: Walters cat., 1909, p. 69, no. 205 (as by Samuel Drummond); Michael Compton, "The Apotheosis of Nelson," *Ferens Art Gallery* (Summer 1964): 5–7.

Jean-Auguste-Dominique Ingres

French: Montauban, 1780 - Paris, 1867

Ingres, the chief advocate of the primacy of line and delineated form in painting, was indisputably successor to J.-L. David as leader of French neoclassicism. For visual inspiration, Ingres turned to the art of Antiquity, notably sculpture and pottery, to painting of the High Renaissance, especially the works of Raphael, and to his contemporary neoclassicists including John Flaxman. Though frequently pitted against Eugène Delacroix and the adherents of the Romantic movement, Ingres' themes were at times as varied and as exotic as were those of these opponents. His subjects were derived from classical mythology and ancient history, the "Celtic" mythology of James MacPherson, the lives of various great artists, the histories of France and Spain, religion and the "Orient." Above all, he was a consummate portraitist. Despite this range, Ingres' subjects were restricted in number and, recurrently throughout his career, he reworked earlier compositions as is evinced in the Walters by the *Oedipus and the Sphinx* and the *Odalisque with Slave.*

In his native Montauban, Ingres received a limited education from the Brothers of Christian Doctrine, as well as training in drawing and music from his father, Joseph Ingres. From 1791 to 1797, he was enrolled in the Academy of Toulouse, studying under J. G. Roques, De Vigan and J. Briant. He then transferred to Paris where he entered the studio of J.-L. David and, two years later, was admitted into the Ecole des Beaux-Arts. After several attempts he won in 1801 the Grand Prix de Rome, though it was not until five years later that he actually received the funds enabling him to travel to Rome. Meanwhile he began to participate without notable success in the Paris Salons and was particularly offended by the harsh criticisms of his entries in 1806. That winter he removed to Rome where he enjoyed the privileges of being pensionnaire at the Academy until 1810. During his first Italian sojourn, he was engaged in copying the old masters and producing several important works, including in 1808 the now lost *Sleeper of Naples,* a prototype for his later odalisques. After the expiration of his stipend, Ingres continued in Rome, completing his *Jupiter and Thetis,* which was unfavorably received at the Académie des Beaux-Arts in Paris in 1811, visiting Naples in 1814 to execute portraits of Queen Caroline Murat and her family, and supporting himself after the fall of the Bonapartes by drawing portraits of foreign visitors to Rome. At the encouragement of his friend, the sculptor Lorenzo Bartolini, Ingres left Rome in 1820 for Florence, where he copied Titian's masterpiece in the Pitti Palace, the *Venus of Urbino,* and worked on his monumental *Vow of Louis XIII.*

Ingres returned to Paris for the exhibition of the *Vow* at the Salon of 1824. The extraordinary reception accorded this work, which had been commissioned four years earlier for the Cathedral of Montauban, proved to be the turning point in his career. In 1825 he received the Cross of the Legion of Honor and was elected a member of the Académie des Beaux-Arts. The following year he was commissioned to paint *The Apotheosis of Homer* for the ceiling of the Charles

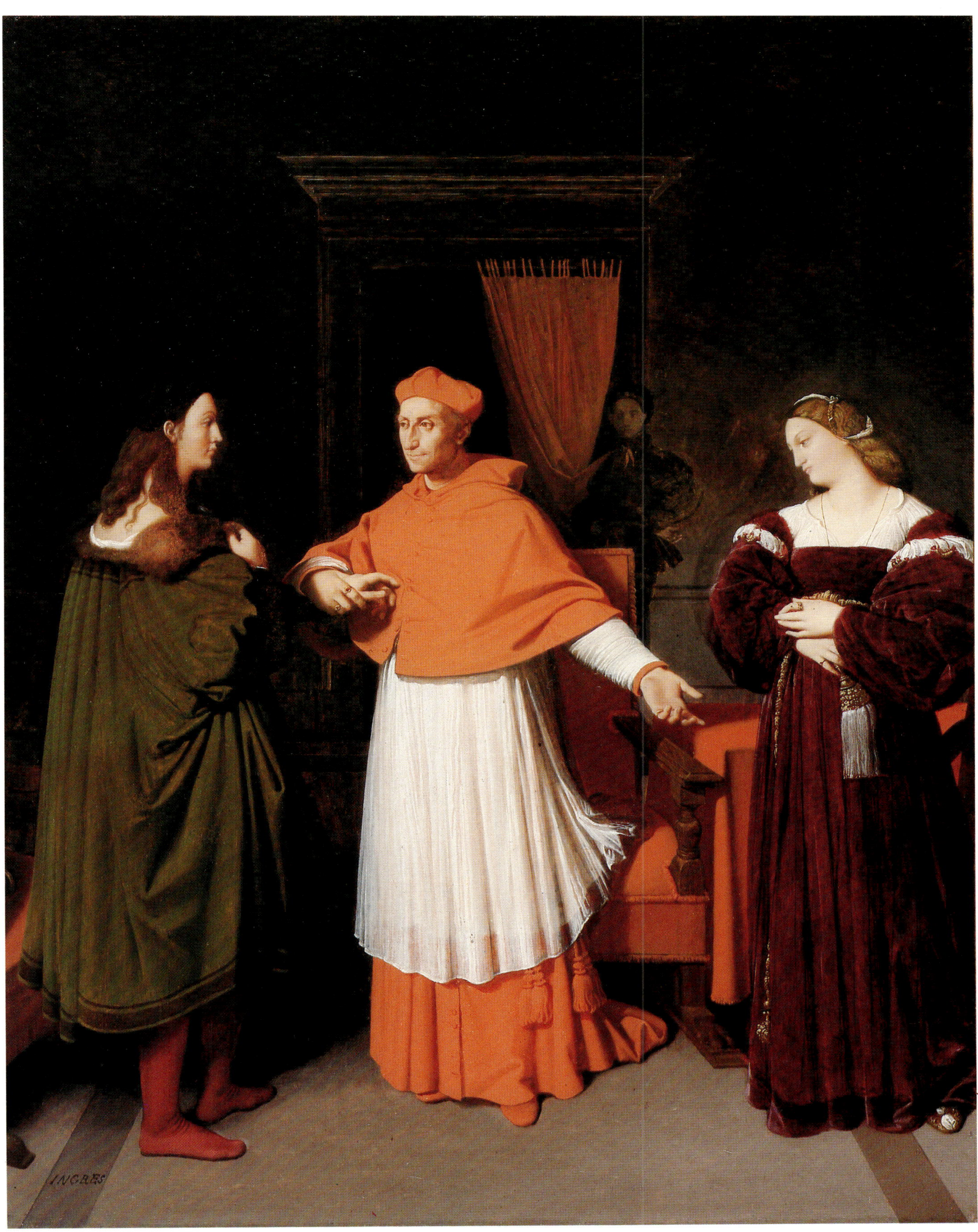

Ingres *The Betrothal of Raphael and the Niece of Cardinal Bibbiena*, no. 4

X Museum at the Louvre. Ingres' position within the Ecole des Beaux-Arts continued to improve—he was appointed professor in 1829, vice-president in 1832, and president in 1833.

Following a mixed reception of his altarpiece, *The Martyrdom of St. Symphorian,* at the Salon of 1834, Ingres returned to Rome where he admirably fulfilled the position of director of the French Academy from 1835 to 1841. Despite heavy administrative responsibilities, he was able to undertake several works, including an *Odalisque with Slave* commissioned by his friend M. Marcotte d'Argenteuil, which was begun in 1834 and completed in 1840.

In 1841 Ingres returned to France, where he enjoyed almost unmitigated success and acclaim for the remainder of his career, marred only by grief over the loss of his first wife in 1849. It was during the 40s that he produced many of his most celebrated portraits including those of the Duc d'Orléans (1842), the Comtesse d'Haussonville (1845) and Mme. Gonse (1845-1852). With the establishment of the Second Empire, Ingres' fortunes continued to grow. He was commissioned in 1853 to paint an *Apotheosis of Napoleon I* for the ceiling of the Salon de l'Empereur of the Paris Hôtel de Ville (destroyed in 1871), and in December that year he was appointed to serve with his rival Eugène Delacroix on the imperial commission for the 1855 Exposition Universelle. A selection of forty-three of his paintings and of twenty-five cartoons for stained-glass windows of the Chapels of Dreux and of Saint Ferdinand at Neuilly were featured in a special gallery at the Exposition. Napoleon III awarded him on this occasion the title Grand Officier of the Legion of Honor. In his later years Ingres was much involved in reworking subjects that he had first treated in his youth. Upon his death, his work was the subject of a vast exhibition at the Ecole des Beaux-Arts and the collections in his studio were transferred according to his wishes to the museum in his native Montauban.

4. The Betrothal of Raphael and the Niece of Cardinal Bibbiena

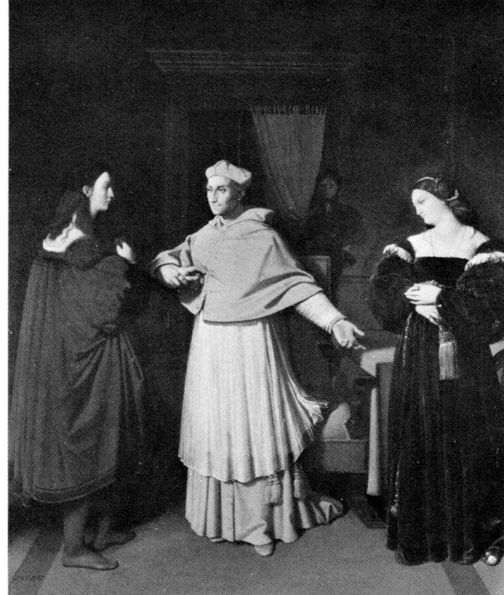

37.13 1813

Bernardo Dovizi il Bibbiena, a friend of Raphael since childhood, was appointed Cardinal by Leo X. Here he is seen offering his niece in marriage to the artist. She, unfortunately, proved frail and died prior to her wedding. A page stands behind them beside a doorway with a drawn curtain.

Ingres intended to produce a series of works illustrating the life of the artist whom he idolized. Eight incidents are cited by Delaborde in his "list of Ingres' projected works" (pp. 327–328): the birth of Raphael; Raphael taking his leave of the Duchess of Urbino; Raphael working on one of Perugino's paintings; Pope Julius II before the *Disputà;* Leo X and Raphael in the Loggia accompanied by Bramante and Bembo; Raphael entering court; Raphael on his deathbed and the Funeral of Raphael. None were realized as completed paintings although five versions of another Raphaelesque subject, *Raphael and La Fornarina,* were executed. The earliest, dated 1813, disappeared in Riga in 1941, whereas the others are located in the Fogg Museum, Cambridge; the Mrs. Francis Kettaneh collection, New York; the Columbus Gallery of Fine Arts (1840), and, in 1961, Knoedler and Company, New York (before 1850-finished 1860–65). In his notebooks, *Cahiers VII* and *IX,* Ingres noted a number of biographical sources for his study of Raphael: Vasari, Baglione, Passeri, Filippo Baldinucci and Conte Baldassare Castiglione. For the story of Raphael's betrothal, Ingres used, in particular, Abbé Angelo Comolli, *Vita inedita di Raffaelo da Urbino,* Rome, 1780, 2nd ed., 1791, excerpts of which are transcribed in his *Cahier VII.*

On May 26, 1814, Ingres mentioned in a letter to his friend, M. Marcotte d'Argenteuil, the pleasure he experienced in completing *The Betrothal of Raphael* within a short time (quoted in Delaborde, p. 227).

Five drawings are related to the Baltimore painting: two sketches in the Musée Ingres, Montauban, catalogued by Jules Momméja in *Collection Ingres au Musée de Montauban.* Inventaire général des richesses d'art de la France, 7, Paris, 1905, nos. 247 and 248; a highly finished drawing heightened with white, dated 1812, in the Louvre, cited by Henri Delaborde, in *Ingres, sa vie, ses travaux, sa doctrine,* Paris, 1870, no. 210; a wash drawing in a Paris private collection listed by Jacques Mathey in *Ingres, dessins,* Paris, 1955, no. 8; and a late replica in watercolor and graphite, dated 1864, in the Fogg Museum, Cambridge, shown in "Ingres Centennial Exhibition," Fogg Art Museum, Cambridge, 1967, no. 115. Several variations occur within these works. Only in the Walters painting does the page pull aside the draped curtain and in the Louvre and Fogg drawings the maiden's hand is clasped by the cardinal. Inscribed in the lintel above the door in the drawing is CARD BIBIANUS.

For his likeness of the young artist Ingres is believed to have drawn from Raphael's portrait of Bindo Altoviti in the National Gallery of Art, Washington, D.C. Ingres bequeathed to the museum in Montauban a rather mediocre copy of this portrait which was formerly identified as representing Raphael rather than Bindo Altoviti (Daniel Ternois, *Montauban-Musée Ingres, Peintures, Ingres et son temps,* Paris, 1965, no. 178). The likeness of the cardinal is based on Raphael's portrait of Bibbiena in the Pitti Palace, Florence.

The Betrothal of Raphael and the Niece of Cardinal Bibbiena was engraved by Réveil for Albert Magimel, *Oeuvres de J. A. Ingres,* Paris, 1851, plate 30.

Support: Oil on paper mounted on a double thickness of fabric with a glue adhesive, .593 x .463 (23⅜" x 18¼"), the paper surface is about .07 (¼") less than the stretcher measurements on all four sides.

Signed lower left: *INGRES.*

Marks: Paper label on stretcher of *DURAND-RUEL/Paris 16 rue Laffite/New York 315 Fifth Avenue/Ingres No. 834/Le Cardinal Bibiena presentant sa niece à Raphael.* Sticker: *66.*

Stencil on canvas lining: *American Art Association/Mrs. S. D. Warren Sale/January 8th, 1903.*

Inscribed in ink on stretcher: *Mrs. S. D. Warren, 67 Mt. Vernon St./Boston.*

Condition: Readily visible are an inverted L tear in the upper right corner and a long vertical tear extending through the Cardinal's hat. Small losses along the bottom edge have been inpainted. Discolored varnishes were removed in 1961. Removal of discolored varnish and previous inpaintings in 1981 revealed remnants of an inscription in the lintel of the door.

Provenance: Painted in 1813 for Caroline Murat, Queen of Naples; Prince of Salerno Sale, Naples, April 19, 1852, no. 118; Collection Giuseppe Tibaldi, Naples; Ch. Blanc Sale, Paris, March 13–15, 1882, no. 33; Collection L. Tabourier; Mrs. S. D. Warren, Boston, Sale, New York, January 8–9, 1903, no. 52.

Exhibitions: "Catalogue des tableaux, études peintes, dessins et croquis de J.-A.-D. Ingres," Ecole impériale des Beaux-Arts, Paris, 1867, no. 581; "From Ingres to Gauguin," Baltimore Museum of Art, 1951, no. 5. "Ingres in American Collections," Paul Rosenberg & Co., New York, 1961, no. 10; "Ingres et son temps," Musée

Ingres, Montauban, 1967, no. 45. "Ingres," Petit Palais, Paris, 1967–68, no. 63.

References: J. A. D. Ingres, *Cahier IX,* ms. (Musée Ingres, Montauban); *Cahier X,* ms. (private collection); Albert Magimel, *Oeuvres de J. A. Ingres.* Paris, Firmin Didot, 1851, plate 30; Henri Delaborde, *Ingres, sa vie, ses travaux, sa doctrine.* Paris, H. Plon, 1870. pp. 226–27, no. 56; Jules Momméja, "La correspondance d'Ingres," *Réunion des Sociétés des Beaux-Arts des Départements* 12 (1888): 737–40; Henry Lapauze, *Les dessins de J. A. D. Ingres du Musée de Montauban.* Paris, J. E. Bulloz, 1901, pp. 129, 216; Walters cat. 1909, no. 13, and subsequent Walters catalogues; Henry Lapauze, *Ingres, sa vie et son oeuvre.* Paris, G. Petit, 1911. pp. 148, 150; Edward S. King, "Ingres as classicist," *JWAG* 5 (1942) : 77, 105, n. 52 and 53; Jean Alazard, *Ingres et l'Ingrisme.* Paris, Michel, 1950. pp. 54–55, plate XLIII; Georges Wildenstein, *Ingres.* London, Phaidon Press, 1954. pp. 176–77, no. 85, plate 37; Norman Schlenoff, *Ingres, ses sources littéraires.* Paris, Presses universitaires de France, 1956. p. 137; Richard H. Randall, Jr., "Ingres and Titian," *Apollo* 82 (1965): 366; *Ingres centennial exhibition, 1867–1967,* Fogg Art Museum, Harvard University (no. 115 is a related watercolor) ; Ettore Camesasca, *L'Opera completa di Ingres.* Classici dell'arte, 19. Milan, Rizzoli, 1968. p. 95, no. 76, illus.; James H. Beck. *Raphael.* Library of great painters. New York, Abrams, 1976. p. 53, fig. 65; Tokiko Suzuki, *Ingres,* 25 great masters of modern art, 1. Tokyo, Kodansha, 1981, p. 115, no. 25, illus., plate 25.

5. Reclining Venus

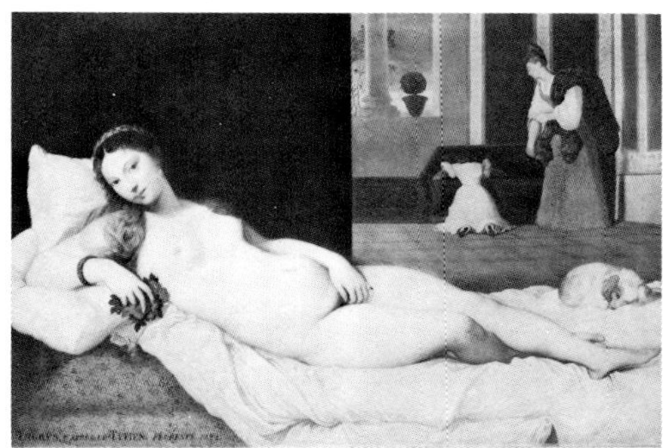

37.2392 1822

Abraham Constantin, a painter of porcelains, relates how Ingres worked at his side in the Uffizi in Florence, copying Titian's *Venus of Urbino.* He alleges that Ingres' copy was intended as an aid for Lorenzo Bartolini, who was engaged in producing a sculpture of the reclining Venus. It was Bartolini, a friend of Ingres since their days together in David's atelier, who had persuaded the young painter to leave Rome for Florence and who had provided him with accomodations. Bartolini's plaster model of the figure is in the Gipsoteca Bartoliniana in Florence and the marble, commissioned by the Marquess of Londonderry, is in the Musée Fabre, Montpellier. Constantin's copy on porcelain is preserved in the Galleria Sabauda, Turin, as noted by R. H. Randall.

Ingres' copy differs from Titian's painting in that the tones are cooler, the swag of drapery above the head of Venus eliminated, the fabric design on the couch emphasized, and the pavement pattern and architectural detail in the background reduced or eliminated.

Support: Canvas, coarse weave, 1.160 x 1.678 (45⅝" x 66⅛")

Signed and dated lower left: *INGRES D'APRES LE TITIEN, FLORENCE 1822*

Condition: Discolored varnishes removed in 1966.

Provenance: Bequeathed by Ingres to Armand Cambon, 1866; sold to the expert Haro, October 6, 1866; Ingres Sale, Paris, May 6–7, 1867, no. 2; Khalil Bey Sale, Paris, January 10–18, 1868, no. 35, 10,000 francs; Wandé collection, Lille (1870); Purchased by Henry Walters prior to 1931.

Exhibitions: "Catalogue des tableaux, études peintes, dessins et croquis de J.-A.-D. Ingres," Ecole impériale des Beaux-Arts, Paris, 1867, no. 25.

References: J. A. D. Ingres, *Cahier IX,* ms. (Musée Ingres, Montauban); *Cahier X,* ms. (Private collection); Théophile Gautier, *Khalil-Bey collection,* sale, Paris, January 16–18, 1868. Introduction and no. 35; Henri Delaborde, *Ingres, sa vie, ses travaux, sa doctrine.* Paris, H. Plon, 1870. pp. 263–64, no. 164; Jules Momméja, *Ingres, biographie critique.* Les grands artistes. Paris, H. Laurens, 1903. pp. 61, 76; A. J. Boyer d'Agen, *Ingres d'après une correspondance inédite.* Paris, H. Daragon, 1909. p. 460; Henry Lapauze, *Ingres, sa vie et son oeuvre.* Paris, G. Petit, 1911. pp. 214, 552, no. 24; Danielle Plan, *A. Constantin, peintre sur émail et sur porcelaine.* Geneva, 1930. p. 61; Georges Wildenstein, *Ingres.* London, Phaidon Press, 1954. p. 193, no. 149 (erroneous measurements) ; Norman Schlenoff, *Ingres, ses sources littéraires.* Paris, Presses universitaires de France, 1956. p. 249, n. 2; Agnes Mongan, "Ingres," *Encyclopedia of world art.* 15 vols. New York, McGraw-Hill, 1959–68. 8: col. 122; Richard H. Randall, Jr., "Ingres and Titian," *Apollo* 82 (1965) : 366–69, fig. 2; Ettore Camesasca, *L'Opera completa di Ingres.* Classici dell'arte, 19. Milan, Rizzoli, 1968. p. 101, no. 108, illus.

6. Odalisque with Slave

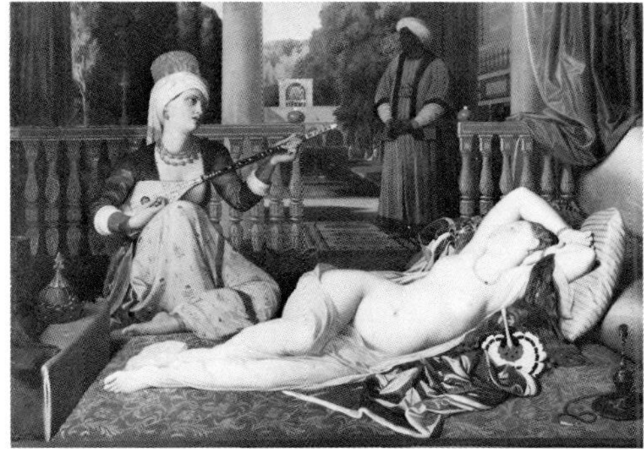

37.887 1842

Ingres' deliberate development of a theme over many years is illustrated by this work. The germ for the painting is thought to have been the so-called *Sleeper of Naples* of 1808 which disappeared with the fall of the French ruling house in 1815. As a pendant for the *Sleeper,* Ingres completed in 1814 *La Grande Odalisque,* Musée du Louvre (R.F. 1158) in which the subject looks over her shoulder with her back to the viewer. The first version of the *Odalisque with Slave* (canvas .716 x .995) in The Fogg Art Museum, Cambridge, Mass. (1943.251) dated 1839, was painted in Rome by Ingres for his friend, Charles Marcotte d'Argenteuil. It has been interpreted as Ingres' response to the orientalism prevalent in the 1830s and in particular to the success of Delacroix's *Women of Algiers in Their Harem* of 1834. In his representation of the langorous odalisque stretched across glistening fabrics, apparently enraptured by the music of her slave, Ingres captured the sensual exoticism that was associated with the eastern harem.

A number of drawings related to the *Odalisque with Slave* have survived. One sketch of the odalisque in the Musée Ingres, Montauban (Inv. 867.2030), bears an inscription identifying the model as Mariuccia, a blonde belle who lived at via Marguta 106, whereas in another sketch in the Petit Palais, Paris (Inv. 1157), she is identified as Mencuccia of via della Vita 58. In a second preliminary sketch in Montauban (Inv. 867. 2029), the odalisque and slave are portrayed with two additional attendants in the foreground. A highly finished drawing of the odalisque's head and torso, perhaps of later date, is preserved in the collection of the Dowager Lady Aberconway, London. Sketches for the slave are to be seen in Montauban, Inv. 867.2032 and 867.2031, and in the British Museum. Replicas of the entire composition include a watercolor belonging to Dr. and Mrs. T. Edward Hanley of Bradford, Pa., (.324 x .407) dated 1839, and a much later drawing in pencil and wash, heightened with white, made for Emile Galichon in 1858 (Louvre, R.F. 4622).

The compositional sketch in Montauban (Inv. 867.2029) bears inscriptions in which the principal figure is alternately identified as a "sultane" and as an Italian woman taking a siesta. This potentially Italian theme spawned another series of works, including three paintings of a sleeping nude, one in the Victoria and Albert Museum, London, another in a Paris private collection and a third now unlocated, and ultimately the *Jupiter and Antiope,* dated 1851, in the Musée du Louvre (R.F. 2521) in which the supine figure of the mythological maiden is identical in pose to that of the odalisque of the *Odalisque with Slave.*

The Walters painting, commissioned by King Wilhelm I of Württemberg and dated 1842, is a variant rather than a replica of the Fogg Art Museum picture. A principal difference is that the background, rather than being closed, opens to a vista of a garden with a pool, arbors, and pavilions. Other variations include a difference in the positioning of the slave in relation to the balustrade, the suppression of the red and green floral pattern brocaded on the silvery garments of the standing attendant, and the substitution of a western carpet with a two-toned floral design for the rectilinear lozenge pattern of the earlier picture. Correspondence between Charles Marcotte, the original owner of the Fogg Museum painting, and Edouard Gatteaux, who managed the artist's financial affairs, has been published by Hans Naef. The patron noted that when Ingres requested permission to paint a replica of the Odalisque he consented with the provision that certain changes be made. He also observed that the replica was not entirely by Ingres (n. 26). Gatteaux, however, consistently alluded to the Baltimore picture as a copy by Paul Flandrin, given final touches by Ingres (n. 31). Lapauze and Thoré concur that Ingres employed the assistance of his pupil Paul Flandrin in this work, particularly in painting the garden vista in the background. That the pupil was responsible for this feature was recently confirmed by the appearance in the Paris art market of an oil sketch on paper (.25 x .33) showing the trees and the pool with the swans but lacking the figures, which was inscribed: *Fait en compagnie d'Ingres/parc du chateau de Dampière/Flandrin.*

Support: Fabric, .76 x 1.054 (30" x 41½")

Signed and dated at lower left: *J. Ingres/1842*

Condition: Discolored varnishes and overpainting were removed in 1948, revealing that the picture's support had been extensively damaged by tears and slashes. The torso of the odalisque had suffered in particular. Other damages included a tear extending from the upper left corner through the odalisque's ankles to the bottom edge, slashes through the knees of the musician and a scratch in the shape of a square in the trees of the background. The paint losses were subsequently inpainted in water-color.

Provenance: Painted for Wilhelm I, King of Württemberg. Collections of Delessert (6,000 francs); Baron Gustave de Rothschild; Sir Philip Sassoon, London; Wildenstein & Co. New York; Henry Walters, 1925, purchased with encouragement of Bryson Burroughs.

Exhibitions: Chez M. Léopold, Boulevard Italien, Paris, ca. 1842; "The 19th century Heritage," Paul Rosenberg & Co., New York, 1950, no. 11; "Diamond Jubilee Exhibition," Philadelphia Museum of Art, 1950–51, no. 51; "From Ingres to Gauguin," Baltimore Museum of Art, 1951, no. 6; "Masterpieces of French Painting," Isaac Delgado Museum of Art, New Orleans, 1953–54, no. 53; "French Pre-Impressionist Painters," Winnipeg Art Gallery, 1954, no. 10; "Inaugural Exhibition," Fort Worth Art Center, 1954, no. 42; "De David à Toulouse-Lautrec," Orangerie, Paris, 1955, no. 37; "Art from Ingres to Pollock," University of California, Berkeley, 1960, pp. 16, 52, illus.; "Ingres in American Collections," Paul Rosenberg & Co., New York, 1961, no. 52; "The Romantic Era," Herron Museum of Art, Indianapolis, 1965, no. 29; "Ingres et son temps," Musée Ingres, Montauban, 1967, no. 114; "An Exhibition of Treasures of the Walters Art Gallery," Wildenstein and Co., New York, 1967, no. 44; "Ingres," Petit Palais, Paris, 1967–68, no. 198.

References: J. A. D. Ingres, *Cahier X*, ms. (Private collection); Théophile Thoré, *Les Salons de T. Thoré, 1844, 1845, 1846, 1847, 1848.* 2nd ed. Paris, Librairie de Ve Jules Renouard, 1870, p. 351; A. J. Boyer d'Agen, *Ingres d'après une correspondance inédite.* Paris, H. Daragon, 1909. pp. 298–300, 349; Henry Lapauze, *Ingres, sa vie et son oeuvre.* Paris, G. Petit, 1911. p. 352; Edward S. King, "Ingres as a classicist," *JWAG* 5 (1942: 79–80; Jean Alazard, *Ingres et l'Ingrisme.* Paris, Michel, 1950. pp. 113–14, plate CVII; Frank Elgar, *Ingres.* Paris, Editions du chêne, 1951. plate XV; Georges Wildenstein, *Ingres.* London, Phaidon Press, 1954. p. 213, no. 237, plate 83; Norman Schlenoff, *Ingres, ses sources littéraires.* Paris, Presses universitaires de France, 1956. plate XLVII; François Fosca, *French painting: XIX century painters, 1800–1870.* New York, Universe Books, 1960. pp. 39 (illus.), 42; Robert Rosenblum, *Jean-Auguste-Dominique Ingres.* The Library of great painters. New York, Abrams, 1967. plate 38; Gaëtan Picon, *Ingres.* The Taste of our time, 47. Geneva, Skira, 1967. pp. 59 (illus.), 60 (illus. of detail); Jacques Paul Dauriac, "'Ingres' au Petit Palais," *Pantheon* 26 (1968): 66 (illus.), 68; Ettore Camesasca, *L'Opera completa di Ingres.* Classici dell'arte, 19. Milan, Rizzoli, 1968. pp. 106 (illus.), 107, no. 128b; Hans Naef, "Odalisque à l'esclave by J. A. D. Ingres," *Fogg Art Museum Acquisitions 1968.* Cambridge, Mass., 1968. pp. 80–98, fig. 2; Toshio Nishimura, ed., *Ingres et Delacroix.* Les grands maîtres de la peinture moderne, 3. Tokyo, Chuokoron-Sha, 1972, plate 7, p. 107, illus.; Barbara H. Cartland, *Barbara Cartland's book of love and lovers.* New York, Ballantine Books, 1978. p. 103 (illus.); Gwendolyn Owens, "Pioneers in American museums: Bryson Burroughs," *Museum News* 57, no. 5 (May-June 1979): 49 (illus.); Gaëtan Picon, *Jean-Auguste-Dominique Ingres.* Discovering the nineteenth century. New York, Skira/Rizzoli, 1980. pp. 69 (illus.), 71 (illus.).

7. Oedipus and the Sphinx

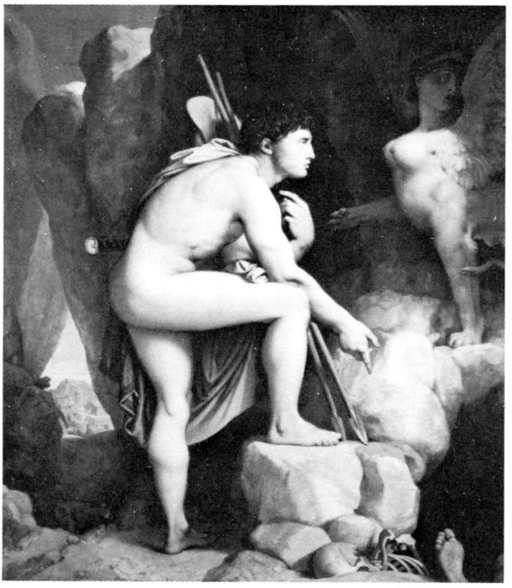

37.9 1864

The story of Oedipus and the Sphinx is told in Apollodorus, *The Library* III, V. 8. The Sphinx has posed her riddle "What is that which has one voice and yet becomes four-footed, two-footed, and three footed?" and Oedipus has replied that it is "man, for as a babe he is four-footed, going on four limbs, as an adult he is two-footed, and as an old man he gets a third support in a staff." Hearing the correct response, the monster turns her head away in surprise and anger and enters into a state of fury that will end with her dashing herself to pieces on the rocks below.

The setting is a rocky cavern. Jutting from the sphinx's lair at the lower right are the macabre remnants of her victims. At the left, two spectators watch the event from a boulder, and visible beyond, through openings in the rocks, are glimpses of the sky above and the town of Thebes below. As for the figure of the nude Oedipus seen in profile, historians differ regarding the artist's source, presumably a piece of ancient statuary or decorated pottery.

This subject was recurrent in Ingres' work. The earliest version, the *Oedipus and the Sphinx* (1.89 x 1.44), dated 1808, in the Louvre (R.F. 218), Ingres' *envoi de Rome,* sent from Rome to Paris according to the regulations of the Ecole des Beaux-Arts in 1808, was expanded on both sides and at the top prior to being exhibited at the Salon of 1827. In it and in two variants in the National Gallery, London, (.178 x .137) and in the Musée d'Angers (1.60 x .95), c. 1829, the scene is reversed. These earlier pictures also vary from the Baltimore work in that Oedipus' left hand is raised as he addresses the Sphinx rather than pointing downward to the beast's lair, and there is but one gesticulating spectator in the middle ground. Since there are no other versions recorded, it is presumably to the Walters painting that Jean Gigoux alluded when he discussed a reduced interpretation seen shortly before Ingres' death. With this work the artist hoped to surpass his first version.

A number of drawings for the Walters painting (nos. 2176–2196) are preserved in the Musée Ingres, Montauban, and in the Ecole des Beaux-Arts, and drawings for the earlier version of the composition are in the Musée Bonnat, Bayonne.

Support: Canvas, 1.055 x .87 (41½" x 34¼")

Signed and dated lower center: *J. Ingres fbat/etatis/LXXXIII/1864*

Condition: Discolored varnishes removed and replaced with synthetic varnish in 1961. Damages include a small loss on Oedipus' left leg and a long crack on his right thigh. Losses also apparent along the contours of Oedipus and in the figure of the spectator climbing the rock.

Provenance: Painted for M. Emile Pereire; Pereire Sale, Paris, 1872, March 6–9, no. 26, 25,600 francs; Secrétan Sale, Paris, July 1–7, 1889, no. 37; P.-A. Chéramy Sale, Paris, May 5–7, 1908, no. 208.

Exhibitions: "Catalogue des tableaux, études peintes, dessins et croquis de J.-A.-D. Ingres," Ecole impérial des Beaux-Arts, Paris, 1867, no. 24; "From Ingres to Gauguin," Baltimore Museum of Art, 1951, no. 8; "Flight: Fantasy, Faith, Fact," Dayton Art Institute and Columbus Institute of Fine Arts, 1953–54, no. 58; "Ingres in American Collections," Paul Rosenberg & Co., New York, 1961, no. 72; "Masterpieces of Art," Seattle World's Fair, 1962, no. 38; "Man: the Glory, Jest and Riddle," California Palace of the Legion of Honor, San Francisco, 1964–65, no. 194; "Neo-Classicism: Style and Motif," Cleveland Museum of Art, 1964, no. 131; "From El Greco to Pollock," Baltimore Museum of Art, 1968, no. 72.

References: Henri Delaborde, *Ingres, sa vie, ses travaux, sa doctrine.* Paris, H. Plon, 1870. p. 212; Jean Gigoux, *Causeries sur les artistes de mon temps.* Paris, Calmann Levy, 1885. p. 92; Henry Lapauze, *Ingres, sa vie et son oeuvre.* Paris, G. Petit, 1911. p. 90; Edward S. King, "Ingres as a classicist," *JWAG* 5 (1942): 70–76, fig. 1; Jean Alazard, *Ingres et l'ingrisme.* Paris, Michel, 1950. p. 42, plate XII; P. H. Polak, "De invloed van enige monumenten der oudheid op het classicisme van David, Ingres en Delacroix," *Nederlandsch kunsthistorisch jaarboek* (1948–1949):301; Georges Wildenstein, *Ingres.* London, Phaidon Press, 1954. p. 173, fig. 32; p. 231, no. 315; Norman Schlenoff, *Ingres, ses sources littéraires.* Paris, Presses universitaires de France, 1956. cover and plate XIII; Daniel Ternois, "Ingres" catalogue, Petit Palais, Paris, 1967–68, p. 60; Ettore Camesasca, *L'Opera completa di Ingres.* Classici dell'arte, 19. Milan, Rizzoli, 1968. p. 40, fig. 50C.

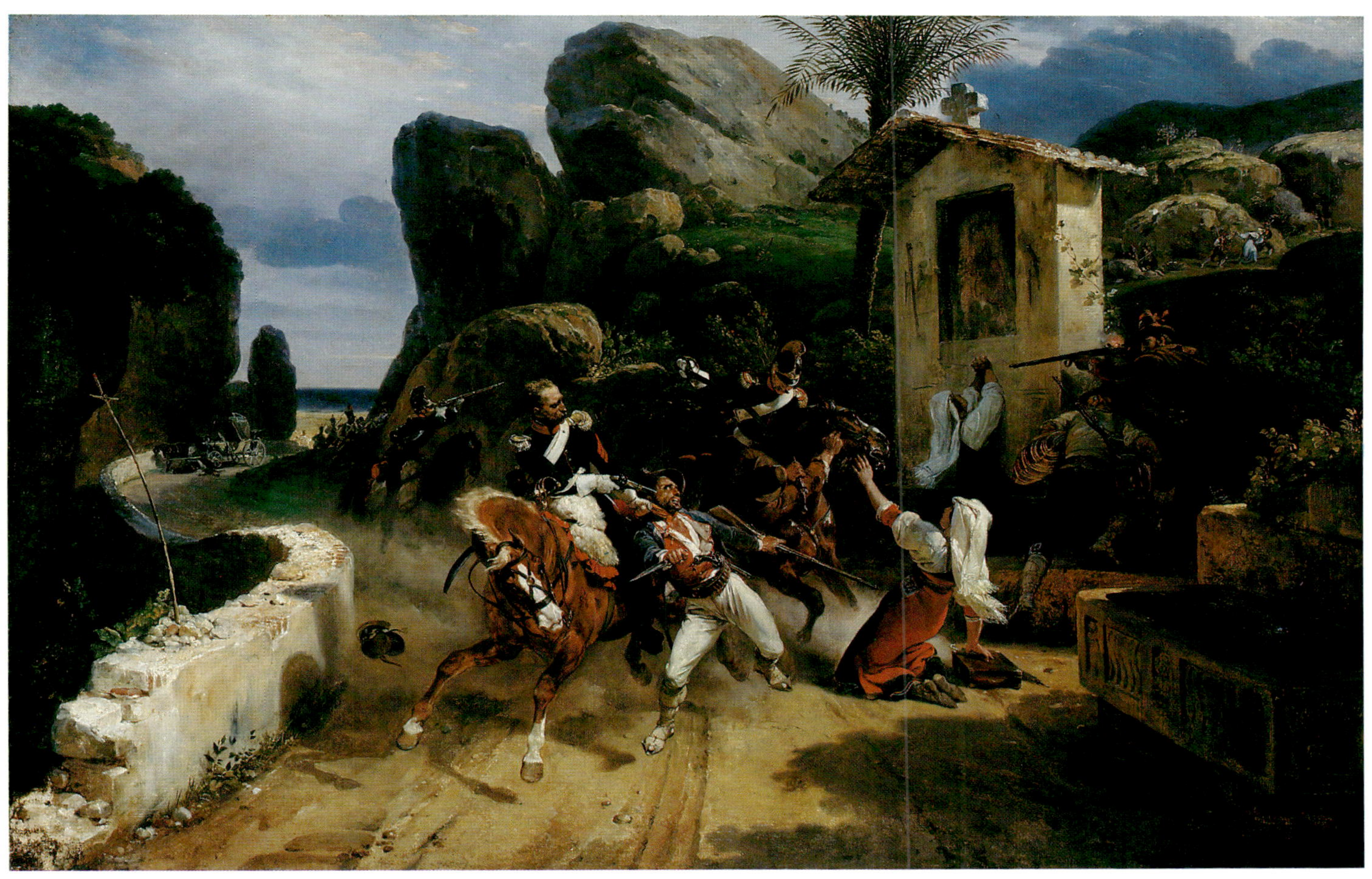

Vernet *Italian Brigands Surprised by Papal Troops,* no. 8

Emile-Jean-Horace Vernet
French: Paris, 1789 - Paris, 1863

Horace Vernet, the *juste milieu* painter of historical subjects, particularly military events, oriental themes and portraits, is remembered chiefly for his monumental battle paintings at Versailles. He represented the third generation of a distinguished family of artists, his grandfather being Joseph, and his father Carle Vernet.

In his youth he trained under his maternal grandfather, Jean-Michel Moreau, and in the studio of François-André Vincent. At the Salon of 1812 he received a first–class medal for several military and equestrian subjects. Two years later Vernet participated in the defense of Paris, was appointed a chevalier of the Legion of Honor and subsequently recorded these experiences in *The Clichy Gate* (Louvre). A confirmed Bonapartist, he was patronized by King Jérôme of Westphalia and by the Empress Marie-Louise. In 1820 he made his first trip to Rome, painting there *The Start of the Riderless Race* (study in The Metropolitan Museum of Art, New York). During his early years he was also active as an engraver and pioneered in the use of lithography.

In 1822, after seven of his paintings were rejected by the Salon jury on the grounds that they were politically seditious, Vernet received the public in his studio initiating the phase of his career that was the most popularly acclaimed. Despite his anti-royalist sentiments, he received commissions from Charles X for a ceiling decoration in the Louvre and for a painting *The Battles of Bouvines and Fontenoy*. His principal patron was the Duc d'Orléans who commissioned a number of battle subjects. In 1826 Vernet was elected a member of the Institut and between 1828 and 1835 he served as director of the French Academy in Rome.

The years following his return from Rome in 1835 were marked by the commissions from Louis Philippe for vast battle paintings for the Hall of Constantine in Versailles and by his numerous travels which took him to Algeria in 1835, 1837, and 1845, to Saint Petersburg in 1836, 1838 and 1842 and to the Middle East in 1839–40. Vernet's production after the 1848 Revolution was one of diminishing returns artistically. He did, however, paint the *Battle of The Alma,* recording an episode of the Crimean War for Prince Napoleon, the Emperor's cousin; was honored with a special exhibit at the 1855 Exposition Universelle and, several weeks before his death, was made a Grand Officier of the Legion of Honor.

8. Italian Brigands Surprised by Papal Troops

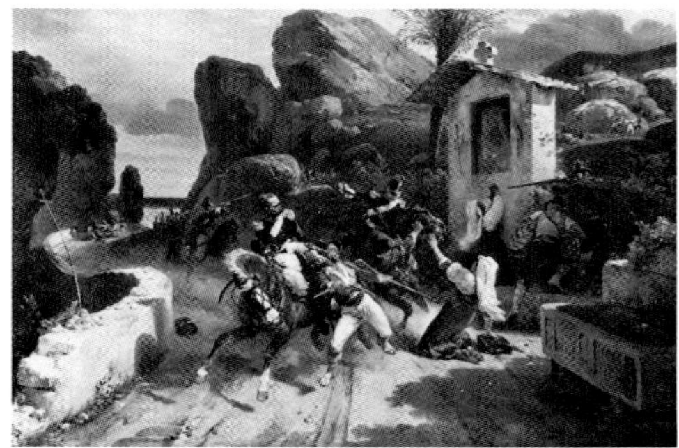

37.54 1831

Papal troops have surprised brigands in the process of looting a carriage. In the central foreground, two dragoons, one with a pistol and the other a saber, are about to despatch a couple of brigands on foot. A peasant woman with a stolen escritoire and umbrella has fallen on her knees, raising a hand in supplication, while a companion desperately prays before a wayside shrine. As a brigand fires his musket from the side of the shrine, he is joined by another who scampers up the slope with a bag and a chest under his arms. Further down the road, to the left, is a dragoon firing his carbine, a detachment of soldiers preparing to ascend the hills, and, in the distance, the coach with a slain horse and postilion. To the right, brigands fire from the rocks, while a lady dressed in blue is being led away as hostage. A strigilated sarcophagus in the immediate right foreground serves as basin for a spring. Such scenes of brigandage remained common in the Apennines until late in the last century.

This work is one of several related paintings executed by Vernet during his tenure at the French Academy in Rome. In an account book entitled *Horace Vernet, marié avec Louise Pujol le 15 Avril 1811/a reçu de travaux executés par lui,* published by Armand Dayot (p. 211), the artist noted for July 31, 1831, *Reçu de M.H. Vernet remis à M. Pigneux Cette somme doit être pour paiement du Combat des brigands et pour la Confession des brigands . . . 9000 fr* and for August 9, that year, he recorded a payment of 1500 francs from M. Jazet for permission to engrave the *Combat des brigands.*

An issue not fully resolved concerns the signature and date of this work which has traditionally been deciphered as reading *H Vernet/Paris 1830.* Since Vernet did not return to Paris that year and because of the difficulty in reading the inscription, which is in an area of the painting that has suffered from abrasion, it may be assumed that originally it read *Roma* rather than *Paris* and that an early restorer incorrectly reinforced the artist's writing. A signed pen and wash drawing of the entire composition (.364 x .521) has recently appeared on the Paris art market.

Support: Fabric, .856 x 1.31 (33 11/16" x 51 9/16")

Signed and dated lower right on sarcophagus end: *H Vernet/Paris (?) 1830*

Condition: Lined prior to 1938. Cleaned and lined in 1969. Some inpainting in bottom right corner near signature. Losses along bottom edges and lower left corner.

Provenance: John T. Johnston Collection, New York, December, 1876, no. 146.

Exhibitions: Paris, Salon of 1831; "The Romantic Circle," Wadsworth Atheneum, Hartford, 1952, no. 10; "War à la Mode," The Walters Art Gallery, 1977, no. W8.

References: Strahan, 1:94; Walters cat., 1878, p. 14, and subsequent Walters catalogues; Armand Dayot, *Les Vernet.* Paris, Magnier, 1898. pp. 127 (illus. with engraving by Jazet), 128, 211; William Hauptman, "Charles Gleyre: Tradition and Innovation" in *Charles Gleyre* (exhibition catalogue), Grey Art Gallery and Study Center, New York, 1980, p. 19, fig. 10.

Jean-Louis André Théodore Géricault
French: Rouen, 1791 - Paris, 1824

Géricault's formal training was limited to brief periods in the studios of Carle Vernet (1808–10) and of the neoclassicist Pierre Guérin (1810–11). He also studied in the Louvre which had temporarily been enriched with Napoleon's spoils from Italy. His first Salon entry, *Officer of the Imperial Guard,* shown in 1812, was followed in 1814 by the *Wounded Cuirassier.* He himself served briefly in the Royal Household Cavalry. Failing to win the Prix de Rome, Géricault traveled to Italy at his own expense, and while in Rome witnessed in February 1817 the horse race that inspired a series of studies intended for a large-scale painting, never realized. He returned to Paris that year, turned to lithography and, in 1818, began work on his masterpiece, *The Raft of the Medusa.* When it was exhibited at the Salon of 1819, the political ramifications of the subject aroused the public's attention more than did artistic considerations. Not until later was it recognized as a landmark in the evolution of French art in which realistic, classical, and romantic trends all converged. Géricault accompanied the picture on a traveling exhibition in Great Britain in 1820–21 and while there developed an interest in English art, as reflected in his lithographs and watercolors. He returned to France in 1822 in failing health, continued working but completed no major projects, though he did paint a number of revolutionary smaller works such as his portraits of the insane. In January 1824 he died of tuberculosis of the spine.

9. Riderless Racers at Rome

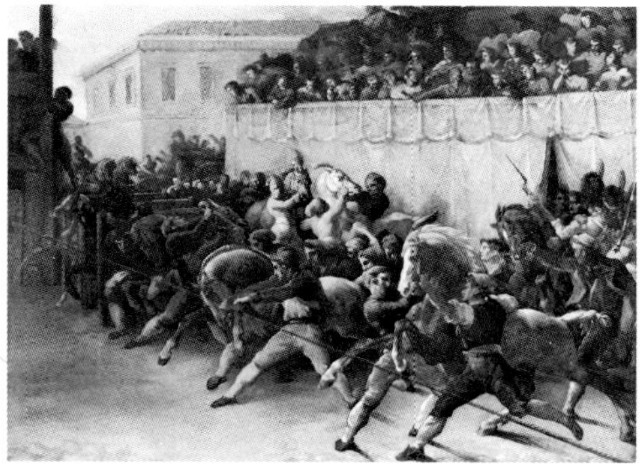

37.189 1817

From the mid fifteenth century until 1874, the Carnival of Rome traditionally closed with the *corsa dei barberi,* the race of the Barbary horses. At the firing of cannons two lines of infantrymen cleared an opening among the revelers and a detachment of dragoons galloped the length of the route on the Via del Corso extending from the Porta del Popolo to the Palazzo di Venezia. The start of the race was announced by the sound of a trumpet and its close by firing of cannons. The riderless horses, decked with plumage and exacerbated by balls of lead spiked with steel tips dangling against their flanks and by strips of metal foil flapping from their backs, usually covered the course in less than two and a half minutes.

The spectacle was described by Goethe in 1788 (*Goethes Werke,* Stuttgart 1860, 20: 176) and by Alexandre Dumas (*Le Comte de Monte Cristo,* Paris, 1888, 2: 291–92) and was recorded by a number of artists: F. Muccinelli painted *La mossa de Barberi* in 1781; David Allan made a drawing now in Windsor Castle; Giuseppe Bossi was author of several drawings (discussed by L. Eitner in *Géricault* (catalogue) Los Angeles, Detroit, Philadelphia, 1971–72, p. 84); G. B. Delera, active at the beginning of the 19th century, showed the start of the races using ancient Rome as the setting; Antoine Thomas was responsible for a lithograph showing the start of the race in a contemporary setting; Horace Vernet, in 1820, painted *La Mossa,* now known only through a lithograph by Peter Wagner and through a study in the Metropolitan Museum of Art, New York, Inv. 87.15.47; and his father Carle Vernet executed the *Riderless Horse Race* in the Musée Calvet, Avignon in 1826.

Géricault, an ardent equestrian, was drawn to the event in February 1817, and undertook a series of studies for a monumental painting of the race, a project abandoned upon his abrupt return to Paris the following autumn. His biographer, Clément, reported that the person who unpacked the artist's materials sent from Rome, recalled seeing over twenty oil sketches related to this subject, all of which had adhered to one another. The known oil studies and numerous drawings related to the project indicate that Géricault was attracted to various aspects of the race, particularly to the confusion surrounding its start and finish, and that the theme was one which evolved from being primarily descriptive, to more idealized and classical.

The surviving oil studies are on paper mounted on fabric and for the most part measure approximately .4 by .6. Two sketches in private collections show a groom struggling with a horse and in a third, belonging to Victor D. Spark of New York, a groom with a large banner is leading his horse. The Walters painting illustrates the preparations for the start of the race, whereas a picture in the Musées des Beaux-Arts, Lille, shows the melee of horses and grooms at its conclusion. Generally associated with the series is a frieze-like classical composition, *Four Ephebes Holding a Running Horse,* in the Musée des Beaux-Arts, Rouen, in which the figures are either nude or in ancient garb. The most abstracted, least narrative, phase in the evolution of the subject, one that is centered on the struggle between men and beasts divorced from a specific time despite the monumental classical buildings in the background, is known through several studies in the Louvre (R.F. 2050), the Hans Buehler collection, Winterthur, and reversed, and in larger format, in a sketch that was left in Italy and is now in a private collection in Paris.

In the Baltimore study, generally considered one of the earliest and most literal, grooms endeavor to restrain the seven horses at the starting line while three remaining animals are led forward into position. The grandstand is filled with spectators. Several soldiers at the extreme right block an opening in the red bunting facing the grandstand. To the left, figures swarm over the wooden construction supporting the starting line. Further in the background, carriages mill about the piazza lined with modern buildings. The scene is dramatically illuminated by the sinking sun.

Although Géricault has included such descriptive details as the plumage on the horses, he has dispensed with the spiked balls and metallic foil devices for goading the animals.

Clément (p. 340, no. 65) listed as related to this study a drawing, measuring .27 x .44, showing Romans holding horses at an oblique starting line, which belonged to M. Sauvé. In the collection of the late Col. Hans Buehler, Winterthur, there was a watercolor of this subject measuring .185 x .208. Drawings in the Museum Boymans–van Beuningen, Rotterdam, and in the Musée des Beaux-Arts, Poitiers, both showing two grooms in modern dress restraining a rearing horse, may be related to the horse and attendants in the right foreground of the Walters painting. Also similar was a pen and ink drawing in the Gobin Sale, Paris, 1935, no. 18.

The Walters painting was lithographed by Eugène Leroux.

Alternative Titles: *La Course des chevaux libres; La Corsa dei Barberi.*

Support: Paper mounted on two layers of fabric with a glue-paste adhesive (now removed), .445 x .595 (17$\frac{9}{16}$" x 23$\frac{3}{8}$")

Condition: The painting was treated for discolored varnish in 1951. In 1958, two old canvas linings were removed and a new fabric support was applied. A slight cleavage in the area of the grandstand bunting was treated in 1965.

Provenance: Géricault estate sale, Paris, November 2–3, 1824, no. 81, *huit tableaux esquisses dont six representent des courses de Rome.* 250 francs (?); A. M. Couvreur, Paris; E. Secrétan, Paris, July 1, 1889, no. 35, 9,200 francs; H. O. Havemeyer; Durand Ruel to H. S. Henry; H. S. Henry Sale, New York, January 25, 1907, no. 21, $3,000.00.

Exhibitions: "French Painting from David to Toulouse-Lautrec," Metropolitan Museum of Art, New York, 1941, no. 58; "The Spirit of Modern France," Toledo Museum of Art and Art Gallery of Toronto, 1947, no. 19; "From David to Courbet," Detroit Institute of Arts, 1950, no. 27; "Diamond Jubilee Exhibition," Philadelphia Museum of Art, 1950–51, no. 53; "From Ingres to Gauguin," Baltimore Museum of Art, 1951, no. 10; "The Romantic Circle," Wadsworth Atheneum, Hartford, 1952, no. 14; "Inaugural Exhibition," Fort Worth Art Center, 1954, no. 36; "The Romantic Movement," Tate Gallery, London, 1959, no. 177; "Sport and the Horse," Virginia Museum of Fine Arts, Richmond, 1960, no. 20; "The Horse in Art," The Fine Arts Gallery of San Diego, 1963, no. 52; "The Romantic Era," Herron Museum of Art, Indianapolis, 1965, no. 30; "An Exhibition of Treasures of the Walters Art Gallery," Wildenstein and Co., New York, 1967, no. 42.

References: Charles Clément, *Géricault, étude biographique et critique.* Paris, Didier, 1879, pp. 93–96, plate 5 (in reverse); Catalogue, p. 296; no. 82; Eitner supplement, p. 452; Richard Muther, *The history of modern painting.* 4 vols. New York, E. P. Dutton, 1907. 1:225, illus. (reversed); Germain Bazin, "La course des chevaux barbes de Géricault," *L'Amour de l'art* (April 1932): 96, fig. 44; Nancy Wynne, "Géricault's riderless racers," *Magazine of art* 31 (1938): 209, illus.; F. Antal, "Reflections on classicism and romanticism-III," *Burlington Magazine* 77 (1940): 78, plate II B; Henry Varnum Poor, "Roots that grow," *Magazine of art* 33 (1940):670; Klaus Berger, *Géricault und sein Werk,* Vienna, Anton Schroll, 1952, pp. 49, 68, nos. 26 and 27, illus.; Walter Friedlander, *David to Delacroix,* Cambridge, Mass., Harvard University Press, 1952, pp. 96–97, plate 53; D. Aimé-Azam, *Mazeppa: Géricault et son temps,* Paris, Plon, 1956. pp. 144, 342; Felicia Schaps, "The race horse in art," *The thoroughbred of California* (October 1961) : 350; Günter Busch, "Kopien von Theodore Géricault nach alten Meistern," *Pantheon* 25 (1967) :182, (illus. of detail), 184; Max Huggler, "Die Bemühung Géricaults um die Erneuerung der Wandmalerei," *Wallraf-Richartz Jahrbuch* 32 (1970) : 156, fig. 115; Lee Johnson, "Géricault in Los Angeles," *The Burlington Magazine* 103 (1971) : 770; Anne Murphy, "Riderless racers at Rome," *WAGB* 24, no. 2 (March 1972) : 1–4, fig. 2; Jacques Thuillier, *L'opera completa di Géricault,* Classici dell'arte, 8. Milan, Rizzoli, 1978, pp. 102–03, no. 106, plate 19; Lynn K. Matteson, "Observations on Géricault and Pinelli," *Pantheon* 38 (1980) : 76, illus.; John Canaday, *Mainstreams of modern art.* 2nd ed. New York, Holt, Rinehart and Winston, 1981. p. 65, illus.

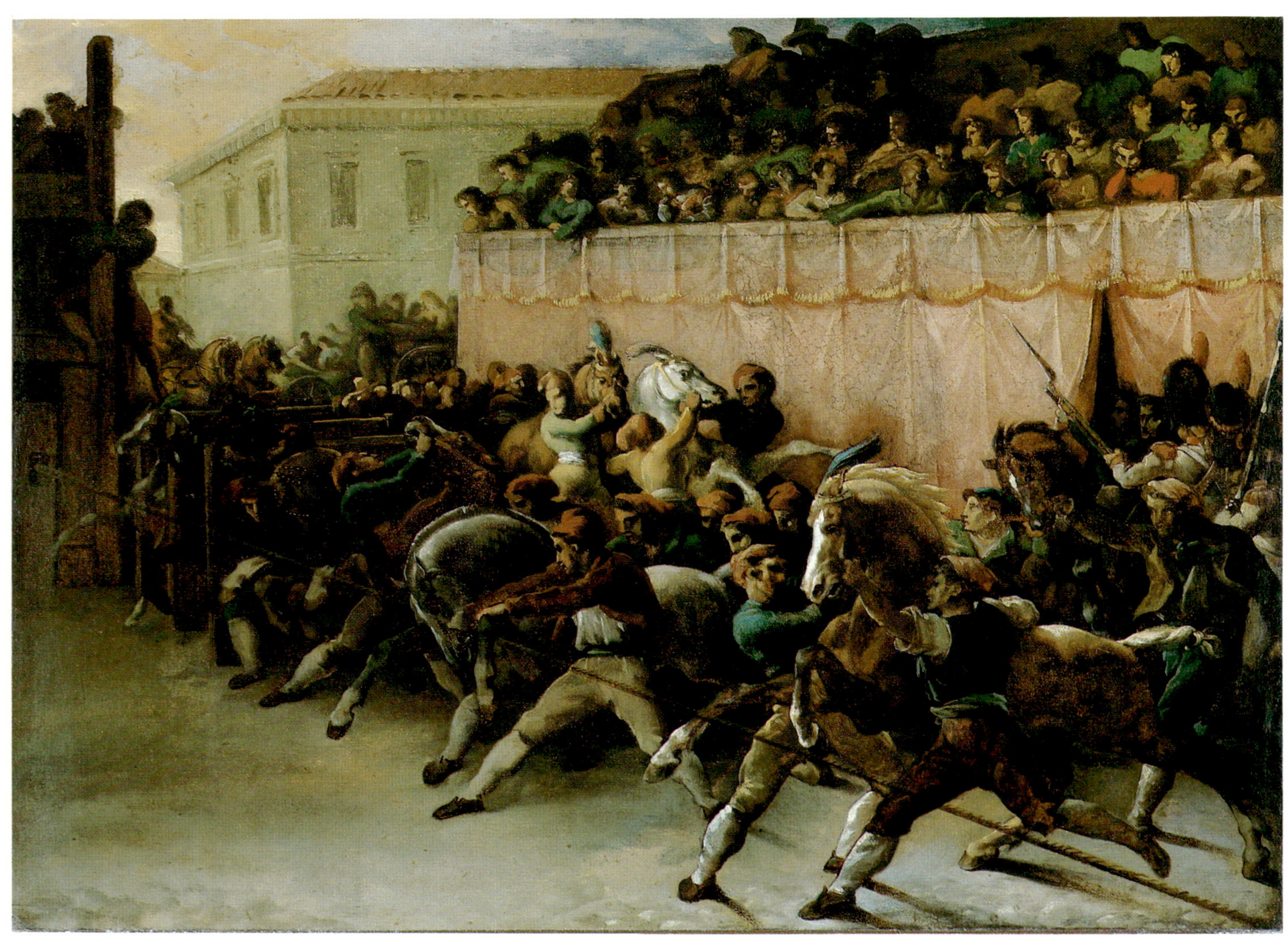

Géricault *Riderless Racers at Rome,* no. 9

Attributed to Géricault

10. Lion in Repose

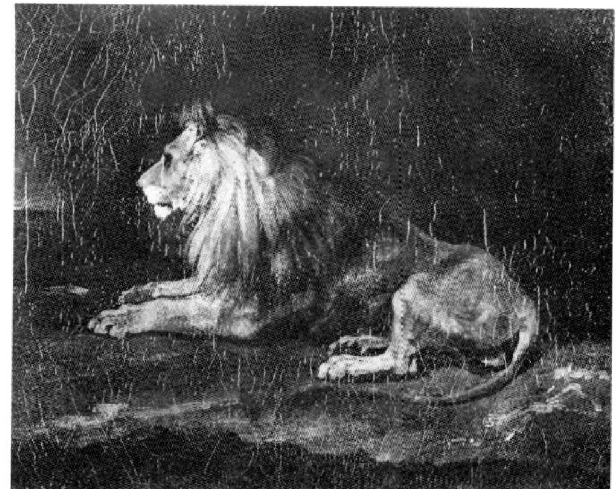

37.882

The reclining lion, facing left, is posed against a dark ground. A number of paintings of resting lions in similar backgrounds have been associated with Géricault. These include *Family of Lions* in which a number of animals rest in a lair, a composition known through two versions, one in the Louvre, R.F. 3962 (.46 x .56) and the other in a private collection, Paris (.47 x .585), as well as the *Head of a Lioness,* The Louvre, MNR 137 (.55 x .65) and *Family of Lions,* formerly collections Schiekler and J. D'Harcourt, Sale, Palais Galliera, Paris, November 28, 1971, no. 18, (.47 x .585). It is known that Géricault painted lions in the London zoo in 1820–21, inspired probably by George Stubbs' and James Ward's animal subjects. One of the lion's heads in a drawing in the Musée Bonnat, Bayonne, no. 2118 (.171 x .218) bears a striking resemblance to the animal in the Baltimore painting.

Support: Canvas, .38 x .47 (15″ x 18½″)

Marks: Label on stretcher inscribed: *Géricault 1816.*

Condition: X-rays taken in 1948 reveal that the lion was painted over a picture of two heads of men.

Provenance: Acquired by William T. Walters from an unknown source between 1887 and 1893.

References: Walters cat., 1893, p. 97, no. 162 and subsequent Walters catalogues until 1929.

Prosper-Georges-Antoine Marilhat

French: Vertaizon, 1811 - Thiers, 1847

Marilhat entered the studio of C. M. Roqueplan in 1829 and two years later made his debut at the Paris Salon with a landscape of his native Auvergne. In 1831 he left Paris to accompany Baron Karl Alexander Hügel of Regensberg on a scientific expedition that took him to Greece, Syria, Palestine and, eventually, to Egypt. He remained in Cairo sketching and supporting himself through portraiture until, compelled by ill health, he returned to France in 1833. The following year he submitted three Egyptian views to the Salon including a *View of the Mosque of Babel-Wasir,* and he continued thereafter to participate in the salons until 1844 when he submitted no fewer than eight works. Dispirited by their reception, he withdrew entirely from public exhibition and three years later, died in his native region in the Auvergne.

Marilhat, one of the earliest "Orientalists", was known as "the Egyptian". Despite the exoticism of his subjects, he worked in an essentially neoclassical style delineating his landscapes and architectural scenes with precision and displaying considerable finesse in his handling of such details as the diminutive figures that populate his scenes.

11. Landscape with Mosque

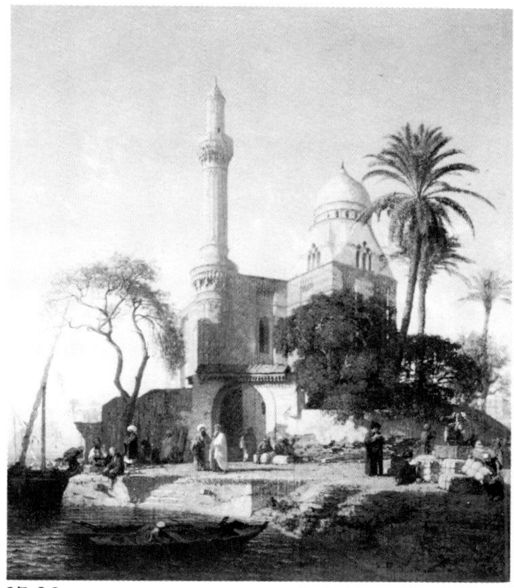

37.96

A small Mameluke-style mosque with an Ottoman minaret, nestled among a few palms and shrubs, stands on the bank of the river. To the left boatmen and merchants ply their trades, and at the right a camel caravan is being unloaded. The setting is believed to be imaginary rather than a specific site and, as is true of many of Marilhat's Egyptian views, the time of day is twilight with its lengthening shadows, limpid atmosphere and mellow tones. A replica of this painting signed by Narcisse Berchère belongs to a private collection in Thiers.

Support: Oil on fabric, .56 x .47 (22″ x 18½″)
Signed at lower right: *P. MARILHAT*

Condition: Lightly cleaned in 1938 and blisters laid down. Blisters laid down along bottom edges in 1974.

Provenance: Purchased together with a F. Thaulow landscape on April 3, 1902, at the Paris dealer Montaignac for a combined price of 22,000 francs.

References: Walters cat., 1909, p. 34, no. 96, and subsequent Walters catalogues; Lucas, 2: 897, 899.

Ferdinand Victor Eugène Delacroix

French: Charenton-Saint-Maurice, 1798 - Paris, 1863

Eugène Delacroix, an easel painter, muralist, lithographer and watercolorist, held a pivotal role in the evolution of French art in the nineteenth century. His paintings such as *The Massacres of Chios* (Salon of 1824) and *The Death of Sardanapalus* (Salon of 1827) are acknowledged masterpieces of Romantic Art. He himself, however, was never unequivocably an adherent of the Romantic Movement. Drawing inspiration from the great colorists Rubens and Veronese, and championing the primacy of color in painting, Delacroix linked past traditions with modern movements. Impressionist and Post-impressionist artists were to formulate theories of color and technique that he had anticipated from his own empirical explorations.

Since his copious correspondence and his *Journal* have been published, Delacroix's career is known in considerable detail. He received a traditional classical education, studying literature at the *Lycée Impérial* from 1806 to 1815, when he entered the studio of the neoclassical follower of J.-L. David, P. N. Guérin. The following year, Delacroix was enrolled in the Ecole des Beaux-Arts and while studying under Guérin, became acquainted with Géricault and Bonington. He, in fact, posed for one of the figures in the former's *Raft of the Medusa* in 1818. Delacroix's first Salon entry in 1822, *Dante and Virgil,* drew considerable attention, was praised by the artists Gérard and Gros as well as by the rising writer and statesman Adolphe Thiers, and ultimately was purchased by the State. More indicative of his subsequent development was *The Massacres of Chios* shown in 1824. In this masterpiece Delacroix revealed his mastery of light and color in dramatizing the topical tragedy. With the sale of the painting to the government, Delacroix was able to visit England where he met Lawrence, Etty and Wilkie, admired the works of John Constable and developed an interest in English literature. *The Death of Sardanapalus,* drawn from a play by Byron, epitomized Delacroix's romantic tendencies, and, when shown in the Salon of 1827, alienated him temporarily from sources of official support. Though out of favor, he painted two history paintings for the Bourbon Monarchy. One of these, *The Battle of Poitiers* commissioned by the Duchesse de Berry, is represented in Baltimore by a vibrant sketch. The change of government in 1830 proved no deterrent to his career and was commemorated by his

Liberty leading the People, a work that when shown in 1831 resulted in his being appointed Chevalier of the Legion of Honor.

In 1832, Delacroix accompanied the diplomatic expedition of the Comte de Mornay to the Sultan Abd-er-Rhaman of Morocco and continued traveling to Spain and Algiers. Paintings inspired by this journey, such as *The Women of Algiers* (Salon of 1834) and *The Sultan of Morocco and his Entourage* (1845), illustrate his avoidance of the exotic bric-a-brac and the "turquerie" approach of most subsequent orientalists. Instead he often sought a "classical dignity" among the inhabitants of North Africa. His exposure to the sun-drenched atmosphere of the region has generally been regarded as a contributing factor to his subsequent explorations in the handling of color. Only one painting in Baltimore, *The Collision of Moorish Horsemen,* an 1844 variant of an 1834 composition, is related to his North African experience.

Although he was to receive major commissions for large-scale decorative works from succeeding governments throughout his career, Delacroix never abandoned easel painting, producing countless pictures illustrating literary, biblical, mythological as well as North African subjects. The *Marphise* of 1852 in the Gallery is one of a number of works, from late in his career, that were drawn from 16th-century Italian literary sources.

Delacroix was never formally a Christian yet he frequently turned to biblical subjects, being attracted in particular to the drama and pathos of the Passion. It is likely an indication of W. T. Walters' inclinations that this facet of Delacroix is represented by two important works, one of the most dramatic versions ever painted of *The Christ on the Sea of Galilee* and *The Christ on the Cross.* The latter is frequently cited as among the most profoundly moving interpretations of the subject, as well as one that exemplifies Delacroix's indebtedness to Rubens.

Late in his life, Delacroix was generally regarded as one of the major painters of his time. In 1855, the year thirty-six of his paintings were exhibited at the Exposition Universelle, he was appointed Commandeur of the Legion of Honor. Despite such honors, he continued to experience the consequences of his early reputation as a radical and romantic, and it was not until his eighth application in 1857 that he received the official recognition of membership in the Institut de France.

12. Sketch for the Battle of Poitiers

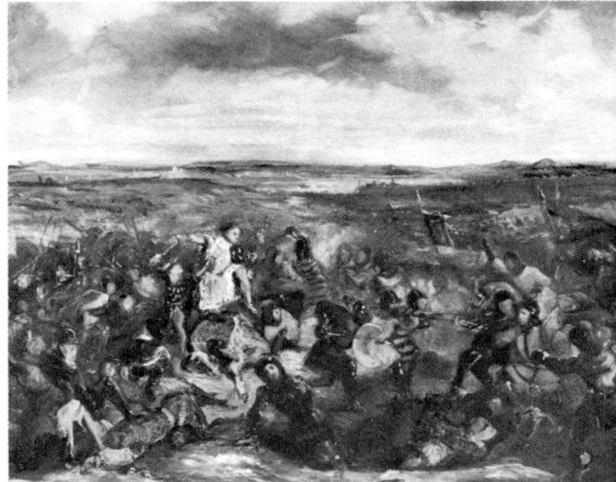

37.110 **1829–30**

The battle is drawing to a close as King John the Good of France, distinguished in the melee of combattants by his ermine-lined surcoat, is about to fall prisoner to the troops of Edward, Prince of Wales, the Black Prince. Fighting at the French king's side is his fourteen year old son, Philip.

This sketch, recording a critical incident of September 19, 1356, in the One Hundred Years' War, was painted in preparation for *King John at the Battle of Poitiers,* The Louvre, canvas (1.14 x 1.46, R.F. 3153), commissioned in 1829 by the Duchesse de Berry and executed over a six month period the following year.

The sketch is marked by a remarkable freedom of facture and an intensity of color that reinforces the drama of the subject. In the final work, Delacroix developed the composition, altering some of the figures and lowering the horizon line so as to silhouette the banners and the head of the King against the sky.

It has been noted by Lee Johnson ("Delacroix," The Art Gallery of Toronto-The National Gallery of Canada, 1962–63, catalogue no. 2) that this picture as well as *The Battle of Nancy,* Musée des Beaux-Arts, Nancy, commissioned by Charles X in 1828, may have been inspired by a copy of Gros' sketch for the *Battle of Nazareth* deposited with Delacroix by Horace Vernet in December, 1828.

Delacroix's sketch for the *Battle of Poitiers* in turn was copied by Degas about 1880 (canvas, collection of Dr. Peter Nathan, Zurich).

Support: Canvas, .52 x .648 (20¾" x 25½")

Signed at lower right: *ED* (scratched in wet paint)

Marks: Paper label of Durand-Ruel on the stretcher.

Condition: In 1963 the painting was prepared for exhibition with limited abraded areas in the lower portion of the sky inpainted in tempera. An examination in 1979 verified the fact that the picture had previously been lined and the original tacking edges removed.

Provenance: Delacroix Sale, Paris, February 16–19, 1864, no. 54, 4,700 francs to Baron de Laage; N. V. Diaz Sale, Paris, January 25, 1877, no. 323, 12,000 francs: Baron de Beurnonville Sale, Paris, April 29, 1880, no. 14, 10,000 francs to Brame; Collection of L. Tabourier (Paris, 1885); Tabourier Sale, Paris, June 20, 1889, no. 19, 18,500 francs; Durand-Ruel, New York, to Henry Walters, June 29, 1899, for $8,000.00 (Invoice 4715).

Exhibitions: Société National des Beaux-Arts Paris, 1864, no. 6; "Delacroix," Ecole des Beaux-Arts, Paris, 1885, no. 214; Exposition Universelle Internationale des Beaux-Arts, Exposition Centennale de l'Art Francais, Paris, 1889, no. 269; "From Ingres to Gauguin," Baltimore Museum of Art, 1951, no. 20; "Delacroix," The Art Gallery of Toronto–The National Gallery of Canada, 1962–63, no. 2; "Centenaire d'Eugène Delacroix," Louvre, Paris, 1963, no. 121; "From El Greco to Pollock," Baltimore Museum of Art, 1968, no. 61; "French Nineteenth Century Oil Sketches: David to Degas," The William Hayes Ackland Memorial Art Center, Chapel Hill, 1978, no. 26.

References: Théophile Silvestre, *Les Artistes français, études d'après nature,* Paris, E. Blanchard, 1855–56, p. 81; Théophile Silvestre, *Documents nouveaux,* Paris, Michel Lévy Frères, 1864, p. 4 f.; A. Cantaloube, *Eugène Delacroix, l'homme et l'artiste,* Paris, Dentu, 1864, pp. 39, 56; Adolphe Moreau, *E. Delacroix et son oeuvre.* Paris, Librairie des bibliophiles, 1873, p. 311; Alfred Robaut and Ernest Chesneau, *L'Oeuvre complet de Eugène Delacroix.* Paris, Charavay, 1885, p. 90, no. 322; Maurice Tourneux, *Eugène Delacroix devant ses contemporains.* Bibliothèque internationale de l'art. Paris, Jules Rouam, 1886, p. 150; Walters cat., 1901, p. 108, no. 180; Etienne Moreau-Nélaton, *Delacroix raconté par lui-même.* 2 vols. Paris, H. Laurens, 1916. 1:102, illus.; Julius Meier-Graefe, *Eugène Delacroix, Beiträge zu einer Analyse.* 2nd ed. Munich, R. Piper, 1922. p. 108, illus.; Raymond Escholier, *Delacroix, peintre, graveur, écrivain.* 3 vols. Paris. H. Floury, 1926. 1:235, 239, illus. opposite p. 238; Louis Hourticq, *Delacroix, l'oeuvre du maître.* Paris, Hachette, 1930. p. 30; R. Huyghe, "Le portrait de Jenny Le Guillou et la bataille de Nancy par Delacroix," *Bulletin des Musées de France.* 3:6; André Joubin, ed. *Journal de Eugène Delacroix.* 3 vols. Paris, Plon, 1932. 3:373; André Joubin, ed. *Correspondance générale d'Eugène Delacroix.* 5 vols. Paris, Plon, 1936–38. 1:234, 258–59; Edward S. King, "Delacroix's paintings in the Walters Art Gallery," *JWAG* 1 (1938): 87, 97–98, fig. 19; Maurice Sérullaz, *Mémorial de l'exposition Eugène Delacroix.* Paris, Editions des Musées nationaux, 1963. p. 84, no. 123: p. 85, illus.; Philippe Verdier, "Delacroix's 'Grandes Machines': 1," *Connoisseur* 156 (1964):232, illus.; Frank A. Trapp, *The attainment of Delacroix.* Baltimore, Johns Hopkins Press, 1971. p. 179, fig. 103; Theodore Reff, "Degas, a master among masters," *The Metropolitan Museum of Art Bulletin* 34, no. 4, Spring 1977: 34 (illus. no. 63), 35; Lee Johnson, *The Paintings of Eugène Delacroix, A critical Catalogue,* Oxford, Clarendon Press, 1981. I:137, 138; 2: plate 122.

13. Collision of Moorish Horsemen

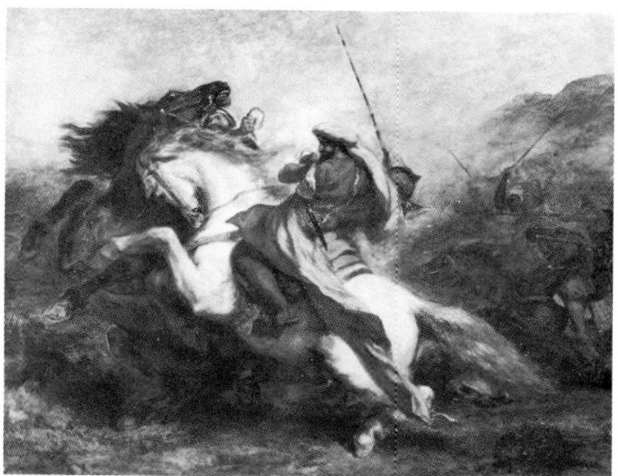

37.6 1843–44

When an earlier version of this composition was exhibited in Nantes in 1839, Delacroix described the scene as follows:

> *During their military exercises which consist of riding their horses at full speed and stopping them suddenly after firing a shot, it often happens that the horses carry away their riders and fight each other when they collide. That is the situation of the two principal figures of this painting.* (André Joubin, ed. *Correspondance générale d'Eugène Delacroix,* 2: 38).

Delacroix witnessed such an incident at Garbia, on March 6, 1832 while he was accompanying the diplomatic expedition of the Count de Mornay from Tangier to Meknes. He described the event in his *Journal* (André Joubin, ed., *Journal de Eugène Delacroix,* 1: 131) and subsequently painted six works recording this or similar actions: *Fantasia arabe,* 1832, .59 x .73, Musée Fabre, Montpellier; *Fantasia arabe,* 1833, .605 x .745, Staëdelscher Museumsverein, Frankfurt; *Exercices militaires des Marocains,* 1847, .66 x .82, Oskar Reinhart Collection, Winterthur; *Fantasia devant la porte de Mequinez,* watercolor, .15 x .27, (ex. collection Comte de Mornay, Sale, Paris, March, 1877, no. 14) The Louvre, R.F. 3372; and the two versions of the *Rencontre de cavaliers maures,* one belonging to the descendants of Salomon Goldschmidt, 1833–34, .805 x 1.005 and the other the Baltimore picture.

In the *Collision,* Arabs on contrasting white and black horses collide. The foreground figure wears a flowing white burnoose rather than a blue garment mentioned by Delacroix in his *Journal.* Behind, to the right, partially concealed in clouds of dust and smoke, are several charging mounted warriors.

Robaut in cataloguing the *Collision* confused the two versions and mentioned in addition a poor copy. This confusion, together with the abraded condition of the Walters picture, led E. S. King in 1938 to conclude that the Baltimore painting was not genuine. However, Lee Johnson, in 1961, identified the Goldschmidt work as one that was rejected by the Paris Salon of 1834 and exhibited in Nantes in 1839 and he noted, in addition, that the extremely thin painting and absence of pronounced contours of the Baltimore picture were consistent with Delacroix's technique of the 1840s, thus reaffirming the authenticity of this version. Subsequently, P. Joannides verified the fact that the Walters painting, which replicates the Goldschmidt picture except for minor details in the shape of the horses' tails and in the position of their veins, was exhibited in the Galerie des Beaux-Arts, 20–22 Boulevard de la Bonne Nouvelle, Paris, between April and November, 1844.

A drawing, in ink, and an etching, both by Delacroix and dated 1834, showing the principal figure reversed, were published by Ernest Chesneau in *L'Art* 29 (1882): 105, 107.

Alternative titles: *Rencontre de cavaliers Maures; Choc de Cavaliers Arabes*

Support: Canvas, .813 x .991 (32″ x 39″)

Signed lower left: *Eug. Delacroix*

Condition: The paint film is extremely thin, especially in the dark areas. The original canvas was glue-lined at an unknown date to a fabric of similar weave. In the process of lining, any raised surfaces may have been accidentally flattened. The surfaces were unevenly cleaned and areas in the sky somewhat abraded at this time.

Provenance: Arnold and Tripp sold the painting to W. T. Walters on May 9, 1883, for 40,000 francs after having acquired it on February 12, 1881 for 9,000 francs (See Arnold, Tripp et Compagnie, *Livre d'entrée,* no. 52 and *Livre de Sortie,* no. 1159, collection of M. Dieterle).

Exhibitions: Galerie des Beaux-Arts, Paris, 1844: "Delacroix," The Art Gallery of Toronto-The National Gallery of Canada, 1962–63, no. 11.

References: "Galeries des beaux-arts," *Bulletin de l'ami des arts* 2 (April 10, 1844): 283; Al. de la Fizelière, "Galerie des beaux-arts, coup d'oeil sur la peinture moderne," *Bulletin de l'ami des arts* 3 (September 1844): 45; Walters cat., 1844, no. 113, and subsequent Walters catalogues; Alfred Robaut and Ernest Chesneau, *L'oeuvre complet de Eugène Delacroix,* Paris, Charavay, 1885. pp. 125, 486, no. 469; André Joubin, ed. *Journal de Eugène Delacroix.* 3 vols. Paris, Plon, 1932: 3: 373; Edward S. King, "Delacroix's paintings in the Walters Art Gallery," *JWAG* 1 (1938): 87, 94, 95, 97, 108, n. 11, 111, n. 60; Lee Johnson "Delacroix's *Rencontre des cavaliers maures,*" *Burlington Magazine* 103 (1961): 417–19, fig. 13; Philippe Verdier, "Delacroix's 'Grandes Machines': 2," *Connoisseur* 157 (1964): 11, fig. 17; Paul Joannides, "Delacroix, the Choc des cavaliers arabes and the Galerie des Beaux-Arts," *JWAG* 35 (1977): 93, 96, 97, fig. 1.

14. Christ on the Cross

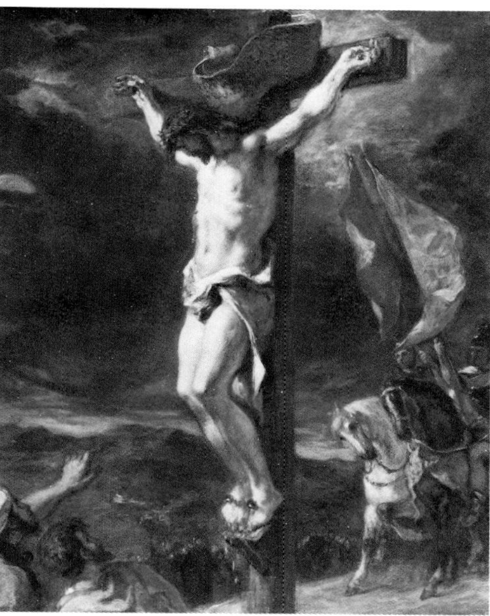

37.62 1846

The body of the expiring, crucified Christ, turned to the left, is sharply illuminated against the darkened sky. Spectators include two figures cut at shoulder-length by the picture margins at the lower left, a pair of mounted Roman soldiers with billowing, yellow and red banners at the right, and a throng of shrouded witnesses discernible down the slope in the middle ground. To the left, the darkened sun is partially obscured by clouds. Christ's side has been pierced and blood flows from the wound and dribbles from his feet to the ground.

The Baltimore painting is one of the most frequently cited versions of the subject to which Delacroix turned on a number of occasions throughout his career. Both Thoré in 1847 and Silvestre in 1855 drew parallels between this painting and Rubens' crucifixions.

In the Boymans-Van Beuningen Museum there is an oil sketch on panel (.37 x .25), dated by Robaut 1847 (no. 995), which is very closely related to the Baltimore picture.

Delacroix's treatment of the subject included elaborate, narrative compositions such as *Christ Between the Two Thieves* (1835) in the Musée Municipal des Beaux-Arts, Vannes, a work said to have been inspired by Rubens' *Coup de Lance,* Antwerp; scenes containing Mary being supported by John the Evangelist and Mary Magdalene as in Robaut nos. 996–997 (1847), in the National Gallery, London, Robaut no. 1223 (1853), and in the Bremen Kunsthalle, Robaut no. 1289 (1856); a work showing Mary Magdalene kneeling before the Cross, Robaut no. 296, (1829); and dramatic representations of the isolated figure of Christ facing either frontally as in Robaut no. 656, (1837); the Musée du Louvre, Robaut no. 1047, (1848); or turned to the right as in Robaut no. 987 (1846); and in a pastel in the National Gallery of Canada. The pair of mounted soldiers in the Baltimore picture also occurs at the left in the London painting and in the right background of the Bremen version of the subject.

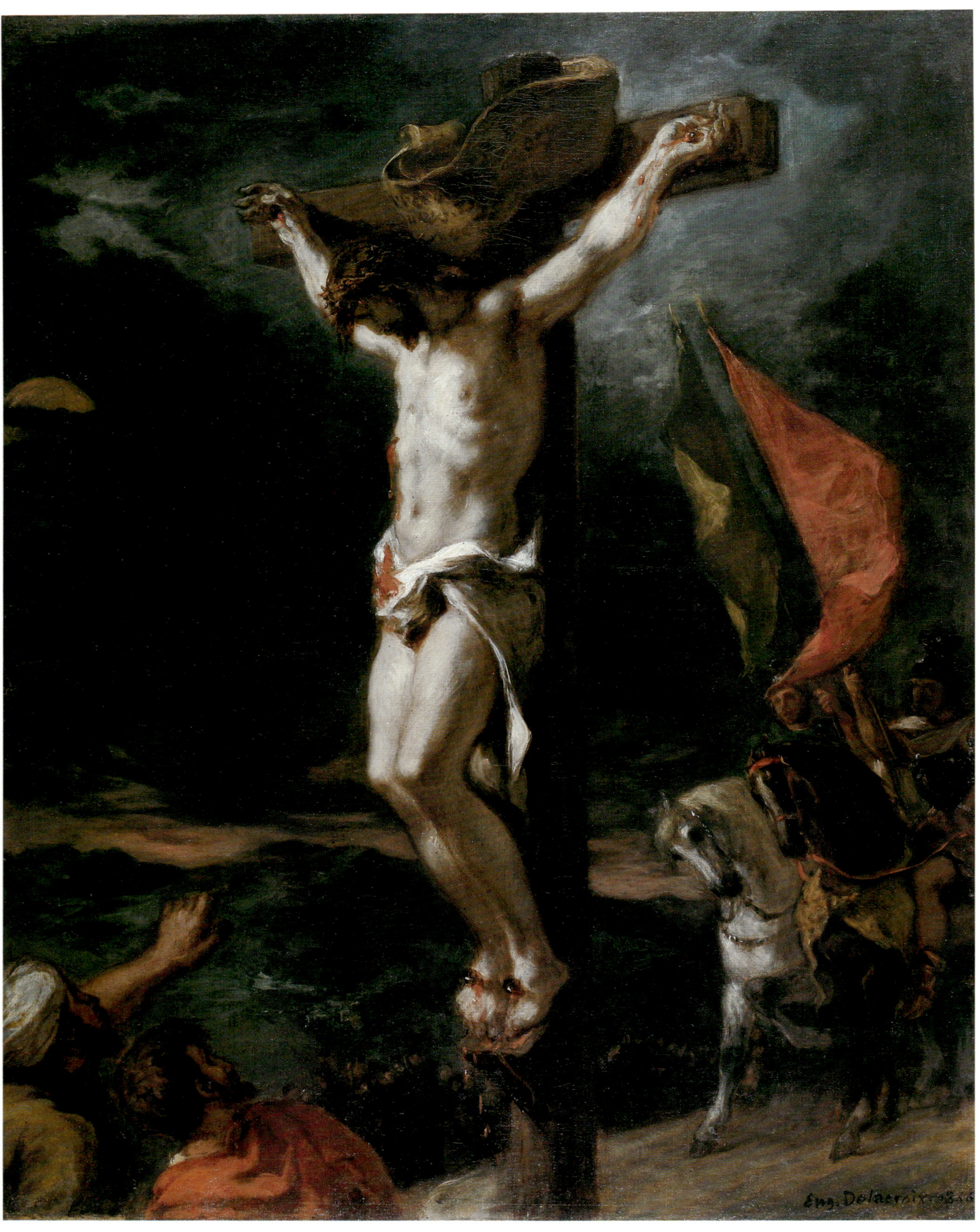

Delacroix *Christ on the Cross,* no. 14

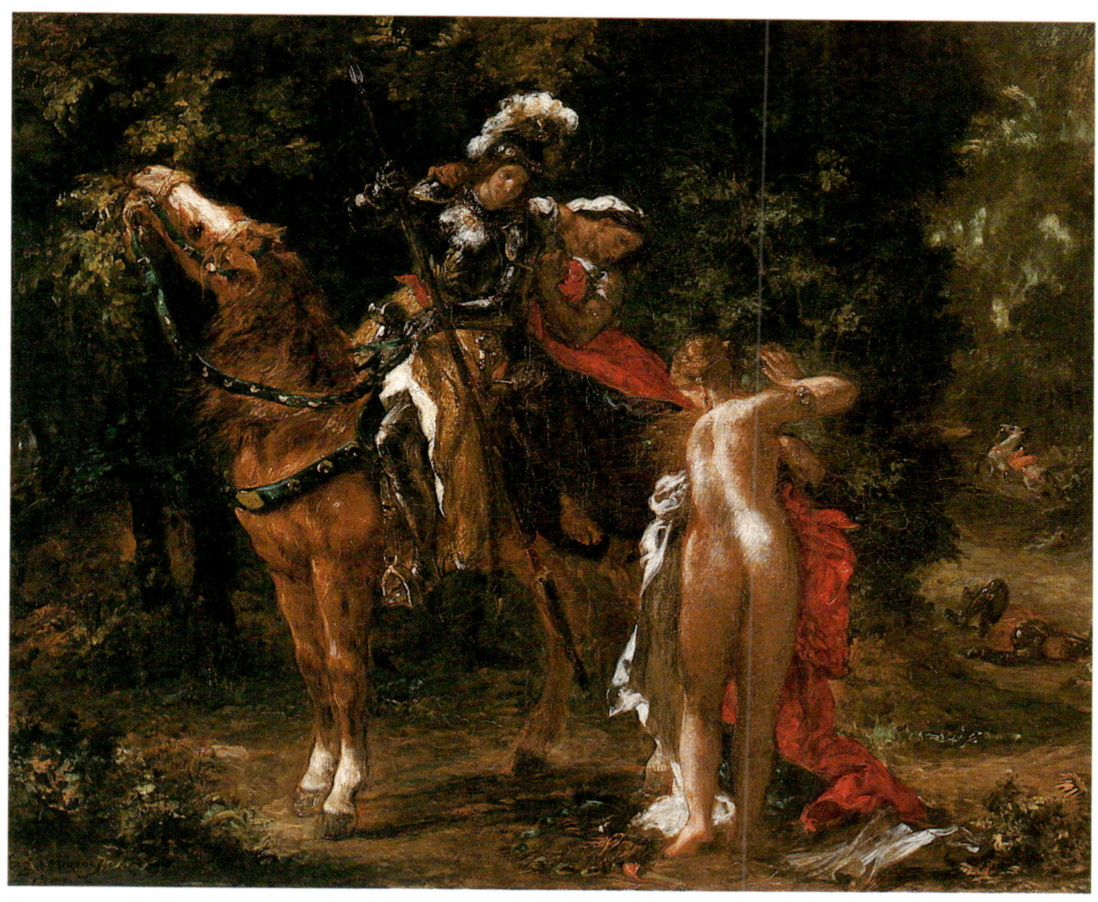

Delacroix *Marphise,* no. 14

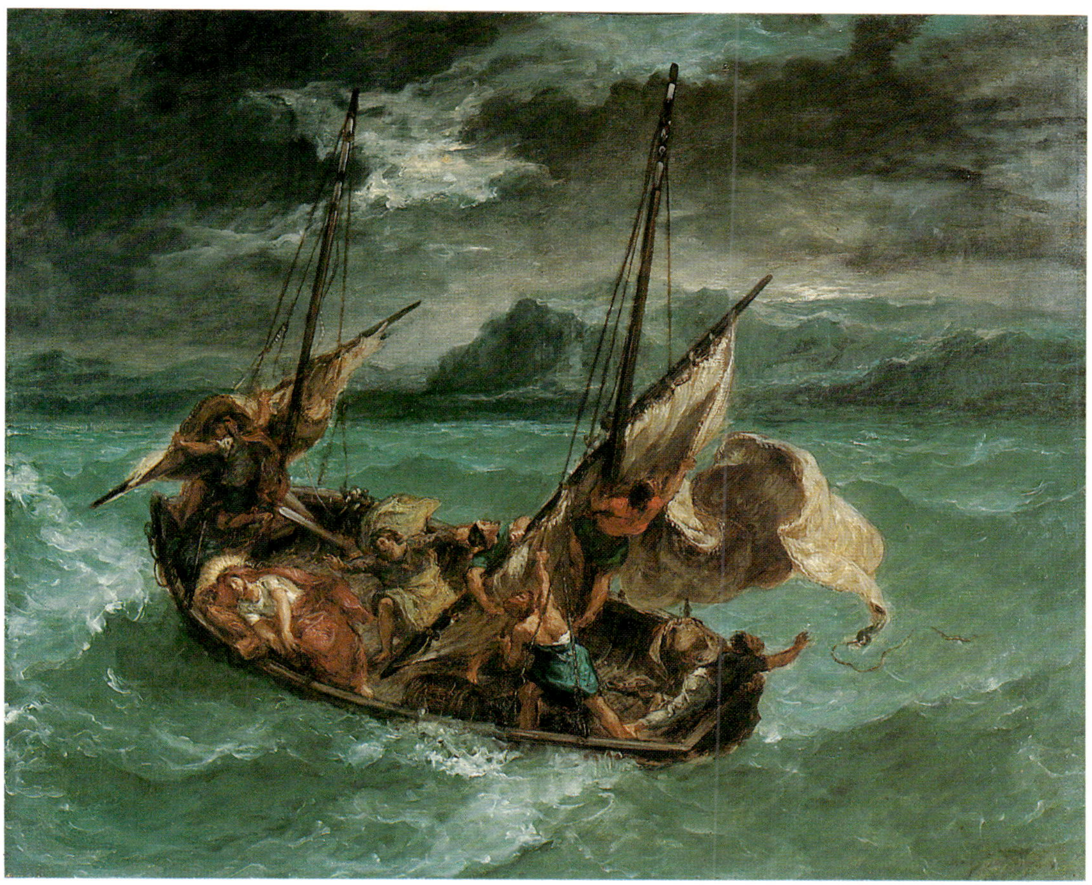

Delacroix *Christ on the Sea of Galilee,* no. 16

Support: Canvas, .8 x .642 (31½" x 25¼")

Signed and dated lower right: *Eug. Delacroix 1846*

Condition: An examination in 1951 revealed minor paint losses along the lower edge. In 1963 an old lining was removed and the picture was relined. In the process, three previous sets of tacking holes became discernible.

Provenance: Sold by the artist together with an *Odalisque* to van Isaker of Antwerp for 1500 francs, March 16, 1847; collection van Cuyck(?); Bonnet Collection Sale, Paris, February 19, 1853, no. 10, 4100 francs; collections of Bréville, Solar, Osiris, Gavet, Fanien; sold to Georges Petit, 7600 francs according to Robaut; collections of Defoer, Sale, Paris, May 22, 1886, no. 16, illus., 29,500 francs; bought by Montaignac for Walters.

Exhibitions: Salon Paris, 1847, no. 459; Exposition Universelle, Paris, 1855, no. 2909; Exposition Alsace-Lorraine, Paris, 1874; "Cent Chefs d'Oeuvre," Galerie Georges Petit, Paris, 1883, no. 27; "Delacroix," Ecole Nationale des Beaux Arts, Paris, 1885, no. 52; Barye Monument Association, no. 535; "French Painting from David to Toulouse Lautrec," Metropolitan Museum of Art, New York, 1941, no. 43; "The Spirit of Modern France," Toledo Museum of Art and The Art Gallery of Toronto, 1947, no. 23; "Forty Masterpieces," City Art Museum, St. Louis, 1947, no. 12; "Masters of Art from 1790 to 1950," Los Angeles County Fair, Pomona, 1950; "From Ingres to Gauguin," Baltimore Museum of Art, 1951, no. 21; "The Life of Christ," Washington County Museum of Fine Arts, Hagerstown, 1951, no. 6; "The Romantic Circle," Wadsworth Atheneum, Hartford, 1952, no. 30; "Religious Paintings, 15th–19th centuries," Brooklyn Museum, 1956, no. 24; "Religious Art of the Western World," Dallas Museum of Fine Arts, 1958, no. 36; "The Face of Christ in Art," Museum of Fine Arts, Little Rock, 1959, no. 8; "Centenaire d'Eugène Delacroix," Louvre, Paris, 1963, no. 363; "An Exhibition of Treasures of The Walters Art Gallery," Wildenstein and Co., New York, 1967, no. 39; "Paris-New York: A Continuing Romance," Wildenstein and Co., New York, 1977, no. 66.

References: Théophile Thoré, *Le Constitutionnel,* March 17, 1847 and April 14, 1847.* (reprinted in *Les Salons de T. Thoré.* 2nd ed. Paris, Librairie de Ve Jules Renouard, 1870); *Le moniteur universel,* March 29, 1847; Theophile Gautier, *La Presse* (Paris) April 1, 1847 (reprinted in *Salon de 1847,* pp. 43–52); L. Clément de Ris, *L'Artiste* 4th series 9 (April 4 and 18, 1847): 75, 107; P. Haussard, *Le National* (Paris) April 8, 1847; E. du Molay Bacon, *La Patrie* 7 (April 11, 1847); Paul Mantz, *Salon de 1847.* Paris, F. Sartorius, 1847. pp. 12–18*; M. de Vaines, *Revue nouvelle,* April 15, 1847, p. 251; P. Petroz, *La Presse* (Paris) June 5, 1855; Charles Perrier, *L'Artiste* 5th series 15 (June 10, 1855): 7; Paul Mantz, *Revue française* 3 (June 10 and October 10, 1855); E. Gebauer, *Les Beaux-arts à l'Exposition Universelle de 1855.* Paris, Librairie Napoléonienne, 1855. p. 41; Éd. About, *Voyage à travers l'Exposition des beaux-arts.* Paris, Hachette, 1855. pp. 178–79; Théophile Silvestre, *Les artistes français, études d'après nature.** Paris, E. Blanchard, 1855–56. p. 24; Adolphe Moreau, *E. Delacroix et son oeuvre.* Paris, Librairie des bibliophiles, 1873. pp. 152?, 182, 187, 260; Albert Wolff, *Cent chefs-d'oeuvre.* New York, Knoedler, 1885. pp. 35–36, illus. opposite p. 4 (engraving by Courtry); Charles Ponsonaille, *L'Artiste* 8th series (March 1885): 167–68; Alfred Robaut and Ernest Chesneau, *L'Oeuvre complet de Eugène Delacroix.* Paris, Charavay, 1885. p. 258, no. 986; Maurice Tourneux, *Eugène Delaroix devant ses contemporains.* Bibliothèque internationale de l'art. Paris, Jules Rouam, 1886. pp. 83–85, 94–98; Walters cat., 1887, p. 49, no. 74, and subsequent Walters catalogues; Etienne Moreau-Nélaton, *Delacroix raconté par lui-même.* 2 vols. Paris, H. Laurens, 1916. 2:57, fig. 272; Raymond Escholier, *Delacroix, peintre, graveur, écrivain.* 3 vols. Paris, H. Floury, 1926–29. 2: 310, illus. opposite p. 314; André Joubin, ed. *Journal de Eugène Delacroix.* 3 vols. Paris, Plon, 1932. 1: 208; André Joubin, ed. *Correspondance générale d'Eugène Delacroix.* 5 vols. Paris, Plon, 1936–38. 3: 139; Michel Florisoone, *Delacroix, 1798–1863.* Paris, Braun, n.d., no. 47. (illus.); Edward S. King, "Delacroix's paintings in the Walters Art Gallery," *JWAG* 1 (1938): 87–90, 108, n. 12, fig. 1; Lucien Rudrauf, *Eugène Delacroix et le problème du romantisme artistique.* Paris, H. Laurens, 1942. plate VI; Philippe Verdier, *L'Art religieux.* Formes de l'art, 2. Paris, Formes et Reflets, 1956. pp. 208–09, illus.; W. R. Juynboll, "Een olieverfschets van Eugène Delacroix," *Bulletin Museum Boymans-van Beuningen* 12 (1961): 1–11, no. 1, fig. 4; *GBA* 6th pér. 59 (1962): Supplément, p. 59, illus. no. 219 (oil sketch on panel, Museum Boymans-van Beuningen, Rotterdam); Katharine Morrison McClinton, *Christian church art through the ages.* New York, Macmillan, 1962. plate XLIV; Raymond Escholier, *Eug. Delacroix.* Paris, Editions Cercle d'art, 1963, p. 183; Maurice Sérullaz, *Mémorial de l'exposition Eugene Delacroix.* Paris, Editions des Musées nationaux, 1963. pp. 267–69; Philippe Verdier, "Delacroix's 'Grandes Machines': 2," *Connoisseur* 157 (1964): illus. opposite p. 9; Denys Sutton, "Connoisseur's haven," *Apollo* 84 (1966): 426, 428 (plate I); Frank A. Trapp, *The attainment of Delacroix.* Baltimore, Johns Hopkins Press, 1971. pp. 237–38, illus.; Mahonri Sharp Young, "The last time I saw Paris," *Apollo* 106 (1977): 415, fig. 8, 416.

* Quoted at length in Maurice Séruallaz, 1963.

15. Marphise

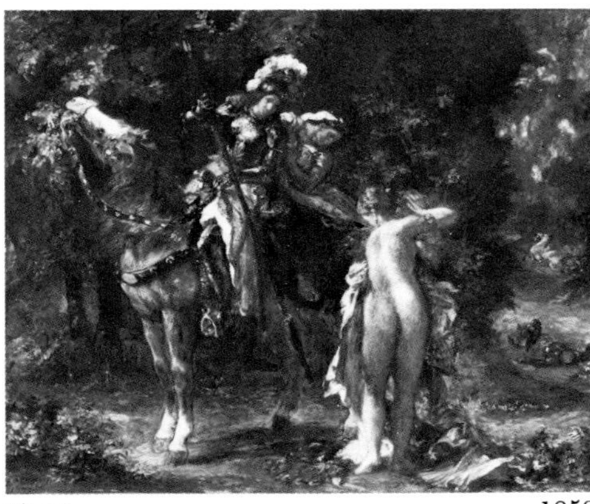

37.10 1852

Late in his career, Delacroix drew a number of subjects from the epic poetry of Ludovico Ariosto and Torquato Tasso. Illustrated here is the aftermath of the encounter between the woman warrior Marfisa and the knight Pinabello as related in Ariosto, *Orlando Furioso*, XX, 108–116. At the extreme right, Pinabello, who has been unhorsed by Marfisa with her sturdy lance, lies stunned on the ground while his horse disappears into the background. In the central foreground, the knight's lady, who had initially provoked the challenge by mocking Marfisa's companion, the old woman Gabrina, is being compelled to disrobe and exchange her finery for the rags of Gabrina. The old woman is seated behind Marfisa on her white horse which is nonchalantly chewing the leaves of a tree.

Sérullaz convincingly interprets the allusion to the "Femme impertinente" that occurs in Delacroix's *Journal* entry for February 14, 1850 (André Joubin, ed: *Journal de Eugène Delacroix,* Paris, 1932, 1: 340) as a reference to this work.

Preliminary studies for this work include a pencil drawing in the Art Institute of Chicago, a crayon drawing in the Musée de Lille (.26 x .195), and a wash drawing illustrated in Raymond Escholier, *Delacroix,* Paris, 1929, 3, opposite p. 145. In these renditions of the subject the lady turns away from Marfisa, disrobing facing the viewer. Another version of the painting, attributed to Delacroix and illustrated in Escholier, 3, opposite p. 146, differs from the Baltimore picture in lacking the figure of Gabrina, but shows the lady from the back.

Alternative Titles: *Marfisa and Pinabello's Lady; La Femme Capricieuse et Marphise.*

Support: Canvas, .82 x 1.01 (32¼" x 39¾").

Signed and dated lower left: *Eug. Delacroix/1852.*

Condition: In 1961 the canvas was lined with wax attachment and was cleaned.

Provenance: Sold by the artist to Bonnet, 1,500 francs; Collection Bonnet, Sale, February 19, 1853, no. 9 to Bulloz, 1,100 francs; Sale, Hôtel Drouot, May 20, 1881, 25,100 francs; Collection Balay, c. 1885; Knoedler & Co. New York, 1904; Henry Walters.

Reproductions: Lithographed by Leroux.

Exhibitions: "Delacroix," Ecole des Beaux-Arts, Paris, 1885, no. 107; "Delacroix," Musée du Louvre, Paris, 1930, no. 148; "Ariosto and Tasso," The Smith College Museum of Art, Northampton, 1946; "From Ingres to Gauguin," Baltimore Museum of Art, 1951, no. 24; "Inaugural Exhibition," Fort Worth Art Center,1954, no. 21; "Delacroix," The Art Gallery of Toronto-The National Gallery of Canada, 1962–63, no. 16; "Centenaire d'Eugène Delacroix," Louvre, Paris, 1963, no. 426.

References: Adolphe Moreau, *E. Delacroix et son oeuvre.* Paris, Librairie des bibliophiles, 1873. pp. 115, 247; Alfred Robaut and Ernest Chesneau, *L'oeuvre complet de Eugène Delacroix,* Paris, Charavay, 1885. p. 321, no. 1198; Étienne Moreau-Nélaton, *Delacroix raconté par lui-même.* 2 vols. Paris, H. Laurens, 1916. 2: 102, fig. 318; Raymond Escholier, *Delacroix, peintre, graveur, écrivain.* 3 vols. Paris, H. Floury, 1926–29. 3: 158; André Joubin, ed. *Journal de Eugène Delacroix.* 3 vols. Paris, Plon, 1932. 3: 438; G. Rouchès, "Eugène Delacroix et la littérature italienne," *Mélanges de philologie, d'histoire et de littérature offerts à Henri Hauvette.* Paris, Les presses françaises, 1934. pp. 602–03; E. Lambert, "Une scène du Roland Furieux traitée par Delacroix," *Bulletin de la Société de l'histoire de l'art français* (1936): 146–52; Michel Florisoone, *Delacroix, 1798–1863.* Paris, Braun, n.d. illus. no. 53; Richard B. K. McLanathan, "Ariosto and Tasso," *Art News* 45, no. 5 (July 1946): 37 (illus.), 56; Lee Johnson, *Delacroix.* Masters and movements. London, Weidenfeld and Nicolson, 1963. p. 94, plate 57; Maurice Sérullaz, *Mémorial de l'exposition Eugène Delacroix.* Paris, Editions des Musées nationaux, 1963. pp. 325–26, no. 429, illus.

16. Christ on the Sea of Galilee

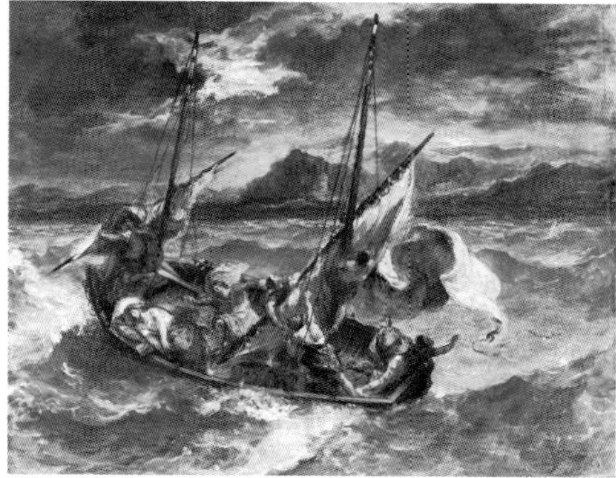

37.186 1854

A two-masted boat battles tumultuous seas. In the prow, a sailor wrestles with the foresail, while further aft three men struggle with the mainsail. In the stern, a figure grasps for a halyard flapping in the wind. Christ, identified by an orange halo and crimson garment, is asleep amidships and is about to be awakened by a disciple who reaches toward him. The light breaking through the clouds reveals an ominous, rocky coast in the background.

Earlier in his career Delacroix had dealt with similar scenes. Notable examples included the *Dante et Virgile aux enfers* (1822), The Louvre; *Naufrage de Don Juan* (1840), also in the Louvre, and *Des naufrages abandonnés dans un canot* (1847), Pushkin Museum.

The series of pictures illustrating the story of Christ stilling the tempest (Matthew 8:23–27; Mark 4:36–40; Luke 8:23–25) painted in the 1850s may, in part, have been inspired by the artist's sojourns at Dieppe in 1851, 1852, and 1854. In a letter to Baroness Forget, September 13, 1852, Delacroix recorded how he had rested, contemplating the ocean for three or four hours at a time (André Joubin, ed. *Correspondence générale d'Eugène Delacroix,* Paris, 1932, 3:124).

The paintings of this subject have been categorized on the basis of whether a rowboat or a sailboat is portrayed. Of the former, there are examples in The Portland Art Museum, Oregon; The Metropolitan Museum of Art, New York; The Museum of Fine Arts, Boston (perhaps a replica by Pierre Andrieu); the Georg Reinhart Collection, Winterthur; the Dr. Peter Nathan Collection, Zurich; the Mrs. Verena Haftner-Reinhart Collection, Zurich; the Fogg Art Museum (drawing); and the late Léon Suzor Collection (drawing). The pictures in which a sailboat is shown fall into two subdivisions, those with one and those with two masts. In the Bührle Collection, Zurich, a painting dated 1853 shows the sailboat, with one mast, directed to the right and away from the viewer, as is also true in a drawing in the Cl. Roger-Marx Collection, Paris, whereas in the Ingersoll Collection, Philadelphia Museum of Art, the vessel is similar though heading in the opposite direction. The two-masted sailboat occurs in the Walters painting; in a preliminary pencil drawing in the Musée du Louvre, R.F. 493 (.223 x .349); and in a related work in the Nasjonalgalleriet, Oslo, (.38 x .46).

In these series, only the Walters picture and the painting belonging to the Bührle Collection are dated. Delacroix, in his *Journal,* noted that he had begun a *Christ dans la tempête* for Count Grzymala, April 30, 1853, finished it on June 29, 1853 and had had it replicated by his pupil Pierre Andrieu, July 3, 1854 (André Joubin, ed., *Journal de Eugene Delacroix,* Paris, 1932, 2:32, 71, 211). Lee Johnson, in "Delacroix," The Art Gallery of Toronto, the National Gallery of Canada, 1962–63, catalogue no. 61, observes that the versions in the Nathan Collection, Zurich, and in the Museum of Fine Arts, Boston, appear most readily as original and replica, and he therefore identifies the former as the first work in the series and as the one painted for Count Grzymala.

Support: Canvas, .598 x .733 (23½" x 28⅞").

Signed at lower right: *Eug Delacroix 54.*

Condition: Cleaned and lined in 1947.

Provenance: Sold by the artist to the dealer Beugniet; Beugniet to Tabourier; Troyon; Viot, Sale, Paris, May 25, 1886, no. 2, 49,000 francs; Levesque; W. T. Walters, 1889.

Reproductions: Engraved by C. Courtry and published in *Galerie Durand-Ruel,* Paris, n.d., 3, no. 161.

Exhibitions: Société des Amis des Arts, Bordeaux, 1855, no. 170; "Exposition des oeuvres d'Eugène Delacroix," Société Nationale des Beaux-Arts, Paris, 1864, no. 33; "Cent chefs-d'oeuvre," Galerie Georges Petit, Paris, 1883; "Exposition Eugène Delacroix," Ecole Nationale des Beaux-Arts, Paris, 1885, no. 229; Barye Monument Association, no. 546; "Centennial Exhibition," Fort Worth Art Association, 1949; "Masterpieces of the 19th Century," Seattle Art Museum, 1951; "From Ingres to Gauguin," Baltimore Museum of Art, 1951, no. 27; XXVII Biennale di Venezia, Venice, 1956, no. 34; "Centenaire d'Eugène Delacroix," Louvre, Paris, 1963, no. 444; "Delacroix," Arts Council of Great Britain, 1964, no. 63; "From El Greco to Pollock," Baltimore Museum of Art, 1968, no. 62.

References: Adolphe Moreau, *E. Delacroix et son oeuvre.* Paris, Librairie des bibliophiles, 1873. p. 262, n. 1; Albert Wolff, *Cent chefs-d'oeuvre.* New York, Knoedler, 1885. illus. opposite p. 28. (engraving by Bracquemond); Alfred Robaut and Ernest Chesneau, *L'oeuvre complet de Eugène Delacroix.* Paris, Charavay, 1885, p. 326, no. 1214; Walters cat., 1887, p. 90, no. 145, and subsequent Walters catalogues; Étienne Moreau-Nélaton, *Delacroix raconté par lui-même.* 2 vols. Paris, H. Laurens, 1916. 2: 115, fig. 334; Raymond Escholier, *Delacroix, peintre, graveur, écrivain.* 3 vols. Paris, H. Floury, 1926–29. 3: 188; André Joubin ed. *Journal de Eugène Delacroix.* 3 vols. Paris, Plon, 1932. 2: 196?, 289?, 290?, 478; Edward S. King, "Delacroix's paintings in the Walters Art Gallery," *JWAG* 1 (1938): 87, 90–92, 109, n. 14, fig. 5; Lee Johnson, "Eugène Delacroix," catalogue, Art Gallery of Toronto and National Gallery of Canada, 1962–63, p. 46; Maurice Sérullaz, *Memorial de l'exposition Eugène Delacroix,* Paris, Editions des Musées nationaux, 1963. pp. 341, 343–44, no. 450, illus.; Gene Baro, "Things to come in London," *Arts* 38, no. 8–9 (May-June 1964): 48–49, illus.; Philippe Verdier, "Delacroix's 'Grandes Machines': 2," *Connoisseur* 157 (1964): 12, fig. 19; Janice Cooper, "Delacroix's Christ on the Lake of Gennesaret in the Metropolitan Museum of Art," *Vassar Journal* 21 (December 1968): 48–55, fig. 2; Shoji Takashina, "Chronologie et sources de la série du 'Christ sur le lac de Genesareth' par E. Delacroix," *Bijutsushi* 19 (December 1969): 89, no. 3, 90, illus.; Frank A. Trapp, *The attainment of Delacroix.* Baltimore, Johns Hopkins Press, 1971. plate 21; Kuno Mittelstädt, *Eugène Delacroix,* Welt der Kunst, Berlin, Henschel, 1974, no. 24, illus.

Artist unknown, formerly attributed to Delacroix

17. Copy after Rubens

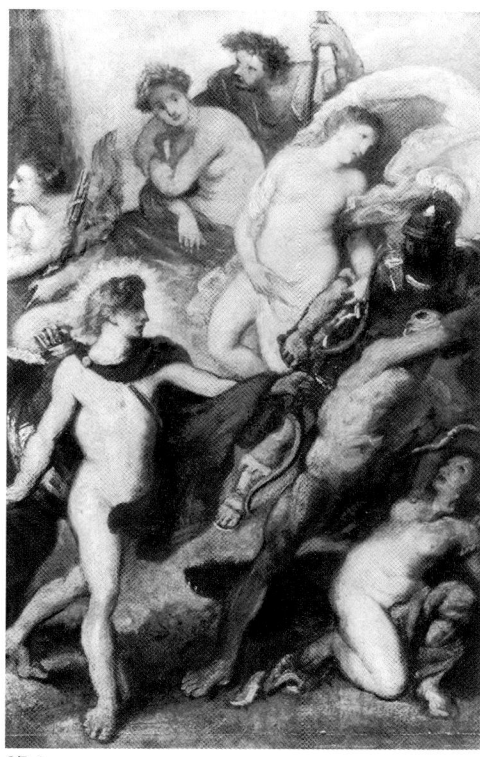

37.1

Rather freely copied is a section of *The Government of the Queen* by P. P. Rubens. The original painting is from the Medici cycle commissioned in 1622 for the Luxembourg Palace by the Dowager Queen, Marie de' Medici, and completed by Rubens and his assistants within three years. When the Palace was presented to the Senate of the Republic in 1808, the twenty-one monumental canvases were transferred to the Louvre where they have since been displayed. Preliminary studies for the cycle are preserved in the Alte Pinakothek, Munich.

The Government of the Queen is set on Mount Olympus. In the Walters copy, a detail from the right side of the original composition, Apollo and Mars are seen in the foreground expelling Discord and Envy. Behind are several Olympian deities, including Venus partially swathed in pink drapery, and Ceres.

The Walters copy bore until treatment in 1937 the signature *E Delacroix* which proved to be spurious. Previously, it was consistently recorded as a work of Eugène Delacroix, an attribution which has not been substantiated by stylistic comparisons or documentary evidence. It is now catalogued as an anonymous work of the first half of the nineteenth century.

Support: Panel, .50 x .325 (19⅝" x 12¾").

Formerly signed at lower left: *E Delacroix.*

Marks: Paper label on reverse of frame: *Millikin/ 35420.*

Provenance: Daniel Cottier, London; E. F. Milliken, New York, American Art Galleries, New York, February 14, 1902, no. 20, illus., $2,700.00.

Exhibitions: International Exhibition of Industry, Science and Art, Edinburgh, 1886, no. 1111 (listed p. 320, as After Rubens, E Delacroix).

References: Walters cat., 1909, no. 1, and subsequent Walters catalogues. Edward S. King, "Delacroix's paintings in the Walters Art Gallery," *JWAG* 1 (1938): 86–87, 109 (illus.), n. 15.

Alexandre-Gabriel Decamps

French: Paris, 1803 - Fontainebleau, 1860

In his review *Les Beaux-arts à l'Exposition universelle de 1865,* Paris, 1855, p. 155, Maxime Du Camp ranked Decamps with Ingres and Delacroix as one of the most outstanding artists of the modern French school. Though his reputation has since diminished, Decamps was esteemed as a major artist during his life. Even more than Delacroix, he was preeminent as a painter of oriental subjects, which he treated with distinctive veracity rather than with the drama associated with the great romantic painter. He did not open his atelier to students, yet he exerted considerable influence upon his successors, both those who borrowed his motifs, and those who emulated his exploitation of the textures of pigments, a feature transmitted by his associates at Barbizon to later nineteenth-century painting.

Decamps was perhaps an incomplete artist, who, torn by "high-minded" intentions, never fully developed his inherent talents as a realist. He was essentially self-taught despite brief sojourns in the studios of Etienne Buhot in 1816 and Alexandre-Denis Abel du Pujol in 1818. His early travels were to Switzerland in 1824 and to the south of France the following year. He made his debut at the Paris Salon in 1827 with an imaginary oriental subject *A Janissary* (Wallace Collection, London, Inv. P304) and a now lost hunting scene. That year he began the travels which took him to Greece and much of Asia Minor and North Africa.

At the 1831 Salon, he revealed his range of interests in five works: *The Turkish Patrol* (Wallace Collection, London, Inv. P307), another oriental scene, a view of Moret, and two kennel subjects which won him a second-class medal and considerable public esteem. At the height of his career in the 1830s, Decamps painted numerous eastern subjects and occasional *singeries* and dog pictures. His most ambitious work, *The Defeat of the Cimbri* (Louvre Museum, Paris) was a classical battle scene set in France which won for him a first-class medal in the 1834 Salon. This inclination toward historical themes, which was probably motivated by a visit to Rome and Florence in 1835, gradually waned in the later 1840s.

Decamps began to frequent the Fontainebleau region, staying at the Cheval Blanc Inn in Chailly in 1846, and visiting his friends Barye, Corot, Huet and Millet in nearby Barbizon. Although his nine large drawings illustrating the life of Samson were favorably reviewed at the 1845 Salon, he received mixed and negative reviews the following year, which led to his becoming somewhat of a recluse. He closed his Paris studio in 1853, and settled at Veyrier near Fontainebleau until 1858, when he bought a large property there. Meanwhile, at the 1855 Exposition Universelle Decamps was given a retrospective exhibition of fifty works and was awarded the Grand Medal of Honor. Though he continued to paint until his death five years later, many of his late works were lost when his widow's house was destroyed during the Siege of Paris.

18. The Suicide

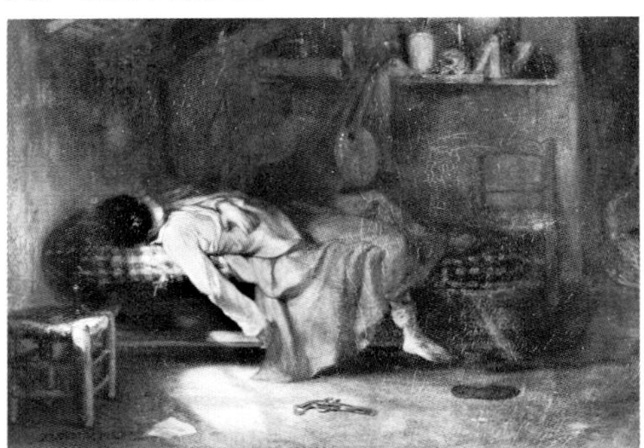

37.42 c.1836

A dead artist lies sprawled across the bed with his foot and hand dangling over the edge. In the foreground a pistol and a note suggest the tragic sequence of events. The interior, a loft, is illuminated by a shaft of light emanating from the left. Barely discernible in the background are a palette and a portable easel resting against a shelf which carries some books, a jar of brushes, and a skull.

Dewey F. Mosby dates the picture about 1836 and relates it to notable suicides of the time, particularly those of Decamps' friend Léopold Robert and Baron Gros. He cites in connection with this work a drawing by Decamps of the dead Robert that belonged to Alfred Arago as well as A. Bouquet's lithograph *Morte!!!* of 1833 based on Decamps' painting of a shrouded corpse in a candle-lit room.

In the Museum of Fine Arts, Boston, is a pastel and crayon preliminary drawing for *The Suicide* that once belonged to Thomas Gold Appleton. It measures .23 x .34 and bears the inscription *sic irat ad astra.* There was once available on the New York art market a now unlocated watercolor by Decamps entitled *The Suicide* (Charles Stewart Smith Sale, New York, 1919, no. 98).

Mosby suggests that Decamps' *Suicide* probably served as an inspiration for Charles Hue's lithograph *La Fin de l'Oeuvre* and Henry Wallis' *Death of Chatterton* (1856) in the Tate Gallery, London.

Support: Canvas, .4 x .56 (15¾" x 22").

Signed at lower left: *DECAMPS.*

Condition: Lined prior to 1934. In 1972, the painting was lightly cleaned and crackle lines in the background right of center were inpainted.

Provenance: Didier (1845); Charles de la Roche (1868); Wm. T. Blodgett Sale, New York, April 27, 1876, no. 88, $2,100.00; John Taylor Johnston Sale, December 22, 1876, no. 86, $2,900.00 to S. P. Avery; Avery to Walters before 1878.

Reproductions: Lithograph by Eugène Leroux.

Exhibitions: Barye Monument Association, no. 541; "The Romantic Circle," Wadsworth Atheneum, Hartford, 1952, no. 38; "Paris-New York, A Continuing Romance," Wildenstein and Co., New York, 1977, no. 63, fig. 56.

References: Auguste de Vaucelles, "Gravures de numéro," *L'Artiste* 5th series 7 (1851): 112; Adolphe Moreau, *Decamps et son oeuvre.* Paris, D. Jouaust, 1869. p. 80, no. 49, p. 119, no. 103; Strahan, 1: 87, illus. (in reverse), 89; Walters cat., 1878, p. 28, and subsequent Walters catalogues; Champlin and Perkins, 1: 382; Francis Wilson, *Joseph Jefferson.* New York, Charles Scribner's Sons, 1906. p. 223; Dewey F. Mosby, *Alexandre-Gabriel Decamps, 1803–1860.* Outstanding dissertations in the Fine Arts. 2 vols. New York, Garland, 1977. 1: 140–43, 261–62; 2: 401, no. 22, plate 38B.

19. The Guardsmen

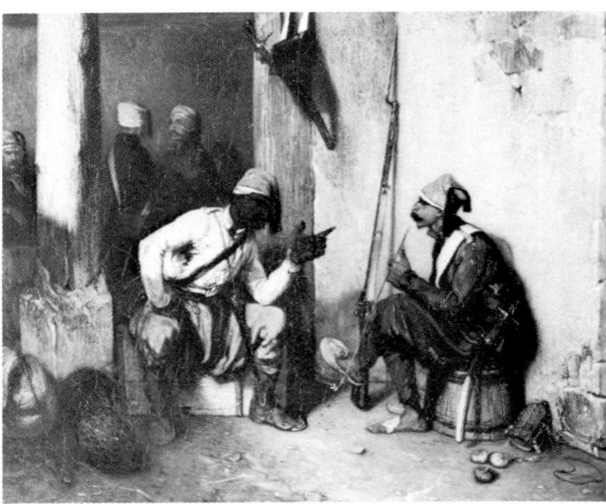

37.849 1841

In a Turkish guardroom or barracks, two soldiers are seated conversing. One with negroid features gesticulates while addressing the other who listens impassively, smoking his long pipe. On the ground beside the speaker, are a cloth-wrapped bundle, a couple of melons, and a pipe. Three other soldiers are discernible in the background. Behind the figure smoking is a crumbling masonry wall, a recurrent motif in Decamps' pictures. A watercolor, *Poste Turc,* has been related to this picture by Adolphe Moreau (p. 239).

Scenes of oriental guardrooms abound in Decamps' work. Perhaps the most ambitious example is *The Road from Smyrna to Magnesia,* dated 1833, in the Musée Condé, Chantilly. One of his last works was *A Corps of Bashi-Bazouk Guards,* in which a soldier stands outside a guardroom filled with men ("Vingt cinq contemporains," *Les Contemporains,* Paris, n.d. p. 13, illus.).

Alternative titles: *Corps-de-Garde; Corps de Garde Turc.*

Support: Canvas, .495 x .598 (19½" x 23½").

Signed at lower left: *DECAMPS 1841.*

Condition: Deep traction crackle pattern mars much of the surface of this picture.

Provenance: Ed L. Jacobson Sale, April 28–29, 1876, no. 22, 12,400 francs; Charles T. Yerkes Sale, American Art Association, New York, April 5, 6, 7, 8, 1910, no. 13, $1,500.00.

Reproductions: Lithograph by Eugène Leroux, engraving by François Flemeng.

References: Julius Meyer, *Geschichte der modernen französischen Malerei seit 1789.* Leipzig Seemann, 1867. illus.; Adolphe Moreau, *Decamps et son oeuvre.* Paris, D. Jouaust, 1869. p. 125, no. 126; *L'Art* 5 (1876): 94 (illus. with engraving by Flameng); Charles Clément. *Decamps.* Les artistes célèbres. Paris, Librairie de l'art, 1887. p. 67 (illus. with engraving by Flameng); Dewey F. Mosby, *Alexandre-Gabriel Decamps, 1803–1860.* Outstanding dissertations in the Fine Arts. 2 vols. New York, Garland, 1977. 1: 167; 2: 400, no. 21, plate 55A.

Artist unknown, after Decamps

20. Sunset, Tombs near Cairo

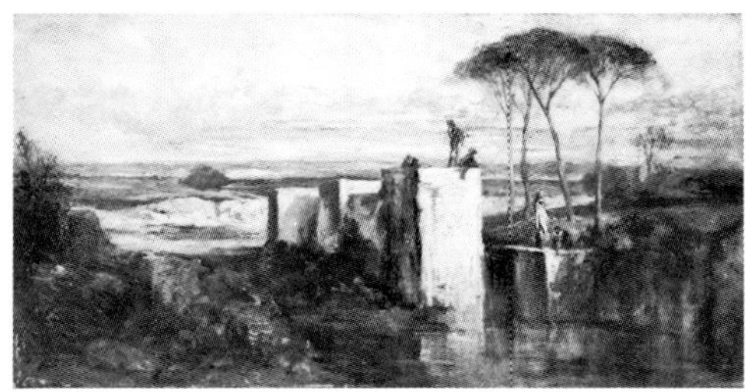

37.8

The composition of *A Well in the East,* dated 1847, canvas, .31 x .42, Wallace Collection, London, Inv. P 263, has been reversed in this picture. The rich coloring of the sunset and the thick impasto of the Walters picture are reminiscent of Decamps' painting. However, the lack of definition of forms at both sides of the picture, the reversal of the composition and the unusual signature in cursive script suggest that the painting is a forgery. Dewey F. Mosby in *Alexandre-Gabriel Decamps, 1803–1860,* dissertation, Harvard University, 1973, illustrates a number of forgeries involving reversal of compositions (nos. 224, 24, and 62).

Alternative title: *Syrian Landscape.*

Support: Panel, .325 x .63 (12¾" x 24¾").

Signed at lower left: *Decamps.*

Provenance: Mrs. S. D. Warren Sale, January 8, 1903, no. 42 illus., $3,000.00.

Exhibitions: Museum of Fine Arts, Boston, 1902, no. 2668.

References: William R. Johnston, "Alexandre-Gabriel Decamps, an Orientalist," *WAGB* 20, no. 7 (April 1968): 2–3; Dewey F. Mosby, *Alexandre-Gabriel Decamps, 1803–1860.* Outstanding dissertations in the Fine Arts. 2 vols. New York, Garland, 1977. 2: 401, no. 23.

Louis-Gabriel-Eugène Isabey

French: Paris, 1803 - Lagny, 1886

Eugène Isabey trained under his father Jean-Baptiste Isabey, portrait miniaturist to the Empress Josephine and to Charles X. In 1823–24, he assisted the senior Isabey with lithographs illustrating a travel-book of the Italian states, and in 1824 made his debut at the Salon, winning a first-class medal in marine painting. The following year he crossed the English Channel, probably in the company of Bonington, Delacroix, and A. Colin, and upon his return, began to paint along the coast of Normandy. Until the mid-thirties, Isabey specialized in oils and watercolors of coastal scenes. In 1830 he was chosen to accompany the French expeditionary force to North Africa, an experience that left no apparent imprint on his subsequent development, though he did draw a view of the fleet on the eve of its departure from Toulon harbor, which was presented to Charles X by the artist's father. Other travels were to Brittany in 1833–34 and 1851, and to the Low Countries in 1839 and 1846. During the reign of Louis-Philippe he turned increasingly to historical genre scenes that were eventually to dominate his salon entries, though he did not abandon marine painting until the mid-sixties. Isabey accompanied Louis-Philippe to Tréport in 1843 to record Queen Victoria's visit to France, an event that he commemorated in two works, one depicting her arrival (Salon of 1844) and the other, her departure (Salon of 1845). In the forties, Isabey became acquainted with two artists who were to establish reputations in coastal scenes, Eugène Boudin, whom he met at Le Havre in 1844, and Jongkind, whom he encountered in the Hague in 1846 and who was subsequently to follow him back to Paris as his pupil. The historical genre subjects produced by Isabey during the Second Empire may most aptly be described as "costume pieces." These were rendered with a distinctive spontaneity of brush stroke, a boldness of color and a theatrical quality that recalled Flemish seventeenth-century and French rococo antecedents.

21. After the Storm

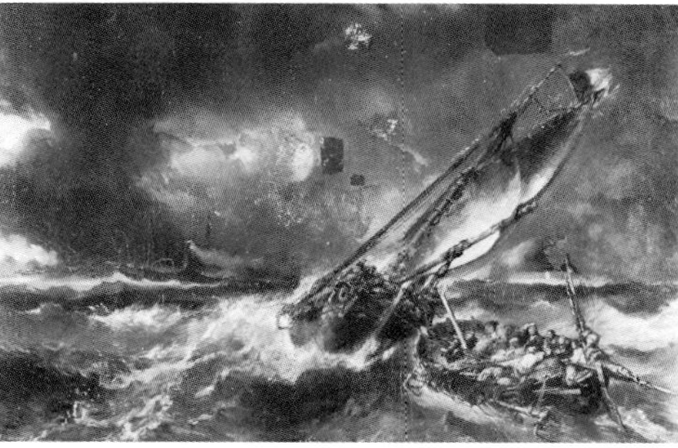

37.63 1844

In high seas, a sailboat heeling to starboard tows another boat that has lost its mast and is crowded with huddling figures and tangled rigging. A paddle-wheel steamer is visible against the horizon. The storm is passing and a ray of light is breaking through the scudding clouds at the left.

Support: Fabric, .76 x 1.155 (30" x 45½").

Signed and dated at lower left: *E. Isabey 1844.*

Condition: An examination of the painting in 1959 revealed that its entire surface was covered with a thick, tinted varnish. Upon its removal, extensive areas of overpainting were discovered in the sky. This overpainting was applied over a water-soluble gesso used as filling in extensive cracks. Further study in 1977 employing microscopic analysis and X-ray photography revealed extensive area of overpainting in the sailboat and its rigging. No treatment was undertaken and this picture is presently unexhibitable.

Provenance: Unknown; acquired by W. T. Walters between 1878 and 1884.

References: Walters cat., 1884, p. 39, no. 62, and subsequent Walters catalogues; Champlin and Perkins 2: 321.

22. The Departure of Elisabeth of France for Spain

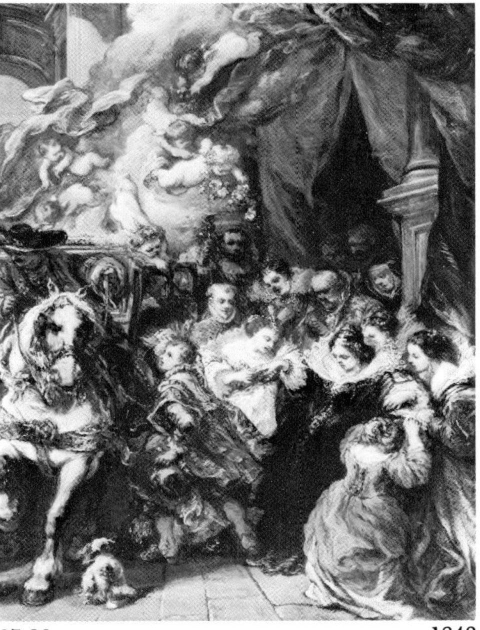

37.90 c.1848

As she is being conducted from the threshold of the palace to the waiting carriage, the princess, overcome by emotion, swoons. She

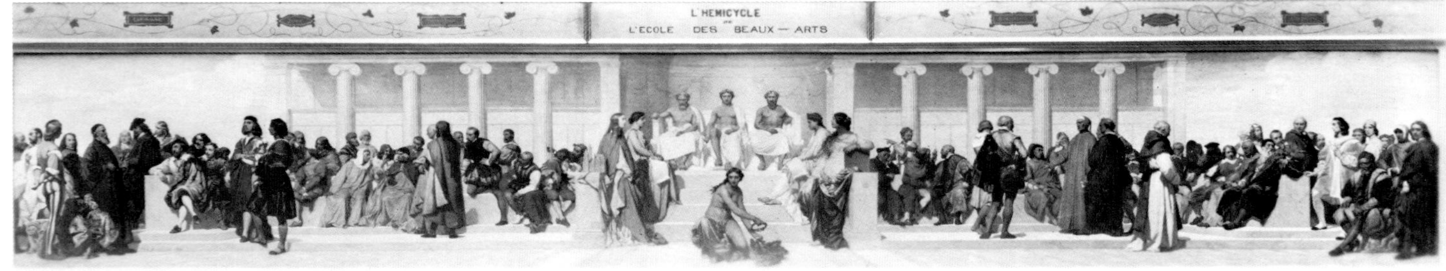

Delaroche: The Hemicycle, no. 23

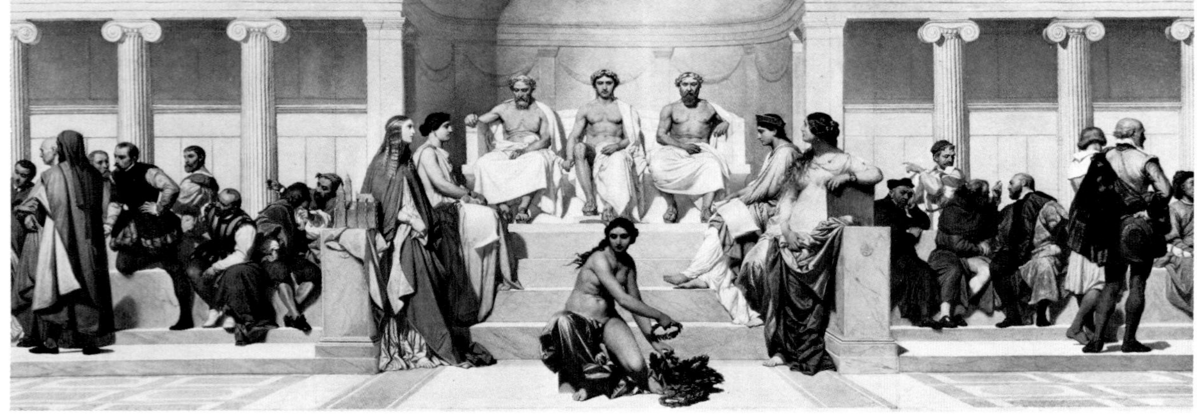

Central detail

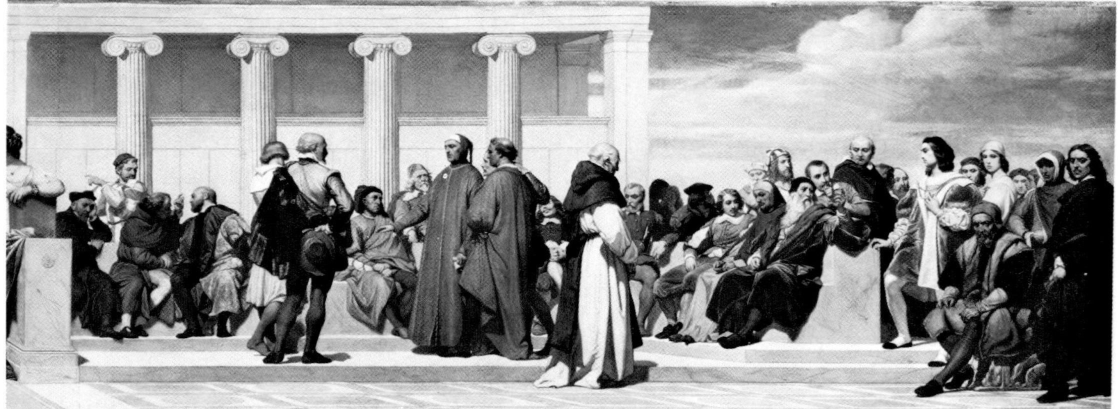

Right detail

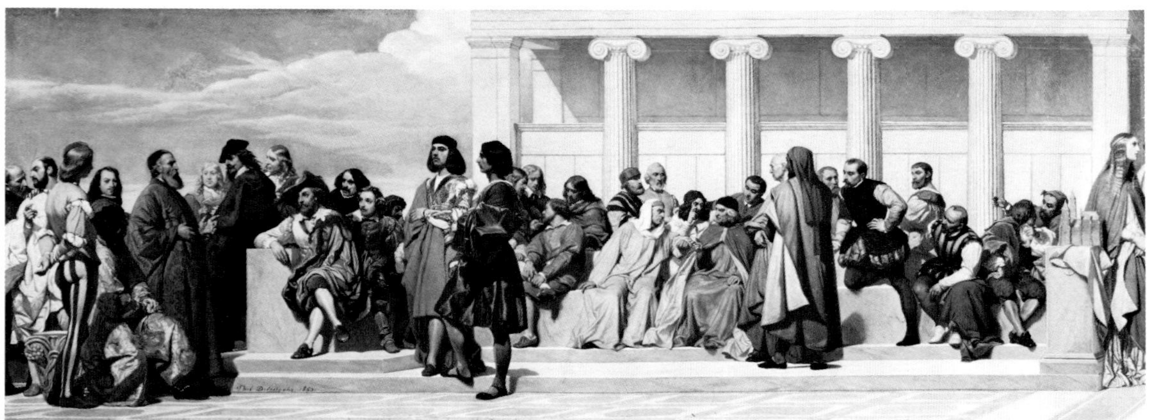

Left detail

is surrounded by various grieving courtiers and maids of honor. Above, in billowing clouds, hover amorini scattering garlands of roses.

Elisabeth (1545–1568), the hapless daughter of Henri II and Catherine de' Medici, was briefly betrothed in 1559 to Don Carlos, Prince of Asturias, but for reasons of state, she was married instead to the prince's father, Philip II of Spain. She and Don Carlos are the subjects of tragedies by J. C. F. von Schiller (1787) and A. M. de Chénier (1789).

The painting exemplifies Isabey's debt to Rubens' "Medici Cycle" executed between 1622 and 1625 for Marie de' Medici. Ironically, Isabey could not have directly known the episode in the Cycle *The Queen taken Prisoner by Order of her Son,* with which his picture most closely corresponds in subject and composition. The Rubens composition, replaced in the Cycle by another scene, survives only as an oil sketch in the Alte Pinakothek in Munich. The author of the Introduction to the exhibition catalogue *Eugène Isabey,* Fogg Art Museum, Cambridge, Mass. 1967, suggests that Isabey's Rubensian works, such as this example and his *Episode du mariage d'Henri IV* (1848) in the Philadelphia Museum of Art, both dating from the reign of Louis Philippe, were intended to aggrandize the monarchy.

Support: Three-ply laminated plywood, cradled, .66 x .5 (26″ x 19 11/16″).

Marks: The reverse of the panel bears the stencil: *VENTE ET LOCATION / DURAND RUEL / Rue de la Paix / pres de la Place Vendome / A Paris / TABLEAUX ET DES. . . .*

Condition: The panel appears to have been reduced on both sides at the time the cradle was applied. Discolored varnish was removed in 1942.

Provenance: Mme. la baronne de Gunzbourg, Sale, Paris, Dec. 12, 1892, no. 16, 6,400 francs.

Exhibitions: "Eugène Isabey," Fogg Art Museum, Cambridge, Mass., 1967, no. 8.

References: Walters cat., 1895, p. 97, no. 163, and subsequent Walters catalogues; Pierre Miquel, *Eugène Isabey, 1803–1886.* 2 vols. Maurs-la-Jolie, Editions de la Martinelle, 1980. 2: 208, no. 1157.

Hippolyte (Paul) Delaroche

French: Paris, 1797 - Paris, 1856

Paul Delaroche was widely acclaimed by the general public of his time. Now he is remembered as the principal painter of the Juste Milieu, the middle course between the romantic and classic camps during the Orléans regime.

Delaroche was the son of a paintings *expert* at the Mont-de-Piété. Initially he studied with the landscape painter L. E. Watelet, then briefly with C. J. Desbordes, and finally in 1818, he succeeded his elder brother as a student in the atelier of A. J. Gros. He made a modest debut at the Salon of 1822, but received wider attention in 1824 with paintings depicting events in the lives of Filippo Lippi, Saint Vincent de Paul, and Jeanne d'Arc. Until 1837 he participated in almost every salon, submitting pictures that illustrated episodes from the modern histories of France and England. Apparent in his output was a romantic preference for the more somber moments in the lives of the monarchs of the two countries. These he portrayed with keen draftsmanship and a conscientious approach to historical accuracy. Among his most widely acclaimed works were the *Death of President Duranti* (1827), *Cromwell and Charles I* (1831), and *The Assassination of the Duke of Guise at the Chateau of Blois* (1834–35). In preparation for some murals for the Madeleine he traveled to Italy in 1834–35 and while there, married Louise Vernet, the daughter of the painter Horace Vernet. Returning to Paris, he rejected the commission for the church murals when he learned that the project was to be shared with the artist Jules Ziègler. Louis Philippe arranged for him to receive instead the commission for the mural of the amphitheater of the Ecole des Beaux-Arts, his one monumental undertaking that occupied him between 1836 and 1841. This project was interrupted by another visit to Italy in 1839 to study Byzantine art in Venice and Ravenna.

After 1837 Delaroche no longer participated in the salons, though he did exhibit abroad. Narrative religious themes abounded in his later production, as did tragic views of Napoleon I. Much of this work is marked by a sense of melancholy that can in part be attributed to a number of grievous experiences, the death of his wife in 1845, the 1848 Revolution, and the loss of a brother and the illness of a son in 1849. He remained an accomplished and fashionable portraitist, painting such noted figures as F. P. G. Guizot (1837); comte de Rémusat (1845); comte de Pourtalès-Gorgier (1846); J.-E. Pereire (1855); and L. A. Thiers (1856).

Throughout his career, Delaroche was showered with official rewards. He became a Chevalier of the Legion of Honor in 1828, the youngest member of the Institut in 1832, a professor at the Ecole des Beaux-Arts in 1833, and an Officier of the Legion of Honor in 1834. Later, he was elected an honorary member of the academies of almost every nation, including America's National Academy of Design.

Delaroche is also remembered in association with the numerous students who worked in his atelier between 1833 and 1843. Over 355 pupils are listed by Henri Delaborde, including such prominent painters as Couture, Gérôme, Hébert, Yvon, Millet, and Robert Fleury.

In part, Delaroche's popularity with the public can be attributed to the engravers, particularly L. P. Henriquel-Dupont, who reproduced his works, and to his publisher of long standing M. M. Goupil et Cie.

23. The Hemicycle

37.83 (see facing page) 1853

This replica of the mural in the Salle des Prix of the Ecole des Beaux-Arts served as a basis for the 1853 engraving by Louis Pierre Henriquel-Dupont. Accounts of its execution vary. William T. Walters believed that the replica was the work of Delaroche alone. Mirecourt stated that it was painted by students and retouched by the master working in front of the original over a three week period one winter. Goddé reported an initial phase in 1841 and Delaroche's extensive reworking of it in 1853. Changes in the allegorical figure of Renaissance Art, including the addition of garments and jewelry, suggest that the final reworking was undertaken after the completion of the print.

Henriquel-Dupont's three-part engraving (.56 x 2.6) which won the medal of honor at the Salon of 1853 (no. 1579), contributed to the mural's fame and probably inspired a number of later works including Nicaise de Keyser's *The Antwerp School of Painters,* 1862–67; H. H. Armstead's and J. B. Philip's friezes for the Albert Memorial, 1864–72; Frank Furness' relief for the Pennsylvania Academy of the Fine Arts, 1872-76; and J. Stortenbeker's *Pantheon* in the Art Gallery at Het Loo, The Netherlands, 1875. It also served as the basis for a cartoon by the German–American artist Thomas Nast, published by Albert B. Paine in *Th. Nast,* New York, 1904, p. 267.

The original mural (3.9 x 25) was painted in encaustic by Delaroche and assistants between 1836 and 1841 and restored by them after a fire in 1855. It shows the assemblage of the great artists of the past for the distribution of recompenses in the hall below them.

Enthroned on a raised dais in the central recess of the Temple of Immortality are Ictinus, the architect of the Parthenon, Apelles the painter, and the sculptor Phidias. To their left, on the steps of the dais, are personifications of Greek and Gothic Art, and to the right, of Roman and Renaissance Art. With the exception of the sensuous Renaissance Art, who is addressing the immortal artists of Antiquity, the personifications appear to be fully self-absorbed. The Genius of Fame, represented by a kneeling, semi-nude figure in the foreground, breaks with the classical unities of space and time to distribute laurel wreaths, presumably to the successful students of the Ecole beyond the bounds of the mural. Grouped to the left of the central niche of the Temple are fourteen great sculptors: Andrea Pisano, Luca della Robbia, Lorenzo Ghiberti, Donatello, Peter Fischer, Pierre Bontemps, Benedetto da Maiano, Baccio Bandinelli, Jean Goujon, Bernard Palissy, Benvenuto Cellini, Pierre Puget, and Gian Bologna, and beyond them a gathering of painters distinguished as colorists and naturalists: Jan van Eyck, Antonello da Messina, Titian, Gian Bellini, Giorgione, Rembrandt, Rubens, Van Dyck, Correggio, Paul Veronese, Murillo, Gerard Terburg, Van der Helst, Velasquez, Caravaggio, Claude Lorraine, Gaspar Poussin, Ruysdael and Paul Potter. To the right of the central triad are the architects: Arnolfo di Lapo, Filippo Brunelleschi, Bramante, Pierre Lescot, Andrea Palladio, Inigo Jones, Robert de Luzarches, Sansovino, Erwin von Steinbach, Philibert Delorme, Baldassare Peruzzi, Jules Mansard and Giacomo da Vignola. Two engravers, M. A. Raimondi and Gerard Edelinck, separate the architects from the painters on the right. That end of the composition is devoted to the nineteen painters "eminent as designers and creators in the highest walks of art": Leonardo da Vinci, Raphael, Michael Angelo, Fra Bartolommeo, Andrea Mantegna, Giulio Romano, Masaccio, Giotto, Cimabue, Andrea del Sarto, Nicolas Poussin, Domenichino, Andrea Orcagna, Albert Dürer, Sebastiano del Piombo, Le Sueur, Hans Holbein and Fra Angelico. Within these groupings, Delaroche attempted to display his historical erudition through a meaningful disposition of the figures.

Preliminary studies for the Hemicycle include two drawings (.65 x 1.65) now belonging to Gérard Coste, Paris; several drawings in the Louvre on one of which is composed a list of thirty-six artists; and an oil study (.35 x 2.12) in the Musée des Beaux-Arts, Nantes, in which the number of artists has been extended to sixty-one. The final selection of great artists ranging in date from the thirteenth through the seventeenth centuries included thirty-nine Italians, thirteen Frenchmen, eight Dutch and Flemish artists, four Germans, two Spaniards and a lone Englishman, Inigo Jones. Delaroche drew the likenesses from well-known self-portraits and from illustrations in Vasari's *Lives of the Artists*.

In *Paris Guide*, Paris, 1867, p. 869, Alexandre Dumas wrote that the Hemicycle was *"le plus beau morceau de peinture moderne,"* an opinion shared by many of his contemporaries. The replica was generally regarded as a highlight of the Walters collection.

Support: Finely woven fabric, three sections attached to an auxilliary canvas.

Painted surface: .416 x 2.573 (16⅜" x 101$\frac{5}{16}$").

Fabric: .546 x 2.579 (21½" x 101$\frac{9}{16}$").

Signed and dated at lower left: *Paul Delaroche, 1853;* Frame made by Dutocq Sept. 28, 1871 (Lucas 2: 347).

Provenance: Delaroche estate sale, Paris, 1857, 43,000 francs, M. M. Goupil et Cie. Purchased at Georges Petit, 80,000 francs (G. A. Lucas *Agenda,* Oct. 3, 1871).

Exhibitions: The First Exhibition of the French School of the Fine Arts in London, 1854, Gallery, no. 121 Pall Mall, no. 38; French Exhibition, Pall Mall, London, 1855.

References: "The exhibition of French pictures," *Art Journal* (London) new series 6 (1854): 187; Eugène de Mirecourt, *Paul Delaroche.* Les contemporains. Paris, Gustave Havard, 1856. p. 60; Henri Delaborde and Jules Goddé, *Oeuvres de Paul Delaroche.* Paris, Goupil, 1858. pp. 18–21, plates 29, 30; Charles Blanc, "L'Hemicycle de Paul Delaroche gravé par Henriquel-Dupont," *GBA* 8 (1860): 354–61; *A Description of the great picture by Paul Delaroche / The Hemicycle.* Privately printed by W. T. Walters, n.d. (1870's); Walters cat., 1878, p. 22, and subsequent Walters catalogues; Strahan, 1:82–87; Clement and Hutton, 1:197; Mathews, p. 5; Lamb p. 245; Karl Baedeker, *The United States.* Leipsic, Karl Baedeker, 1893, p. 247; Stranahan, p. 217; Reizenstein, p. 553, illus. p. 554–55; H. Mireur, *Dictionnaire des ventes d'art.* 7 vols. Paris, Ch. de Vincenti, 1911–12. 2:432; E. P. Richardson, *The way of western art.* Cambridge, Mass., Harvard University Press, 1939. p. 143 (illus. no. 123—detail); Dorothy Weir Young, *The life and letters of J. Alden Weir.* New Haven, Yale University Press, 1960. p. 64; Francis Haskell, "Un monument et ses mystères," *Revue de l'art* 30 (1975): 61–62 (illus.); Francis Haskell, *Rediscoveries in art.* Ithaca, N.Y., Cornell University Press, 1976. pp. 9–10, plates 2, 5–7;David Van Zanten, "Félix Duban and the buildings of the Ecole des Beaux-Arts," *Journal of the Society of Architectural Historians* 37 (1979): 170–73, fig. 9; Lucas, 2:343, 345–47, 349–50; J. M. W. Van Voorst tot Voorst, "De Kunstzaal in Paleis Het Loo," *Antiek* 15 (1980): 71, fig. 3.

24. The Christian Martyr

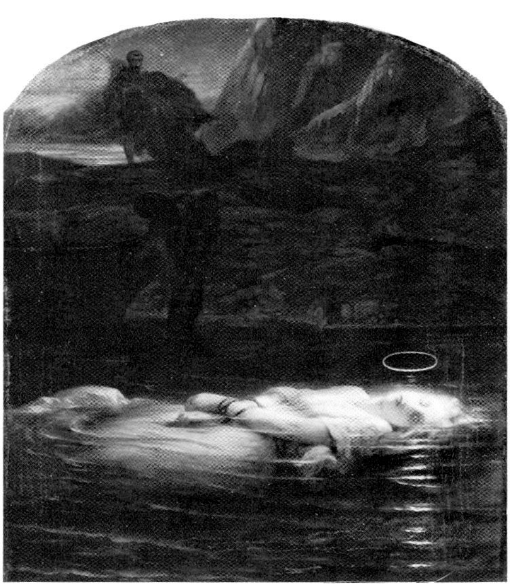

37.188 after 1853

This replica of Delaroche's *A Martyr of the Reign of Diocletian,* 1853 (1.705 x 1.48) Louvre, Paris, inv. 1038, was begun by the master and completed by his pupil C. F. Jalabert.

Portrayed is the body of a young Roman girl, who, refusing to sacrifice to pagan deities, was thrown into the River Tiber with her hands bound. A halo denotes her martyrdom. Two fellow Christians standing on the river bank and a moored boat are discernible in the waning evening light. The subject, inspired by a dream the artist experienced during an illness in December 1853 (Louis Ulbach, "Paul Delaroche," *Revue de Paris* 36, April 1857, p. 91), occurs several times in Delaroche's work: a preliminary oil sketch, dated 1853, Hermitage Museum, Leningrad, (.33 x .25); a version cited in H. Mireur, *Dictionnaire des ventes d'art,* Paris, 1911, 2:433 (1895, 1887), is now in the Samuel and Mary R. Bancroft Collection in the Delaware Art Museum, Wilmington, Del. (.519 x .437). Another replica, attributed to Delaroche and Lucien Prziaporski (.945 x 1.22), was exhibited in "The Goddess and the Slave," Hammer Galleries, New York, 1977.

Support: Canvas, lined, .556 x .467 (21⅞" x 18⅜").

Signatures: *Esquisse Delaroche* in pencil, top left, *finit par Jalabert* in pencil, top right, *D'apres P. Delaroche Ch. Jalabert* in paint, bottom left.

Marks: Stretcher: Cross bears stencil *GOUPIL & Cie / 9 Rue CHAPTAL, Paris,* and *3217* inscribed in ink.

Condition: The picture was cleaned and lined in 1972.

Provenance: Acquired by W. T. Walters before 1884.

References: Clement and Hutton, 1:197; Walters cat., 1884, p. 8, and subsequent Walters catalogues.

Ary Scheffer

Dutch/French: Dordrecht, 1795 - Argenteuil, 1858

Born in Dordrecht of a Rhenish father and a Dutch mother, Ary Scheffer was eligible for French citizenship because of an agreement between the "Batavian Republic" and the French government. He trained with his father Johann Bernhard Scheffer and submitted to the 1807 Amsterdam Exhibition a Rembrandtesque *Portrait of an Old Man* that drew the attention of the reigning Louis Bonaparte. Following the death of the senior Scheffer, the family moved to Paris. Ary studied briefly with P.-P. Prudhon before enrolling in the Ecole des Beaux-Arts. In the studio of his professor P.-N. Guérin, he became acquainted with Géricault and met Delacroix and Delaroche. His early works, including his first Salon entry of 1812, a painting of Abel singing a hymn of praise, were in the neoclassical manner of J.-L. David but a romantic vein emerged progressively in the *Orpheus and Eurydice* (Salon of 1814); *The Patriotism of Six Burghers of Calais* (Salon of 1819); *Francesca da Rimini* (Salon of 1822) and *Gaston de Foix Found Dead at Ravenna* (Salon of 1824). In the meantime he turned to producing a series of sentimental genre scenes beginning with *The Soldier's Widow* (Salon of 1822), which were popularized through his lithographic copies.

A liberal and an anti-Bourbon partisan in politics, Scheffer championed the Philhellenic movement along with such writers and painters as Delacroix and Victor Hugo and in support of this cause he painted the *Young Greek Women Imploring the Protection of the Virgin During Battle, Suliote Women,* and *The*

Last of the Garrison at Missolonghi exhibited in 1827. He was closely associated with the liberal Orléans house, serving as drawing master to Princess Marie. He witnessed both the beginning and the close of Louis-Philippe's reign, having accompanied Thiers to Neuilly in 1830 to inform the monarch of his election and assisting in 1848 in the royal family's flight. Many of the most eminent liberal figures of the reign sat to Scheffer for their portraits. He also contributed large historical scenes to the King's Galerie des Batailles at Versailles.

Scheffer was the most literary artist of his time. Byron's *The Giaour* and *The Corsair,* Walter Scott's *The Antiquary,* and the poems and plays of Dante, Shakespeare and Schiller provided him with subjects, but it was to Goethe's *Faust* and *Wilhelm Meister* that he turned most frequently in the 1830s. Apart from the poem "L'Orage" of his friend P. J. de Béranger, which inspired his *The Round of Children* (Salon of 1831), he ignored contemporary French literary sources.

In his later career, Scheffer grew increasingly isolated and, after 1846, ceased to exhibit, with one exception in 1855. An intense religious fervor manifested itself in a series of images of Christ. Undoubtedly these were affected by his Dutch Protestant background and his close associations with Augustin Thierry and the Saint Simonian movement. Included among these religious themes were the *Christus Consolator* (1836) originally acquired by the Duchesse d'Orléans, and its companion the *Christus Remunerator, Christ Carrying the Cross* (Salon of 1846), *Christ Entombed* (1845), the *Temptation of Christ* (1856) and the *Kiss of Judas* (1857), all rendered in an extremely idealized static style imbued with heavy sentiment. The polished surfaces and muted colors of these works have been attributed to the influence of Ingres, though the latter's definition of contours is less readily apparent in Scheffer's work.

Despite his rapidly failing health he journeyed to England in the spring of 1858 to attend the funeral of his friend and patroness the Duchesse d'Orléans and perished from exhaustion shortly afterward. A retrospective exhibition of his works held the following year was received with restrained enthusiasm, suggesting that Scheffer's highly personal Juste Milieu compromise between the romantic and classic traditions had become outmoded.

25. Christ Weeping Over Jerusalem

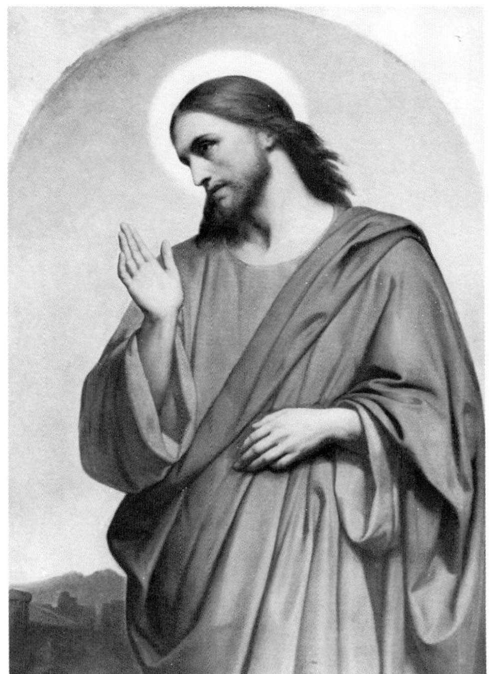

37.111 1851

Christ weeps as he foretells the destruction of Jerusalem as recounted in Luke 19: 41. He stands alone, almost three-quarter length, with his head turned to the left. One hand is raised as he speaks and the other is pressed to his side. An aureole of light emanates from his head. Visible below the low horizon in the left background are the walls and roof-tops of the doomed city. The picture is topped by a curved arch with the upper spandrel areas left in a greyish ground streaked with diagonal hatch lines in blue.

In this lachrymose picture of Christ, the artist has suppressed the narrative elements, thus producing a devotional image rather than a religious genre scene. This trait distinguishes his work from the noted *Christ Lamenting Over Jerusalem,* exhibited by Sir Charles Eastlake at the Royal Academy in 1847, no. 75, in which Christ's three followers as well as several rustic genre details are included in the scene.

The Baltimore painting is one of a number of versions of this composition. Marthe Kolb, in her biography of the artist, cites a date of 1848 for the initial composition without giving its location. In the *Art-Journal,* London, 1849, p. 289, reference is made to a *Christ Weeping* painted for J. C. Grundy of Manchester in 1849. It was presumably the same painting that was exhibited by Robert Barnes at the "Exhibition of Works by Modern Artists," Royal Manchester Institution, 1855, no. 12, and at the "Manchester Art Treasures," Manchester, 1857, no. 665. Pictures of the same title occurred in the "French Gallery," London, 1870, no. 17, and at the L. Pocock Sale, Christie's, London, May 1873, no. 87. These references may allude to the *Christ Weeping Over Jerusalem,* given by a Mrs. Murray Miller to the Victoria and Albert Museum, London, (.843 x .66) dated 1849. The London painting differs from the Walters picture in that it has a rectangular format, the figure is shown waist-length and there are variations in the rendition of the city's roofs and in the positioning of Christ's left hand. Also, a picture listed as *Christ the Consoler,* though apparently identical in composition to the Victoria and Albert Museum version, is mentioned in the *Catalogue of the European Pictures,* Baroda Picture Gallery, Baroda, 1935, p. 24, no. 106. (.915 x .685).

Support: Fabric, 1.076 x .735 (42$\frac{3}{8}$" x 28$\frac{15}{16}$").

Signed and dated, lower left: *Ary Scheffer 1851.*

Marks: Inscribed in ink on the reverse of the frame on several members is *8125 Walters.* A paper sticker with the number 527 is on the stretcher.

Condition: The picture was lined at an unknown date.

Provenance: Acquired by W. T. Walters before 1878.

Exhibitions: "The Life of Christ," Washington County Museum of Fine Arts, Hagerstown, 1951, no. 7; "Christian Imagery in French Nineteenth Century Art, 1789–1906," Shepherd Gallery, New York, 1980, no. 38.

References: Charles Lenormant, *Ary Scheffer.* Paris, 1859. p. 470; Mrs. H. Grote, *Memoir of the life of Ary Scheffer.* London, J. Murray, 1860. p. 162; Walters cat., 1878, p. 34, and subsequent Walters catalogues; Strahan, 1: 94; Marthe Kolb, *Ary Scheffer et son temps.* Paris, Boivin, 1937. pp. 378–79, 477.

Simon Saint-Jean

French: Lyons, 1808 - Ecully, 1860

Saint-Jean was a prominent still life painter during the second quarter of the nineteenth century. Though born in Lyons, he spent considerable time in the village of Millery, the birthplace of his parents.

Initially he studied in the studio of François Lepage and at the Lyons Ecole des Beaux-Arts. Dedicating himself to flower painting early in his career, he won a gold medal in this field in 1826 while working in Lyons under Augustin Thierriat. In 1834 Saint-Jean received a third-class medal for his first Paris Salon entry, *Flowers in a hat hanging from the branch of an oak tree* (Musée de Rouen). His growing reputation was enhanced by a *Bouquet of Flowers on a Tomb* (Salon of 1835), *The Flower Girl* (Salon of 1839) now in the Musée de Rouen, and *The Medici Vase* (Salon of 1841) in the Musée des Beaux-Arts, Lyons. That year, in which he received another second-class medal, he and his bride traveled to Holland where he was drawn to the seventeenth and eighteenth-century still life traditions and especially to the flower paintings of Jan van Huysum. In 1842, the year he exhibited *Christ with the Symbols of the Eucharist,* subsequently reproduced in a woven fabric by the firm of Lamy and Giraud, a *Virgin Surrounded by Flowers* and an *Offering to the Virgin,* he was made Chevalier of the Legion of Honor. As his fame grew, he was patronized by such collectors as Lord Hertford (1845), and the princes Galitzin (1850), Demidoff (1851), and Radziwill (c. 1852). At the 1851 International Exhibition several of his paintings were included by special decree in the Lyonnais Industrial Arts section in the Crystal Palace because of their influence on the silk weaving industry, and in 1855 he served as a member of the jury for the silk industry. Following the loss of his wife, he grew despondent and died in 1860.

26. Still Life with Fruit

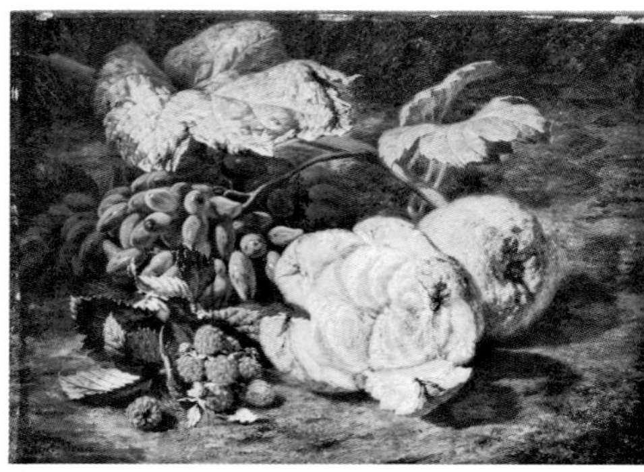

37.168 c.1850

Lying on the ground are two oranges, one of which is opened, some raspberries and a bunch of Tokay grapes still attached to a vine branch. Similar in composition is *Flowers and Fruit,* a still-life of 1853, showing grapes, raspberries and roses in the Wallace Collection, London, P601.

Support: Panel, mahogany, beveled edges, .343 x .483 (13½″ x 19″).

Signed at lower left in black: *Saint-Jean;* remnants of an earlier signature *St. Jean* appear above the existing signature as pentimenti.

Provenance: Unrecorded.

References: *Walters cat.,* 1878, p. 21, and subsequent Walters catalogues; Strahan, 1:94.

27. Still Life with Flowers

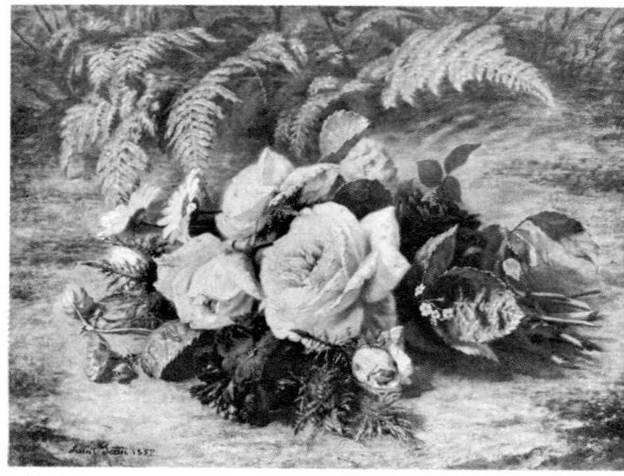

37.166 1852

A bouquet of red, white and pink roses, juniper, buttercups and a sprig of forget-me-nots lies on the ground. Behind grow some ferns.

Support: Canvas: .367 x .455 (14½″ x 17⅞″).

Signed and dated in brown paint at lower left: *Saint Jean 1852.* Although the date now appears to read *1857,* discernible under close scrutiny is a dash of brown paint that may complete the *2.* Early catalogues consistently transcribe the date as 1852.

Provenance: Unrecorded.

References: Walters cat., 1878, p. 24, and subsequent Walters catalogues; Strahan, 1:94; Champlin and Perkins, 4:102.

Auguste-Antoine-Ernest Hébert

French: La Tronche (Isère), 1817 - La Tronche, 1908

Hébert, working in the classical tradition during the Second Empire and Third Republic, distinguished himself as a painter of Italian genre scenes, religious subjects and portraits.

His training was unusually varied. He attended a lycée in Grenoble and studied drawing under Benjamin de Rolland, a disciple of J.-L. David. At the age of sixteen Hébert went to Paris, where he enrolled in both the Faculté de Droit and the Ecole des Beaux-Arts. He received his training in art in the studio of the sculptor David d'Angers and from the painter R. R. J. Monvoisin. By 1839 he was an *avocat,* and had studied briefly in Delaroche's atelier. That year his first salon entry, *Tasso in Prison,* was purchased for the museum in Grenoble and his *The Cup Found in Benjamin's Sack* won for him the Prix de Rome. In Rome he was cordially received at the Villa Medici by Ingres, who was director until succeeded by Victor Schnetz in 1841, and established a friendship with the composer Charles Gounod. While a pensionnaire, Hébert traveled about Italy for four years, sending to the Ecole des Beaux-Arts such *envois* as the *Slave dreaming on the tomb of a Freeman,* painted under Ingres' supervision, the two *Odalisques* and *Sibylla Delphica.* As the result of a knee injury he received returning to France, he remained in Marseilles for two years to recuperate and did not participate again in the Paris salons until 1848.

Hébert's reputation was established in the 1850 Salon, in which he exhibited his *La Mal'aria,* a melancholic view of plague victims being conveyed on a raft through the Pontine Marshes, and confirmed by such successes as *The Kiss of Judas,* Salon of 1853, and *The Women of Cervaro,* Salon of 1859, all three of which were acquired for the Luxembourg Gallery.

During the 1860s, he painted a number of portraits, including those of Prince Napoleon and his wife Princess Clotilde (1863) and Princess Mathilde (1867), executed murals for the library of the Louvre, and produced numerous figurative works. In 1867 Hébert returned to Rome as director of the Académie de France, a post he held until 1873 and again from 1885 to 1890.

Hébert's religious paintings included the *Virgin of the Deliverance,* painted for the church of La Tronche in 1873, and a mural for the apse of the Pantheon completed in 1884. For the latter he undertook additional studies in Venice, Ravenna, Rome and Palermo.

Over a long career Hébert received all the awards of French officialdom, winning medals at the expositions of 1855, 1867 and 1889, and rising through the ranks of the Legion of Honor from Chevalier in 1853 to Grande Croix in 1903. In addition he was elected a member of the Institut in 1874.

28. Going to the Well

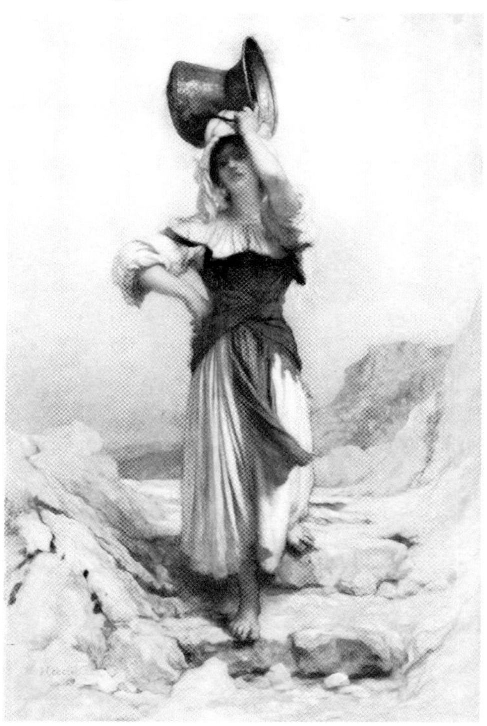

37.133 after 1859

In a rocky terrain a young Italian peasant, carrying an empty copper container on her head, descends some roughly-hewn steps. She is a replica of the principal figure in *The Women of Cervaro,* Salon of 1859. In the large work (2.88 m. x 1.75 m.), three inhabitants of Cervaro, a hamlet outside Rome, a child, the young woman, and an older woman, representing the different stages of life, are shown mounting and descending a spiral staircase in a grotto. Drawings of the head and full figure of the girl, identified as Adela or Adelaide, have been published in George Lafenestre, "M. Ernest Hébert,"

Gazette des Beaux-Arts 3rd pér. 18 (1897): 355, 359. Another drawing of her, entitled *L'Orfanella* (the orphan) is reproduced in Jules Clairtie, "Ernest Hébert, notes et impressions, artistes contemporains," *La Revue de l'art ancien et moderne* 20, (1906): 411.

Copper vessels similar to that carried by the woman in this work are preserved in the Musée Hébert, Paris.

Support: .705 x .447 (27¾" x 17⅝").

Signed lower left: *Hebert.*

Condition: The picture was cleaned and lined in July 1975.

Provenance: Purchased May 11, 1883 at M. Gavet's residence, Paris, by W. T. Walters and G. A. Lucas (See Lucas, 2:563).

References: Walters cat., 1884, p. 47, no. 70.

A young peasant girl ascends a hill carrying a water jug on her head and another on her left hip. The sun is setting on the low horizon, and since it is twilight, the colors are muted. In an engraving of this painting entitled *The Water Bearer,* by J. Levasseur, published by D. Appleton and Co., New York, the flowers are disposed differently at the girl's feet and it does not have the lone bird in the sky.

Alternative title: *The Water Bearer.*

Support: Three-ply panel, .407 x .267 (16" x 10½").

Signed at lower right: *H.*

Marks: Stamped on reverse: *Tachet/Brevete/ a Paris;* paper labels *13.7111,* in chalk: *III.*

Condition: Removal of some discolored varnishes in 1981. Revarnishing with synthetic resin. Replacement of central panel in three-ply support with rag matboard sheet.

29. Returning from the Well

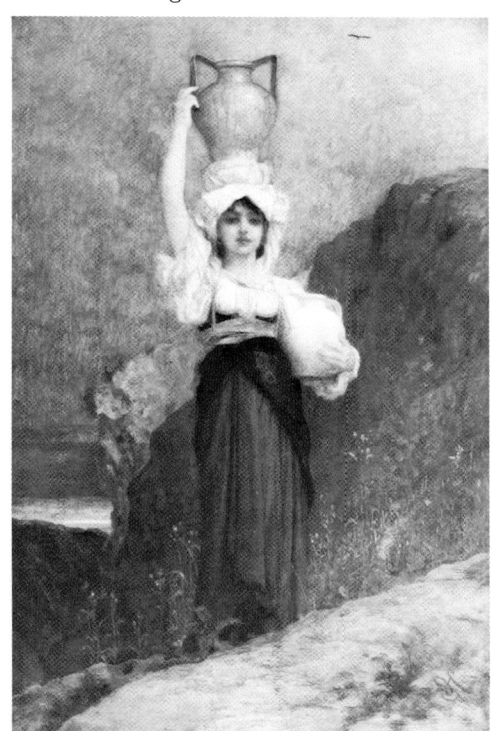

37.2 c.1860

Provenance: Acquired by W. T. Walters between 1878 and 1884, source unknown.

References: Walters cat., 1884, p. 60, no. 90.

30. Virgin of the Deliverance

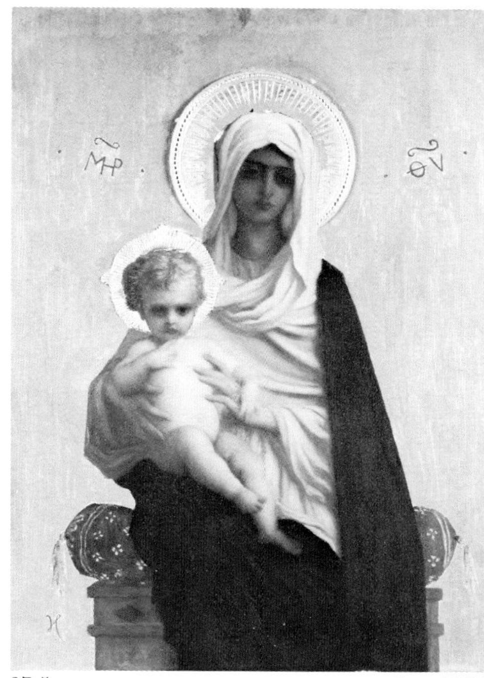

37.5 after 1873

This work is a reduced version of *The Virgin of the Deliverance,* an ex-voto painting dedicated to the Virgin by Hébert upon his safe return to La Tronche, his native village, in 1873. The Virgin, seated on a cushioned throne, holds the naked Christ Child in her lap. Affirming an interest in Byzantine art that culminated during the eighties in the Pantheon mural, Hébert substituted in this version a gold ground for the velvet panel woven in the pomegranate pattern seen in the La Tronche painting. Other archaisms include the inscription in the gold background of the Greek letters Mu, Rho, Theta and Upsilon, the abbreviation of *Maria Theotokos* found in numerous Byzantine mosaics, and the rendering in relief of the Virgin's halo. The representation of the infant Christ is almost identical to that in *The Virgin of the Kiss,* 1883 (Collection of the Marquise Landolfo Carcano, Sale, Galerie Georges Petit, Paris, June 1, 1919).

Support: Panel, beveled edges .405 x .281 (15$\frac{15}{16}$" x 11$\frac{1}{16}$").

Signed at lower left: *H.*

Marks: Stencil on reverse: *Toiles Tableaux & couleurs/Encadrements Latouche Paris 34 Rue de La Fayette 34.*

Condition: Cleaned and minor losses inpainted in January 1967.

Provenance: Collection of Mrs. Mary J. Morgan, Sale, New York, March 3, 4, 5, 1886, no. 12.

References: Walters cat., 1887, p. 23, no. 27, and subsequent Walters catalogues; Reizenstein, p. 548, illus.

Antoine-Louis Barye

French: Paris, 1795 - Paris, 1875

Barye, the pre-eminent *animalier* of the nineteenth century, painted in both watercolors and oils. His works in the latter medium were never exhibited during his life and have remained the least known facet of his oeuvre. After his death, over ninety-nine oil paintings were dispersed at auction (*Oeuvres de feu Barye,* Paris, Hôtel Drouot, 5/6 février, 1876). These were mostly small works, many measuring about .14 x .24 or .25 x .32. As in his watercolors, exotic animals were frequently portrayed in settings within the Forest of Fontainebleau.

Initially Barye worked for the metal engraver Fourier. He received early training in the studio of the neoclassical sculptor F. J. Bosio (1816) and in that of the proto-romantic painter Baron Gros (1817). While a student at the Ecole des Beaux-Arts from 1818 to 1824, he befriended the landscapists Paul Huet, R. P. Bonington and P. Comairas. In 1823 he became an artisan in the firm of the fashionable goldsmith Fauconnier. That year he also began his practice of sketching and studying the anatomy of animals at the Jardin des Plantes. He was accompanied there in 1828 by his friend Eugène Delacroix.

Barye made his debut as a sculptor at the Salon of 1827 and as a watercolorist in 1831. In 1833, he was nominated a Chevalier of the Legion of Honor and was named Inspecteur des Beaux-Arts. The following year he received a major commission for a *Surtout de Table* from the Duc d'Orléans, but when his models were rejected at the 1837 Salon, he ceased to participate in the exhibitions.

Following the 1848 revolution, he again received official recognition, being appointed a member of the new jury for the salons and obtaining the posts of *Chef de l'atelier de moulages* and *Conservateur de la galerie des plâtres* at the Louvre. In 1854, he also was made *maître de dessin pour la zoologie* at the Muséum d'histoire naturelle de Paris.

As early as 1849, Barye joined the painter Diaz at Barbizon, a village he frequently visited in the fifties, residing at the Auberge Ganne. In 1859–60 he purchased a house in the village at 26 Grande rue. There he enjoyed the camaraderie of the painters A. G. Decamps, H. Daumier, N. V. Diaz, T. Rousseau and C. F. Daubigny, and executed his oils and watercolors.

31. Tiger at Rest

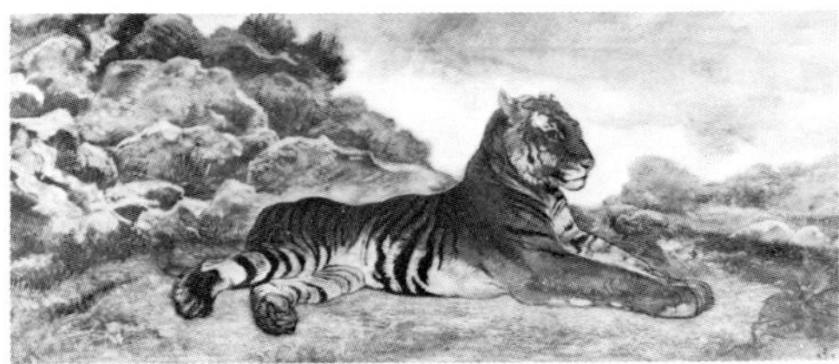

37.833 after 1859

As was his practice in both oils and watercolors, Barye juxtaposed the beast against a rocky terrain characteristic of that found in the Gorges d'Apremont near his residence in the village of Barbizon. The rich pasty handling of the pigments recalls the technique of Barye's associate in Barbizon, A. G. Decamps.

The unusual size of this picture distinguishes it from the other works dispersed at the 1876 estate sale.

Support: Canvas, .487 x 1.14 (19¼" x 44⅞").

Signed lower right: *BARYE;* wax seal on stretcher: *VENTE BARYE.*

Provenance: *Oeuvres de feu Barye,* Sale, Paris, February 5–6, 1876, no. 95, 1,720 francs to Brame; Brame to a private collector in Rheims; G. A. Lucas paid the dealer Montaignac for this painting on Nov. 28, 1884.

References: W. R. Johnston, "The Barye Collection," *Apollo* 100 (1974): 47, fig. 4; Lucas 2: 598.

32. Tiger Asleep

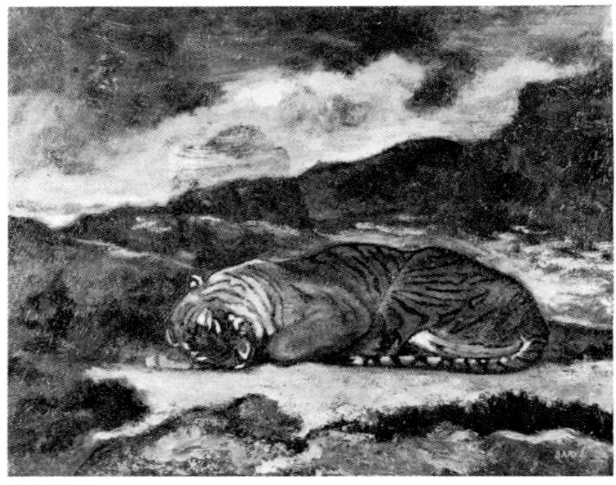

37.813 after 1859

Sleeping tigers in similar poses occur in Barye's watercolors in the collection of Georges Wildenstein, New York, and the Musée Bonnat, Bayonne (Ch. O. Zieseniss, *Les Aquarelles de Barye,* Paris, 1956, pp. 62–63, nos. B 1 and B 2). An oil painting showing the tiger resting his head on his paws though with his eyes open, was exhibited at the Ecole des Beaux-Arts, Paris, in 1889 (no. 750 *Tigre au repos,* panel, .25 x .33).

Support: Panel, .32 x .42 (12⅝" x 16½").

Signed at lower right in red: *BARYE.*

Marks: Red seal on reverse: *Vente Barye.*

Provenance: *Oeuvres de feu Barye,* Paris, February 5–6, 1876, no. 67, *Tigre dormant,* to Barye family. 1,160 francs; purchased by G. A. Lucas for W. T. Walters, January 17, 1885.

Exhibitions: Barye Monument Association, no. 469.

References: Lucas, 2:601.

Honoré Daumier

French: Marseilles, 1808 - Valmondois, 1879

Information pertaining to Daumier's early career is scant. When imprisoned in Sainte-Pélagie for political reasons in 1832 he registered himself as an "artist-painter." In 1848, at the urging of his friends Courbet and François Bonvin, he entered a competition presented by the Ministry of Fine Arts to produce a figure symbolic of the Republic, a project that he never developed beyond the sketch, *The Republic,* now in the Louvre. The following year, Daumier received a commission from the Ministry to execute a religious painting suitable for a provincial church; a project that was also abandoned, though in 1863 the Government accepted another picture, the *Drunkenness of Silenus.* Daumier entered oils in two salons, showing *The Miller, his Son and their Ass* (Burrell Collection, Glasgow) in 1849; and *Two Nymphs pursued by Satyrs* (Montreal Museum of Fine Arts), *Don Quixote* (Paine Collection, Boston) and *The Drunkenness of Silenus* (Musée des Beaux-Arts, Calais) in 1851. His comrades at this point included Diaz, whom he had known since the early thirties, Millet, Daubigny, François Bonvin, and Meissonier. In the summer of 1853 he registered at the Auberge Ganne in Barbizon and three years later he served there as witness at the baptism of Millet's son Jean-François (Mme. Daumier was the child's godmother). Beginning in 1863 he began to spend his summers away from Paris, at Valmondois.

While Daumier's early paintings tended to be devoted to mythological and allegorical subjects rendered in a monumental, perhaps sculptural style, his later pictures dealt with everyday subjects. The caustic wit of so many of his cartoons was replaced in his paintings by a sense of pathos concerning the human condition. The chronology of his later paintings has never been satisfactorily ascertained, though many works are believed to have been produced between 1860 and late 1863, a period when he was no longer illustrating *Le Charivari.* In 1878, a year before his death, Daumier's friends organized an exhibition of his works at Durand-Ruel, which featured ninety-four oils, one hundred and forty watercolors and drawings, and some sculpture and caricatures.

K. E. Maison, Daumier's most recent biographer, has catalogued about three hundred oils, fifty-three of which he regards as having seriously deteriorated in appearance. Apparently the artist's lack of technical expertise in painting and his inability to complete many of his pictures has resulted in his work's suffering the ravages of time, sometimes augmented by the efforts of overly zealous restorers and finishers.

33. The Prison Choir

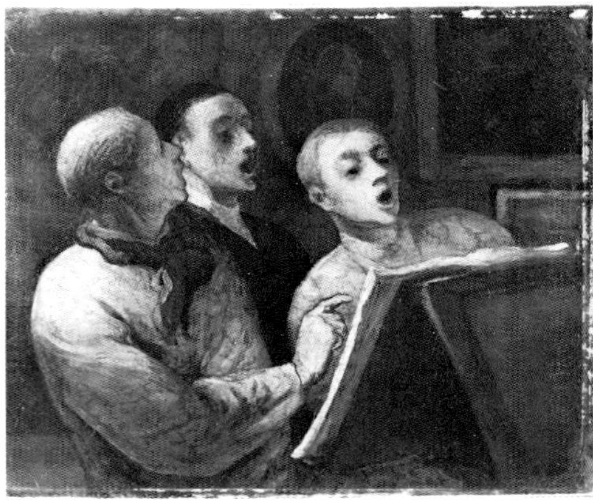

37.7

Three figures, facing right, read music held on a lectern as they sing. Visible in the background are a number of framed paintings suggesting that the scene transpires in the artist's studio rather than in a prison. In the 1878 exhibition, the picture was listed simply as *Chanteurs.*

Alternative title: *Les Chanteurs au Lutrin.*

Support: Canvas, .502 x .612 (19¾" x 24").

Signed lower left: *h.D.*

Condition: This painting is no longer exhibited because of its condition. Considerable controversy has arisen regarding the treatment undertaken in 1939. K. E. Maison admits that the picture's deterioration began at a very early date. However, he also regards the conservator's treatment in 1939 as the "virtual destruction of a genuine" work. Prior to commencing the treatment the painting was thoroughly examined by X-rays and infra-red photography. This examination revealed that the painting had been extensively damaged and treated in the past: two fabric liners had been applied to the back of the original canvas, and an extensive system of wide cracks had developed, probably as a result of the artist's use of bitumen. The latter had been concealed by overpainting. Further study revealed the use of tinted varnishes and "fillers" applied in the interstices between the ridges of impasto. In some areas the pigments were five layers thick. As a result of the complexity of the painting's state, treatment was halted.

Provenance: Latouche (1878); Mme. Bureau; Mrs. S. D. Warren, New York, 1903, no. 110; H. Williams; Henry Walters.

Exhibitions: "Exposition des Peintures et Dessins de H. Daumier," Galerie Durand-Ruel, Paris, 1878, no. 18; "Exposition de Peintures, Aquarelles, Dessins et Lithographies de Maîtres Français de la Caricature et de la Peinture de Moeurs au XIXe siècle," Ecole des Beaux-Arts, Paris 1888, no. 365; "Daumier, 1808–1879," Pennsylvania Museum of Art, Philadelphia, 1937, no. 7.

References: Arsène Alexandre, *Honoré Daumier, l'homme et l'oeuvre.* Paris, H. Laurens, 1888, p. 374; Walters cat., 1909, p. 4, no. 7; Erich Klossowski, *Honoré Daumier.* 2nd ed. Munich,

R. Piper, 1923, no. 337 A; Eduard Fuchs, *Der Maler Daumier.* Munich, A. Langen, 1927, no. 280 B; Francis Henry Taylor, "What Baltimore will do with the Walters bequest," *American Magazine of Art* 27, (1934): 264; K. E. Maison, *Honoré Daumier, catalogue raisonné.* 2 vols. Greenwich, Conn., New York Graphic Society, 1967. 1: 14, 200, no. II 32, figs. 5–11, plate 192.

Jean-Baptiste-Camille Corot
French: Paris, 1796 - Paris, 1875

Not until the age of twenty-six did Corot cease working in a dry goods shop to become an artist. He entered the studio of the narrative landscape painter, Achille-Etna Michallon, but upon the latter's untimely death in 1822 Corot turned for instruction to another landscape painter, Jean-Victor Bertin, who had served as Michallon's teacher. Imbued with classicizing tendencies by his instructors, Corot first traveled to Italy in the autumn of 1825. He remained there for three years, sketching out-of-doors during the warm seasons and expanding his sketches into larger compositions in the winter in his studio in Rome. While there, he received significant encouragement from the classicizing landscape painter Claude-Félix-Théodore d'Aligny and in 1827 he sent two works to the Paris Salon, *The Bridge at Narni* (National Gallery of Canada) and *Roman Campagna.* He returned to France in the autumn of 1828 after visiting Naples and Venice. In France he traveled extensively throughout the countryside, adhering to the pattern of seasonal activity that he had established while in Italy. Frequently he returned to his family's country house at Ville-d'Avray on the outskirts of Paris. Subsequent travels abroad included a six-month visit to Italy in 1834 with stops at Volterra and Florence, a third journey to Italy, principally to Rome, in 1843, numerous trips to Switzerland beginning with one to Montreux and Geneva in 1842, a Dutch tour in 1854, and a one-week stay in London during the International Exhibition in 1862.

Fortunately Corot received a stipend from his parents, for only gradually did his paintings gain recognition. He received a second-class medal in the 1833 Salon for a Fontainebleau forest scene, another in 1848 for an Italian view and several French subjects, and a first-class medal in 1855. In 1846 he was awarded the rank of Chevalier of the Legion of Honor and in 1867 he was promoted to Officier. Following the 1848 Revolution, Corot's fortunes improved. He frequently served on the now more liberal salon juries and he received another first-class medal at the Exposition Universelle of 1855 at which he exhibited six paintings, including the *Remembrance of Marcoussy Montlhéry,* purchased by the Emperor. His paintings began to be eagerly sought by the public and on April 11, 1858, he sold through the Hôtel Drouot thirty-eight paintings for 14,233 francs. At the 1855 Salon he was nominated for the medal of honor, an award that was ultimately given to Cabanel; in 1865 he exhibited an etching and two paintings, one of which, *La Solitude* was purchased by Napoleon III. At the Exposition Universelle of 1867 where he was represented by seven paintings, including the Walters *Saint Sebastian* that had been reworked since its first appearance in the 1853 Salon, he received a second-class medal and was promoted to Officier of the Legion of Honor. Corot was now working in association with such colleagues as Charles Daubigny, L. A. Hervier, Stanislaus Lépine and H.-J. Harpignies as well as with a host of pupils and followers whose works he was reputed to have occasionally signed with his own name as an act of charity, thus confounding later historians. During his life he was most noted for his *machines* and for his lyrical landscapes painted with their distinctively limited range of tones and harmonious balance of values. Subsequently, attention has been focused on his brilliant early studies from nature, one of which, *Rome The Coliseum seen from the Farnese Gardens* of 1826 (Louvre) he showed as early as the 1849 Salon, and also on the figurative works associated with his later years when failing health limited his out-of-door activities.

34. Two Italian Peasants

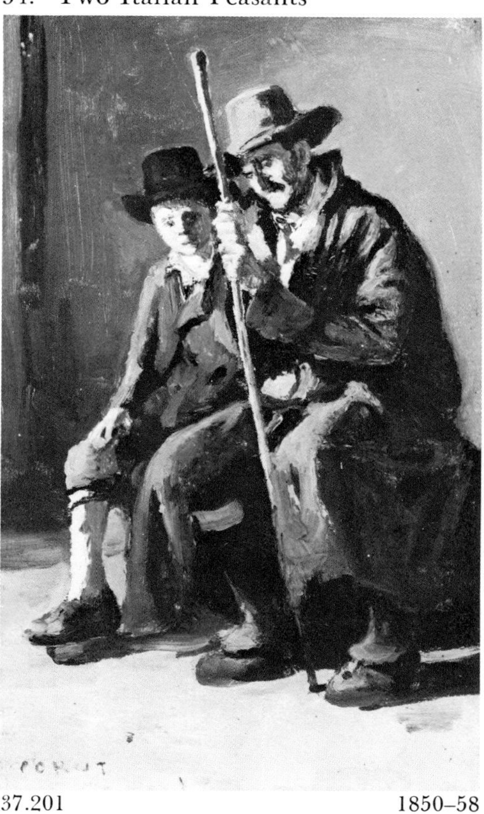

37.201 1850–58

Robaut, the first owner of this small painting of a seated old man and a youth, catalogued it as a work executed by the artist in his studio in Paris between 1850–1858. He thus distinguishes it from a series of figure studies (Robaut nos. 57–64 and 107–113) painted by Corot during his first trip to Rome and retained in his studio throughout his life.

Alternative titles: *Youth and Old Age; Mendiants jeune et vieux (étude); Mendiants; Italiens (Deux); Vieillard et jeune garçon.*

Support: Fabric, .295 x .178 (11⅝" x 7").

Signed at lower left: *COROT.*

Provenance: Sold by Corot to Alfred Robaut in 1858; since 1886 P. A. Chéramy, Sale, Paris, 1908, no. 138 to Henry Walters for 1150 francs. (Early Walters catalogues, without foundation, list as early owners Constant Dutilleux and Etienne Moreau-Nélaton) .

Exhibitions: "Exposition de l'oeuvre de Corot," Ecole des Beaux-Arts, Paris, May 1875, no. 228; "Exposition centenaire Corot," Palais Galliéra, Paris, May-June, 1895, no. 32; "Corot," The Philadelphia Museum of Art, 1946, no. 36; "From Ingres to Gauguin," The Baltimore Museum of Art, 1951, no. 36; "Corot," The Art Institute of Chicago, 1960, no. 72.

References: Alfred Robaut, *L'Oeuvre de Corot.* 4 vols. Paris, H. Floury, 1905. 2:318, no. 1040, 319 (illus.); 4:277, no. 228; Walters cat., 1909, no. 201; F. C. Watkins, "Jean Baptiste Camille Corot," *Magazine of Art* 39 (1946): 373, illus.

35. Saint Sebastian Succored by Holy Women

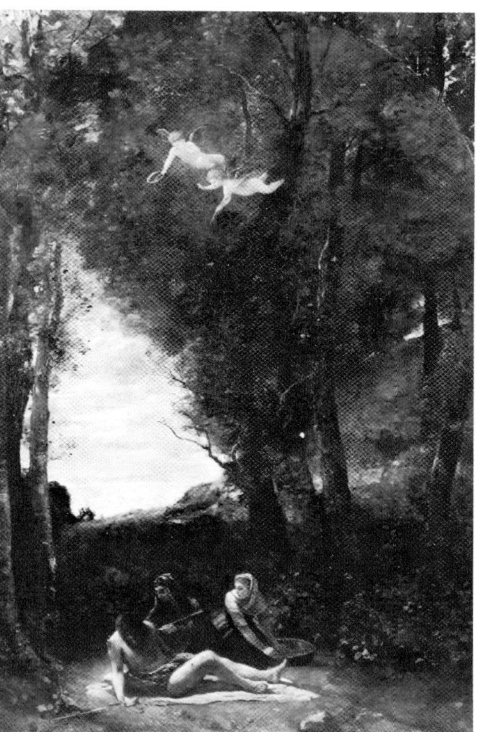

37.192 1851–73

In the foreground, two Christian women tend the wounded saint who has been left as dead by Diocletian's archers (See William Caxton, *The Golden Legend,* London, 1900, 2: 243). The women, Irene, a widow of one of his martyred friends, and her companion, are withdrawing arrows and preparing to dress his wounds. Overhead hover two small angels, one holding a wreath and the other a palm frond. The scene is set in a glade. Through an opening in the trees on the left side of the picture several soldiers ride over the crest of a hill into the sunset.

In a letter to his friend H. J. C. Dutilleux, dated November 23, 1851, Corot noted that he was in the process of painting an historical landscape embellished with a Saint Sebastian assisted by holy women (Robaut, *L'Oeuvre de Corot,* Paris, 1905, 1: 132). He mentioned it again on October 29 the following year (Robaut, *L'Oeuvre de Corot,* Paris, 1905, 1: 140) and on January 13, 1853 (Robaut, *L'Oeuvre de Corot,* Paris, 1905, 1: 145–46), he observed that it was nearly finished. The painting, as exhibited in the Paris Salon of 1853, is illustrated by Robaut, (*L'Oeuvre de Corot,* Paris, 1905, 1: 238–39). It was reworked by Corot prior to its being shown at the 1867 Exposition Universelle. There it appeared in a "style aggrandi" and with "expression plus profonde." Changes occurred in the forms of the trees, the positioning of the saint's head and of the head of the woman withdrawing the arrow, and in the view of the mounted troops in the background. After the painting had been acquired by Messrs. Robaut and Durand-Ruel, it was again altered by Corot in his studio on the rue Fontaine in Paris in 1873. At this time, according to Robaut (*L'Oeuvre de Corot,* Paris, 1905, 2: 330) the arch at the top of the painting was suppressed, a change that is not readily apparent, although the foliage appearing beneath the spandrels when the frame is removed may have been added at this time.

A smaller replica of the Saint Sebastian measuring 1.89 x .85 and utilizing a rectangular rather than an arched format, was prepared by Alfred Robaut and Louis Desmarest in Corot's studio and completed by the master in October 1874 (Robaut, *L'Oeuvre de Corot,* Paris, 1905, 3: 360, no. 2316). Numerous studies can be associated with the composition. Robaut identified as a *premier projet* of about 1853 a charcoal drawing showing the saint being untied from the tree of execution by two holy women (*L'Oeuvre de Corot,* Paris 1905, 1: 133). A drawing for the recumbent saint as he appeared in 1853, inscribed: *On m'a recommandé de ne pas trop les monter . . . M. Cibot, peintre histoire,* and another drawing showing the figures in a wooded setting, identified as Le Charlemagne in the Fontainebleau Forest, are illustrated by Etienne Moreau-Nélaton in *Histoire de Corot et ses oeuvres,* Paris, 1905, p. 143, figs. 122 and 121. In the collection of the Walters Art Gallery are two related works, a watercolor, 37.1286, (.25 x .13), showing the scene in a tall slender format with the foliage at the left reduced and the rise of land to the right eliminated, and a crayon drawing, 37.1582, on cardboard (.348 x .25), representing the 1853 composition. The latter is probably the drawing made by Corot in Arras in 1852 for his friend Dutilleux to which Robaut alluded in a fragment of a letter of October 15, 1883, published in the early catalogues of the Walters collection. Another crayon drawing mentioned by Robaut in this letter may be the rectangular rather than arched composition that he illustrated in his *L'Oeuvre de Corot,* 1: 310. Finally, in his 1883 letter Robaut noted that Corot incorporated the "Saint Sebastian group" into a sketch made at the Carrefour of Charlemagne in the Forest of Fontainebleau. He also mentioned a wood engraving executed by M. H. Lemaire for Durand-Ruel in 1873–74.

Support: Fabric, moderately fine weave; a strip of coarsely woven fabric $5\frac{1}{4}''$ wide added along the bottom edge; 2.58 x 1.68 ($101\frac{5}{8}''$ x $66\frac{1}{8}''$).

Signed in yellowish brown at bottom left: *COROT.*

Condition: In 1935–36, the painting was cleaned and lined with extensive areas of alligator crackle in the darker sections of the picture inpainted. By 1971, pockets of air had developed between the original and the lining fabrics. These were then treated and the painting was lightly cleaned and revarnished.

Provenance: Corot donated the painting to the Loterie au profit des Orphelins des victimes de la guerre held in 1871. It was purchased jointly by Alfred Robaut and Durand-Ruel for 9,000 francs. At the instigation of these owners, the painting was reworked by the artist and offered for sale for 15,000 francs to the Administration des Beaux Arts in February 1874. When the offer was rejected, the picture was sold to Samuel Barlow of Stakehill, Lancashire. William Walters purchased the picture through the London dealer Tom Wallis on August 11, 1883 for 50,000 francs.

Exhibitions: Salon of 1853, no. 287; Exposition Universelle, Paris, 1867, no. 161; Barye Monument Association, no. 528.

References: Walters cat., 1884, pp. 10–12, no. 13, and subsequent Walters catalogues; E. Durand-Gréville, "La peinture aux Etats-Unis," *GBA* 2nd pér. 36 (1887): 72–73; Champlin and Perkins, 1: 335; Mathews, p. 5; Lamb, pp. 245–46; Reizenstein, pp. 551, 553; Étienne Moreau-Nélaton, *L'Histoire de Corot et de ses oeuvres.* Paris, H. Fleury, 1905. pp. 135–36, 145, 153 (fig. 127); Alfred Robaut, *L'Oeuvre de Corot.* 4 vols. Paris, H. Floury, 1905. 1: 132, 140, 145–46, 238–39, 311; 2: 330, no. 1063, 331 (illus.); 4: 169, 171, 333, 334, 365; Everard Meynell, *Corot and his friends.* London, Methuen, 1908. p. 256; *Corot raconté par lui-même et par ses amis.* 2 vols. Vésenaz-Geneva, P. Cailler, 1946, 1: 60; André Coquis, *Corot et la critique contemporaine.* Paris, Dervy-Livres, 1959. p. 63; Lucas, 2: 573, 574, 576, 578, 580–81, 583.

36. Very Early Spring

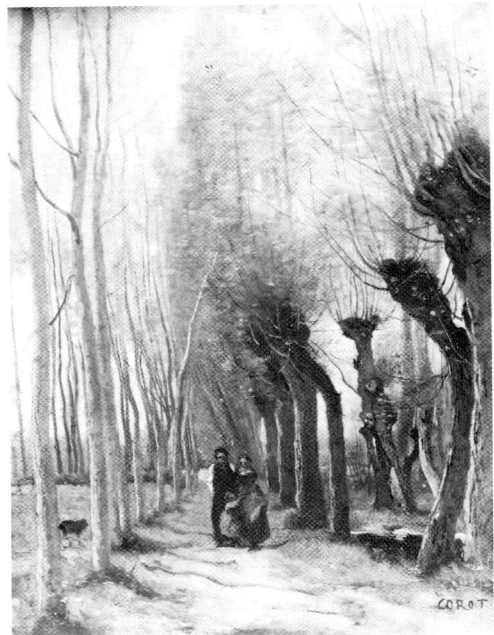

37.194 c. 1857

A man, woman and child, accompanied by a dog, are walking down a path towards the viewer. The path is flanked on the left by tall slender poplars and on the right, by willows with knobbly, pruned trunks.

Corot visited the village of Marissel, located within twenty kilometers of Beauvais, on several occasions: presumably, though briefly, in June 1857, when he was invited to Beauvais by M. Badin, director of the tapestry manufactory; again in the spring of 1866 when he executed the famous *The Church in Marissel,* in the Louvre, and finally, possibly, in April 1872. Since the painting allegedly belonged to Constant Dutilleux (1806–1865), it must date from the first of these visits. Robaut associated several works with this trip (nos. 1003–1014), though only one, no. 1011, *Marissel près Beauvais — prairie entourée d'arbres* involves similar parallel rows of poplar and willow trees.

Robaut referred to a copy of *Very Early Spring,* with some changes, which bore Corot's signature though it was executed by Célestin Lépollart of Douai between 1860 and 1865.

A number of authorities, most recently Hélène Toussaint and Pierre Dieterle of Paris, have informally expressed reservations regarding the authenticity of the Walters picture despite its seemingly impeccable provenance and the frequency with which it has been exhibited. Their doubts, based on the construction of the signature as well as on stylistic grounds, presuppose the possibility that Robaut had deliberately or mistakenly confused the Lépollart copy with Corot's painting. Until further evidence, either documentary or stylistic, arises, the present attribution is being maintained.

Alternative title: *Les Saules de Marissel.*

Canvas: .553 x .394 ($21\frac{3}{4}''$ x $15\frac{1}{2}''$).

Signed in dark brown, at lower right: *COROT.*

Condition: The painting was cleaned in 1951 and lined in 1959. No losses were recorded.

Provenance: Constant Dutilleux collection, Sale, March, 1874, no. 24, sold for 2,450 francs according to an annotated catalogue in the Walters Art Gallery (withdrawn from the sale according to Alfred Robaut). Acquired from Alfred Robaut between 1878–84.

Exhibitions: "Exposition de l'oeuvre de Corot," Ecole des Beaux-Arts, Paris, 1875, no. 101; "Exposition rétrospective de tableaux et dessins de maîtres modernes," Galerie Durand-Ruel, Paris, 1878, no. 97; Barye Monument Association, no. 532; "Corot," Philadelphia Museum of Art, 1946, no. 32; "From Ingres to Gauguin," Baltimore Museum of Art, 1951, no. 39; "Paintings by J. B. C. Corot," Paul Rosenberg & Co., New York, 1956, no. 20; "The Barbizon School," Walters Art Gallery, 1957; "Corot and his Contemporaries," The Museum of Fine Arts of Houston, 1959; "Corot," The Art Institute of Chicago, 1960, no. 85; "Landscape into Art," Atlanta Art Association, 1962, no. 37; "An Exhibition of Treasures of the Walters Art Gallery," Wildenstein and Co., New York, 1967, no. 31; "Corot," Wildenstein and Co., New York, 1969, no. 40.

References: Walters cat., 1884, pp. 36–37, no. 56, and subsequent Walters catalogues; Etienne Moreau-Nélaton, *L'Histoire de Corot et de ses oeuvres*. Paris, H. Fleury, 1905. p. 182, fig. 145; Alfred Robaut, *L'Oeuvre de Corot*. 4 vols. Paris, H. Floury, 1905. 2: 308, no. 1006; 309 (illus.).

37. The Evening Star

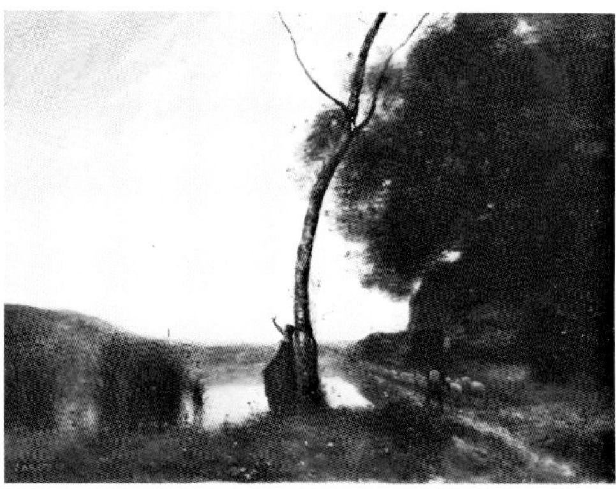

37.154 1864

A woman stands beside a leafless tree on the bank of a still body of water. She gestures toward a star shining brilliantly in the twilight sky. To the right a shepherd and his flock proceed along a path bordered by densely foliaged trees and a house.

This painting is a replica of *L'Etoile du Berger* (1864) in the Musée des Augustins, Toulouse. The larger work, measuring 1.29 x 1.6, was purchased by the town for 3,000 francs at the Exposition de l'Union Artistique de Toulouse in 1864. Robaut, in *L'Oeuvre de Corot,* Paris, 1905, 1:222, related how W. T. Walters visited the artist's studio while the original work was in process and after hesitating over the price, ordered the replica in its stead. In his diary, George A. Lucas recorded this purchase at length. On February 8, 1864, Lucas ordered the replica of the *L'Etoile du Berger* for 1,000 francs, a commission confirmed the following day when both he and Walters were together at Corot's studio. Lucas on this occasion did try to persuade the artist to part with a total of four works for 2,000 francs rather than the 2,100 francs initially asked. On May 31, 1864, Lucas again went to examine the painting and on January 17, 1865, he took possession of the picture for Walters and had it varnished by Alexis Ottoz.

In *Hommage à Corot,* Orangerie des Tuileries, Paris, 1975, pp. 90–91, no. 80, the cataloguer, Hélène Toussaint, gave as the inspiration for the original composition the following lines from Alfred de Musset's "Le Saule" of 1830:

> Pâle étoile du soir, messagère lointaine,
> Dont le front sort brillant des voiles du couchant.

She also referred to Daniel Baud-Bovy's biography, *Corot,* Geneva, 1957, p. 193, in which it is related how Corot, during a sojourn at the Château de Gruyères in Switzerland in 1864, had been moved by hearing the daughter of the Bovy family singing the lines from de Musset to the music of Bovy-Lisberg. On this occasion, the artist, according to Baud-Bovy, made the following statement: *Ah Musset, quel poète! . . . vous rappelez-vous les Stances qu'il a consacrées à la pauvre et grande Malibran (. . .) Lui aussi a bien souffert. Il m'a signalé jadis à l'attention, alors que personne ne me connaisait. Je dois un souvenir à sa mémoire.* Toussaint concluded that *L'Etoile du Berger* was a "souvenir" in which Corot associated his memory of Maria Malibran, the celebrated singer who died tragically from a fall from a horse in 1836, with his recollection of Alfred de Musset, the poet who mourned the singer's death in his *Stances à la Malibran* written the same year. Malibran had figured in Corot's sketchbooks as early as 1822 (Robaut, 1: 26–27). Another replica of *L'Etoile du Berger* was sold at the Henri Rouart Sale, Paris, 1912, no. 146.

Alternative title: *L'Etoile du Berger.*

Support: Fabric, 60 threads to the inch, .709 x .9 (27 15/16" x 35 7/16").
Signed lower left: *COROT.*

Condition: The painting was lined at an unknown date. In 1947 discolored varnish was removed and the surface coated with a mastic varnish and a special wax. In 1978 the painting was again cleaned, with the discolored varnish being removed and replaced by a synthetic varnish.

Provenance: Purchased from the artist in 1864 for 1,000 francs.

Exhibitions: Barye Monument Association, no. 529; "A Baltimorean in Paris, George A. Lucas, Art Agent, 1860–1909," The Walters Art Gallery, 1979.

References: Walters cat., 1878, pp. 24–25, and subsequent Walters catalogues; Strahan, 1: 94; Champlin and Perkins, 1:335; Alfred Robaut, *L'Oeuvre de Corot.* 4 vols. Paris, H. Floury, 1905. 1: 222; 3: 134, no. 1623; 135 (illus.); Etienne Moreau-Nélaton, *Histoire de Corot et de ses oeuvres.* Paris, H. Fleury, 1905. p. 235; "Hommage à Corot," Orangerie des Tuileries, Paris, 1975, p. 91; Lucas, 2: 171, 173, 179, 191.

38. Landscape with Bridge

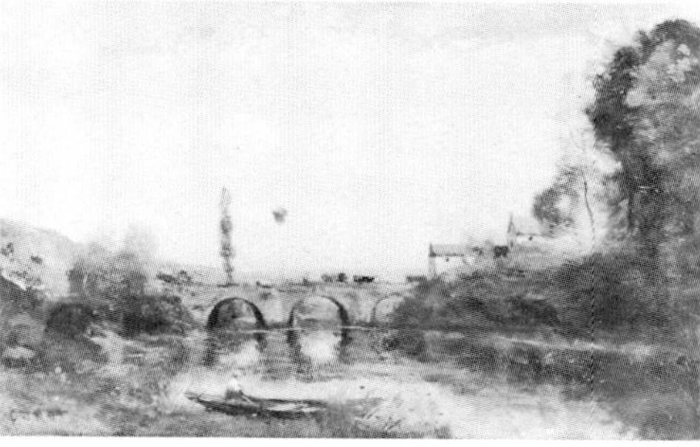

37.152 1865–70

Characteristic of Corot's later work is this small river scene with its silvery tonalities. Several of the artist's paintings have been associated with the site, a small village, eleven kilometers from Fontainebleau, which was frequented by artists and fishermen alike. Robaut catalogued a *Grez-sur-Loing, pont et église,* of 1850–60 (Robaut, no. 895) showing the bridge and the 12th–century church without the fisherman and boat in the foreground and a *Grez-sur-Loing, pêcheur en barque, le matin* of 1867–68 (Robaut, no. 1451), in which a stretch of the river and fisherman appear without the structures, in addition to the Walters composition that he dated between 1865 and 1870.

Alternative titles: *Souvenir de Grez-sur-Loing.*

Support: Panel, cradled, .278 x .434 (11" x 17 1/8").

Signed in brown, lower left: *COROT.*

Provenance: Sold by the artist to M. Painel; sold by Painel to M. Surville; Purchased by Henry Walters from Knoedler and Co., New York, March 3, 1903 for $9,000.00.

Exhibitions: "Exposition de l'Oeuvre de Corot," Ecole des Beaux-Arts, Paris, 1875, no. 106 (Belonging to M. Surville).

References: Alfred Robaut, *L'Oeuvre de Corot,* 4 vols. Paris, H. Floury, 1905, 3: 68, no. 1448, (illus. by a sketch by A. Robaut) 4: 273, no. 106 (with the erroneous measurements .6 x .76); Walters cat., 1909, p. 50, no. 152, and subsequent Walters catalogues.

39. The Fisherman's Cottage

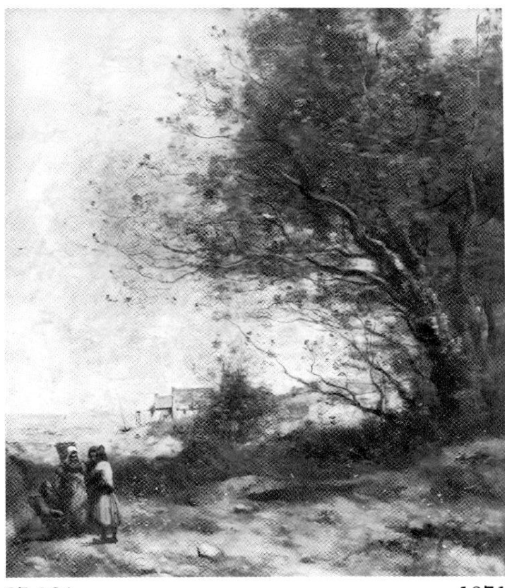

37.164 1871

At the left, four women are conversing. Behind them are discernible the sea and beach, a couple of fishing boats, and cottages. An expansive blue sky is dotted with warmly tinted clouds. At the right are gnarled trees with silvery, wispy foliage.

As Corot passed 1871 in Paris and the North near Arras and Douai, this painting must have been inspired by recollections or sketches of an earlier trip to the Normandy coast.

Alternative title: *Une Famille de pêcheurs au bord de la mer.*

Support: Fabric, .76 x .655 (30" x 25¾").

Signed and dated in dark brown at lower right: *COROT 1871.*

Condition: Cleaned and lined in 1957.

Provenance: Sold by Corot to the dealer M. Breysse; Collection Faure (?); purchased by W. T. Walters between 1878 and 1893.

Exhibitions: "Exposition de l'Oeuvre de Corot," Ecole des Beaux-Arts, Paris, 1875, no. 54 (collection Breysse); "The Men of 1830," Walters Art Gallery, 1957.

References: Walters cat., 1893, p. 96, no. 159; Alfred Robaut, *L'Oeuvre de Corot.* 4 vols. Paris, H. Floury, 1905. 3: 336, no. 2214, 337 (illus.); 4: 271, no. 51.

Jean Achille Benouville

French: Paris, 1815 - Paris, 1891

In their youth Jean Achille Benouville and his brother Léon (1821–1859) were regarded as two of the most promising painters of their time. In 1834, the year J. A. Benouville made his first appearance at the Salon with landscapes painted near Versailles and Ville d'Avray, the critic Laviron wrote in *Le Salon de 1834,* p. 337:

> *Plusieurs artistes, tels que Benouville, Desgoffe, Diaz, Marilhat, dont les noms n'avaient pas encore été remarqués, ont paru au Salon de cette année, d'une manière très brillante et ont conquis du premier coup, une réputation à laquelle d'autres n'arrivaient pas toujours après plusieurs expositions.*

In the following salons Benouville exhibited views executed in the vicinity of Paris at St. Cloud, Bougival, Marly and Compiègne. He came second in the Prix de Rome in 1837, and in 1845 won Grand Prix in the category of *paysage historique* with *Ulysses and Nausicaa.* That year, he left for Rome with his brother, who had won the prize in history painting. Benouville remained in Italy for twenty-five years, submitting regularly to the Paris salons idealized landscapes produced in Rome and the surrounding Campagna. In the 1840s the two Benouvilles were listed with Cabanel, Busson, Ricard, Chenavard and Bidinier in a circle of artists that had gathered around M. Moor, a Frenchman of Irish extraction residing in Rome (Henri de Curzon, *Alfred de Curzon, peintre,* Paris, 1914, p. 36). The elder Benouville was also closely associated at this time with Louis Cabat, the classical landscape painter, and with Corot, to whom he offered his house in 1843. In the 1870s Benouville turned to painting views in the Pyrenees, Venetian scenes, and the occasional French subject.

40. Landscape with Buffalo

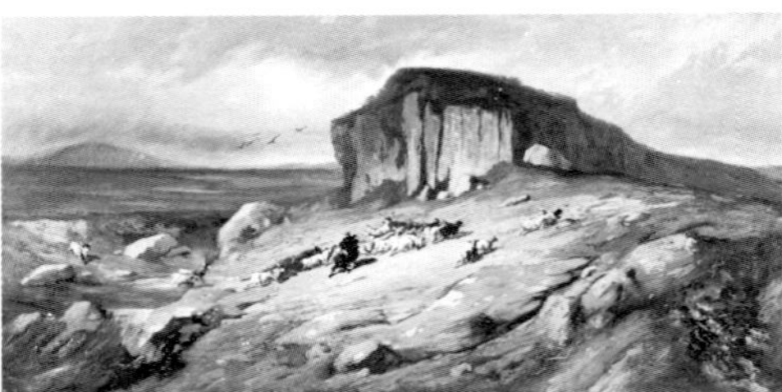

37.1209 c. 1865–68

Long-horned buffalo or oxen are being herded across a desolate stretch of the Roman Campagna. In the center of the scene juts a high outcrop of rock. Overhead, reeling in the dark sky, are some vultures.

The artist has applied the pigments in high impasto, utilizing a palette knife. The surface is further enriched with squiggly indentations made with the end of a brush-handle.

Giovanni Costa, an Italian artist noted for his views of the Campagna, listed in *Quel che Vidì e Quel che Intesì,* Trèves, 1927, p. 122, a number of colleagues also drawn to the region including Böcklin, David, Plock, George Mason, Zäner, Lenbach, Wilde, and Charles Coleman as well as Benouville.

The Walters picture is attributed to Benouville on the basis of similarities it exhibits in technique and format to a pair of landscapes belonging to the Heim Gallery, London (1978). The London pictures (.390 x .9), also showing views of the Campagna, one with an aqueduct and the other with a herd of buffalo, are inscribed with the artist's monogram *J A B* (conjoined) and are identified: *Rome 68* (in red).

Support: Canvas, preprimed, loose, irregular weave. .4 x .806 (15¾" x 31¾"). Inscribed on stretcher: *Mass. 843 100* (in pencil).

Condition: Discolored varnishes were removed in 1977 to reveal a grimy surface which was cleaned. The picture was then lined and treated with synthetic varnish.

Provenance: This painting was acquired by Henry Walters in 1902 as part of the Massarenti Collection, Rome. It is not, however, listed in the Massarenti catalogue of 1897.

References: *Catalogue d'une collection de tableaux de diverses écoles,* Rome, 1881, p. 81, no. 309, attributed to Bourlard (?), "Vue de Tor di Quinto, près de Rome" (?)

Virgile Narcisse Diaz de la Peña

French: Bordeaux, 1808 - Menton, 1876

Following the death of his parents, Spanish exiles residing in Bordeaux, Diaz was reared by a Protestant minister. He lost a leg at an early age as a result of a snake bite, a handicap that had no apparent effect on his genial disposition.

Initially Diaz worked as a shop boy, but by 1825 was serving an apprenticeship as a decorator in a porcelain factory operated by Arsène Gillet, Jules Dupré's uncle. There he received instruction in drawing from François Souchon, a former pupil of J.-L. David. He also began to copy works in the Louvre, particularly those of Correggio.

In 1830 Diaz abandoned porcelain decorating and turned seriously to painting, seeking advice from Xavier Sigalon. At the 1831 Salon he submitted several landscape sketches and a *Love Scene.* In the early thirties, he was drawn to the paintings of Eugène Delacroix and became acquainted with the romantic artist A. G. Decamps, H. Daumier and P. Huet. To support himself, Diaz produced lithographs of troubadour scenes and numerous small paintings of various themes. A trip to the Pyrenees in 1832 resulted in several Spanish subjects, one of which drew the attention of the critics at the 1834 Salon.

For the next twenty-five years, he exhibited regularly, though his only academically ambitious work was the *Battle of Medina-Coeli,* submitted in 1835. About this time he first visited the village of Barbizon in the Fontainebleau Forest. He returned to the region every year for increasing lengths of time, painting near Barbizon, Chailly, le Bas-Bréau and in the Gorges d'Apremont, and participating in the artistic and social milieu of the Auberge Ganne in Barbizon. Though working out-of-doors Diaz continued to exhibit historical subjects that reflected an indebtedness to both Decamps and C.-F.-T. d'Aligny, fellow habitués of Barbizon. Ultimately more significant for the development of his style, particularly as regards color and the handling of pigment, was the influence of Théodore Rousseau, to whom Diaz had turned for advice.

The course of Diaz's career as a mature artist was marked by its regularity and continuity. He was a prolific painter, producing over the years innumerable paintings of Venuses and Amors, Dianas, Oriental women, Spanish scenes, gypsies and bohemians, as well as his landscapes. Though he continued to participate in salons until 1859, winning a third-class medal in 1844, a second-class in 1846, and a first-class in 1848, and being appointed a Chevalier of the Legion of Honor in 1851, Diaz eventually came to rely upon privately organized sales for the distribution of his works. One such sale, held in 1849. was remarkable in that it was entirely comprised of out-of-doors sketches. In addition to working in the Fontainebleau forest and Paris, Diaz also began to spend time on the Normandy coast, at Etretat, which he visited as early as 1854, and at Honfleur. As his reputation as the principal colorist of his generation grew, he acquired numerous admirers and followers. Among the most prominent were Adolphe Monticelli who worked with him at Barbizon in the fifties; the future impressionists Monet, Renoir, Bazille, and Sisley who sought him out in the Fontainebleau forest in the early sixties, and his friend Courbet who joined him at Etretat in 1869. Though his later years were saddened by the loss of his closest friends, Rousseau in 1867 and Millet in 1874, Diaz continued, despite his own failing health, to satisfy the ever-increasing requests for works until his death at Menton in 1876.

41. The Assumption

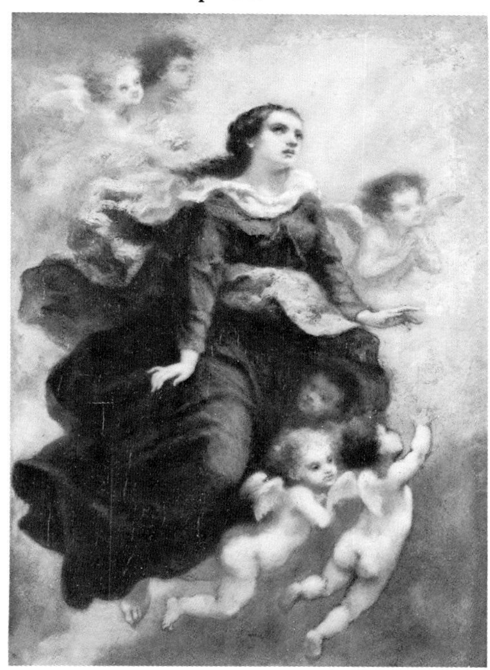

37.145 1850

The Virgin, with her eyes raised, and her arms extending gracefully from her sides, ascends heavenward accompanied by six cherubs. Diaz has dispensed with the overt religious symbolism, the crescent moon, the clasped hands and the histrionic gestures associated with 17th-century Italian and Spanish precedents for this subject.

By 1851 Diaz was engrossed in an *Assumption of the Virgin* in compliance with an official commission as noted by Pierre Miquel in *Le Paysage francais au XIXe siècle*, Maurs-la-Jolie, 1975, 2: 299. His ultimate development of the theme, *The Last Tears*, was exhibited at the Exposition Universelle of 1855, no. 2974. As Miquel notes, p. 302, Diaz was unsuccessfully attempting to demonstrate in such works an ability to rival his friend Ary Scheffer as a painter of religious and historical themes.

Support: Canvas, .392 x .274 (15½" x 10¾").

Signed and dated at lower right: *N. Diaz 50.*

Marks: Reverse: Paper sticker of Georges Petit, *Georges Petit, 12 Rue Godot de Mauroy, Paris 31 janvier 1887, Je certifie que le tableau ci-contre peint sur bois, measurant haut 0.40 c.-larg. 0.27c. et représentant "L'Assomption de le Vierge" par N Diaz est bien le même que j'ai-vendu le 4 mars 1878 dans la vente de M.E." Georges Petit.* Panel stenciled: *5082.*

Condition: Discolored varnishes removed in 1950, revealing overpainting along edges of picture.

Provenance: Collection de M. W[olf], Sale, Paris, April 11, 1877, no. 15; Collection M.E. . . . until 1878; Georges Petit; Albert Spencer Sale, Chickering Hall, New York, February 28, 1888; acquired by W. T. Walters between 1887 and 1888.

Exhibitions: Barye Monument Association, no. 543.

References: Walters cat., 1888, p. 84, no. 133, and subsequent Walters catalogues.

42. Cupid Disarmed

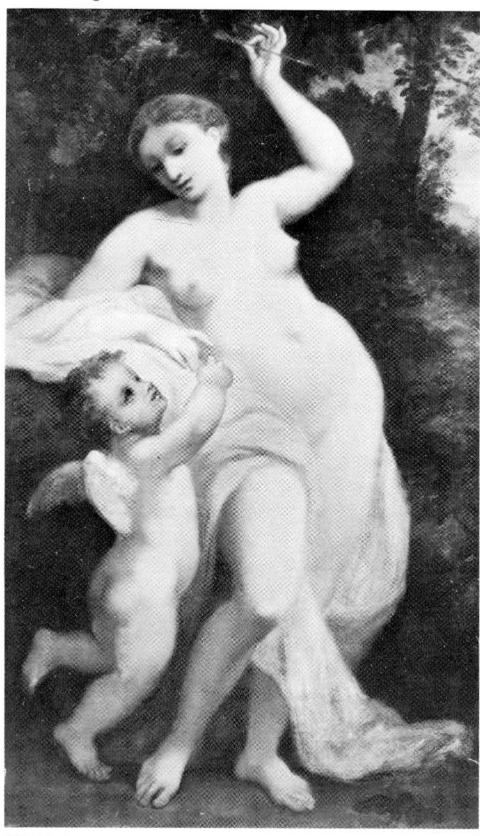

37.114 1850–1855

A voluptuous, fair-haired Venus teases her son Cupid by dangling his arrow beyond his reach.

As early as November 1847 it was recorded in *L'Artiste*, p. 127, that Diaz was engaged in painting several Venuses and Amors: *Venus et Adonis, L'Amor désarmé, Venus et L'Amour,* and *L'Amour et Venus.* In 1850 he exhibited at the Salon a *Love Disarmed* (.95 x .85). The Wallace Collection, London, includes a pair of small paintings, *Venus Disarming Cupid* (P266), and *The Education of Cupid* (P268), both measuring .19 x .12. *Venus Disarming Cupid* resembles the Walters composition and has been described by F. J. B. Watson in *Wallace Collection Catalogues, Pictures and Drawings*, London, 1968, pp. 92–93, as a sketch for the *Cupid Disarmed* of 1855, .685 x 394, sold at the Yerkes Sale, New York, April 5–10, 1910, no. 44. The Yerkes picture, which differs slightly from the Baltimore painting in that a fawn appears to the right of Venus, may be the *Love Disarmed* sold in the Diaz Sale, Paris, 1857, no. 2. Other versions were recorded in the Petit Sale, Paris, May 27, 1910, no. 27 and the J. Fau Sale, Paris, 1861.

Support: Canvas, .678 x .393 (26¾" x 15½").

Signed at lower left: *N Diaz.*

Condition: The painting was lined and discolored varnishes were removed in 1952.

Provenance: Acquired by W. T. Walters before 1878.

Exhibitions: Barye Monument Association, no. 549a.

References: Walters cat., 1878, p. 28, and subsequent Walters Catalogues; Strahan, 1:94.

43. Effect of Autumn, Fontainebleau

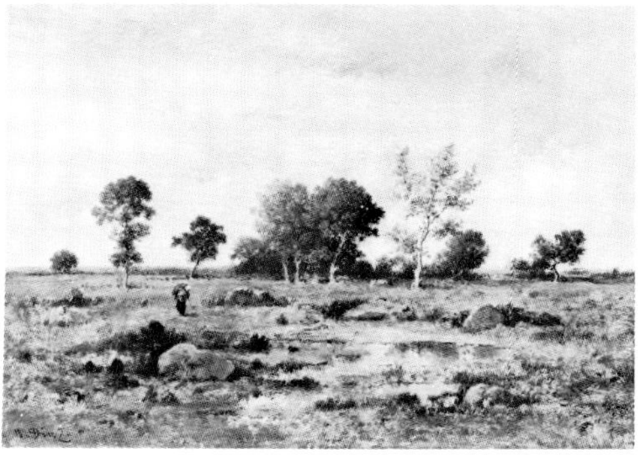

37.43 c. 1870

A solitary peasant woman bearing a heavy bundle makes her way across a marshy plain under an overcast sky. This melancholy autumn scene employs a restricted range of colors.

Support: Mahogany panel, .298 x .417 (11¾" x 16⅜").

Signed in black at lower left: *N. Diaz.*

Condition: Discolored varnishes removed in 1971.

Provenance: Acquired by W. T. Walters before 1878.

Exhibitions: Barye Monument Association, no. 542.

References: Walters cat., 1878, p. 45, and subsequent Walters catalogues; Strahan, 1:94.

44. Forest of Fontainebleau, Autumn

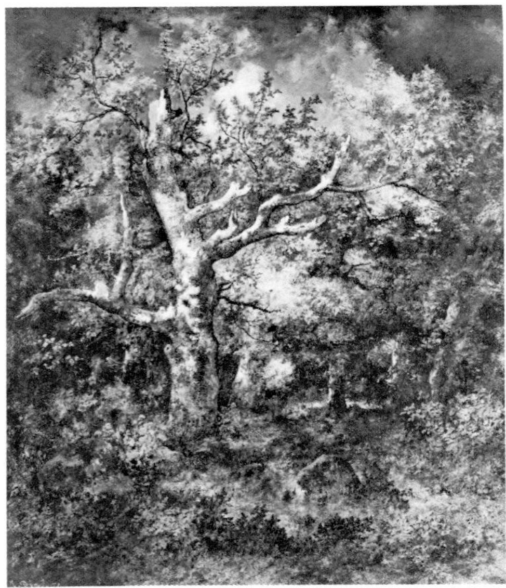

37.64 1871

Diaz's reputation as the colorist of his generation is confirmed by this painting of an ancient tree with broken limbs in the Fontainebleau Forest. The artist has achieved the appearance of a tapestry, dabbling and scumbling the russets, ochers, golden yellows and olive tints of the autumnal foliage with the various greens and greys of the lichen and moss-covered boulders. Reflected in a small marshy pond in the foreground are various blues and purplish greys of the partially clouded sky overhead.

Support: Mahogany panel, beveled edges, .780 x .647 (30¾" x 25⅜").

Signed in red at lower left: *N. Diaz. 71.*

Marks: Reverse: wax seal impressed *FV* (?); pencil: *4;* red chalk: *M;* blue chalk: *38.*

Condition: Discolored varnishes removed in 1957.

Provenance: Acquired by W. T. Walters before 1878.

Exhibitions: Barye Monument Association, no. 540.

References: Walters cat., 1878, p. 6, and subsequent Walters catalogues; Strahan, 1:94.

45. The Storm

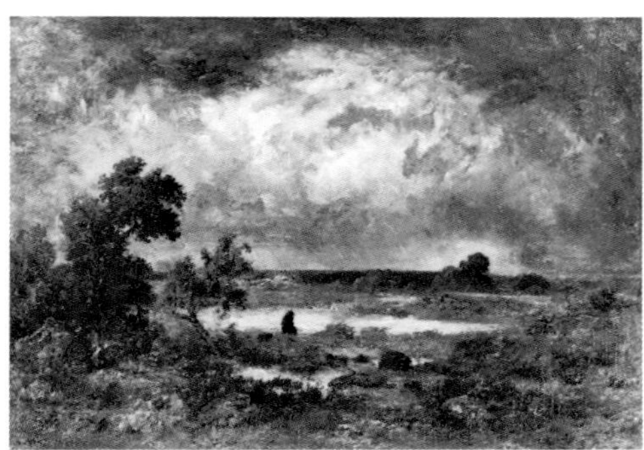

37.121 1872

A single figure accompanied by a dog is buffetted by a violent wind as he makes his way across the plain. Sunlight penetrating the scudding cloud-cover illuminates a patch of terrain in the central ground. The stormy sky is reflected in a pond in the foreground.

Diaz repeated this composition several times in the early 1870s, altering the weather conditions. Variants listed in the Witt Library, University of London, include *Before the Storm,* dated 1872, Guasco Sale, Paris, June 11, 1900 (.46 x .67); a *Sunset after a Storm,* Sale, New York, January 24, 1912, (.665 x .863); *A Stormy Landscape,* dated 1875, oil on panel, Sale no. 1654, Parke-Bernet, February 29, 1956, no. 50; *The Storm,* dated 1873, canvas, .825 x 1.092, Sale, Sotheby, London, November 7, 1962, no. 101, and *The Storm,* Art Gallery of Ontario, Toronto, .85 x 1.065. In *The Storm* in the National Gallery, London, dated 1871, panel, the composition differs in that the figure and his dog are placed toward the right side.

Support: Panel, cradled, .59 x .859 (23¼" x 33$^{13}/_{16}$").

Signed and dated at lower left: *N. Diaz. 72.*

Condition: Extensive overpainting concealing a broad alligator crackle pattern was revealed in 1972 when discolored varnishes were removed. The overpainting was removed, the losses inpainted and the picture coated with synthetic varnish.

Provenance: Acquired by W. T. Walters between 1878 and 1884.

Exhibitions: Barye Monument Association, no. 537.

References: Walters cat., 1884, pp. 62–63, no. 97, and subsequent Walters catalogues; Mathews, p. 7; Reizenstein, p. 560 (illus.).

Artist unknown, formerly attributed to N. Diaz

46. Fête Galante

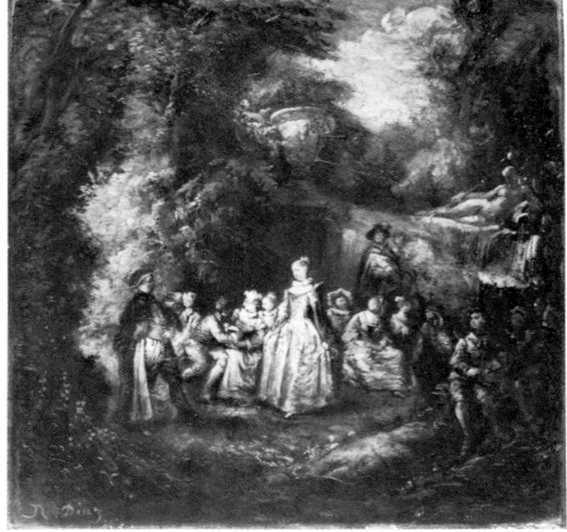

37.177

This small painting, a rather free copy of Watteau's *Fêtes Vénitiennes* of 1716–18 (.577 x .464), in the National Gallery of Scotland, Edinburgh, has traditionally been identified as a work of N. Diaz. It differs from the original painting principally in the pose of the fountain statue in the background. Since Watteau's picture left France in 1777, when it was acquired by Allan Ramsay at the Randon de Boisset Sale, the copyist, were he French, would have been obliged to work from an engraving or from a painted replica. The *Fêtes Vénitiennes* was copied by Crépy the Younger in an edition for the dealer, Gersaint, in 1725, and it was engraved in reverse in 1732 by Laurent Cars for Jean de Jullienne, the owner.

The question of authorship for the Walters copy is complicated by the nature of the painting's ground: a circular piece of canvas mounted on strips of fabric with additional cloth added in the spandrels. Upon examination the painted surface of the central patch and that of the spandrels do not appear contemporaneous. Furthermore, the name in the lower left corner does not conform orthographically to Diaz's usual signatures.

Although Diaz was a prolific painter who occasionally treated rococo themes, there does not appear to be sufficient evidence at present to confirm the attribution of this painting to Diaz.

Support: Fabric, .19 x .19 (7½" x 7½").

Signed at lower left: *N Diaz.*

Condition: Extensive crackle pattern with areas of inpainting.

Provenance: Acquired by Henry Walters between 1903 and 1909 from an unknown source.

References: Walters cat., 1909, p. 59, no. 177, and subsequent Walters catalogues.

Constant Troyon

French: Sèvres, 1810 - Paris, 1865

Troyon represented the third generation of his family to work at Sèvres. Apart from instruction received from employees of the Manufactory, most notably from D. D. Riocreux, his godfather and curator of the ceramic museum, Troyon was never able to benefit from formal training in painting. He did, however, receive advice from the landscape painter Camille Roqueplan, whom he encountered in the forest of St. Cloud in 1831, as well as from Théodore Rousseau. Two years later he made his debut at the Paris Salon with three undistinguished views painted in the vicinity of Sèvres. He traveled extensively in the mid to late thirties, painting in Brittany, Touraine and Limousin, and won a third-class medal at the 1838 Salon. With the encouragement of Dupré, whom he had known since 1833, Troyon began to frequent Barbizon and the Fontainebleau Forest, deriving advice from Rousseau, Français and the other habitués of the Auberge Ganne. He also visited Normandy as early as 1841, painting with the specialist on farm animal subjects J. R. Brascassat. Perhaps as a result of Brascassat's example, or because of the encouragement of his colleagues Louis Robert and Ad. Charropin, Troyon began to introduce animals into his land-

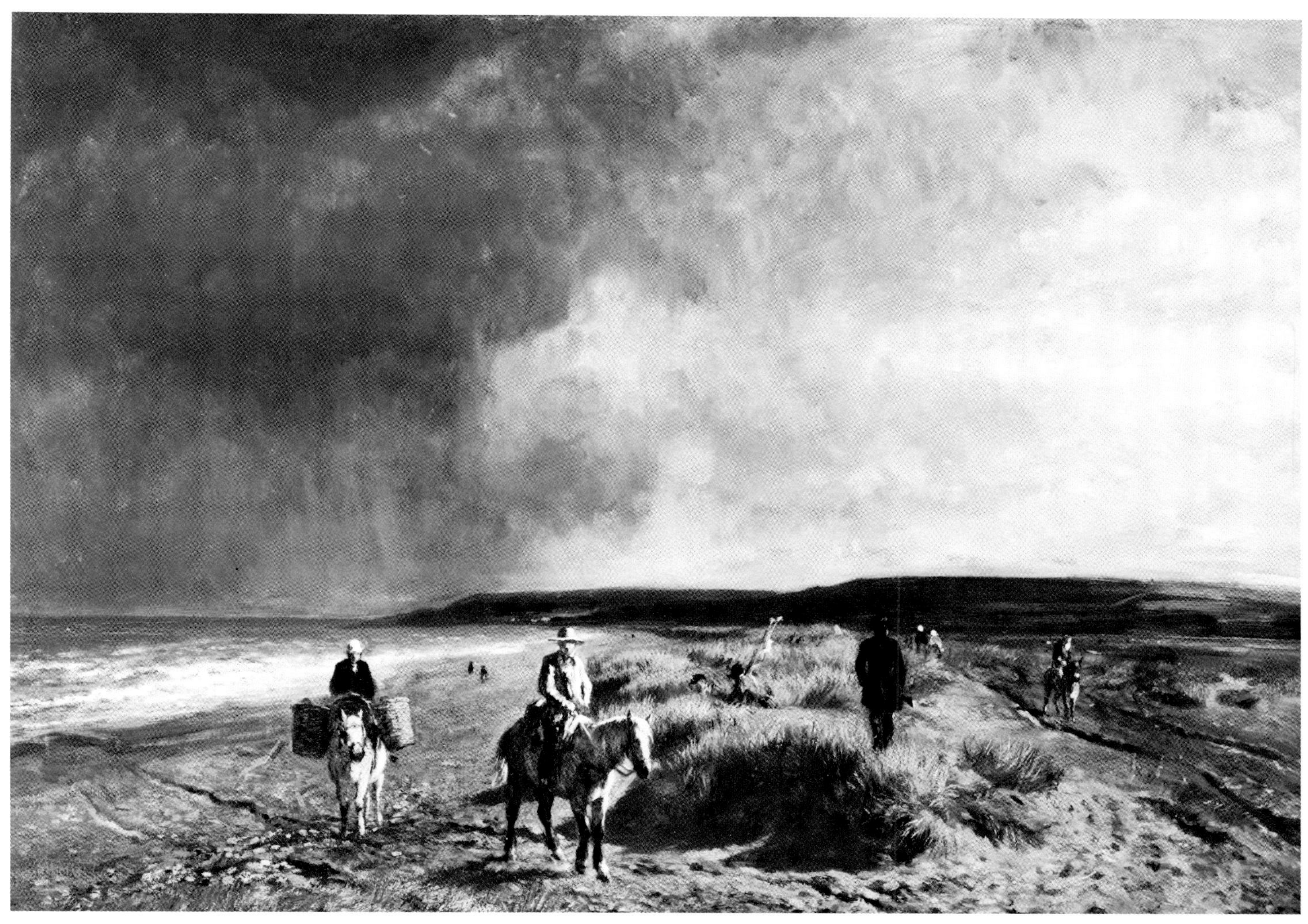

Troyon *Coast near Villers,* no. 49

scapes early in his career. A turning point occurred in 1847 when he visited Holland and Belgium, where he was captivated in particular by the animal subjects of Paul Potter and Albert Cuyp. Back in France, he now devoted himself to representing farm animals in landscape contexts, winning recognition both in his own country and abroad. He received a first–class medal at the 1848 Salon and was appointed Chevalier of the Legion of Honor the following year. Throughout the fifties he worked extensively in Normandy, befriending Jongkind and Boudin and acquiring a number of followers, most notably E. L. van Marcke. In 1858 he worked at the Saint-Siméon farm on the Côte de Grâce, which served as a gathering point for numerous artists on the Normandy coast, much as the Auberge Ganne had in Barbizon. After 1859 Troyon ceased to enter works in the Paris salons, though he continued to participate in regional shows in Bordeaux, Le Havre, Marseilles, and Besançon, and to submit paintings to exhibitions held abroad in Brussels, Rotterdam, and London. At his death in 1865 he was acclaimed the principal animal painter of his era.

47. Cattle Drinking

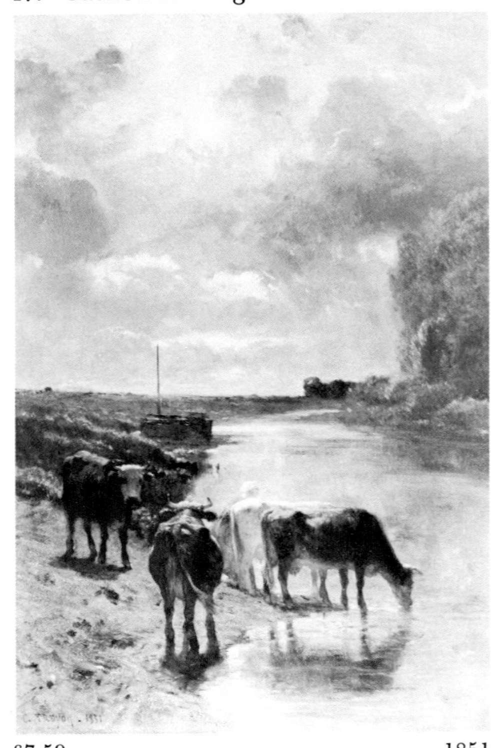

37.59 1851

Though the sun directly overhead is obscured, light penetrating the storm cloud bathes the scene below of cattle drinking at a river's edge tended by a woman. Upstream the mast of a moored boat stands out against the horizon. Pierre Miquel identified the location as the banks of the Touques, which flows into the sea between Trouville and Deauville (1980 visit).

Alternative Titles: *The Drinking Place; L'Abreuvoir.*

Support: Panel, oak, cradled, .784 x .518 (30⅞" x 20⅜").

Signed and dated in black at bottom left: *C. Troyon. 1851.*

Marks: Reverse: old wax seal.

Condition: Discolored varnishes replaced with mastic varnish in 1948. An examination in 1979 revealed that a half-inch wide strip of mahogany had been added to the right edge.

Provenance: Suermondt Collection, Sale, February 1877, 35,000 francs; Narischkine Collection, Sale, 1883, no. 82, 80,000 francs; Gustave Viot Collection, Sale, Paris, May 25, 1886, no. 9, 71,000 francs.

Reproductions: Engraved by R. de Los Rios for Albert Wolff in *Cent Chefs-d'oeuvre,* Paris, 1883, p. 72; etched by Léopold Flameng; engraved by Boulard fils.

Exhibitions: "Cent Chefs-d'oeuvres," Galerie Georges Petit, Paris, 1883, no. 87; Barye Monument Association, no. 533.

References: Albert Wolff, *Cent chefs-d'oeuvre.* New York, Knoedler, 1885. illus. opposite p. 72 in engraving by R. de Los Rios; Walters cat., 1887, p. 41, no. 58, and subsequent Walters catalogues; Cook, 1:226, illus.; Mathews, p. 7; A. Hustin, *Constant Troyon.* Les artistes célèbres. Paris, Librairie de l'art, 1893, p. 76 (illus. in engraving by Flameng), 81.

48. Repose

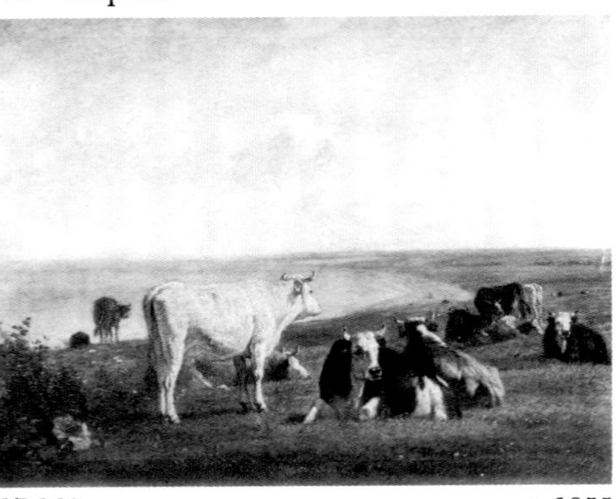

37.160 c. 1855

A sense of serenity permeates this scene of cattle at rest during a sunny day on the Normandy coast.

Alternative title: *Seashore and Cattle.*

Support: Canvas, .72 x .885 (28⅜" x 37⅞").

Signed at lower left: *Troyon.*

Provenance: Acquired by W. T. Walters before 1878.

Exhibitions: Barye Monument Association, no. 68.

References: Walters cat., 1878, and subsequent Walters catalogues; Strahan, 1: 94.

49. Coast near Villers

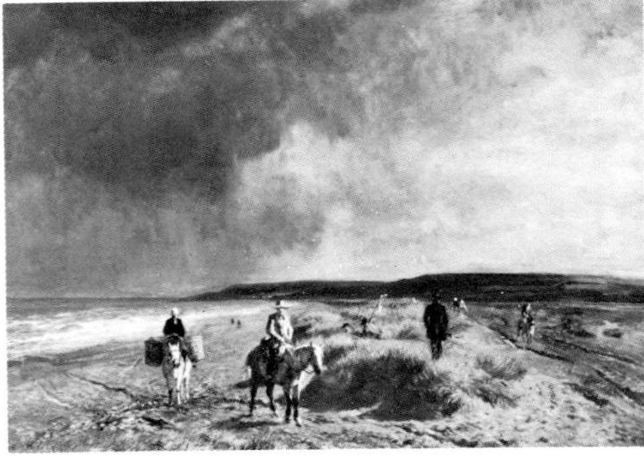

37.993 c. 1859

The artist has skillfully incorporated into this coastal setting a number of figures: a peasant couple mounted on white ponies, a sportsman, hunters with fowling nets, and some less clearly defined individuals. It is a dramatic scene in which a storm moving ashore threatens to obscure the sunlight that still illuminates the figures and casts long shadows across the beach. Ominously silhouetted against the horizon is an estuary lost in shadow.

The motif of the woman riding a donkey occurs frequently in Troyon's work and is seen for example in *Woman on a Donkey* in the Kunsthalle, Hamburg, no. 1873 and in *Homeward,* 1859, ex. Alexander Young Collection.

Alternative title: *Plage au Villers sur mer Calvados.*

Support: Canvas, .674 x .957 (26½" x 37¾").

Signed in black at lower left: *C. Troyon.*

Marks: Stretcher inscribed on reverse: *Plage au Villers sur mer Calvados.*

Condition: Discolored varnishes removed in 1947, mastic varnish applied. Picture lined and mastic varnish replaced with AW2 in turpentine in 1968.

Provenance: Mrs. Mary J. Morgan Sale, New York, March 3, 4, 5, 1886, no. 72. $8,100.00; Mrs. S. D. Warren Sale, Boston, 1903, no. 115, $8,100.00 to Henry Walters.

References: A. Hustin, *Constant Troyon,* Les artistes célèbres, Paris, Librairie de l'art, 1893, p. 79.

Jules-Louis Dupré

French: Nantes, 1811 - Paris, 1889

In the 1830s Dupré helped to transmit the influence of the English landscape tradition to the French naturalist school that eventually came to be associated with Barbizon, though he was never himself a regular habitué of the Fontainebleau village. He was also closely linked with Théodore Rousseau, as well as with such colleagues as Delacroix, Lami, Decamps, Scheffer and Barye, who were in the vanguard of the Romantic movement.

After receiving initial training from his father, a painter turned porcelain manufacturer in Parmain near L'Isle-Adam, Dupré joined an uncle in Paris and eventually enrolled in the studio of Jean-Michel Diebolt, a specialist in animal subjects and landscapes rendered in gouache. He professed at this point a keen admiration for the works of Claude Lorraine and Géricault. When his father was appointed director of the Coussac porcelain factory near Limoges in 1827, Dupré availed himself of the opportunity to sketch in the Haute Vienne region. Returning to Paris he supported himself as an artisan painting "clock pictures" in which mechanical movements were actually inserted behind the canvases. He did however, become acquainted with Delacroix, Charlet, Decamps and Roqueplan and through the enthusiasm of the landscape painter, Louis Cabat, he was introduced to the works of the seventeenth-century Dutch masters, Ruysdael, Hobbema, and Van Ostade. His first Salon in 1831 proved relatively fortunate in that one of his three entries was allegedly sold to a member of the Royal family and another to Baron Ivry. Later that year the English collector Lord Graves invited him to London. Dupré's preference at this time for low horizons, fluid brush strokes and limpid atmosphere has been attributed to this English trip. Throughout the thirties he flourished, painting the landscapes of Berry, Limousin, and l'Indre. At the Salon of 1833 he entered five works, winning a second-class medal, ironically for genre rather than for landscape painting. In 1836 he collaborated with Eugène Lami on an historical subject, *The Battle of Hondschoote* that was not favorably received, and also produced his first lithographs. His reputation as one of the foremost landscape painters was confirmed at the Salon of 1839 in which he showed no less than seven works.

In the summer of 1841, Dupré was accompanied to the L'Isle-Adam forest by Théodore Rousseau whom he had met seven years earlier. During the decade of the forties the two artists worked together, to each other's benefit, at L'Isle-Adam and in the Landes region. This close rapport ended however in 1849, the year Dupré was awarded the Legion of Honor. Thereafter Dupré grew increasingly reclusive, isolating himself at L'Isle-Adam and after 1852 withdrawing from the salons, not exhibiting again until 1867. He gradually turned away from dramatic forest scenes to more generalized rustic landscapes. Beginning in 1865, he spent the summer months each year at Cayeux-sur-Mer on the English Channel, painting marines and coastal scenes. Millet and his family joined him there in 1868 and in 1870, Gustave Courbet, a fellow refugee from the Franco-Prussian War, made his appearance in the same coastal town. In the meantime Dupré exhibited twelve pictures at the 1867 Salon winning a second-class medal, and within three years was elevated to the rank of Officier of the Legion of Honor. His financial standing was somewhat ameliorated in 1872 when he was introduced by Corot to the collector Stumpf, who immediately commissioned several works. Though the seventies and eighties were marred for Dupré by the deaths of his associates Millet, Diaz, and Corot he continued to work in increasing isolation, painting in a broader, looser technique that was particularly adaptable to the rendering of atmospheric effects in his skies. He last exhibited in 1883, showing eight works.

50. A Bright Day

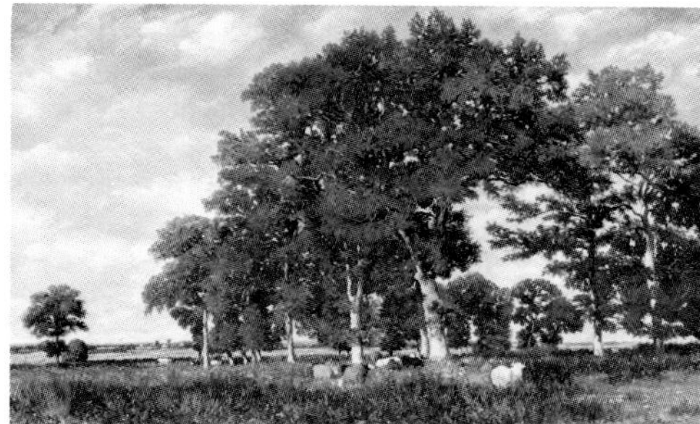

37.38 1835–40

Sunlight piercing the cloud-cover lights this flat, expansive landscape in which cattle graze beneath tall trees. This painting illustrates the continuing impact on Dupré of English precedents, most notably the landscapes of Constable with their dramatic skies.

The date and signature are no longer fully decipherable. Early Walters catalogues recorded a date of 1870, a possibility in so far as the artist's stylistic development was irregular and since some of his late landscapes, such as the *Pastoral Scene,* dated 1876, in the Brooks Memorial Gallery, Memphis, recall much earlier works. Aubrun assigned a date of 1835 and Pierre Miquel, during his 1981 visit, suggested that the picture was executed about 1840 though recording a scene of the early thirties.

Support: Fabric, .285 x .45 (11⅛" x 17¾").

Signed and dated in dark brown at lower right: *Dupré 40* (?).

Marks: Frame inscribed: *Dupré Mons. Lucas.*

Condition: Blisters laid down in 1939. Discolored varnishes removed in 1943 and the painting revarnished and waxed. Picture lined and small puncture hole near bottom edge at right inpainted in 1971.

Provenance: Gavet collection; purchased by W. T. Walters, April 11, 1883.

Exhibitions: "The Men of 1830," Walters Art Gallery, 1957.

References: Walters cat., 1884, p. 76, no. 121, and subsequent Walters catalogues; Champlin and Perkins, 1: 435; Lamb, p. 247; Edward S. King, "The men of 1830," *BWAG* 9, no. 6 (March 1957): 1 (illus.); Marie-Madeleine Aubrun, *Jules Dupré, 1811–1889.* Paris, Laget, 1974. pp. 56, no. 62; 71 (illus.); Lucas, 2: 563.

51. The Old Oak

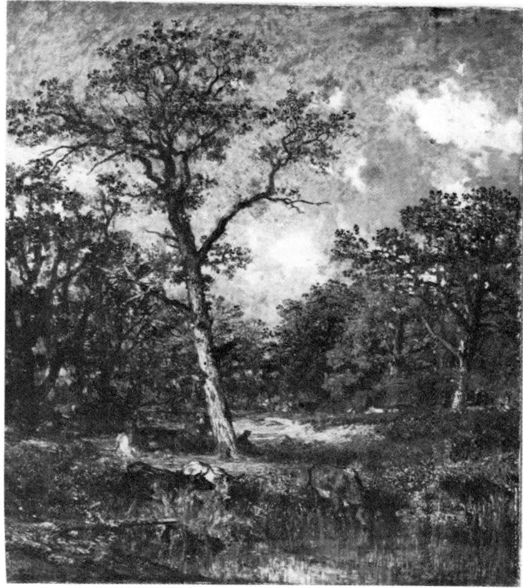

37.61 1850–55

The center of this landscape is dominated by an old oak tree at the base of which is seated a solitary figure. Cattle drink from a pond in the immediate foreground. The foliage of the surrounding trees is touched with warm tones suggesting that it is an autumnal scene. A most distinctive feature of this landscape is the cerulean sky.

Aubrun assigns this work to the 1845–50 period on the basis of the rich paint texture and the not-too-subtle modulation in the color values.

Support: Fabric, .72 x .615 (28¾" x 24¼").

Signed at lower left: *Jules Dupré.*

Condition: Discolored varnishes removed, revarnished in 1957.

Provenance: Marquis de la Roche Bousseau, Paris, 1873, no. 20, 25,000 francs; Gavet collection; purchased by W. T. Walters on April 11, 1883.

Reproduction: Engraved by Gustave Greux for the Gazette des Beaux-Arts.

Exhibitions: Barye Monument Association, no. 538.

References: Walters cat., 1884, p. 62, no. 102, and subsequent Walters catalogues; Champlin and Perkins, 1:435; Lamb, p. 246; Marie-Madeleine Aubrun, *Jules Dupré, 1811–1889.* Paris, Laget, 1974. pp. 96, no. 201; 111 (illus.); Lucas, 2:563.

52. At Sea

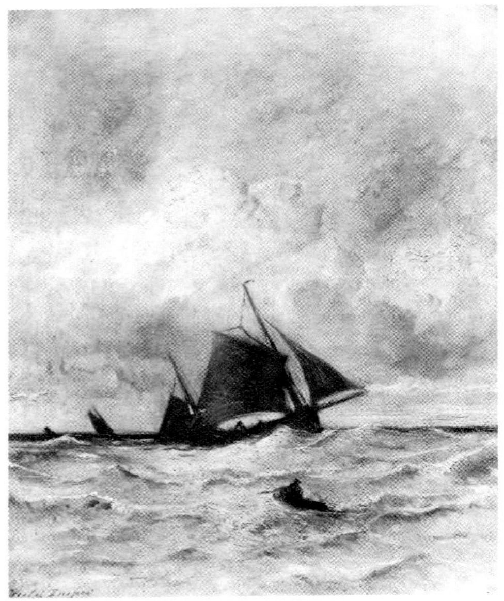

37.135 c. 1870

Several small fishing boats are sailing on choppy seas. A single figure is rowing a small boat near the foreground. The sky is heavily overcast.

Support: Fabric, .818 x .657 (32¼" x 25¾").

Signed at lower left: *Jules Dupré.*

Marks: Canvas stenciled: *M. DEFORGE CARPENTIER / COULEURS FINES / ET TOILES à PEINDRE / BOULEVARD MONTMARTRE 8 / Paris / METIER RUE LEGENDRE 62 Batignolles.*

Condition: Lined and cleaned in 1957.

Provenance: Acquired by W. T. Walters before 1884.

Exhibitions: Barye Monument Association, no. 547.

References: Walters cat., 1884, p. 43, no. 69, and subsequent Walters catalogues; Champlin and Perkins, 1: 435; Marie-Madeleine Aubrun, *Jules Dupré, 1811–1889.* Paris, Laget, 1974. p. 201, no. 562.

53. Sunset on the Coast

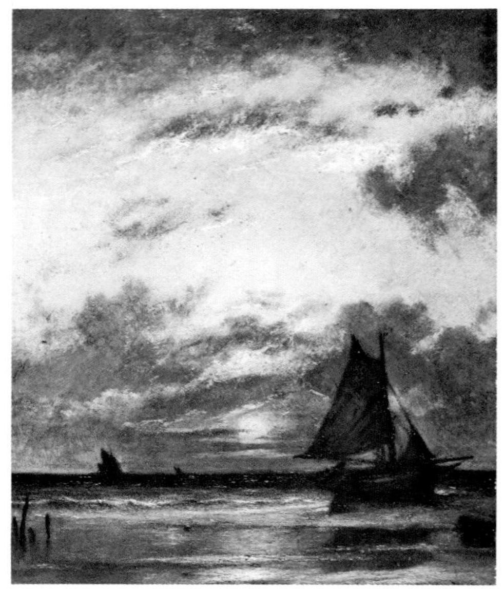

37.120 c. 1870–75

Beginning in 1865, Dupré spent the summer months at Cayeux-sur-Mer on the Normandy coast painting coastal scenes and seascapes. In this example, executed with the pasty texture distinctive of his work in the seventies, the sun is seen as a golden orb behind a bank of clouds, setting low on the horizon, with its light dramatically reflected off higher, darker clouds. Several fishing boats are silhouetted against the horizon.

Support: Fabric, .741 x .608 (29¼" x 23⅞").

Signed at lower right: *Jules Dupré.*

Marks: canvas stenciled: *TABLEAUX MODERNES TEDESCO / M. DEFORGE CARPENTIER / COULEURS FINES / ET TOILES A PEINDRE / BOULEVARD MONTMARTRE 8 / PARIS / METIER RUE LEGENDRE 62 (BATIGNOLLES).*

Provenance: Acquired by W. T. Walters between 1884 and 1889.

Exhibitions: Barye Monument Association, no. 549.

References: Walters cat., 1889, p. 87, no. 135, and subsequent Walters catalogues; Marie-Madeleine Aubrun, *Jules Dupré, 1811–1889.* Paris, Laget, 1974. pp. 203, no. 582; 224 (illus.).

Pierre Etienne Théodore Rousseau

French: Paris, 1812 - Barbizon, 1867

Rousseau, a draper's son, was encouraged in art by his mother's cousin, P. A. Pau de Saint-Martin, who introduced him to sketching in the forest of Compiègne. He acquired a taste for more dramatic scenery while visiting the Franche-Comté in 1825 with a friend of his father who ran a sawmill. Back in Paris, he enrolled in the studio of the classical landscape painter, J. C. J. Rémond, an experience that apparently proved unsatisfactory, for Rousseau later listed himself instead as the pupil of G. Guillon-Lethière, a professor at the Ecole des Beaux-Arts who probably offered private tutoring. In the meantime he frequented the galleries of the Louvre, being particularly drawn to the works of Claude Lorraine, Karel Dujardin and the Van de Veldes, and he continued to sketch in the forests of Compiègne and Fontainebleau.

The year 1830 was passed in the barren countryside of the Upper Auvergne. After receiving some notice for a *Landscape in the Auvergne,* submitted to the 1831 Salon, he traveled to Normandy where he met Paul Huet, who introduced him to the paintings of the English artists Constable and Bonington. In the early thirties, he also became acquainted with Decamps, Diaz, Raffet, Alexandre Dumas and George Sand. One of his pictures accepted at the 1834 Salon, *Edge of a Clearing, Forest of Compiègne,* brought him a third-class medal and was acquired by the Duc d'Orléans. In 1836 however, his most ambitious work to date, *Descent of Cattle in the Mountains of the Upper Jura,* was rejected, and from 1837 until after the liberalization of the jury selection in 1848 his works were systematically excluded from the annual salons. Despite the lack of official support, Rousseau's merits became recognized by an increasing number of colleagues and critics, including Delacroix, Théophile Gautier, and Théophile Thoré.

In the autumn of 1836 Rousseau first visited Barbizon, the village in the Fontainebleau Forest that eventually lent its name to the movement of Naturalism of which he was the leading exponent. There he passed the winter in the company of Diaz and C.-F.-T. d'Aligny. It was with his close friend Jules Dupré that he first visited the region of L'Isle-Adam in 1841. During the decade of the forties, he tended to be attracted to less dramatic, more tranquil scenery. Together with Dupré, he traveled in the Berry in 1842, the Landes in southwestern France in 1844, L'Isle-Adam again in 1846, returning to Barbizon between these travels. As a result of an argument involving his engagement to the adopted daughter of George Sand, Rousseau severed relations with Dupré and later formed a more enduring friendship in Barbizon with Millet.

Rousseau's travels in the 1850s were substantially reduced as a result of the mental instability of his common-law wife. He passed his time in Barbizon and Paris, exhibiting frequently at the salons. Although his works were still criticized, they attracted a number of important admirers, including the collector Fréderick Hartmann, the Belgian dealer Arthur Stevens and the critic Théophile Silvestre. At the Exposition Universelle of 1855 thirteen of his paintings were shown, confirming his reputation as one of the principal landscape painters of the age and bringing him a first class-medal. In the fifties Rousseau's paintings grew increasingly "finished," reflecting the continuing influence of Dutch seventeenth-century tradition on his work, a trait which pleased many collectors though it incurred the disparagement of those who had admired his earlier, more spontaneous representations of nature.

For Rousseau the early sixties were marred by his wife's instability and by financial deprivation. In 1861 a sale of twenty-five of his pictures brought prices ranging from only 560 to 3,200 francs, and in 1863 another sale organized to pay his debts realized comparable sums. However, he was able to form a modest collection of graphics that included a number of Japanese wood-block prints,

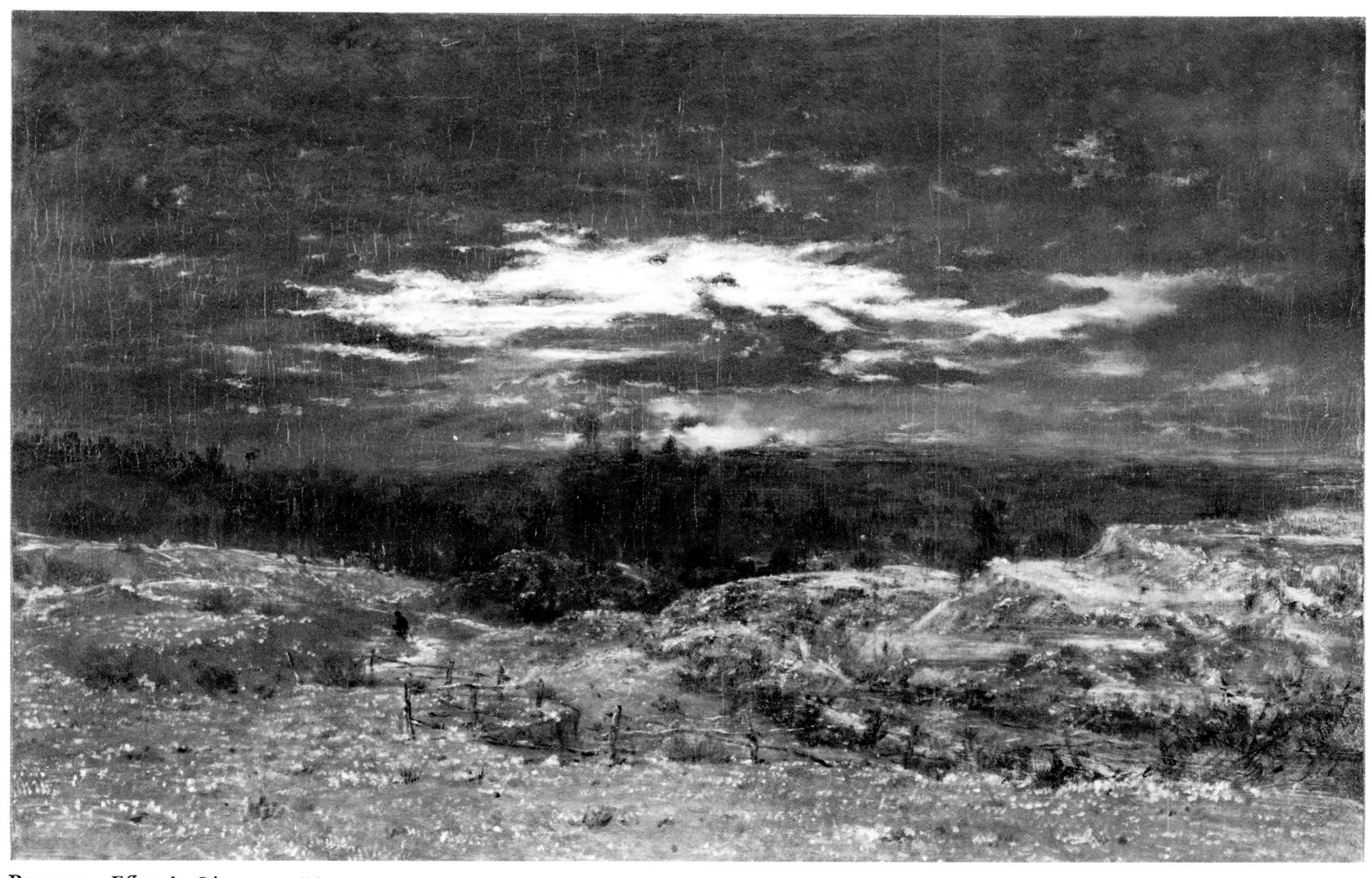

Rousseau *Effet de Givre,* no. 54

which apparently influenced his own painting at this time. In the autumn of 1865 Rousseau was invited to the Imperial Court at Compiègne, where he seized the opportunity to plead for the preservation of the Fontainebleau Forest in its natural state, a cause of abiding concern to him. Late in life, circumstances continued to improve for him. In 1866 the dealers Brame and Durand-Ruel offered 100,000 francs for his early studies as well as an additional 40,000 francs for a group of later works, thus alleviating his financial worries; that year Rousseau's *Le Givre* (Walters Art Gallery) fetched 9,800 francs at the Troyon Sale, an unprecedented sum for one of his pictures. In 1867 he served as president of the jury at the Exposition Universelle which featured thirteen of his pictures. Though Rousseau was acknowledged on this occasion as *"le premier paysagiste de l'Europe,"* he was not promoted to the rank of Officier of the Legion of Honor, an oversight remedied only in August, four months before he died.

54. Effet de Givre

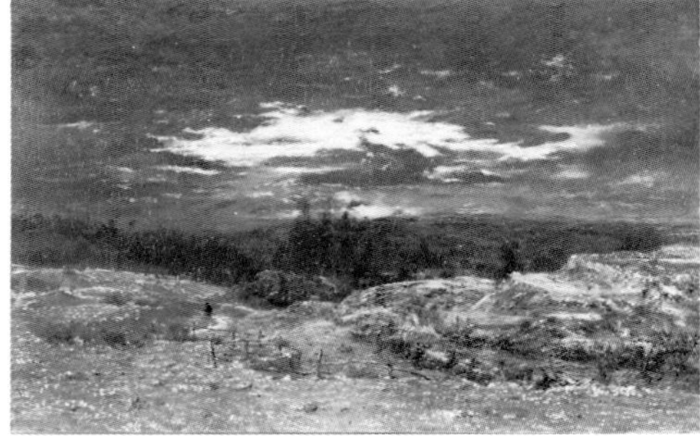

37.25 1845

In the center, near the horizon in this rural scene, reddish golden light breaking through the cloud formations illuminates the hoarfrost glistening on the rocky greyish-green hillocks of the foreground. Interrupting the horizon-line are some rather evanescent poplar trees. A solitary figure is discernible on a winding path to the left.

In the winter of 1845–46 Rousseau shared quarters with Jules Dupré at L'Isle-Adam on the Oise River northeast of Pontoise. Alfred Sensier, Rousseau's biographer, identified the site of this picture as "the hills of the Valmondois as seen slightly over a mile away, across the river, along the Des Forgets road" and he recorded how the artist feverishly painted the scene directly from nature on an unprepared canvas, completing the feat within eight days. Because of this spontaneous treatment, involving the elimination of the traditional division between the *ébauche* and the definitive painting, *Le Givre* has frequently been cited as a harbinger of later nineteenth-century *plein-air* painting.

The subsequent history of the picture is fraught with problems. Evidently two versions were produced: one, measuring .41 x .63, was acquired by the singer Baroilhet from Jules Dupré and was last recorded at the Laurent-Richard Sale of 1878, no. 58, whereas the other, now in Baltimore, was given at one point by the dealer Durand-Ruel to Troyon in exchange for a sheep picture. Hence the latter version was designated by Rousseau as the "tableau de Troyon" in a letter of July 10, 1861, cited in the Laurent-Richard Sale catalogue, April 7, 1873, p. 46, no. 44. A further confusion arises in that several authors have erroneously identified *Le Givre* as *Terrains d'automne*, one of the artist's entries in the 1849 Salon that actually measured .55 x .7 inclusive of the frame.

Alternative titles: *Le Givre; Uplands in the Valmondois near L'Isle-Adam; Sur les hauteurs de Valmondois.*

Support: Fabric, .635 x .98 (25" x 38⅝").

Marks: Canvas stenciled *AN . . . OTTOZ / 2 Rue de la Michodier / Paris.*

Condition: A comparison between the painting in its present state and an engraving by Henry Defort reproduced in the Laurent-Richard Sale catalogue of 1873 indicates that the condition of *Le Givre* has deteriorated, a result either of inherent faults or of efforts of overly zealous restorers. Particularly apparent are losses in the definition of the poplar trees in the middle ground and of the thicket of bushes in the right foreground. The rail fence winding across the foreground has also deteriorated. In 1947 deeply discolored varnishes were removed, revealing that the painting had been treated previously and that cracks appearing across the surface had been inpainted. In the process of this work in 1947, the conservator removed what he considered to be overpainting and reinforcing of contours dating from the earlier, unidentified treatment, thus leaving the picture with its present appearance. In defense of the earlier restorations, it should be noted that Rousseau was notorious for reworking his paintings and that the conditions under which *Le Givre* was executed set it apart within his oeuvre. Examinations subsequent to the 1947 treatment, including one in 1957 when the picture was lined, and another in 1962, failed to verify whether the overpainting removed in 1947 was solely the work of a later restorer or whether it could have included, in part, reworking by the artist.

Provenance: Sold by Rousseau to Paul Casimir-Périer; Durand-Ruel; Troyon; Troyon Sale, Paris, 1866, no. 568; Collection Bocquet, Lille; Laurent-Richard Sale, Paris, 1873, no. 44, to Durand-Ruel, 60,100 francs; Collection Febore; Beurnonville Sale, Paris, 1880, no. 45, 74,100 francs; Goupil; bought by W. T. Walters, December 26, 1882 for 112,000 francs.

Reproductions: Engraved by H. Lefort in *Galerie Durand Ruel, Recueil d'estampes,* Paris, 1873, plate 280.

Exhibitions: Barye Monument Association, no. 539; "Barbizon Revisited," San Francisco, Toledo, Cleveland, Boston, 1962–63, no. 96; "Théodore Rousseau," Louvre, Paris, 1967–68, no. 33.

References: A. Baschet, "Les ateliers de Paris," *L'Artiste* (May 1854): 98; Philippe Burty, "Théodore Rousseau," *GBA* 24 (1868): 314–15; Alfred Sensier, *Souvenirs sur Th. Rousseau.* Paris, Léon Techener, 1872. pp. 151–52, 259; R. Ménard, "La collection de Laurent-Richard," *GBA* 2nd pér. 7 (1873): 194; H. Perrier, "De Hugo van der Goes à John Constable," *GBA* 2nd pér. 7 (1873): 260; E. Fromentin, *Les maîtres d'autrefois.* 2nd ed. Paris, Plon, 1876. p. 281; Philippe Burty, *Maîtres et petits maîtres.* Paris, G. Charpentier, 1877. p. 138; A. de Lostalot, "La collection Laurent-Richard," *GBA* 2nd pér. 17 (1878): 466; Philippe Burty, "Théodore Rousseau paysagiste," *L'Art* 28 (1882): 170–71; Walters cat., 1884, p. 62, no. 103, and subsequent Walters catalogues; Albert Wolff, *Cent chefs-d'oeuvre.* New York, Knoedler, 1885. p. 55; J. W. Mollett, *The painters of Barbizon: Millet, Rousseau, Diaz, Corot, Daubigny, Dupré.* London, S. Low, Marston, Searle & Rivington, 1890. p. 122; Lamb, p. 246; Jules Breton, *Nos peintres du siècle.* L'art et les artistes. Paris, Société d'édition d'artistique, 1899. p. 57; G. Lanoé and T. Brice, *Histoire de l'école française de paysage depuis Le Poussin jusqu'à Millet.* Paris, A. Charles, 1901. p. 185; D. C. Thomson, *The Barbizon school of painters.* London, Chapman and Hall, 1902. pp. 123, 164; W. Gensel, *Millet und Rousseau.* Bielefeld, Velhagen & Klasing, 1902. p. 88; H. Marcel, *La peinture française au XIXe siècle.* Paris, A. Picard & Kaan, 1905. p. 160; E. Michel, *Les maîtres du paysage.* Paris, Hachette, 1906, p. 428; E. Michel, *La Forêt de Fontainebleau.* Paris, H. Laurens, 1909. p. 155; Prosper Dorbec, *Thèodore Rousseau.* Paris, H. Laurens, 1910. pp. 88, 123; Prosper Dorbec, "L'oeuvre de Théodore Rousseau aux Salons de 1849 à 1867," *GBA* 4th pér. 9 (1913): 110; Prosper Dorbec, *L'art du paysage en France.* Paris, H. Laurens, 1925. pp. 89, 107; H. Focillon, *La peinture au XIXe siècle.* Manuels d'histoire de l'art. Paris, H. Laurens, 1927. p. 348; L. Venturi, *Les archives de l'impressionisme.* 2 vols. Paris, Durand-Ruel, 1939. 2: 205; Raymond Escholier, *La Peinture française, XIX siècle.* Bibliothèque artistique. 2 vols. Paris, Floury, 1941–43. 2: 132; Ch. Léger, *La Barbizonnière.* La petite histoire des grands artistes. Paris, René Julliard, 1946. pp. 87, 104; M. Boudot-Lamotte, "Théodore Rousseau, essai de biographie critique," *Revue palladienne* (1951): 208–10; (1952): 349–50; Nina V. Iavorskaia, *Paysages de l'école de Barbizon.* Moscow, Iskusstvo, 1962. p. 107; Jean Bouret, *The Barbizon School and 19th century French landscape painting.* Greenwich, Conn., New York Graphic Society, 1973. p. 132 (illus.); Pierre Miquel, *Le paysage français au XIX siècle.* L'école de la nature, 1–6. 6 vols. Maurs-la-Jolie, Editions de la Martinelle, 1975– 3: 446; Lucas, 2: 555, 556.

55. A Swamp in the Landes

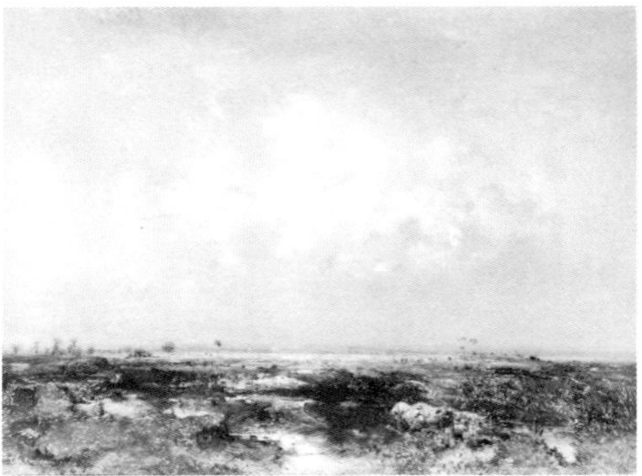

37.991 after 1844

Though known initially as *Plaine et Marais,* this desolate scene has generally been identified as a locale in The Landes in southwestern France. Rousseau accompanied Jules Dupré to this region, noted for its vast swampy wastes, in the summer of 1844. The experience proved conducive to Rousseau's experiments in painting in the manner of the seventeenth-century Haarlem school. The expanse of sky, low horizon, and rendering of the flat terrain in muted ochers, greens and greys, are reminiscent of Hobbema's landscapes. In this scene, Rousseau portrays a moment at which sunlight, penetrating the cloud formations in the center of the picture, illuminates expanses of the terrain below.

Support: Panel, .417 x .567 (16⅜" x 22¼").

Signed in red in lower left: *Th. Rousseau.*

Condition: Untreated since 1934.

Provenance: Boyard collection; Laurent-Richard collection, Sale, Paris, April 7, 1873, no. 51 (illus.) for 30,000 francs; Laurent-Richard collection, Sale, Paris 1886, no. 60 (illus.); William H. Fuller Sale, New York, 1898, no. 24; Isidor Wormser Sale, New York, 1917, no. 109 to Henry Walters for $10,000.00.

References: Walters cat., 1929, p. 68, no. 204 C, and subsequent Walters catalogues.

56. Early Summer Afternoon

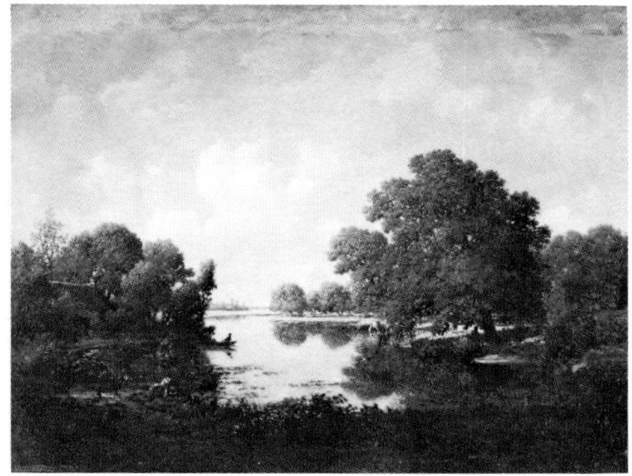

37.137 1855–60

Warm sunlight breaks through the clouds in this tranquil scene. To the left, nestled in foliage on a point of land, is a cottage with a thatched roof. Nearby, partially obscured in the reflections of the trees, is a man in a punt. An oak tree dominates the right bank. Further upstream a horse is drinking and on the shores beyond are clusters of trees.

The relative attention to detail and degree of finish is characteristic of Rousseau's works of the late fifties, a period when the influence of Hobbema and other Dutch seventeenth-century landscape painters dominated his production.

Support: Panel, cradled, .56 x .74 (22¹⁄₁₆" x 29⅛").

Signed bottom left: *THEODORE ROUSSEAU.*

Marks: Reverse: Label for Lincoln Safe Deposit Co., N.Y.

Condition: Discolored varnish removed in 1951. Thorough examination in 1979 revealed signs of warping and rupturing as a result of pressure from cradle, traces of inpainting along the edges; minimal cleaning undertaken.

Provenance: Henry Probasco (Cincinnati) Sale, New York, 1887, no. 9 to William Schaus for $2,100.00; Schaus to W. T. Walters 1887–88.

Exhibitions: Barye Monument Association, no. 536; "From Ingres to Gauguin," Baltimore Museum of Art, 1951, no. 48; "An Exhibition of Treasures of the Walters Art Gallery," Wildenstein and Co., New York, 1967, no. 49.

References: Walters cat., 1888 p. 63, no. 93 and subsequent Walters catalogues.

Artist unknown, formerly attributed to T. Rousseau

57. Woodland Scene

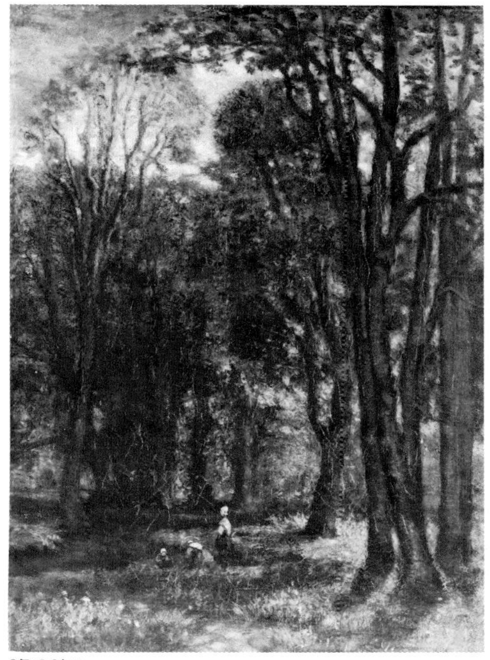

37.2378

Three figures — a child, a kneeling woman wearing a wide-brimmed hat, and a girl — are picking flowers or fruit in a wooded glen. Sunlight breaking through the foliage creates patterns of light and shadow on the ground. Though dating from the 19th century, this picture has been extensively reworked with a false signature added.

Support: Fabric, .35 x .246 (13¾" x 9⅝").

Signed at lower right: *T. H. ROUSSEAU.*

Condition: The painting was treated and lined prior to 1960. Both the signature and much of the foliage in the upper areas appear to have been applied over earlier painting marred by crackle.

Provenance: Bequest of Philip B. Perlman, 1960.

Exhibitions: "Landscape Painting and the Point of View," The Walters Art Gallery, 1944.

Charles-Emile Jacque

French: Paris, 1813 - Paris, 1894

Jacque's early training was limited to copying lithographs, particularly those of Léon Cogniet, and to working in the engraving shop of a map printer. Finding time for his art in the course of military service (1831–1836), he submitted two prints to the 1833 Salon. In the late thirties, while visiting England and Burgundy, Jacque was active as an engraver and illustrator. Early in the forties he painted near Montmartre, drawing inspiration from the landscapes of a predecessor, Georges Michel. By 1843, the year he took a residence on the rue de Rochechouart in Paris, Jacque had gained a reputation as a major realist through his etchings. Two years later, he began to paint in earnest, working in Montmartre and on the plains of Clignancourt. As a result of an outbreak of cholera in 1849, Jacque and his neighbor on the rue de Rochechouart, J.-F. Millet, moved with their families to the village of Barbizon, where they painted together in the nearby forest. In the fifties, Jacque divided his time between Paris and Barbizon, which had by now become his home. His small paintings of poultry and pigsties were already in demand. An abiding interest in fowl led him to practice poultry husbandry and to produce a book, *Le Poulailler, monographie des poules indigènes et exotiques* (1852). In the later fifties, when he was exceedingly active both as a painter and an etcher, Jacque gradually severed his relations with Millet, though he remained on good terms with his neighbors Théodore Rousseau and A.-L. Barye. His pictures at this point were mainly sold through the Belgian merchant Couteaux.

After 1868, Le Croisic on the Bay of Biscay was one of his favorite haunts, particularly in the autumn. He found a ready market for his pictures of sheep and poultry in England in the seventies, selling them through the dealers Durand–Ruel and Georges Petit. Among his later projects was the heading of the Société des animaliers français, which held exhibitions in 1882 and 1883. Jacque died in 1894, having outlived all his colleagues in Barbizon.

58. Chickens

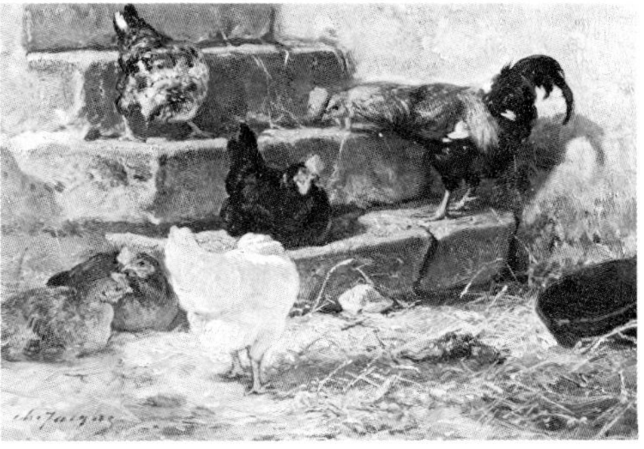

37.80 1860s

A shaft of sunlight illumines this scene in which five hens and a rooster are portrayed on masonry steps in the corner of a straw-strewn yard. The artist has carefully delineated the variations in the poultry. As early as the late 1840s Jacque began to produce these small poulaillers. A major example of his work in this genre was *La Sieste,* (.65 x .53) illustrated in Jules Claretie, *Catalogue des tableaux, études peintes,* Galerie Georges Petit, Paris, November, 1894, no. 24.

Support: Panel, chestnut, beveled edges, .18 x .26 (7⅛" x 10⅜").

Signed lower left: *ch. Jacque.*

Marks: Oval stamp *LE. . . GANNE/PANNEAUX DU CHENE/RUE. . .*

Provenance: Felix Ziem; purchased by W. T. Walters between 1878–84.

References: Walters cat., 1884, p. 64, no. 100.

59. Chickens

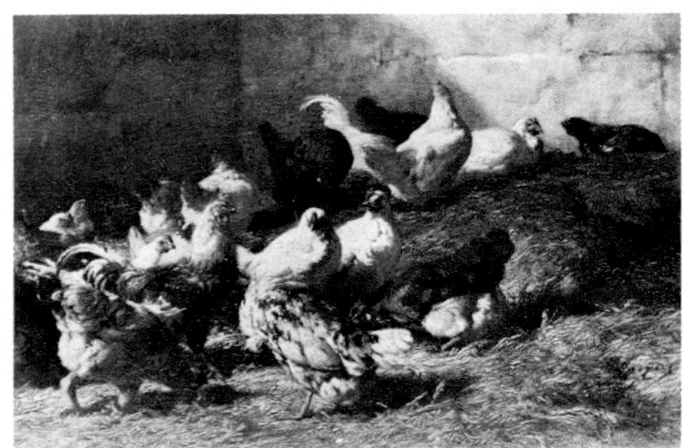

37.81

In a sunlit corner of a yard poultry of various colors are perched on a mound of steaming straw.

Support: Panel, .204 x .309 (8" x 12⅛").

Signed lower right: *ch. Jacque.*

Marks: Paper sticker on frame: *50.*

Provenance: purchased by W. T. Walters between 1878 and 1884.

References: Walters cat., 1884, p. 98, no. 98, and subsequent Walters catalogues.

Jean-François Millet

French: Gruchy, 1814 - Barbizon, 1875

Millet, a son of prosperous peasants, received an education in classical and modern literature from the curate of the village of Gréville, Normandy. His early training in painting in Cherbourg, under a pupil of J.-L. David named Mouchel, was interrupted by periods of toil on the family farm. In 1835 Millet became a student of L.-T.-A.-S. Langlois de Chevreville, who had once studied with Baron Gros. Langlois de Chevreville was the curator of the Thomas Henry Collection of Spanish, Dutch and French art, the foundation of Cherbourg's art museum. Two years later, a stipend from the municipality of Cherbourg enabled Millet to enroll in the atelier of Paul Delaroche at the Ecole des Beaux-Arts, Paris. There Millet remained for two years until, disheartened by the rejection of his entry for the *prix de peinture,* he withdrew from the Ecole and began to frequent the Académie Suisse and the picture galleries of the Louvre. After 1840, when one of his entries, a portrait, was accepted at the Salon, Millet spent four years in Paris and Cherbourg, submitting occasional oils and pastels to the salons. When his first wife died in 1844 after only three years of marriage, he established a liaison with Catherine Lemaire who eventually became his second wife and who accompanied him in 1845 to Le Havre, where he produced some portraits of sailors and captains. Back in Paris the following year, he established contacts with Rousseau, Jacque, Troyon, and Diaz as well as with Barye and Daumier, artists whose names were subsequently linked with his within the context of the "Barbizon School." During the later forties, however, he painted in his *manière fleurie,* executing vigorously sculptural figurative compositions, frequently imbued with erotic overtones.

When an outbreak of cholera threatened Paris in 1849, Millet, using proceeds from his first government commission, *Gleaners at Rest,* in the Louvre, joined Charles Jacque in establishing a residence in the village of Barbizon where he remained for most of his later life, portraying in his oils and pastels the lives of the villagers and farmers. At the 1850 Salon, his *The Sower* (Provident National Bank, Philadelphia) and *The Hay Balers* (Louvre) were acclaimed as profound social statements by the avant-garde critics who associated him in this regard with the realist Courbet. The following year, Alfred Sensier, the artist's supplier of materials, quasi-dealer, and eventual biographer, sent to Litchfield House, London, *Breaking Flax* (Walters Art Gallery), the first work by Millet to be exhibited abroad. This composition figured in 1853 in a collection of ten engravings drawn by Millet, printed by A. Lavieille and published in *L'Illustration.* His salon entries that year drew a second-class medal as well as the attention of William Morris Hunt and several of his compatriots from Boston, who were to become Millet's most avid supporters.

Though Millet was too much of a fatalist to be strongly motivated politically, his paintings continued to be interpreted in socialist terms. *The Gleaners* (Louvre), shown in 1857, was as violently attacked by the conservative critics as it was praised by the liberals, most notably Castagnary. A similar controversy was engendered by *Man with the Hoe* (private collection, U.S.A.) in 1863. Millet's fatalism likewise precluded any deeply religious convictions, though when his *The Angelus* (1855–57) was first exhibited at the Cercle de l'union artistique in 1865, it, too, was misinterpreted by the public which, oblivious to the artist's agnosticism, acclaimed it as a profoundly religious statement.

Nine of Millet's paintings, including *The Potato Harvest* and *The Sheep Fold,* now in the Walters Art Gallery, were shown in the Exposition Universelle in 1867 and the following year he was appointed Chevalier of the Legion of Honor.

In the autumn of 1871, Millet sought refuge from the Franco-Prussian War in Normandy where he remained for over a year, producing many of his finest landscapes and coastal scenes. During his later years Millet worked at an unabated pace, not only in oils but in pastels, a medium in which he excelled. A commission received in 1874 to execute a series of scenes from the life of Saint Geneviève for the Panthéon was unrealized when he died in January 1875.

60. Breaking Flax

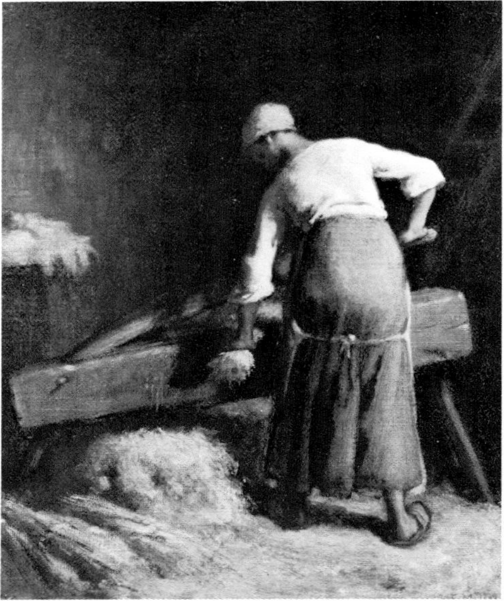

37.87 1850–51

In a murky interior one can discern a woman with her back to the viewer, clad in a blue skirt and light blouse, crushing flax. She holds a sheaf of dried flax against the block, and lowers the beetle. Additional sheaves and a hamper are visible at the left, and to the right is a ladder.

A drawing of this composition, entitled *Peasant Woman Cleaning Out a Trough* is published in facsimile by Léonce Bénédite in *The Drawings of Jean François Millet,* London, 1906, no. 31. The composition also figured as *L'arracheuse de lin* in a series of ten subjects devoted to rural labor, drawn by Millet and engraved by Adrien Lavieille in 1852 and published in *L'Illustration* 16 (February 7, 1853): 93, no. 519.

Support: Fabric, finely woven, .464 x .38 (18¼" x 14 15/16")

Signed in dark brown at lower right: *J. F. Millet.*

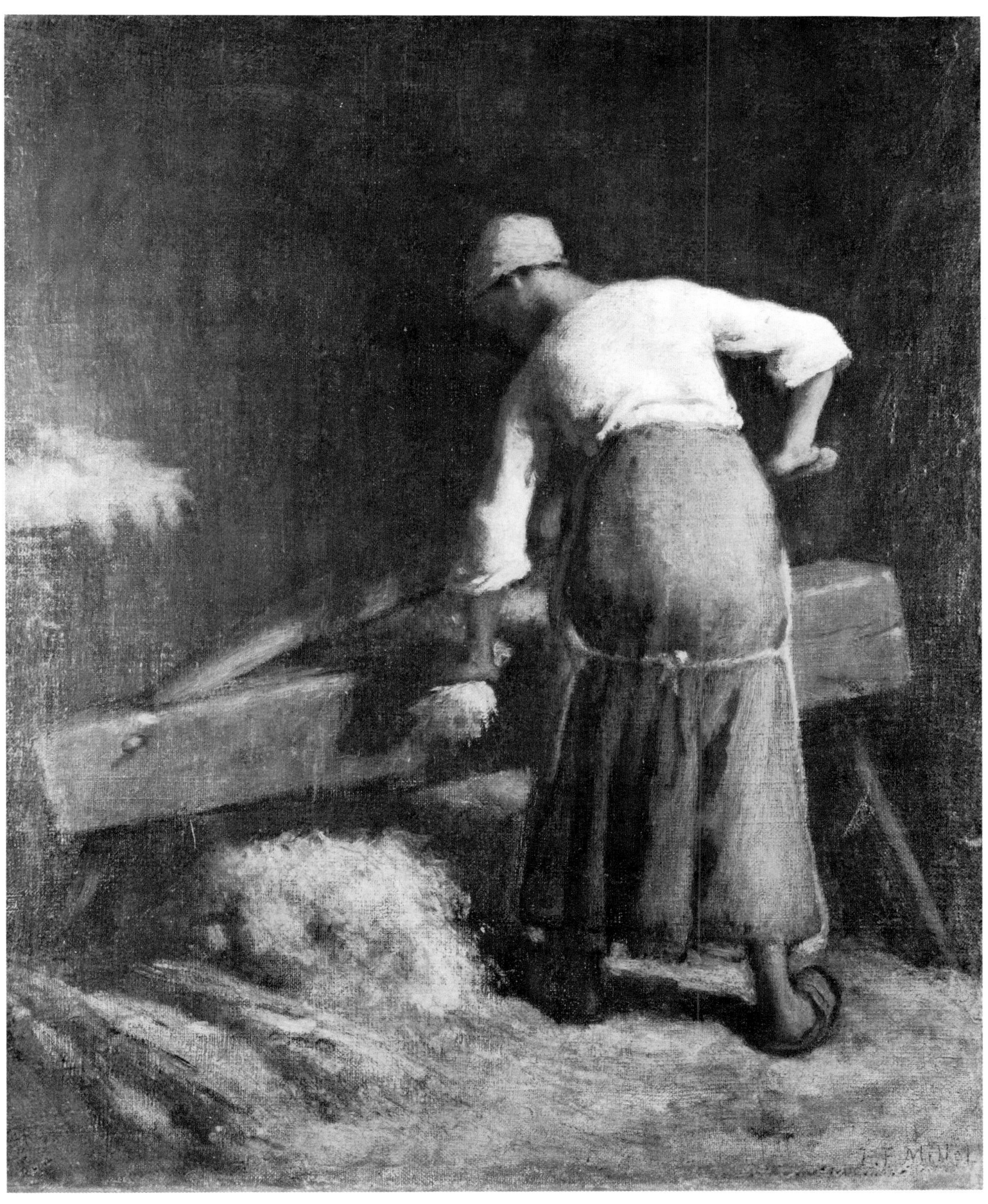

Millet *Breaking Flax,* no. 60

Condition: The picture was lined with a coarsely woven fabric at an unknown date. A 1978 treatment revealed slight areas of overpainting near the "J" of the signature and in the foot of the block. The surface was partially cleaned at this time.

Provenance: Millet to Sensier for sale in February 1851 (E. Moreau-Nélaton, 1: 92); Purchased by W. T. Walters from Henry Wallis, London, prior to 1878.

Exhibitions: "General Exhibition of Pictures by Living Artists," Litchfield House, London, May 1851 (as *La paysanne normande);* "Twenty-first Annual exhibition in London of Pictures, the Contributions of Artists of the Continental Schools," The French Gallery, London, 1874; "From Ingres to Gauguin," The Baltimore Museum of Art, 1951, no. 50.

References: Strahan, 1:93–94; Walters cat., 1878, p. 41, and subsequent Walters catalogues; Stranahan, p. 375; Etienne Moreau-Nélaton, *Millet raconté par lui-même.* 3 vols. Paris, H. Laurens, 1921. 1:90, 92, fig. 65; "Jean-François Millet," Grand Palais, Paris, 1975–76, pp. 25, 31.

61. The Potato Harvest

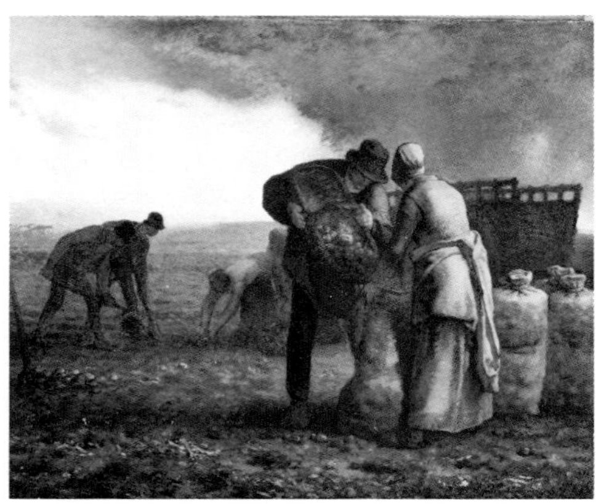

37.115 1855

On the right a farmer is pouring a basket of potatoes into a sack held open by a woman. Beside the couple are three full sacks and a cart. Further back, at the left, two men are digging potatoes which are being gathered by women. The sky at the left is suffused with warm sunlight, whereas the right side is darkened by a glowering, low-lying rain cloud.

In the Louvre are two preliminary compositional sketches, as well as two drawings for the foreground figures. In addition there is a study with a horse in black crayon bequeathed by Léon Bonnat. Related to the last is a charcoal drawing heightened with blue and white, sold at Adam A. Weschler and Son, Washington, D.C. May 22–24, 1970.

A lithographic stone showing *The Potato Harvest* was acquired by Messrs. Brown and Phillips from a member of the artist's family and was printed by Leicester Galleries in an edition of 200 in 1921.

Support: Fabric, finely woven, .54 x .652 (21¼" x 25⅝")

Signed at lower right in black: *J. F. Millet.*

Marks: Stretcher: paper sticker inscribed 4.380; paper label with numbers 1234; red seal with no decipherable marks.

Condition: Discolored varnish removed in 1937, revealing some overpainting. In 1975 an early glue lining was replaced with a wax lining. Very slight losses were inpainted.

Provenance: Papeleu (before 1863); Baron Goethals (before 1867); acquired by W. T. Walters before 1878.

Exhibitions: Exposition Universelle, Paris, 1867, no. 478; Barye Monument Association, no. 534; "Corot and his Contemporaries," Houston Museum of Fine Arts, 1959; "Jean François Millet," Grand Palais, Paris, 1975–76, no. 64.

References: E. Wheelwright, "Personal recollections of Jean François Millet," *Atlantic monthly* 38 (1876): 264; Walters cat., 1878, pp. 7–8, and subsequent Walters catalogues; Strahan, 1: 94; Alfred Sensier, *La vie et l'oeuvre de J.-F. Millet; manuscrit publié par Paul Mantz.* Paris, 1881. p. 301; D. C. Thomson, *The Barbizon school of painters.* London, Chapman and Hall, 1891. p. 241; Lamb, p. 246; Stranahan, p. 375; E. Staley, *Jean François Millet.* London, G. Bell, 1903. p. 67; Etienne Moreau-Nélaton, *Millet raconté par lui-même.* 3 vols. Paris, H. Laurens, 1921. 3:19, fig. 243; "Drawings by Jean François Millet," The Arts Council of Great Britain, 1956. pp. 36, 50; Roseline Bacou, *Millet, one hundred drawings.* New York, Harper & Row. 1975. p. 208; André Fermigier, *Jean-François Millet.* Geneva, Skira, 1977. p. 52 (illus.).

62. The Sheepfold, Moonlight

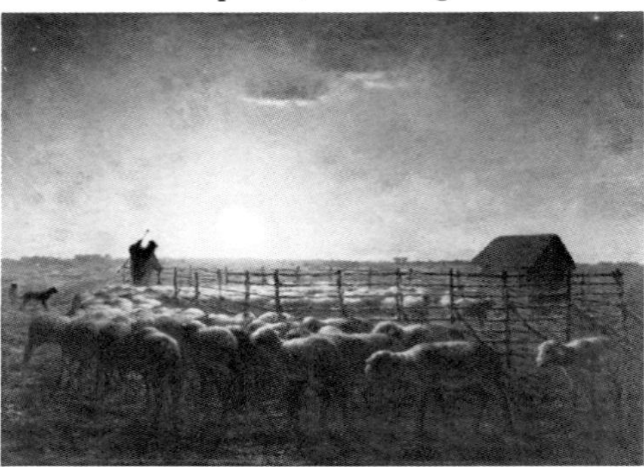

37.30 1856–60

A shepherd and his dogs are herding a flock of sheep into a pen on the Barbizon plain. Light emanating from the partial moon low on the horizon illuminates this tranquil nocturnal scene.

In the context of the solitary shepherd at night, Sensier quotes Millet as saying:

Oh, how I wish I could make those who see my work feel the splendors and terrors of the night! One ought to be able to make people hear the songs, the silences and murmurings of the air. They should feel the infinite. Is there not something terrible in thinking of these lights which rise and disappear, century after century, without varying? They light both the joys and sorrows of men, and when our world goes to pieces, the beneficent sun will watch without pity the universal desolation.

A variation on this composition with differences in the pattern of light on the backs of the sheep and in such details as the positioning of the rail fence and the shack, was delivered by Millet to his agents Messrs. Blanc and Stevens in August, 1861 (E. Moreau-Nélaton, 2:103). The later work, a reduction on panel, measuring .395 by .577, passed through the collections of Montenacken, Emile Gavet, Adolphe Bellino, and Chauchard to the Louvre in 1881.

Recorded related works include drawings in the J.-F. Millet Sale, Paris, 1875, and the Mme. Vve. Millet Sale, Paris, 1894, and two pastels in the Emile Gavet Sale, Paris, 1875, nos. 1 and 81. In the Glasgow Art Gallery is a *Flock of Sheep by Moonlight* in pencil and pastels. An engraving of the composition by Larguillermie (.46 x .63), was also published by Galerie Durand-Ruel in Brussels in 1873.

Support: Panel, chestnut, .453 x .634 (17⅞" x 24⅞")

Signed at lower right: *J. F. MILLET.*

Marks: Inscribed in ink on reverse of panel: *Au Ch. de Knyff;* Stenciled on reverse of panel: *2694.*

Condition: Discolored varnish removed in 1941.

Provenance: Chevalier A. de Knyff; vente C (Carlin), Paris, 29 April 1872, no. 19 to Mme. William Hooper for 20,000 francs; purchased by W. T. Walters between 1884 and 1887.

Exhibitions: Exposition Universelle, Paris, 1867, no. 477; "Cent chefs-d'oeuvre" Galerie Georges Petit, Paris, 1883, no. 69; Barye Monument Association, no. 545.

References: Alfred Sensier, *La vie et l'oeuvre de J.-F. Millet; manuscrit publié par Paul Mantz.* Paris, 1881. pp. 168–70; Albert Wolff, *Cent chefs-d'ouevre.* New York, Knoedler, 1885, illus. opposite p. 8, 20 (illus. in engraving by Damman); Walters cat., 1887, p. 88, no. 141, and subsequent Walters catalogues; Mathews, p. 7; Lamb, p. 246; Stranahan, p. 375; Reizenstein, p. 549; Julia Cartwright, *Jean François Millet, his life and letters.* 2nd ed. London, Swan Sonnenschein, 1902. p. 207; Etienne Moreau Nélaton, *Millet raconté par lui-même.* 3 vols. Paris, H. Laurens, 1921. 2: 79–80, fig. 150; 3: 85.

63. The Goose Girl

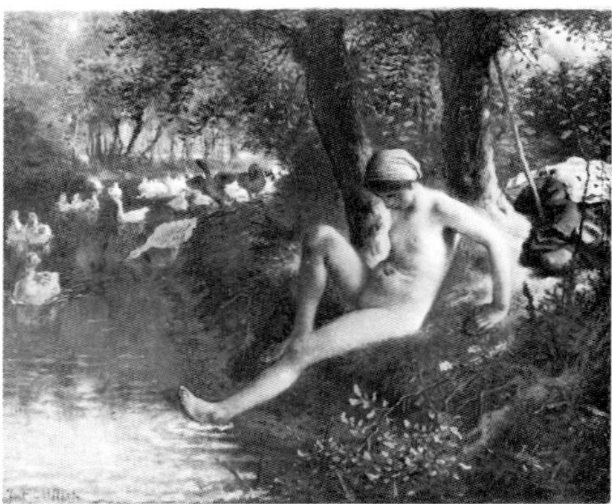

37.153 1869

A nude adolescent girl seated beside a couple of trees on the bank of a stream dangles her heel in the water. Her clothing is heaped behind her. Slightly upstream at the left swim her geese, and, scarcely discernible through an opening in the foliage at the right, is a grazing cow. Sunlight penetrating through the foliage illumines patches of terrain otherwise shaded by the trees.

Goose girls with their gaggles were recurrent in Millet's work: namely, *La gardeuse d'oies,* Salon of 1867; another painting of the subject in the Mrs. L. A. Frothingham collection exhibited at the Museum of Fine Arts, Boston, in 1923; a watercolor of a girl separating fighting geese of about 1865, formerly in the Durand-Ruel collection; a chalk drawing of a standing goose girl illustrated by Clarence Cook in *Art and Artists of Our Time,* New York, 1888, 1:246; and a drawing, *Gardeuse d'oies,* in the Marmontel Sale, Paris, Hôtel Drouot, March 1898. Nudes, however, seldom occurred after the 1840s. An exception, apart from the Walters picture, is the *Baigneuses,* a pastel of about 1863–65, in the Musée des Beaux-Arts, Lille, in which the artist has transferred a composition of one nude assisting another from a studio painting of the same title of 1848, in the Louvre (R.F. 141), to an outdoor setting on the banks of a stream somewhat comparable to that in *The Goose Girl.*

Directly related to the Walters picture are four drawings in chalk, three in the Louvre, and the fourth in the Musée des Beaux-Arts, Dijon. In addition, there are a sketch, *The Bather,* in the Gallery of Modern Art, Dublin, no. 180; a pencil drawing by Etienne Moreau-Nélaton in *Millet raconté par lui-même,* Paris, 1921, 2, fig. 185; a pencil drawing in a private collection in Iowa and a charcoal drawing, *La baigneuse,* Paris, Hôtel Drouot, May 27, 1926, no. 122.

Camille Pissarro adopted the theme of Millet's paintings in *Woman Washing her Feet* in the Metropolitan Museum of Art, New York (A. F. Janson, *100 Masterpieces of Painting, Indianapolis Museum of Art,* Indianapolis, 1980, p. 196.

Alternative titles: *The Bather; Le bain de la gardeuse d'oies.*

Support: Fabric, fine twill weave, .369 x .464 (14½" x 17 13/16")

Signed at lower left: *J. F. Millet.*

Marks: Reverse: Stretcher marked *E* (stencil) 865 (ink) *PARIS* (stencil) 366 (incised); Inscribed in ink: *GE 11199,* nine wax seals on stretcher; In addition, the cross bar of the stretcher bore on its face, covered by the fabric, the name *Sidelmeyer* (sic) written in white chalk.

Condition: The picture was lined prior to 1934. A thorough examination of the picture in 1975 revealed that in the initial lining a thin fabric interleaf had been employed. Two sets of tack holes were discovered on the stretcher corresponding to holes in the tacking edge of the fabric, suggesting that the stretcher was original. The painting was relined and partially cleaned at this time.

Provenance: Millet to the dealer Ennemond Blanc for 800 francs in 1865 (see letter from Millet to Blanc, August 23, 1863, reproduced by E. Moreau-Nélaton, 2: 141–42); Van Praet, Brussels; J. Saulnier, Bordeaux; Mme. Vve. Saulnier Sale, Paris, 1886, no. 64, illus. 29,100 francs; Sedelmeyer Sale, Paris, March 25, 1892, no. 10, illus.; Henri Heugel Sale, Paris, May 26, 1905, no. 12; Henry Walters.

Exhibitions: "Jean-François Millet" Ecole des Beaux-Arts, Paris, 1887, no. 51; "From Ingres to Gauguin," Baltimore Museum of Art, 1951, no. 53; "Birth of Impressionism," Wildenstein and Co., New York, 1963, no. 55; "Man, the Glory, Jest and Riddle," California Palace of the Legion of Honor, San Francisco, 1964–65, no. 203; "An Exhibition of Treasures of the Walters Art Gallery," Wildenstein and Co., New York, 1967, no. 47; "Jean-François Millet," Grand Palais, Paris, 1975–76, no. 160.

References: T. H. Bartlett, "Barbizon and Jean-François Millet," *Scribner's Magazine* 7 (1890): 746; W. J. Mollett, *The Painters of Barbizon: Millet, Rousseau, Diaz, Corot, Daubigny, Dupré.* London, S. Low, Marston, Searle & Rivington, 1890. p. 114; H. Naegely, *J. F. Millet and rustic art.* London, E. Stock, 1898. p. 118; *Jean-François Millet.* Masters in art. Boston, 1900. p. 33; L. Soullié, *Peintures, aquarelles, pastels, dessins de Jean-François Millet.* Les grands peintres aux ventes publiques. Paris, L. Soullié, 1900. p. 17; Walther Gensel, *Millet und Rousseau.* Bielefeld, Velhagen & Klasing, 1902. p. 47, fig. 33; Julia Cartwright, *Jean-François Millet, his life and letters.* 2nd ed. London, Swan Sonnenschein, 1902. pp. 245–46; H. Marcel, *J.-F. Millet.* Les grands artistes. Paris, H. Laurens, 1904. p. 88; E. Michel, *La Forêt de Fontainebleau.* Paris, H. Laurens, 1909. pp. 187–88; P. M. Turner, *Millet.* London, T. C. & E. C. Jack, 1910. pp. 21–22; Kenyon Cox, *Artist and public.* London, G. Allen & Unwin, 1914. pp. 66–68, illus.; Etienne Moreau-Nélaton, *Millet raconté par lui-même.* 3 vols. Paris, H. Laurens, 1921. 2:140–44, fig. 184; Edward S. King, "The men of 1830," *BWAG* 9, no. 6 (March 1957): 4 (illus.); A. Reverdy, *L'école de Barbizon, l'évolution du prix des tableaux de 1850 à 1960.* Paris, Mouton, 1973, p. 124; "Peasant painter," *MD medical newsmagazine* 8, no. 8 (August 1964): 165; Eldon N. Van Liere, "Solutions and dissolutions: the bather in nineteenth-century French painting," *Arts magazine* 54 (May 1980): 108, fig. 13.

Charles-François Daubigny

French: Paris, 1817 - Paris, 1878

Charles-François, a proponent of out-of-door painting and a pioneer print maker, was the son of Edme Daubigny, also a landscape painter who had trained under the academic landscapist Jean–Victor Bertin and had made his Salon debut in 1819.

A sickly child, the young Daubigny was sent from Paris to the countryside of the Valmondois, a region to which he was later drawn as a painter. In his youth, he supported himself by decorating jewelry boxes and clock-faces. For several years beginning in 1834 he served as a restorer in the Louvre under F. M. Granet, and worked as a decorative painter at Versailles. He became a pupil of P.-A.-T. Senties in 1835, but interrupted his training the following year to travel to Rome with a companion, Henri Mignan. Returning from Italy in 1837, he continued his studies with Senties and in 1838 he became associated with a group of young artists, his brother-in-law J. L. Trimolet, L. Steinheil, and A. V. Geoffroy-Dechaume, sharing quarters and pooling resources. Daubigny began to exhibit at the Salon that year, entering a *View of Notre Dame and the Ile Saint Louis.* He and his associates now primarily supported themselves by illustrating books with engravings. The favorable reception accorded his *Saint Jerome in the Desert* in the Salon of 1840 encouraged him to prepare for the Prix de Rome by enrolling in the studio of Paul Delaroche. This endeavor was abandoned in 1841 after he had been rejected for a technical oversight midway through the competition.

During the forties Daubigny continued to earn his livelihood preparing illustrations for the popular press. He also traveled in the countryside and regularly submitted landscapes to the Paris Salons. In 1848, at the non-juried Salon, he submitted five landscapes, receiving his first award, a second–class medal.

His wanderings continued in the fifties. In 1852 he befriended Corot and together they accompanied A. F. Ravier to the Isère. The following summer he was again with Corot in Dardagny, Switzerland, where they stayed with the family of the painter Armand Leleux. Daubigny first visited Villerville on the Channel coast in 1854 and in the summer of that year he joined Corot at Auvers-sur-Oise, where they were surrounded by a coterie of pupils. Daubigny met with moderate success at the 1855 Exposition Universelle, exhibiting four canvases and receiving a third–class medal. In 1857 the course of his annual wanderings was altered when he purchased a small, flat-bottomed boat equipped with a cabin which he named *Le Botin,* "the little box," to serve as a floating studio. Corot was honorary admiral, Daubigny captain, and his son Karl cabin boy. He cruised the French rivers every summer sketching out of doors, accompanied by a crew of admirers and followers. By 1859 Daubigny was generally acclaimed a major landscape painter, being appointed Chevalier of the Legion of Honor, winning a first–class medal at the Salon and receiving a commission for decorative panels for the Chamber of the Ministry of State in the Louvre.

He purchased a plot of land in 1860 at Auvers-sur-Oise where he built and furnished a cottage with the assistance of Corot and Oudinot and his son Karl. The "Villa des Vallées," as it was known, provided a winter mooring for *Le Botin* and was a gathering point for his many colleagues. In the later sixties Daubigny began to travel further afield, accompanying Alfred Cadart to London in 1865, that year visiting Trouville where he met Courbet, and going to Spain with the dealer Brame in 1869.

Though he distinguished between his études executed out-of-doors and his less spontaneous salon paintings prepared in his studio, Daubigny occasionally submitted to exhibitions large pictures painted entirely *en plein air.* An example of such was the *Villerville-sur-mer* (Mesdag Museum, The Hague), shown in 1864. When he was elected to the Salon jury he used his position to further the interests of the *plein-air* painters. In 1866 he had Pissarro's entry accepted, though he was unsuccessful in his defense of Cézanne's and Renoir's submissions. Again when he served on the Jury in 1868, works by a number of the future Impressionists were included. The rejection of Monet's entry in 1870 led to Daubigny's resignation from the Jury.

With the outbreak of the Franco-Prussian War, Daubigny and his family sought refuge in London, where the dealer Durand-Ruel had recently established a gallery that dealt in the works of the French refugee painters. He returned to France upon the cessation of hostilities and resumed his customary itinerary, sketching from *Le Botin* every summer, and exhibiting regularly at the Salons until his death in 1878.

64. Beach Scene

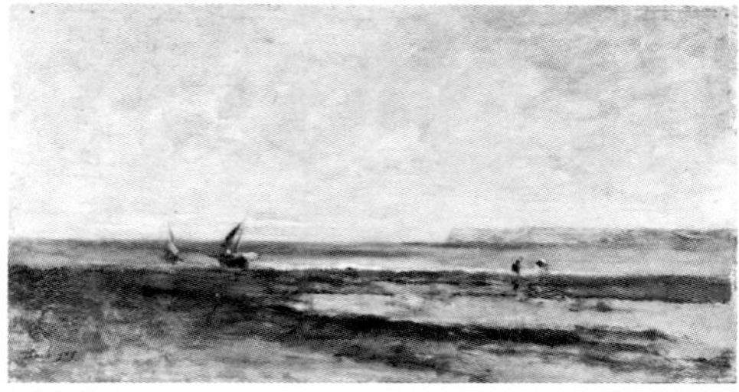

37.2379 after 1854

Several fishing boats have been stranded on the beach of Villerville at low tide. Across the bay loom the cliffs of Sainte-Adresse. Daubigny first visited this region in June 1854, and returned to it frequently thereafter.

Alternative titles: *Villerville; Vue sur les Falaises de Sainte-Adresse.*

Support: Coarse panel, perhaps poplar, .167 x .317 (6⅝" x 12½").

Signed at lower left: *Daubigny.*

Provenance: Bequest of Philip B. Perlman, 1960.

References: Robert Hellebranth, *Charles-François Daubigny, 1817–1878.* Morges, Editions Matute, 1976. p. 214, no. 644, illus.

65. Landscape with Gleaners

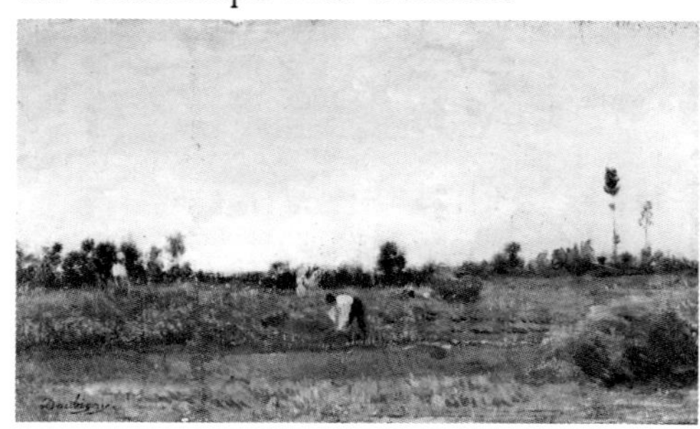

37.35

Throughout his career Daubigny dealt with harvest scenes. Most similar to the Walters panel is a *Summer Landscape with Harvesters,* panel (.255 x .48) in the Ateneumin Taidemuseo, Helsinki.

Support: Coarse panel with grain running vertically, .149 x .242 (5⅞" x 9½").

Signed in dark brown at lower left: *Daubigny.*

Condition: Left of center is a vertical disjoin partially obscured by some inpainting.

Provenance: Mrs. P. C. Hanford of Chicago, Sale, American Art Gallery, New York, January 30, 1902 to Henry Walters for $975.00.

References: Walters cat., 1909, p. 12, no. 35, and subsequent Walters catalogues; Robert Hellebranth, *Charles-François Daubigny, 1817–1878.* Morges, Editions Matute, 1976. p. 327, no. 1000, illus.

66. Sunset on the Coast in France

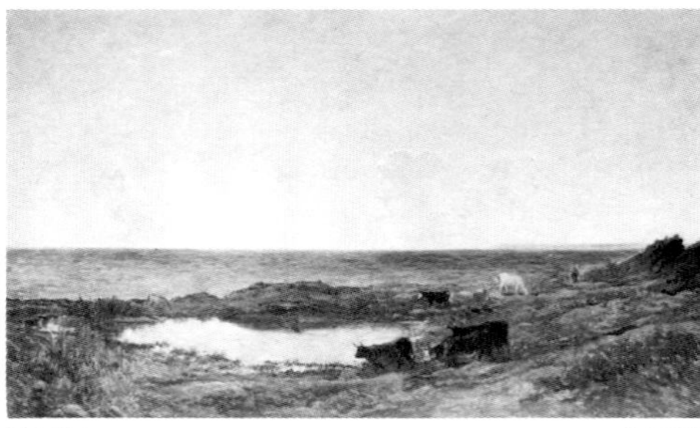

37.17 1865?

The sun is setting on the horizon, leaving the sky suffused with a pinkish glow. In the central foreground is a tidal basin. Amidst rocks and tufts of herbage graze cattle and two horses attended by a solitary figure. The date of the painting is problematic. Hellebranth, on the basis of similarities between this work and *Return of the Fishing Fleet at Sunset* (1873) in the Chrysler Collection, and *Beach at Villerville at Low Tide* (1874) in the Mesdag Collection, The Hague, assigns a date of 1874 to the Baltimore picture. The previous year, Daubigny exhibited *Beach at Villerville at Sunset* at the Salon and in the Vienna International Exhibition. However, the Walters picture appears to be dated 1865. Both the signature and the two digits of the date have been partially obscured by an early reworking of the paint surface.

Alternative titles: *Coucher de Soleil sur la côte normande; La Mare à Villerville.*

Support: Canvas, .934 x 1.505 (36¾" x 59¼").

Signed and dated: *Daubigny 65.*

Marks: On stretcher: large paper label: *38/VERNON;* large paper label: *VERNON/1/au HA . . .;* small label inscribed: *222;* paper sticker: *17.582.*

Condition: Lined prior to 1934. The surface is obscured by a thick layer of discolored varnish.

Provenance: Acquired between 1878 and 1884.

Exhibitions: Barye Monument Association, no. 544.

References: Walters cat., 1884, pp. 84–85, no. 137, and subsequent Walters catalogues; Champlin and Perkins, 1:375; Mathews, p. 7; Robert Hellebranth, *Charles-François Daubigny, 1817–1878.* Morges, Editions Matute, 1976. p. 208, no. 620, illus.

67. Twilight

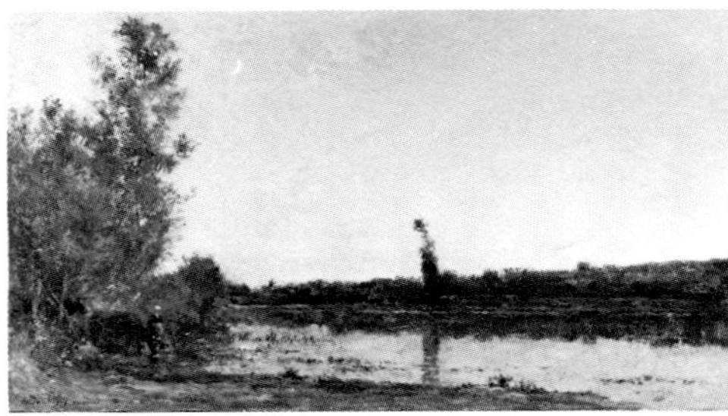

37.128 1866

In this subdued view of the Seine near the village of Andrésy, Daubigny has indicated the time of day by the crescent moon shining in the sky. Against the golden opalescent sky is silhouetted a single tall tree. At the left, a couple of cattle are drinking, tended by a peasant woman.

Crepuscular scenes were recurrent in Daubigny's work, a preference he shared with his colleague Corot.

Alternative title: *Un soir à Andrésy, bords de Seine.*

Support: Thick mahogany panel, .45 x .815 (17⅝" x 32").

Signed and dated in dark brown at lower left: *Daubigny 1886.*

Condition: A technical examination in 1952 revealed that the picture had been extensively overpainted to conceal a wide crackle pattern. Discolored varnishes and overpainting were removed on this occasion and the picture was coated with dammar varnish.

Provenance: M. Coing (?); John Taylor Johnston Sale, National Academy of Design, New York, December 19–22, 1876, no. 54 to W. T. Walters for $1,450.00.

Exhibitions: Paris Salon, 1867; Barye Monument Association, no. 531.

References: P. Mantz, "Salon de 1867," *GBA* 22 (1867): 539; Strahan, 1:94; Walters cat., 1878, p. 32, and subsequent Walters catalogues; Champlin and Perkins, 1:375; Madeleine Fidell-Beaufort and Janine Bailly-Herzberg, *Daubigny.* La vie et l'oeuvre, 1. Paris, Geoffroy-Dechaume, 1975. pp. 24, 157, fig. 89; Pierre Miquel, *Le paysage français aux XIXe siècle.* L'école de la nature, 1-6. 6 vols. Maurs-la-Jolie, Editions de la Martinelle, 1975– 3: 692–93; Robert Hellebranth, *Charles-François Daubigny, 1817–1878.* Morges, Editions Matute, p. 22, no. 49, illus.

68. The Coming Storm, Early Spring

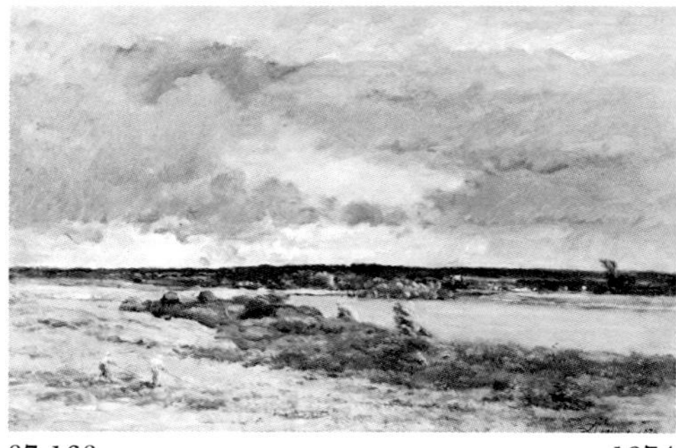

37.163 1874

Sunlight breaking through the clouds illuminates the emerald green and golden fields and the winding river below. Two peasant women in the left foreground scythe their crop. Other figures are visible among the bushes growing along the banks. Across the river plains extend to the horizon lost in deep blue shadows.

Daubigny painted in his floating studio, *Le Botin,* on both the Yonne and the Seine rivers in 1874. This vibrantly colored scene dating from the year of the first "Impressionist" exhibition may reflect an indebtedness on the part of Daubigny to Claude Monet.

An almost identical scene, *La Fenaison,* panel, .45 x .68 (17¾" x 26¾") was in the Gerbeau Sale, Hôtel Drouot, May 18, 1980, no. 9.

Support: Panel, .444 x .694 (17½" x 27⁵⁄₁₆").

Signed and dated in brown paint at lower right: *Daubigny 1874.*

Condition: Discolored varnishes removed in 1943, mastic varnish applied.

Provenance: Purchased by Henry Walters between 1887 and 1895.

Exhibitions: Barye Monument Association, no. 548; "From Ingres to Gauguin," The Baltimore Museum of Art, 1951, no. 57; "An Exhibition of Treasures of the Walters Art Gallery," Wildenstein and Co., New York, 1967, no. 33.

References: Walters cat., 1888, pp. 93–94, no. 153, and subsequent Walters catalogues; Madeleine Fidell-Beaufort and Janine Bailly-Herzberg, *Daubigny.* La vie et l'oeuvre, 1. Paris, Geoffroy-Dechaume, 1975. p. 189, no. 140, illus.; Robert Hellebranth, *Charles François Daubigny, 1817–1878.* Morges, Editions Matute, 1976. p. 324, no. 987, illus.

Henri-Joseph Harpignies

French: Valenciennes, 1819 - Saint-Privé, 1916

During a career spanning six decades, Harpignies pursued an independent course. Though he was only five years junior to Millet and seven to Rousseau, his artistic output was that of a later generation. He expressed little interest in the grandeur of Nature, dwelling instead upon its enduring qualities. Likewise, he was not particularly concerned with those accidental aspects of Nature upon which the later Impressionists concentrated. His vision, though subdued and austere, was one of remarkable vigor and freshness.

Harpignies was educated in the Valenciennes communal college, distinguishing himself only in the classes of drawing and geography. He seemed destined to enter the family's sugar-beet mill, but after working as a sales agent for six years he decided to become an artist.

In 1846 he became a pupil and friend of Jean-Alexis Achard, a rigorous teacher who encouraged his pupil to sketch out-of-doors and to record his observations with meticulous fidelity. Harpignies' early travels included a visit to Belgium at the time of the 1848 Revolution, a trip to Germany in 1850, and a prolonged stay in Italy in 1851–52. There he sketched in the vicinities of Rome and Naples. Back in Paris in 1852 he established a studio and began to frequent the cafés in the company of Gérôme and his followers. About this time he became acquainted with Corot, who was to leave an indelible impression upon the younger painter's work.

Harpignies made his debut at the Paris Salon in 1853 with a *View on the Isle of Capri, Gulf of Naples* and with a Valenciennes view. He was a regular participant at the salons, exhibiting landscapes painted in the areas bounded by the tributaries of the Seine and the Loire, interspersed with an occasional Italian scene. In the 1863 Salon one of his entries received an honorable mention and the other three were rejected and subsequently shown in the Salon des Refusés. A second Italian sojourn followed, during which he again worked in Rome and further south. After his return to France in 1865, his continuing success was assured. He received medals in 1866, 1868 and 1869; was rated by the critics along with such artists as Chintreuil, Flers, and Daubigny; and even elicited a favorable response from Count Nieuwerkerke with a series of watercolors submitted for the Superintendent's approval. By the end of the decade Harpignies was acknowledged to be a principal proponent of watercolor painting in France and was attracting a number of pupils.

While visiting the family of a follower at the château of Montais in the Département of Allier in 1869, he came across the village of Hérisson. He found it so attractive that he returned every summer for a decade and it was there, in the service of the National Guard, that he spent the winter of 1870. Some paintings and watercolors of the region, shown in the Salon of 1875, brought him the rank of Chevalier of the Legion of Honor. That year he submitted for sale at the Hôtel Drouot thirty-four paintings, studies, and decorative panels and fifty watercolors that fetched over 23,000 francs, a remarkable sum for the time. At the 1878 Exposition Universelle, he received a second-class medal.

In the autumn of 1879 Harpignies bought a house at Saint-Privé near Bléneau, Yonne, where he spent most of his remaining summers. The winter months he now passed in the south of France, often at Nice. Despite his advancing age, Harpignies continued to pursue an active career, joining the Société des artistes français in 1887; being elected a member of the jury in 1889; winning the Grand Prix in 1900, and in 1901 being invited by Whistler to exhibit at the Royal Institute in London with such diverse artists as Manet, Lautrec, Segantini, and Klimt in the International Society of Painters, Sculptors and Graveurs.

He was ninety-seven when he died at Saint-Privé in 1916.

69. Landscape

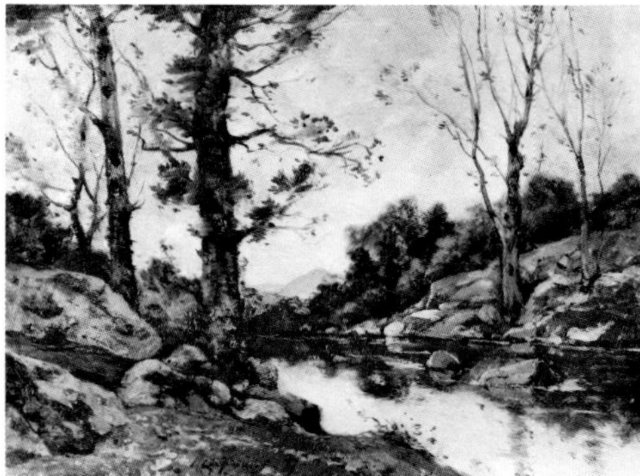

37.181

A river cuts through a lightly wooded landscape. The terrain is rocky with mountains appearing against the horizon in the background. An inscription on the reverse of the stretcher identifies the location as being near the village of Hérisson on the Aumance River, in the Département of Allier on the Massif Central.

Alternative title: *Vue prise, Hérisson Allier.*

Support: Canvas, .24 x .324 (9½" x 12¾").

Signed and dated in dark brown paint in center of bottom edge: *h. harpignies. 75.*

Marks: Stretcher inscribed in ink: *Vue Prise: Herisson / Allier.* Also marked in ink: *6098, EG. 247 / N.Y. 588;* Paper sticker on stretcher: *4046* in rectangle; *16.872* in rectangle; *88.819 B / 24 / Glaenzer* in circle.

Condition: Discolored natural varnish was removed and the surface recoated with a synthetic resin varnish in 1966. The picture was lined for the first time. The picture was relined in 1978. Minor losses were inpainted.

Provenance: Purchased by Henry Walters at Eugene Glaenzer and Co., 303 Fifth Avenue, New York, November 29, 1904. The firm's invoice is numbered 425 and dated December 1, 1904.

Exhibitions: "Henri-Joseph Harpignies, 1819–1916," The Dixon Gallery and Gardens, Memphis, 1978–79, no. 4.

References: Walters cat., 1909, p. 60, no. 181; William R. Johnston, "Harpignies' landscape," *BWAG* 19, no. 7 (April 1967): 1–2, illus.

Camille Hippolythe Delpy

French: Joigny, 1842 - Paris, 1910

In the salon *livrets,* Delpy was listed as a pupil of Corot and Daubigny. His earliest entry, a still life, was shown in 1869. The following year, however, he exhibited a view of Ville d'Avray, Corot's pied-à-terre, and at his next Salon in 1873, his subject was a scene near Auvers, the town where Daubigny moored his floating studio, *Le Botin*. Thereafter Delpy exhibited regularly, participating in later years in the salons of the Société des artistes français. He met with moderate success, receiving an honorable mention in 1881, a third–class medal in 1884, an honorable mention again in 1889, and a second–class medal in 1900. His paintings were featured in retrospective exhibitions in Paris in 1890 and again in 1908.

Delpy is remembered for landscapes, especially river-scapes, that recall the works of his teacher Daubigny. Occasionally he painted views in the Fontainebleau Forest. His preference was for tranquil, inhabited stretches of the French countryside.

70. The House of M. Lucas

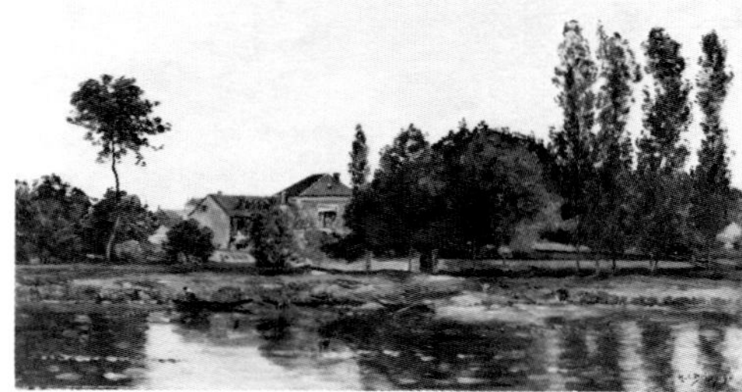

37.1157 1890

From across the water one sees the summer residence of George A. Lucas at Boissise-la-Bertrand. Near the opposite bank are several fishermen in boats. Lucas purchased this house on the Seine near Melun on May 10, 1868.

Another painting by Delpy of Lucas' house, in which the owner appears on the river bank, is preserved in the George A. Lucas Collection, The Maryland Institute College of Art, oil on canvas, .547 x .425.

Lucas never alluded in his diary to Delpy's views of his house. On September 1, 1890, the year the Walters picture was dated, he did, however, record a visit to Boissise of Delpy and his daughter with M. and Mme. M. J. Montaignac. Delpy may have presented the pictures as gifts on this occasion.

Support: Panel (possibly poplar) .285 x .531 (11¼" x 20⅞").

Signed at lower right: *H. C. Delpy . 90.*

Marks: Inscribed in pencil on reverse: *Boissise la Bertrand / La Maison de M. Lucas / H. C. D.;* Paper sticker: *1239 bis*; Inscribed in black ink: *A / 598;* Stamped in panel: *H. C. D.*

Condition: Two horizontal disjoins were reattached in 1968. The picture was cleaned on this occasion.

Provenance: In the Gallery's files is a certificate dated July 27, 1922, guaranteeing the authenticity of the Delpy landscape under paragraph 652, Tariff Act, October 3, 1913.

Exhibitions: "A Baltimorean in Paris, George A. Lucas, Art Agent, 1860–1909," Walters Art Gallery, 1979.

Emile-Lecumen Van Marcke

French: Sèvres, 1827 - Hyères, 1890

Emile Van Marcke, a noted painter of cattle, was born in Sèvres, where his father Jean-Baptiste (1798–1849), a Fleming, had studied with C. J. Watelet, and was attached to the porcelain manufactory. In 1831 the Van Marcke family returned to Belgium, to Liège. There Emile was eventually enrolled in drawing classes and in the local academy. After marriage to the daughter of a director at Sèvres, he returned to France and from 1853 to 1862 served as a decorator at the Sèvres manufactory. While there he was encouraged by Constant Troyon, the landscape painter also employed at Sèvres, to sketch from Nature and to work in oil paints, and in 1857 he entered two works at the Paris Salon. After studying at the agricultural schools of Villeneuve-L'Etang and Grignon, Van Marcke journeyed to the various regions of France, painting cattle in the Landes, the Pyrenees, Normandy, Brittany and Sologne. Preferring as subjects the cattle of Normandy, he settled for seven years in the valley of Tréport and eventually bought a farm house at Bouttencourt in the valley of Bresle where he remained, apart from the winter months passed in Paris.

Van Marcke won medals at the 1867, 1869, and 1870 Salons and was appointed a Chevalier of the Legion of Honor in 1872. At the 1878 Exposition Universelle he exhibited a number of earlier works, winning a first–class medal. Following the death of his mentor Troyon in 1865, Van Marcke came to be esteemed by many collectors, particularly Americans, as the foremost painter of cattle.

71. The Approach of a Storm

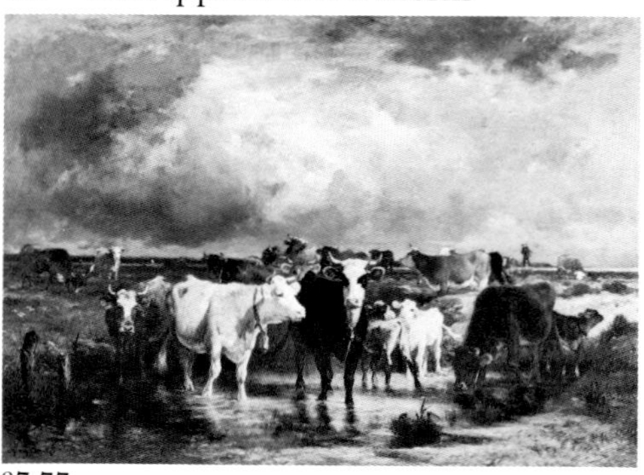

37.77

Cattle are grazing in marshy terrain. The foreground is dominated by several cows and calves standing in a pool of water. In the far distance a cowherd mounted on stilts watches over the herd while his dog pursues a stray animal. The sky is heavily overcast.

The identification of this picture is problematical. Early Walters catalogues noted that the painting was exhibited in the 1873 Paris Salon even though the titles of the works submitted by Van Marcke that year, *The Rope Yard* and *The Mill*, do not readily apply. In 1872 a *Landes du bassin d'Arcachon (Gironde)*, no. 1477, was shown in the Salon and listed as belonging to Mr. Walters. The cowherd's use of stilts suggests that the scene was set in that region of France. The Walters painting, however, corresponds to the Félix Bracquemond etching after Van Marcke's *Troupeau de vaches passant un gué*, rather than to the Ch. Country print after Van Marcke's *Landes du bassin d' Arcachon*, 1872, both published in Armand Silvestre, *Galerie Durand-Ruel*, Brussels, 1873, vol. 2, nos. 197 and 111 respectively.

Alternative title: *Troupeau de vaches passant un gué.*

Support: Canvas, 1.46 x 2.01 (52½" x 79⅛")

Signed in black at lower left: *Em. Van Marcke.*

Marks: Inscribed in pencil on frame: *2431, Van Marcke.*

Provenance: G. A. Lucas paid 12,448 francs for the painting and frame on June 8, 1872. The picture, however, was listed in the *livret* of the 1872 Salon that opened on May 1 as already belonging to Mr. Walters.

Exhibitions: Paris, Salon, 1872, no. 1477(?)

References: Walters cat., 1878, p. 23, and subsequent Walters catalogues; Emile Bellier de la Chavignerie and Louis Auvray, *Dictionnaire générale des artistes de l'école française*. 2 vols. Paris, Renouard, 1882–85. 2:629; Strahan, 1:94; Champlin and Perkins, 3: 194; Lamb, p. 247; Reizenstein, p. 556; Lucas, 2: 363.

72. Early Morning

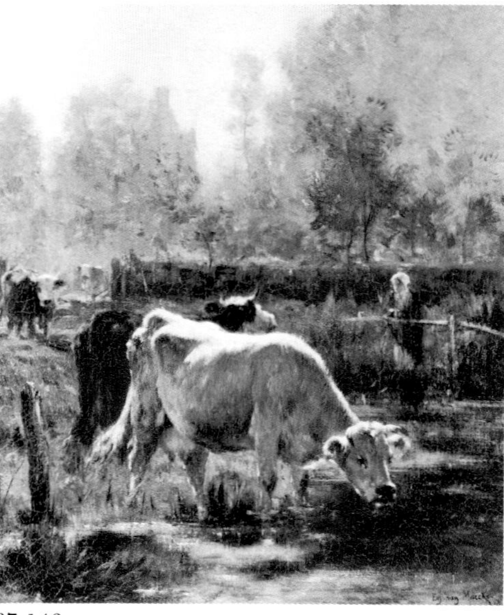

37.143

A white cow drinking in the foreground is about to be joined by three other cows progressing at intervals toward the pool. They are tended by a girl leaning against a gatepost. The scene is drenched by early morning sunlight.

Support: Canvas, .63 x .505 (24 13/16" x 19 7/8")

Signed in black at lower right: *Em. van Marcke.*

Marks: Stenciled on stretcher cross-bar: *Goupil & Cie/9 rue Chaptal/Paris;* Frame bears paper sticker: *Thomas A. Wilmurt/Mirror Picture Frames/54 East 13th Street/New York;* Inscribed on frame in crayon: *GC 16070.*

Provenance: Acquired by W. T. Walters between 1878 and 1884.

References: Walters cat., 1884, p. 31, no. 40, and subsequent Walters catalogues; Champlin and Perkins, 3: 194.

73. The Pool

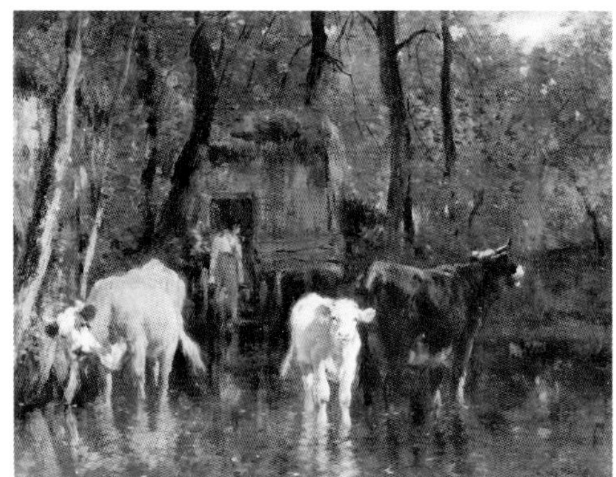

37.65

Two cows and a white calf stand in a pool of water surrounded by woods. In the background is a girl holding a bucket. Sunlight breaking through the verdure illuminates the scene.

Support: Canvas, .506 x .615 (20" x 24 1/4")

Signed in black at lower right: *Em. van Marcke.*

Marks: On reverse of frame are the remnants of a paper sticker of the New York framing establishment, Thomas A. Wilmurt.

Provenance: Acquired by W. T. Walters between 1878 and 1887.

References: Walters cat., 1884, p. 37, no. 50; Champlin and Perkins, 3: 194.

Jules-Jacques Veyrassat
French: Paris, 1828 - Paris, 1893

Thiébault-Sisson observed in 1893 that Veyrassat, though not a major master, was in the first rank of the "petits maîtres" (Preface to *Catalogue des tableaux, études esquisses . . .par M. Veyrassat,* Paris, December 12–13, 1893, p. 4). This assessment proved enduring, for as late as 1934, it was noted in Edouard-Joseph, *Dictionnaire biographique des artistes contemporains,* Paris, 1934, 3:386, that the artist's pleasant landscapes, so much in demand at the end of the last century, were again in vogue.

Veyrassat's father, a jeweler of Swiss origin, wished his son to pursue the family business and therefore enrolled him in the state school for industrial drawing on the rue de l'Ecole de Médecine, Paris. The 1848 upheaval in France ruined the jewelry business, leaving young Veyrassat free to pursue his inclinations as an artist. To support himself he at first painted copies of works in the Louvre and made etchings, some of which appeared in *L'Artiste.* Before becoming known as a painter, he gained distinction as a graphic artist, winning medals in the 1866 and 1869 Salons. He produced etchings after the paintings of Frère, Fortin, Decamps, Daubigny, and Rembrandt, as well as a series of prints based on religious subjects by Bida. In painting, Veyrassat was reported to have studied under H. Lehmann and F. Besson before moving to Ecouen where he consulted Edouard Frère. His long career as a landscape and genre painter appears to have been relatively uneventful and was not recorded in any detail. The titles of his salon entries provide *post facto* clues as to the chronology of his production and his range of travels. In the salon *livret* of 1851 there are references to Normandy, of 1859 to Morlaix in Brittany, of 1861 to Valvins near Fontainebleau, of 1863, 1864, and 1865 to the Lower Pyrenees, and of 1869, to Samois, a picturesque village on the Seine four miles from Fontainebleau, where he established residence. Later, in 1883 and 1885, there are references to Algerian subjects based on a visit to North Africa in the early years of the decade, and in 1888 and 1889 there is again mention of Normandy. Veyrassat received a second–class medal in painting in 1872 and was appointed Chevalier of the Legion of Honor in 1878. Though he exhibited in Chicago in the World's Columbian Exposition in 1893, he was never widely known in this country where his pictures are relatively rare.

74. Harvest Scene

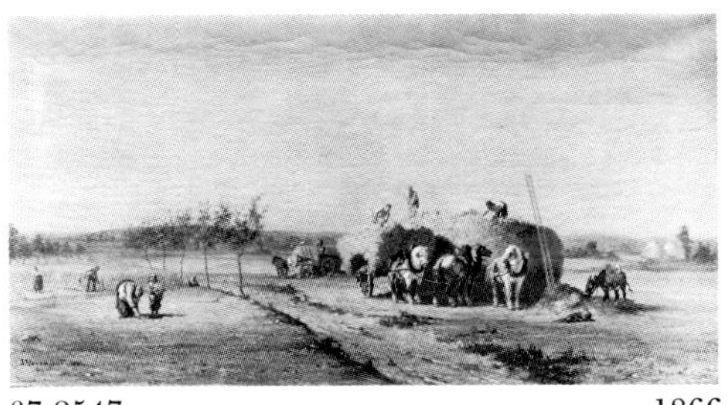

37.2547 1866

This work is characteristic of Veyrassat in both the subject and its treatment. The catalogue of the artist's estate sale, Hôtel Drouot, Paris, December 12 and 13, 1893, listed five oils and three watercolors entitled *La Moisson,* all varying in dimensions. In the Walters picture, hay is being unloaded from two carts to form haystacks. At the left the grain is being scythed and gathered, and at the right in the background several stacks have been completed. The artist has displayed his adroitness as an animal painter in the rendering of the draft horses and the donkey grazing beside the nearest stack. Also characteristic of Veyrassat is the sense of expanse, created in part by the low horizon, the unusually wide format of the picture, and the foreshortened row of trees receding into the background.

A replica of this painting, measuring .457 x .838 and dated 1867, was offered on the art market by M. Newman, Ltd., London, (*Connoisseur* 160 (1965): XLV).

Support: Canvas, .77 x 1.5 (30 1/8" x 56 1/16")

Signed and dated in dark brown at lower left: *J Veyrassat 1866.* Signed on reverse in black painted letters. *J. VEYRASSAT.*

Condition: Discolored varnishes removed in 1981, revealing an early small tear in the lower right quadrant. A coarse fabric backing was removed, uncovering the artist's signature. The picture was lined and treated with synthetic varnish.

Provenance: Sale, Paris, Hôtel Drouot, March 13, 1914; Collection Gary-Roche (1934); gift of Mrs. William S. Hilles, 1977.

References: René Edouard-Joseph, *Dictionnaire biographique des artistes contemporains, 1910–1930.* 3 vols. Paris, Art & édition, 1930–34. 3:386 (illus).

Eugène Fromentin
French: La Rochelle, 1820 - Saint Maurice (La Rochelle), 1876

Fromentin completed studies in law prior to pursuing a dual career of writing and painting. In 1843 he briefly entered the studio of J. C. J. Rémond, an academic landscape painter, and then turned to N. L. Cabat, whom he subsequently acknowledged as his master. Fromentin's earliest trip to Algeria in 1846 was to attend a wedding. He returned for a longer stay in 1847–48 traveling to Biskra and Constantine and spending a month in the oasis of Zaatcha. His last visit was on his honeymoon in 1852–53 when he stopped at Mustapha, Algiers, and Blidah, and passed two months in the oasis of El Aghouat. These experiences provided him with subjects for the remainder of his career.

Fromentin first appeared at the Paris Salon in 1847, showing a farm scene near La Rochelle, said to reflect the influence of his teacher Cabat, as well as two Algerian views that were inspired in part by the works of the Orientalist Prosper Marilhat. Other artists said to have influenced his development were Delacroix and Corot. Fromentin's paintings of Arab horsemen in repose or galloping across the plains, and his broad vistas of the Sahara and the Sahel, executed with great sensitivity to color and atmosphere, were readily appreciated. He received a second-class medal in 1849, a *rappel* in 1857, and first-class medals at the 1859 Salon and at the 1867 Exposition Universelle and he rose through the ranks of the Legion of Honor from Chevalier in 1859 to Officier in 1869. Later travels were to Egypt to attend the opening of the Suez Canal in 1869, to Venice in 1870, a trip that resulted in several Venetian views exhibited in the 1872 Salon, and to Belgium and to the Netherlands in 1875 to study Old Master painting.

Fromentin as a painter eludes ready categorization. E. C. Bénézit, (*Dictionnaire critique et documentaire des peintres, sculpteurs . . .* Paris, 1951, 4:100) in contrasting him with his colleagues concluded that Fromentin was an *artiste hors série* (an artist without context).

As a writer Fromentin is chiefly remembered for *Un été dans le Sahara* (1857), *Une année dans le Sahel* (1858), and *Dominique* (1863), that led to his being ranked as a creator of the French psychological novel, and *Maîtres d'autrefois, Belgique, Hollande* (1876), recording his studies of 1875.

75. An Encampment in the Atlas Mountains

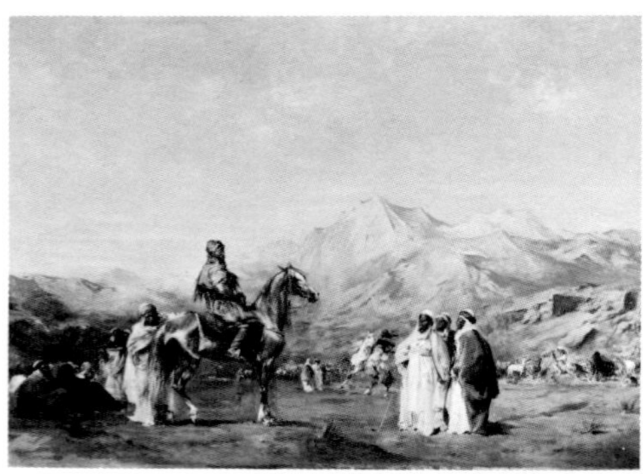

37.195 c.1865

Prosper Dorbec in "L'Hellénisme d'Eugène Fromentin," *Gazette des Beaux-Arts,* 5th pér. 9 (1924): 30–31, singled out Fromentin as a classicist among Orientalists. For the painter-writer, according to Dorbec, the desert and the ramparts of Aïn Mahdy became the plains of Ilium. In this spacious view, characteristic of the artist's production in the mid-sixties, the bold silhouettes of the horsemen, their generalized treatment and the essentially static composition reaffirm the classical character of Fromentin's painting. Shown are a group of Arabs examining a horse being displayed for sale. A rather similar composition, *Horse Market in Algeria,* dated 1867, 1.035 x 1.485, appeared on the New York art market in 1913. Related studies include a view similar to the group of would-be purchasers in the Walters scene, *Five Standing Arabs,* dated 1874, panel, .318 x .405, The William Hayes Ackland Memorial Art Center, 76.36.1; a smaller subject sold in the Verdé-Delisle Collection, Paris, Hôtel Drouot, May 29, 1879, no. 35; and a three-figured composition sold at the Hôtel Drouot, Paris, March 12, 1943, no. 26.

Support: Canvas, 1.05 x 1.433 (41⅜" x 56½")

Signed at lower left: *Eug. Fromentin*

Provenance: Unknown, Purchased by W. T. Walters between 1878 and 1884.

Condition: Discolored varnishes were removed in 1968 revealing extensive areas of overpainting particularly in the sky. The overpainting was removed and the picture was lined and coated with synthetic varnish. Pentimenti such as those visible beneath the forelegs of the horse abound in Fromentin's thinly painted canvases.

Reproductions: Engraved and published by Goupil et Cie.

References: Walters cat., 1884, p. 48, no. 81, and subsequent Walters catalogues; J. Eugene Reed, ed. *The gallery of contemporary art, an illustrated review of the recent art productions of all nations, by A. Silvestre and other writers,* 2 vols. Philadelphia, Gebbie, 1884–85. 2: plate 20. Champlin and Perkins, 2: 96.

76. The Halt

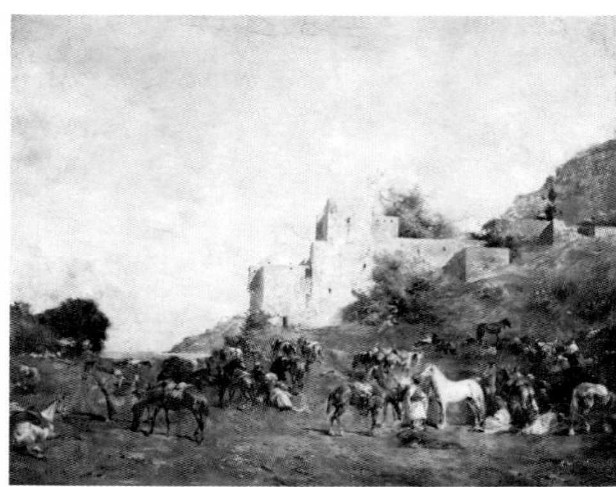

37.126 1872

At the base of a slope, presumably a foothill of the Tell Mountains, a caravan of mules has come to rest. At the right are the muleteers and their horses. A fortified building stands out against the sky and stretching beyond is the sea.

Alternative titles: *Un campement; Halte de muletiers.*

Support: Panel, mahogany, beveled edges, .498 x .627 (19⅝" x 24¾")

Signed and dated: *1872* (lower left) *-Eug. Fromentin-/Algérie,* (lower right).

Marks: Label on reverse of panel: *William Schaus/Tableaux modernes/749 Broadway/New York.*

Provenance: Lepel-Cointet Sale, Hôtel Drouot, Paris, June 9–10, 1881, no. 12, 30,600 francs; William Schaus, New York; acquired by W. T. Walters before 1884.

Reproductions: Engraved by Courtry.

References: Louis Gonse, *Eugène Fromentin, peintre et écrivain.* Paris, A. Quantin, 1881. p. 99; Walters cat., 1884, no. 57, and subsequent Walters catalogues; Champlin and Perkins, 2: 96.

77. At the Well

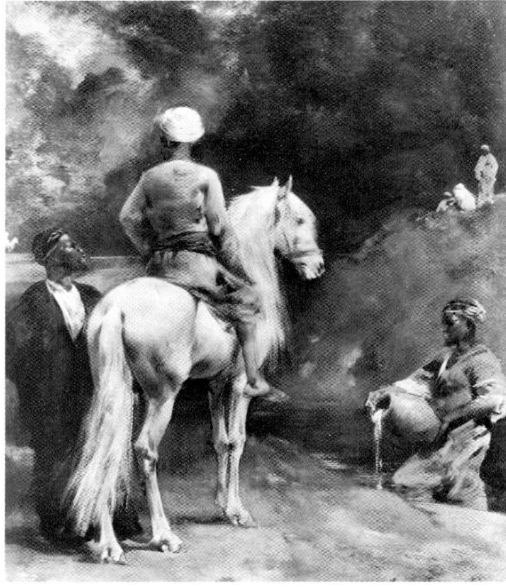

37.100 1875

The Arab and his horse is a recurrent theme in Fromentin's painting and writing. This scene is painted in the small scale and with the delicate harmonies of tone characteristic of the artist's later work.

Rather similar in subject is *A la fontaine,* panel, .355 x .267 M. C. D. Borden Sale, New York, 1913, no. 45.

Support: Panel, .26 x .215 (10¼" x 8½")

Signed and dated, lower right: *-75- Eug. Fromentin.*

Provenance: Unknown. Acquired by W. T. Walters prior to 1884.

References: Walters cat., 1878, p. 20 (as *Arabs and horse* ?) and subsequent Walters catalogues; Champlin and Perkins, 2: 96.

Jean Désiré Gustave Courbet

French: Ornans, 1819 - La Tour de Peilz, 1877

Courbet, the famous realist and socialist, was born in Ornans (Doubs) in the Jura, a region to which he remained attached throughout his career. His parents, prosperous landowners, enrolled him in a seminary in Ornans, where he was taught to draw from Nature by a Father Beau, a former pupil of Baron Gros. In 1837 he entered the Collège Royal in Besançon. There the courses in drawing were given by a M. Flajoulot, a follower of David. Late in 1839 or early in 1840 Courbet moved to Paris, ostensibly to study law, though he soon enrolled in the studio of Baron Charles Steuben and in the Académie Suisse, where he met François Bonvin, a fellow realist. He also went to the Louvre to copy works by the Dutch, Flemish, and Venetian Old Masters as well as by the modernists Ziegler, Schnetz, Géricault, and Delacroix. In addition he sought the advice of N. A.

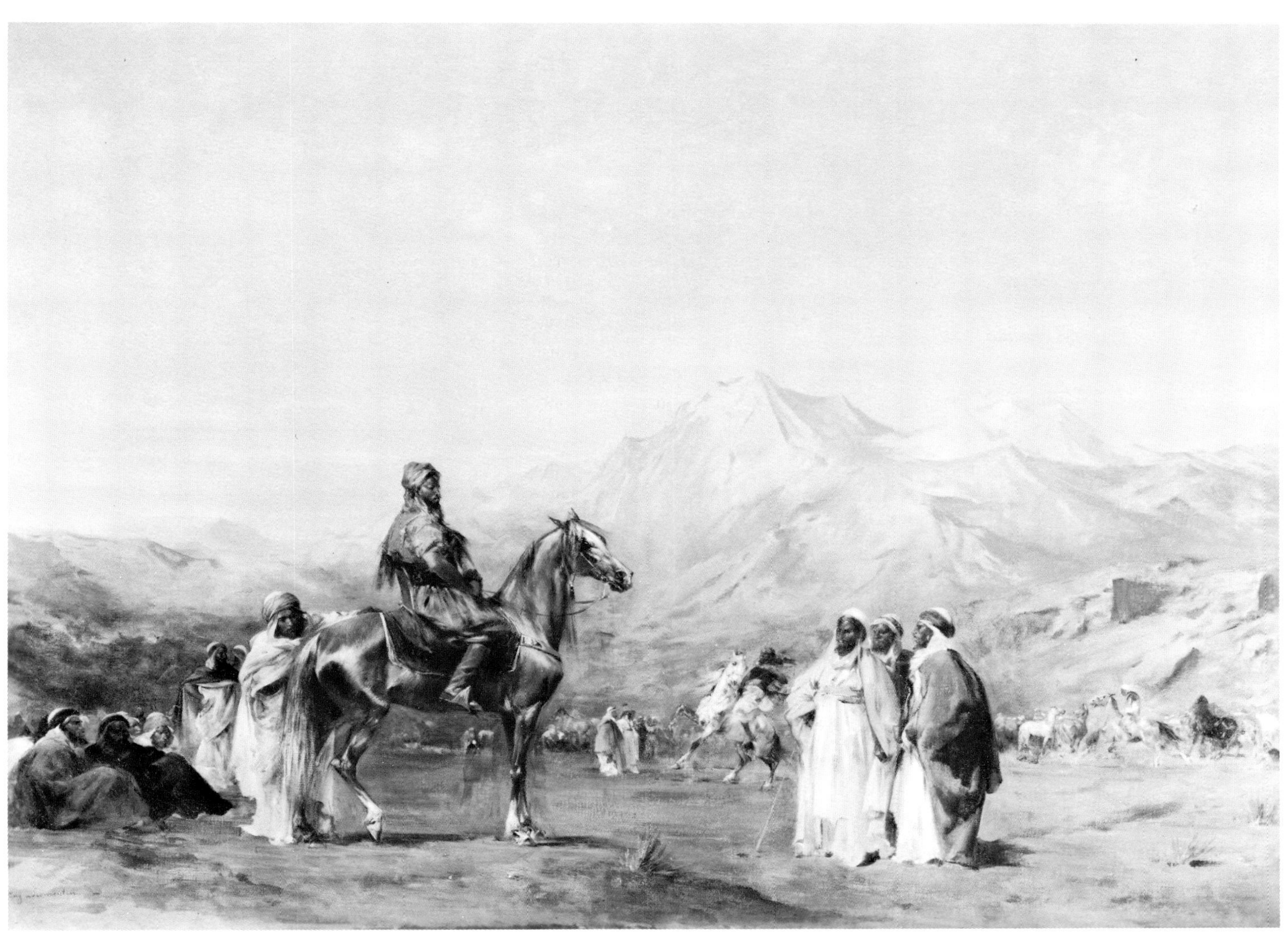

Fromentin *An Encampment in the Atlas Mountains,* no. 75

Hesse, whom he listed in the salon *livrets* with Steuben as his teacher.

Beginning in 1841 Courbet submitted pictures to the salons, but it was not until 1844 that one, a self-portrait, was accepted. The following year, another self-portrait, *Guittarero,* was accepted and four other paintings rejected. In 1848 *Walpurgis Night* elicited a favorable response from the critic Champfleury who was to become his most ardent defender. Later that year a *"temple du réalisme,"* composed of Courbet, Champfleury, A. L. Schanne, H. Murger, A. Promayet and Max Bouchon, formed at the Brasserie Andler on the rue Hautefeuille. Courbet's *Afternoon at Ornans,* shown in 1849, was purchased by the State for the Lille Museum and resulted in the artist's receiving a second–class medal. In 1850, eight paintings, including two of his most controversial works *The Burial at Ornans* and *The Stone–Breakers,* were shown. Subsequently, he exhibited a number of equally controversial paintings, now regarded as masterpieces of realism. Among them was the *Bonjour, Monsieur Courbet* (1854) commemorating the friendship of Courbet and his patron, Bruyas, and *The Atelier* (1854–55). At the 1855 Exposition Universelle a number of his more important pictures were accepted for exhibition, but when *L'Atelier* and *The Burial* were rejected, Courbet decided to open his own exhibition in a pavilion facing the Palais de l'Exposition. Above its entrance a sign read: *DU REALISME.G. Courbet. Exposition de quarante tableaux et de ses oeuvres,* and accompanying the show was a pamphlet that was to serve as a veritable manifesto of the realist movement. Courbet began to spend increasing amounts of time outside Paris, in 1858–59 visiting Frankfurt, where he was enthusiastically received. In 1860 he returned to Paris and opened his studio to a number of pupils, including Fantin-Latour. In 1865 and 1866 he spent summers on the Normandy coast, joined at one point by the American, Whistler. Again, during the Exposition of 1867, he opened a private pavilion at the Rond-Point du Pont de l'Alma in which he assembled 115 paintings, drawings, and several sculptures, a precedent adopted by another realist, Manet, who opened a one-man show nearby.

By 1870 Courbet was at the height of his success. In June he was nominated to the rank of Chevalier of the Legion of Honor, an award he refused. In September of that year, he was elected president of the Commission of Artists established to safeguard works of art. The following year he joined the Commune. Subsequently Courbet was implicated in the destruction of the Vendôme Column and was sentenced to six months in prison. The decision to rebuild the column led to his property being confiscated and a fine of 300,000 francs being levied to meet construction costs. Overwhelmed by these disasters, Courbet fled to Switzerland and settled at La Tour de Peilz near Vevey, where he died four years later.

To meet his financial obligations in his last years Courbet resorted to the unfortunate practice of relying on assistants to supplement his own production. Marcel Ordinaire, Jean-Jean Cornu, and Chérubino Pata are thought to have been responsible for many of the later works mass produced for foreign markets. In addition, at La Tour de Peilz, Courbet trained his neighbor and fellow refugee Auguste Morel to assist in painting. Such practices gave rise to the thriving commerce in outright forgeries both before and after the master's death.

78. Landscape

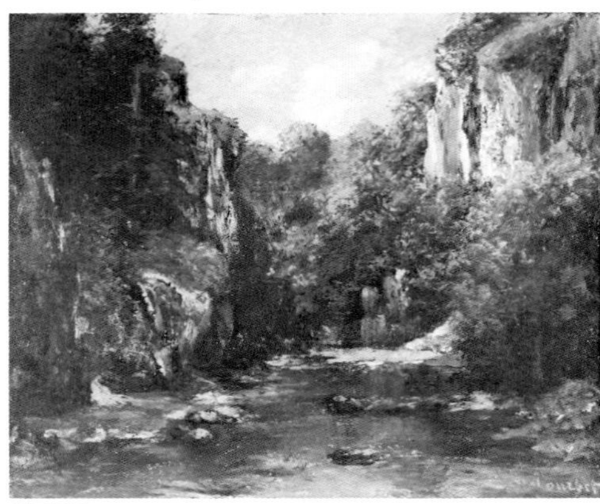

37.203

A shallow stream, La Plaisir Fontaine or Le Puits Noir, meanders between high rocky banks overgrown with foliage. Courbet first painted this site from nature in 1855 *(Le Ruisseau du Puits Noir,* 1.04 x 1.38; National Gallery of Art, Washington, D.C.) and returned to it many times thereafter. One of the best known versions of the subject is *Le Ruisseau couvert* of 1865 (.94 x 1.35) in the Louvre. During his last stay in Ornans in 1872 he painted no less than four landscapes at the site (letter from Courbet to his sisters, dated July 26, 1872, published in Charles Léger, *Courbet selon les caricatures et les images,* Paris, 1920, pp. 123–24) .

The Walters painting represents an attractive, though inconsequential version of the subject. In *La Vie et l'oeuvre de Gustave Courbet,* Lausanne, 1977–78, Robert Fernier intended to catalogue the Walters version as a late work executed in collaboration with a follower, Auguste Morel or Chérubino Pata. Fernier died before his monumental study was completed and the Walters painting, as a result, appears in the index under no. 5C, but not in the text.

Support: Canvas, .465 x .555 (18⅜" x 21⅞")

Signed at lower right: *G Courbet*

Provenance: Purchased from Alfred Prunaire by G. A. Lucas for Henry Walters on June 18, 1903, for 1,000 francs.

References: Walters cat., 1909, p. 68; Lucas, 2: 917.

Follower of Courbet

79. Hind Forced Down in the Snow

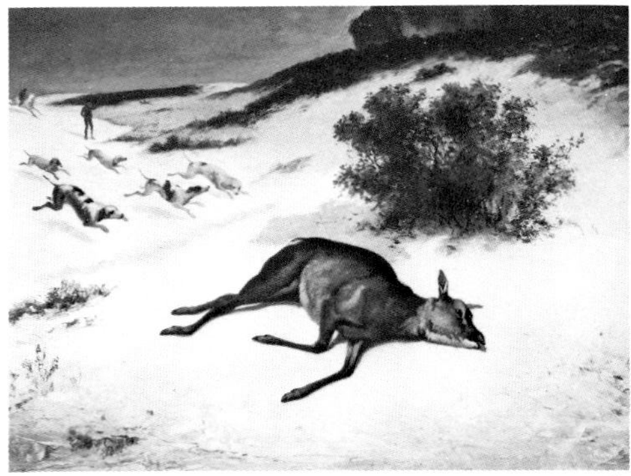

37.2422 after 1857

In the 1857 Salon Courbet showed his celebrated *Hind Forced Down in the Snow,* (.925 x 1.47). Though the artist was an avid hunter, the painting probably doesn't record a specific incident since hunting in the snow had been outlawed thirteen years earlier.

The Baltimore painting freely replicates in reverse the 1857 work, its principal difference being the diminution of distance between the deer in the foreground and the figures in the background. It poses the question of whether the artist would have reversed a major composition: an issue analagous to that raised by the relationship between the two reversed studies for *The Stonebreakers* in the Oskar Reinhardt Collection, Winterthur, and the Salon painting, *The Stonebreakers* (1849), formerly in the Dresden Gemäldegalerie. In a study of 1857, *Chevreuil mort,* Oran Museum, Courbet portrayed a fallen doe facing the same direction as in the Walters picture. The positioning of the animal's limbs and ears differs, however, from that in the 1857 Salon painting and in the Baltimore version.

After an examination of the Walters painting in 1972, Robert Fernier concluded that it had been produced by a follower of Courbet, who adopted the Master's technique of applying the pigments with slashing strokes of the palette knife, and that it was based on Armand Gautier's lithograph of the 1857 picture published in reverse that year in *L'Artiste.*

Support: Canvas, .62 x .825 (27$\frac{7}{16}$" x 32½")

Signed and dated at lower left: *Gustave Courbet/66.*

Condition: Cleaned and lined in 1966.

Provenance: This painting, which does not appear in any Walters inventories, was found in W. T. Walters' town residence in 1965.

Follower of Courbet

80. View of Lake Geneva

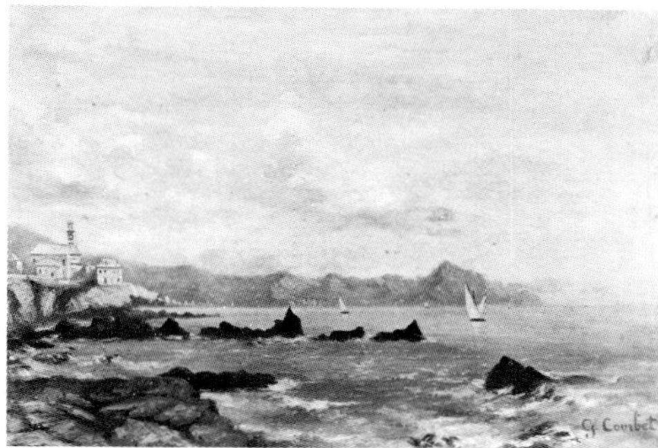

37.876 before 1881

The viewer looks across a stretch of water from a rocky shoreline. At the left, on a promontory, is a cluster of buildings. Though the architecture and the terrain are in keeping with a site on Lake Geneva, the specific scene has not been identified.

The rather crude handling of the pigments has little in common with the work of Courbet. Robert Fernier, president of the Amis de Courbet, concluded in a letter to the Gallery of 1972, that this work might have been painted by the master's follower from Ticino, Chérubino Pata (1827–1899), who is known to have been responsible for a number of forgeries dating from Courbet's last years in Switzerland.

Support: Canvas, .378 x .543 (14⅞" x 21⅜")

Signed at lower right: *G. Courbet.*

Marks: Canvas stenciled: *Brachard et Fils, Geneva.*

Provenance: Acquired by Henry Walters with the Massarenti Collection, 1902.

References: *Catalogue d'une collection de tableaux de diverses écoles, spécialement des écoles italiannes,* Rome, 1881, p. 82, no. 312; *Catalogue du musée de peinture, sculpture et archaeologie au Palais Accoramboni,* 2 vols. Rome, Imprimerie du Vatican, 1897, 1: 145, no. 844.

François–Saint Bonvin

French: Vaugirard, 1817 - Saint-Germain-en-Laye, 1887

François Bonvin, an early realist, was noted for his paintings and etchings of domestic interiors, religious genre scenes, and still lifes that recalled seventeenth– and eighteenth–century precedents. Though he attracted a small circle of admirers among avant-garde critics and prominent collectors, he failed to win wide recognition and endured as a consequence deprivations both early and late in his career. Bonvin's father, a former soldier, held various posts before opening a simple cabaret in Vaugirard, then a rural suburb of Paris. His mother, a seamstress, died when he was aged four. François initially earned a livelihood as a clerk for the mairie of Vaugirard, then as a typesetter for publishers in Versailles and Paris, and finally as a supernumerary for the Bureau of Prisons and Hospices. In his spare time he received instruction in art at the Ecole de Dessin on the rue de l'Ecole de Médecine, from 1828 to 1830, and again about 1842. He also attended evening classes at Gobelins under a Professor Mulard and drew after the model at the Académie Suisse. Of greater consequence was the advice received from the then noted painter and art historian from Aix, François Marius Granet, to whom he showed the studies of seventeenth-century Spanish and Dutch paintings that he made in the Louvre. Through friendship with the museum director P.-A. Jeanron, Bonvin received special access to the galleries, where apparently he was also drawn to the works of the Le Nain brothers and to those of Chardin. Bonvin's first salon picture, a portrait, appeared in 1847, but his entries the following year included two paintings of women eating by lamplight, subjects more characteristic of his work.

By the end of the decade his career appeared promising. He received a third-class medal in 1849, a second-class in 1851; his *Charity,* shown in 1852 was acquired for the Museum of Niort, and *Regimental School* was commissioned that year by the Prince-President. He was at this point figuring prominently in realist circles. Emile Bouvier (*La Bataille réaliste,* Paris, n.d. p. 233) recorded his presence at the Brasserie Andler in the late forties with Champfleury, Castagnary, Courbet, and Chenavard. Etienne Moreau-Nélaton (*Bonvin raconté par lui-même,* Paris, 1927, pp. 31–32) cited, in addition, his membership in a circle known as "Les Mercredis" that included his friends Courbet and Champfleury among others, who assembled regularly in 1849 on the Ile Saint-Germain du Bas-Meudon. He also had become acquainted with Laurent Laperlier, who became his principal patron and who, with the artist's encouragement, assembled a collection of eighteenth-century art rich in the still lifes of Chardin. Significant events in Bonvin's career in the fifties included visits to Brittany in 1853, and to Tréport the following year, and commissions from the State for *A Low Mass,* a scene set in Saint Germain-des-Prés exhibited in the 1855 Exposition, and *The Letter of Recommendation,* shown in 1859 and presented to the Museum of Besançon.

In the sixties Bonvin's fortunes began to wane. A second marriage in 1860 proved unfortunate, and in 1862 precarious finances compelled him to find employment with the Prefecture of Police as a custodian of the markets. In 1866, however, he left the police and that autumn undertook his first trip to the Lowlands, visiting Belgium in 1866 and proceeding to The Netherlands in January 1867. Two years later he again visited The Netherlands, where he was particularly drawn to the works of Rembrandt, Vermeer, De Hooch, Metsu, and Teniers. In 1870 he was made Chevalier of the Legion of Honor after the award had been rejected by his former friend G. Courbet. He continued to study Dutch master paintings in the public collections in London, where he sought refuge during the Franco-Prussian War. This interest was further pursued during a third visit to The Netherlands in 1873. By 1877 his health was beginning to decline, and in 1881 he underwent surgery for gallstones. He survived the operation but continued to deteriorate. In 1886 a retrospective exhibition of his paintings and drawings was held in the Galerie Rothschild and several months before his death a number of his associates, including Detaille, Bonnat, Gérôme, Boulanger, and Duez, organized a benefit sale at the establishment of the commissaire-priseur, Me. Boussaton.

81. Drawing Water

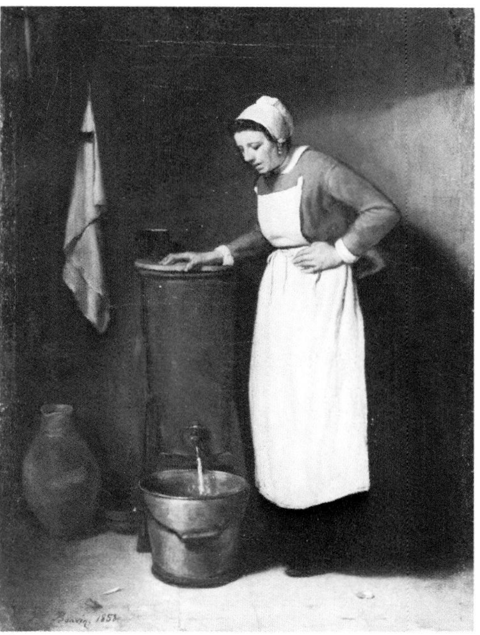

37.199 1858

A servant stands to the right of a copper urn drawing water into a bucket. At the left a towel is suspended on the wall and on the floor are placed a large ceramic jug and a small bowl. Weisberg (1979) suggested that the artist, in this instance, drew inspiration from Chardin's *La Pourvoyeuse* or from *La Fontaine de cuivre.*

This subject is recurrent in Bonvin's work. In later versions such as the *Servant Drawing Water* (Louvre, R.F. 462), painted in 1861 for the actor P. Bressant, and *The House Maid,* J. S. Inglis Sale, American Art Association, March 11–12, 1909, no. 101, dated 1867, the artist included vistas of a kitchen in the right background, recalling the compositions of Dutch seventeenth-century masters, notably those of Pieter de Hooch.

Alternative title: *Femme à la fontaine.*

Support: Fabric, tightly woven, preprimed, .445 x .324 (17½" x 12¾")

Signed at lower left: *F. Bonvin, 1858.*

Marks: Stenciled on reverse: *J. BOVARD* (top center).

Condition: The surface endured some abrasion in the past, revealing a reddish underpaint. X-rays indicate pentimenti in the positions of the servant's elbow and bonnet. The picture was lightly cleaned and varnished in June 1976.

Provenance: Acquired by Henry Walters between 1895 and 1899.

References: Walters cat., 1899, p. 100, no. 165, and subsequent Walters catalogues; Gabriel P. Weisberg, "François Bonvin and an interest in several painters of the seventeenth and eighteenth centuries," *GBA* 6th pér. 76 (1970): 362–63, fig. 5; Gabriel P. Weisberg, *Bonvin.* La vie et l'oeuvre, 2. Paris, Editions Geoffroy-Dechaume, 1979. pp. 56 (illus. 17), 58; p. 173, no. 25 (illus.).

82. Interior of a Tavern

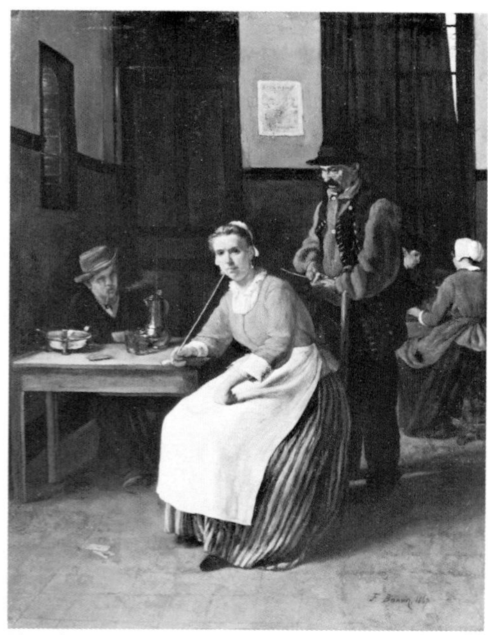

37.837 1867

The principal figure in this tavern interior is a woman seated at a table smoking a long-stemmed clay pipe. She wears a white cap, red jacket, striped homespun skirt and white apron. Behind the woman stands a peasant filling his pipe and seated at the left is another man, also smoking. A conversing couple are at a table in the background. Various accessories include a beer stein, two glasses, and a chafing dish placed on the table-top, and a couple of playing cards lying on the floor in front of the table. Hanging on the wall in the background is a placard bearing the title "GOODWIN," a cryptic allusion to either the artist's name or to the sign inscribed "A bon vin" that was displayed in the Bonvin cabaret at Vaugirard, cited by Etienne Moreau-Nélaton in *Bonvin raconté par lui-même,* Paris, 1927, p. 51.

This painting was executed after Bonvin's journey to The Netherlands in January 1867. However, as has been observed by both Gabriel Weisberg and P. Ten Doesschate Chu, the disposition of the figures in this composition most closely approximates that of Pieter de Hooch's *The Cardplayers* in the Louvre. A connection between the two paintings is substantiated by the presence of playing cards lying on the floor in the foregrounds of both.

Alternative title: *Cabaret Flamand.*

Support: Panel, cradled, .501 x .372 (19¾" x 14⅝")

Signed and dated at lower right: *F Bonvin, 1867.*

Condition: In 1948 the painting was cleaned, revealing some cracks resulting from the use of non-drying pigments. The affected areas were primarily in the floor. In removing the overpaint the presence of the cards on the floor was discovered.

Provenance: A. Bellino Sale, Paris, May 20, 1892; Charles T. Yerkes Sale, American Art Association, New York, April 5, 6, 7 and 8, 1910, no. 11.

Exhibitions: "The Realist Tradition; French Painting and Drawing, 1830–1900," Cleveland, Brooklyn, St. Louis, Glasgow, 1980–82, no. 13.

References: Etienne Moreau-Nélaton, *Bonvin raconté par lui-même.* Paris, Henri Laurens, 1927. p. 69, fig. 46; Gabriel P. Weisberg, "François Bonvin and an interest in several painters of the seventeenth and eighteenth centuries," *GBA* 6th pér. 76 (1970): 363–64, fig. 6; Petra ten-Doesschate Chu, *French realism and the Dutch masters.* Utrecht, Haentjens Dekker & Gumbert, 1974, p. 41, fig. 63; Gabriel P. Weisberg, *Bonvin.* La vie et l'oeuvre, 2. Paris, Editions Geoffroy-Dechaume, 1979. pp. 84, 86–87 (illus. 45, 45bis, 45ter); p. 181, no. 40 bis (illus.).

Léon Bonvin

French: Vaugirard, 1834 - Meudon, 1866

Léon, the younger half brother of François Bonvin, painted flowers, working primarily in watercolors rather than oils. His brief career ended, when, overtaxed emotionally and overburdened financially, he took his life at the age of thirty-two.

As a youngster, Léon received encouragement from François and enrolled briefly in the Ecole de Dessin, rue de l'Ecole de Médecine, under Lecocq de Boisbaudran. After his marriage in 1861 he was compelled to restrict his painting to early morning and evening, and to earn a livelihood for his family by operating the Bonvin Cabaret during the day. He was also gifted as a musician and drew a clientele at the cabaret with his playing of the harmonium organ (F. Henriet, *Les Campagnes d'un paysagiste,* Paris, 1891, pp. 188–90). Léon portrayed flowers either growing in his garden and on the plains of Vaugirard, or cut and arranged in vases. He also painted several landscapes as well as the occasional domestic interior, such as the cabaret scene showing his wife behind the bar illustrated in Philippe Burty, "Léon Bonvin," *Harper's New Monthly Magazine* 72 (December 1885): 45. It was in such works as this interior that he most closely approximated the paintings of his half brother. Léon never participated in the salons. Instead, he sold his watercolors directly to customers at the Cabaret or in shops such as the Dessins de Siècle in the galleries of the Ecole des Beaux-Arts for as little as ten to fifteen francs apiece. As the plains of Vaugirard were developed, other cabarets appeared, and he was eventually reduced to toiling as a carter for the stone wagons.

83. Still-Life, Daisies and Violets

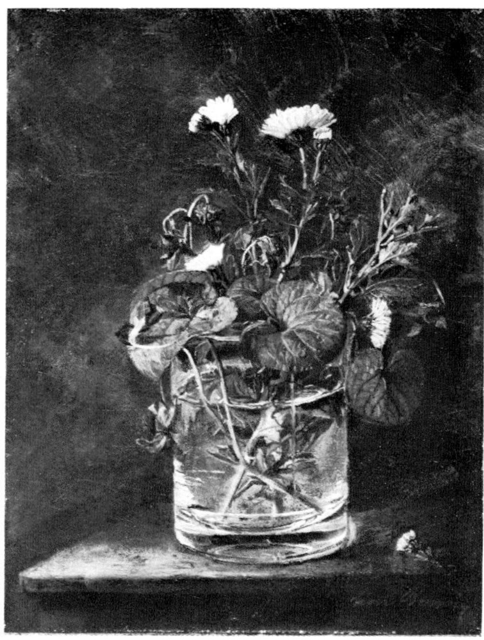

37.1049 before 1866

White daisies and wilting blue violets have been arranged in a glass beaker and placed on a table top. Similar arrangements abound among the artist's watercolors. The directness of approach exhibited in this painting distinguishes the pictures of Léon from those of his half brother, who had more fully immersed himself in the traditions of seventeenth- and eighteenth-century still life painting, and particularly in the art of Chardin.

Support: Canvas, .27 x .2 (10⅝" x 7⅞")

Signed in red at lower right: *Léon Bonvin.*

Marks: Stencil on reverse of canvas reads: *TABLEAUX MODERNES / G. TEMPELAERE / 28. Rue Lafitte. 28 / Paris.*

Provenance: Unknown. There are no references to this canvas in any of the early literature pertaining to the Walters collection. Presumably the picture was acquired by W. T. Walters, who also assembled an album of watercolors of flowers and landscapes by this artist.

Théodule Augustin Ribot

French: Saint-Nicolas d'Attez (Eure), 1823 - Colombes, 1891

Ribot was a naturalist painter who specialized in domestic genre subjects and religious themes. He initially studied geometry to become a civil engineer and subsequently worked as an assistant surveyor in Breteuil and as a bookkeeper for a textile firm in Elbeuf. After his marriage in 1844 Ribot moved to Paris where he eked out a living decorating mirror frames. Eventually he entered the studio of A.-B. Glaize, whom he assisted in the rendering of architectural backgrounds in paintings. In 1848, however, he left Paris for Algeria to pass three years as foreman of a construction crew. Returning to Paris, Ribot undertook such prosaic tasks as the coloring of lithographs, decorating window shades, and producing copies of Watteau's paintings for the American market. Working at night, a factor that may have contributed to his restricted color range and selection of subjects, mostly domestic scenes, he began to paint in earnest. His entries to the Salon were rejected in 1857, but two years later, a supporter, François Bonvin, showed in his studio Ribot's paintings along with those of Vollon, Fantin-Latour, and Whistler. Ribot first appeared at the Salon in 1861 with five kitchen subjects and one poultry scene. Subsequently he showed etchings, which were published by the Société des Aqua-Fortistes.

Beginning with a painting of Saint Sebastian shown in 1865, Ribot turned to religious subjects. Undoubtedly significant sources of inspiration for Ribot were the works by the seventeenth-century Dutch, Spanish, and French masters, particularly the Le Nain brothers, which he could have seen in the Louvre and in the collection of Louis La Caze. His masterly exploitation of a limited palette, dominated by blacks, whites and greys, was admired by a number of collectors and critics, most notably Théophile Gautier.

Ribot was appointed Chevalier of the Legion of Honor in 1878 and elevated to Officier in 1887. His works were shown in the shop of Louis Martinet and in the gallery of Alfred Cadart. He was also featured in an exhibition at the gallery of the journal *L'Art* in 1880, and in that of Bernheim-Jeune in 1887 and 1890.

84. The Young Cook

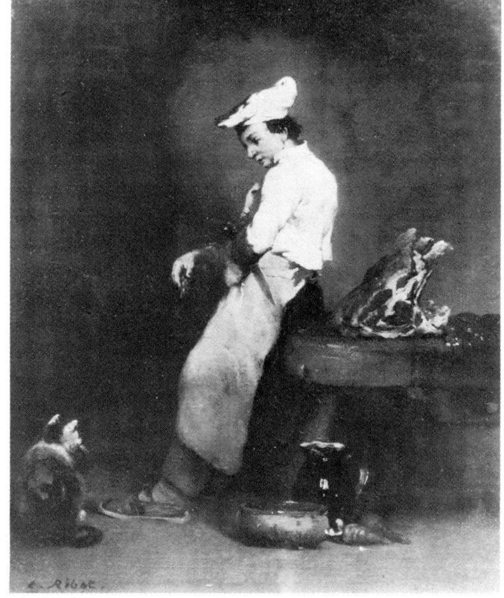

37.3

A young cook, resting against a chopping block on which has been placed a large roast, tempts a cat with a piece of meat. This small painting exemplifies the artist's preference for dramatic lighting and a limited range of colors, inspired in part by Spanish seventeenth-century painting. He painted numerous similar scenes of young male cooks treated with gentle humor.

Support: Canvas, .35 x .275 (13¾" x 10¾")

Signed at lower left: *t. Ribot.*

Condition: Discolored varnishes removed in 1966 revealing some abraded areas in background. Minute losses along edges were inpainted, and the painting revarnished.

Provenance: Purchased by Henry Walters at the P.-A. Chéramy Sale, Paris, May 6–7, 1908, no. 231, for 2,000 francs.

Jules-Adolphe-Aimé-Louis Breton

French: Courrières, 1827 - Paris, 1906

Jules Breton was born in Courrières (Pas-de-Calais) in comfortable circumstances, his father being the steward of the Duc de Duras and one time mayor of the village. Jules' first drawing master was Father Wallet at the College of Douai. Later, he trained in the studio of Félix de Vigne in Ghent and, very briefly, in the Belgian Academy in Antwerp under Baron Wappers. In 1847, failing health compelled him to return briefly to Courrières. Breton then proceeded to Paris to study in the studio of Michel-Martin Drölling. As a result of the 1848 Revolution, his family became financially distressed and Breton was forced to earn a living. Early salon entries, *Misery and Despair* (1849), and *Hunger* (1851) reflected his awareness of the plight of the laboring classes. In his later rustic scenes he turned from such expressions of social realism to a more idealized naturalism that was readily appreciated by his urban clientele though it incurred the criticism of a number of more liberal critics and fellow artists. Millet, for example, acidly observed that Breton's models were invariably the girls who left the farm.

Breton returned to his native Courrières where he eventually married Elodie de Vigne, the daughter of his teacher. Later travels included a trip to the south of France in 1862 and a series of visits to Brittany beginning in 1865. Breton was never lacking in official recognition: he received a third–class medal in 1855, a second–class two years later, and first–class in 1859, 1861 and at the Exposition Universelle in 1867. He was awarded a Medal of Honor in 1872 and was appointed Chevalier of the Legion of Honor in 1861, Officier in 1867 and Commandeur in 1885. In addition, Breton was elected to the Institut de France in 1886.

Breton was also a writer, publishing *La Vie d'un artiste* in 1890, *Un Peintre paysan* in 1896, and *Nos Peintres du siècle* in 1899, as well as some poetry.

85. The Close of Day

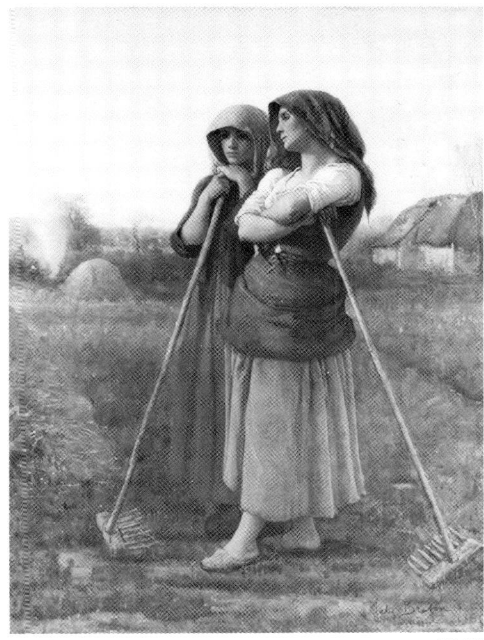

37.57 1865

Two statuesque peasant women are resting on their rake handles. It is twilight and a bonfire has been lit in the left background. This composition approximates the central grouping in one of Breton's chefs-d'oeuvres, *La Fin de la journée,* exhibited in 1865 and again at the Exposition Universelle of 1900. In the larger work, which confirmed the artist's reputation as "le maître de la peinture rustique," there is a mother nursing an infant, a sleeping woman, and a squatting child at the left, and a couple of figures pre-

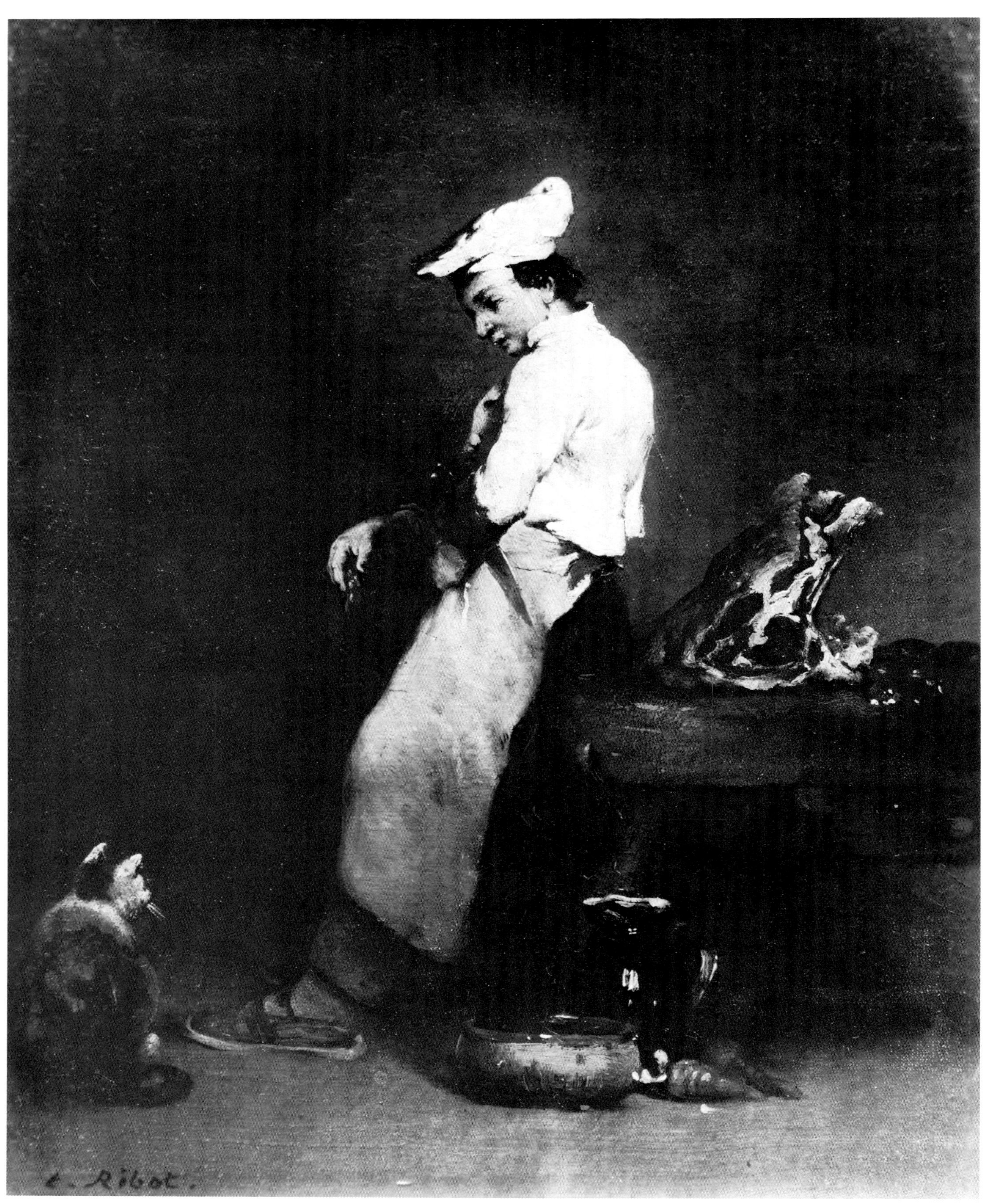

Ribot *The Young Cook,* no. 84

paring to rest at the right. The bonfire in the Salon version was removed to the extreme right background.

Support: Canvas, .655 x .485 (25¾" x 19")

Signed and dated at lower right: *Jules Breton/ Courrières 1865.*

Marks: Stretcher inscribed: *8 rue Ventadour, chez W. R. Redon, Emballeur.*

Condition: Discolored varnishes removed and surface revarnished in 1938. The canvas was lined in 1957.

Provenance: Purchased from the artist (according to early Walters catalogues).

References: Walters cat., 1878, pp. 10–11, and subsequent Walters catalogues; Strahan, 1: 94; Clement and Hutton, 1:91; Champlin and Perkins, 1: 203.

86. Returning from the Fields

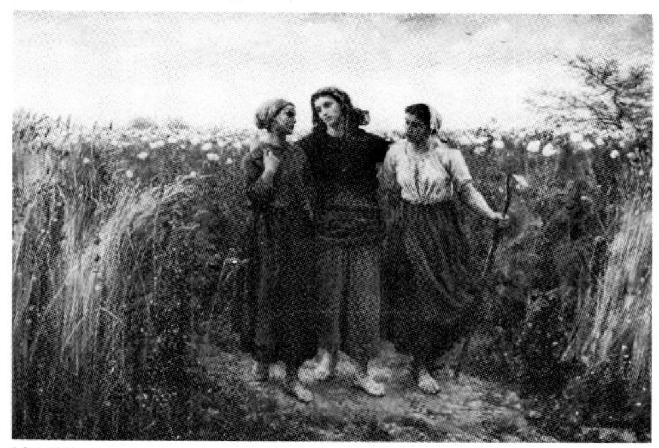

37.58 1871

Three barefoot young women are returning home through the fields at the close of day. Lining their path are burgeoning stalks of wheat, and in the background is a field of poppies. This attractive triad of young women is recurrent in the artist's work. Perhaps the most familiar example is the three gleaners in *The Recall of the Gleaners,* purchased by Napoleon III at the 1859 Salon and now in the Arras Museum. In Breton's estate sale, *Catalogue des tableaux . . . par Jules Breton,* Galerie Georges Petit, Paris, June 2–3, 1911, there was a composition very similar to the Walters picture, no. 193, *Dans les oeillettes, le soir* (.22 x .38), in which the models were identified as sisters.

Support: Finely woven canvas, 6.95 x 1.04 (27⅜" x 41")

Signed and dated: *Jules Breton 1871.*

Condition: In 1977 the painting was lined and the discolored varnishes removed and replaced with synthetic varnish. A pentimento became visible where the artist had changed the staff to a hoe.

Provenance: Mrs. Mary J. Morgan Sale, American Art Galleries, New York, 1886, no. 158.

References: Champlin and Perkins, 1: 203; Walters cat., 1887, p. 86, no. 136; George A. Smith, *The laurelled chefs-d'oeuvre d'art from the Paris Exhibition and Salon, also from the Royal Academy of London and other public galleries of Europe and America.* Philadelphia, Gebbie, 1889. plate 6 (gravure by Gebbie and Husson Co., Ltd.); Mathews, p. 7.

Marie-Rosa Bonheur

French: Bordeaux, 1822 - Le By (Seine-et-Marne), 1899

Though she was one of the most celebrated animal painters in France during the Second Empire, Rosa Bonheur's renown was more widespread in Britain and America than in her own country. Her fame rested primarily on several large works executed early in her career.

Her father, Raymond Bonheur, a social radical and an adherent of Saint Simonianism, painted portraits and landscapes and taught drawing in Bordeaux. His other children included Auguste and Juliette, both painters, Isidore the sculptor, and Germain, a son by a second marriage who also turned to painting. In 1828 Raymond Bonheur moved to Paris to further his career and was followed there by his family the next year.

Rosa proved precocious and began to study with her father at an early age. She sketched in the Paris parks, copied Old Masters in the Louvre, including Pourbus' *Henry IV* and Poussin's *The Shepherds of Arcady,* and studied animal anatomy in the Roule slaughterhouse, where she first adopted male attire for its greater convenience. After exhibiting a painting of two rabbits and one of goats and sheep at the 1841 Salon, she continued to participate in the salons throughout the decade, winning a third–class medal in 1845 and a first–class in 1848. Her *Ploughing in the Nivernais,* commissioned by the State in 1848, entered the Luxembourg Museum in 1849, the year she succeeded her father as director of the Paris Free School of Design for Young Girls. Her early travels included visits to the Auvergne in 1846, and to southern France, the Pyrenees and Germany in 1850. About 1852, work commenced on *The Horse Fair* (Metropolitan Museum of Art, New York, inv. 87.25) which was shown at the 1853 Salon at which the artist was exempted from further competition by special decree. This enormous painting of rearing and thrashing horses at the Paris Horse Market, which remained unsurpassed in her work for grandeur of composition and directness of observation, was eventually purchased by Ernest Gambart, who featured it in the 1855 "French Exhibition" in his Pall Mall gallery. The following year the Belgian dealer conducted Rosa Bonheur on a triumphal tour of England and Scotland, during which she was befriended by Queen Victoria and met Sir E. H. Landseer, whose pictures of animals she had previously known only through engravings.

After exhibiting in 1855 *Hay Making in the Auvergne,* also acquired for the Luxembourg, she ceased almost entirely to enter works in the salons, although she was represented in the 1867 Exposition Universelle by nine works, including *Sheep by the Sea,* belonging to the Empress Eugénie. In 1858–59, Rosa Bonheur bought a château in the hamlet of By, near Fontainebleau, which provided her with adequate space for the large menagerie of animals that she used as models. There she remained with her constant companion, the still life painter Nathalie Micas, producing her animal subjects, many of which were sold abroad through her dealer Gambart. Late in her career she turned to American western subjects, inspired by the 1889 visit to France of Colonel William F. Cody (Buffalo Bill) and his traveling show. Among her many awards was the cross of the Chevalier of the Legion of Honor presented to her personally in her studio in 1865 by the Empress Eugénie, membership in the Antwerp Institute offered in 1868, the Leopold Cross, and the Commander's Cross of the Royal Order of Isabella the Catholic, both presented in 1880, and elevation in 1894 to the rank of Officier of the Legion of Honor.

87. Ploughing Scene

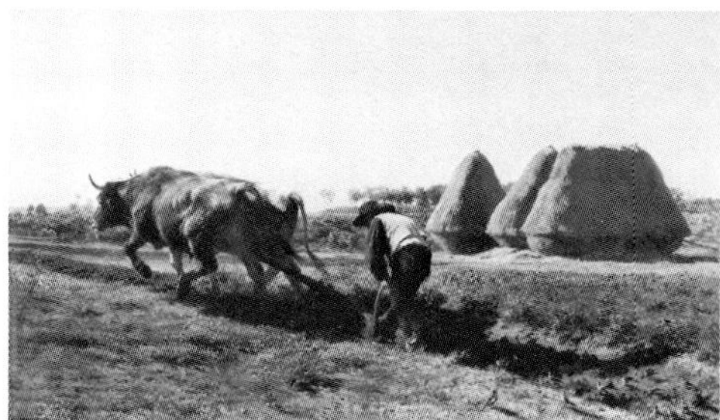

37.836 1854

Foreshortened and moving away from the viewer are a peasant and his plough drawn by a yoke of oxen. A flock of birds in the right foreground peck for food in the freshly turned furrows. In the background are the three haystacks that were denigrated by John Ruskin as the "awkwardest" in France. It is apparently evening, as the shadows are lengthening.

Ploughing scenes were recurrent in Rosa Bonheur's production. She received a third-class medal at the 1845 Salon, in which she exhibited *Le Labourage,* showing a team of horses drawing a plough toward the viewer, and in 1848 she received a commission from the State for *Labourage nivernais,* which was exhibited in 1849 and then presented to the Luxembourg Museum. The latter, now in Fontainebleau, was said to have been inspired by a reading of George Sand's *La Mare au Diable* (1846–48).

Support: Canvas, .495 x .805 (19½" x 31¾")

Signed and dated lower right: *Rosa Bonheur/ 1854.*

Provenance: Ernest Gambart; entry of this painting into the collection is undocumented, pre-

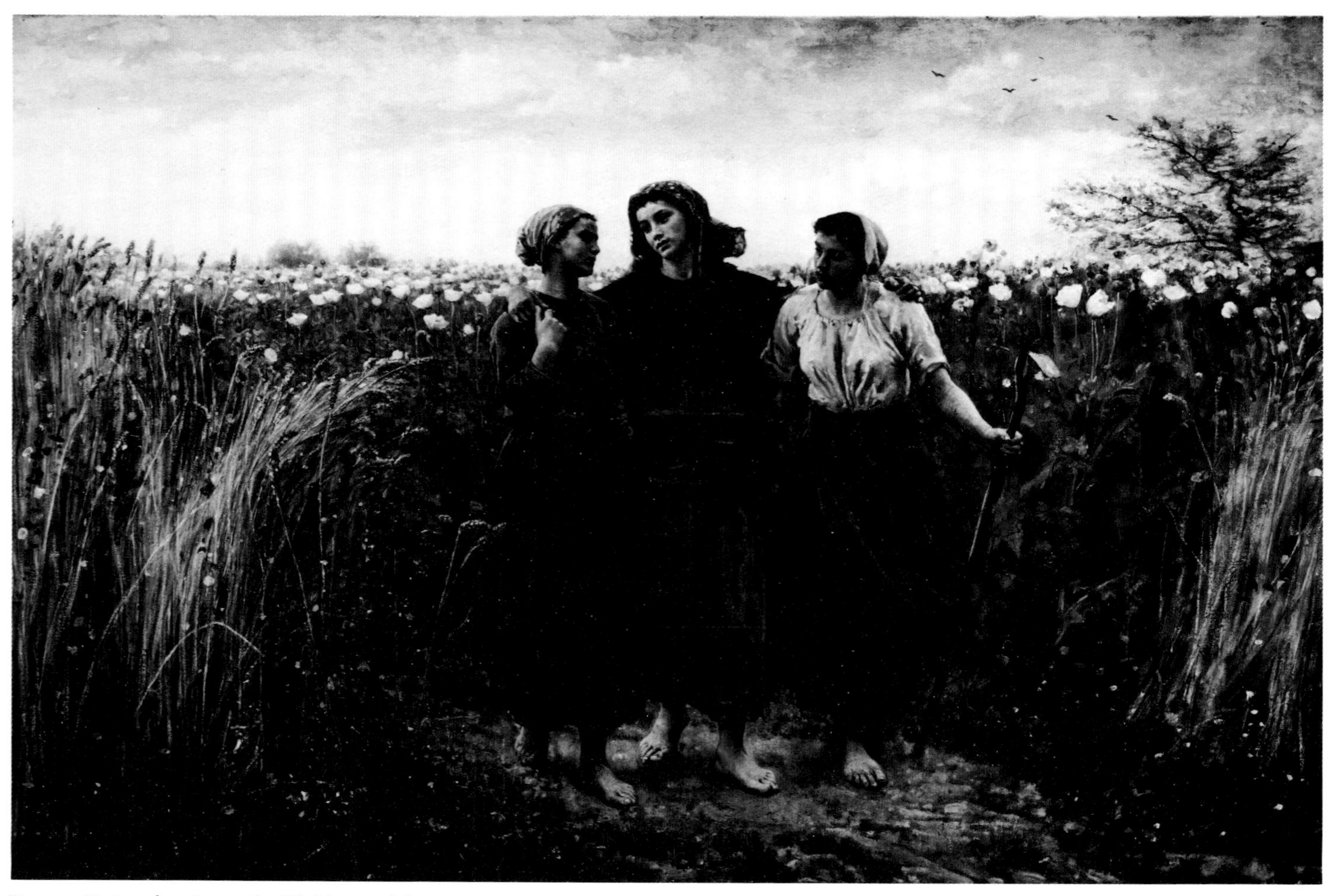

Breton *Returning from the Fields,* no. 86

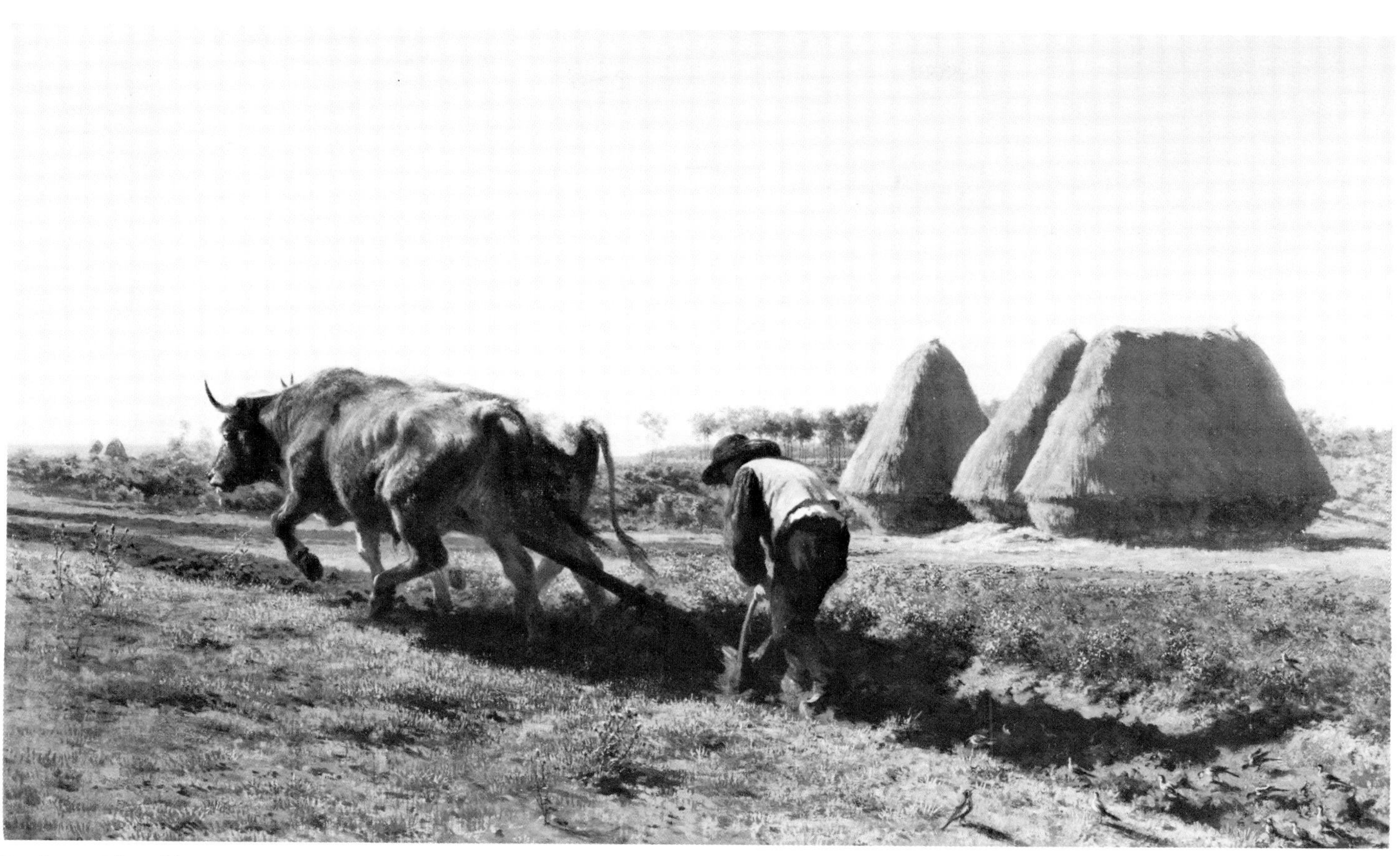

Bonheur *Ploughing Scene,* no. 87

sumably acquired by Henry Walters after 1929, date of the last complete catalogue of the collection.

Exhibitions: "The French Exhibition", 121 Pall Mall, London, 1858, no. 7; "Old Mistresses, Women Artists of the Past", Walters Art Gallery, 1972, no. 22; "The Realist Tradition: French painting and drawing, 1830–1900," Cleveland, Brooklyn, St. Louis, Glasgow, 1980–82, no. 53.

References: John Ruskin, "Academy Notes," *The Complete Works of John Ruskin,* edited by E. T. Cook and Alexander Wedderburn. 39 vols. London, G. Allen, 1903–12. 14: 173.

Pierre-Edouard Frère

French: Paris, 1819 - Ecouen, 1886

Frère's intimate, often sentimental scenes of rural childhood appealed particularly to English viewers and came to be as highly admired in Britain and America as in France. Initially Frère trained under Paul Delaroche at the Ecole des Beaux-Arts, but after an early marriage he was compelled to earn a livelihood executing wood-engraved vignettes for such publications as *L'Histoire de Paris, Mystères de Paris* and *Veillées littéraires. The Beggars of Dunkirk* represented his Salon debut in 1842, and in 1848 he exhibited no less than seven small pictures of children which, subsequently reproduced as prints, contributed to his popularity. He received a third–class medal in 1851, a second–class the following year, and in 1855 was appointed Chevalier of the Legion of Honor. About 1854 Frère became associated with the Belgian dealer Ernest Gambart, who opened an exhibition of modern French painting that April at 121 Pall Mall, London, an event which fortuitously coincided with the growing rapprochement between Britain and France, allies in the Crimean War.

The English public and critics were particularly fascinated with Frère's works. John Ruskin, commenting on the French artist's view of children exhibited in 1857, queried in his *Academy Notes:* "Who could have believed it possible to unite the depth of Wordsworth, the grace of Reynolds, and the holiness of Angelico." The following year he elaborated upon these views, explaining that by "depth" he meant the manner in which the artist approached the simplest subject with perfect feeling for its greater humanity, by "grace" he was alluding to Reynolds' hitherto unrivaled rendering of the momentary loveliness of childhood, and by "holiness" he was referring to the purity from sensual taint ("Academy Notes", *The Complete Works of John Ruskin,* London, 1904, 14: 143, 174).

Frère, a highly industrious artist, participated regularly in the annual salons in Paris, in Gambart's commercial shows abroad, and from 1868 to 1885 submitted paintings to the Royal Academy, London. Though interior settings dominated his early work, he was increasingly drawn to working out-of-doors and had constructed for winter sketching a sledge equipped with a foot-warmer and wicker hood. As his fame grew, Ecouen, the small town about eight miles north of Paris, in which he had originally settled for reasons of economy, emerged as a distinctive colony of genre painters inhabited by such artists as Frère's son Charles, the English still life painter George Todd, the Swiss artist Luigi Chialiva, and the Dane A. F. A. Schenck.

88. Going to School

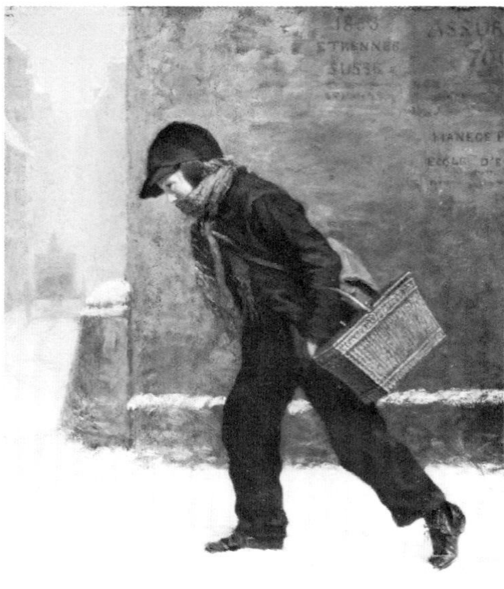

37.20 1853

Trudging through the snow on his way to school is a boy with a scarf wrapped over his mouth and his hands shoved into his pockets. He carries a wicker lunch basket and a satchel is strapped over his shoulder. Several decaying posters can be deciphered pasted on the wall in the background, and around the corner a cab disappears into the falling snow.

Support: Panel, mahogany, beveled edges, .31 x .248 (12¼" x 9¾")

Signed and dated lower left: *Ed. Frère 53.*

Provenance: Before 1878, unrecorded.

Exhibitions: "The Realist Tradition: French Painting and Drawing, 1830–1900" Cleveland, Brooklyn, St. Louis, Glasgow, 1980–82, no. 2.

References: see his *The Little Housekeeper* 37.18.

89. The Little Housekeeper

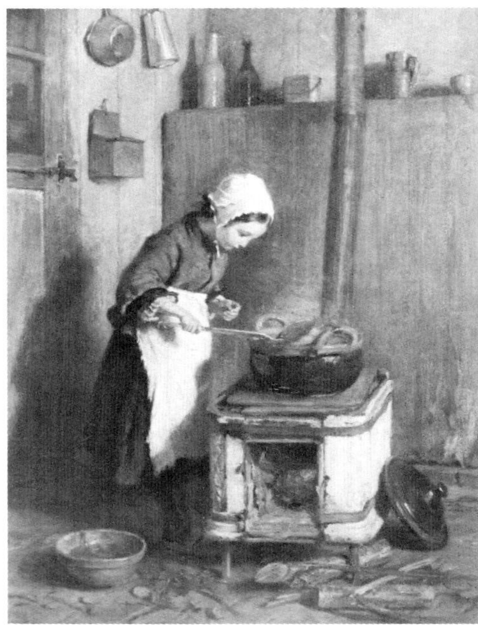

37.18 1857

A young village girl bends over a stove to peer into a large marmite, the contents of which she stirs with a strainer. She wears a white cap and apron, a casaque, and petticoat, wool stockings and sabots. At her feet is an earthenware bowl, some kindling and firewood. In the background are various utensils including a salt box and dust basket, wine bottles, milk can, water jug and basin.

Support: Panel, .327 x .24 (12⅞" x 9½")

Signed and dated in black paint at lower left: *Ed. Frere. 57.*

Provenance: Purchased by W. T. Walters for $400.00 at the "French and English Exhibition of Pictures," National Academy of Design, New York, October 29, 1859.

Exhibitions: Preserved in the Gallery's archives is an unidentified nineteenth–century newspaper clipping showing a wood engraving by W. Thomas of this painting. It is described as no. 72 in the French Exhibition (E. Gambart's Pall Mall Gallery).

References: Walters cat., 1878, pp. 17–18, and subsequent Walters catalogues; Champlin and Perkins, 2: 91; Cook, 1: 79.

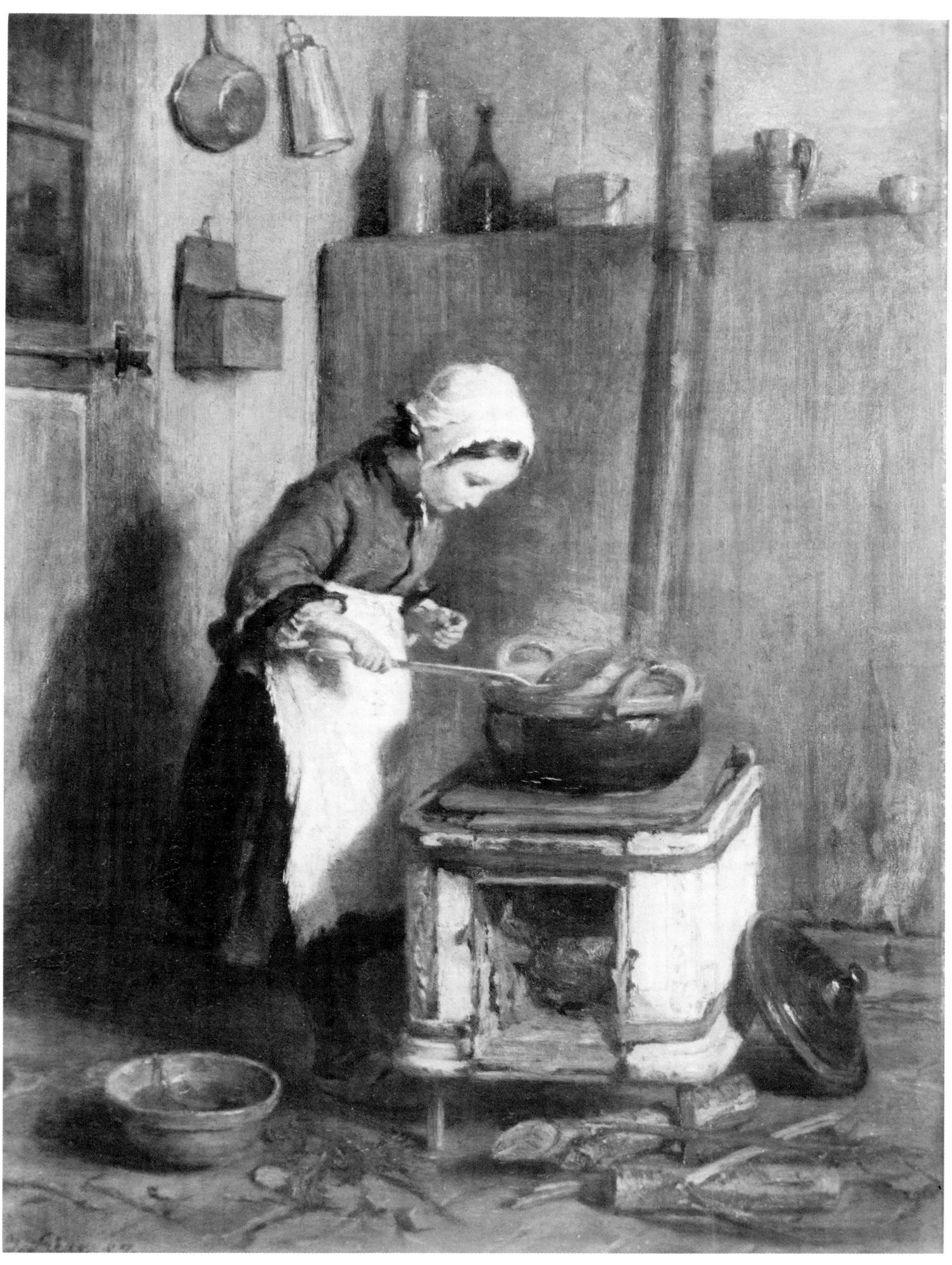

Frère *The Little Housekeeper,* no. 89

90. The Little Dressmaker

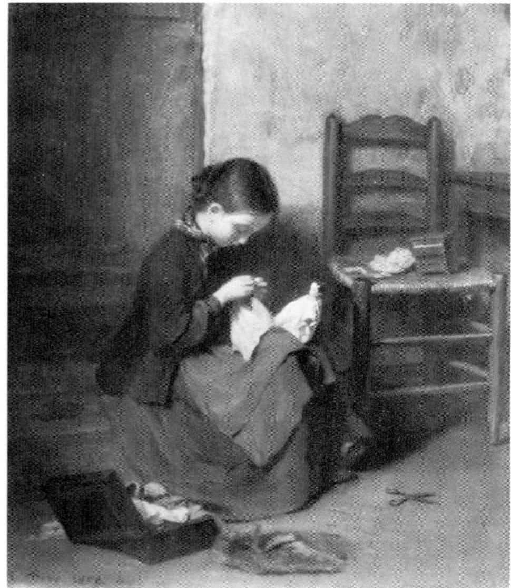

37.24 1858

A young girl is seated on a step in front of a doorway making a dress for a doll resting on her lap. At her left is a chair on which she has placed a miniature chest of drawers and some clothes, and on the floor is an open sewing box and a pair of scissors.

Support: Panel, mahogany, beveled edges, .273 x .219 (10¾" x 8⁹⁄₁₆")

Signed and dated lower left: *Ed. Frère. 1858.*

Marks: Panel stenciled on reverse: 542.

Provenance: Purchased by W. T. Walters at the "French and English Exhibition of Pictures" National Academy of Design, New York, October 29, 1859, for $300.00.

References: see entry for *The Little Housekeeper* 37.18.

91. Preparing Dinner

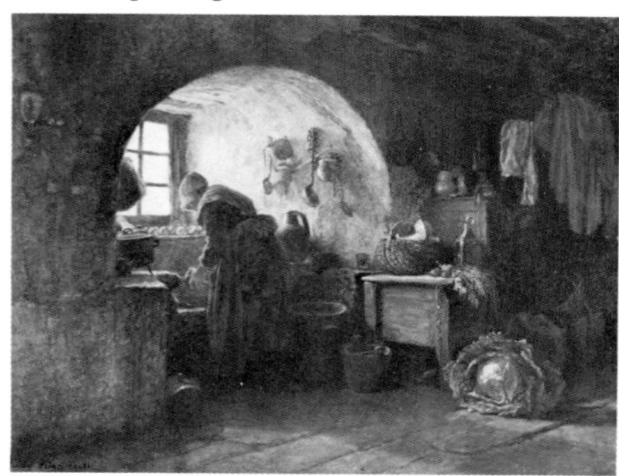

37.27 1858

In an alcove of an Ecouen kitchen a peasant woman stands stooped over a bowl with her back to the viewer. Light streaming through the window illuminates the alcove, showing the onions and apples on the sill, the beets and a wicker basket containing a section of squash on a chest, and an exceptionally large cabbage lying on the floor, as well as various utensils, a wicker hamper, a keg, an iron pot, a large ceramic pitcher and various strainers and ladles hanging from pegs on the wall. Discernible within the dimly lit interior are a chest, several pots, and the wash hung to dry.

Support: Fabric, .41 x .53 (16⅛" x 20⅞")

Signed and dated in black paint at lower left: *Edouard Frère. 1858.*

Condition: Cleaned and lined, May 1977.

Provenance: Acquired by W. T. Walters before 1878.

Exhibitions: "The Realist Tradition; French Painting and Drawing, 1830–1900" Cleveland, Brooklyn, St. Louis, Glasgow, 1980–82, no. 76.

92. The Cold Day

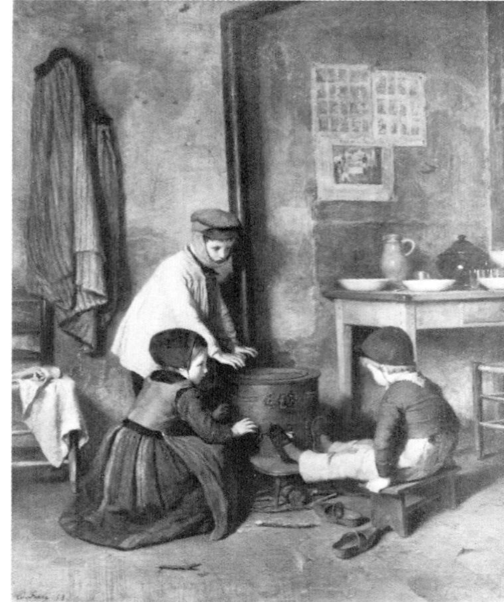

37.29 1858

Three children are huddled around an iron stove. One boy is seated on a bench at the right warming his feet on the hearth, a squatting girl warms her hands, and a boy standing behind her does likewise. The furniture in this interior includes a couple of chairs with rush seating and a table set with three bowls, an earthenware tureen, a pitcher and several glasses. Several prints, showing figures in red and blue uniforms, perhaps of Napoleonic subjects, are tacked to the wall, and a striped cloak hangs from pegs at the left.

Support: Panel, mahogany, beveled edges, .413 x .317 (16¼" x 12½")

Signed and dated lower left: *Ed. Frère. 58.*

Provenance: Purchased by W. T. Walters at M. Knoedler, successor to Goupil and Co., New York, June 26, 1860, for $750.00.

References: see his *The Little Housekeeper* 37.18.

93. Helping Herself

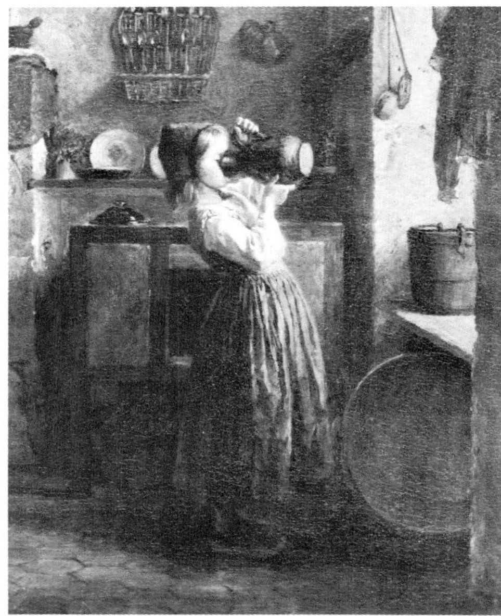

37.22 1859

A young girl stands in a larder drinking milk directly from a pitcher. Light from a window at the right illuminates the interior, revealing various utensils, including a rack of pewter spoons hanging on the back wall, a shelf of dishes, a cupboard, a wooden dairy bucket, and several strainers. The floor is laid in earthenware hexagonal tiles.

Support: Panel, .27 x .21 (10⅝" x 8¼")

Signed and dated in black paint at lower left: *Ed. Frère 59.*

Provenance: Acquired by W. T. Walters before 1878. Unrecorded.

References: see entry for his *The Little Housekeeper* 37.18.

Félix-François-Georges-Philibert Ziem

French: Beaune, 1821 - Paris, 1911

Ziem, the most peripatetic of nineteenth-century artists, is remembered for his prolific Venetian views produced during a long career spanning almost seven decades. He was born in Beaune, Burgundy, of French parentage, his unusual Polish surname being that adopted by his paternal grandfather, an Armenian who reached France by way of Kwidzyn on the Vistula. Ziem's family settled in Dijon in 1831 and six years later the future artist entered the town's Ecole des Beaux-Arts, where he distinguished himself in architectural and landscape drawing. In 1839 he left Dijon for Marseilles to become a construction-site manager. By this time he was painting in watercolors and giving private lessons in drawing. Having a sociable nature, he proved most adept at attracting wealthy prominent pupils. Among his earliest admirers was the Grand Duchess Stéfanie, niece of the Empress Josephine.

In 1842 Ziem embarked on his first extensive tour, traveling to Italy, where he visited Venice before continuing to Austria and Germany. The following year he went even further afield, accompanying a Prince and Princess Gagarin to Odessa, Kiev, and Moscow and then continuing to Saint Petersburg, where he remained until the autumn of 1844. Ziem was back in Italy in 1846, and the following year he settled briefly in Florence, where he offered drawing lessons to the nobility. In 1850 he joined Théodore Rousseau, who was to remain a lifelong friend, in painting woodland scenes in the village of Barbizon. Following the advice of Alexandre Gabriel Decamps, he also traveled that year to Holland. There he was profoundly moved by the paintings of Rembrandt. In 1852 Ziem made his first trip to England and Scotland. His reputation as an Orientalist was initiated by visits to Egypt in 1854, Constantinople in 1855, Turkey, Rhodes and Egypt again in 1856, and to Algeria in 1858. For much of the remainder of his career, Ziem's travels continued at an unabated pace. Stopping points included his studio built on rue Lepic, Montmartre, in 1852, a mosque-like studio erected in 1861 in Martigues on the Mediterranean coast, and a villa acquired in Nice in 1877. An interruption in his routine occurred in 1866 when he settled in Barbizon for a couple of years, buying a house on the edge of the forest from Charles Jacque.

As an artist Ziem defies ready categorization. It has been suggested that in his marine and landscape paintings this essentially self-taught artist sought to combine classical composition inspired by the paintings of Claude Lorrain with a dynamic technique derived from the works of Rembrandt. Other artists cited as influencing his development included Delacroix, Huet, Isabey, his friends Rousseau and Diaz, and the English painter Turner, equally famed for Venetian views. Ziem's influence as one of the great colorists of his time, was, in turn, reflected in the works of his friend Monticelli, and further afield in the paintings of Van Gogh. Although sharing little in common with the Impressionists, he did precede them in working *in situ,* contriving a floating studio in Venice and employing a caravan in the Fontainebleau Forest.

Ziem participated in the salons from 1849 to 1868 and again in 1888, receiving a third-class medal in 1851, a first-class in 1852, and a third-class again at the 1855 Exposition Universelle. He rose through the ranks of the Legion of Honor from Chevalier in 1857, to Officier in 1878, and to Commandeur in 1908.

94. Venice, Morning

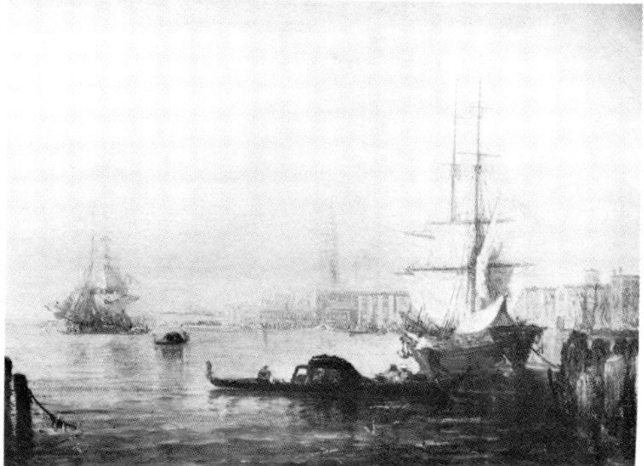

37.157 c.1864

Dominating the right foreground are a gondola and a moored sailing vessel. Left, in the middle ground, are other craft. The buildings of the Riva degli Schiavoni are visible in the background.

Support: Finely woven canvas, .43 x .555 (17" x 21⅞")

Signed in dark brown at lower left: *Ziem.*

Marks: Stenciled on reverse: ... *ARPENTIER - DEF... / Me. de Couleurs/Boulevard Montmartre Paris;* Inscribed in white chalk on reverse: *Me Ziem 72;* Paper sticker on reverse: *322.*

Provenance: Purchased from the artist in 1864; See *Catalogue des tableaux exécutés et sortis de l'atelier de M. Félix Ziem né à Beaune, Côte d'Or, le 25 Février 1821,* 1864, no. 89, Mr. Walters—"Venise matin" turquoise beau. 1500 F.

References: Walters cat., 1878, p. 21, and subsequent Walters catalogues; Pierre Miquel, *Félix Ziem, 1821–1911.* L'Ecole de la nature, 7, 8. 2 vols. Maurs-la-Jolie, Editions de la Martinelle, 1978. 2: 16.

95. Venice, Evening

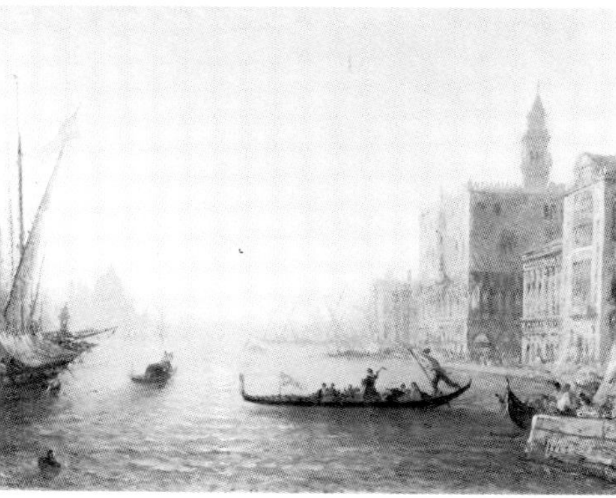

37.158 c.1865

The sun is setting in the west, illuminating the entrance to the Grand Canal. At the left, silhouetted against the sky, is the dome of Santa Maria della Salute. The right is dominated by the Ducal Palace and beyond it, the Campanile. Crossing from the Riva degli Schiavoni is a gondola laden with passengers. Several sailing vessels are moored at the right.

Support: Canvas, finely woven, .433 x .55 (17$\frac{1}{16}$" x 21⅝")

Signed in dark brown at lower right: *ZIEM.*

Marks: Stenciled on reverse: *R. N.DAME DE LORETTE, 46/ OTTOZ FRERES/ Mds DE COULEURS FINE/& TOILES à TABLEAUX/ PARIS.*

Condition: The painting was treated for discolored varnishes and was lined in 1975.

Provenance: Purchased from the artist in 1865. See *Catalogue des tableaux exécutés et sortis de l'atelier de M. Félix Ziem né à Beaune, Côte d'Or, le 25 février 1821,* 1864, no. 104 Mr. Walters—"Soleil couchant Venise," assez bien. 1.500 F. (reproduced in Pierre Miquel).

References: Walters cat., 1878, p. 21, and subsequent Walters catalogues; Pierre Miquel, *Félix Ziem, 1821–1911.* L'Ecole de la nature, 7, 8. 2 vols. Maurs-la-Jolie, Editions de la Martinelle, 1978. 2: 16, 117, no. 650.

96. Venice, Midday

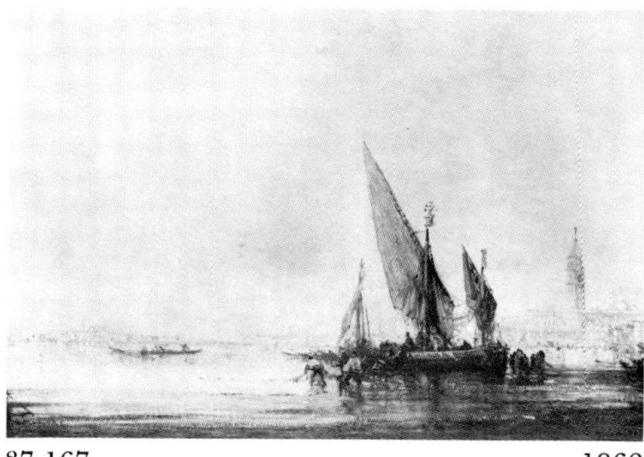

37.167 1868

From a vantage point to the east, one looks across the Bacino di San Marco toward Santa Maria della Salute on the left and to the Ducal Palace and Campanile on the right. Moored fishing boats occupy the foreground.

Support: Panel, .422 x .594 (16⅝" x 23⅜")

Signed and dated in dark brown at lower right: *Ziem 68.*

Marks: Stenciled in red on reverse: *MULLER/ PARIS;* Inscribed in red crayon: *627.*

Provenance: Purchased by W. T. Walters between 1878 and 1884.

References: Walters cat., 1884, p. 20, no. 30, and subsequent Walters catalogues; Pierre Miquel, *Félix Ziem, 1821–1911.* L'Ecole de la nature, 7, 8. 2 vols. Maurs-la-Jolie, Editions de la Martinelle, 1978. 2: 112, no. 608.

97. Venice, Sunset

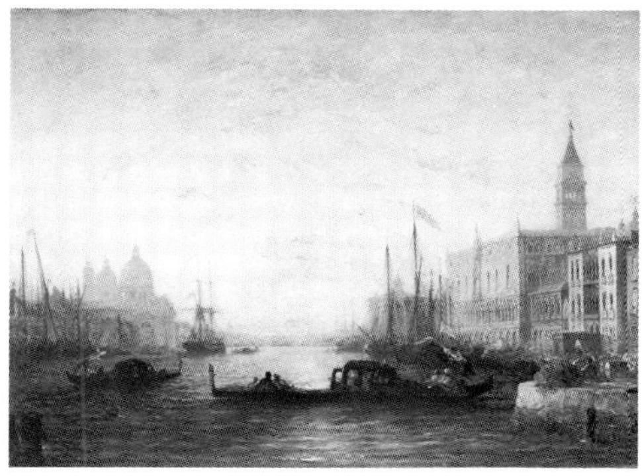

37.26

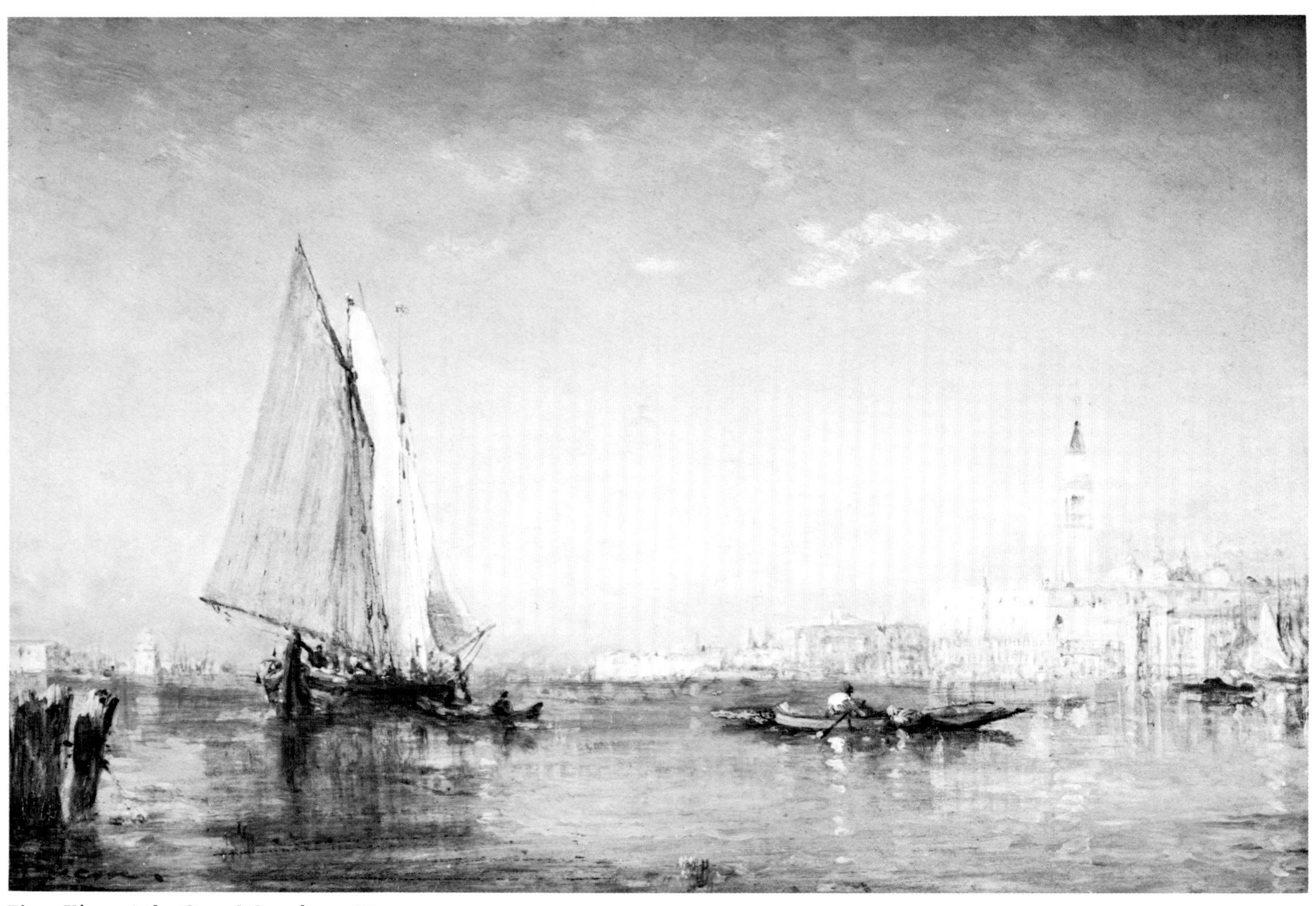

Ziem *View of the Grand Canal,* no. 98

From the artist's usual vantage point, the viewer looks westward into the sunset. On the right are the Ducal Palace and the Prison, and on the left in the middle ground is Santa Maria della Salute. Gondolas cross the Bacino di San Marco in the foreground.

Support: Canvas, fine weave, .995 x 1.365 (39¼" x 53¾")

Signed in dark brown at lower right: *Ziem.*

Provenance: Goldschmidt Sale, Paris, May 17–22, 1888, no. 53, illus., 26,000 francs to M. Montaignac, Paris; M. Montaignac to Walters.

References: Louis Fournier, *Un grand peintre, Félix Ziem; notes biographiques.* Beaune, H. Lambert, 1897. p. 87; illustrated by an engraving by Kratké opposite p. 87, and by a photograph by Ad. Braun et Cie, opposite p. 118.

98. View of the Grand Canal

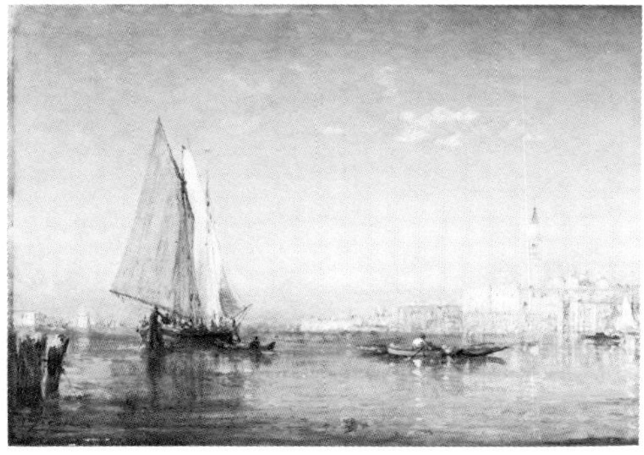

37.2481

This painting, characteristic of many of Ziem's Venetian views, looks toward the Grand Canal from the Canale di San Marco. The scene is suffused with a warm, golden sunlight.

Support: Panel, cradled, .27 x .394 (10⅝" x 15½")

Signed in brown at lower left: *ZIEM.*

Marks: Paper sticker: *Scott and Fowles, 295 Fifth Avenue, no. 245;* Stenciled: *2079;* Inscribed: *No. 5 Library.*

Provenance: The inscription "No. 5 Library" would suggest that the painting originally belonged to Henry Walters and that it was hung in the Library of the Walters town house at 5 West Mount Vernon Place, Baltimore. Bequest of Miss Laura F. Delano (niece of Henry Walters), 1972.

Artist unknown, formerly attributed to Ziem

99. Canal Scene, Holland

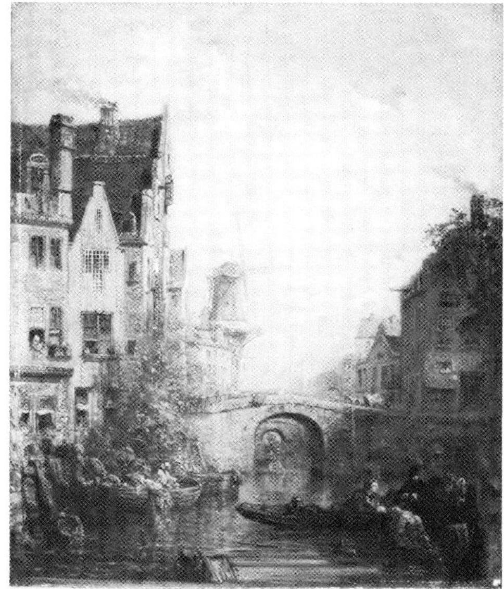

37.997

A canal is lined with town houses and a windmill. In the foreground people in boats are engaged in washing fabrics in the water, perhaps an allusion to Amsterdam's numerous textile industries in the nineteenth century. Attempts to identify the actual site have proved unsuccessful.

Ziem, on the advice of his colleague A.-G. Decamps, visited The Netherlands in 1850 and again in the summers of 1852 and 1853. Usually, he portrayed windmills along banks of rural waterways.

In 1980 Pierre Miquel rejected the authenticity of this painting because of the highly atypical subject matter.

Support: Canvas, coarse weave, .695 x .56 (27⅜" x 22")

Signed in red at lower right: *Ziem.*

Marks: Paper sticker on reverse: *MAISON POTTIER, FONDEE EN 1802, CH. POTTIER, M. BALLEUR-PACKER, SPECIALIATE POUR TABLEAUX ET OBJETS D'ART, 14 rue GAILION, PRES AVENUE DE L'OPERA, PARIS;* Paper sticker: *22.541;* Paper sticker: *5673.*

Condition: In 1981 the picture was cleaned and examined. The signature appeared to be early in date and placed directly on the painted surface without an intervening layer of varnish. Also, it was determined that the canvas had been restretched on a stretcher that was slightly smaller than the original one. The new stretcher had been expanded with half-inch wooden strips on the vertical sides. Repainting had been performed to mask the original tacking holes. In the process of the expansion the tacking holes on the left side were lost.

Provenance: Purchased by Henry Walters from Georges Petit in 1922, customs declaration dated July 27, 1922.

References: Pierre Miquel, *Félix Ziem, 1821–1911.* L'Ecole de la nature, 7, 8. 2 vols. Maurs-la-Jolie, Editions de la Martinelle, 1978. 2: 192, no. 1347 (as questionable).

Marc-Charles-Gabriel Gleyre

Swiss-French: Chevilly, 1806 - Paris, 1874

Gleyre was not a consistent exhibitor at the Paris salons and never received any major commissions from French officialdom. As a result, posterity has emphasized his role as the head of a major atelier and ignored his painting and his leadership in the Néo-grec movement.

From the age of nine Gleyre was raised in France by his uncle, a textile merchant in Lyons. About 1825 he went to Paris to study painting, entering the studio of Louis Hersent for about a year and then adopting a regimen that included mornings at the Ecole des Beaux-Arts, afternoons working in watercolors with R. P. Bonington, and evenings at the Académie Suisse. In 1828 he departed for Italy, visiting Florence and settling in the via Condotti area of Rome for four years. Six years later a Bostonian, John Lowell, Jr., commissioned him to record a tour of the East. They traveled together to Greece and Turkey, stopping at Constantinople and Smyrna, continued to Egypt, and journeyed up the Nile where they eventually separated, Lowell returning to Cairo and Gleyre staying among the Sudanese. Shattered health compelled him to return to France to convalesce in 1837. In Paris Gleyre produced several works inspired by the Italian sojourn which he exhibited at the 1840 Salon. The same year he was commissioned by the Duc de Luynes to execute murals for the Château de Dampierre. These were subsequently effaced, to be replaced by Ingres' celebrated *Age d'or.*

Recovering from the humiliation, Gleyre won a second-class medal for *Evening* in 1843, the year he also inherited from Delaroche the directorship of a private atelier. Although of conservative disposition, Gleyre proved to be a flexible teacher. His list of pupils, which numbered more than five hundred over a span of two decades, included such diverse figures as the Néo-grecs Hamon, Gérôme, Picou and Aubert; the future Impressionists Monet, Sisley, Bazille, and Renoir; the Swiss artists Bocion and Anker, and the Anglo-Saxons Whistler, Poynter, and Du Maurier.

During the forties Gleyre again visited Italy and went to England and Spain. Among his major works at this point were two religious pictures: *The Departure of the Apostles* (1845) for the church of Montargis and *Pentecost* (1848–55) for the church of Sainte Marguerite; his last salon entry, *Dance of the Bacchantes* (1849); and a Swiss theme, *Major Duval* (1850), painted for his native canton of Vaud. That government also commissioned his most ambitious historical subject, *The Helvetians put the Conquered Romans under the Yoke* (1853–58). In his later years he continued to produce religious and historical subjects and the occasional portrait. At his death he was working on a mystical religious picture, *Morning* or *Earthly Paradise,* which was probably intended as a pendant for *Evening.*

The influence of Gleyre's painting was explored in an exhibition, *Charles Gleyre ou les illusions perdues,* Winterthur, Lausanne, 1974–75. It was demonstrated that he was a pivotal figure not only for the Néo-grecs, who treated everyday subjects in classical guise, but also for the Impressionists, the members of the British Aesthetic Movement, and for followers of a number of other later nineteenth-century trends.

100. Lost Illusions

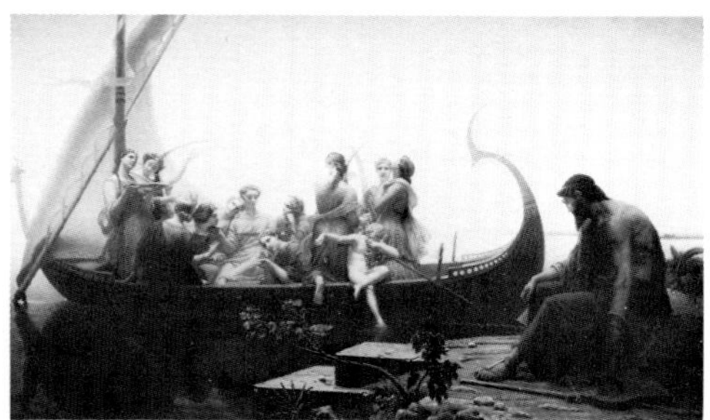

37.184 1865–67

Charles Clément, in *Gleyre, étude biographique et critique,* Paris, 1878, p. 399, records that this work, a replica of the celebrated *Evening* exhibited at the Paris Salon of 1843, no. 512, was rendered as an ébauche by Léon Dussart (born 1824) and considerably reworked by Gleyre.

Portrayed is a vision experienced by the artist on the banks of the Nile near Abydos on the evening of March 21, 1835. The scene is rendered in ancient costume. At the river's edge, an aging poet, resigned in his reveries, watches as a wondrous bark carries away his youthful dreams and illusions, personified by music-making maidens and a cupid strewing flowers. The rigging of the vessel approximates that of a dahabieh, a Nile river boat. A crescent-shaped moon and a flight of birds are visible in the evening sky.

The original painting (1.565 x 2.38) was acquired by the Luxembourg Gallery and is now in the Louvre, inv. 10039. Preliminary studies include a pencil sketch of the composition (.252 x .376) in Lausanne, Musée Cantonal des Beaux-Arts, inv. D. 1083; an oil study of the figure of the poet (.225 x .2) also in Lausanne, inv. 1368; and a black chalk drawing of this figure nude (.54 x .41) in the same collection, inv. 1.232. Clément, pp. 399–400, mentions another version, differing in details, that belonged to Mme. Cornu.

Among the replicas are *The Evening Hymn* (.975 x 1.55) in the Walker Art Gallery, Liverpool, and another (.395 x .675), dated 1866, in the Kunstmuseum, Wintherthur, inv. 1004.

The title *Lost Illusions* came to be associated with the composition through the engraved copies by J. P. M. Jazet. The fame of this composition gave rise to a series of barque themes which included Lodovic Piette's chalk drawing *Les Fantômes,* reproduced in *L'Artiste* 7 (1859), opposite p. 80.

Support: Canvas, lined 1967, .865 x 1.505 (34" x 59¼")

Provenance: The replica was commissioned by W. T. Walters from Gleyre through the firm of Goupil prior to October 1865, and was completed by January 1867. An undated letter from the dealer to Mr. Walters reads: "Mr. Gleyre has finally nearly finished his reproduction of his picture, "Les Illusions Perdues". It has lasted some time but we are happy to be able to tell you that this reproduction is beautifully done. It has taken a long time and has required more trouble from the painter than he thought. The price had not been definitely fixed but now we can tell you that it is impossible to estimate it at less than ten thousand francs."

References: Charles Clément, *Gleyre, étude biographique et critique,* Paris, Didier, 1878, p. 399, no. 38; *Walters cat.,* 1878, pp. 33–34, and subsequent Walters catalogues; Strahan, 1: 89–90, 94; Cook, 1: 10; Champlin and Perkins, 2: 153; Lamb, p. 251; Karl Baedeker, *The United States,* Leipsic, Karl Baedeker, 1893, p. 247; Stranahan, p. 287; Reizenstein, pp. 551; E. P. Spencer, "Academic French Painting," *Magazine of Art,* 31 (1938): 382; Lucas, 2: 203, 209, 210, 212, 223, 232–34; William Hauptman, "Allusions and Illusions in Gleyre's Le Soir," *Art Bulletin* 60 (1978): 321; H. Barbara Weinberg, "American Impressionism in Cosmopolitan Context," *Arts Magazine* 55, no. 3 (November 1980): 162, fig. 5.

Thomas Couture

French: Senlis, 1815 - Villiers-le-Bel, 1879

Thomas Couture was a member of the Juste Milieu, the group of artists who strove to reconcile progressive and conservative tendencies. A complex individual, he ultimately was hampered by an inability "to reconcile reality and idealism and to bridge the gap between sketch and finished work" (Albert Boime, "Thomas Couture and the Evolution of Painting in Nineteenth Century France," *The Art Bulletin,* March 1969, p. 53). In painting, he evolved a personal technique that imparted a greater degree of spontaneity to his finished works than did the prevailing academic practice. He also recommended to his pupils modern subjects such as locomotives and construction workers, though he himself usually worked in an allegorical vein. He recorded his views in *Méthode et Entretiens d'Atelier,* published in French in 1867, and in English in 1879.

Thomas Couture was the son of a Senlis shoemaker. In 1826 his family migrated to Paris and four years later he was enrolled in the studio of Baron Gros, where he remained until the latter's death in 1835. Three years later he briefly entered the studio of Paul Delaroche. His formal training was supplemented by frequent visits to the Louvre, where he studied the Italian collection, especially Veronese and the Venetian School. Couture's three attempts in 1837, 1838 and 1839, for the first place in the Prix de Rome proved unsuccessful. Beginning in 1840 he exhibited at the salons, entering such works as *Young Venetian after an Orgy* (1840), *The Troubadour* (1843), and *The Love of Gold* (1844), all marked by a moralizing tone. Their fresh colors and originality of concept won for the artist the approbation of the critics. His role as a leader among the younger artists was confirmed by the appearance at the 1847 Salon of the enormous *Romans of the Decadence.* It was interpreted by many viewers as a comment on Louis Philippe's government, couched in classical guise. That year he opened his studio to pupils, thus providing them with an alternative to academic training at the Ecole des Beaux-Arts. Two other large-scale works, never completed, were the *Enrollment of the Volunteers,* commissioned during the Second Republic, and the *Baptism of the Prince Imperial,* begun in 1856. In both works contemporary and idealized imagery were rather unconvincingly combined. After 1847 he exhibited intermittently at the salons, submitting smaller, more marketable easel paintings and portraits. Until the late sixties he continued to receive the encouragement of the government and the Imperial family. In 1859 he left Paris for his native Senlis and in 1869 settled at Villiers-le-Bel.

Couture trained a number of artists including Manet, with whom he fought because of the latter's unorthodox realism, and a host of foreigners, especially Americans. Among his American pupils were Daniel Huntington, Thomas Hicks, and William M. Hunt.

101. Horace and Lydia

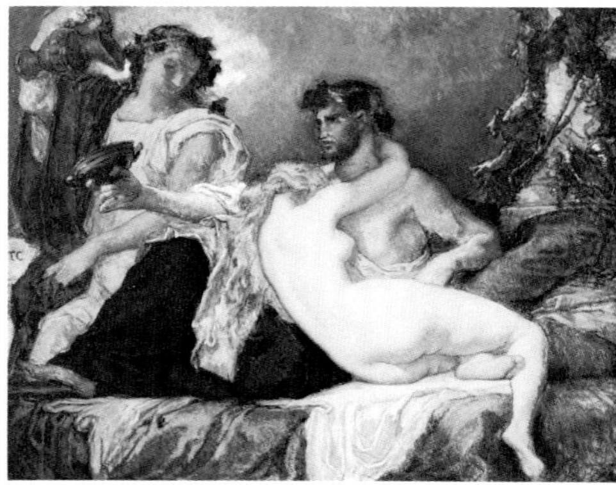

37.23 after 1843

A nude woman clasps her arms around the neck of a man reclining on a draped bench. He is being served wine by a kneeling servant. At the extreme right is a column entwined with grape vines.

The subjects of the Walters picture have traditionally been identified as the Roman poet, Quintus Horatius Flaccus, 65 - 8 B.C., and Lydia, a Roman courtesan, who figures prominently in the poet's *Odes*. An identical composition, though distinguished by more dramatic illumination, is in the Wallace Collection, London, inv. P340, oil on canvas, (.38 x .46), dated 1843, listed as *A Roman Feast*.

The composition is generally described as an essay preliminary to the celebrated *Romans of the Decadence*, Louvre, R.F. 3451, shown in the Salon of 1847. Superficial similarities can be cited between the poses of the figures in the small composition and those of the reclining couple at the left side of the Salon picture, and also between the laurel-wreathed male head in the Walters picture and the head of the second figure witnessing the orgy at the extreme right in the Louvre painting. Drawings related to the London and Baltimore pictures were sold at the Hôtel Drouot, Paris, 1970, November 23 (.28 x .315), and again June 25, 1973, (*A Roman Feast*, .117 x .133).

Support: Panel, .215 x .27 (8½" x 10⅝")

Signed mid left: *TC*

Provenance: Sedelmeyer Sale, Paris, April 30-March 2, 1879, no. 13. Purchased by W. T. Walters from S. P. Avery, New York, March 10, 1885.

Condition: Discolored varnishes and some overpainting removed in 1980; revarnished with synthetic varnish.

References: Walters cat., 1887, p. 6, no. 5, and subsequent Walters catalogues; Roger-Ballu, *Catalogue des oeuvres de Th. Couture exposées au Palais de l'Industrie.* Paris, A. Quantin, 1880. p. 2, no. 10; Georges Bertauts-Couture, *Thomas Couture, 1815–1879; sa vie, son oeuvre, son caractère, ses idées, sa méthode, par lui-même et par son petit-fils.* Paris, Le Garrec, 1932. p. 40; Jane Van Nimmen et al., *Thomas Couture: Paintings and Drawings in American Collections.* College Park, University of Maryland, 1970. p. 49; Albert Boime et al., *Thomas Couture, 1815–79; drawings and some oil sketches.* New York, Shepherd Gallery, 1971 (no. 10 is a possibly related drawing).

102. The Prodigal Son

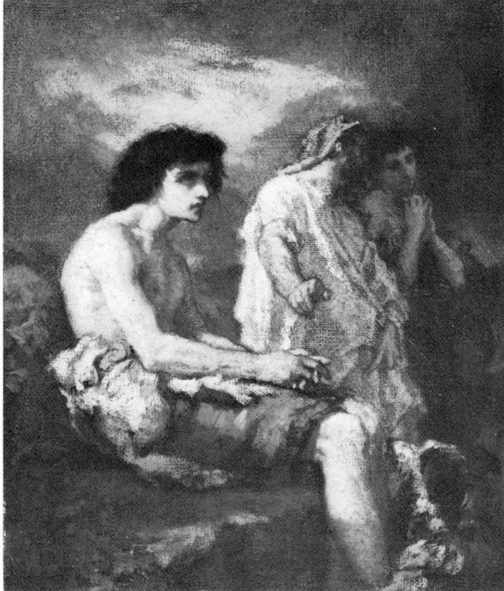

37.848 1850

A partially clad youth with a forlorn expression is slouched on a rock. At his side is his dog and behind, a man gestures toward him while addressing a young woman who clasps her hands. This painting is a replica of a work shown in the 1841 Salon. The original, subsequently acquired by G.P.A. Healy, was destroyed in the 1871 Chicago fire. A larger, more finished, replica, *L'Enfant prodigue*, oil on canvas, .81 x .65, was presented to the Havre Museum in 1843. The Walters picture has been described by Roger-Ballu as a "première composition" and by G.P.A. Healy as a "spirited sketch" for the Salon picture. Albert Boime, in a letter to the cataloguer in 1969, noted the dubious nature of the signature and referred to the painting as a "studio" product.

Jerome Willard Howe, Jr. has identified a drawing in the Valentine Museum, Richmond, Inv. OM. 106.3, black chalk, .407 x .365, as a preliminary study for the youth's head.

Support: Canvas, .335 x .26 (13¼" x 10¼")
Signed at left: *T. Couture/1850*

Provenance: E. L. Jacobson (The Hague) Sale, Paris, 1876, no. 21, illus.; M. Barbedienne Sale, Paris, 1892, no. 27, illus., 5800 francs.

Exhibitions: "Exposition Thomas Couture," Palais de l'Industrie, Paris, 1880, no. 7;"Exposition des oeuvres de Thomas Couture," Galerie Levesque, Paris, 1913, no. 7.

References: Roger-Ballu, *Catalogue des oeuvres de Th. Couture exposées au Palais de l'Industrie,* Paris, A. Quantin, 1880, p. 2, no. 7; G. P. A. Healy, "Thomas Couture," *Century Magazine* 44 (May 1892): 7; G. P. A. Healy, *Reminiscences of a Portrait Painter*. Chicago, A. C. McClurg, 1894, p. 84; Jane Van Nimmen et al., *Thomas Couture: Paintings and Drawings in American Collections.* College Park, University of Maryland, 1970, pp. 49, 53.

103. Day Dreams

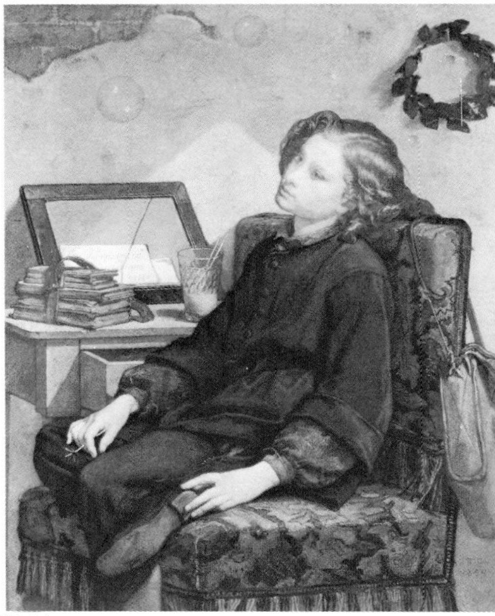

37.44 1859

A young boy is languidly seated, with his legs crossed, on a Turkey work covered chair, blowing bubbles, which drift upward. On a table at his side are a bundle of school books strapped together, a glass of soapy water, and a framed mirror. A laurel wreath hangs behind him on a nail driven into a masonry wall with crumbling plaster. The picture has been interpreted as an allegory of vanity with the soap bubbles connoting ephemeral existence, the wreath symbolizing glory, and the decaying wall referring to the transience of existence.

In a larger variant of this picture, *Soap Bubbles*, Metropolitan Museum of Art, New York, Inv. 87.15.22, oil on canvas, 1.358 x .979, undated, a dark, rather than fair haired, model is portrayed. In the Walters picture, a sheaf of papers, inserted in the frame of the mirror on the table, bears the inscription: *Le Parasseux/indigne/de vivre* (The lazy one, unworthy of living), whereas a similar paper in the New York painting is inscribed: *immortalité de l'un.* (immortality of one.) Moreover, the Walters painting differs from the New York picture in that it lacks a purse and additional papers lying on the tabletop, and the table drawer is shown pulled open rather than partially closed. Although the varying conditions of the two works hinder direct comparison, the Baltimore picture appears to be suffused by a more warm, glowing light.

The Fogg Museum, Cambridge, possesses a highly finished drawing, *Day Dreaming*, Inv. 1943.792, .595 x .451, dated 1859, which is directly related to the Walters painting, whereas a drawing of the boy's head in the Valentine Museum, Richmond, Inv. OM. 106.14, black and white chalks, .528 x .413, is a preliminary study for the Metropolitan Museum's picture. It is dated 1859, indicating that the two versions of the composition are probably contemporaneous.

Boime cites as prototypes for this *vanitas* theme Hendrik Goltzius' engraving *Quis Evadet?* (1594) and J.B.S. Chardin's paintings of boys blowing bubbles.

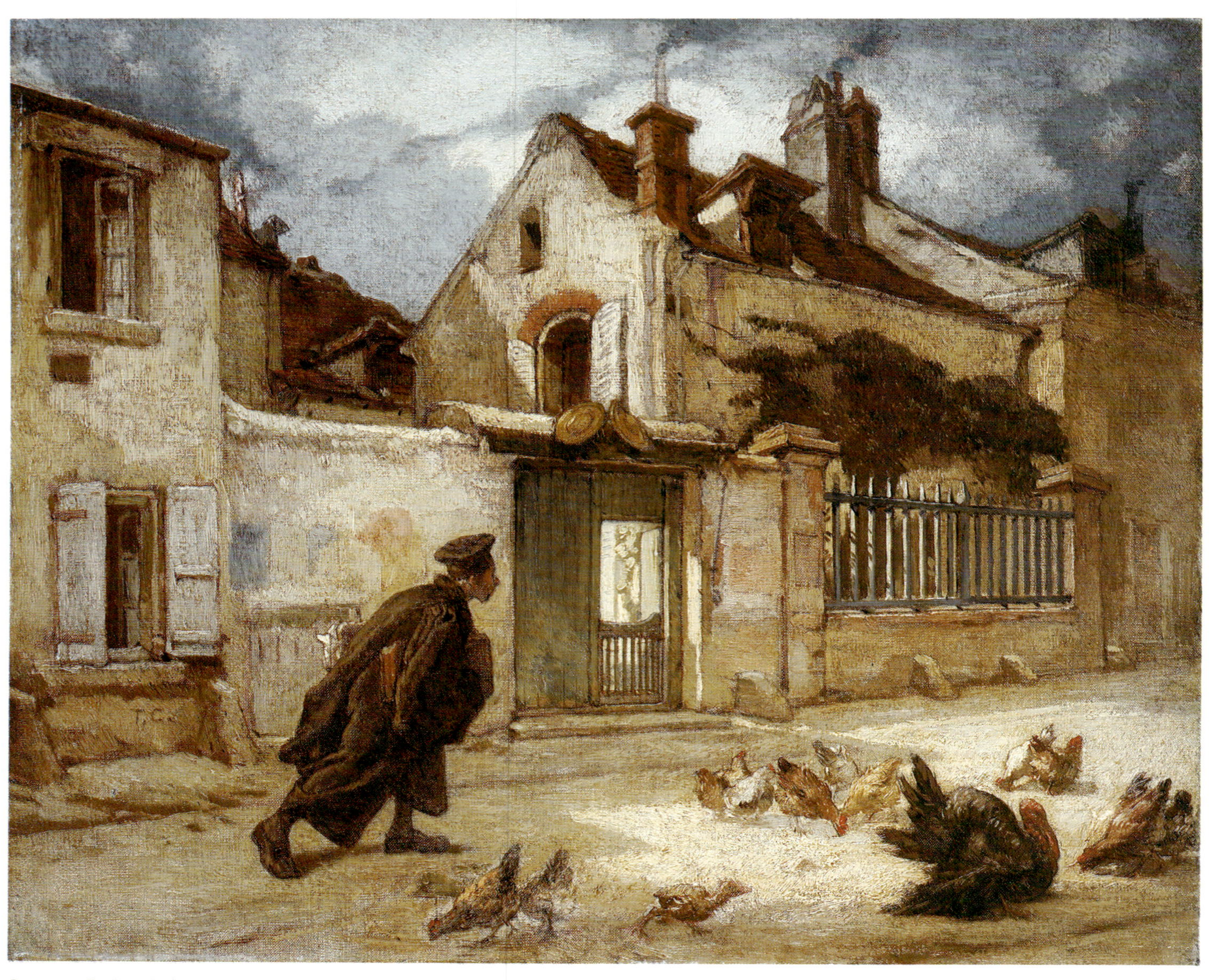

Couture *Judge Going to Court,* no. 104

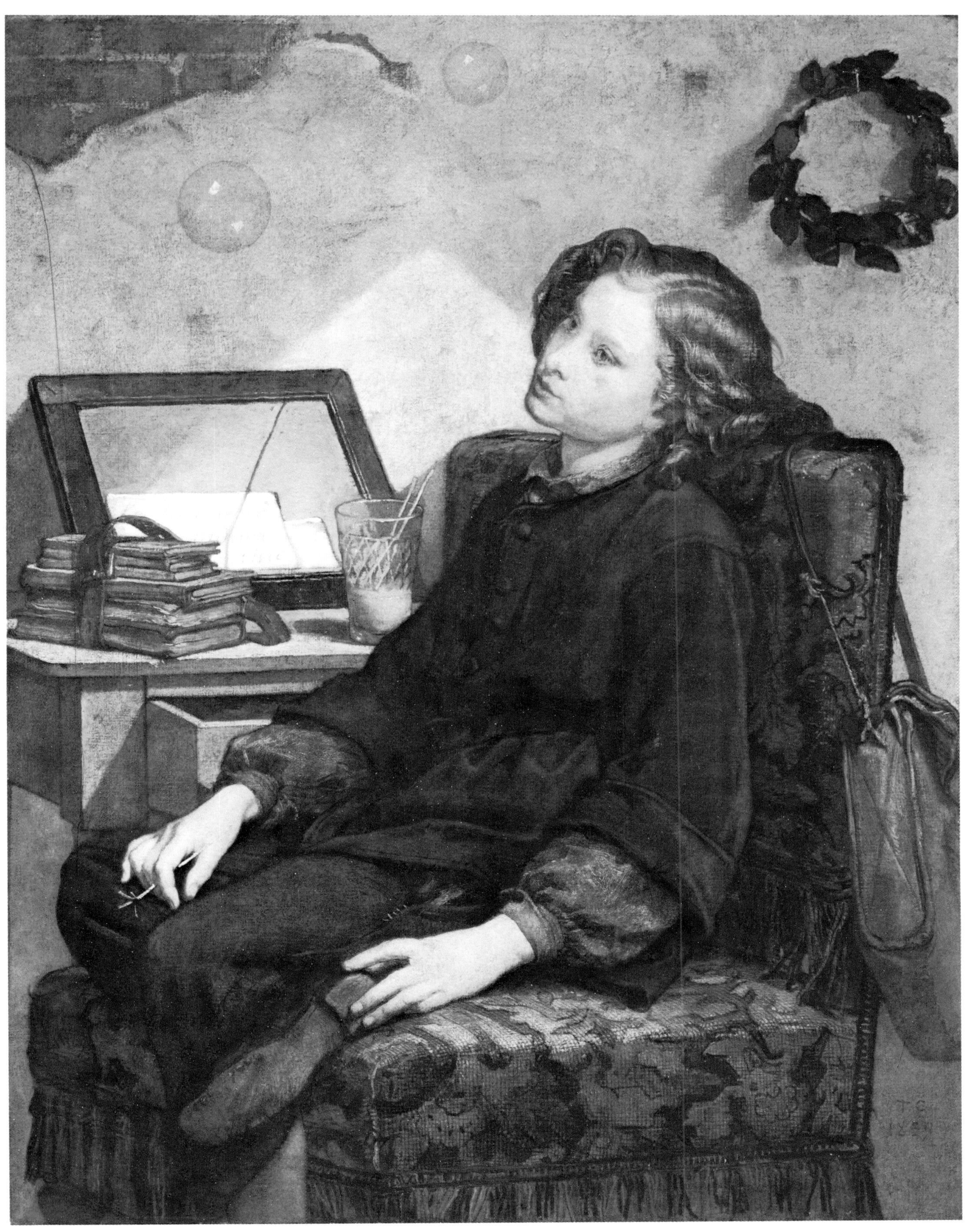

Couture *Day Dreams,* no. 103

Alternative title: *Blowing Bubbles.*

Support: Canvas, 1.18 x .903 (46$\frac{7}{16}$ x 35$\frac{1}{2}$)

Signed lower right: *TC/1859*

Provenance: Henry Probasco (Cincinnati) Sale, New York, April 18, 1887, no. 45, $3,000.00.

References: Edward E. Hale, *G.T.T.; or The Wonderful Adventures of a Pullman,* Boston, Roberts Brothers, 1877, p. 43; Walters cat., 1893, p. 93, no. 151; Stranahan, p. 292; George Boas, *Courbet and the naturalistic movement.* Baltimore, Johns Hopkins Press, 1938, p. 50; George Boas, "Courbet and the naturalistic movement," *Parnassus* 10 (April 1938): 10–11 (illus. p. 11); Charles Sterling and Margaretta M. Salinger, *French paintings II, the Metropolitan Museum of Art.* New York, 1966, pp. 147–48; Jane Van Nimmen et al. *Thomas Couture: paintings and drawings in American collections.* College Park, University of Maryland, 1970, pp. 50, 58.

104. Judge Going to Court

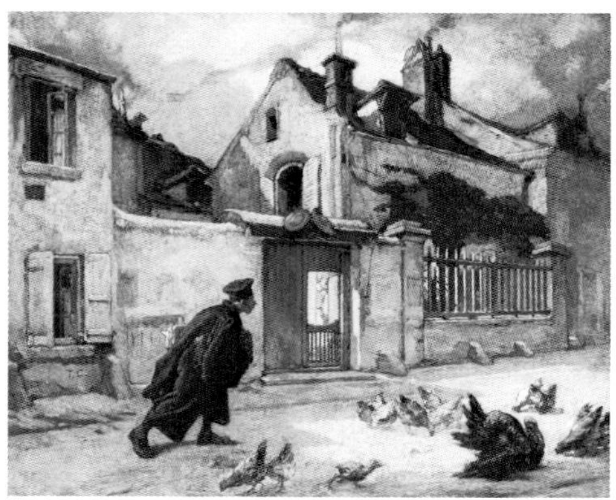

37.1204 c.1860

A judge in cap and gown, stooping because of the weight of the tomes which he carries under each arm, trudges along a village street. In his path a turkey-cock and a flock of fowl peck for food in the street. A pair of shields suspended above the gate leading into a yard denote the ownership of the house in the background as that of a notary. In this choice of a contemporary subject Couture appears to have followed the precedent of Daumier. The painting also demonstrates the artist's technique of emphasizing the freshness of his colors by utilizing exposed areas of the white, primed canvas.

Reputedly a larger version of this composition, *The Belated Judge,* oil on canvas, .584 x .725, dated 1867, belongs to the descendants of Robert Hoe of New York. In the Musée Haubergier, Senlis, there is a study, *Rentrant de l'audience,* showing the same scene without the fowl in the foreground. Illustrated in Bertauts-Couture, *Thomas Couture: 1815-1879; sa vie, son oeuvre, son caractère, ses idées, sa méthode, par lui-même et par son petit-fils,* Paris, 1932, opposite p. 113, is a drawing inscribed *Senlis* and dated *1860,* in which the fowl are limited to a cock and a hen. Related drawings include *Lawyer on his Way to Court* in the Metropolitan Museum of Art, New York, Inv. 60.142.14, chalk on beige paper mounted on cardboard (.318 x .478), which shows two figures of the judge, one with books under both arms, and the other with books under one arm only, as well as the outlines of the garden gate, and *A Lawyer* in the Santa Barbara Museum, Inv. 59.45, charcoal, .178 x .3, which repeats the figure with the books under one arm in the New York drawing.

Support: Canvas, .38 x .462 (15″ x 18$\frac{3}{16}$″)

Signed at left beneath the windowsill: *T. C.*

Provenance: Unknown. The picture was formerly erroneously listed as coming from the Barbedienne Collection sold in Paris, 1892. No record of the painting appears in the catalogues of William and Henry Walters published as late as 1909. Presumably the picture was acquired subsequently by Henry Walters.

Exhibitions: "Exposition Thomas Couture," Palais de l'Industrie, Paris, 1880, no. 116 (listed as belonging to the family of the artist) "Exposition des Oeuvres de Thomas Couture," Galerie Levesque, Paris, 1913(?); "From David to Courbet," Detroit Institute of Arts, 1950, p. 98, illus.; "From Ingres to Gauguin," Baltimore Museum of Art, 1951, no. 81, illus.; "An Exhibition of Treasures of the Walters Art Gallery," Wildenstein and Co., New York, 1967, no. 32; "Small Paintings from Famous Collections," The Taft Museum, Cincinnati, Ohio, 1981, pp. 40, 41 (illus.).

References: Roger-Ballu, *Catalogue des oeuvres de Th. Couture exposées au Palais de l'Industrie.* Paris, A. Quantin, 1880, p. 37, no. 116; Georges Bertauts-Couture, *Thomas Couture, 1815–1879; sa vie, son oeuvre, son caractère, ses idées, sa méthode, par lui-même et par son petit-fils.* Paris, Le Garrec, 1932, p. 37; Jane Van Nimmen et al., *Thomas Couture: Paintings and Drawings in American Collections.* College Park, University of Maryland, 1970, pp. 50, 58–59; Albert Boime, *Thomas Couture and the eclectic vision.* New Haven, Yale University Press, 1980, p. 328, illus. IX.41.

Jean-Léon Gérôme

French: Vesoul, 1824 - Paris, 1904

In painting historical and ethnographic subjects, Gérôme assiduously strove for an appearance of verisimilitude and he has therefore been classified as an objective realist. His imaginative and frequently brilliant compositions were widely circulated as photogravures. Through his own achievements as well as through the promotional activities of Adolphe Goupil, his dealer, publisher and father-in-law, Gérôme emerged as one of the most successful artists of the third quarter of the century. He was fated, however, to outlive the vogue for his art, and, until recently, historians have tended to neglect Gérôme's contributions to nineteenth–century imagery and to forget his associations with such contemporaries as Degas and Manet. Instead they have emphasized his vociferous opposition to Impressionism in his later years.

Gérôme, the son of a Vesoul silversmith, received his initial four years of training in the studio of Paul Delaroche. When his teacher closed his studio and withdrew to Rome in 1843, Gérôme accompanied him for a year. Returning to Paris in 1845, he briefly enrolled as a pupil of Charles Gleyre, and, together with several fellow students, notably J. L. Hamon, H. P. Picou, A. M. F. Jobbé-Duval, and A. Toulmouche, initiated the Néo-grec movement, specializing in sentimental genre subjects rendered in classical guise. His major work in this vein, *The Cock Fight* of 1846, was extravagantly praised by Théophile Gautier at the Salon of 1847. Thus launched on a successful career, Gérôme received a number of important commissions for portraits and decorative programs in the following decade, culminating in *The Age of Augustus, the Birth of Christ.* Shown with this colossal neoclassical allegory at the 1855 Salon was a small painting, *Recreation in a Camp, Souvenir of Moldavia,* his earliest exercise in realistic genre.

Gérôme was an inveterate traveler. His first trip to the East had been in 1854, when he visited Greece and Turkey with the actor F. J. E. Got. In preparation for *The Age of Augustus,* he traveled through the Balkans, and in 1856 went to Egypt, Constantinople, and French North Africa. These journeys and subsequent trips to the Near East, including those of 1867, 1869, 1875, and 1881, resulted in a number of paintings of oriental subjects, some of which were highly romantic, whereas others have proven to be of significant ethnographic value.

He also altered his treatment of historical subjects, replacing the rather light-hearted classicism of the Néo-grecs with a more convincing, archeologically accurate approach, first apparent in *Ave Caesar, Morituri Te Salutant,* 1859 (Yale University Art Gallery). Following the precedent of his teacher Delaroche, he also drew subjects from French history, particularly from the seventeenth century, which he rendered with the same sense of accuracy.

A regular and successful exhibitor at the Paris salons and at the international expositions, Gérôme was the recipient of most official honors, becoming a Chevalier of the Legion of Honor in 1855, an Officier in 1867, and a Commandeur in 1878, and a member of the Institut in 1865. In 1863 he was appointed one of three professors of painting at the Ecole des Beaux-Arts, a position in which he exerted considerable influence not only on his French pupils but on many foreigners, notably Americans, who preferred his instruction.

In his later years, particularly after 1878, Gérôme turned increasingly to sculpture rather than painting, producing marble, bronze, and chryselephantine works.

105. The Duel after the Masquerade

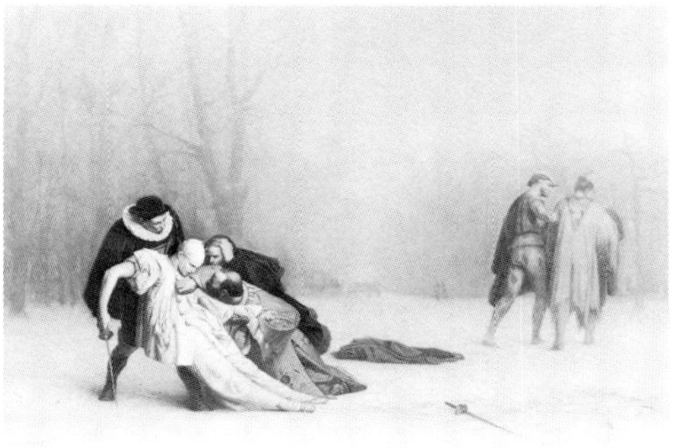

37.51 after 1857

The wintry scene is set at daybreak in the Bois de Boulogne, Paris, with the duellists and their attendants still dressed in their costumes for a masquerade ball. Mortally wounded, Pierrot succumbs in the arms of the Duc de Guise. The Venetian Doge examines the victim's chest wound, while Domino grasps his head in dismay. To the right, the victor, an American Indian, departs with Harlequin. Discernible through the lurid morning mists are the waiting cabs of the protagonists.

This painting is a replica of *Suite d'un bal masqué* (.5 x .72) painted for the Duc d'Aumale in 1857 and now in Chantilly (Inv. 258). It differs slightly from the earlier work in the rendering of the background and in the direction in which Harlequin's head is facing. Another replica (.68 x .99), commissioned in 1859 by Prince Alexander of Russia, is now in the Hermitage, Leningrad.

The subject has been associated with an actual duel that took place in the winter of 1856–57 between Deluns-Montaud and Symphorien-Casimir-Joseph Boittelle (Coleman A. Parson's "The Wintry Duel: A Victorian Import," *Victorian Studies,* London, 1959. 2: 317–23) and also draws on French pantomime (Francis Haskell, "The Sad Clown: Some Notes on a 19th–century Myth," *French 19th–century Literature and Poetry,* Manchester, 1972, pp. 2–16). Its possible precedents in French painting, P. R. Vigneron's *Les suites d'un bal,* 1822, Musée Massey, Tarbes, and Thomas Couture's *Duel After The Ball,* 1857, Wallace Collection, London, are discussed by Gerald M. Ackerman in *Jean-Léon Gérôme,* Dayton Art Institute, Dayton, 1972, no. 7, pp. 40–41.

This cabinet painting can also be related to the small paintings of historical subjects of Gérôme's master Paul Delaroche, who painted *After the Ball* in 1827 and *The Assassination of the Duke of Guise* in 1834.

The initial painting, rather than the Walters replica, was reproduced in lithograph by A. Sirony (published by E. Gambart, London) in 1859 and later, in photogravure, by Goupil et Cie. One of these reproductions inspired Thomas Nast's satire, *A Duel after a Spat,* published in *Harper's Weekly,* July 17, 1869.

Alternative titles: *Duel after the Ball; Le Duel après le bal masqué.*

Support: Canvas, .391 x .563 (15⅜" x 22⅛")

Provenance: William T. Walters paid $2,500.00 for the picture at the National Academy of Design, New York, October 1859.

Signed lower left: *J. L. GEROME*

Marks: Stretcher stenciled: *693;* Canvas stenciled: *2 Exposition de 1849 . . . . / Premières Medailles . . . . / . . . GENIE DES ARTS . . . HARO/HARO FILS Succ: Chimiste Fab*[r] *de COULEURS FINES/Restaurateur & TABLEAUX . . . . Nouveau Systèm/20 Rue Bonaparte E St G., Paris.*

Condition: Discolored varnishes removed in 1943. Picture lined with wax adhesive in 1958.

Exhibitions: "Collection of English and French Paintings," Second Annual Exhibition, National Academy of Design, New York, 1859; "From Ingres to Gauguin," The Baltimore Museum of Art, 1951, no. 88; "The Two Sides of a Medal," Detroit Institute of Arts, 1954; "Harlequin and the Arts," Denver Art Museum, 1957; "Masks and Masquerades," Isaac Delgado Museum of Art, New Orleans, 1968, no. 208; "Jean-Léon Gérôme," The Dayton Art Institute, The Minneapolis Institute of Arts, The Walters Art Gallery, 1972–73, no. 7.

References: Walters cat., 1878, p. 29, and subsequent Walters catalogues; Strahan, 1: 44 (illus.), 87–88; Mathews, p. 6; Fanny Field Hering, *Gérôme; the life and works of Jean Léon Gérôme.* New York, Cassell, 1892, pp. 68, 75; Lamb, p. 250; Stranahan, pp. 318–19; Reizenstein, p. 550 (illus.); John Canaday, "From Salon to cellar—and back?" *Horizon* 2, no. 4 (March 1960): 57, 68 (illus.); Frank A. Trapp, "An aged lion returns: Jean-Léon Gérôme," *Burlington magazine* 115 (1973): 347, fig. 114; Ruth K. Meyer, "Jean-Léon Gérôme: the role of subject-matter and the importance of formalized composition," *Arts magazine* 47 (February 1973): 31 (illus.); Albert Boime, *Thomas Couture and the eclectic vision,* New Haven, Yale University Press, 1980, p. 313, fig. IX 23; John Canaday, *What is Art?* New York, Alfred A. Knopf, 1980, p. 75 (illus.); E. A. Carmean, *Picasso and The Saltimbanques,* Washington, D.C., National Gallery of Art, 1980, p. 23, illus. 8.

106. The Death of Caesar

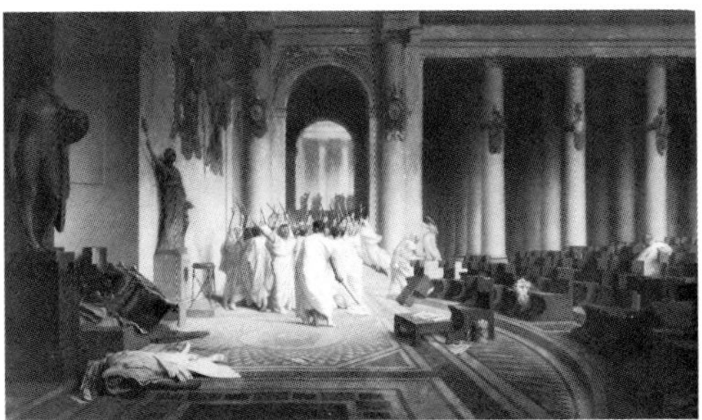

37.884 1859

The assassination of Julius Caesar on the Ides of March, 44 B.C., as narrated in Plutarch, *Brutus,* XIV-XVIII, is the subject of this painting. The setting is the dimly lighted curia of the Theater of Pompey, Rome. Flanking a dais on the left wall are statues of Pompey and Roma. It is characteristic of Gérôme that he should depict, not the incident itself, but its immediate aftermath. The body of the emperor lies beside the blood-smeared base of the statue of Pompey. An overturned chair and scattered scroll petitions are suggestive of the sequence of events. A lone senator, seated on the right, is apparently overcome by the deed, while the assassins depart brandishing their swords. Beyond an archway still other figures can be seen fleeing from the scene.

The reconstruction of the interior is extraordinarily convincing and is probably based on various literary and archeological sources. Such details as trophies displayed on the columns occur in J.A. Léveil's engraving of "L'interieur d'une basilique" published in Charles Dezobry's *Rome au siècle d'Auguste,* Paris, 1846, plate VIII, a publication Gérôme is known to have consulted. In "The Second Empire, Art in France under Napoleon III," Philadelphia, 1978, pp. 308–09, Gerald Ackerman is cited as listing Vicenzo Camuccino's *The Death of Caesar* (1798) as a probable source for this composition.

The figure of the dead Caesar lying beside the base of the statue first appeared in *César,* a large painting (2.185 x 3.175) shown at the Salon of 1859 and later acquired by the Corcoran Gallery, Washington, D.C. (now lost). An engraving (.11 x .19) of this work was published in Anatole France's *Sonnets et eaux-fortes* (edited by Philippe Burty) Paris, 1867, (Henri Béraldi, *Les graveurs du XIX siècle,* Paris, vol. 7, p. 103, no. 3). A drawing for the engraving (.147 x .32) is in the David Daniels collection, New York. Either a preliminary study or the unfinished Walters picture was seen in 1858 in Gérôme's studio by Théophile Gautier ("A travers les ateliers," *L'Artiste* 14 (May 16, 1858): 177).

The Death of Caesar was one of Gérôme's most widely acclaimed compositions. That the foreshortened figure of the dead Caesar served as an inspiration for Edouard Manet's *Dead Toreador* (National Gallery of Art, Washington, D.C.) was first noted by Bates Lowry. *The Death of Caesar* also inspired such diverse works as Thomas Nast's *The Death of the Bogus Caesar,* a political satire on Andrew Johnson's termination of the presidency published in *Harper's Weekly,* Spring 1869, and *Flight and Pursuit* painted by William Rimmer in 1872, now in the Museum of Fine Arts, Boston.

Support: Canvas, .855 x 1.455 (33$\frac{11}{16}$" x 57$\frac{5}{16}$")

Signed and dated lower left: *J.L. GEROME MDCCCLIX* [last two digits abraded]

Condition: Lined in 1971.

Provenance: M. J. Allard; John Taylor Johnston Sale, New York, 1876, no. 188; John Jacob Astor; Boussod Veladon et Cie; James B. Haggin et al. Sale, New York, April 5, 1917, no. 148, $7,200.00.

Exhibitions: Exposition Universelle, Paris, 1867; Fifth Annual Exhibition of the Yale School of Fine Arts, New Haven, 1872, no. 12; "Jean-Léon Gérôme," The Dayton Art Institute, The Minneapolis Institute of Arts, The Walters Art Gallery, 1972–73, no. 20; "The Second Empire, 1852–1870," Philadelphia, Detroit, Paris, 1978–79, no. VI-60.

References: Théophile Gautier, "A travers les ateliers," *L'Artiste* 14 (1858): 177; "Bulletin bibliographique, photographies," *GBA* 8 (1860): 386; A. Arago, *Oeuvres choisis de J.L. Gérôme.* Paris, Goupil, n.d., plate 14. Strahan, 2: 3–5; Edward Strahan, ed., *Gérôme; a collection of the works of J.L. Gérôme in one hundred photogravures.* 10 sections. New York, Samuel L. Hall, 1881–83. section 9, plate 5; Champlin and Perkins, 2: 129;

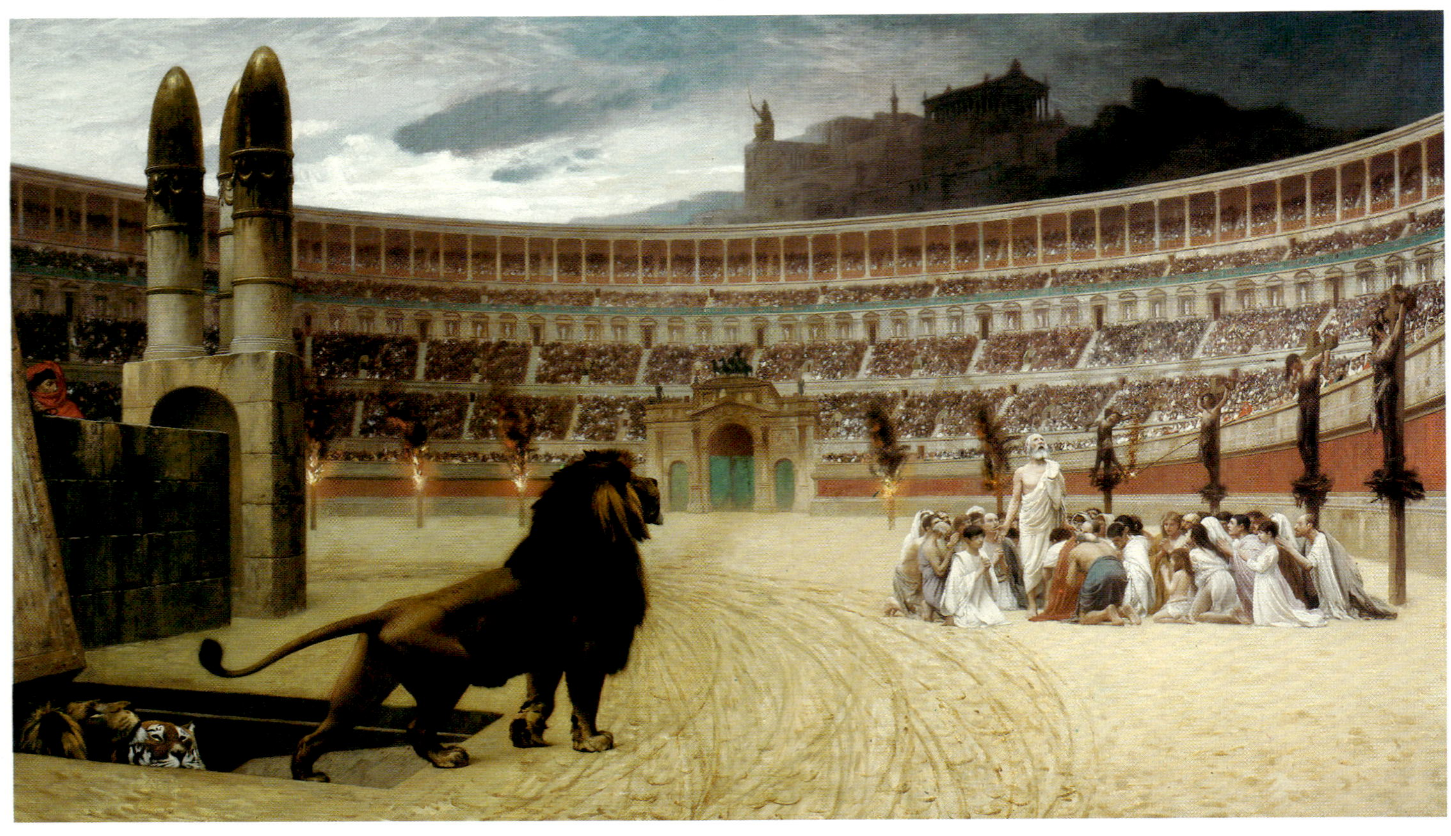

Gérôme *The Christian Martyrs' Last Prayer,* no. 108

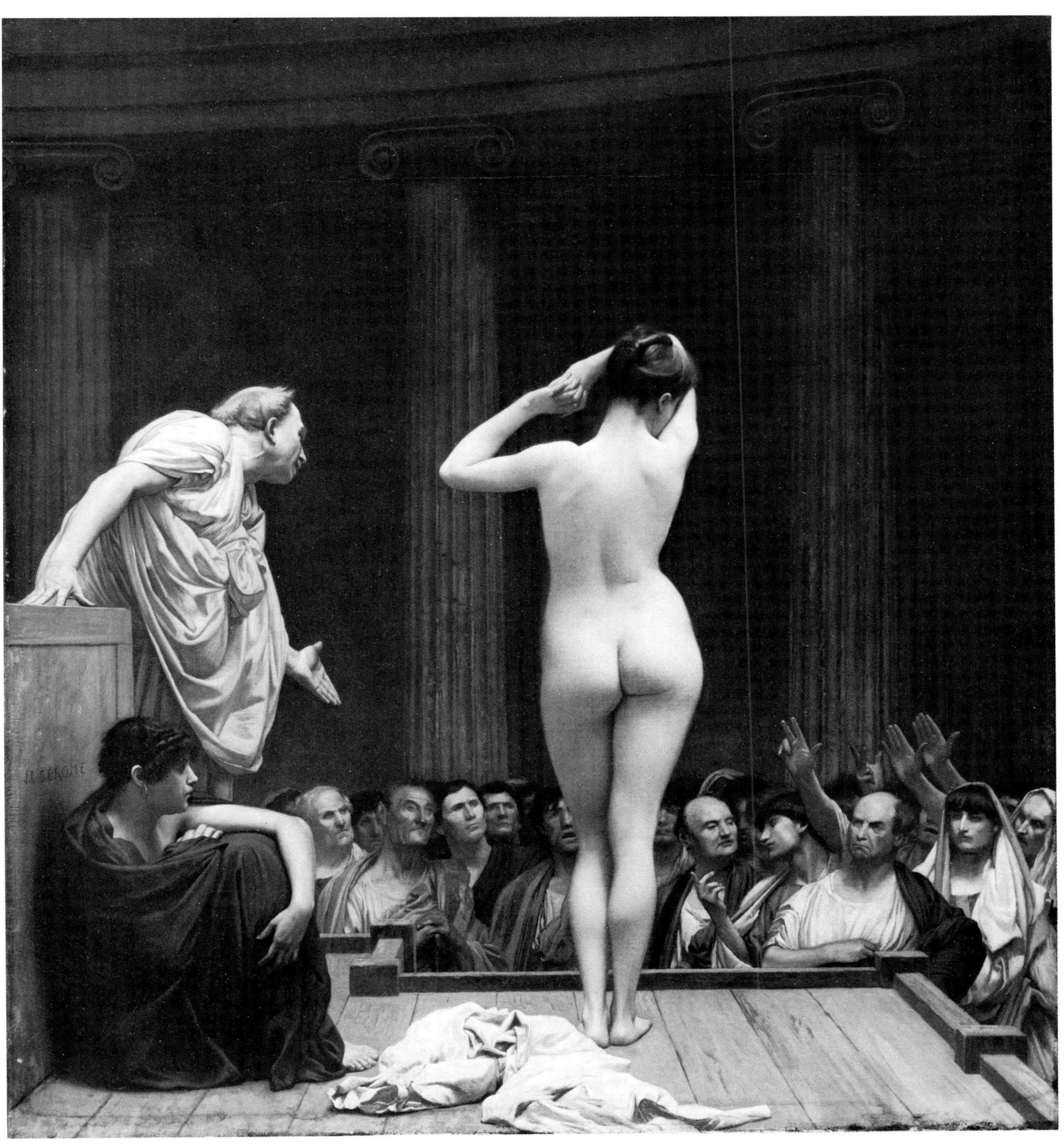

Gérôme *Roman Slave Market,* no. 111

Cook, 1: 30–31; Fanny Field Hering, *Gérôme; the life and works of Jean Léon Gérôme.* New York, Cassell, 1892. pp. 88 (illus.) , 92, 115–16; Dorothy Weir Young, *The life and letters of J. Alden Weir.* New Haven, Yale University Press, 1960. p. 45; "Muse or ego; Salon and independent artists of the 1880's", 75th anniversary exhibition, Pomona College Gallery, Claremont, Calif., 1963, p. 33 (no. 33 is a study for the Walters painting); Gerald M. Ackerman, "Gérôme and Manet," *GBA* 6th per. 70 (1967): 165–68, fig. 3; Mary Lee Bennett and Agnes Mongan, *Selections from the drawing collection of David Daniels.* Cambridge, Mass., 1968. p. 9, no. 43; Albert Boime, "Jean-Léon Gérôme, Henri Rousseau's *Sleeping Gypsy* and the Academic Legacy," *Art quarterly* 34 (1971): 4, 17, fig. 2; Ruth K. Meyer, "Jean-Léon Gérôme: the role of subject-matter and the importance of formalized composition," *Arts magazine* 47 (February 1973): 33 (illus.), 34; James Harding, *Artistes pompiers, French Academic Art in the 19th century,* London, Academy Editions, 1979, p. 42; Brown University, Department of Art. "Edouard Manet and the *Execution of Maximilian.*" Exhibition catalogue, 1981. pp. 33, 146 (illus.) , 215.

107. Diogenes

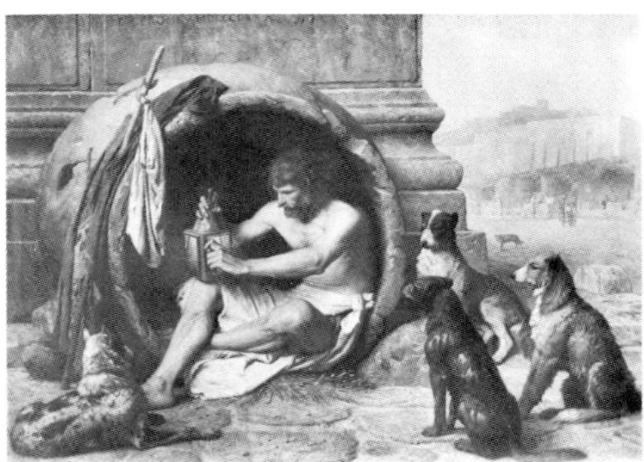

37.131 1860

Diogenes (404–323 B.C.) is shown with his attributes, the staff and wallet (Diogenes Laertius, *Lives of Eminent Philosophers,* Loeb Classical Library, 2:25), seated in his abode, the tub, in the Metroön, Athens, lighting the lamp in daylight with which he was to search for an honest man. Surrounding him are the dogs, his companions in austerity, and the emblems of his "Cynic" philosophy that derives its name from the Greek word for "dog."

This painting differs from a preliminary oil sketch (.19 x .254) formerly belonging to Pierce Rice, Washington, D.C., both in the background and in the placement of the dogs. Also, in the Walters painting the tub is clearly depicted as having been mended, a reference to a passage in Juvenal, *Satire IV,* 305–310. Gérôme's composition probably inspired the 1885 *Diogenes in a Barrel* of Julian Russell Story (Parke-Bernet Sale, New York, October 10, 1973, no. 94).

Support: Linen, .74 x .999 ($29\frac{1}{2}$" x $39\frac{15}{16}$")

Signed and dated upper left: *J. L. GEROME MDCCLX*

Condition: Lined in 1967.

Provenance: Acquired at August Belmont Sale, New York, November 12, 1872, no. 31.

Exhibitions: "Exposition universelle de Besançon," Besançon, 1860 (see "Correspondence de Besançon," *GBA* 8 (1860) : 59) ; "Exhibition for the Benefit of the U. S. Sanitary Commission," The Belmont Gallery, New York, 1864, no. 51; "Hommage à Baudelaire," University of Maryland, College Park, 1968, p. 34, plate 69; "Jean-Léon Gérôme," The Dayton Art Institute, The Minneapolis Institute of Arts, The Walters Art Gallery, 1972–73, no. 11.

References: A. Arago, *Oeuvres choisis de J.L. Gérôme.* Paris, Goupil, n.d. plate 18; Strahan, 1: 85 (illus.), 88; Walters cat., 1878, p. 6, and subsequent Walters catalogues; Clement and Hutton, 1: 290; Edward Strahan, ed. *Gérôme; a collection of the works of J.L. Gérôme in one hundred photogravures.* 10 sections. New York, Samuel L. Hall, 1881–83. section 9, plate 3; Mathews, p. 7; Lamb, p. 250; Gerald M. Ackerman, "Gérôme and Manet," *GBA* 6th pér. 70 (1967): 163–76; Albert Boime, "Thomas Nast and French art," *American art journal* 4(1972): 43–65; Ruth K. Meyer, "Jean-Léon Gérôme: the role of subject-matter and the importance of formalized composition," *Arts magazine* 47 (February 1973): 31 (illus.), 32.

108. The Christian Martyrs' Last Prayer

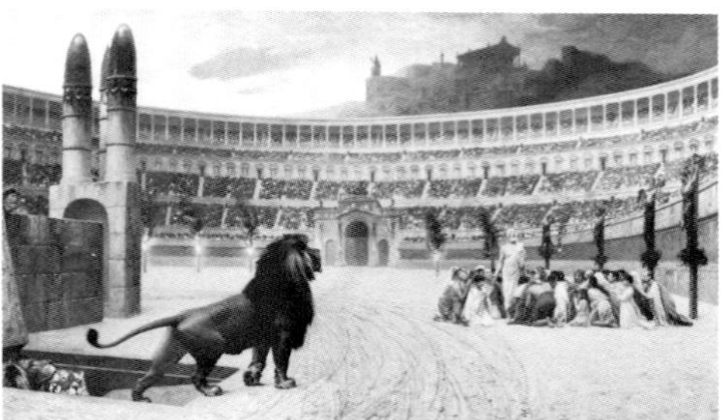

37.113 1863–1883

Gérôme has illustrated the dramatic moment at which the animals appear before the public. In the left foreground a fearsome lion has emerged from a subterranean chamber, soon to be followed by another lion and a tiger. To the right Christians of various ages are huddled in prayer around a patriarchal figure. Further back other Christians, bound to crosses and smeared with pitch, are being burned, a method of execution practiced during Nero's reign.

In a letter to William Walters, July 15, 1883, Gérôme identified the architectural setting as that of the Circus Maximus, Rome, noting such details as the *meta,* the brazen-capped goal posts, and the chariot tracks in the dirt. However, the architecture resembles far more closely that to be seen in the artist's depictions of the Colosseum, as in the *Ave Caesar, Morituri Te Salutant,* 1859, Yale University Art Gallery, and the *Pollice Verso,* 1874, Phoenix Art Museum, than it does the structures in his other representation of the Circus Maximus, *The Chariot Race,* 1866–76, George F. Harding Museum, Chicago. In the latter considerable archeological erudition is displayed. In the background of the Walters picture a citadel, topped by a temple and a colossal statue, is silhouetted against the evening sky.

In his 1883 letter, Gérôme tells how he reworked the composition three times over twenty years. An oil sketch (.9 x 1.15) on the Paris art market in 1973 shows an early stage in the evolution of the composition in which the goal posts are not rounded but pointed as in most early archeological publications, and the colossal statue on the citadel is of a standing rather than a seated deity. A sketch for a praying male martyr, *Chrétien livré aux bêtes,* was published in Charles Timball, "Gérôme, étude biographique," *Gazette des beaux-arts,* 2d pér. 14(1876): 228 (illus.) , 346. William Macleod records that Gérôme consulted the noted *animalier,* Antoine-Louis Barye, regarding the representation of the beasts.

In comparing this work to later representations of the subject such as Eugène Romain Thirion's *Les martyrs au cirque* (Armand Silvestre, *Galerie Durand-Ruel,* Paris, 1873, vol. 4, plate CXCIV), it becomes evident that Gérôme relied upon his masterly composition for dramatic effect, rather than on the exploitation of the savagery of the subject. The composition was later utilized by Charles Dana Gibson in "America's Tribute," *Life* (January 1980): 138–39.

Alternative title: *The Last Prayer.*

Support: Canvas, .879 x 1.501 ($34\frac{5}{8}$" x $59\frac{1}{16}$")

Signed: *J. L. GEROME*

Condition: Lined in 1967.

Provenance: The painting was commissioned in 1863 and received by W. T. Walters in 1883.

Exhibitions: "Jean-Léon Gérôme," The Dayton Art Institute, The Minneapolis Institute of Arts, The Walters Art Gallery, 1972–73, no. 36; "Romans and Barbarians," The Museum of Fine Arts, Boston, 1976–77, no. 282.

References: William Macleod, "The public and private collections," *American art review* 1 (1880): 18; Walters cat., 1884, no. 63, and subsequent Walters catalogues; Champlin and Perkins, 2: 129; Mathews, p. 6; Fanny Field Hering, *Gérôme; the life and works of Jean Léon Gérôme.* New York, Cassell, 1892. p. 8 (illus.), 242–43; Lamb, p. 250; Stranahan, p. 314; Reizenstein, pp. 552 (illus.), 554–55; Albert Boime, "Jean-Léon Gérôme, Henri Rousseau's *Sleeping Gypsy,* and the Academic Legacy," *Art quarterly* 34 (Spring 1971): 13–14; Ruth K. Meyer, "Jean-Léon Gérôme: the role of subject-matter and the importance of formalized composition," *Arts magazine* 47 (February 1973): 34; W. R. Johnston, "Gérôme—an archaeologist?" *BWAG* 25, no. 7 (April 1973): 1–4, illus. p. 1.

109. On the Desert

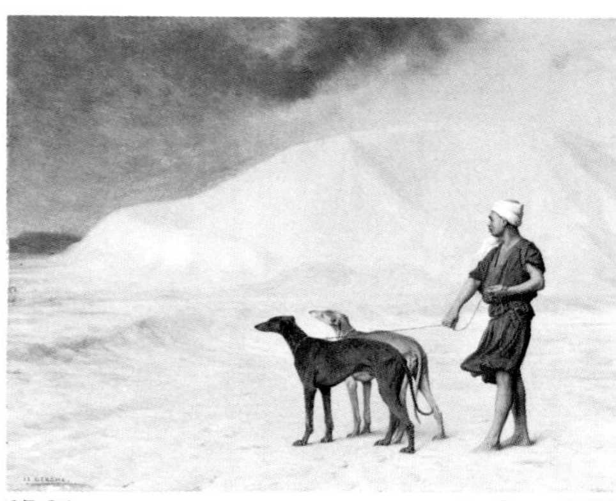

37.34 before 1867

Two whippets are being walked by a Nubian in a barren wind-swept desert. The small meticulously painted panel was apparently commissioned by W.T. Walters and altered at his request. On September 9, 1867, G.A. Lucas saw this painting at Goupil et Cie, and noted a change in the rendering of one of the dogs. Walters recorded in his early catalogues the artist's particular satisfaction with this picture. The theme of this picture was also adopted by Henri Regnault in *Arabe dans la montagne tenant en laisse deux levriers* (*Gazette des Beaux Arts* 2nd pér. 25 (1882) : 431, illus.) .

Alternative titles: *Leash of Hounds; Relais de chiens dans le désert.*

Support: Panel, .212 x .269 (8⅜" x 10⁹⁄₁₆")

Signed lower left: *J.L. GEROME*

Provenance: Purchased from the artist by W. T. Walters in 1867 (Lucas 2: 249) .

Exhibitions: "Jéan-Léon Gérôme," Dayton Art Institute, The Minneapolis Institute of Arts, The Walters Art Gallery, 1972–73, no. 19.

References: A. Arago, *Oeuvres choisis de J.L. Gérôme,* Paris, Goupil, n.d. plate 39; Walters cat., 1878, p. 35, and subsequent Walters catalogues; Stranahan, 1: 84 (with engraving by F. Faust), 88; Edward Strahan, ed., *Gérôme; a collection of the works of J.L. Gérôme in one hundred photogravures.* 10 sections. New York, Samuel L. Hall, 1881–83. section 4, plate 2; Champlin and Perkins, 2: 129; Lamb, p. 250; Stranahan, pp. 318–19.

110. Bashi-Bazouk Singing

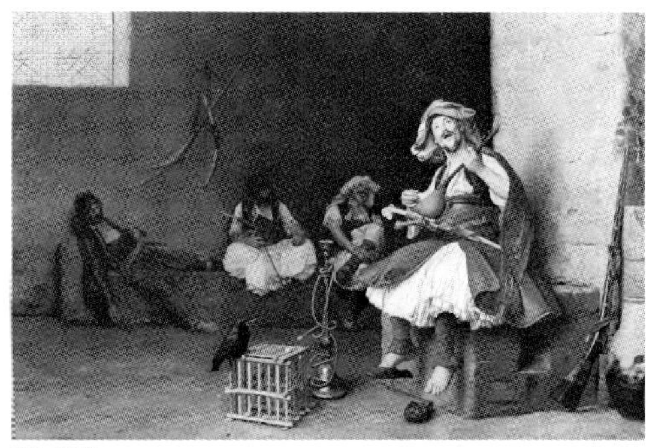

37.883

An Arnaut, an Albanian soldier, is seated with his hookah and pet ravens playing an oud and singing. Behind him are three other men, all Bashi-Bazouks, members of the Ottoman Empire's irregular troops noted for their ferocity. A replica drawing of the composition is located in the Sterling and Francine Clark Art Institute, Williamstown, Massachusetts.

Alternative title: *Arnaut Singing.*

Support: Canvas, .463 x .66 (18³⁄₁₆" x 26")

Signed lower right: *J. L. GEROME*

Provenance: Goupil et Cie., Paris; Acquired at the James B. Haggin et al. Sale, New York, 1917, no. 40, $1,400.00, R. H. Lorenz agent.

Exhibitions: "Jean-Léon Gérôme," The Dayton Art Institute, The Minneapolis Institute of Arts, The Walters Art Gallery, 1972–73, no. 10; "Americans Abroad, Painters of the Victorian Era," San Jose Museum of Art, San Jose, Cal., 1975–76.

References: Edward Strahan, ed., *Gérôme; a collection of the works of J.L. Gérôme in one hundred photogravures.* 10 sections. New York, Samuel L. Hall, 1881–83. section 6, plate 5; Gerald M. Ackerman, "Thomas Eakins and his Parisian masters, Gérôme and Bonnat," *GBA* 6th pér. 72 (1969): 255, fig. 24, no. 10.

111. A Roman Slave Market

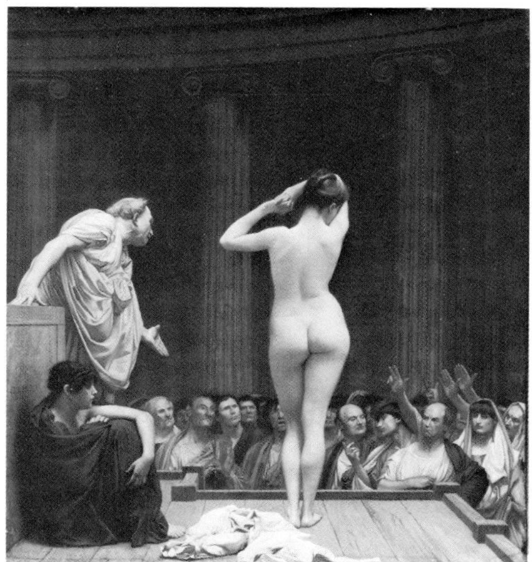

37.885 c.1884

Gérôme's slave-market subjects afforded him the opportunity to produce both figurative studies of sensual beauty and interesting exercises in physiognomy. Usually he depicted such subjects in Near Eastern settings, but in this instance he chose ancient Rome.

The pose of the slave, seen from the back, is reminiscent of that found in the *Phryne before the Tribunal,* Gérôme's masterpiece of 1861 (Hamburger Kunsthalle, Inv. 1910). The auctioneer is leaning forward to exhort the bidders, an adroit illustration of Gérôme's masterly foreshortening. The Walters picture was apparently a pendant for a larger painting shown at the 1884 Salon, *Le marché d'esclave* (.92 x .74) bought by Grand Duke Serge of Russia (The Hermitage, Leningrad). In the latter, approximately the same scene as in the Walters picture is portrayed frontally. Most of the protagonists are identical in both pictures, although shown from the opposite vantage point.

Support: Canvas, 64.1 x 56.9 (25³⁄₁₆" x 22⅜")

Condition: Strips of canvas four inches wide have been added to the upper and left sides, suggesting that Gérôme expanded the composition.

Provenance: Boussod Valadon et Cie; James B. Haggin et al. Sale, as *Sale of Circassian Slave,* New York, 1917, no. 119, $3,000.00.

Exhibitions: "The Nude in Painting," Wildenstein & Co., New York, 1956, no. 25. "Fortuny and his Circle," Walters Art Gallery, Baltimore, 1970, no. 27; "Jean-Léon Gérôme," The Dayton Art Institute, The Minneapolis Institute of Arts, The Walters Art Gallery, 1972–73, no. 37; "Paris-New York: a continuing romance," Wildenstein and Co., New York, 1977, no. 68.

References: Fanny Field Hering, *Gérôme; the life and works of Jean Léon Gérôme.* New York, Cassell, 1892, p. 244; Frederic Masson, "J.-L. Gérôme," *Les Arts* 3, no. 26 (1904): 17 (illus.); W. R. Johnston, "Roman slave market," *BWAG* 22, no. 6 (March 1970): 1–2, illus.; Joachim Heusinger von Waldegg, "Jean-Léon Gérômes 'Phryne vor den Richtern'," *Jahrbuch der Hamburger Kunstsammlungen* 17 (1972): 129 (fig. 6), 130; Ruth K. Meyer, "Jean Léon Gérôme: the role of subject-matter and the importance of formalized composition," *Arts Magazine* 47 (February 1973) : 33.

Hugues Merle

French: Saint-Marcellin (Isère), 1823 - Paris, 1881

Merle trained under Léon Cogniet at the Ecole des Beaux-Arts and made his debut at the 1847 Salon. He exhibited consistently at the salons from 1847 to 1880, winning a second-class medal in 1861, with *rappel* in 1863, and being appointed Chevalier of the Legion of Honor in 1866. As a painter of life-size genre and historical subjects, he was regarded as a rival to W. Bouguereau, with whom he shared a sentimental approach and a highly finished academic style (C. H. Stranahan, *A History of French Painting,* New York, 1893, p. 398). Critics praised his correct drawing but occasionally questioned his lachrymose compositions and weak palette (Jules Clarétie, *L'Art et les artistes français contemporains,* Paris, 1876, p. 153). He was also a fashionable portraitist.

Major works included *Rebecca's Adieus to Lady Rowena* (Salon of 1855) from Walter Scott's *Ivanhoe; The Beggar Woman* (Salon of 1861) and *The Assassination of Henry III* (Salon of 1863) both bought by the State; and *Charlotte Corday* (Salon of 1878). Merle's principal patron was probably the Bonapartist Duc de Morny, who acquired his *The First Thorns of Knowledge,* and for whom he painted *Portraits of the Sons of the Duc de Morny* (Salon of 1865). Evidently he also had an extensive clientele in the United States, since Strahan could cite as many as fifty-two works by Merle in American collections in 1878–79.

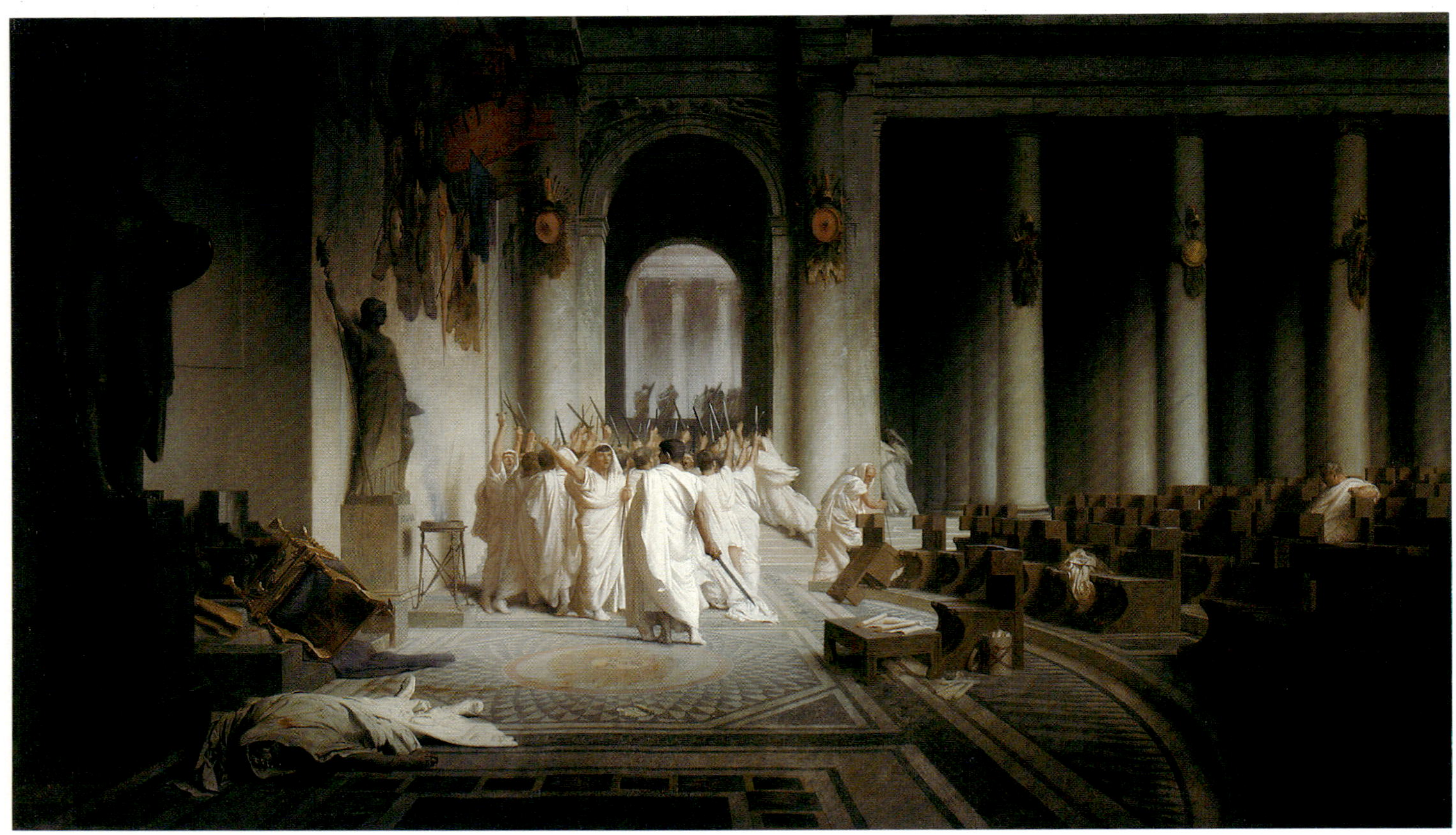

Gérôme *Death of Caesar,* no. 106

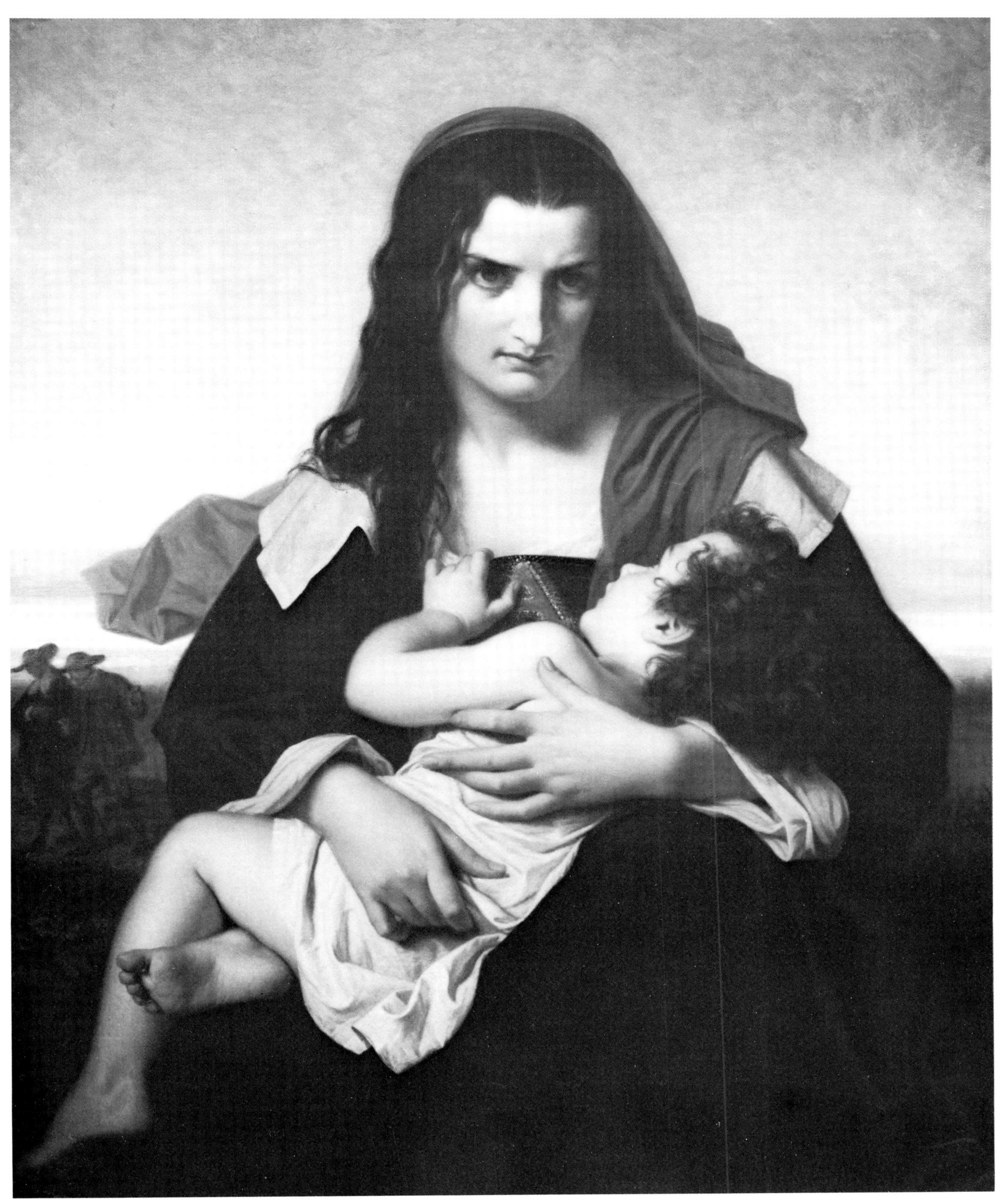

Merle *The Scarlet Letter,* no. 112

112. The Scarlet Letter

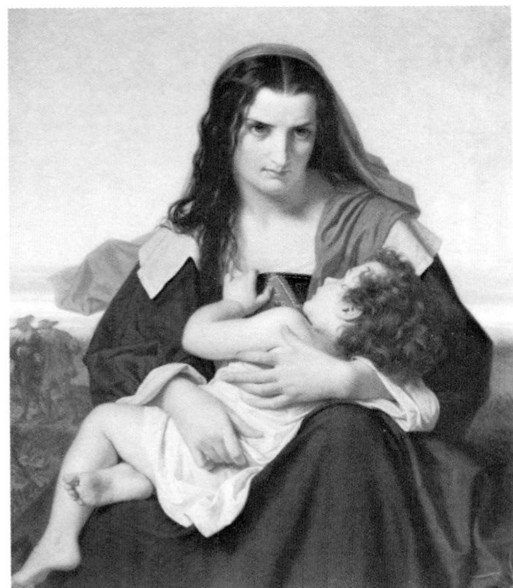

37.172 1861

Portrayed is a scene from Nathaniel Hawthorne's novel *The Scarlet Letter* published in English in 1850 and translated into French in 1853. The setting is Puritan Boston. An anguished Hester Prynne clutches her illegitimate daughter Pearl to her bosom. The infant fingers the embroidered scarlet A, the symbol of her mother's shame. Visible in the background are two Puritans passing by, one of whom points to Hester and Pearl.

It is noted in the 1878 W. T. Walters Collection catalogue that Hawthorne regarded this painting as the finest illustration of his story. A replica in oils of this composition (.245 x .187) was acquired by G. A. Lucas, the advisor to W. T. Walters in Paris, and is now in a private collection in Baltimore.

Alternative title: *Hester et Perle*

Support: Finely woven fabric, 1 x .81 (39⅜" x 31⅞")

Signed lower right: *HUGUES MERLE*

Condition: Lined before 1934.

Provenance: The painting was commissioned by W. T. Walters on November 1, 1859. On March 9, 1861, George A. Lucas, acting on behalf of W. T. Walters, paid Merle 2,000 francs for it.

Exhibitions: Paris, Salon of 1861; "The Second Empire," Philadelphia, Detroit, Paris, 1978–79, no. 254.

References: Walters cat., 1878, p. 19, and subsequent Walters catalogues; Strahan, 1: 94; Clement and Hutton, 2: 111; Emile Bellier de la Chavignerie and Louis Auvray, *Dictionnaire général des artistes de l'école française*. 2 vols. Paris, Renouard, 1882–1885, 2: 74; Lamb, p. 253; Reizenstein, p. 556; Lucas, 2: 104, 111.

Paul-Jacques-Aimé Baudry

French: La Roche-sur-Yon (Vendée), 1828 - Paris, 1886

Baudry was a prominent decorative painter and accomplished portraitist during the Second Empire and early Third Republic.

Of rural background, he trained with a local artist, Antoine Sartoris, and then, with the aid of a scholarship from the Département of Vendée, he joined the Paris studio of the classicist and painter of religious subjects Michel-Martin Drölling and also entered the Ecole des Beaux-Arts. In 1850 he won, concurrently with William Bouguereau, the Premier Grand-Prix de Rome. In Italy he was particularly drawn to the masters of the High Renaissance in Rome and to the Venetian School. These interests were sustained by later trips to Italy in 1863–64 and 1869.

Upon his return to Paris in 1857, Baudry met with immediate success, winning that year a first-class medal. Noted successes at subsequent salons included *Charlotte Corday* shown in 1861, the year he was appointed Chevalier of the Legion of Honor, and the 1863 *The Pearl and the Wave* acquired by Napoleon III.

As a decorative painter Baudry is chiefly remembered for his decoration of the Grand Foyer of the Paris Opera (1865–1874). Other projects were formerly to be found in the hôtels of M. Chevreux-Guillemin (1856), Achille Fould (1858), Mme. la comtesse de Nadaillac (1859), the Duc de Galliera (1861) and the Comte de Henckel Donnersmarck (1865), as well as in the Cour de Cassation, Paris (1881), and in the Château of Chantilly (1882 and 1884).

113. Diana Reposing

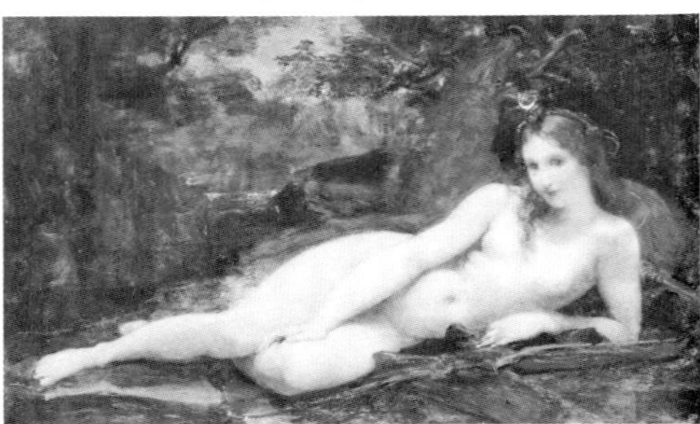

37.12 c.1859

The nude goddess, identified by the crescent moon in her hair and the bow and quiver at her side, reclines on a blue drapery in front of a recumbent stag in a wooded glade. An early inscription identifies this painting as a variant sketch for an overdoor in the hôtel of Achille Fould, the Minister of State. The hôtel, on the rue du Faubourg-Saint-Honoré, was acquired by the Duc d'Aumale in 1872, and its decor was transferred to the Château of Chantilly six years later. The overdoor, *Diane au repos,* and another, *Venus jouant avec l'Amour,* were both mounted in the Galerie des Cerfs. The actual overdoor is painted *en grisaille* unlike the Walters sketch which is in naturalistic colors. In the overdoor the majestic stag is an integral part of the composition, whereas in the Walters sketch he is barely discernible in the right background.

This composition illustrates the artist's practice of imparting to his traditional subjects an air of modishness or coquetry, that may have resulted from his occasional use of professional beauties as models. The figure of Diana reposing in the sketch and the overdoor bears a striking resemblance to Blanche D'Antigny, an actress who at the age of eighteen modeled for Baudry's famous *The Penitent Madeleine,* painted about the same time and acquired by the State at the 1859 Salon for the Nantes Museum.

Support: Thick mahogany panel, .353 x .597 (14" x 23½")

Signed lower right: *PB* (conjoined) in gold paint

Marks: Inscribed along left margin in ink: *57 sur 35 esquisse d'un dessus (variante) de porte de l'hotel du ministre d'etat 1859;* Reverse: stenciled: *Berne Bellecour/tableaux/ . . . Paris;* Paper sticker: *No. 744 Baudry;* black paint: *2127.*

Provenance: Théophile Gautier Sale, Hôtel Drouot, Paris, January 14, 15 and 16, 1873, no. 5, 6,000 francs (described as a première pensée de la Diane au repos); François Thiébault-Sisson, Paris, 1903, 20,000 francs.

References: Walters cat., 1909, p. 5, no. 12, and subsequent Walters catalogues; W. R. Johnston, "La Diane au repos de Paul Baudry," *Le Musée Condé* 15 (October 1978): 1–3, fig. 1; Lucas, 2: 916.

Charles-François Jalabert

French: Nîmes, 1819 - Paris, 1901

Jalabert, a devoted follower of Delaroche, was praised for his subtle refined renderings of historical genre subjects. Théophile Gautier, in *Les Beaux-Arts en Europe, 1855,* Paris, 1856, p. 8, described Jalabert's talent as having "quelque chose de tendre, de delicat, de feminin qui charme et vous empêche de lui désirer plus de force." Later Charles Blanc in *Les Artistes de mon temps,* Paris, 1876, p. 474, commented on the profound tenderness and contained melancholy characteristic of Jalabert's work.

Initially Jalabert studied with Alexandre Colin at the Ecole de Dessin in his native Nîmes and then he departed for Paris where he entered Delaroche's studio in 1839. Becoming a veritable disciple of Delaroche, Jalabert followed him to Rome in 1843. His Italian paintings included such historical and genre subjects as *Rome in the Age of Augustus, Virgil, Titus-Livy,* and *Maria Pasqua.*

He returned to Paris in 1846 and continued to work in Delaroche's house, winning a third-class medal at the 1847 Salon with *Virgil, Horace and Varius at the Home of Maecenas,* subsequently acquired for the Luxembourg Museum.

He exhibited regularly at the salons for sixteen years, winning a first-class medal in 1853, the year he submitted the *Orpheus* now in the Walters Art Gallery and an *Annunciation* bought by the Empress Eugénie for the Tuileries but destroyed with the building in 1871.

After 1853 he turned increasingly to religious subjects and to portraiture and undertook the occasional decorative project. Jalabert sold his works through the dealer Goupil who provided him with a residence in 1858. He continued to participate in the salons until 1882.

114. Orpheus

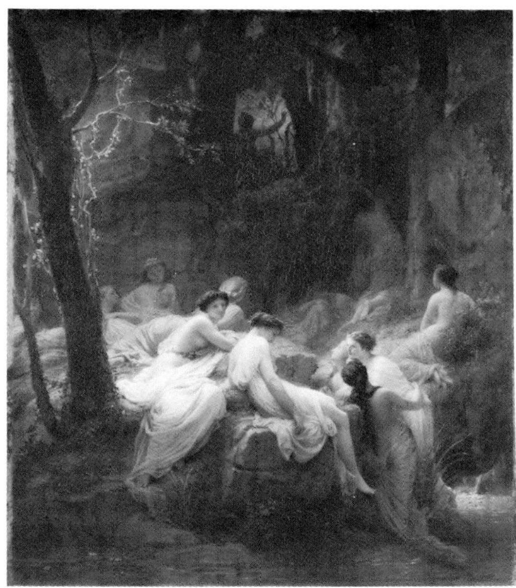

37.37 1853

Assembled on the rocky bank of a stream are dryads, oreads, and other nymphs listening enthralled to the music of Orpheus, who is playing his lyre in a forest glade. The subtle rendering of the sunlight permeating the forest and the sensitive treatment of the lightly clad figures illustrate the elegance and delicacy associated with Jalabert's painting. This picture ranks, together with the 1847 *Virgil,* among the artist's major classical subjects, a genre he abandoned after 1853.

The painting was initially shown in an arched frame (removed after 1878). The areas in the top corners originally covered by the frame's spandrels differ slightly in texture and tonality. Emile Reinaud noted that the *Orpheus,* begun in 1851 and completed in 1853, was to be shown in the 1855 Exposition Universelle. However, Goupil sold it beforehand to a collector in Liège and from there it entered one of the Rothschild collections. H. Mireur cited a .4 x .9 painting of the same title, with an arched frame, sold at the 1863 Gilkinet Sale for 8,900 francs (*Dictionnaire des ventes d'art,* Paris, 1911, 4:35).

Alternative title: *Nymphes écoutant les chants d'Orphée.*

Support: Finely woven fabric, 1.118 x .918 (44" x 36⅛")

Signed and dated lower left: *ch. Jalabert. 1853*

Marks on frame: *Avery* in white chalk; paper label of frame maker: *Thos. A. Wilmurt / Mirrors and Picture Frames / 54 E. 13th St., New York; 355* on paper sticker, *86 36* in ink.

Provenance: Goupil et Cie; Unknown collector in Liège; Rothschild (?); Alexanter White, Chicago; Samuel P. Avery to W. T. Walters in 1878 or earlier.

Exhibitions: Paris, Salon of 1853, no. 646; "The Second Empire," Philadelphia, Detroit, Paris, 1978–79, no. VI–73.

References: *La Presse* (Paris), June 28, 1853; Walters cat., 1878, p. 7, and subsequent Walters catalogues; Strahan, 1: photogravure, Goupil et Cie., opposite p. 93 (showing arched frame); Clement and Hutton, 2: 8; Emile Bellier de la Chavignerie and Louis Auvray, *Dictionnaire général des artistes de l'école francaise.* 2 vols. Paris, Renouard, 1882–85. 1, pt. 3: 330; Champlin and Perkins, 2: 330; Lamb, p. 251; M. K. Halévy, *Mythology and the Siege of Troy,* Philadelphia, G. Barrie, 1892, 2: 110 (illus.); Stranahan, p. 396.

115. Italian Girl

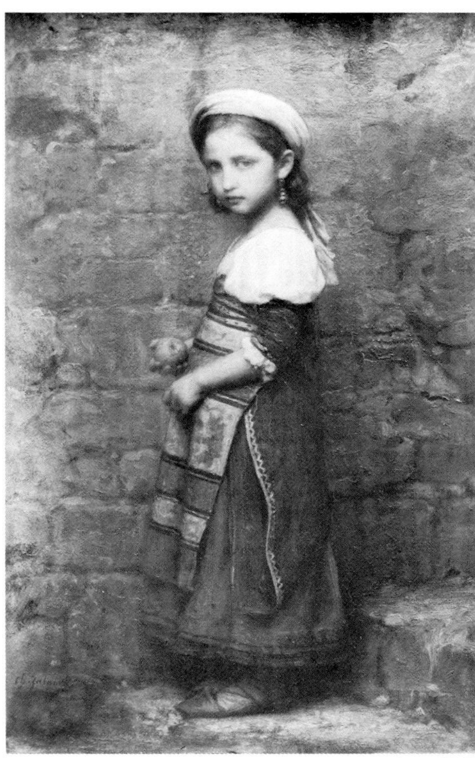

37.91 after 1863

A young girl in Italian peasant costume stands in front of a masonry wall. She holds in her right hand what appears to be a green apple. This picture is a replica of the *Maria Abruzeze* exhibited at the Paris Salon of 1863, no. 986.

Emile Reinaud identified the subject as Maria Pasqua, a blue-eyed child from Abruzzi, who posed for Jalabert on four occasions and also for the artists A.A.E. Hébert, Curzon, and L.-J.-F. Bonnat. Reinaud lists two versions of this subject, one presented by the artist to his city of birth, Nîmes, and another that once belonged to Goupil et Cie and was later sold by Jalabert to a son of Achille Fould. However, Reinaud illustrated in his biography of Jalabert what is evidently the Walters picture distinguished by the fact that the girl holds an apple rather than a stick of bread as in the Salon painting.

Alternative titles: *Maria Abruzeze; Maria Pasqua.*

Support: Mahogany panel with beveled edge, .38 x .237 (15" x 9¼"). The painting does not extend fully to the edges of the panel.

Signed at lower left: *ch. Jalabert.*

Marks: Stenciled on panel: *H. DEFORGE CARPENTIER / couleurs . . . / Boulevard Montmartre / Paris.*

References: Strahan, 1: 94; Walters cat., 1878, p. 43; Champlin and Perkins, 2: 330; Emile Reinaud, *Charles Jalabert, l'homme, l'artiste d'après sa correspondance.* Paris, Hachette, 1903, p. 62 (illus.)

116. The Morning

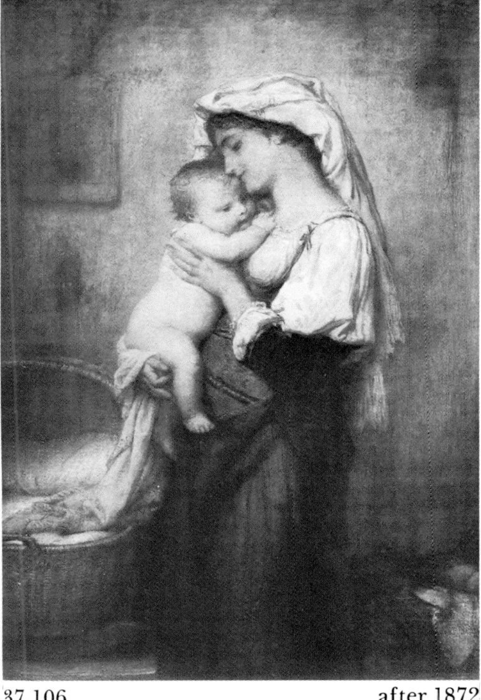

37.106 after 1872

A girl in Italian costume stands beside a wicker cradle pressing an infant to her body. This small panel is a replica of *Le Réveil* exhibited in the Salon of 1872, no. 849. The artist has made some modifications, adding in the Walters picture a religious painting adorned with a sprig of greenery, a wall sconce and a flask all mounted against the wall in the background, whereas in the salon version the figures are posed beneath a shallow archway.

Emile Reinaud in *Charles Jalabert, l'homme, l'artiste,* Paris, 1903, pp. 151–52, described the subject as a "souvenir de Rome" and listed a copy painted for the daughter of Don Pedro, Emperor of Brazil, as well as a modified replica executed for a Mr. Stewart.

Support: Canvas, .331 x .233 (13" x 9$\frac{1}{16}$")

Provenance: Acquired by William Walters before 1878.

References: Walters cat., 1878, p. 18 (as *Mother and Child*), and subsequent Walters catalogues; Strahan, 1: 94.

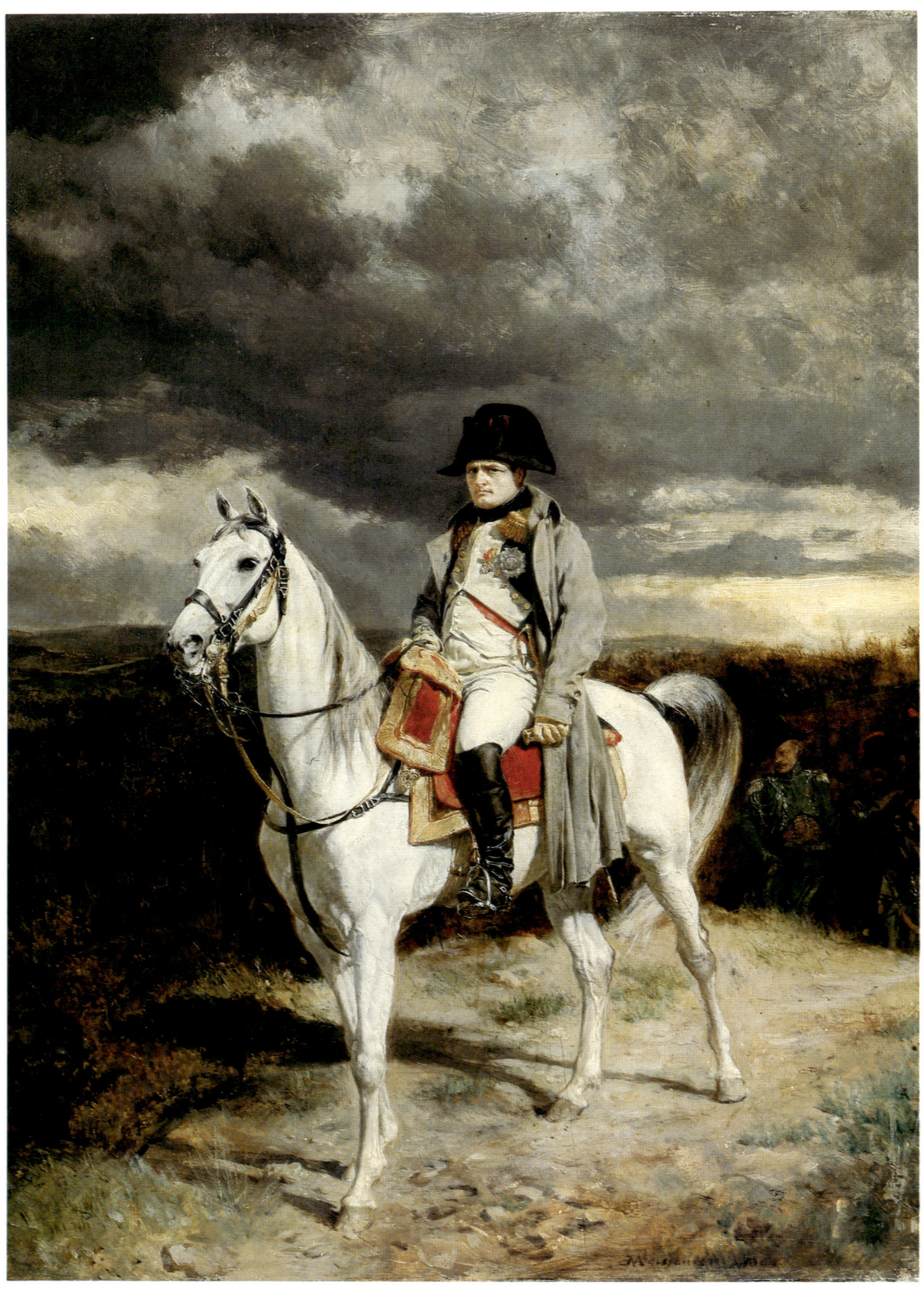

Meissonier *1814,* no. 117

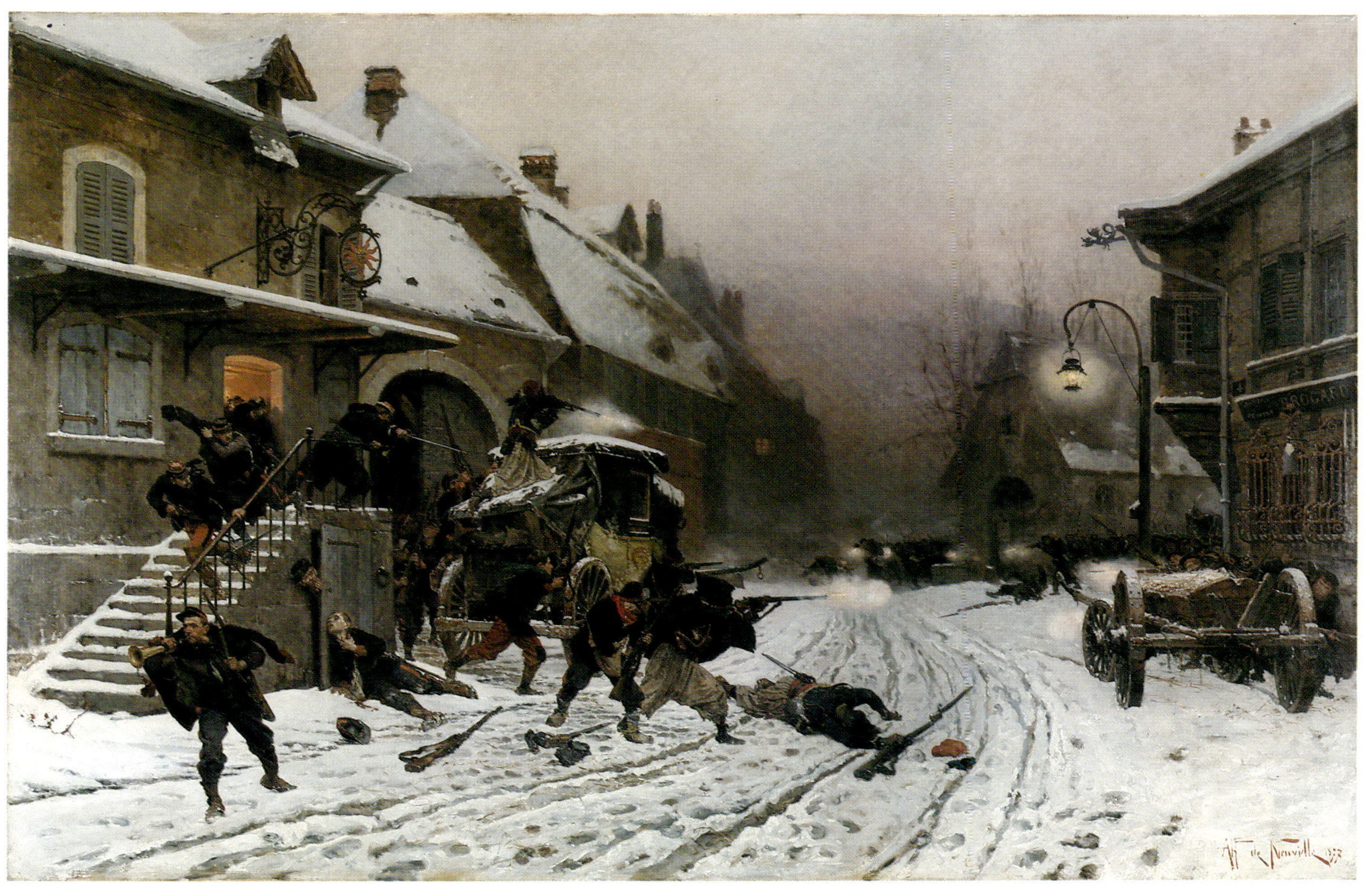

De Neuville *Attack at Dawn,* no. 127

Jean-Louis-Ernest Meissonier
French: Lyons, 1815 - Paris, 1891

The adverse conditions which curtailed Meissonier's formal training may have indirectly contributed to his singular development independent of the prevailing classical and romantic schools of painting. Lacking sufficient funds to enroll in Delaroche's atelier, the principal one of the period, he turned to a minor artist, Julien Potier, who eventually directed him to Léon Cogniet. In five months in the latter's studio he received little instruction, though he did at this point become closely associated with a coterie of young artists that included L. J. Trimolet, C. F. Daubigny, L. G. A. Steinheil, and H. Daumier. It was Trimolet who first directed him to copy the seventeenth-century Dutch masters in the Louvre. At the 1834 Salon Meissonier entered an oil, *Dutch Burghers* (Wallace Collection, London, inv. P369) and a watercolor, and two years later he first drew public notice with *Chess Players*. When a visit to Rome in 1834–35 had to be abandoned because of an outbreak of cholera, Meissonier returned to Paris to pursue a successful career as an illustrator for the publisher L. Curmer. The artist P. M. J. Chenavard, also from Lyons, convinced Meissonier that he should specialize as a painter of small meticulously rendered genre scenes showing figures in historical costume that range in date from the Renaissance to the Directory. Though obviously inspired by Dutch seventeenth-century precedents, the miniature scenes of card players, musicians, smokers and duelists exhibited by Meissonier were distinguished by a distinctively theatrical character, resulting in part from the animated gestures and facial expressions of his subjects. These works rapidly won for the artist the awards of official success and a growing clientele of admirers. By 1845 he was able to acquire the remains of an abandoned abbey at Poissy near the Forest of Saint-Germain for a residence and studio. Later he bought, in addition, an Italianate mansion on the Boulevard Malesherbes, Paris.

The outbreak of the Austro-Italian War of 1859 was a turning point in his career. Meissonier accompanied the French army and recorded its exploits at Solferino (*The Emperor at Solferino*, Versailles, 1863). L.-A. Thiers' *Histoire du Consulat et de l'Empire*, published between 1840 and 1855, subsequently inspired him to execute a cycle of works dramatizing the rise and fall of Napoleon I: *1796: Castiglione; 1807: Friedland* (Metropolitan Museum of Art, inv. 87.-20.1); *1808: Erfurt; 1814: The Campaign of France* (Louvre, R.F. 1862) and *1815: Bellerophon*. Only the second and fourth of these works were fully realized. In preparation for this project and other Napoleonic subjects Meissonier amassed a major collection of military paraphernalia and consulted with such survivors of the First Empire as Napoleon's valet Hubert and his groom Pillardeau. He was also able to demonstrate in his military subjects the thoroughness of his studies of horses in motion and his knowledge of horsemanship in general. During the Franco-Prussian War Meissonier joined the Army of the Rhine, and in the Siege of Paris he served as colonel of a corps of artists. The powerful studies, *The Siege of Paris*, Louvre, R.F. 1249, and *The Ruins of the Tuileries* (Salon of 1883) date from this period. Though chiefly remembered for these battle subjects and for his interior genre scenes, Meissonier also painted portraits and out-of-door scenes. His *plein-air* sketches of views of Poissy, Antibes, Evian, and Venice exhibit a verve and freedom of technique contrasting sharply with the painstaking finish of his salon pictures. Though Meissonier succeeded Abel du Pujol in the Institut in 1861, he never taught at the Ecole des Beaux-Arts. He received a major retrospective exhibition at Galerie Georges Petit in 1884, and in 1889 was acclaimed the president of the international jury for the Exposition Universelle. That year he also became the first artist to receive the Grand Cross of the Legion of Honor. In 1890 he was elected the first president of the recently established Société Nationale des Beaux-Arts.

117. 1814

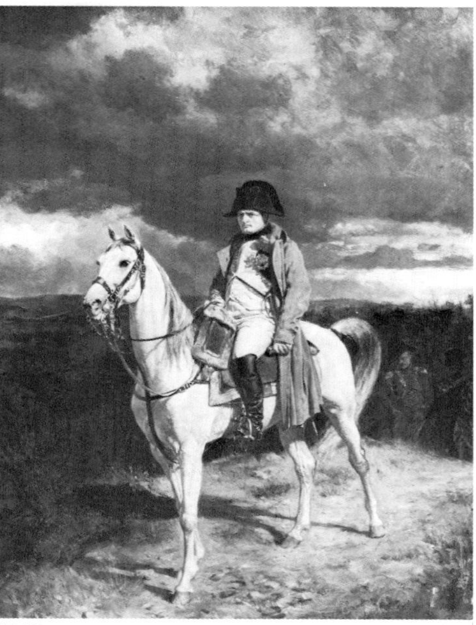

37.52 1862

On a hillock overlooking a desolate wooded landscape, Napoleon is shown mounted on his white horse. Behind him are an officer and a member of the Chasseurs de l'Escadron des Guides de la Garde Impériale. The Emperor's gloomy expression, the somber evening lighting of the scene, and the heavy cloud-laden sky all impart a sense of foreboding. The scene was identified by John Ruskin as Napoleon on the Chausée de Vitry just after the Battle of Arcis-sur-Aube (1814).

C.C. Hungerford relates the *1814* to two paintings by Meissonier, *1814: The Campaign of France*, (.515 x .765), Louvre, R.F. 1862, painted between 1860 and 1863 and showing Napoleon and his army in a wintry landscape after the Battle of Lâon, and to *Napoleon I* (.16 x .12), unlocated, in which the Emperor appears on foot. In addition, variants of the *1814* and the Louvre's *1814: The Campaign of France* were painted in grisaille. In the grisaille version of the former, executed for the engraver Noller in 1863, the positions of the officers in the background are reversed and the sky, particularly on the right side, appears more overcast. The grisaille painting of *1814*, entitled *L'Empereur Napoléon* (.458 x .385) was purchased at the Palais Galliera, Paris, June 5, 1974, no. 56, for 33,000 trancs for the Musée de l'Armée, whereas the grisaille version of the larger work remains unlocated. An oil sketch of the white horse inscribed by Meissonier: *Mon pauvre Bachelier pris par l'armée de la Loire, 1871* was sold at the Coll. Pierre Bezine et autres amateurs sale, Galerie Fievez, Brussels, June 14–15, 1927, no. 257.

The Walters picture originally belonged to Prince Napoleon, son of Jérôme Bonaparte, who was responsible for editing his uncle's correspondence and who lent the artist the Emperor's saddle to ensure veracity of detail in executing the Louvre picture. Subsequently, the English critic John Ruskin acquired the *1814* and displayed it over the mantel of the turret-room of his residence, Brantwood.

Although admiring the execution of the horse and rider, he dismissed the rendering of the landscape as "nearly unintelligible" and therefore disposed of the picture rather than presenting it to St. George's Schools, as was his original intent.

One of W.T. Walters' favorite paintings, *1814* was originally shown separately, mounted on an easel in the center of the picture gallery at 5 West Mount Vernon Place.

Alternative title: *Napoleon I in 1814*

Support: Panel, .324 x .242 (12¾" x 9½")

Signed and dated lower right: *E* (conjoined) *MEISSONIER 1862.*

Provenance: Prince Napoléon, Vente publique de vingt-six tableaux . . ., Paris, April 4, 1868, no. 18, Bouruet-Aubertot, 1,000 guineas; J. Ruskin, London, Sale, June 3, 1882, no. 111; 5,900 guineas; Defoer Sale, Paris, May 22, 1886, no. 23, 128,000 francs (See G. A. Lucas diary, May 22, 1886).

Exhibitions: International Exhibition, London, 1862, no. 190; Paris, Studio of the photographer M. Bingham, January 1863; Royal Institution, London, 1869; "Exposition Meissonier," Galerie

Georges Petit, Paris, 1884, no. 70; "War à la Mode," Walters Art Gallery, 1977, no. W1.

References: "Nouvelles," *Chronique des arts et de la curiosité* (January 25, 1863): 103; John W. Mollett, *Meissonier.* New York, Scribner and Welford, 1882, p. 44; Lionel Robinson, *J. L. E. Meissonier, his life and work.* London, Art Journal, 1887, pp. 11 (illus.), 29; Mathews, p. 6; Lamb, p. 248; Walters cat., 1893, p. 94, no. 154, and subsequent Walters catalogues; Reizenstein, p. 550; Valéry C. O· Gréard, *Meissonier, his life and his art.* New York, A. C. Armstrong, 1897, pp. 284, 370; John Ruskin, "Notes on Prout and Hunt," *The Complete Works of John Ruskin,* edited by E. T. Cook and Alexander Wedderburn. 39 vols. London, G. Allen, 1903–12. 14: 381; 438, n. 1; 439; Lucas, 2: 630; Constance Cain Hungerford, "Ernest Meissonier's first military paintings II: 1814, the campaign of France," Arts magazine 54, no. 5 (January 1980): 98, 100 (illus.); Philippe Guilloux, *Meissonier: trois siècles d'histoire.* Peintres témoins de l'histoire. Paris, Copernic, 1980, p. 97, fig. 27.

118. The Jovial Trooper

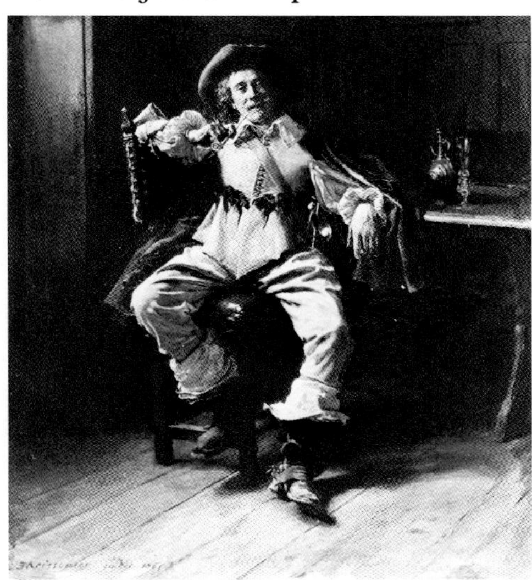

37.151 1865

A gentleman in Louis XIII costume is seated, smoking a clay pipe in an interior illuminated from the left. Beside him is a table on which stands a clay jug and an empty wine glass. The same model and utensils occur in *After Lunch,* "Exposition Meissonier," Galerie Georges Petit, Paris, 1884, no. 116.

Support: Panel, .267 x .214 (10½" x 8⅜")

Signed and dated lower left: *E* (conjoined) *MEISSONIER juillet 1865.*

Provenance: Acquired by W. T. Walters before 1878.

Exhibitions: "Hommage à Baudelaire," University of Maryland, College Park, 1968, pp. 34–35, illus. p. 69.

References: Walters cat.,' 1878, and subsequent Walters catalogues; Strahan, 1: 94; Champlin and Perkins 3: 235; Stranahan, p. 344; Valéry C. O. Gréard, *Meisonnier, his life and his art.* New York, A. C. Armstrong, 1897, p. 371.

119. The End of the Game of Cards

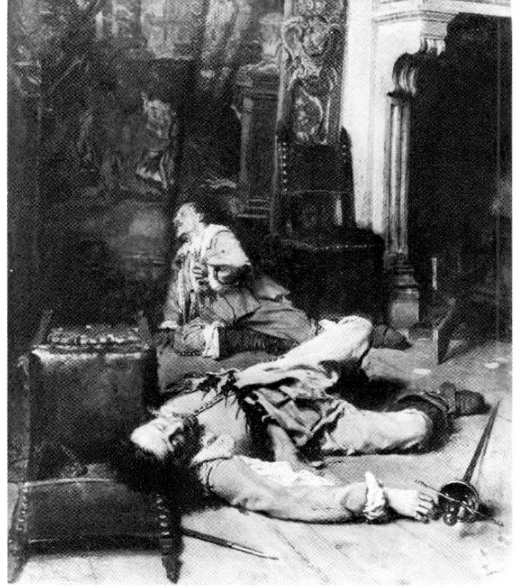

37.149 1865

Two gentlemen in Louis XIII attire have quarreled over a game of tarot and fought. One lies dead with his head resting on an overturned chair and the other, clasping his chest, expires in the background. Strewn across the floor are the cards with the two swords and three coins visible in the right foreground. The setting is actually Meissonier's richly furnished studio at Poissy. This picture, which illustrates Messonier's mastery of foreshortening and his ability to express dramatic action in a miniature scale, was conveyed to Rome in 1869 by its first owner W. H. Stewart, to be studied by the Spanish artist, Mariano Fortuny, at the latter's request.

Alternative title: *The Sequel of a Gambling Quarrel.*

Support: Panel, .222 x .18 (8¾" x 7⅛")

Signed and dated lower right: *E* (conjoined) *MEISSONIER 1865.*

Provenance: William Hood Stewart Sale, New York, 1898, no. 110.

Exhibitions: Vienna, International Exhibition, 1873; "Exposition Meissonier," Galerie Georges Petit, Paris, 1884, no. 68; "Fortuny and his Circle," Walters Art Gallery, 1970, no. 28.

References: John W. Mollett, *Meissonier.* New York, Scribner and Welford, 1882, p. 72; Lionel Robinson, *J. L. E. Meissonier, his life and work.* London, Art Journal, 1887, p. 21; Valéry C. O. Gréard, *Meissonier, his life and his art.* New York, A. C. Armstrong, 1897, pp. 370–71; Walters cat., 1899, p. 102, no. 170; W. R. Johnston, "W. H. Stewart, the American patron of Mariano Fortuny," *GBA* 6th pér. 77 (1971): 183; 187, n. 8.

Victor-Joseph Chavet

French: Pourcieux (Var), 1822 - Creusot, 1906

Though known as a pupil of Meissonier, Chavet received his early training from E. C. J. Loubon, P.-H. Revoil, and C. J. E. Roqueplan. Before establishing himself in Paris, he taught drawing, worked with the decorative painter P. L. C. Ciceri, and served in the army. His first two Salon entries, *Young Man Reading* and *A Smoker,* shown in 1846, confirmed his reputation as a follower of Meissonier. Thereafter, he exhibited small paintings showing figures in eighteenth-century costume that were widely admired during the Second Empire and brought him a third-class medal in 1853, a second-class medal in 1855 with *rappel* in 1857, and resulted in his being appointed a Chevalier of the Legion of Honor in 1859. He also received a commission to paint a full-length portrait of Admiral Bergeret for Versailles in 1859, and, during Queen Victoria's visit to France in 1855, he painted watercolors recording her trip for a volume that was presented to the monarch by Napoleon III. With the fall of the Second Empire, he removed to Geneva, where he continued to paint, specializing in portraiture.

120. The Amateur

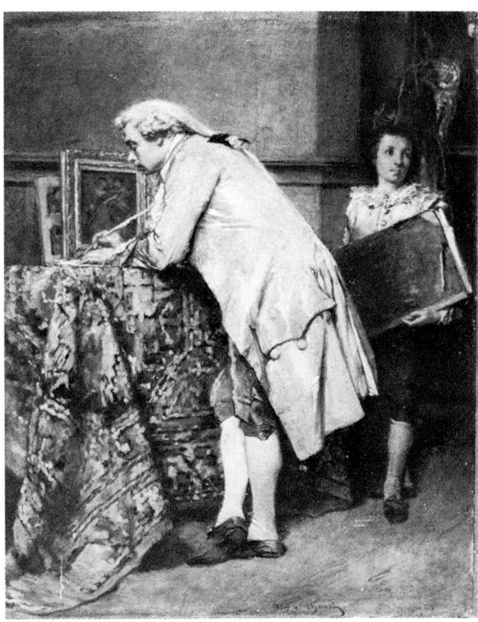

37.204 1859

A gentleman in eighteenth-century dress leans against a high, rug-covered table while writing with a quill. A painting in a gilt frame and a framed drawing have been placed upright on the table resting against the wainscot of the wall. Behind him a page is holding a portfolio of drawings or prints.

Alternative title: *The Connoisseur*

Support: Panel, thin, unbeveled, .215 x .16 (8½" x 6⅜")

Signed and dated at bottom right: *1859 V. Chavet.*

Marks on reverse: Stenciled *32;* in pencil *G9462;* on paper sticker *567.*

Condition: The panel has become bowed, resulting in a small crack forming at the bottom left.

Provenance: Acquired by W. T. Walters before 1878.

References: Walters cat., 1878, p. 20, and subsequent Walters catalogues; Strahan, 1: 94; Champlin and Perkins, 1: 277–78.

Charles Chaplin

French: Les Andelys, 1825 - Paris, 1891

Chaplin was born to a French mother and an English father and was not naturalized French until he reached the age of sixty-one. He studied in the atelier of Michel-Martin Drölling and at the Ecole des Beaux-Arts. Chaplin's first appearance at the Paris Salon was in 1845 when he entered a portrait of a woman. His works in the forties, which were of a decidedly realistic bent, included a number of genre scenes set in the Auvergne, one of which was exhibited at the Royal Academy, London, in 1849. During the fifties, Chaplin emerged as a modish painter, specializing in portraits and brightly colored decorative genre scenes reminiscent at times of the eighteenth-century rococo artists. He received a third-class medal in 1851, a second-class the following year, and a medal of distinction in 1865, the year he also was appointed Chevalier of the Legion of Honor. Fourteen years later, he was promoted to Officier. *Bryan's Dictionary,* in 1903, (1:282) listed as his best known works *Evening in the Bruyères* (1849) in the Bordeaux Museum, and *Soap Bubbles,* acquired for the Luxembourg Gallery in 1864. Chaplin's decorative projects included the ceiling and overdoors for the Salon des Fleurs in the Tuileries (1861), the salon of the Hemicycle in the Elysée Palace (1861), panels and overdoors painted on glass for the Empress Eugénie's bathroom, also at the Elysée (1864), and a panel for the ceiling of Prince Demidoff's palace (1861). Chaplin was also an etcher.

121. Devotion

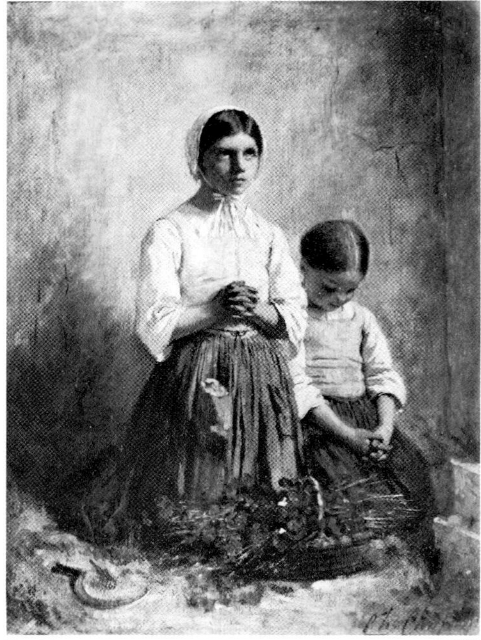

37.46 1857

Two peasant girls are kneeling in prayer. In front of them is a basket of flowers and a sickle.

Alternative title: *At the Shrine*

Support: Canvas, .273 x .217 (10¾" x 8½")

Signed and dated at lower right: *Ch. Chaplin 57.* Stretcher stenciled: *475;* canvas stenciled: *3.*

Provenance: This picture, which is listed in the early catalogues as having been being purchased from the artist, may have been acquired as early as 1863, when W. T. Walters was accompanying his friend G. A. Lucas to various artists' studios. At the time Walters was forming a collection of drawings of a devotional nature.

References: Walters cat., 1878, p. 43 (as *Girls kneeling at a shrine);* Strahan, 1: 94; Clement and Hutton, 1: 129; Champlin and Perkins, 1: 269.

Antoine-Emile Plassan

French: Bordeaux, 1817 - Paris, 1903

Plassan was a painter of intimate, domestic genre scenes that were much in vogue about 1860 in France and England. Little is known of his early life other than that he left Bordeaux at the age of eighteen and settled in Paris, where he apparently fell under the influence of Meissonier. He exhibited a portrait at the 1846 Salon; a view of the artist in his studio the following year; and in 1848 several landscapes recording a visit to Algeria, as well as a still life, a portrait, and a genre scene. He participated regularly in the Salons until 1889, winning a third-class medal in 1852, with *rappel* in 1857 and 1859, and also being elected a Chevalier of the Legion of Honor in 1859. In London his small paintings of eighteenth-century and contemporary interiors were shown at Ernest Gambart's "French Exhibitions" on Pall Mall. At the 1854 opening exhibition of this gallery, Queen Victoria purchased *The Foot Bath,* an eighteenth-century scene in which a servant girl is washing the feet of a lady. The critic John Ruskin, in reviewing the 1857 "French Exhibition," characterized Plassan's painting no. 130, *The Music Lesson,* as "lighter and softer in laying of colour than Frère's work and more refined in colour than Meissonier's." (*The Complete Works of John Ruskin,* Editors: E. T. Cook and Alexander Wedderburn, London, 1904, 14:180). The Empress Eugénie and Napoleon III each acquired two works by Plassan and exhibited them in the 1867 Exposition Universelle. In the 1876 Philadelphia Centennial Exhibition Plassan's *Before the Mirror* earned him a medal.

122. Devotion

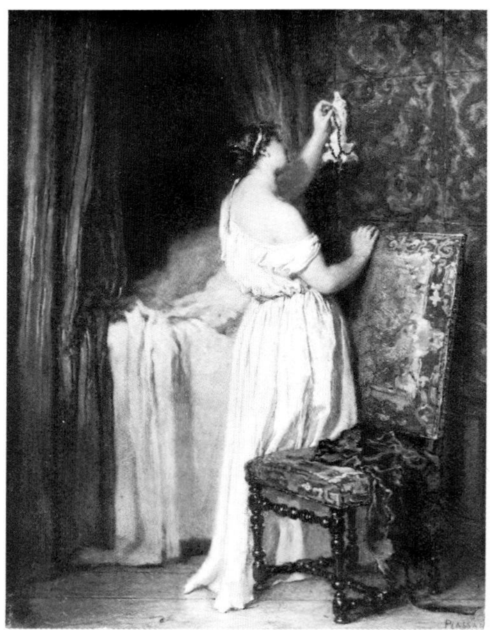

37.45 c. 1863–64

A woman, wearing a nightgown with her shoulder exposed, places a strand of rosary beads on a devotional image mounted on the wall beside her bed. In this instance Plassan suggests a late seventeenth-century interior, showing a high-backed chair upholstered in needlepoint and a Spanish embossed leather wall-covering.

Alternative title: *Contemplation*

Support: Panel, mahogany, beveled, reverse painted brick red, .245 x .188 (9⅝" x 7⅜")

Signed at lower right in block letters: *PLASSAN.* Reverse: illegible stencil.

Provenance: One of two pictures of "Prayer"

ordered by W. T. Walters directly from the artist, December 5, 1863, for 3,500 francs; payment made April 9, 1864 (See Lucas, 2: 175).

References: Walters cat., 1878, p. 32, and subsequent Walters catalogues; Strahan, 1:94; Champlin and Perkins, 3: 451.

123. Prayer

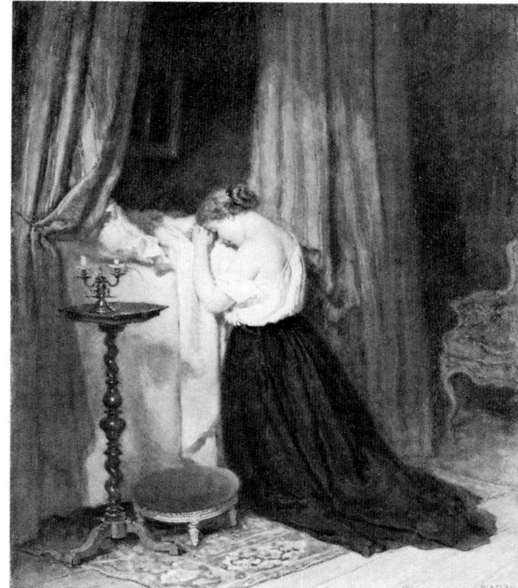

37.47 c. 1863–64

A young woman, wearing a white blouse with her shoulders bared and a long black skirt, kneels in prayer beside her bed. The furnishings of this contemporary bourgeois interior include a colorful oriental rug, a turned mahogany candlestand carrying a brass double candleholder, and an upholstered Louis XV-style armchair. Partially concealed by the pink silk bed curtains is a framed crucifix.

Single-figured boudoir scenes, such as this work, were the mainstay of Plassan's oeuvre. A very similar composition, with the same figure and candlestand, entitled *La Prière,* was sold at Sotheby's, London, July 21, 1976, no. 45, dated 1862, .28 x .21.

Alternative title: *Evening Prayer*

Support: Panel, three-ply laminated wood, .27 x .22 (10⅝" x 8$\frac{1}{16}$")

Signed at lower right in block letters: *PLASSAN.* Reverse of panel impressed: *TACHET / BREVETTE / A PARIS.*

Condition: In 1971 the picture was cleaned and the layers of wood which had become detached were reaffixed.

Provenance: One of two pictures of "Prayer" ordered by W. T. Walters directly from the artist, December 5, 1863, for 3,500 francs; payment made April 9, 1864 (See Lucas, 2: 175).

References: See his *Devotion,* 37.45.

124. Disappointment

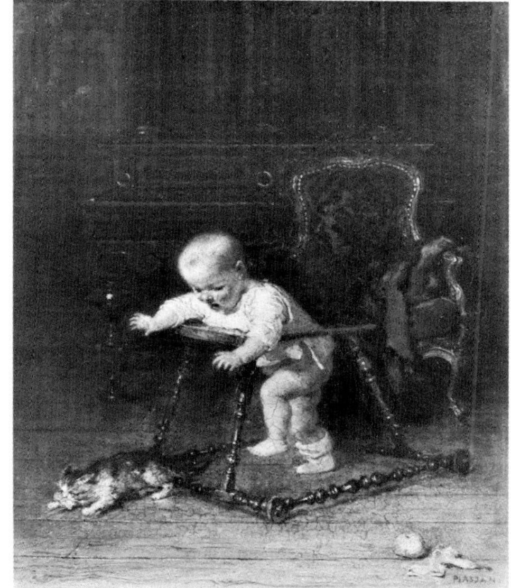

37.56

A red-haired infant boy, enclosed in a wheeled wooden walker, angrily pursues a cat across the floor. In the right foreground lies an apple and one of the child's stockings. In the background appear a rococo-style armchair and a baroque-style cupboard, rendered in light wood with contrasting panels of black ebony, raised on baluster legs.

Support: Panel, thick mahogany, beveled edges, .184 x .154 (7⅛" x 6⅛")

Signed at lower right in block letters: *PLASSAN.*

Provenance: Acquired from the artist before 1884.

References: Walters cat., 1884, p. 45, no. 66, and subsequent Walters catalogues; Champlin and Perkins, 3: 451.

Jehan-Georges Vibert

French: Paris, 1840 - Paris, 1902

Vibert is usually associated with small, brightly colored easel paintings showing clerical or secular subjects of a satirical nature. Among his most frequently cited works of this nature are *A Committee on Moral Books* (formerly in the Wm. H. Vanderbilt Collection) in which clerics read with obvious relish the proscribed literature, and *The Missionary's Tale* (Metropolitan Museum of Art, New York, Inv. 25.110.140) showing a bedraggled missionary reporting to his complacent superiors.

Vibert received his early training from his maternal grandfather, the engraver J. P. M. Jazet, and then entered the studio of Félix Barrias. At age sixteen, he was enrolled in the Ecole des Beaux-Arts where he studied for six years. In 1863 he received an honorable mention for his first Salon entries, two genre subjects, *Repentance* and *Siesta,* and a portrait. At this point, he sought to further his career by exhibiting historical themes, including in 1865 a *Christian Martyrs in the Lion's Den,* which was surely one of the most sanguinary renditions of the subject in French painting. By 1866 he had turned to contemporary genre subjects set in Spain, among the first of which was the *Entry of the Toreadors,* painted in collaboration with Eduardo Zamacoïs, a pupil of J.-L.-E. Meissonier and a friend of the popular Catalan artist, Mariano Fortuny y Marsal. It was the successful exhibitions of Fortuny's watercolors at Goupil et Cie that encouraged Vibert and four other young French painters, who shared quarters in Montmorency, to establish the Société des aquarellistes français in 1867.

After serving during the Franco-Prussian War in the artists' battalion with Regnault, Clairin, Detaille, and others, Vibert resumed his highly productive career, producing apart from his Salon entries innumerable oils and watercolors of amusing genre subjects many of which were illustrated in his autobiographical deluxe publication, *La Comédie en peinture,* Paris, London, New York, 1902. His more ambitious projects, the 1878 *Apotheosis of M. Thiers,* and a five meter high *Assumption of the Virgin,* painted for the chapel of Saint Denis in the Church of Saint-Bernard, were not, apparently, particularly successful. Vibert's Paris residence, which housed an important collection of Japanese and Near Eastern artifacts until divorce proceedings in 1886, served as a gathering point for many of the younger artists who banded together to form a social club, the Cercle de St. Arnaud. Not only did Vibert express his inclinations as a dramatist in his anecdotal paintings but he also wrote several comical theatrical productions in the 1870s.

125. Entry of the Toreadors

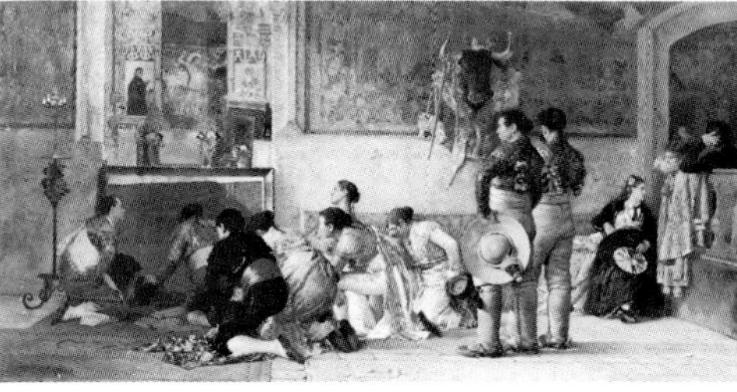

37.197 1866

This work was exhibited at the 1866 Salon as a collaborative effort on the part of Vibert and Eduardo Zamacoïs. The scene is a chapel located beneath the galleries of an arena. A number of toreadors are shown kneeling in prayer before an altar unpropitiously placed in an embrasure of the *arcade condamnée.* The altar is adorned with several vases of paper flowers and some religious paintings. At the right stand a couple of picadors, unable to kneel because of their protective padding, and further to the side is seated a woman who is conversing with several figures leaning over the balustrade. Suspended on the wall in the background is a bull's head adorned with various trophies. A replica of this painting, dated 1871, and showing minor variations in the altar decoration was illustrated and described by Vibert along with a number of related subjects in the chapter "Les Courses de Taureaux" in *La Comédie en peinture.* It has not proved possible to distinguish Vibert's contribution to this work from that of Zamacoïs. In another collaborative work, *Les deux Ennemis,* sold by auction April 22–28, 1886, Vibert is listed as having painted a figure and Zamacoïs a parrot on its perch (Paul Endel, *L'Hotel Drouot 1886/7,* Paris, 1888, p. 184).

Alternative title: *Toreadors before entering the Arena.*

Support: Canvas, .454 x .844 (17⅞" x 33¼").

Signed lower left: *G. Vibert.*

Condition: Cleaned and lined in 1951.

Provenance: Acquired between 1878 and 1884, source unknown.

Exhibitions: Paris Salon, 1866; "Fortuny and his Circle," Walters Art Gallery, 1970, no. 31.

References: Pierre Larousse, *Grand dictionnaire universel du XIXe siecle.* 17 vols., Paris, Larousse, 1865–1890, 15: 981; Walters cat., 1884, p. 17, no. 17, and subsequent Walters catalogues. Champlin and Perkins, 4: 365; Gustave Vapereau, *Dictionnaire universel des contemporains.* Paris, Hachette, 1893. p. 1561; Jehan Georges Vibert, *La comédie en peinture. Paris,* 1902. p. 81 (1871 version only).

Alphonse Marie Deneuville

French: Saint-Omer, 1835 - Paris, 1885

Though remembered chiefly for such paintings as *The Last Cartridges* and *Le Bourget* extolling French resistance in the Franco-Prussian War, Deneuville also drew subjects from the Crimean War, the Italian campaign of Napoleon III, and the British-Zulu Wars. The son of a candle manufacturer of Saint-Omer, Deneuville (whose name is sometimes spelled De Neuville or de Neuville) may have studied in the local école des beaux-arts under Hippolyte Cuvelier. His earliest sketches, however, were influenced by the lithographs of J. L. H. Bellangé. While visiting Belgium, Switzerland, and Germany with his father in 1850, he sketched his first military subjects. In 1852–53 Deneuville enrolled in the lycée of Lorient to prepare for the Ecole Navale, but in 1854 he turned instead for about three years to the study of law in Paris. Finally, in 1858, on the advice of Bellangé, he entered the studio of F. E. Picot, where he received only nominal formal training. He regarded the counsel of Eugène Delacroix as more decisive for his subsequent development. In addition, he was drawn to the work of Jules Breton, a Juste Milieu realist, who was widely acclaimed at the 1859 Salon, at which Deneuville made his successful debut, winning a third-class medal with two works recording the siege of Sebastopol. That year Deneuville traveled to southern Italy to record Garibaldi's capture of Naples for the Cercle artistique de la rue de Provence. In 1861 he received a second-class medal, and two years later was made *hors concours.* During the sixties, in addition to his military subjects, he worked on some illustrations reproduced as wood-engravings in various publications and produced several posters for operas in conjunction with Ludovic Halévy, and in 1865 entered in the Salon a subject taken from Goethe's *Faust.* With the outbreak of war in 1870, Deneuville was enrolled in the army engineers, serving as a lieutenant in the Génie Auxiliaire under General Caillié in the Belleville sector. Ironically ths period of military service was briefly followed by a series of non-military genre paintings of life in coastal Normandy before his return to his most celebrated military subjects. His *The Last Cartridges,* recording an incident at Bazeilles on August 31, 1870, was enthusiastically received at the Salon of 1873, the year he received the Legion of Honor. In the mid-seventies the dealer Goupil began to handle his works with success abroad as well as in France. After his works were exhibited in London in 1880, Deneuville turned to British military subjects. In addition to his easel paintings, Deneuville collaborated with Detaille and a number of assistants on several vast mural paintings, a panoramic view of the battle of Champigny (1882) and one of Rezonville (1883).

126. Information

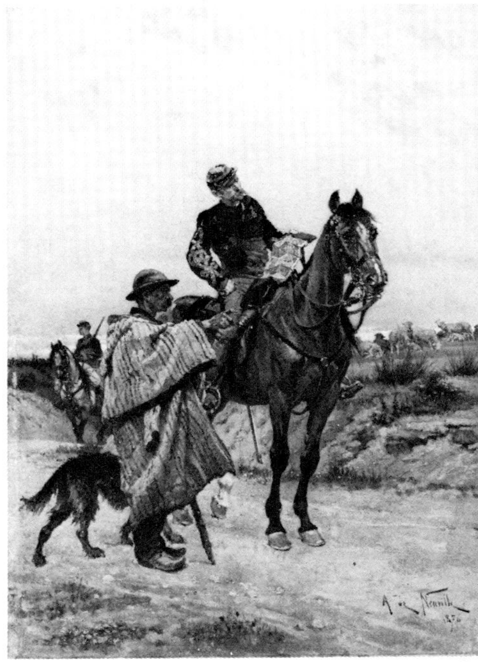

37.93 1876

A mounted officer of the Engineers with map in hand is seeking directions from a peasant tending his flock with a dog. Another mounted soldier is visible in the background.

A pen and ink drawing of this subject (.37 x .28), now in a private collection in Boulogne-sur-Mer, dated 1876, was published by Deneuville in *Croquis Militaires,* Paris, 1876, plate 16. This drawing may be the *Paysan donnant des renseignements à des officiers français,* listed in the Deneuville Sale, Paris, 1886, no. 256.

Support: Canvas, .466 x .33 (18⅜" x 13")

Signed and dated lower right: *A de Neuville / 1876.*

Provenance: Acquired by W. T. Walters before 1878.

Condition: Cleaned in 1942.

Exhibitions: "War à la mode," Walters Art Gallery, 1977, no. W7.

References: Walters cat., 1878, p. 42; Strahan, 1: 94; Philippe Chabert, *Alphonse de Neuville: l'épopée de la défaite.* Peintres témoins de l'histoire. Paris, Copernic, 1979, p. 19 (illus.)

127. The Attack at Dawn

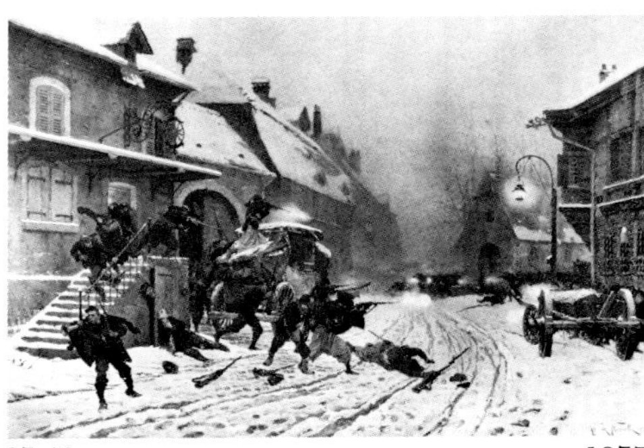

37.40 1877

As a bugler sounds the alarm, French soldiers rush from an inn to defend themselves against an advancing Prussian column. Several men are firing from a diligence parked outside the inn, whereas others already lie fallen in the snow. The French soldiers, Algerian riflemen (*turcos*), and members of the Garde Mobile (*mobiles*), belong to the Army of the East led by General Bourbaki, which by January 1871 had been pushed back to the Swiss border. The setting, a village in the Jura, is indicated by a mountain silhouetted against the dimly lit sky.

This work may have resulted from a trip to Montbéliard and Basle undertaken by Deneuville and his companion Detaille in the summer of 1876. A somewhat similar village scene is the *Attaque par le feu d'une maison barricadée et crénelée,* about 1875, in the Louvre, which shows an incident involving the same armies at Villersexel.

The Attack at Dawn was among the battle paintings intended for exhibition at the 1878 Exposition Universelle, eventually withdrawn for diplomatic reasons, and displayed instead in the gallery of the dealer Goupil, in the rue Chaptal.

Support: Canvas, 1.465 x 2.22 (57⅝" x 7' 3½")

Signed and dated lower right: *Alf. de Neuville 1877.*

Provenance: Goupil et Cie, before 1878.

Condition: Discolored varnish removed in 1943.

Exhibitions: Goupil et Cie, Paris, 1878; "War à la Mode," Walters Art Gallery, 1977, no. W6.

References: Walters cat., 1878, pp. 11–13, and subsequent Walters catalogues; Eugène Montrosier, "La peinture militaire en 1878," *L'Art* 14 (1878): 29–37; illus. opposite p. 34, gravure by Bellenger; Strahan, 1: 90 (illus.), 92, 94; Edward Strahan, ed., *The chefs-d'oeuvre d'art of the International Exhibition, 1878*. 24 parts. Philadelphia, Gebbie & Barrie, 1878–80. part 2: 22; Gustave Goetschy, *Les jeunes peintres militaires: De Neuville, Detaille, Dupray*. Paris, Ludovic Baschet, 1878. p. 29; Jules Richard [T. J. R. Maillot] *En campagne*. 2nd sér. Paris, n.d. pp. 10–11, illus.; Reizenstein, p. 553; *Revue historique de l'Armée* 4 (1955): 149 (illus.); Philippe Chabert, *Alphonse de Neuville: l'épopée de la défaite*. Peintres témoins de l'histoire. Paris, Copernic, 1979, p. 26, fig. 20.

128. In the Trenches

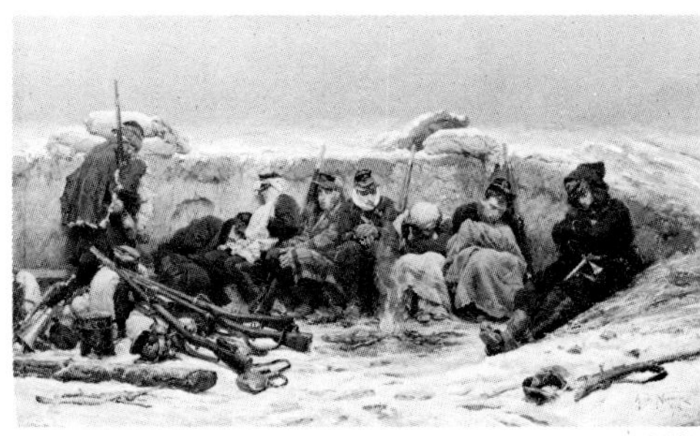

37.118 1874

In the early dawn of a winter's day seven soldiers of the Garde Mobile doze, huddled in a shallow trench before a smoldering fire. Standing beside a stack of rifles and military paraphernalia, an eighth soldier keeps watch.

Though the general misery and tedium experienced by the men in the 1870–71 War was portrayed by Deneuville in such noted pictures as *Bivouac before Le Bourget,* about 1872, now in Versailles, and *Concert at the Advanced Post,* 1882, unlocated, it is in the Walters painting that these themes are perhaps most graphically shown. In a letter to his father, published by Philippe Chabert, Deneuville complains that his dealers Goupil and Boussod prefer more flattering, less troubling subjects and will therefore offer him only 6,000 francs for this picture.

Alternative title: *Une tranchée sous Paris*

Support: Canvas, .574 x .965 (22¾" x 38")

Signed and dated lower right: *A de Neuville / 1874.*

Provenance: Goupil et Cie., Paris (Photograph no. 1405); Henry Wallis, London.

Condition: Lined prior to 1943.

Exhibitions: "War à la Mode," Walters Art Gallery, 1977, no. W6.

References: "In the trenches," *Art journal* new series 1 (1875): 22 (illus.), 23; Walters cat. 1878, p. 25, and subsequent Walters catalogues; Strahan, 1:94; Gustave Goetschy, *Les jeunes peintres militaires: De Neuville, Detaille, Dupray.* Paris, Ludovic Baschet, 1878. p. 29, illus.; Jules Richard [T. J. R. Maillot] *En campagne*. 2nd sér. Paris, n.d. p. 3, illus.; Francis Wilson, *Joseph Jefferson*. New York, Charles Schibner's Sons, 1906. pp. 224–25; Philippe Chabert, *Alphonse de Neuville: l'épopée de la défaite*. Peintres témoins de l'histoire. Paris, Copernic, 1979. pp. 23, 72, fig. 13.

Jean-Baptiste-Edouard Detaille
French: Paris, 1848 - Paris, 1912

Detaille was the principal artist to record both the Franco-Prussian War and the post-war French army, the "armée nouvelle." Though his works are frequently compared with those of Deneuville, he was less prone than his colleague to dramatize particular incidents in battle and more inclined to recreate with painstaking accuracy general scenes of military life in war and peace. His exacting academic realism was backed with personal military experience recorded in sketch books, occasionally supplemented by photographs, careful study of the actual sites of action, and a conscientious attention to detail.

Detaille was born in comfortable circumstances and was encouraged by his father, an architect, in his artistic career. At the age of seventeen he entered the Poissy studio of J.-L.-E. Meissonier, the highly successful realist painter, with whom he evidently maintained a close rapport. In 1867 Detaille submitted his first work to the Paris Salon, a view of his teacher's studio, and in 1869 and 1870 he received medals for military subjects. Traveling in Spain and Algeria with his friends Vibert, L. Leloir, and E. Berne-Bellecour when the Franco-Prussian War erupted, he returned to France to serve in the Eighth Batallion of the Mobiles, seeing action at Bondy, Châtillon, and Villejuif. He was later attached to the secretariat of General Appert and was given the mission of delineating enemy positions. His sketches executed during the battle of the Marne and Champigny proved invaluable in his later career. Important works based on his war experiences included *The Conquerors* and *A German Convoy,* submitted to the 1872 Salon but withdrawn for diplomatic considerations, *Salute to the Wounded* (1876), *The Faron division at Champigny* (1879), and two vast panoramas executed in collaboration with Deneuville and assistants, the *Panorama of the Battle of Champigny* (1882), and the *Panorama of the Battle of Rezonville* (1883).

Following the cessation of hostilities, Detaille continued to participate in military maneuvers, serving in the reserves of the Chasseurs à Pied in 1876 and 1880, and in 1881 accompanying the Vincendon Expeditionary Brigade to Tunisia. The post-war army was extolled in such celebrated works as *The Passing Regiment* (1875) and *The Dream* (1888).

He also turned to historical military subjects, drawing from the Napoleonic tradition in *Long Live the Emperor* (1891); *Victory is Ours* (1894); and *General Lasalle at Wagram* (1912); and from the more remote past in *Count Montgomery Wounding Henri II in a Tournament* (1906) and *Fontenoy, May 11, 1745* (1912).

In addition to producing easel paintings and panoramas, Detaille participated regularly in the salons of the Société des Aquarellistes français, executed murals for the Panthéon (1905) and the Hôtel de Ville (1908), and was involved with several publications devoted primarily to military campaigns and uniforms.

For his efforts he received a second-class medal at the Salon of 1872, a Medal of Honor in 1888, Grand Prizes at the Expositions of 1889 and 1900, became an Officier of the Legion of Honor in 1881 and was elected to the Institut in 1892.

Detaille's importance lay in his quasi-official role as painter to the French army. Critically he outlived his time and toward the end of his career his painting appeared as outmoded as later proved the colorful designs for army uniforms that he proposed in 1912.

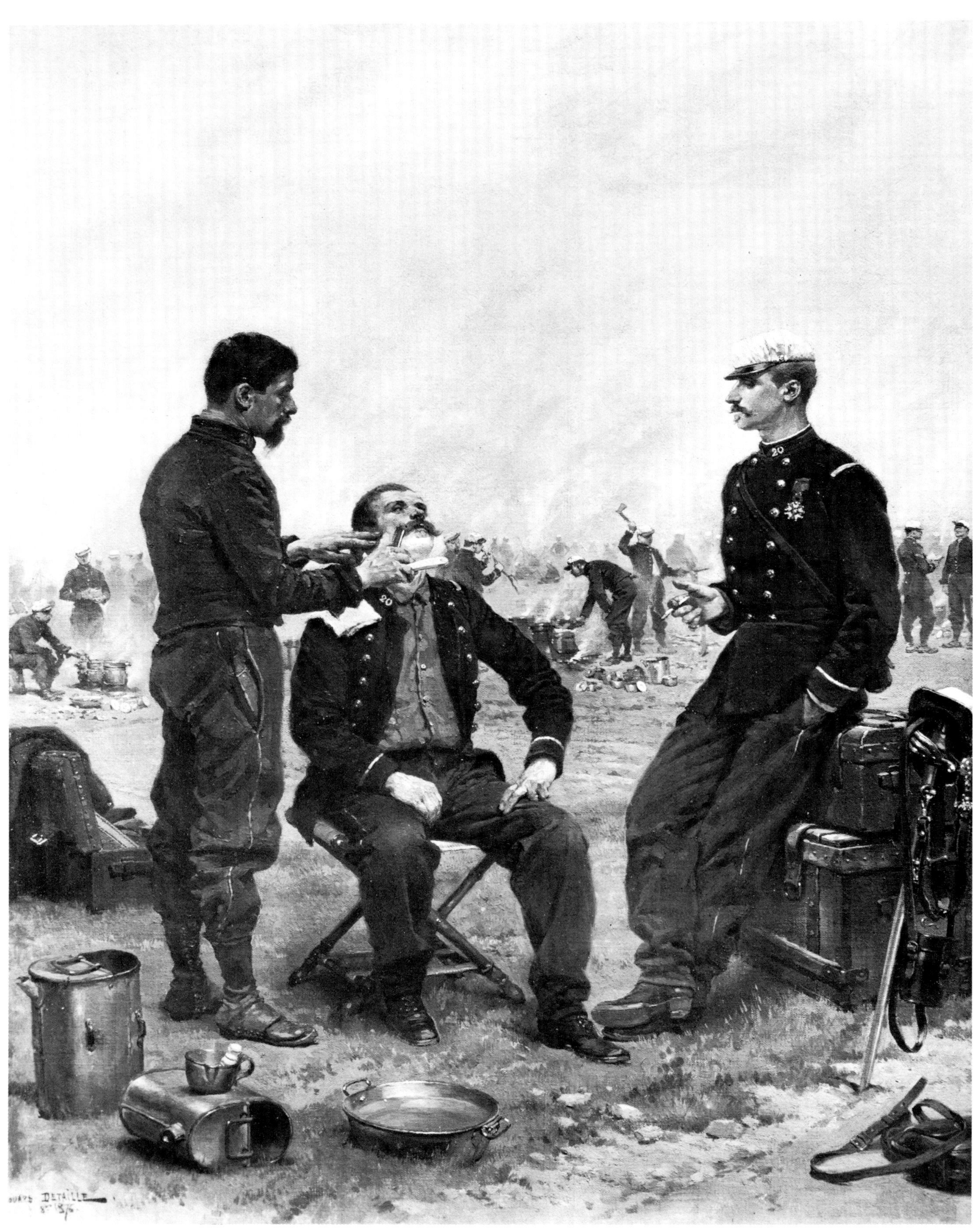

Detaille *The Camp Barber,* no. 130

129. The Picket

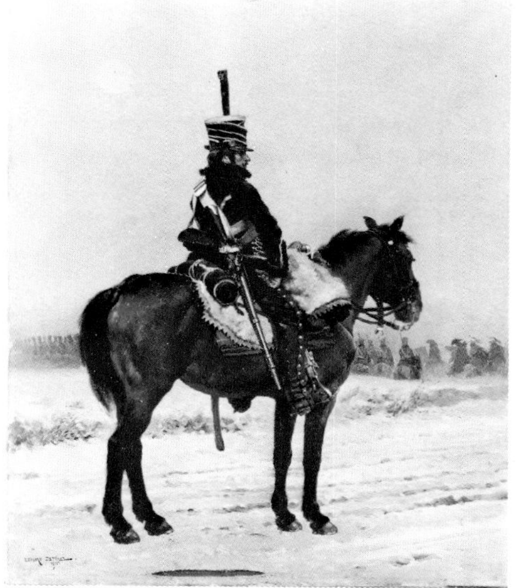

37.92 1875

On watch in a wintry scene is a mounted hussar of about 1800. In the background troops file past. The foreground figure has been identified as a member of the Eleventh Hussar Regiment, which was formed in 1793 and converted to Dragoons in 1803. This work may be the *Hussard en vedette* listed by Montrosier as being among those works withdrawn from the Exposition Universelle and exhibited at Goupil's gallery on the rue Chaptal in 1878.

Alternative title: *Hussard en vedette*

Support: Canvas, .464 x .381 (18¼" x 15")

Signed and dated lower left: *EDOUARD DE-TAILLE / 1875*

Provenance: Acquired by W. T. Walters before 1878.

Condition: Small tear in lower center repaired in 1938; lined and cleaned in 1942.

Exhibitions: Goupil et Cie, Paris, 1878 (?); "War à la mode," Walters Art Gallery, 1977, no. W4.

References: Walters cat., 1878, p. 1, and subsequent Walters catalogues; Eugène Montrosier, "La peinture militaire en 1878," *L'Art* 14 (1878): 36; Strahan, 1: 94.

130. The Camp Barber

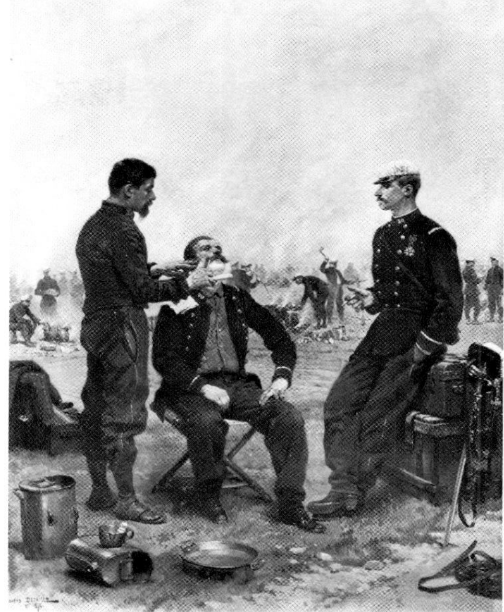

37.190 1876

A soldier is being shaved by the camp barber while a soldier smoking a cigarette waits at the right. In the background men prepare breakfast. The figure at the right has been identified by Jean Humbert as Detaille himself. In 1876 the artist served as a sub-lieutenant of the reserve in the Twentieth Batallion of the Chasseurs à Pied during maneuvers of the Third Corps of the Army on the plains of the Eure.

Alternative title: *Le Barbier au bivouac, octobre 1876*

Support: Canvas, .355 x .273 (14" x 10¾")

Signed and dated lower left: *EDOUARD DE-TAILLE / 8bre 1876.*

Provenance: Henry R. Bishop Sale, New York, 1906, no. 25, to Henry Walters for $1,150.00.

Condition: Lightly cleaned in 1966.

Exhibitions: "War à la mode," Walters Art Gallery, 1977, no. W3.

References: Jean Humbert, *Edouard Detaille: l'héroisme d'un siècle.* Peintres témoins de l'histoire. Paris, Copernic, 1979, pp. 18 (illus.), 85.

Alexandre Cabanel

French: Montpellier, 1823 - Paris, 1889

Cabanel, a precocious youth, became a drawing master at the College of Saint Pons at the age of fourteen, and two years later received a scholarship to study in Paris. He entered the atelier of the classicist F. E. Picot in 1839 and enrolled in the Ecole des Beaux-Arts the following year. In 1845 he shared first place in the Prix de Rome contest with Léon Benouville. Although the prize was awarded to Benouville, Cabanel, too, went to Rome, where he remained five years studying the works of the High Renaissance, particularly those of Raphael and the Carracci. Upon his return to Paris he received commissions for a number of important decorative projects: The *Months* for the Salon de Caryatids, Hôtel de Ville (destroyed 1871), the *Senses* and the *Hours* for the Hôtel Pereire (1858), and *Dream of Life* and the *Four Elements* for the Hôtel Say.

Cabanel enjoyed a rapid rise to success, first appearing at the Salon in 1844, receiving a second-class medal in 1852, and in 1855 obtaining a first-class medal and an appointment as Chevalier of the Legion of Honor. Among his most ambitious works were the *Glorification of Saint Louis,* commissioned in 1853 by the State at Delaroche's instigation for the Chapel of Saint Louis, Château de Vincennes, and *Paradise Lost,* painted for the King of Bavaria and first shown at the 1867 Exposition Universelle. Cabanel enjoyed the patronage of Napoleon III, who purchased Cabanel's *The Rape of the Nymph* and *The Birth of Venus* for his private collection and who commissioned an official portrait in 1865.

After the Exposition of 1867, Cabanel worked primarily as a portraitist of the Paris *haute monde.* Georges Lafenestre, "Alexandre Cabanel," *Gazette des Beaux-Arts* 3d pér. 1 (1889) : 278, mentions, in particular, a series of paintings of beautiful partially clad women, such as Baltimore's *Pandora,* portrayed in various mythological, historical and literary guises.

After succeeding Horace Vernet as a member of the Institut in 1863, Cabanel was appointed professor at the Ecole des Beaux-Arts, where, because of his relatively liberal teaching, he drew a considerable number of pupils, including J. Bastien-Lepage, Benjamin Constant, Raphael Collin, F. Cormon, H. Gervex, A.-M. Morot, and his own son Pierre Cabanel.

131. Napoleon III

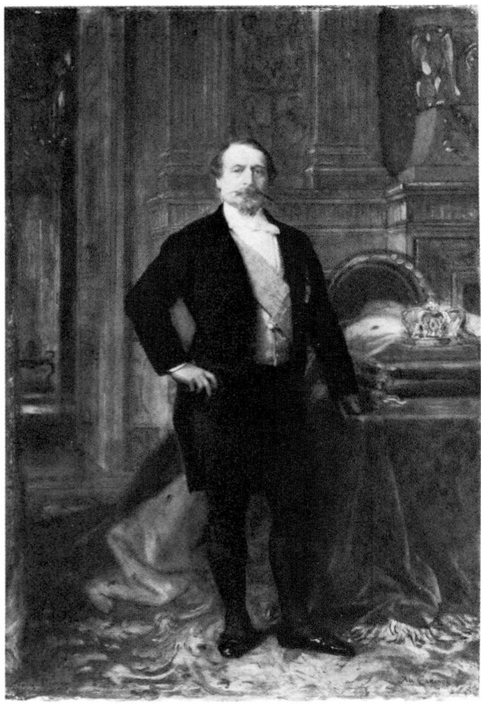

37.146 c. 1865

The Emperor is posed with his right hand on his hip and his left on a table. He wears prescribed court attire: black court suit, breeches, and white waistcoat. Across his chest is the red Grand Cordon of the Legion of Honor and pinned to his breast are medals, indecipherable in this sketch. Resting on a cushion at his right is the Imperial Crown. His robes of office lie across a chair behind him. In the background is a chimneypiece decorated with an Imperial Eagle and at the left a vista into another room.

This small painting is a replica of Cabanel's large portrait commissioned in 1865 for the apartments of the Empress in the Tuileries and exhibited at the 1867 Exposition Universelle. The large work, the location of which is presently unknown (Cabanel's official portrait of the Emperor was purported in 1981 to belong to a private collector in Lucca, Italy), was intended to rival H.-J. Flandrin's famous portrait showing the Emperor in the uniform of a General of Division that was exhibited in 1863 and is now in Versailles. In both portraits the figure is posed before the same chimneypiece. Philippe de Chennevières recorded that Napoleon preferred the more flattering Cabanel portrait to Flandrin's picture which he thought gave him a melancholy appearance. Within artistic circles, however, the more pleasing Cabanel painting was mockingly discussed as the "portrait du maître d'hôtel."

Support: Panel, hardwood, painted red, beveled on sides and bottom, .41 x .32 (16⅛" x 12⅝").

Signed at lower left in black cursive lettering: *Ale Cabanel;* Signed at lower right in brown block letters: *Al. Cabanel.*

Provenance: Unknown, purchased between 1887 and 1893. Perhaps it was the Cabanel "sketch" purchased by G. A. Lucas at Chevalier's for 350 francs, May 27–28, 1889.

Exhibitions: "The Second Empire, 1852–1870," Philadelphia, Detroit, Paris, 1978–79, no. VI-17.

References: Philippe de Chennevières, "Souvenirs d'un directeur des beaux-arts," 5 parts, *L'Artiste* (1883–89). Part 2 (1885): 8–9; Walters cat., 1893, p. 97, no. 161, and subsequent Walters catalogues.

132. Pandora

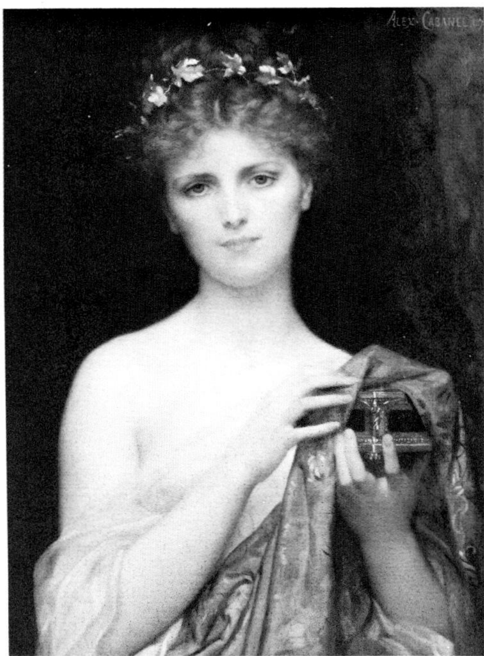

37.99

Pandora, the first woman according to classical mythology, is shown half-length. She is in the process of removing an embroidered silk cloth to reveal the fatal box given to her by Zeus, which, when opened, would inundate the world with troubles. About her head is a gold floral diadem. Her diaphanous white garment reveals the contours of her body. The artist has carefully rendered the flesh tones in dense pigments that contrast with the brown glazes of the background.

Early Walters catalogues suggest that the model was Christine Nilsson (1843–1921), the celebrated Swedish soprano to whom Georges Bizet dedicated his *Tarentelle* in 1862. By 1873, the year of this painting, she had been married to Auguste Rouzaud for a year and had therefore abandoned her role of leading prima donna of Paris. Cabanel painted a full length picture of Pandora (1.016 x .724), dated 1881, that appeared on the New York art market in 1980.

Alternative title: *Portrait of Mlle. Nilsson*

Support: Canvas, .732 x .521 (28⅞" x 20½")

Signed at upper right in yellow letters: *ALEX. CABANEL 1873.*

Condition: Cleaned and lined in 1972.

Provenance: Purchased directly from the artist by G. A. Lucas, for 10,000 francs on October 26, 1873.

References: Strahan, 1: 92, 94; Walters cat., 1878, p. 40, and subsequent Walters catalogues; Champlin and Perkins, 1: 225; Mathews, p. 8.

Adolphe Yvon

French, Eschviller (Moselle), 1817 - Paris, 1893

In 1834 Adolphe Yvon resigned from the Garde à cheval dans les eaux et forêts du domaine royale to become a pupil of Paul Delaroche and to enroll in the Ecole des Beaux-Arts. His early paintings included portraits, such as *le portrait de M.H.P.* . . . shown in 1841, and biblical subjects such as *Saint Paul in Prison baptizing the Gaoler and his Family,* Salon of 1843, and *Christ driving out the Money-Changers from the Temple,* Salon of 1845. A trip to Russia in the mid-forties resulted in numerous drawings of Russian subjects which were sent to the Salons as well as a large historical work, *The Battle of Kulikovo,* shown in 1850 and acquired by the Tsar in 1857. With the fall of the Second Republic Yvon turned to the military exploits of the First and Second Empires. His *The First Consul Descending the Saint-Bernard Pass in Italy* was acquired for Compiègne in 1853, and a painting depicting Marshall Ney's retreat from Moscow was sent to Versailles in 1855. Also commissioned for Versailles were three monumental canvases documenting the French assault at Malakoff near Sebastapol on September 8, 1855. In 1859 Yvon participated in the Italian campaign which he recorded in *The Battle of Solferino* and in *Magenta, June 4, 1859,* two works which were shown at the Salons of 1861 and 1863 respectively, and then mounted at Versailles. Among his last large-scale paintings was an allegory, *The United States of America,* exhibited in 1870 and bought by A. T. Stewart, the New York collector. During the Third Republic Yvon flourished as a fashionable portraitist.

This artist's reputation as a principal military painter of the Second Empire was enhanced by popular engravings after his monumental battle scenes. In discussing this aspect of his work, the critic Paul Mantz associated Yvon with Horace Vernet and his followers and questioned his preoccupation with detail and also his lack of vitality, in "Salon de 1859," *Gazette des Beaux-Arts* (1859): 140.

Yvon was also a professor at the Ecole des Beaux-Arts and was author of *Méthode de dessin à l'usage des Ecoles et des Lycées,* Paris, 1867.

133. Portrait of Napoleon III

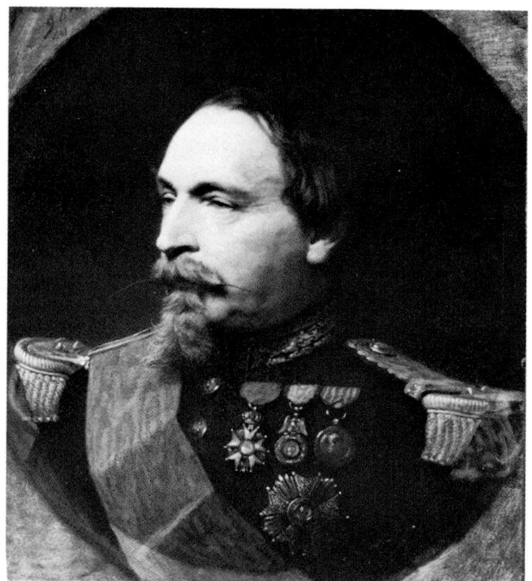

37.95 1868

The Emperor is shown at shoulder-length with his head turned slightly to the left. He is in military uniform with a red moiré sash of the Legion of Honor over his right shoulder and wears, from left to right, the Badge of the Legion of Honor, the Military Medal, and the Medal of Italy. Pinned below is the Star of the Legion of Honor.

Early Walters catalogues, ignoring the 1868 dating of the picture, state that it was painted from life for the *Battle of Solferino* which was exhibited in 1861. Despite the fact that the Emperor is bare headed in the small portrait whereas he wears a cap in the battle scene, the images are very similar. Both show the subject in his prime, suggesting that the Walters picture may have been based on an earlier preliminary study for the monumental painting at Versailles.

The Walters portrait is oval-shaped on a rectangular canvas. Concealed by the rabbet of the frame is a border of underpainting and the painted ground of the spandrels.

Support: Canvas, .557 x .467 (22″ x 18⅜″)

Signed and dated at the right just above the epaulet: *AD. YVON / 1868.*

Marks: Painted in the left spandrel area are the numerals *96;* The frame bears an old paper sticker: *761.* L

Provenance: Henry Walters inscribed in an 1884 catalogue of the collection that this work was acquired from S. P. Avery in 1876.

Condition: Lined in 1959.

Exhibitions: "War à la Mode," Walters Art Gallery, 1977, no. W13.

References: Strahan, 1: 94; Walters cat., 1878, p. 4, and subsequent Walters catalogues; Lamb, p. 251.

Georges-Jules-Victor Clairin

French: Paris, 1843 - Belle-Ile-en-Mer, 1919

Clairin was a prominent painter of Islamic themes, portraits, and murals in the last third of the nineteenth century. He began to train in 1861 in the Ecole des Beaux-Arts, where he studied with F. E. Picot and A. A. Pils. His first salon entry, an illustration for the Erckmann-Chatrian romance, *Histoire d'un conscrit de 1813,* was shown in 1866, and his second, *Panel for a Dining Room,* a collaborative work in which he was assisted by H. Regnault and E. T. Blanchard, appeared the following year. In 1868, after exhibiting several Breton subjects at the Salon, Clairin departed with Regnault for an extended visit to Spain and Morocco. The trip was cut short by the Franco-Prussian War and the subsequent Siege of Paris, during which the two painters served together in the Garde Nationale. Following the death of the latter at the Battle of Buzenval, June 1871, Clairin returned to Morocco for a year and a half, working for some time with the Spanish painters Mariano Fortuny, B. Ferrandiz, and José Tapiro.

Back in France, Clairin completed in 1874 four panels begun by Pils for the staircase of the Opera. Other important decorative projects later undertaken were for a theater at Cherbourg, the Eden Theater in Paris, and the Casino at Monte Carlo. As a genre painter, he occasionally portrayed contemporary events. It was his usual practice however, to paint dramatic quasi-historical scenes set in fifteenth-century Moorish Spain, utilizing the experiences garnered during his early travels reinforced with those of subsequent journeys in the nineties. He sometimes participated in the *Japonisme* movement of the 70s and 80s, producing a number of figurative works involving models attired in kimonos. In portraiture Clairin was noted for his paintings of theatrical figures, the most famous of which is his formidable portrait of Sarah Bernhardt shown lounging *en déshabillé* which is now in the Petit Palais, Paris.

134. Entering the Harem

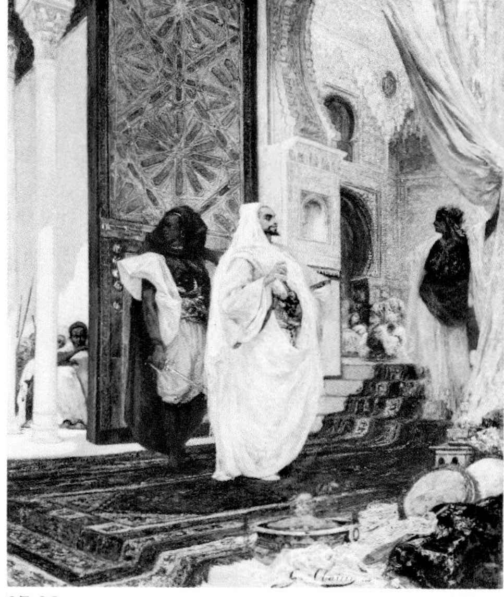

37.82 1870s

The center foreground of the painting is dominated by the imposing figure of a sheik, shown with his yataghan in his girdle, standing on a carpeted landing leading to the steps of the harem beyond. A female attendant draws aside a curtain to reveal a glimpse of the interior of the harem with its rich, Mudéjar-style vaulting and its inhabitants seated in the background. Behind the sheik stands a guard with drawn sword, while several men are squatting at the left in what appears to be a sunlit courtyard. In the immediate right foreground have been placed a smoking copper brazier, several cushions, a lute, and some porcelain vessels on a wooden stand. Stylistically the architecture approximates that of the Alcazar at Seville and the tall, ornately carved and inlaid door in the harem entrance appears to be almost identical to that made for the Hall of the Ambassadors of the Alcazar in 1366.

The painting displays the richness of colors and textures characteristic of Clairin. Its facture varies from careful finish in the principal figure to bravura in the sketchily rendered secondary figures and the setting. Affinities should be noted between this work and the more sanguinary paintings stemming from Clairin's sojourn in Morocco and Spain. The model for the sheik, for example, appears as a central figure in *Massacre of the Abencerrages at Granada* (1874), Musée des Beaux-Arts, Rouen, in which he is surrounded by followers displaying several heads. In *After the Victory of the Moors in Spain,* Salon of 1885, the mounted leader enters a courtyard, passing through the same doorway as in the Baltimore picture, though from the opposite direction. Possibly the archetype for *Entering the Harem* was the celebrated *Execution Without Trial under the Moorish Kings of Granada* painted by Clairin's companion Henri Regnault in Tangier in 1870. Regnault, who appears from contemporary accounts to have been the more innovative of the two artists, shows in his dramatic composition, now in the Louvre (R.F. 22), the executioner towering over his victim on a flight of steps leading into a Mudéjar-style interior.

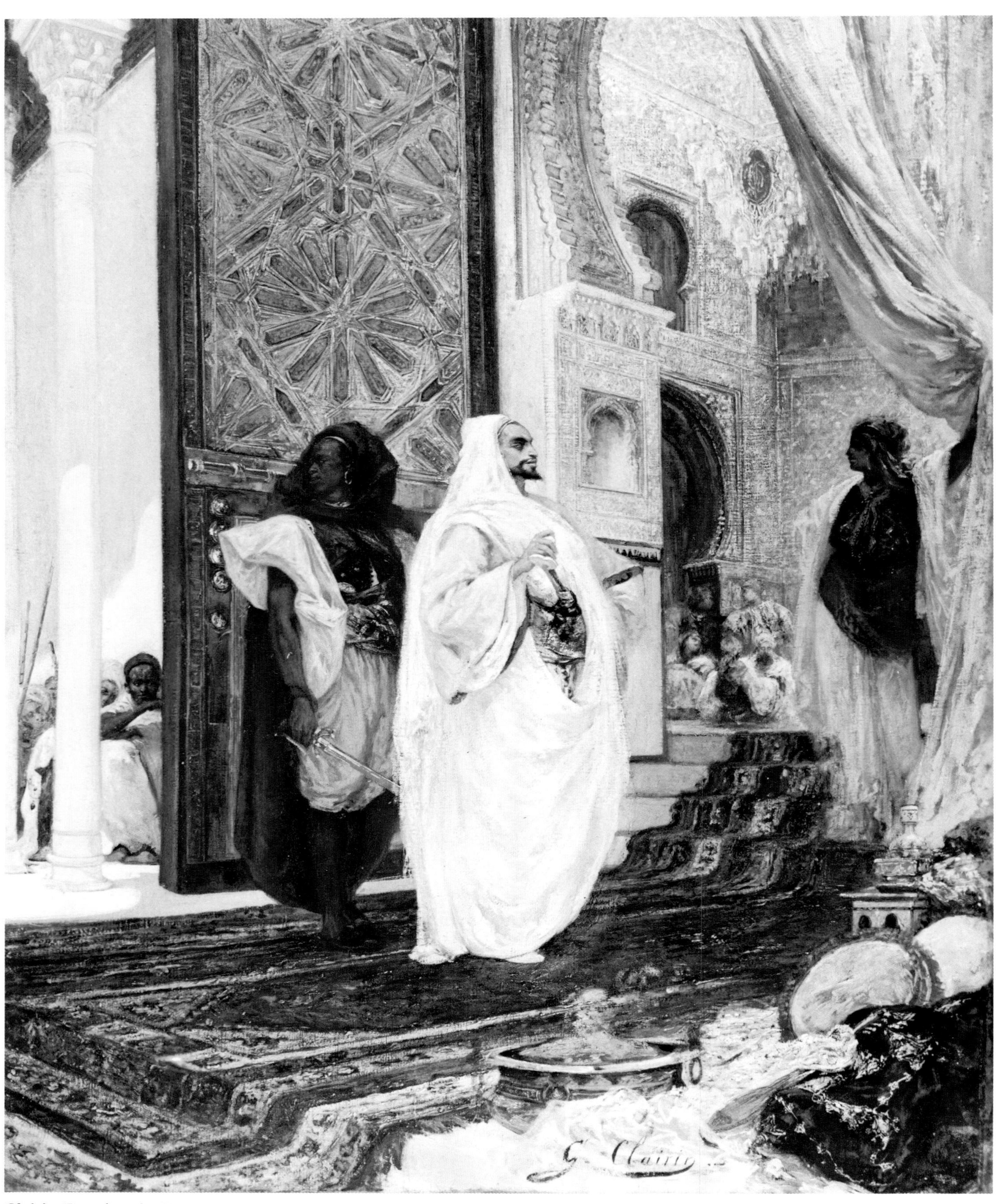

Clairin *Entering the Harem,* no. 134

Alternative title: *A Moorish Sheik entering his Seraglio*

Support: Canvas, thin priming, .815 x .651 (25⅛" x 25⅝")

Signed lower right: *G. Clairin.*

Condition: Cleaned and lined in 1969.

Provenance: Catalogue of Mr. John Wolfe's Gallery of Valuable Paintings, New York, April 5 and 6, 1882, no. 16, $500.00.

Exhibitions: "Fortuny and his Circle," Walters Art Gallery, 1970, no. 20.

References: Strahan, 1: 60–61, 64; Walters cat., 1884, p. 84, no. 144; Stranahan, p. 326; W. R. Johnston, "Califs and captives," *M* 13 (June 1972): 15–16, fig. 4.

Charles Louis Lucien Muller (Müller)

French: Paris, 1815 - Paris, 1892

This artist, who worked in historical and religious genre, portraiture and decorative programs, is chiefly remembered as the author of *The Roll Call of the last Victims of the Terror,* an enormous lachrymose machine that was exhibited at the 1850 Salon and subsequently acquired by the State for the Luxembourg Gallery. "Muller de Paris," as he was known, received his training in the Ecole des Beaux-Arts as a pupil of Léon Cogniet and in the studio of Baron Gros. His earliest entry in the Salons was in 1834, the year he submitted *The Promenade.* Thereafter he entered works regularly, and though overshadowed by the brilliance of Delaroche, Muller pursued a successful, albeit not highly innovative, career, richly rewarded with official recompenses. He received a third-class medal in 1838, a second-class in 1846 and first-class medals in 1848 and again at the Exposition Universelle in 1855. About this time Muller was portrayed by Eugène Delacroix as an extremely self-satisfied individual, mired in Thomas Couture's school of painting *(Journal de Eugène Delacroix,* Paris, 1932, 1:177–78, "février 3, 1847"). Muller, nevertheless, rose through the ranks of the Legion of Honor from Chevalier in 1849 to Officier in 1850, the year he was also appointed artistic director at the Gobelins manufactory, and in 1864 he succeeded H. Flandrin as a member of the Institut. Muller's decorative projects for the Louvre included *Aurora,* painted from sketches by Lebrun for the vault of the Galerie d'Apollon, a ceiling for the Salle des Etats representing the *Apotheosis of France* dated 1855, *Glory Distributing Palms and Crowns* completed in 1866 for the Escalier Mollien, and four large panels of the same date representing the arts in France during the reigns of Saint Louis, Francis I, Louis XIV, and Napoleon, for the Salon Denon. In America Muller's reputation was based on the *Roll Call of the Last Victims of the Terror,* a reduction of his 1850 chef-d'oeuvre that passed through the J. T. Johnston and J. J. Astor collections and for a *Charlotte Corday in Prison* of 1875, formerly in the Corcoran Gallery of Art, Washington, D.C.

135. A Portrait

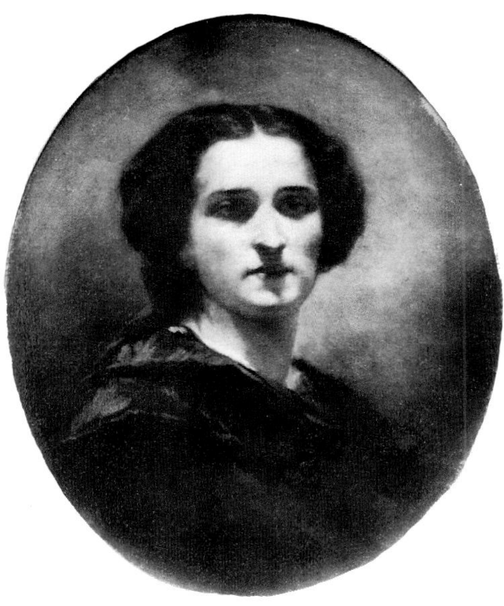

37.75 1852

A black-haired woman, clad in black with a red scarf, is shown shoulder-length posed against a neutral greenish grey, shadowy ground. The lighting is from overhead, leaving the eyes in shadow. The subject's identity has not been ascertained.

Support: Canvas, oval, .61 x .495 (24" x 19½")

Signed and dated at lower right: *C. L. Müller / 1852*

Marks: Stencil on reverse: *Atelier Bro. Clichy, no. 7; DEFORGE; Mn. de Couleurs; Boulevard Montmartre.8.*

Condition: Prior to 1934 the picture had received damages and had been lined and overpainted. At this point the original tacking edges were removed. In 1981 discolored varnishes and overpainting were removed, revealing losses in the right nostril, the center of the nose-ridge, and in the lower neck region.

Provenance: Possibly this picture is the "Head of Muller" bought at Delaroche's by G. A. Lucas, December 16, 1865 (See Lucas Diaries, 2: 208).

References: Walters cat., 1878, p. 40, and subsequent Walters catalogues; Champlin and Perkins, 3: 311 (as *Purity*).

Léon-Joseph-Florentin Bonnat

French: Bayonne, 1833 - Mouchy-en-Brie (Oise), 1922

In his youth in Madrid, Bonnat assisted his father in the family workshop during the day and followed Federico de Madrazo's courses in drawing at the Academy of San Fernando in the evening. During these studies he developed a life-long admiration for the paintings of Velasquez. Receiving a municipal scholarship, he went to Paris to enroll in the Ecole des Beaux-Arts under Léon Cogniet. In 1857 Bonnat submitted three portraits to the Salon and competed for the Prix de Rome, winning a second-class prize. The following year he traveled to Rome to the Villa Medici, where he remained for three years studying Renaissance and Baroque art. This experience resulted in a number of large religious paintings such as *The Good Samaritan* (1859), *Adam and Eve finding Abel Dead* (1861), *Martyrdom of Saint Andrew* (1863), and the *Pilgrims at the Foot of Saint Peter's Statue in St. Peters, Rome* (1864) bought by the Empress, as well as a number of Italian peasant subjects including *Mariuccia* (1861) *Pasqua Maria* (1864) and *Neopolitan Peasants in front of the Farnese Palace* (1866), that recalled similar works by Jalabert and Hébert. In 1868–69 Bonnat accompanied J.-L. Gérôme on a tour of the Holy Land and Egypt, painting numerous oil studies that were never exhibited.

Back in Paris Bonnat entered in the Salons a number of orientalist subjects including *A Fellah Woman and her Child* (1870), *View of Jerusalem* (1870), *Sheiks of Akkaba* (1872), *Turkish Barber* (1873) and *Negro Barber at Suez* (1876). In addition he continued to produce religious paintings, generating considerable controversy with his harshly realistic *Christ* painted in 1869 for the Court of Assizes in the Palace of Justice and exhibited in 1874. In preparation for this work, which represented his triumph as a naturalist, Bonnat studied a cadaver attached to a cross in the Ecole de Médecine. He was also one of twelve painters commissioned to decorate the Panthéon with murals.

Today Bonnat is primarily remembered as one of the foremost portraitists of the Third Republic. His forte lay in vigorous, dramatically illuminated representations of men, in which his study of Spanish and Italian seventeenth-century masters was obviously reflected. His portrait of L. A. Thiers, exhibited in 1877, the year of the statesman's death, assured his reputation in this genre. In the ensuing years many of France's most eminent political leaders, artists, and clerics posed for him, including Victor Hugo (1879), Léon Cogniet (1881), Puvis de Chavannes (1882), Alexandre Dumas (1887), and President Carnot (1890).

Bonnat was the recipient of the highest official awards, rising through the ranks of the Legion of Honor from

Chevalier in 1867 to Officier in 1874 and to Commandeur in 1882, as well as receiving the Grand Cross after the Exposition Universelle of 1900. He succeeded his teacher Cogniet as a member of the Institut, became a director of the Ecole des Beaux Arts and honorary president of the Société nationale des Beaux-Arts. His portraits, however, were increasingly criticized for their emphasis on technical virtuosity and external appearances rather than on penetrating character analysis.

Among Bonnat's pupils were Béraud, Toulouse-Lautrec, and Roll. A particularly close association developed among Bonnat, William Walters, and his Paris agent G. A. Lucas, because of their shared interests in the sculpture of A. L. Barye. Along with Lucas, Henry Havard, and Ferdinand Barbedienne, Bonnat was a member of a committee formed in Paris to erect a monument to the deceased animalier. William Walters was responsible for establishing a similar committee in the United States. Bonnat lent sixty-two sculptures to the Barye benefit exhibition held in the Ecole des Beaux-Arts, Paris, in 1889.

136. An Arab Sheik

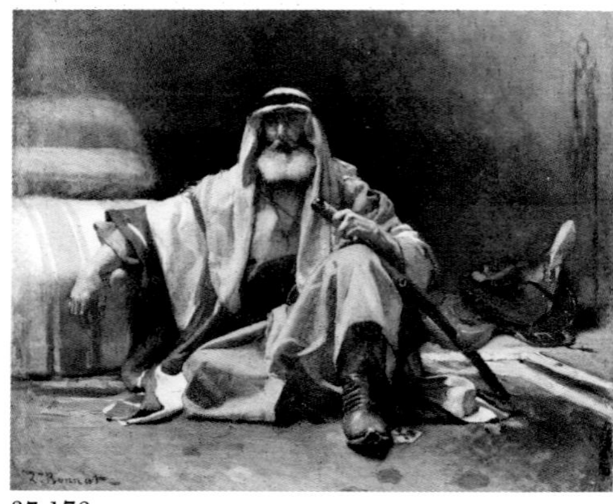

37.173

A bearded Arab in a crimson caftan and a striped beige burnoose is seated on a carpet holding a sword in one hand and resting his elbow on a divan. Behind him is a saddle.

Bonnat's 1868–69 trip to the Near East resulted in a number of paintings with Oriental subjects. Related works include the *Arab removing a Thorn from his Foot,* the *Arab Chief* in the Mrs. Mary J. Morgan collection Sale, New York, 1886, no. 152, *A Gate to Jerusalem* (1870), and the *Job* in the Musée Bonnat, Bayonne, in which the same bearded model is represented.

Support: Canvas, .65 x .725 (25½″ x 28½″)

Provenance: The history of this work is problematical. In the archieves of the Gallery there is preserved the following letter:

Paris
12 December 1884

Dear Walters–

Arnold [Arnold and Tripp] *still has the / little picture Arab Cheik / red Bornous — very good / and very cheap — BONNAT .. 5500 francs*
Size: 10½ x 14¼ inches / Cable if you want it / Truly yours G A Lucas

Neither the vertical format, the color of the burnoose, nor the measurements correspond to the above picture. However, since there is no other reference to a similar purchase in the Gallery records, it is possible that Lucas was mistaken on these points.

Exhibitions: "The Master Artist," American Federation of Arts, New York, 1967–68.

References: Walters cat., 1887, p. 87, no. 139, and subsequent Walters cat.; Cook, 1: 172.

---

137. Portrait of William T. Walters (1819–1894)

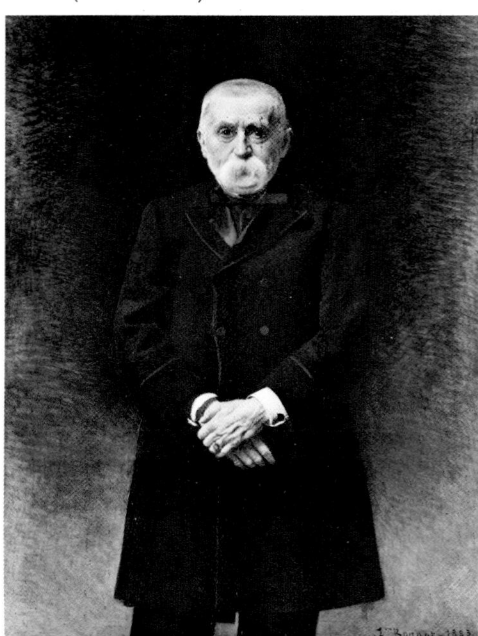

37.758 1883

The sixty-five year-old railroad financier and founder of the Walters collection is portrayed three-quarter length with his hands folded in front. A remarkable sense of presence is conveyed by this life-size portrait. The subject's face and hands are dramatically illuminated from above and his black-clad figure is silhouetted against a neutral ground consisting of hatched strokes of grays, blacks, umbers, dark reds and blue, graduated in intensity, with a considerable amount of the underpainting left exposed, particularly in the lower section of the picture.

Bonnat commenced the portrait on March 30, 1883, and completed it on June 5, 1883. Its completion was delayed by the subject's absences from Paris on visits to Italy and the Netherlands and by postponements resulting from bouts of rheumatism (Lucas Diaries 2: 560–66) .

Support: Canvas, finely woven, 1.432 x 1.022 (56⅜″ x 40¼″)

Signed and dated lower right: *Leon Bonnat — 1883*

Condition: The picture was lined and discolored varnishes removed and replaced with synthetic varnish in 1973.

Provenance: Commissioned from the artist in 1883 for 15,000 francs.

Exhibitions: "A Baltimorean in Paris, George A. Lucas, Art Agent," Walters Art Gallery, 1979.

References: Walters cat., 1884, p. 37, no. 49, and subsequent Walters catalogues; R. B. Gruelle, "Mariano Fortuny and Léon Bonnat"; notes on their pictures in the Walters Collection, Baltimore," *Modern Art* 1 (1893); Reizenstein, p. 545, illus.; Lucas, 2: 560–66.

138. Portrait of the Artist

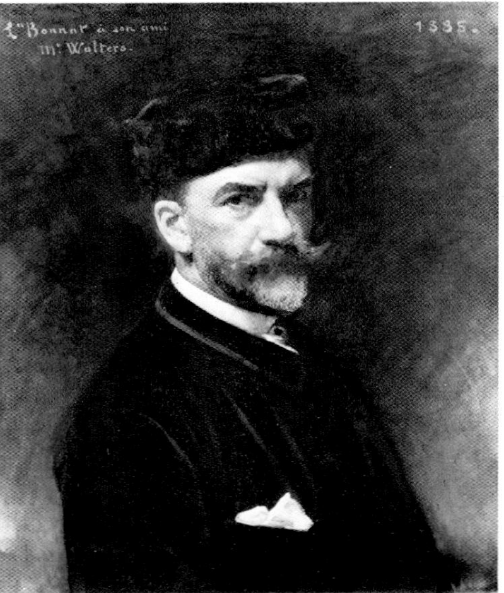

37.74 1885

In his self-portraits, which were recurrent in his oeuvre, Bonnat presented a sense of intimacy rarely encountered in his other works. Here he appears at the age of fifty-two, shoulder-length, turned to the right and dressed in working attire. Other examples of self-portraits are to be found in the Louvre, one showing him at the age of twenty-two (R.F. 2684) and two at eighty-three (R.F. 2425 and INV. 20034), a portrait in the Ecole des Beaux-Arts shows him at eighty-four; another in the Musée Bonnat, Bayonne, at forty-one (no. 676); and in the Petit Palais he appears at age twenty-seven (charcoal drawing). In addition, there is an unlocated self-portrait bearing a dedication to a Dr. A. Doyen painted in 1899.

Support: Canvas, .736 x .606 (29″ x 23⅞″)

Signed and inscribed upper left: *Ln Bonnat à Son ami / Mr. Walters.*

Marks: Dated upper right: *1885.*
Canvas marked in black: *J Ottoz.*

Condition: The canvas was lined and discolored varnishes replaced with synthetic varnish in 1972.

Provenance: Gift of the artist to W. T. Walters.

Exhibitions: "A Baltimorean in Paris, George A. Lucas, Art Agent," Walters Art Gallery, 1979.

References: Walters cat., 1887, p. 53, no. 80, and subsequent Walters catalogues; R. B. Gruelle, "Mariano Fortuny and Léon Bonnat; notes on their pictures in the Walters collection, Baltimore," *Modern Art* 1 (1893), illus.; Lucas, 2: 601.

---

139. Portrait of George Aloysius Lucas (1824–1909)

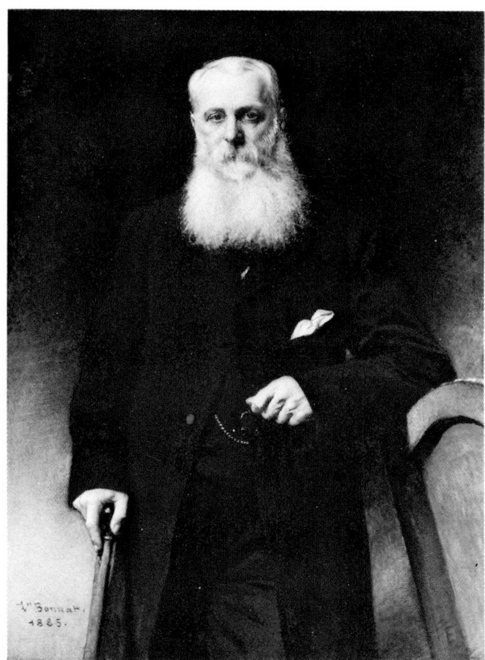

37.759 1885

This life-size three-quarter length portrait was commissioned together with the posthumous portrait of Barye for the "Barye Room" of the Walters residence in Mount Vernon Place, Baltimore. In his preface to *Antoine-Louis Barye: From the French of Various Critics,* Baltimore, 1885, p. 7, W. T. Walters wrote: *The debt I owe him* [G. A. Lucas] *for his good judgment, mature experience and cheerful cooperation in nearly all I have accomplished as amateur and collector, I find only less than the value I place upon his sterling truth, and upon his worth as a man and a friend.* He went on to thank Bonnat for setting aside more important work to complete the portraits of Barye and Lucas for the "Barye Room."

Lucas sailed to Europe in 1857, never to return to the United States. He resided in Paris, serving as a gentleman-agent to a number of American collectors, and played a particularly influential role in the formation of the Walters Barye collection. In addition he was responsible for directing a number of clients to Bonnat's studio and he also assisted the portraitist in the formation of a collection of Barye bronzes. The cordial relations that existed between the American and the portraitist may be surmised by this undated letter preserved in the Gallery:

> *My dear friend,*
> *What's the matter? I think by the portrait of you done by my new concierge that it is you hou kame twice or three times—I am very sorry not to have been home.*
> *Qu'est ce que vous dites de mon anglais? Demain matin je serai chez moi toute la matinée de huit hrs à midi, et mon concierge a ordre d'ailleurs, de vous laisser monter toutes les fois que ça vous plaira.*
> *Bien affectueusement a vous*
> *Ln Bonnat*
> *Lundi*

This portrait was executed between March 22 and May 18, 1885, in seventeen sittings averaging three hours in length.

Support: Canvas, 1.292 x .921 (50⅞" x 36½")

Signed and dated, lower left: *Ln Bonnat / 1885.*

Marks: Canvas stenciled: *EMANUEL CHENOZ, Rue de Conde 29, PRES du MUSEE du LUXEMBOURG, Paris, Mn. DE COULEURS FINS TOILES . . . DIMENSIONS.*

Condition: The painting was lined and discolored varnishes were removed and replaced with synthetic varnish in 1972.

Provenance: On May 18, 1885, Bonnat received 40,000 francs for the portraits of Lucas and Barye.

Exhibitions: "A Baltimorean in Paris, George A. Lucas, Art Agent," Walters Art Gallery, 1979.

References: Walters cat., 1887, p. 92, no. 149, and subsequent Walters catalogues; *The diaries, 1871–1882, of Samuel P. Avery.* Edited from the manuscript by Madeleine Fidell Beaufort, Herbert L. Kleinfield and Jeanne K. Welcher. New York, Arno Press, 1979, fig. 18; Lucas, 2: 605–08.

140. Portrait of A.-L. Barye

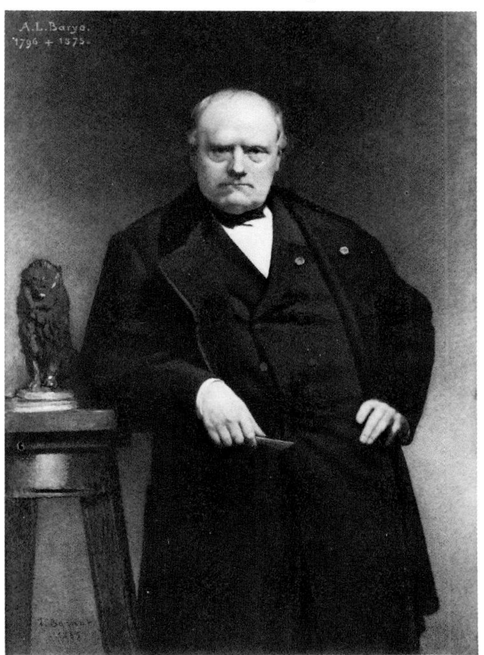

37.757 1885

The sculptor is standing with his left hand on his hip and his right elbow resting on a pedestal bearing a model of the *Seated Lion.* He is clad in black and wears in his lapels two rosettes of the Legion of Honor. In his hand is a wooden scalpel.

William T. Walters commissioned this portrait through G. A. Lucas for the "Barye Room" in his town residence. Bonnat undertook the commission on November 18, 1884, but did not actually commence its execution until April 9, 1885 when he was visited by Mme. Barye and her daughter in the company of Lucas (Lucas Diaries, 2: 597, 606). Lucas lent the portraitist a wax model of the *Seated Lion* on May 12, 1885 and two months later, on July 17, the painting was shipped to America (Lucas Diaries, 2: 608, 612).

In 1889 Bonnat made the following admission: *Je n'ai jamais vu Barye. Et cependant j'ai toujours eu pour lui un vrai culte. Barye a été resté une de mes grandes adorations* ("Barye," *Gazette des Beaux-Arts* 3rd pér. 1 (1889): 375). In this portrait Bonnat worked from a photograph of the elderly sculptor taken by Nadar that was probably provided by Lucas (Lucas Diaries, 2: 595).

Subsequently Bonnat painted another portrait, dated 1889, showing Barye as a younger man, which is now in the Musée Bonnat, Bayonne, no. 52, (1.31 x .825). It was the Bayonne portrait that Lucas presumably saw the artist retouching on the morning of the public opening of the Barye Exhibition at the Ecole des Beaux-Arts, Paris, 1889 (Lucas Diaries, 2: 691).

Support: Canvas, fine weave, 1.295 x .92 (51" x 36¼")

Signed and dated lower left: *Ln Bonnat / 1885.*

Marks: Inscribed upper left: *A. L. Barye / 1791 + 1875;* Original canvas stenciled: *E Ottoz / 9 rue Fontaine.*

Condition: Discolored varnishes removed and replaced with synthetic varnishes and picture lined in 1972.

Exhibitions: "A Baltimorean in Paris, George A. Lucas, Art Agent," Walters Art Gallery, 1979.

References: W. T. Walters, "Preface," *Antoine-Louis Barye, from the French of various critics.* Baltimore, 1885. p. 7; Walters cat., 1887, p. 92, no. 150, and subsequent Walters catalogues; Cook, 1: 172; R. B. Gruelle, "Mariano Fortuny and Léon Bonnat; notes on their pictures in the Walters collection, Baltimore," *Modern Art* 1 (1893); Louis Réau, *L'art français aux Etats-Unis.* Paris, Laurens, 1926. p. 160; Lucas, 1: fig. 39; 2: 597, 598, 606, 608, 612.

141. Hand of A. L. Barye

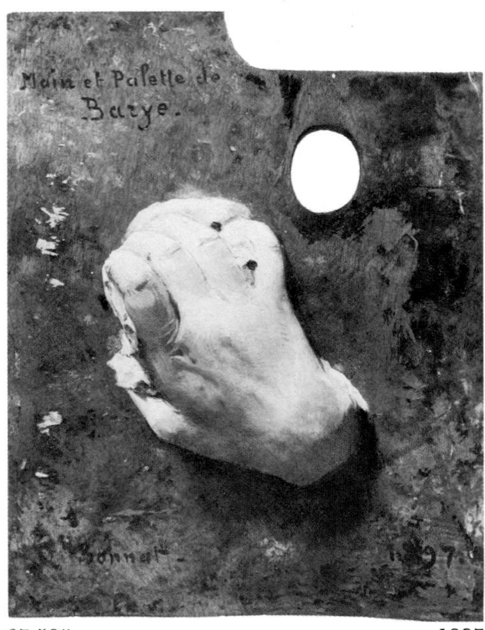

37.595 1897

Credit for the creation of this memento should be given to G. A. Lucas, who assembled a collection of more than seventy-two artists' palettes now belonging to the Maryland Institute College of Art.

Lucas borrowed a plaster cast of Barye's hand from Mme. Peronne-Barye, the animalier's daughter, on April 13, 1897 and delivered it to Bonnat's studio on May 4 the same year (Lucas Diaries, 2: 844–45). The following November 18, Lucas urged Bonnat to paint the hand on the palette that he had provided (Lucas Diaries, 2: 854). The partially cleaned palette bears the inscription: *Main et Palette de / Barye.*

The cast of Barye's hand is presently preserved in the Musée Bonnat, Bayonne (no. 461).

Support: Panel, .355 x .273 (14" x 10¾")

Signed and dated: *Ln Bonnat* (lower left); *1897* (lower right).

Marks: Reverse inscribed: *avec laquelle le portrait du Cardinal Lavigerie a ete fait / L. Bonnat 1888.*

Provenance: When the palette was given by G. A. Lucas to the Walters collection has not been ascertained.

Exhibitions: "A Baltimorean in Paris, George A. Lucas, Art Agent," Walters Art Gallery, 1979.

References: Lucas, 1: fig. 122; 2:844–45.

Pascal-Adolphe-Jean Dagnan-Bouveret

Paris, 1852 - Quincey (Haute-Saône), 1929

Dagnan-Bouveret, though born in Paris, was raised by his maternal grandfather in the village of Melun. His career began in 1869 when he rented a room in Corot's Paris residence on the rue Faubourg-Poissonnière and enrolled in the Ecole des Beaux-Arts, briefly under Cabanel, and subsequently in Gérôme's studio.

He began producing pictures of mythological subjects in a neoclassical vein, submitting an *Atalanta* to the Salon of 1875, and winning the second-class Prix de Rome the following year with *Priam Begging Achilles for the Body of Hector.* At the end of the decade he turned to realistic scenes of contemporary peasant and bourgeois life. These were at first set in the Franche-Comté, which he had first visited with his life-long friend and fellow artist Gustave C. E. Courtois in 1876, but after 1885 they were usually of Brittany subjects. The later paintings were frequently marked by feelings of religious fervor or mysticism not unlike that found in the works of his friend Jules Bastien-Lepage.

The year 1889 marked the apogee of Dagnan-Bouveret's career. He received Medals of Honor at the Exposition Universelle, and the Salon of the Société des Artistes Français and gold medals at exhibitions held in Munich and Ghent.

In the following years Dagnan-Bouveret enjoyed remarkable public success, exhibiting regularly at the salons of the Société nationale des Beaux-Arts and being made an honorary member of virtually every important foreign academy. Later works include ambitious religious paintings, such as *Christ at Gethsemane* (1894), a number of large decorative projects, notably an *Apollo and the Muses* for the Amphitheatre Richelieu of the Sorbonne (1903), and a *Justice* for the Palais de Justice, Paris (1921). During the Third Republic he was also highly esteemed as a portraitist. Most frequently cited are his portraits of Pedro Gil, La Comtesse de Grammont, Marshal Joffre, and Marshal Foch.

Much of the appeal of Dagnan-Bouveret's pictures can be attributed to his consummate draftsmanship, a quality which was readily appreciated by his contemporaries. His studies and drawings were featured in an exhibition at the Société Nationale des Beaux-Arts, Paris, in 1909.

142. An Accident

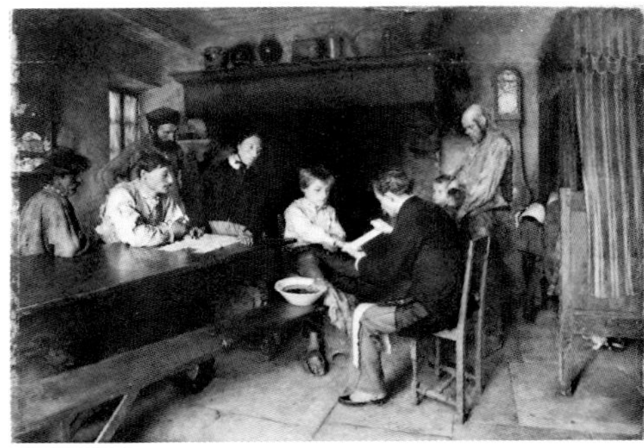

37.49 1879

In a rustic interior a doctor bandages the hand of a pale twelve-year-old boy. Beside them is a basin, filled with bloody water and some rags. On the left are four onlookers, one of whom, a woman, has been cutting bandages, and on the right are a child, a balding peasant, and a crouching woman who has buried her face in her dress. The simply furnished room reveals the artist's keen observation of detail. Arsène Alexandre recorded that Dagnan-Bouveret was traveling with a doctor friend when he witnessed this incident.

This picture was one of the artist's first realistic genre works and serves as a valuable document of nineteenth-century rural life. The following year Dagnan-Bouveret painted a variation with the same title showing the mother and sister on the left, and on the right the father seated with his head buried in his hands (illustrated in George William Sheldon, *Ideals of Life in France,* New York, 1890, facing p. 56). A preliminary study, *L'Enfant blessé,* is cited in H. Mireur, *Dictionnaire des ventes,* Paris, 1911, 2:337, Vente X, 1895.

The theme was further developed in *The Vaccination,* 1882, a painting showing a doctor innoculating some children in a cheerful urban interior.

Support: Canvas, seamed .115 from the top, backed with burlap; .925 x 1.3 (35⅝" x 58⅛")

Signed and dated lower right: *P.A.J. DAGNAN-B 1879 /Pasavant-sur-cones (Haute-Saône).*

Marks: Frame with label of *William Schaus, Tableaux modernes, 749 Broadway.*

Condition: Discolored varnishes removed in 1975; burlap backing removed; relined.

Provenance: William H. Stewart, Paris (not in Stewart Sale, New York, 1898) William Schaus, New York.

Exhibitions: Salon, Paris, 1880, no. 951, *médaille 1re classe.*

References: Lucy H. Hooper, "Art-notes from Paris," *The Art Journal* new series 6 (1880): 253; Walters cat., 1884, no. 107; Champlin and Perkins, 1: 363; Cook, 1: 117–18; Arsène Alexandre, "P.A.J. Dagnan-Bouveret," *Les lettres et les arts* 4 (1889): 395–96; Lamb, p. 251; Reizenstein, p. 556; "Les dessins du Musée du Luxembourg," *Les Maîtres du dessin* 1 (1900): plate VII (engraved by J. Chauvet); *Catalogue des oeuvres de Dagnan-Bouveret (peintures)* Paris, Institut de France, 1930. plate IV.

143. The Musician

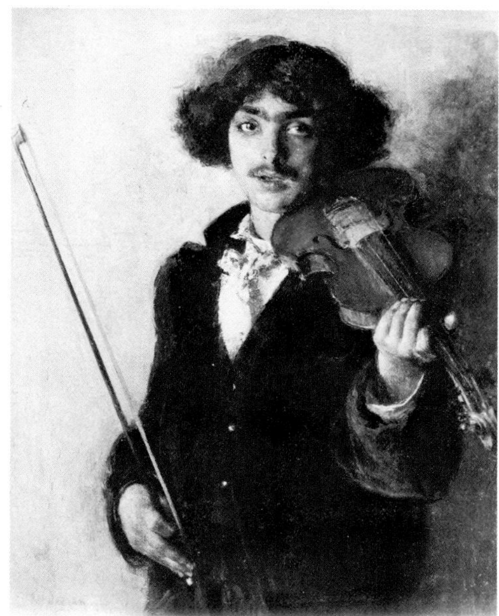

37.28 1884

A young musician is shown from slightly below the waist, posed with his violin and bow. The picture is thinly painted, allowing the wood ground to appear, particularly in the background. A couple of pictures entitled *Petit joueur de violon* of 1884–85 are mentioned in *Catalogue des oeuvres de Dagnan-Bouveret (peintures),* Paris, Institut de France, 1930.

Alternative title: *Le violoniste.*

Support: Thick panel, mitered on three sides, .252 x .195 (9⅞" x 7⅝")

Signed and dated lower left: *P.A.J. Dagnan-B / 1884.*

Marks: Original label on reverse: *Gustav Reichard's Art Room, N.Y.*

Provenance: Gustave Reichard's Art Room, New York; Mrs. Mary J. Morgan Sale, New York, 1886, no. 81.

References: Walters cat., 1884, no. 88, and subsequent Walters catalogues; H. Mireur, *Dictionnaire des ventes.* 7 vols. Paris, Ch. de Vincenti, 1911–12. 2: 336.

Jean-Jacques Henner

French (Alsatian), Bernwiller, 1829 - Paris, 1905

Before going to Paris in 1847, Henner received guidance and training from Charles Goutzwiller, teacher of drawing at the college of Altkirch, and from Gabriel-Christophe Guérin, professor at the Ecole de Dessin, Strasbourg. In Paris he became a pupil of a fellow Alsatian Michel Martin Drölling, at the Ecole des Beaux-Arts. Between 1855 and 1856 Henner was compelled by ill health to leave Paris and recuperate in Bernwiller, where he painted several portraits of family members and of villagers, revealing his talents as a realist. Returning to Paris in 1857, he enrolled in the studio of François Edouard Picot and the following year won the Prix de Rome with *Adam and Eve finding Abel's Body.* During his six-year sojourn at the Villa Medici, he visited Florence, Parma, and Venice in 1860, and Naples in 1862. Preserved in the Musée J. J. Henner, Paris, are landscape studies painted in Italy as well as copies after works by Fra Angelico, Andrea del Sarto, Filippo Lippi, Benozzo Gozzoli, Giovanni Bellini, Titian, Tintoretto, and Correggio. After his return to Paris in 1864, he acquired a studio at 11 Place Pigalle in which for the next four decades he pursued a prosperous career marked by few events of singular significance. His predilection for paintings of nudes, that can be traced to such works as *Young Bather Asleep,* Salon of 1863, and *The Chaste Susannah,* Salon of 1865, gave rise to a proliferation of similar subjects painted for his extensive private clientele. They were executed according to a formula in which the nacreous, pale figures were juxtaposed against a dark wooded background with sharply contrasting azure sky and occasional pools of water. Almost as numerous were his profile portraits of models with auburn hair frequently identified as *The Magdalen.* Although the proliferation of such works detracted from his posthumous reputation, his vigorous talent was clearly manifested at the Paris salons in such religious paintings as *The Dead Christ* (1876), and *Christ at the Tomb, Eclogue* (1879), recalling Holbein's celebrated predella of 1551 in Basel, as well as in his realistic portraits.

144. The Nymph

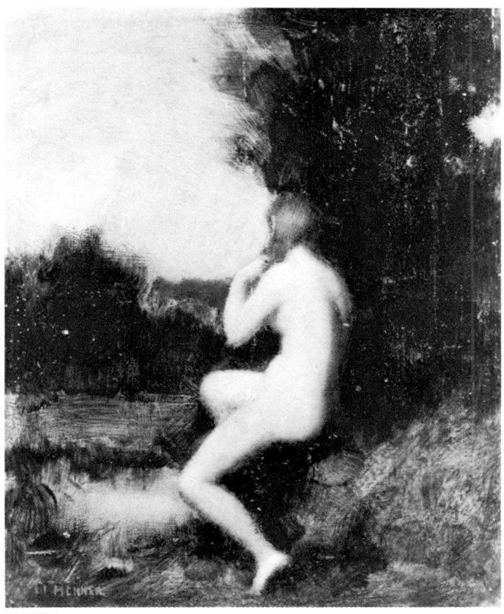

37.89

A nymph, crouching on a rock and combing her auburn hair with her face turned from the viewer, appears to evanesce into the setting. Both the background, composed of several tree shapes, and the immediate foreground are rendered in umber and umber glazes of varying intensity which leave exposed the blonde tonality of the ground in small areas. The sky is of calamine blue, also reflected in a small pool at the nymph's side, with a band of azure stretched across the horizon line.

Support: Thick, blonde, panel, beveled edges .271 x .218 (10⅝" x 8⅝")

Signed at lower left in brown: *J J HENNER*

Provenance: Acquired by W. T. Walters between 1878 and 1884.

References: Walters cat., 1884, p. 61, no. 92, and subsequent Walters catalogues; Champlin and Perkins, 2: 236; Mathews, p. 8.

Léon Jean Basile Perrault

French: Poitiers, 1832 - Royan, 1908

Though little known abroad, Perrault enjoyed a considerable following in France as a painter of genre subjects and portraits. After studying with Picot and Bouguereau he made his first appearance at the Paris Salon in 1861 with *The Old Man and the Three Young Men.* In 1864, the year he received his first medal, Perrault exhibited *Terror,* which was bought by Princess Mathilda. During the upheavals in France in 1870–71, he evidently sought refuge in England and entered the painting *Hide-and-Seek* in the Royal Academy in 1871, listing a Soho address. Resuming his career in France, he entered *Maternal Joys* in the 1873 Salon and also participated that year in the Vienna International Exhibition, receiving a diploma of honor. He was awarded a second-class medal in the 1876 Salon and was appointed a Chevalier of the Legion of Honor in 1887, the year he showed *The Toilet of Venus* and *Portrait of a Child.* In addition to easel paintings he also produced some decorative works, including a ceiling decoration showing the *Triumph of Hymen* for the Marriage Chamber of the city hall of his native Poitiers.

145. Maternity

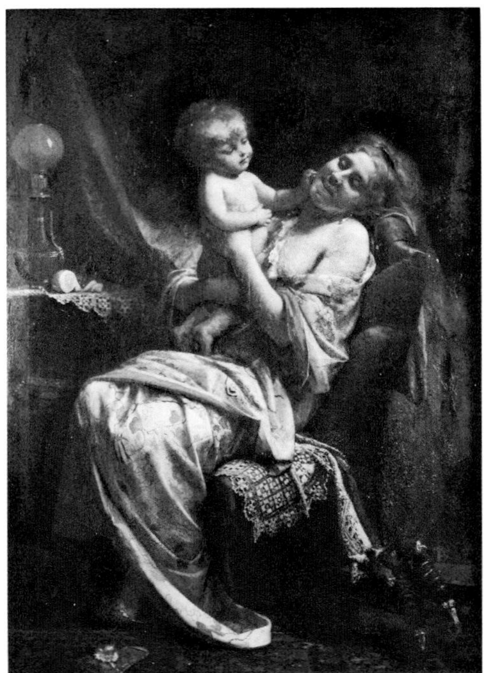

37.2560 1873

A pretty smiling mother, seated in her boudoir, clasps a young boy. He is naked and her shoulder is exposed. The artist has excelled in achieving a remarkable richness of colors and textures: the embroidered saffron-colored silk of the mother's kimono contrasting with the rich purple velvet upholstery of the chair. The vibrantly colored, strongly patterned oriental rug contributes further variety. On a Japanese carved teak bench rests a punchinello doll.

Perrault occasionally returned to such domestic subjects, showing *Tendresses maternelles* at the 1878 Salon. An *Affection maternelle* was sold in the Vente X, Paris, February 15–16, 1906, for $1500.00.

Alternative title: *Les joies maternelles.*

Support: Canvas, 1.703 x 1. 114 (67⅛" x 45¼")
Signed and dated lower right: *L. PERRAULT - 1873.*

Condition: Prior to 1979 the painting had been treated for the crackle resulting from the use of bitumen. Many areas, including the woman's arms and the child's legs, had been extensively over-painted to conceal the damage. In 1979-81 the discolored varnishes and overpainting were removed. An attempt is now being made to reform the surface, especially in the background where the crackle is particularly disfiguring.

Provenance: Aguado Sale, Paris, 1883, *Les Joies maternelles* (6,100 francs ?); Mr. and Mrs. R. Denison Frick; Gift of Mrs. R. Denison Frick, 1978.

Exhibitions: Paris, Salon of 1873, no. 1177.

Jean Béraud

French: St. Petersburg, (Russia), 1849 - Paris 1936

Béraud was born in St. Petersburg, the son of a French sculptor who died about 1853. He was subsequently raised in Paris, attended the Lycée Bonaparte, and began to study law. During the 1870–71 Siege of Paris, he interrupted his studies to serve in the Garde Mobile. Turning to art Béraud became a pupil of Léon Bonnat and began to exhibit at the Paris salons in 1873. His earliest entries were portraits. However, in 1876 he entered *The Return from the Funeral,* a street-scene showing a couple leaving a church after a funeral, the wife disconsolately weeping while the husband nonchalantly lights a cigarette. Béraud soon emerged as a principal chronicler of the Third Republic, recording life on the boulevards as well as more intimate social gatherings. To facilitate his out-of-door painting, he had a fiacre adapted to serve as a mobile studio. Very much part of the "la vie moderne" depicted in literature by Marcel Proust, Béraud served as the author's second in a duel with Jean Lorrain in 1897, and acted again that year in the same capacity in a duel between Robert de Montesquiou and Henri Regnier.

In the 1890s he shocked critics by producing such paintings as *Christ Carrying The Cross (*1894), *Magdalen in a Parisian House* (1900) and *Descent from the Cross* (1900), in which he treated religious subjects in contemporary settings, a practice also adopted by the Hungarian Munkacsy.

Béraud was a member of the Société des artistes français, and also of the breakaway group, headed by Meissonier and Puvis de Chavannes, that founded the Société Nationale des Beaux-Arts which sponsored salons at the Champs de Mars. Though he was never directly linked with the Impressionists, his name was occasionally associated with theirs by the less discerning contemporary critics, who were prepared to accept his appealing realism while castigating the art of the more avant-garde painters ("L'Impressionisme au Salon," *L'Artiste,* July 1, 1877, pp. 32–39). Béraud was appointed Chevalier of the Legion of Honor in 1887 and Officier in 1894, and he received a gold medal at the 1889 Exposition Universelle.

146. Paris Kiosk

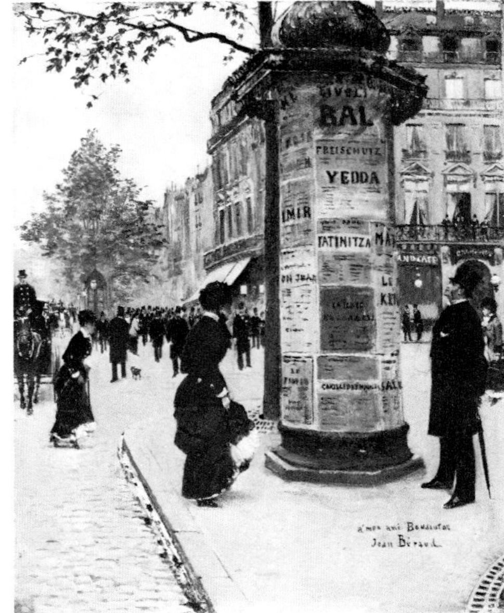

37.1055 early 1880s

Standing on either side of a Morris column are a lady and a gentleman studying posters. In the background are several fiacres and milling crowds of formally attired individuals. Identifying the specific site is a sign above a window of the large corner building which reads *(GR)AND CAFE,* designating the establishment at 14 Boulevard des Capucines near the Opéra. Among the posters are advertisements for the *TIVOLI BAL;* Weber's opera *DER FREISCHUTZ,* and Franz Suppé's comic opera *FATINITZA* that opened in Paris at the Théâtre de Nouveauté in 1879. The style of the costumes suggests a date in the early 1880s.

Alternative title: *Le kiosque des affiches.*

Support: Canvas, .355 x .265 (13$^{15}/_{16}$" x 10⅜")

Marks: Inscribed at lower right: *à mon ami Boussaton / Jean Béraud.* Me. Boussaton was the celebrated *commissaire-priseur* whose collection of modern paintings, including eight by Béraud, was sold on May 5, 1891.

Condition: Cleaned and lined in 1967.

Provenance: Me. Boussaton Sale, Georges Petit, Paris, May 5, 1891, no. 6 (7800 francs); Received by G. A. Lucas at Maurice Mallet's gallery on June 11, 1901 (George A. Lucas / Henry Walters account book, ms.)

Exhibitions: "Paris in the Belle Epoque: People and Places," Museum of Fine Arts, St. Petersburg, Florida, 1980, no. 5, illus.

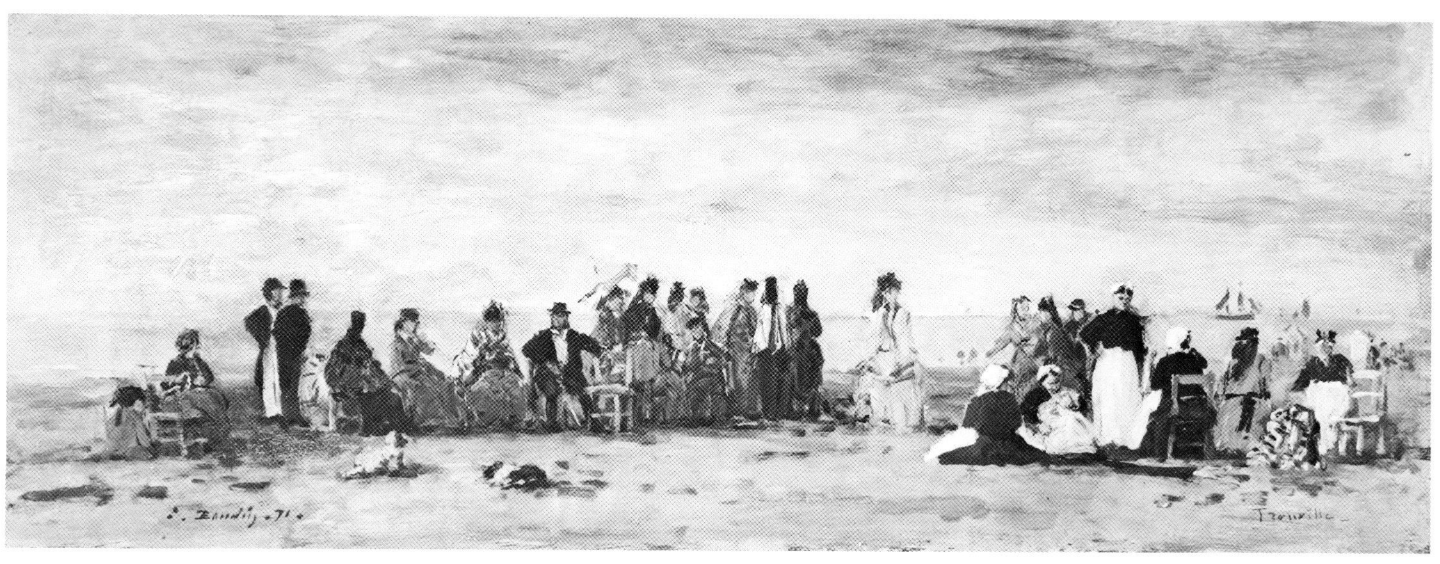

Boudin *Trouville,* no. 148

147. A Female Fencer

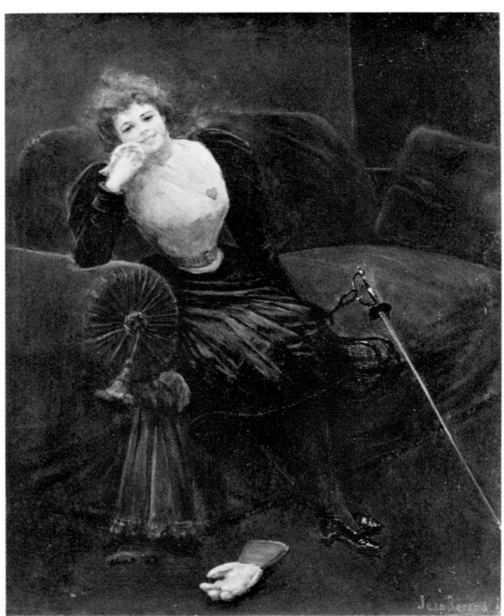

37.2484 1890s

An attractive smiling fencer is seated on an ottoman with her foil at her side and her gauntlet lying on the floor. Béraud, who delighted in depicting the Parisienne in her divertisements, produced numerous fencing subjects. Sold from the collection of Jacques Kugel of Paris, in the Sotheby Parke-Bernet Sale no. 4336, New York, January 25, 1980, was a panel painting of a standing fencer entitled *L'Escrimeuse*.

Support: Mahogany panel, .4 x .324 (15¾" x 12¾")

Signed at lower right: *Jean Béraud.*

Marks: Panel stenciled: *6 / DUPRE.*

Provenance: Gift of Louis E. Schecter, 1972.

Louis-Eugène Boudin

French: Honfleur, 1824 - Deauville, 1898

Boudin, the painter of Normandy beaches and harbors, bathed his paintings with light and atmosphere without fully adopting the color theories of Monet and his colleagues. In 1883 the critic Gustave Geffroy ranked Boudin along with Corot and Jongkind as an immediate precursor of Impressionism.

Boudin was the son of the captain of a coastal boat. His own maritime career ended when, falling off his father's boat at the age of ten, he narrowly escaped drowning. The Boudins settled in Le Havre in 1835, where young Eugène worked as a clerk, initially in a printer's shop and later in a stationer's store. He eventually opened a stationer's and frame-maker's shop in partnership with a Jean Archer. In their establishment were exhibited paintings by artists working in the vicinity, notably Couture, Millet, Isabey, and Troyon. To raise funds to buy himself free from military service, Boudin sold his share in the shop in 1847 and the following year he visited Belgium, where he studied Flemish art. A grant from Le Havre in 1851 enabled him to spend three years studying in Paris and working in Honfleur. He spent the following years in Normandy and Brittany, encountering Monet in Honfleur in 1858, and Courbet at Le Havre the following year. He introduced Monet to plein-air painting and formed a lifelong friendship with Courbet. Boudin's first salon entry was a Breton scene, the *Pilgrimage of Sainte-Anne-la-Palud,* shown in 1859.

In Paris in the early sixties he supported himself by assisting Troyon in laying out large compositions and painting the skies. It was at this point that he encountered Corot, whose works he greatly admired. He met J. B. Jongkind at Honfleur in 1862, and about then began to portray fashionable gatherings on the Normandy beaches. Throughout the decade he was active in the summers at such towns as Trouville, Deauville, Villerville, Dieppe, and also in Brittany. During the 1870–71 War and the Commune he settled in Brussels and worked for a while in Antwerp painting market scenes. Upon his return to France, Boudin continued his summer wanderings in Normandy and Brittany, painting views of the harbors. Though he continued to exhibit at the official salons he also participated in 1874 in the first Impressionist exhibition in Nadar's studio.

In the eighties Boudin's fortunes improved as he began to acquire a following. Belatedly, he was awarded a third-class medal at the Salon of 1881 for his *The Meuse at Rotterdam.* That year the dealer for the Impressionists, Paul Durand-Ruel, became sole distributor of his works and in 1883 an exhibition of his paintings held in this dealer's new gallery in Paris was a marked success. In 1884 Boudin built a villa at Trouville but continued his travels, which were now extended to the south of France. At the 1889 Exposition Universelle Boudin exhibited five paintings, winning a gold medal. Beginning in 1890, he participated in the "new" salons of La Société Nationale des Beaux Arts. In the nineties Boudin shared in the general recognition being accorded the surviving Impressionists and in 1892 he was elected Chevalier of the Legion of Honor. One departure from his customary routine was a visit to Venice in 1895, which resulted in several lagoon scenes. Thereafter, until his death, his output was limited by his failing health.

148. Trouville

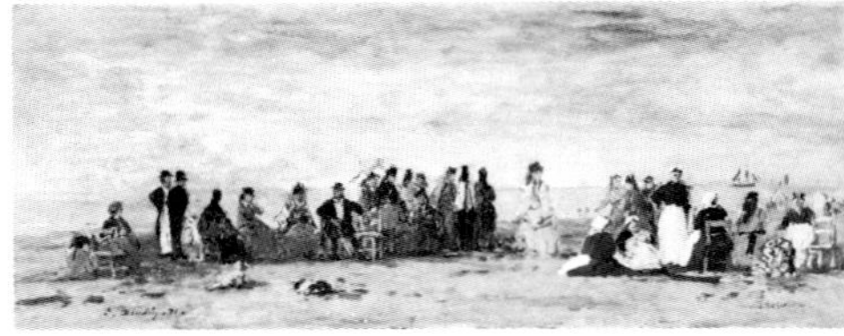

37.840 1871

The mainstay of Boudin's work in the 1860s had been small wide paintings of crowded beaches at such fashionable resorts as Trouville and Deauville. As this work exemplifies, not even the calamities of the Franco-Prussian War of 1870–71 deterred visitors. Boudin had initially been encouraged to pursue this genre by E. Isabey. Though Boudin grew dissatisfied with its limitations, he did not fully abandon it until the eighties. Boudin presumably painted this scene in September 1871 after his return from Antwerp to France.

Support: Panel, oak, carved on reverse with rocaille motif (presumably from a piece of furniture). .18 x .464 (18¼" x 7¼"), grey lead ground.

Signed and dated: *E. Boudin . 71.* (lower left) *Trouville* (lower right).

Condition: Cleaned, discolored varnishes removed in 1935.

Provenance: Cyrus J. Lawrence Sale, New York, January 21, 1910, no. 53 for $875.00 to Henry Chester (for Henry Walters).

Exhibitions: "An Exhibition of Treasures of the Walters Art Gallery," Wildenstein and Co., New York, 1967, no. 30.

References: Ruth L. Benjamin, *Eugène Boudin,* New York, Raymond and Raymond, 1937, p. 185; Edward S. King, "Episodes in collecting," *WAGB* 23, no. 8 (May 1971): 1 (illus.); Robert Schmit, *Eugène Boudin.* 3 vols. Paris, The author, 1973. 1: 225, no. 623, illus.

149. Bordeaux, the Harbor

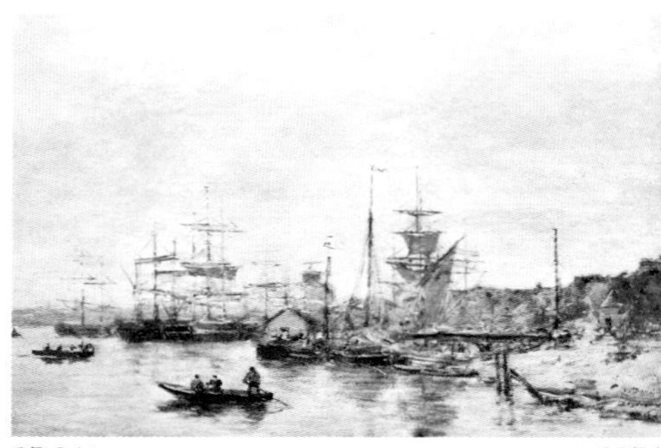

37.841 c. 1874

Boudin visited Bordeaux for six weeks during the autumn of 1874 and returned briefly to the city in 1876. Here the port is viewed at twilight, judging from the warm tones lingering in the sky. Several skiffs are seen and beyond are a jetty and a number of moored sailing vessels.

Support: Canvas, fine weave, .303 x .463 (12" x 18¼")

Signed at lower right: *E. Boudin / Bordeaux;* (Partially obscured by a paint film is an earlier signature slightly above the present signature).

Condition: The picture was lined and given a coat of synthetic varnish in 1959.

Provenance: Cyrus J. Lawrence Sale, New York, January 21–22, 1910, no. 58 for $450.00 to Henry Chester (for Henry Walters).

References: Ruth L. Benjamin, *Eugène Boudin,* New York, Raymond and Raymond, 1937, p. 185; Edward S. King, "Episodes in collecting," *WAGB* 23, no. 8 (May 1971): 2; Robert Schmit, *Eugène Boudin.* 3 vols. Paris, The author, 1973. 1: 355, no. 1002, illus.

Jacob-Emile-Edouard Brandon

French: Paris, 1831 - Paris, 1897

Brandon, an artist of the Jewish faith, is remembered as a painter of religious genre subjects. In 1849 he began to train at the Ecole des Beaux-Arts, studying successively with F. E. Picot, A. A. Monfort and J. B. Corot. His reputation rested primarily on a cycle of mural paintings illustrating the life of Saint Bridget executed for the Oratory of St. Bridget, Rome. These works were shown separately at the Paris Salons of 1861, 1863, 1864 and 1865. In the later 1860s and early 1870s he produced works specifically treating Jewish religious themes, including a *Scene in Synagogue* in the John G. Johnson Collection, Philadelphia. Brandon was among the artists who exhibited in the Société Anonyme des Artistes Peintres, Sculpteurs, Graveurs, etc. (first Impressionist exhibition) in 1874, and in his later years he participated in the salons of the Société Nationale des Beaux-Arts.

150. Portuguese Synagogue at Amsterdam

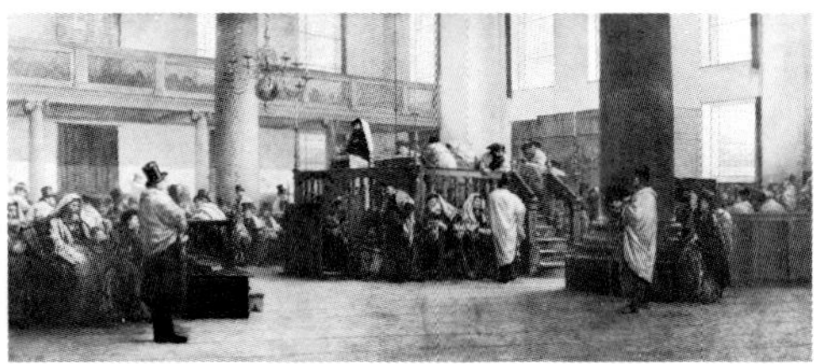

37.33 1867

Brandon received a medal at the Paris Salon of 1867, the year this work was shown as *Le Sermon du daian Cardozo; synagogue d'Amsterdam, le 22 juillet, 1866.* It is a dramatically lighted interior view of one of Europe's most famous and picturesque synagogues (consecrated 1675). The sermon is being delivered by the distinguished Talmudist David de Jahacob Lopez Cardozo (1808–1890), who was appointed *ab bet din* of the Portuguese Synagogue in 1839. Another painting of this interior, *La synagogue portugaise d'Amsterdam,* is cited by H. Mireur (Vente Brandon, Paris, 1897, *Dictionnaire des Ventes d'Art,* Paris, 1911, 1:440).

Support: Canvas, .755m x 1.743m (29¾" x 65⅝")

Condition: Prior to 1934 the picture was lined and numerous losses in the lower portion of the picture inpainted.

Signed at lower right: *Ed. Brandon / 1867.*

Marks: Paper label on frame: *329.*

Exhibitions: Salon, Paris, 1867.

References: Walters cat., 1878, p. 9, and subsequent Walters catalogues; Strahan, 1: 92 (illus.), 94; Clement and Hutton, 1: 89; Théophile Gautier, "Salon de 1869," in *Tableaux à la plume.* Paris, G. Charpentier, 1880. p. 300; Gustave Vapereau, *Dictionnaire universel des contemporains.* Paris, Hachette, 1880. p. 292; Emile Bellier de la Chavignerie and Louis Auvray, *Dictionnaire général des artistes de l'école français.* 2 vols. Paris, Renouard, 1882–85. 1: 160; *The Jewish encyclopedia.* 12 vols. New York, Funk & Wagnalls, 1901–06. 3: 354; Gustave Geffroy, "Edouard Brandon," in Ulrich Thieme and Felix Becker, *Allgemeines Lexikon der bildenden Künstler.* 37 vols. Leipzig, E. A. Seemann, 1907–50. 4: 534; Mozes Heiman Gans, *Memorboek.* Baarn, Bosch & Keuning, 1971. p. 363.

Hilaire-Germaine-Edgar Degas

French: Paris, 1834 - Paris, 1917

Degas, one of the foremost avant-garde artists of his era, was born into cultivated bourgeois circumstances. His grandparents, royalist sympathizers, had emigrated from France at the time of the Revolution: his father's family settling in Naples, where they became bankers, and his mother's family, the Mussons, going to New Orleans via Port-au-Prince. After attending the Lycée Louis-le-Grand, the young Degas briefly followed courses in law. His early interest in art surfaced in 1853 when he began to work with Félix Joseph Barrias and to study Old Master prints in the Cabinet des Estampes. The following year he became a pupil of Louis Lamothe, through whom he met Ingres, and in 1855 he enrolled in the Ecole des Beaux-Arts. Rejecting the formal training of the Ecole, he traveled extensively in Italy from 1856–59, studying Renaissance and Baroque masters. Upon his return to Paris he began to evolve a personal manner of painting based on a synthesis of the opposing styles of Ingres and Delacroix, the modern artists he most admired.

Degas' early paintings were either portraits or themes drawn from traditional history subjects, though handled distinctively. A commitment to equestrian themes, apparent as early as 1855, when he made drawings of casts of the horsemen of the Parthenon frieze during a visit to Lyons, was confirmed six years later, when he visited the stables of the Valpinçon family at Ménil-Hubert near Ornans, Normandy. Thereafter, though not personally a devotee of the track, Degas continued to draw subjects from the world of racing. At his first Salon in 1865 he showed his last history painting, a scene from a war of the Middle Ages, and at his second Salon the following year, he entered a steeplechase subject. Until 1870 Degas exhibited regularly, entering portraits for the most part. At this time he frequented the Café Guerbois, where he became acquainted with the realist writer Edmond Duranty as well as with a number of modernist painters including Manet and a number of future Impressionists. Among them Degas was perhaps the most innovative in deriving inspiration from the Japanese woodcuts recently introduced into France. While serving in the artillery during the Franco-Prussian War, he experienced the inflamation of the eyes to which he attributed his eventual loss of vision. In the fall of 1872, Degas accompanied his brother René to New Orleans. In America he confined his painting to family portraits, including several of his blind sister-in-law and cousin Estelle de Gas, and a couple of group portraits, most notably *The Cotton Market,* showing the family's business, acquired in 1878 by the Museum of Pau.

Back in Paris in 1873 Degas renewed his acquaintance with the former habitués of the Café Guerbois and out of those discussions there emerged in April 1874 the first exhibit of the Société Anonyme des Artistes Peintres, Sculpteurs, Graveurs, etc. in the studio of the photographer Nadar. Degas participated in all but the seventh of the eight Impressionist exhibitions, assuming a significant role in their organization, although he did not share the preoccupations with plein-air painting and instantaneity of vision, commitments to which the landscape painters were bound. Instead he endeavored to expand the group to include a number of realists, who shared his concern for modern, urban subjects. He failed, however, to persuade Manet, Tissot, and Legros to join, though he was responsible for the memberships of his pupil Mary Cassatt, and for those of Zandomenghi, De Nittis, Raffaelli, and others.

In his later years Degas inexhaustibly continued to explore such subjects as ballet dancers, milliners, bathing women, and the track. As his eyesight failed in the eighties, he turned from oils to pastels, gradually perfecting a technique in which he superimposed them, layer upon layer, in an almost sculptural manner. Apart from his oils and pastels, he also modeled in wax, exhibiting *The Little*

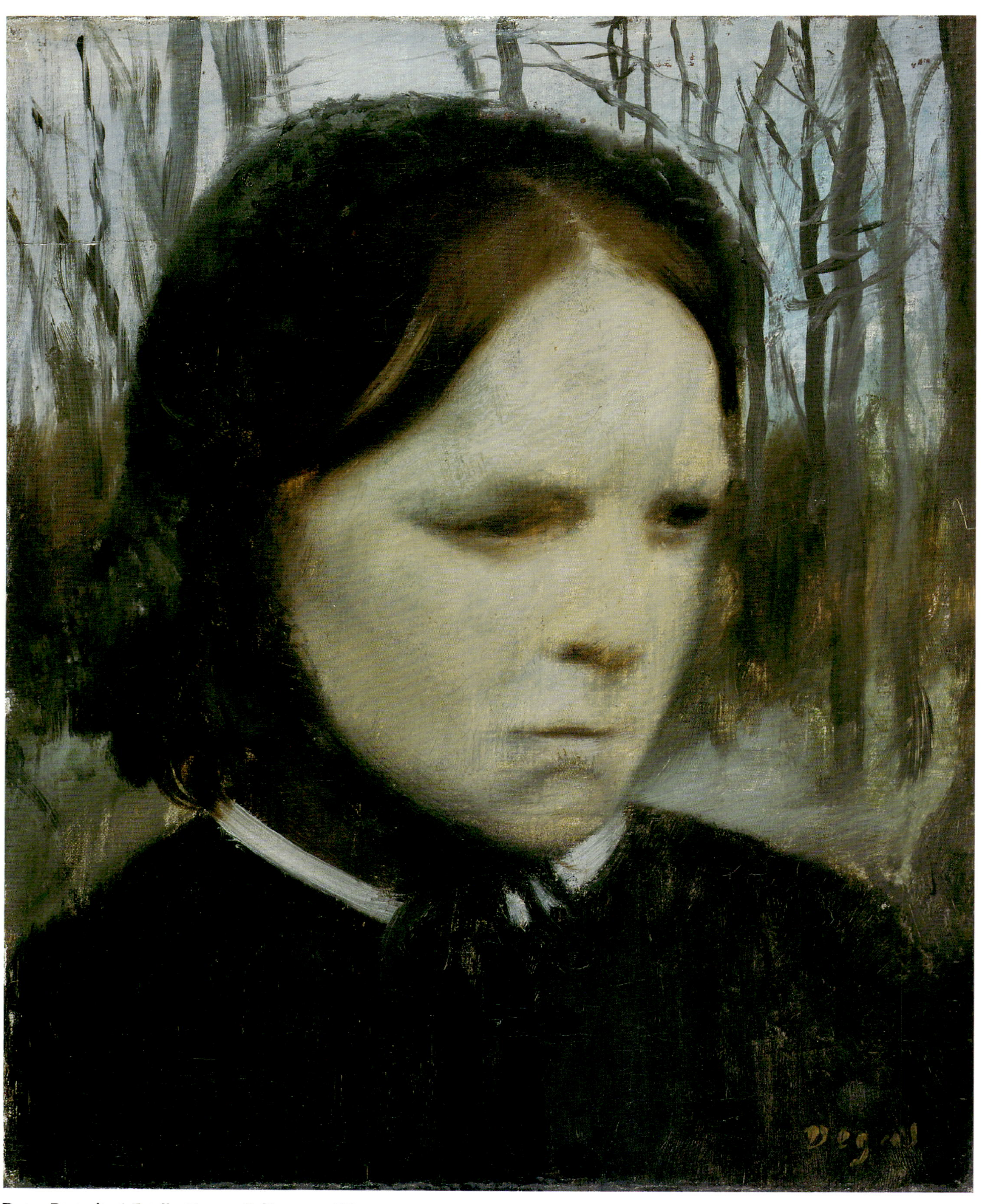

Degas *Portrait of Estelle Musson Balfour,* no. 151

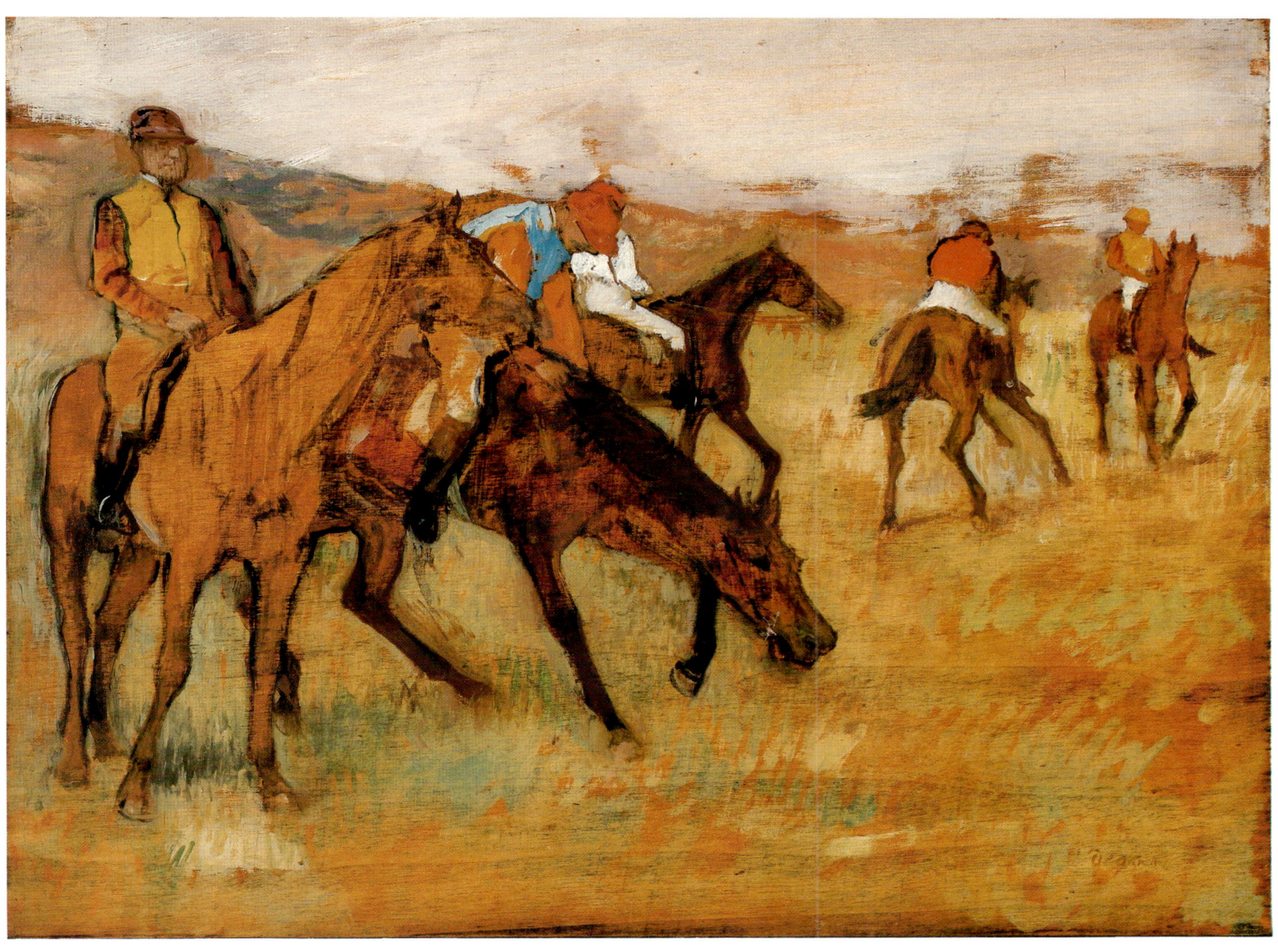

Degas *Before the Race,* no. 152

Dancer at the Sixth Impressionist exhibition in 1881, though none of his waxes were cast in bronze until after his death. He continued to exhibit at his dealer, Durand-Ruel, until 1893 and was able to work intermittently until 1908.

151. Portrait of a Woman (Estelle Musson Balfour)

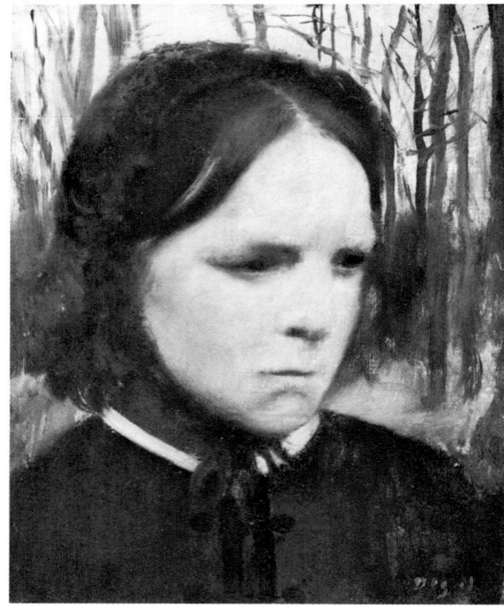

37.179 1863–65

In this small enigmatic portrait, a woman of indeterminite age, dressed in mourning, is seen against a somber background of leafless trees. Her head is turned slightly to the right and her eyes averted or masked in shadow.

The subject has been identified by Jean Sutherland Boggs as Estelle Musson Balfour (1843–1909), the artist's cousin and one-time sister-in-law. She was the daughter of Degas' maternal uncle, Michel Musson of New Orleans. In January 1862 she married Joseph Lazare Davis Balfour who was killed while serving in the Confederate Army at the Battle of Corinth on October 6th that year. The following June, Estelle, her infant daughter, Estelle Josephine, her sister Desirée, and her mother departed New Orleans for France, where they took up residence in Bourg-en-Bresse until the spring of 1865. When they returned to New Orleans at the close of the Civil War, they were accompanied by René de Gas, the artist's brother, who eventually, in partnership with another brother, Achille, established De Gas Frères, a wine-importing business. In 1869 Estelle and her cousin René were married. Nine years later, she was deserted and in succeeding years she lost four of her six children through various illnesses.

Compounding the ill-fortune of this luckless woman was her loss of sight. Exactly when this tragedy occurred is not known. James B. Byrnes in "Edgar Degas, his paintings of New Orleanians Here and Abroad," *Edgar Degas, His Family, and Friends in New Orleans* (exhibition catalogue), New Orleans, 1965, p. 40, n. 9, cited a family tradition that she made a pilgrimage to Lourdes because of her failing vision during the family's sojourn in France at the time of the Civil War. John Rewald, on the other hand, in "Degas and His Family in New Orleans" in the same catalogue, p. 17, attributed her blindness to an attack of ophthamalia that occurred in August 1866. In a letter to P.-A. Lemoisne, Degas' first biographer, cited by Byrnes (pp. 40-41, n. 11), the subject's daughter Odile stated that her mother lost the sight of her left eye in 1868 and that of the right, although it had been previously very feeble, in 1875. Degas, alluding to his cousin's affliction in a letter of November 11, 1872, wrote: "my poor Estelle, René's wife, she is blind as you know. She bears it in an incomparable manner; she needs scarcely any help about the house. She remembers the rooms and the position of the furniture and hardly ever bumps into anything. And there is no hope" (*Degas Letters,* edited by Marcel Guerin, translation by Marguerite Kay. Oxford, Bruno Cassirer, 1947, p. 15).

On the basis of costume the Walters painting has been attributed to the period of 1863–65 when the Mussons were in France. Of his cousin, who was at this point in mourning for her husband Balfour, Degas noted: *Quant à Estelle, pauvre petite femme, on ne peut la regarder sans penser que cette tête a devant elle les yeux d'un mourant* (P.-A. Lemoisne, *Degas et son oeuvre,* Paris, 1946, 1: 73, 234, n. 84).

Other representations of this subject by Degas include a pencil and wash drawing, *Mme. Musson and her two Daughters,* .355 x .26, in the Art Institute of Chicago, dated 1865; a pencil on paper preliminary drawing, .228 x .28, in the Freddy and Regina T. Hamburger Collection, Dedham, Mass.; an oil on canvas, *Mme. René de Gas,* .726 x .92, of 1872–73 in the Chester Dale Collection, National Gallery of Art, Washington, D.C.; a *Femme à la Potiche,* dated 1872, .651 x .54, in the Louvre; and an *Estelle Musson De Gas* of 1872–73, 1 x 1.372, in the New Orleans Museum of Art, Louisiana. The *Femme assise prés d'un balcon,* pastel, .642 x .762, 1872–73, in the Ordrupgaard collection, Copenhagen, and the *Portrait of the Artist's Cousin,* dated 1873, pastel, .627 x .571, in the Metropolitan Museum of Art, New York, thought by P.-A. Lemoisne to represent Estelle Musson are now believed to show instead her sister Mathilde Musson Bell.

It has been suggested that the artist may have been so attracted to his cousin Estelle as a subject because he shared with her the loss of sight (James B. Byrnes, op cit, pp. 43–44).

Support: Canvas, .269 x .218 (10⁹⁄₁₆" x 8⅝")

Signed in light brown at lower right: *Degas.*

Condition: An old lining was removed and the fabric was attached to a masonite panel in 1942. Discolored varnishes were removed at this time and again in 1951.

Provenance: Purchased together with Monet's *Springtime,* from Mary Cassatt, May 7, 1903 for a combined price of 25,000 francs (H. Walters/ G. A. Lucas Account Book, ms.).

Exhibitions: "Works by Edgar Degas," Cleveland Museum of Art, 1947, no. 9; "From Ingres to Gauguin" Baltimore Museum of Art, 1951, no. 101; "Degas," 1955, Marion Koogler McNay Art Institute, San Antonio; "An Exhibition of Works by Edgar Hilaire Germain Degas, 1834–1917," Los Angeles County Museum, 1958, no. 10; "Loan Exhibition: Degas," Wildenstein and Co., New York, 1960, no. 6; "Paintings, Drawings and Graphic Works by Manet, Degas, Berthe Morisot and Mary Cassatt," 1962, Baltimore Museum of Art, no. 47; "Edgar Degas: His Family and Friends in New Orleans," 1965, Isaac Delgado Museum of Art, New Orleans, p. 49.

References: Walters cat., 1909, p. 59, no. 179; Jean Sutherland Boggs, *Portraits by Degas.* Berkeley, University of California Press, 1962. p. 21, plate 41; James B. Byrnes, "Degas and his paintings of New Orleanians here and abroad," in *Edgar Degas: his family and friends in New Orleans.* New Orleans, 1965. p. 40, plate V.

152. Before the Race

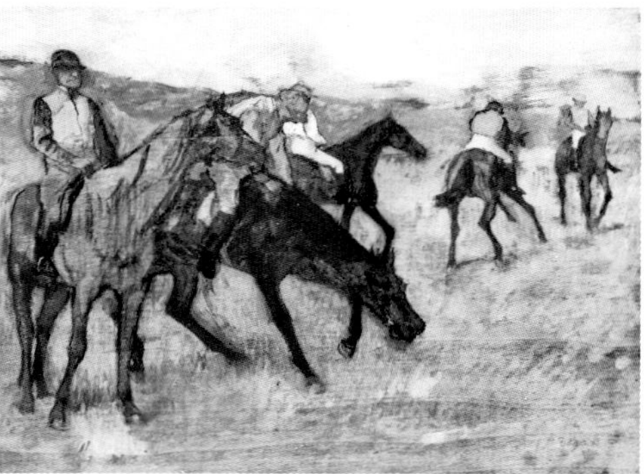

37.850 1875–77 or after

Five horses being prepared for the post are seen in diagonal recession. The setting in this little sketch is most cursorily indicated.

Among the jockey subjects recurrent throughout Degas' work are two panel paintings closely related to the Walters picture. In *Avant la course,* oil on panel, .29 x .46, in the Collection Gallimard, Paris, the positions of the three jockeys and horses furthest to the left are identical to those in the Walters panel, though the figures at the right and in the background vary. Even closer in composition is the *Before the Race,* oil on panel, .27 x .35, in the Sterling and Francine Clark Art Institute, Williamstown. Pickvance cites the Clark and Walters sketches as an example of Degas' ingenious variation on a theme contrasting the "sensuous quality of the paint" in the former with the "thin, stained effect—the wood graining showing through"—in the latter. In the Clark panel the horse and jockey in the extreme left foreground are cropped by the picture's margin, whereas in the other work they are shown in their entirety. The colors of the jockeys' silks also differ markedly in the two works, those in Williamstown being from left to right: blue and red, orange and red, pink, green, blue with white spots and red, whereas those in Baltimore are brown and yellow, orange and blue, white, red and brown and yellow. A pastel drawing for the Walters picture, measuring .255 x .415, entitled *Jockeys* was exhibited in "Edgar Degas," Durand-Ruel, Paris, 1960, no. 9. It was tentatively dated 1866–72. Comparisons have been drawn by Theodore Reff (*The Note-*

books of Edgar Degas, Oxford, 1976, 1: 124) between sketches in a notebook (Notebook 26, p. 27 and p. 28) and the second and third figures of riders and horses from the right in the Clark panel. On the basis of the similarities, Reff (p. 151) rejects the "circa 1882" date that Lemoisne gave to the panel (P.-A. Lemoisne, *Degas et son oeuvre,* Paris, 1945–47, 2: 398, no. 702) and places it instead in 1875–77 when the notebook was probably compiled. Given the similarities in the works involved, the Walters picture could therefore date from as early as 1875–77.

Support: Two panels laminated together with cradle, .264 x .349 (10⅜" x 13¾")

Signed in lower right: *Degas.*

Condition: The picture was cleaned at an early date in the Gallery's history and again in 1979. Losses are confined to some abrasion beneath the rabbet of the frame.

Provenance: Durand-Ruel to Cyrus J. Lawrence, New York, Cyrus J. Lawrence Sale, New York, January 21, 1910, no. 62 to Henry Walters.

Exhibitions: "Works by Edgar Degas," Cleveland Museum of Art, 1947, no. 21; "From Ingres to Gauguin," Baltimore Museum of Art, 1951, no. 104; "Paintings, Drawings and Graphic Works by Manet, Degas, Berthe Morisot and Mary Cassatt," Baltimore Museum of Art, 1962 no. 47; "Degas," Wildenstein and Co., New York, 1967, no. 38; "Degas' Racing World," Wildenstein and Co., New York, 1968, no. 11.

References: Ronald Pickvance, Introduction, "Degas' Racing World," (exhibition catalogue), Wildenstein and Co., New York, 1968, p. 6.

Edouard Manet

French: Paris, 1832 - Paris, 1883

Manet, leader of the avant-garde, was raised in prosperous bourgeois circumstances in Paris. Only after failing to enter France's naval academy was he allowed to pursue his interest in painting. In 1850 he entered the studio of Thomas Couture and began to follow the courses of the Académie Suisse. Though Couture may have asserted more influence on Manet's development than is generally acknowledged, relations between the two artists were never cordial. Manet's realist bent resulted in Couture's famous quip that his pupil would never be more than the Daumier of his time and in Manet's retort that such a role was preferable to being the Coypel of one's era. To supplement his formal training Manet copied seventeenth-century masters in the Louvre, traveled in 1853 to Florence, where he executed drawings after Ghirlandaio and Fra Angelico, and visited Belgium, the Netherlands, Germany, and Italy in 1856, the year he left Couture's studio.

Manet's first submission to the Salon, the *Absinth Drinker,* was rejected in 1859 despite the endorsement of Eugène Delacroix. He did, however, receive an honorable mention two years later, for the *Guitar Player* and *Portrait of the Artist's Parents.*

In the early sixties Manet began to frequent the Café Guerbois, a gathering point for young realist painters and writers on the Avenue Clichy. At this point he also exhibited regularly at the Galérie Martinet and became associated with the Société des Aquafortistes, founded in 1862. Subjects in his prints and paintings now included Spanish dancers, most notably Lola de Valence, who performed at the Paris Hippodrome.

Manet's subsequent career was marked by controversies engendered by a sequence of paintings that were neither fully understood nor appreciated by the public and the majority of the critics of the time, though they have since been acknowledged as masterpieces in the evolution of nineteenth-century realist painting. Included in this category were the *Déjeuner sur l'herbe* exhibited at the Salon des Refusés in 1863, and the *Olympia* that appeared at the 1865 Salon. In the summer of that year he briefly visited Spain, professing keen admiration for the portraits of Velasquez and more restrained enthusiasm for Goya's paintings. Following the rejection of his works from the 1867 Exposition Universelle, Manet followed Courbet's precedent in opening a private pavilion on the Place d'Alma. For political considerations he was not permitted to include in his exhibition his *Execution of Maximilian.* In 1868 he showed his *Portrait of Emile Zola,* painted in gratitude for the critic's favorable review published two years earlier in *l'Evénement.* Berthe Morisot entered his studio the same year to become both a pupil and model, posing for the central figure of *The Balcony* of 1869. She was followed by Eva Gonzales who likewise posed for a number of paintings. During the Franco-Prussian War, Manet served with Degas in the Artillery of the National Guard. His colonel, ironically, was the academic realist J.-L.-E. Meissonier.

Following the War, Manet's fortunes slowly improved. In 1871 the dealer Durand-Ruel paid 35,000 francs for a lot of twenty-two paintings. At the 1873 Salon *Le Bon Bock* was favorably received. This painting, a portrait of the engraver Emile Bellot, manifested Manet's admiration for the works of Frans Hals, which he had seen during a visit to The Netherlands the previous summer.

Manet had long been closely associated with the artists who were to form the Impressionist Movement. He had made tentative experiments in plein-air painting as early as the late sixties, and had adopted the practice for several paintings, most notably for the *Game of Croquet* of 1871, and for marine subjects executed at Berck in the summer of 1873. However, he declined to participate in the Impressionist group exhibitions which began in 1874, though he did join Monet that summer in Argenteuil on the Seine, the gathering-point for the Impressionists. His continuing efforts to pursue success within the framework of the Salons met with only partial recognition: rejected were his *Masked Ball* and *Swallows* in 1874, the *Washing Day* and *The Artist* in 1876, the *Nana* in 1877, and all his entries to the Exposition Universelle in 1878.

In 1878–79, Manet painted several works, including the Walters *At the Café,* showing scenes in the Cabaret de Reichshoffen on the Boulevard Rochechouart. The following year he began to develop symptoms of a degenerative disease since identified as locomotor ataxia. As this disease progressed, he was compelled to work on a less ambitious scale, producing a number of still lifes in oils and pastel portraits of women. He was, however, able to undertake his major cabaret scene in 1881–82, the *Bar at the Folies-Bergère,* now in the Courtauld Institute, London.

153. At the Cafe

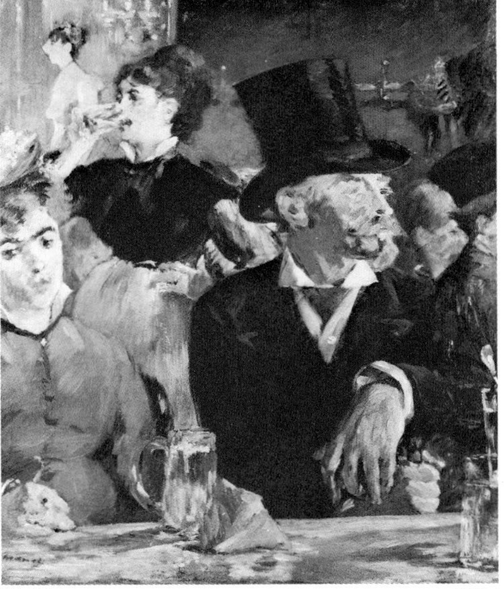

37.893 — 1879

Seated behind a counter that cuts diagonally across the picture is an elderly gentleman who rests his arm on the pommel of his cane. He sports a pointed grey-flecked moustache and goatee. Beside him a young woman, wearing a puce-colored dress and a flowered bonnet, sits smoking a cigarette, lost in thought. Behind are seated customers and a barmaid who swigs a tankard of beer, and reflected in the mirror in the corner, is a singer in low decolletage.

Manet's earliest café scene, *Le Bon Bock* of 1873, bears witness to the artist's admira-

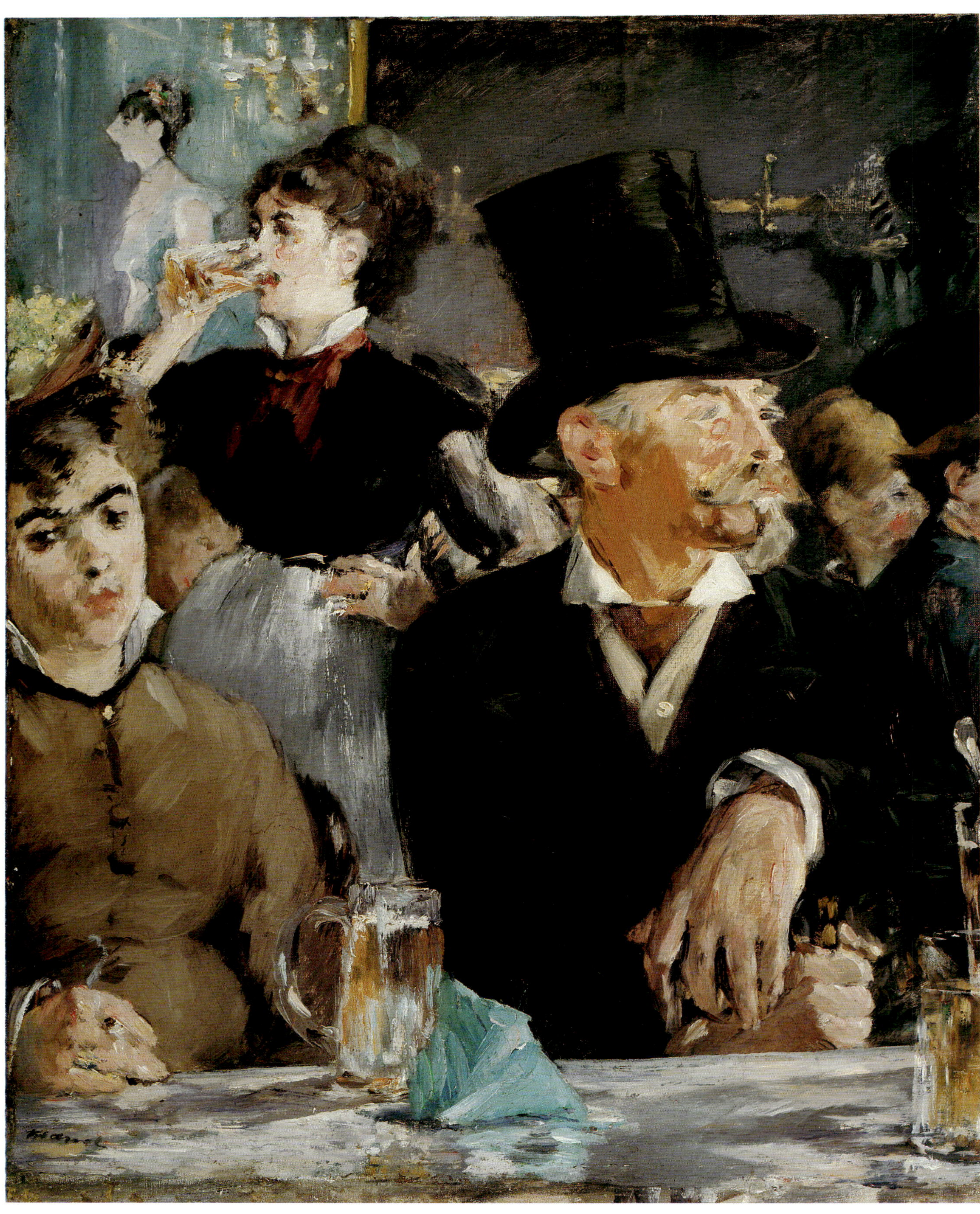

Manet *At the Cafe,* no. 153

tion for the works of Frans Hals. In 1878–79 he returned to the theme, painting a number of outdoor and indoor scenes inspired perhaps by Edgar Degas' precedent, *The Absinth Drinker,* of 1876, in the Metropolitan Museum, New York, or by illustrations in the popular press. Among his outdoor scenes of these years are *Le Bouchon* in the Pushkin Museum, Moscow; *Chez le Père Lathuille,* dated 1879, in the Musée de Tournai; the *Chanteuse de Café-Concert,* formerly in the C. Steinberg collection, St. Louis; and an oil of the same title once in the Rouart collection. His principal indoor café composition was *La Brasserie de Reichshoffen,* which he dismembered and reworked to constitute the *Au Café* dated 1878, in the Oskar Reinhart collection, Winterthur, and *La Serveuse de Bocks* of 1879, in the National Gallery, London. Related to the former fragment is a small oil sketch, *Au Café,* in the Josse Bernheim Jeune collection until 1944, and connected with the latter is *La Serveuse de Bocks* in the Musée du Louvre, Jeu de Paume collection. Other indoor scenes apart from the Walters picture are *La Prune* in the National Gallery of Art, Washington, and *George Moore au Café,* in the Metropolitan Museum of Art, New York. In addition, there is in the Ordrupgaard collection, Copenhagen, an *Au Café* .46 x .33, in which the field of vision has been dramatically cropped by the picture's edges. This picture, however, has now generally been rejected.

The Walters painting has traditionally been associated with the Winterthur and London fragments of *La Brasserie de Reichshoffen.* The seated gentleman and woman of the Walters picture are similar to, but not identical with, figures in the Winterthur painting. The models in the latter, the engraver Henri Guérard and his companion Ellen Andrée, who had also posed for Degas' *Absinth Drinker,* appear younger and have brown hair, whereas the man's hair in the Walters picture is whiter and the woman's blacker. The barmaid in the Walters picture and in the London work bear close resemblance and may in fact be the same model, the brasserie's most proficient waitress, whom, according to Duret, Manet enticed to pose in his studio.

The Walters painting is a fully developed composition and may, therefore, postdate the Winterthur and London canvases. In its exploration of mirrored images it anticipated the masterpiece of the artist's last years, *The Bar at the Folies-Bergère* of 1882, in the Courtauld Institute, London. The Walters painting was included in an exhibition of twenty-five works, four of which dealt with cafes, shown in the Gallery of the newspaper *La Vie Moderne* in the spring of 1880. The cafe scenes met with a mixed reception, G. Goetschy praising them for their veracity and Bertall criticizing their crudeness of execution ("Les petits salons à côte du grand salon," *L'Artiste* (July 1880) : 31–32).

Manet's other renditions of the Walters composition include a Chinese ink and white drawing, *Au Café,* .235 x .195, in the Burrell collection, Glasgow, and a montotype, *La Servante de Bocks* .345 x .255, sold in the Fischer Sale, Lucerne, Nov. 30, 1971, no. 1484. Denis Rouart and Daniel Wildenstein, in *Edouard Manet, catalogue raisonné,* Lausanne/Paris, 1975, 2: 182–83, nos. 511–15, catalogued several drawings showing singers similar to the image reflected in the mirror of the Walters painting. Closest is no. 514, *Chanteuse de Café-Concert,* Chinese ink wash on yellow paper, .51 x .44, that was sold in Mme. Veuve Manet: vente Manet, Hôtel Drouot, Paris, February 4–5, 1884, no. 152. This image also appeared in the transfer lithograph, *La Belle Polonaise,* .285 x .265, published by M. Guérin, *L'Oeuvre gravé de Manet,* Paris, 1944, no. 83.

Alternative titles: *Le café-concert; La serveuse de Bocks.*

Support: Preprimed fabric, .475 x .392 (18$\frac{11}{16}$" x 15$\frac{7}{16}$")

Signed at lower left: *Manet*

Condition: Picture lined with linen and a glue adhesive in 1936 (?) and lightly cleaned in 1941. Discolored varnishes removed in 1951.

Provenance: Manet to Boussaton, 1881; Sale Boussaton, Galerie Georges Petit, Paris, May 15, 1891, no. 61; A. M. Haviland, Limoges; J. B. Faure, Paris; Collection J. B. Faure Sale, Paris, 1902, no. 38; Durand-Ruel, Paris, 1907; Henry Walters, 1909–10, for $25,000.00.

Exhibitions: "Oeuvres nouvelles d'Edouard Manet," La Vie Moderne, Paris, 1880, no. 3; "Works in Oil and Pastel by the Impressionists of Paris," National Academy of Design, New York, 1886, no. 223; "Les Manet de la collection Faure," Durand-Ruel, Paris, 1906, no. 18; "Paintings by Manet from the Collection of M. Faure of Paris," Sulley's, London, 1906, no. 16; "French Paintings from David to Toulouse Lautrec," Metropolitan Museum of Art, New York, 1941, no. 86; "The Spirit of Modern France," The Toledo Museum of Art, Art Gallery of Toronto, 1946–47, no. 43; "Loan Exhibition of Manet," Wildenstein and Co., New York, 1948, no. 25; "Fort Worth Centennial," Fort Worth Art Association, 1949; "Masterpieces of Painting, 1500 to 1900," Columbus Gallery of Fine Arts, 1950; "From Ingres to Gauguin," Baltimore Museum of Art, 1951, no. 94; "Pictures of Everyday Life," Carnegie Institute, Pittsburgh, 1954, no. 80; "French Painting, David to Rouault," Art Association Gallery of Atlanta, Museum of Art of Birmingham, 1955, no. 16; "Paintings, drawings and graphic works by Manet, Degas, Berthe Morisot and Mary Cassatt," Baltimore Museum of Art, 1962, no. 7; "Olympia's Progeny," Wildenstein and Co., New York, 1965, no. 24; "Edouard Manet," Philadelphia Museum of Art, The Art Institute of Chicago, 1966–67, no. 174; "An Exhibition of Treasures of the Walters Art Gallery," Wildenstein and Co., New York, 1967, no. 45; "From El Greco to Pollock, Early and Late Works by European and American Artists," The Baltimore Museum of Art, 1968, no. 76.

References: "Les petits salons à côté du Grand Salon," *L'Artiste* (July 1880) : 30–32; Théodore Duret, *Histoire d'Edouard Manet et de son oeuvre.* Paris, H. Floury, 1902. p. 250, no. 230; Cl. Phillips, "Pictures by Manet," *Daily Telegraph* (London) June 21, 1906; Julius Meier-Graefe, *Edouard Manet.* Munich, R. Piper, 1912. p. 258, n. 1, plate 151; Antonin Proust, *Edouard Manet; souvenirs publiés par A. Barthélemy.* Paris, H. Laurens, 1913. p. 324; Antonin Proust, "Erinnerungen an Edouard Manet, VI," *Kunst und Künstler* (March 1913), illus.; André Fontainas and Louis Vauxcelles, *Histoire général de l'art français de la Révolution à nos jours.* 3 vols. Paris, Librairie de France, 1922. 1: 124, illus.; Etienne Moreau-Nélaton, *Manet raconté par lui-même.* 2 vols. Paris, H. Laurens, 1926. 2: 50, fig. 243; Paul Jamot and Georges Wildenstein, *Manet.* Paris, Les Beaux-Arts, 1932. no. 303; "Speaking about art," *American Magazine of Art* 27 (1934): 685, illus.; *Handbook of the collection.* Baltimore, The Walters Art Gallery, 1936. p. 167 (illus.); Edgar P. Richardson, *The Way of Western Art, 1776–1914.* Cambridge, Mass., Harvard University Press, 1939. pp. 107 (illus.), 111; G. Jedlicka, *Edouard Manet.* Erlenbach-Zurich, E. Rentsch, 1941. plate 170; Samuel Rocheblave, *French Painting, XIXth century.* New York, Hyperion Press, 1941. plate 65; Raymond Mortimer, *Edouard Manet: Un bar aux Folies-Bergére in the National Gallery, London.* 2nd ed. London, Percy Lund Humphries, 1943. pp. 5, 11 (illus.); Marcel Guérin, *L'oeuvre gravé de Manet.* Paris, Librairie Floury, 1944. no. 83. Edward Alden Jewell and Aimée Crane, *French Impressionists and their Contemporaries represented in American Collections.* New York, Hyperion Press, 1944. p. 50; Hans Huth, "Impressionism comes to America," *GBA* 6th pér. 29 (1946): 239, n. 22; Michel Florisoone, *Manet.* Monaco, Documents d'art, 1947. p. 74 (illus.); Adolphe Tabarant, *Manet et ses oeuvres.* Paris, Gallimard, 1947. pp. 329–30, no. 300; *WAGB* 1, no. 1 (October 1948): 4 (illus.); S. Lane Faison, Jr., *Edouard Manet.* The library of great painters, portfolio ed. New York, Harry N. Abrams, 1953. pp .20, 21 (illus.); Georges Bataille, *Manet.* The taste of our time, 14. New York, Skira, 1955. pp. 100 (illus.), 113; Jacqueline Bouchot-Saupique, "Manet dessinateur," *La Revue du Louvre* 11 (1961): 72; Pierre Courthion, *Edouard Manet.* The library of gerat painters. New York, Harry N. Abrams, 1962. p. 133, illus.; Malcolm Vaughan, "The Connoisseur in America," *Connoisseur* 151 (1962): 66 (illus.); John Canaday, "Manet, the reluctant revolutionary," *Horizon* 6, no. 1 (1964): 93, 95, 99 (illus.); Denys Sutton, "Connoisseur's haven," *Apollo* 84 (1966): 429, illus. facing p. 430; Anne Coffin Hanson, "Manet's subject matter and a source of popular imagery," *Museum Studies* (Art Institute of Chicago) 3 (1968): 67 (fig. 4), 68; Pierre Schneider, *The world of Manet, 1832–1883.* New York, Time-Life Books, 1968. pp. 141, 149 (illus.); Jean C. Harris, *Edouard Manet: graphic works, a definitive catalogue raisonné.* New York, Collectors Editions, 1970, no. 87, fig. 172; Denis Rouart and S. Orienti, *Tout l'oeuvre peint d'Edouard Manet.* Les classiques de l'art. Paris, Flammarion, 1970. no. 267; Germain Bazin, *Edouard Manet.* Gli impressionisti. Milan, Fabbri, 1972. p. 83, illus.; Anne Coffin Hanson, "Popular imagery and the work of Edouard Manet," in *French 19th century painting and literature, with special reference to the relevance of literary subject-matter to French painting.* Edited by Ulrich Finke. Manchester studies in the history of art, 1. Manchester, Manchester University Press, 1972. pp. 152, no. 90, 154; Denis Rouart and Daniel Wildenstein, *Edouard Manet; catalogue raisonné.* 2 vols. Lausanne, La Bibliothèque des Arts, 1975. 1: 224, no. 280; *Edouard Manet: Das graphische Werk. Meisterwerke aus der Bibliotheque Nationale und weiterer Sammlungen.* Ingelheim am Rhein, Stadtverwaltung, 1977. p. 135, no. 106; Theodore Reff, "Degas, a master among masters," *Metropolitan Museum of Art Bulletin* n.s. 34, no. 4 (Spring 1977): 17, illus. no. 29; Kirk Varnedoe, "The artifice of candor: Impressionism and photography reconsidered," *Art in America* 68 (1980): 72, 74 (illus.), 75.

Oscar-Claude Monet

French: Paris, 1840 - Giverny, 1926

Monet's youth was spent in Normandy,

at Le Havre, where his father had joined a brother-in-law in a ship chandlery and grocery business. The future artist was educated at a communal college in which drawing was taught by a former pupil of J.-L.-David, François-Charles Ochard. Young Monet proved to be a recalcitrant student but a precocious caricaturist. About 1856–58, he became acquainted with Eugène Boudin, who introduced him to out-of-door oil painting and instilled in him a commitment to immediacy in the recording of one's vision. With Boudin's encouragement Monet moved to Paris in 1859, sought the advice of Constant Troyon, and enrolled briefly in the Académie Suisse, where he first met Pissarro. He was conscripted into the army in 1861 and served for two years in Algeria in the Premier régiment de chasseurs d'Afrique. When his military duties were cut short because of ill health, Monet returned to Le Havre to paint. Here he met with Jongkind, who reinforced the training that he had previously received from Boudin. Returning to Paris, Monet entered the atelier of Charles Gleyre, an experience that proved uncongenial although it afforded him the opportunity to meet with fellow pupils Sisley, Renoir, and Bazille. He painted with them at Chailly in the Fontainebleau Forest in the spring of 1863, and in the summer of 1864 he was again with Bazille at the Ferme Saint-Siméon near Honfleur. The following year he made his debut at the Salon with two coastal scenes, *The Mouth of the Seine at Honfleur* and *The Cape of La Hève at Low Tide,* the merits of which were immediately recognized by the critics. At this time he was occupied with *Le Déjeuner sur l'Herbe,* an enormous picnic scene measuring fifteen by twenty feet, inspired by Manet's chef d'oeuvre of the same title. Serving as models for the preliminary studies executed out-of-doors were Monet's friends, the painters Bazille and Lambron, and a young companion, Camille-Léonie Doncieux (1847–1879), who became his wife in 1870. Camille served as a model on a number of later occasions beginning with *The Green Dress* that caught the attention of Zola and Thoré at the 1866 Salon and ending with the *Camille Monet on her Death Bed,* in which the artist objectively recorded transformations in facial coloring occurring after death.

The later sixties were marred for Monet by severe financial difficulties, resulting in part from his having been disowned by his family and the increasing rejection of his paintings by the salon juries. With the outbreak of the Franco-Prussian War in 1870–71, he sought refuge with his family in London where he met the dealer Paul Durand-Ruel who was also assisting Pissarro, also in England at this time.

Returning from London, Monet stopped during the summer of 1871 in Zaandam, situated on the Zaan river six miles north of Amsterdam. The prosperous town of 12,000 people with its colorful small houses and over four hundred windmills in the surrounding countryside provided the artist with limitless subjects.

Back in France, he divided his time until 1878, between Paris and the suburb of Argenteuil northwest of Paris, where he was frequently joined by Renoir, Sisley, and Caillebotte.

Monet, the consummate Impressionist, was a principal organizer of the Société Anonyme des Artistes Peintres, Sculpteurs, Graveurs, etc., later known as the "Indépendents," that first met in the former studio of the photographer Nadar on the boulevard des Capucines in April and May, 1874. One of his entries, *Impression, soleil levant* (Paris, Musée Marmottan), painted from his hotel window at Le Havre in 1872, gave its name to the movement when it was inadvertently publicized by Louis Leroy in his caustic review of the exhibition for *Le Charivari.* Monet lent his full support to the first, second, third, fourth and seventh Impressionist exhibitions, but declined to show his works in the others because of differences between him and Degas and his followers. Except for an entry in 1880, he did not participate in the Paris Salons, exhibiting instead with his dealers Durand-Ruel, Georges Petit, and eventually Bernheim-Jeune. In 1883 he moved to the village of Giverny near Vernon with the family of a former patron, Ernest Hoschedé, whose wife Alice he eventually married. Seven years later he acquired an estate in the village, where he built a studio and planted flower beds, and in 1893 he began work on his water-garden with its "Japanese style" bridge that figured in his most celebrated late paintings, the *Nymphéas* series.

154. Windmills near Zaandam

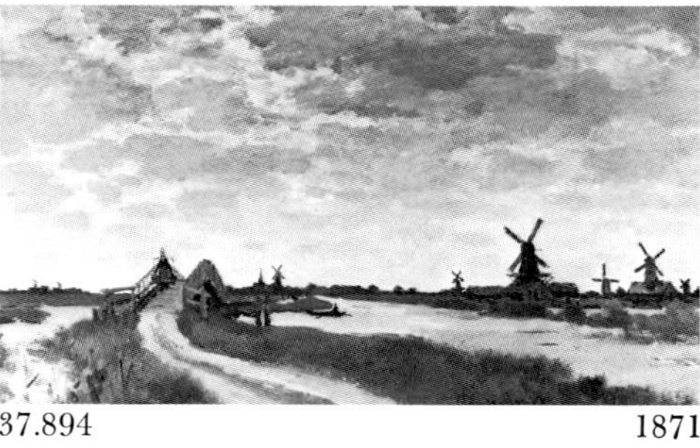

37.894 1871

Monet's five month stay in Zaandam in mid 1871 proved highly productive, resulting in one commissioned portrait and over twenty small paintings or studies of river and canal scenes with windmills and gaily painted houses.

The Walters picture is a view of the footpath, the Weerpad, between Oostzaan and Zaandam. It is somewhat atypical in that most of his Dutch views are devoid of figures, whereas in this scene a girl wearing regional costume and carrying buckets suspended from a yoke is crossing a bridge, and beyond is a person in a rowboat. Across the stretch of water to the right are several windmills, the nearest and largest of which has been identified as De Korff, the biggest in the vicinity. William C. Seitz in *Claude Monet,* New York, 1960, p. 90, has cited the Dutch views as an example of how Monet associated motifs with the style of an artist he admired, in this instance, the Dutch painter whom he had known at Le Havre, Johan Jongkind.

Support: Canvas, .4 x .72 (16″ x 28½″)

Signed at lower right: *Claude Monet*

Marks: Paper label: *DURAND-RUEL. Moulins En Hollande 1874.*

Condition: Yellowed varnish removed and replaced with dammar varnish in 1951. The painting was lined and placed on a new stretcher in 1958. Discolored varnish was removed and replaced with synthetic varnish.

Provenance: Sale, Hôtel Drouot, Paris, January 18, 1873, no. 45 (*Moulins de Zaandam*) (?); bought for Portier, Paris by Boussod Valadon et Cie and sold to Guyotin, Paris in 1887; Erwin Davis, New York; Durand-Ruel, 1899; Henry Walters after 1909.

Exhibitions: "Monet," Durand-Ruel, New York, 1902, no. 1; "Paintings by Impressionists and Post-Impressionists," Virginia Museum of Fine Arts, Richmond, 1950; "From Ingres to Gauguin," Baltimore Museum of Art, 1951, no. 117; "Man and His Years," Baltimore Museum of Art, 1954, no. 117; "Collectors' Firsts," Atlanta Art Association Galleries, 1959, no. 50; "Claude Monet, Seasons and Moments," Los Angeles County Museum, 1960, no. 11; "An Exhibition of Treasures of the Walters Art Gallery," Wildenstein and Co., New York, 1967, no. 48.

References: Georges Lanoë, *Histoire de l'école française de paysage depuis Chintreuil jusqu'à 1900.* Nantes, Société Nantaise d'Editions, 1905. p. 292; Oscar Reuterswärd, *Monet, en konstnär-historik.* Stockholm, Bonnier, 1948. p. 282; Daniel Wildenstein, *Claude Monet, biographie et catalogue raisonné.* 3 vols. Lausanne, La Bibliothèque des Arts, 1974– 1: 194, no. 170; 195 (illus.); John House, *Monet,* Oxford, Phaidon Press, 1981, fig. 24.

155. Springtime

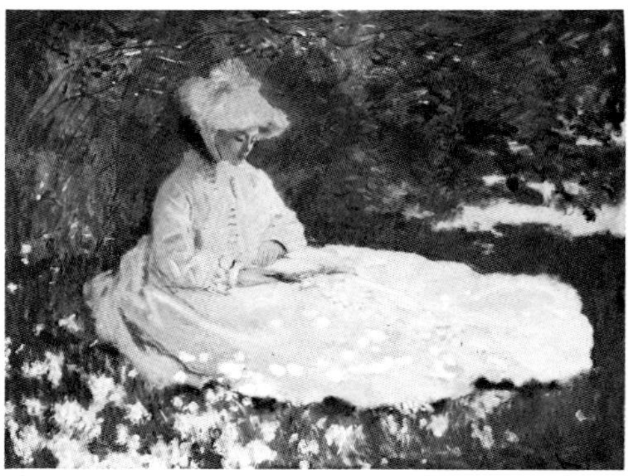

37.11 about 1872

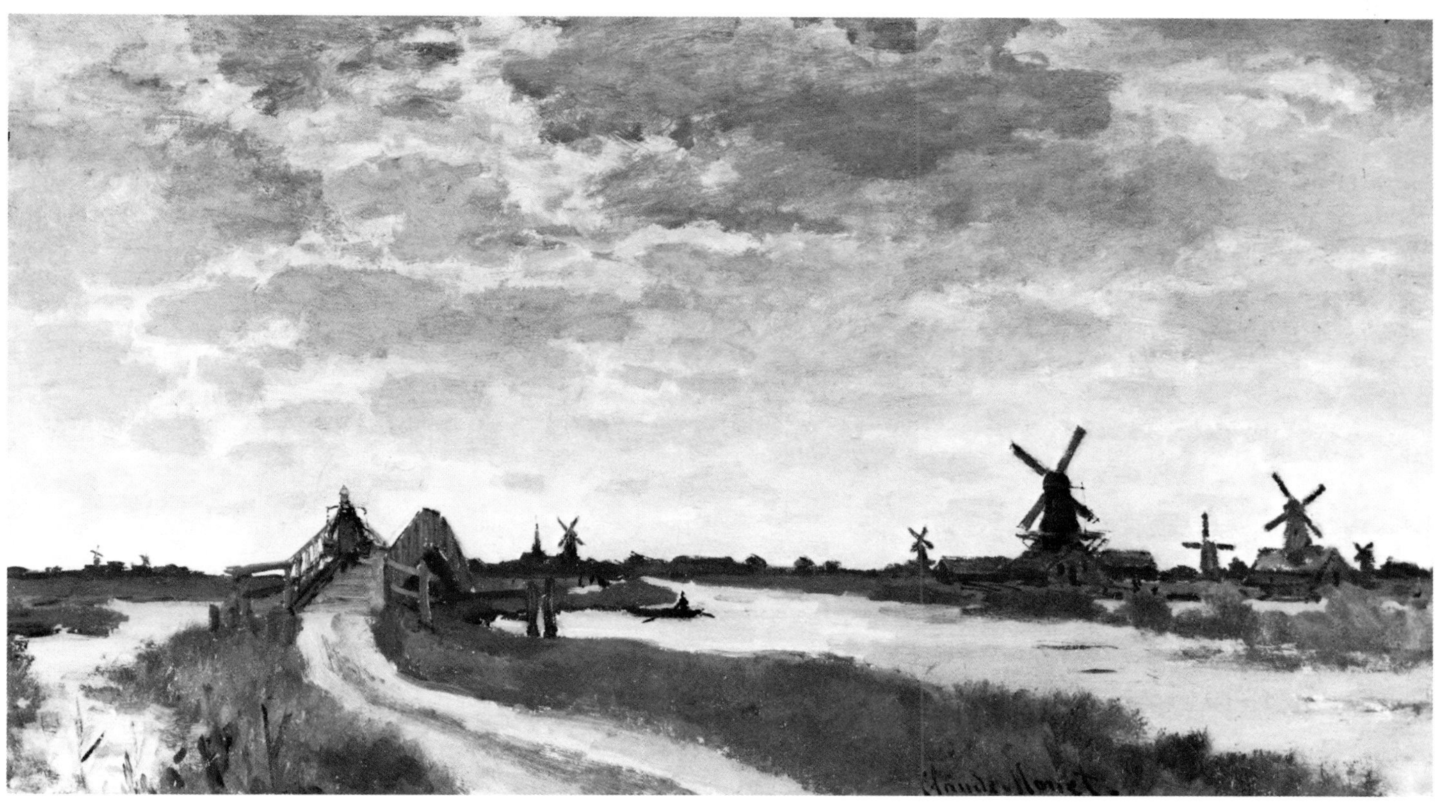

Monet *Windmills near Zaandam,* no. 154

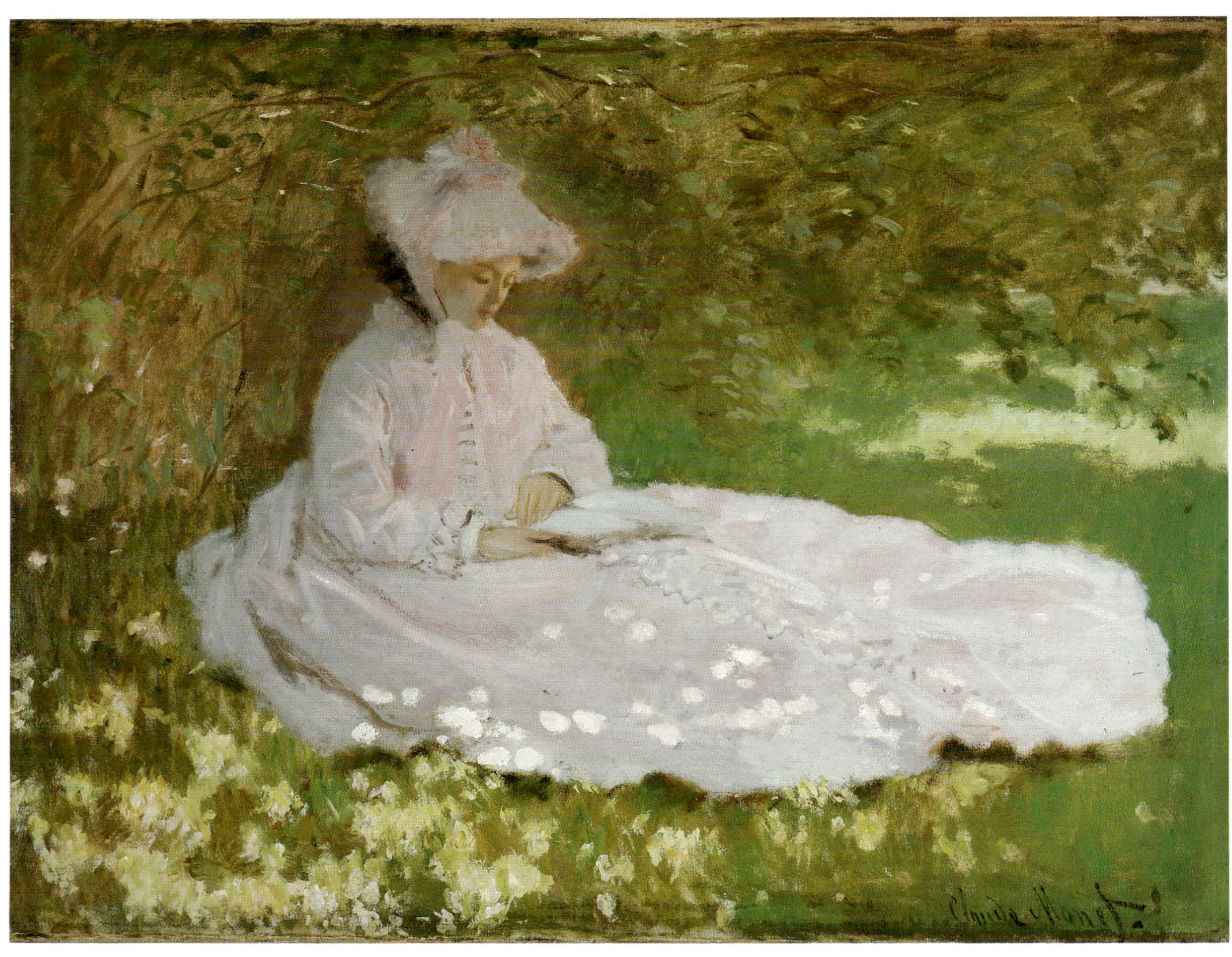

Monet *Springtime,* no. 155

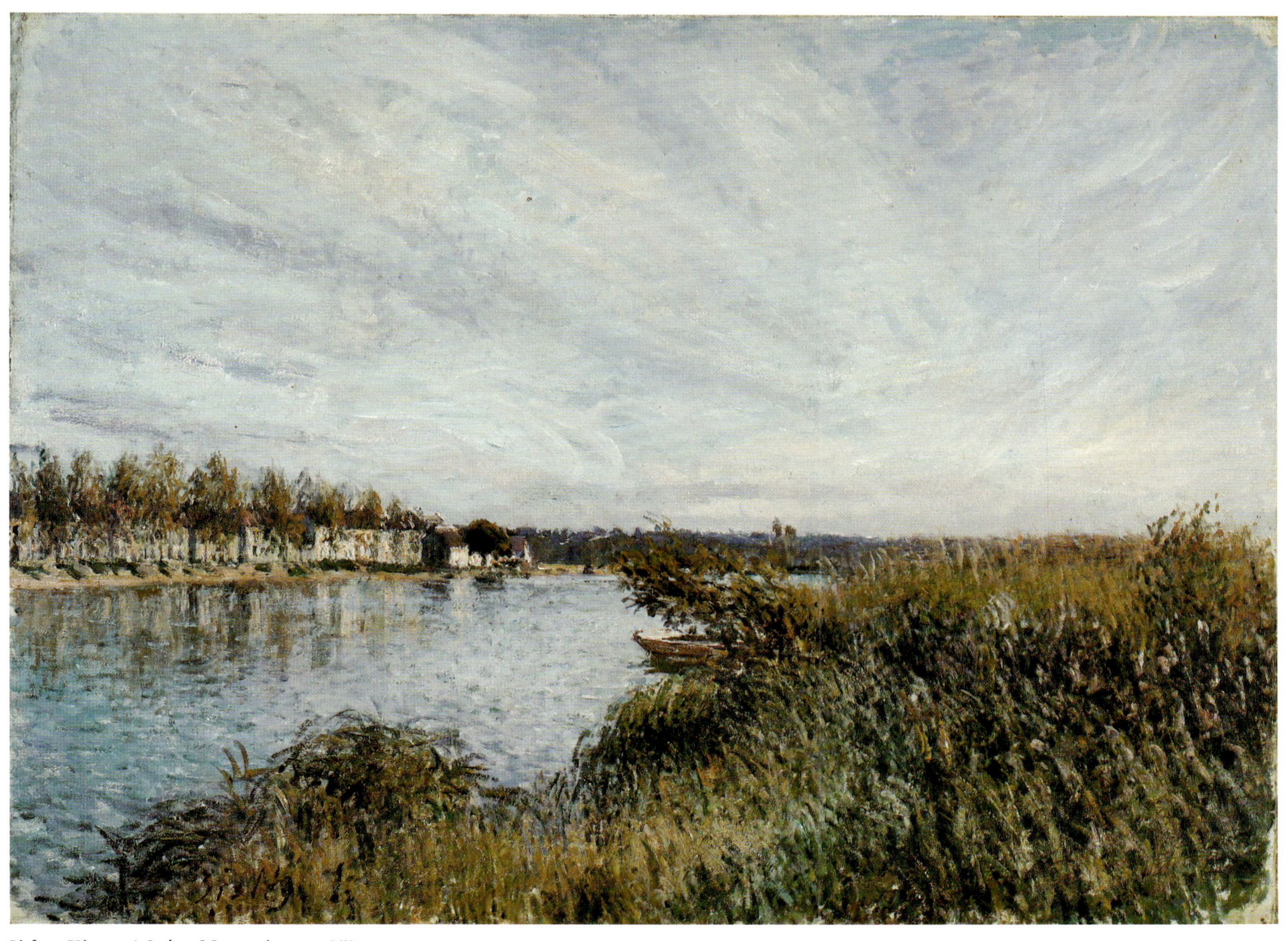

Sisley *View of Saint-Mammès,* no. 157

A young woman seated on the ground is reading a book held in her lap. Sunlight penetrating through is reflected from the foliage and blossoms overhead, to create dappled patches of light on the grass and the woman's garments.

Intermittently in his career Monet produced figurative works employing his acquaintances as models. The subject in this instance was once thought to be Mary Cassatt, an early owner of the picture, but has subsquently been identified by Blanche Hoschedé-Monet as the artist's first wife Camille.

Closely related to the Walters picture is *Madame Monet dans un jardin,* oil on canvas .515 x .66, which was purchased by the Duchesse d'Ayen from the artist's family and most recently sold as part of the Ritter collection in Sotheby Parke Bernet Sale no. 3424, New York, October 25, 1972.

In the latter painting, which does not appear in Daniel Wildenstein's catalogue raisonné of Monet's work, but which is discussed at length by John House in "The New Monet Catalogue," *The Burlington Magazine* 120 (1978) : 680–81, an additional figure of a woman clad in pale blue is seen reclining on the ground gazing upward with a vacant expression. The lighting of the foliage in this work is more dappled and less blended than in the Walters painting.

In the catalogue, "Hommage à Claude Monet," Grand Palais, Paris, 1980, p. 116, nos. 31–32, mention is made of Monet's practice early in his career of occasionally painting his compositions in pairs with one rendition being executed directly from nature and the other being developed in the studio, with or without modifications. Given the simplification in its lighting and its more harmonious composition, one can deduce that the Walters painting would postdate the former Ritter picture in such a sequence. Ironically, in the Grand Palais catalogue, the Walters canvas is cited as a prime example of how Monet chose to preserve the spontaneity of his initial vision by imparting to his work the appearance of a sketch rather than of a finished painting, thus incurring the disapproval of the critics.

An analagous pair of paintings is *Les lilas, temps gris,* oil on canvas, .48 x .64, in the Louvre, and *Lilas au soleil,* dated 1873 though probably painted in 1872, oil on canvas, .5 x .65, Pushkin Museum, Moscow, which likewise show individuals seated beneath shrubbery in bright sunlight. The figures have tentatively been identified as Camille, and Sisley and his wife, and the site accepted as the garden of the Maison Aubry, Argenteuil. It was in the garden of this house, Monet's first address in the town and the former residence of Théodule Ribot, that the artist presumably painted the Walters and the former Ritter pictures.

One other painting, *Le Jardin,* dated 1872, oil on canvas, .64 x .81, private collection, U.S.A., is also closely related to the above works.

Alternative title: *La liseuse.*

Support: Canvas, thinly primed, .485 x .651 (19⅝" x 25¾")

Signed at lower right: *Claude Monet.*

Marks: On stretcher: gummed label: *2319* / stencil on crossbar: *2159* / penciled on crossbar: *2123* / Blue chalk on cross bar: *Miss Cassatt;* Canvas stenciled: *TOILES TABLEAUX COULEURS / LA TOUCHE / 4 RUE de La Fayette 34 / ENCADREMENTS;* Frame: paper sticker *ce tableau appartient / a Mlle Cassatt;* Paper sticker: *Exposition d', Pottier EMBALLEUR, de Tableaux objets d'art, 14 Rue Gaillon-Paris, Walters* (in ink); Paper sticker: *L 130-50-26* (typed); *16 B* (pencil).

Provenance: The painting was purchased from Mary Cassatt together with the Degas *Portrait of a Woman* for a combined price of 25,000 francs by George A. Lucas acting as agent for Henry Walters on May 7, 1903 (Lucas Diary, 2: 914) ; The previous history of the picture is problematical. D. Wildenstein reconstructs its provenance as follows: *Either,* Sale (Monet) Hôtel Drouot, Paris, February 4, 1873, no. 55 *(Jeune femme assise)* to Durand-Ruel; *or,* bought from Monet by Durand-Ruel, November 1872 and resold before 1877 *(La femme en rose);* Hoschedé, Paris; *either,* Sale (Hoschedé) Hôtel Drouot, Paris, June 5–6, 1878, no. 54 *(Jeune femme assise dans un parc)* to Lussac(?); *or,* bought at Hoschedé in 1881 for 50 francs by Durand-Ruel and resold by Durand-Ruel between 1884–1888 *(Femme assise dans l'herbe)* and bought by Mary Cassatt about 1889; Henry Walters, 1903. In the catalogue of the 1980 Grand Palais, exhibition, no. 33, it is recorded that Monet made the following notation in a nôtebook in May 1879: *vendu Mlle Cassatt / Toile printemps 300* (f) (Carnet, Paris, Musée Marmottan, MM 5160 (2) fol. 25v°) . Although this passage might allude to other landscapes it is noteworthy that the French caption corresponds to the traditional English title of the Walters painting.

Exhibitions: "2e Exposition de Peinture," 11, rue Le Peletier, [Durand-Ruel], Paris, 1876 (as *Le printemps*); "Monet-Rodin," Galerie Georges Petit, Paris, 1889, no. 23 (lent by Mary Cassatt as *La Liseuse*); "Contrasts in Impressionism," Baltimore Museum of Art, 1942, no. 18; "Themes and Variations," Baltimore Museum of Art, 1948, no. 83; "Monet and the Beginnings of Impressionism," Currier Gallery of Art, Manchester, N. H., 1949, no. 45; "Paintings by Impressionists and Post-Impressionists," Virginia Museum of Fine Arts, Richmond, 1950; "From Ingres to Gauguin," Baltimore Museum of Art, 1951, no. 118; "Inaugural Exhibition," Fort Worth Art Center, 1954, no. 68; "Turn of the Century," Denver Art Museum, 1956; "Claude Monet" Saint Louis City Art Museum and Minneapolis Institute of Arts, 1957, no. 27; "The Image Lost and Found," Institute of Contemporary Art, Boston, 1960, no. 4; "Hommage à Claude Monet," Grand Palais, Paris, 1980, no. 33.

References: Emile Zola, "Deux expositions d'art au mois de mai," *Messager de l'Europe* (St. Petersburg) June 1876 (reprinted in his *Mon Salon. Manet. Ecrits sur l'art.* Paris, Garnier-Flammarion, 1970. p. 279); Walters cat., 1909, p. 5, no. 11 (as *Springtime*), and subsequent Walters catalogues; Marthe de Fels, *La vie de Claude Monet.* Paris, Gallimard, 1929. p. 236; Oscar Reutersward, *Monet, en konstnärhistorik.* Stockholm, Bonnier, 1948. p. 280; F. W. J. Hemmings and R. J. Niess, *E. Zola: Salons.* Publications de la Société de Publications Romanes et Françaises, 63. Geneva, Droz, 1959. p. 195; J. P. Hoschedé, *Blanche Hoschedé-Monet, peintre impressioniste.* Rouen, Lecerf, 1961. pp. 8–9; John Rewald, *The history of impressionism.* Rev. and enl. ed. New York, Museum of Modern Art, 1961. pp. 386–87; Frederick A. Sweet, *Miss Mary Cassatt, impressionist from Pennsylvania.* Norman, University of Oklahoma Press, 1966. p. 141; Daniel Wildenstein, *Claude Monet, biographie et catalogue raisonné.* 3 vols. Lausanne, La Bibliothèque des Arts, 1974– 1:206, no. 205; 207 (illus.); John House, "The new Monet catalogue," *The Burlington Magazine* 120 (1978): 680; John Canaday, *Mainstreams of modern art.* 2nd ed. New York, Holt, Rinehart and Winston, 1981. pp. 229, 230 (illus.) .

Alfred Sisley

French-English: Paris, 1839 -
Moret sur-Loing, 1899

Sisley's parents were English with ancestral roots on both sides of the English Channel. His father operated a business exporting artificial flowers to South America that enabled him to raise his family in comfortable means. In 1857 Alfred was sent for four years to England, ostensibly to study commerce. He was, however, distracted by the English galleries with their holdings of paintings by Turner and Constable. Returning to Paris, he abandoned a business career and enrolled in October 1862 in the atelier of Charles Gleyre, where he remained until the following March.

At Easter in 1863 Sisley and several former students from Gleyre's atelier, Auguste Renoir, Claude Monet, and Frédéric Bazille, went to Chailly in the Fontainebleau forest to paint together. Early in 1865 Sisley was again in this region at Marlotte, where he was joined by Renoir, Monet, and Camille Pissarro, and later by Renoir at Celle-Saint-Cloud. His first works at the Paris Salon, *Women going to the Woods* and *Street in the Village of Marlotte* (Albright Knox Art Gallery), shown in 1866, recalled the landscapes of Corot and Daubigny. He exhibited again in 1868 but was rejected the following year. At this time he frequented the Café Guerbois, a meeting place for the future Impressionists, Manet, and the realist writers and critics.

Until the upheavals in France in 1870–71, Sisley had received assistance from his parents but with the collapse of the family business during the war and the death of his father shortly thereafter, he was compelled to support himself and his own family through his art. Paul Durand-Ruel had included a view of the Seine by Sisley in his exhibition of French painting at the German Gallery in London in 1871 and subsequently became the artist's principal dealer, though he was himself hard pressed financially in the seventies. In 1874 Sisley submitted five paintings to the first Impressionist exhibition and participated afterwards in the second, third, and seventh exhibitions of this independent group though he did unsuccessfully attempt to exhibit again in the official Salon in 1879. During the seventies Sisley worked primarily in the villages to the west and north of Paris, in Louveciennes where he had joined Renoir during the Commune, at Argenteuil, Marly-Le-Roi, and in the vicinity of Sèvres, specializing in landscapes with stretches of rivers or village roadways. At the invitation of Jean-Baptiste Faure, one of his few early patrons, he visited England in the autumn of 1874, painting some of his most brilliantly Impressionistic river views near Hampton Court. Among his more distinctive works of the seventies were a number of winter scenes.

In 1880, probably for reasons of economy, he moved to the region of Moret-sur-Loing, on the southern flank of the Fontainebleau forest, where he remained except for several brief excursions until his death. He moved from village to village in this area beginning with Veneux in 1880, Moret in 1882, Les Sablons in 1883, and back to Moret in 1889, painting numerous views of the Loing and the Seine. His works were included in Durand-Ruel's various exhibitions both in France and abroad, and beginning in 1887 he began to deal with Georges Petit. He was elected in 1890 an associate member of La Société Nationale des Beaux-Arts that held its salons in the Champs de Mars. In the early nineties Sisley painted a number of views of Moret cathedral that invite comparison with Monet's Rouen cathedral series, though in the former the building retains its architectonic qualities, whereas in the latter the façade appears to dissolve in light and atmosphere. Remaining in Moret, in an ever precarious financial state, Sisley grew increasingly isolated and failed to achieve the recognition being accorded both Monet and Renoir. Immediately after his death, ironically, the prices paid for his paintings began to soar.

Among the Impressionists Sisley was perhaps the most consistent in pursuing his objectives, which were in themselves restricted. His range of subjects was limited; he avoided, for example, figurative compositions. His landscapes are marked by the sense of immediacy and familiarity.

156. La Terrasse de Saint-Germain, Printemps

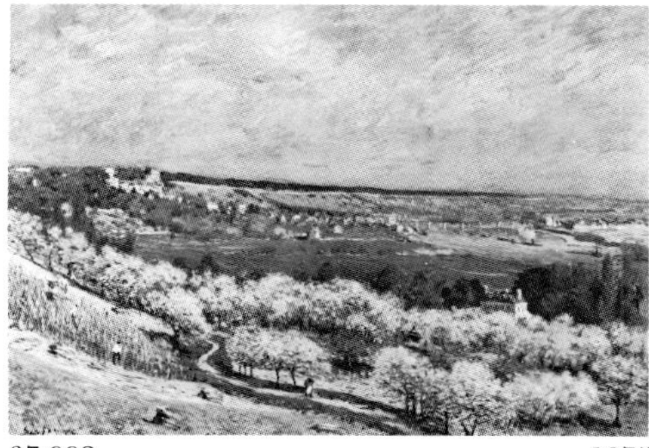

37.992 1875

While living in Marly-Le-Roi from 1875 to 1877, Sisley painted a number of street scenes in the village as well as several panoramic views of the Seine Valley.

In this instance he showed a view overlooking a loop in the river facing toward the town of Saint-Germain-en-Laye, thirteen miles west of Paris. On the slopes in the foreground workmen toil in a vineyard as a solitary woman trudges along a roadway winding through an orchard. To the right is a villa and beyond on the river a tugboat emitting clouds of smoke pulls barges. In the background is the town of Saint-Germain and on the heights to the left the remnants of the château founded in the twelfth century. The terrace, noted for its vista, and the Forest of Laye extend across the horizon line.

As illustrated by this view, Sisley stands apart from his Impressionist colleagues in emphasizing in his compositions a sense of depth and distance.

A closely related, though less dramatic, scene is to be found in *Printemps à Saint-Germain-en-Laye,* dated 1876 (.38 x .56), private collection (Daulte no. 214).

Support: Canvas: .736 x .996 (29″ x 39¼″); originally 27″ x 38¼″.

Signed and dated lower left: *Sisley 75*

Condition: Partial cleaning in 1935. Lined, with some loss of impasto prior to 1951. Discolored varnish removed and replaced with dammar varnish in 1951. Old lining removed and fabric relined with use of glue.

Provenance: Purchased from Sisley by Durand-Ruel in 1880; J. B. Faure, Paris; Charles Guasco Sale, Georges Petit, Paris, June 11, 1900, no. 67 for 12,000 francs to Durand-Ruel; Durand-Ruel to E. J. Blair, Baltimore, July 9, 1900; Blair to Henry Walters, date unknown.

Exhibitions: "Tableaux par P.-A. Besnard, J.-C. Cazin, C. Monet, A. Sisley et F. Thaulow," Galeries Georges Petit, Paris, 1889, no. 62; "Loan Exhibition of Paintings by Alfred Sisley," Paul Rosenberg & Co., New York, 1961, no. 7; "An Exhibition of Treasures of the Walters Art Gallery," Wildenstein and Co., New York, 1967, no. 50.

References: François Daulte, *Alfred Sisley: catalogue raisonné de l'oeuvre peint.* Lausanne, Durand-Ruel, 1959. no. 164, illus.; Elisabeth Packard, "La Terrasse de Saint-Germain," *WAGB* 4, no. 6 (March 1952): 1 (illus.), 3.

157. View of Saint-Mammès (formerly View of the Marne)

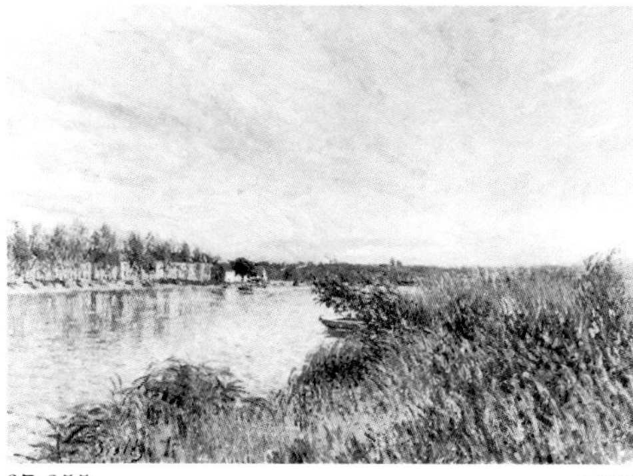

37.355 c. 1880

Though his approach was more intuitive and less systematic than Monet's, Sisley shared his colleague's practice of returning to a particular site to record it in varying seasonal and weather conditions. One of the sites to which he was most frequently drawn in the early eighties was the village of Saint-Mammès, located at the confluence of the Loing and the Seine rivers.

In this work one looks from a densely reeded bank across the water toward the houses of the village. In the distance are the isolated chestnut tree that occurs in the related paintings as well as in a number of views showing the village's sawmill seen from the oppsite direction (François Daulte, *Alfred Sisley, catalogue raisonné,* Lausanne, 1959, nos. 368–372), and the row of poplar trees that separated the village street from the river (Daulte, no. 367). This painting illustrates Sisley's technique of varying the nature of his brushwork from long flowing strokes in the light, scudding clouds to short staccatto strokes in the dense overgrowth in the foreground.

Closely related views include *La Berge à Saint-Mammès* (.5 x .65), the Pitcairn collection, Bryn Athyn, Pennsylvania, and the erroneously entitled *Village sur les bords de la Marne,* (.54 x .73), The Carnegie Art Institute, Pittsburgh. The Walters painting, which has traditionally been known as *Les Bords de la Marne,* and the Pittsburgh picture, both showing Saint-Mammès from slightly different viewpoints, belonged to Durand-Ruel, New York, in the 1890s and may have received their misnomers at that time.

Support: Canvas, .54 x .73 (21½″ x 29⅛″)

Signed at lower left: *Sisley.*

Marks: Canvas stenciled: *MAISON DESPERZ* / . . . / . . . Paper sticker: *Sisley No. 1064* / *Les bords de* / *la Marne* / *NASS;* Crossbar of stretcher: *D.R.N.Y.* / *1064* (ink); *39* (chalk); *279* (chalk); *19* (chalk); *D.R.N.Y. 934* (pencil); *2489;* ink on circular paper sticker; *Photo* / *A489* (pencil).

Condition: Prior to 1934 the painting was lined and a small slit in the sky was over-painted. In 1951 the painting was relined and the discolored varnish removed and replaced with dammar varnish.

Provenance: Durand-Ruel, Paris, to Sir William Van Horne, Montreal, May 6, 1892; Van Horne to Durand-Ruel, New York, April 15, 1893;

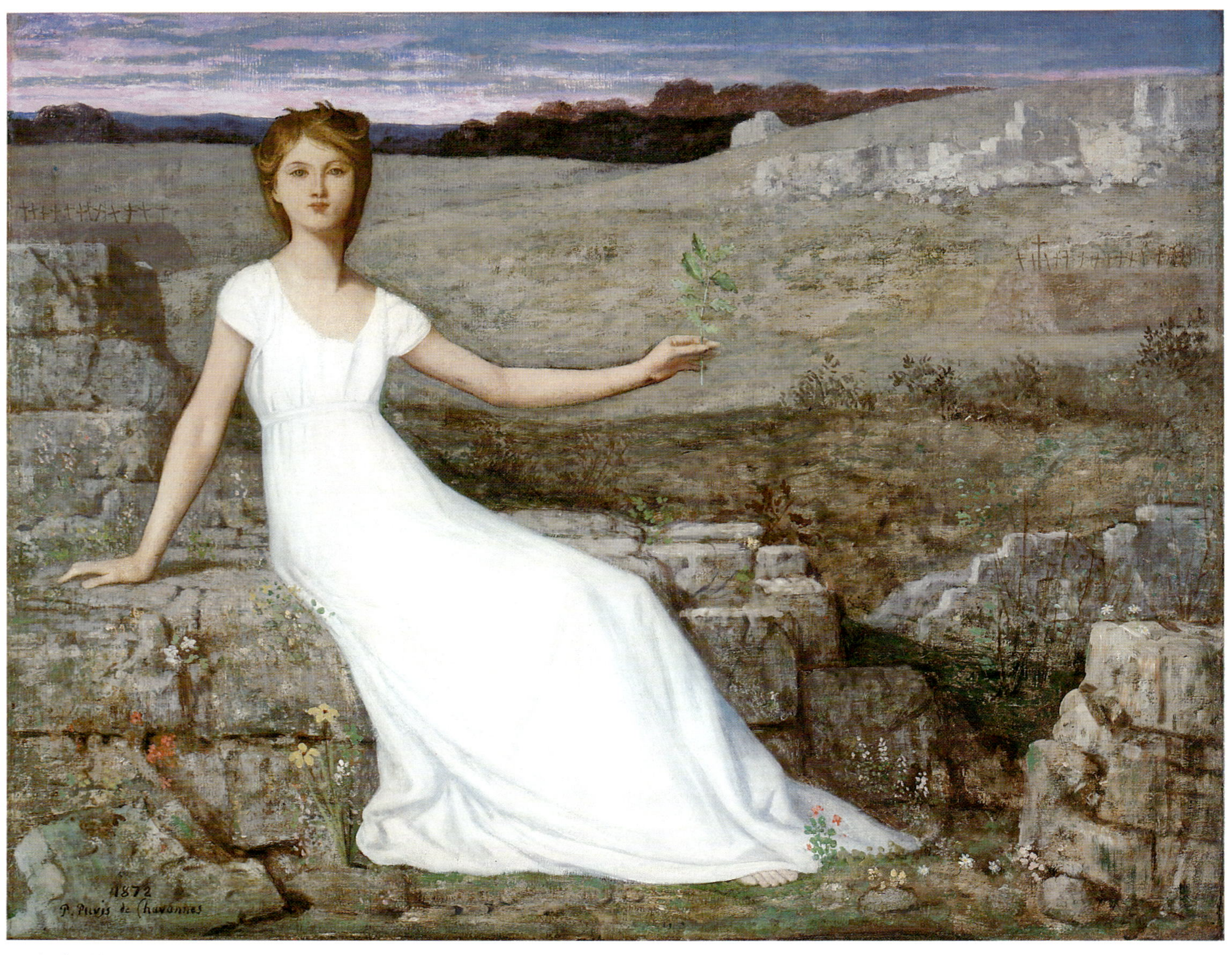

Puvis de Chavannes *Hope,* no. 160

Durand-Ruel to Henry Walters, January 12, 1909.

Exhibitions: "Paintings by the French Impressionists," The Albright Gallery, Buffalo, 1907, no. 78; "From Ingres to Gauguin," Baltimore Museum of Art, 1951, no. 116; "Französische Malerei von Delacroix bis Picasso," Volkswagenwerk, Stadthalle, Wolfsburg, 1961, no. 58.

References: François Daulte, *Alfred Sisley: catalogue raisonné de l'oeuvre peint.* Lausanne, Durand-Ruel, 1959, no. 426, illus.

Stanislas-Victor-Edmond Lépine

French: Caen, 1835 - Paris, 1892

Scant information is available pertaining to the life of this artist, who followed an independent, somewhat secondary course in later nineteenth–century French painting. He was born in Caen, in humble circumstances, his father being an *ébéniste*. It has been conjectured that Lépine was awarded a municipal stipend, enabling him to study in Paris, although this possibility must remain unconfirmed in view of the destruction of the town records. In 1859 he settled in Montmartre and remained in this district, which was incorporated into the city four years later, occasionally painting its streets and alleys.

Although Lépine exhibited regularly in the Salons beginning in 1859, he did not list himself in the *livrets* as a pupil of Corot until 1866. Corot's biographer, Robaut, made no mention of the young artist in his publication but did include Lépine's name in a manuscript (Bibliothèque Nationale) in a list of painters to whom the master had lent works to be copied. Lépine's subsequent career apparently remained relatively uneventful as he pursued his work portraying the waterways of Paris and the occasional Normandy port. He became involved with the Cercle Mogador centered around the dealer Pierre Firmin Martin on the rue Mogador and through this contact he met a number of discerning collectors and progressive artists. Among the former was the Count Armand Doria, who became his principal patron, as well as Lutz, Delineau, Choquet, Rouart, and Tavernier, all of whom acquired examples of his work. His closest associates among the artists were Th. Ribot and A. F. Cals. In 1873 he participated in the Salon des Refusés and the following year he joined the Impressionists, exhibiting three paintings, *Le Canal Saint-Denis,* (collection M. Sporck), *La rue Cortot* (collection M. Brullé) and *Bords de la Seine* (collection M. M. . . .) in their first group showing in Nadar's studio. Although he did not participate in the seven subsequent shows, two of his paintings, *The Bridge of Saint Michel* and *Moonlight in Paris,* were included in Durand-Ruel's Impressionist exhibition held in New York in 1886.

In 1891, the year of the schism in the Salon, Lépine sided with the more progressive Société Nationale des Beaux-Arts. During his life time Lépine obtained only modest recognition. He received an honorable mention at the 1884 Salon, a first–class medal at the 1889 Exposition Universelle, a third–class medal at the Salon the same year, and a second–class award in Madrid in 1891. To support himself between the mid-seventies and mid-eighties, he resorted to holding six sales at the Hôtel Drouot. Nevertheless, he died in relative obscurity and poverty.

In retrospect, Lépine distinguished himself in his dedication to portraying a limited range of subjects, concentrating on the effects of atmosphere and light. His works are devoid of any romantic overtones, and human figures, when they occur, are subordinated to the settings.

158. Pont de L'Estacade

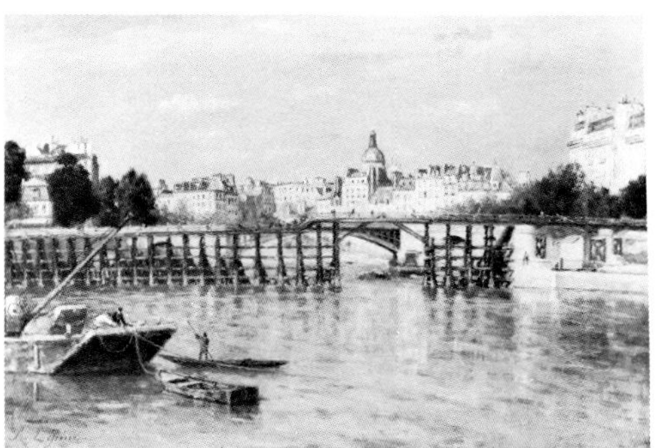

37.2551 c. 1880

In this small painting Paris and the Seine are shown bathed in warm sunlight. Extending across the river in the middle ground is the small foot bridge carried on timbers known as L'Estacade, erected in 1818 and removed in 1938. Slightly beyond is the Pont Sully, constructed in 1874–76, connecting the Ile Saint Louis with the Right Bank. The artist apparently painted the view from a quai near the Port-aux-Vins.

Lépine returned to this site on numerous occasions: no. 1561, *Le pont de l'Estacade à Paris* appeared in the 1885 Salon; *Vue de Paris: le pont de l'Estacade* (.2 x .325) was sold at the Nunès Sale, Paris, 1894, and *L'estacade à Paris* (.31 x .45) and *Autre vue de l'Estacade* (1.4 x .23) were auctioned in the Comte A. Doria Sale, Paris, in 1899. Presently belonging to The Norton Simon Museum of Art is *Pont de l'Estacade, Paris,* (.26 x .4) bearing a dedicatory inscription: *à M. de Fourcade.*

Support: Canvas, .318 x .464 (12½" x 18¼")

Signed at lower left: *S. Lépine.*

Condition: Prior to 1977, the painting was cleaned, lined on fiberglass and coated with synthetic varnish.

Provenance: Acquired by John Leonard Power in the New York art market; bequest to the Walters Art Gallery of John Leonard Power, December 1977.

159. Bassin de La Villette

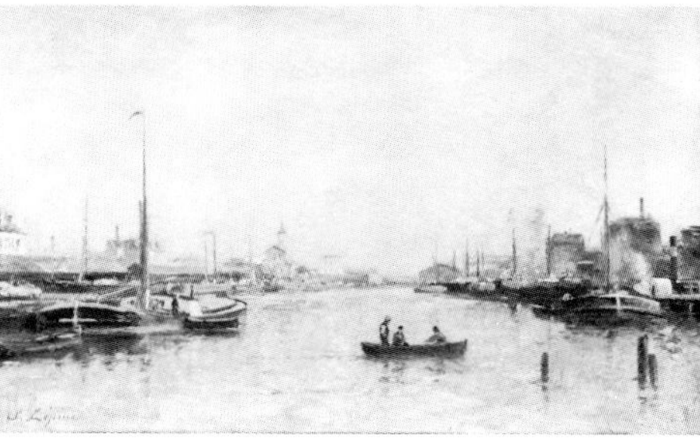

37.892

The Bassin was constructed in the former village of La Villette between 1806 and 1809 to provide a harbor and a reservoir. It was formed from the Canal d'Ourcq connecting the Ourcq, a tributary of the Marne, with the Seine.

Lépine produced a number of paintings of this waterway conveniently located east of Montmartre. Here he shows it on a sunny, though hazy and apparently humid day. Flanking the waterway are numerous barges and warehouses.

A similar view, *Le Bassin de La Villette,* canvas (.34 x .665) is illustrated in John Couper, *Stanislas Lépine, sa vie, son oeuvre,* Paris, 1969, fig. 31.

Support: Canvas, .384 x .613 (15⅛" x 24⅛")

Signed at lower left: *S. Lépine.*

Condition: Discolored varnishes removed and replaced with dammar varnish in 1956.

Provenance: Durand-Ruel; Cyrus J. Lawrence Sale, American Art Association, New York, Jan. 21–22, 1910, no. 61.

References: Edward S. King, "Episodes in collecting," *WAGB* 23, no. 8 (May 1971): 2.

Pierre-Cécile Puvis de Chavannes

French: Lyons, 1824 - Paris, 1898

Puvis de Chavannes, creator of numerous monumental murals and some easel paintings, pursued an independent though pivotal career in the later nineteenth century. His schematized compositions with their rhythmically positioned abstracted figures, served as points of departure for many subsequent artists.

Puvis was essentially self-taught, having trained with Henri Scheffer for less than a year, with Delacroix for only two weeks, and with Couture for three months. An early interest in murals may have been sparked by two trips to Italy, the first in 1846, and the second in the company of the painter Bauderon de Vermeron in 1848.

In 1850 his *Dead Christ* was exhibited at the Salon though not until 1859 was another of the artist's works accepted. In the meantime he discovered his forte, mural painting, in decorating the dining room of his brother's house at Le Brouchy (Saône-et-Loire) in 1854–55 with a series of biblical scenes that also alluded, appropriately, to the seasons and the staple foods.

His *Bellum* and *Concordia* received second–class medals at the 1861 Salon. When the latter was purchased by the state for the Napoleon Museum (Musée de Picardie) at Amiens, Puvis, not wishing to have his compositions separated, donated the other to the city. As a sequel he painted *Repose* and *Work,* shown in the 1863 Salon, and undertook a vast *Ave Picardia Nutrix,* symbolizing the fecundity of the region, all executed in oil and wax media.

His next major project was a pair of murals, *Massilia, colonie grecque* and *Marseille, porte de l'Orient,* symbolizing ancient and modern Marseilles, executed in 1867–69 for the grand staircase of the City's new Palais Longchamp. About this time he befriended Berthe Morisot, through whom he met Manet and a number of more progressive artists.

In the 1870 Salon, Puvis entered two small religious pictures *The Magdalen in the Desert* and *The Beheading of Saint John the Baptist.* The latter, exemplifying the same simplification of planes, forms, and colors encountered in his murals, aroused the ire of most critics. During the War of 1870 he served with Meissonier, Manet, and Tissot in the National Guard. Two pictures, *Le Ballon* and *Le Pigeon voyageur,* allude to the conflict, and a third, *Hope,* existing in two versions, the larger in the Walters and the smaller in the Louvre, refers to the nation's regeneration.

Though he had been commissioned in 1870 to paint decorative panels for the new city hall of Poitiers, it was not until four years later that Puvis was able to show at the Salon his two completed works depicting scenes from the lives of Charles Martel and Saint Radegonde. That year he was also among twelve painters commissioned to execute murals for the church of Saint Genevieve (after 1885, the Panthéon) in Paris. In 1876 he exhibited cartoons for his four major segments of the Saint Genevieve project. He was also elevated from Chevalier, a rank he had received ten years earlier, to Officier of the Legion of Honor.

Puvis received a commission in 1880 to execute a mural showing young Picardians practicing the javelin throw to decorate the north stairwell of the Musée de Picardie in Amiens as a complement to his *Ave Picardia Nutrix.* The resulting *Pro Patria Ludus* has generally been acknowledged as one of his principal achievements.

At the Salon the following year, Puvis exhibited *The Poor Fisherman* which generated considerable controversy and came to serve as a touchstone for the emerging symbolists.

Puvis' later years saw an ever-increasing flow of orders for murals, including decorations for Léon Bonnat's residence (1882); the Palais des Arts, Lyons (1883); the Musée des Beaux-Arts, Rouen (1888); the Sorbonne (1889); the Escalier du Préfet de la Seine in the Paris Hôtel de Ville (1892); the Boston Public Library (1891) and finally, in 1893, he assumed responsibility for a wall painting in the Panthéon originally assigned to Meissonier.

As early as 1873 Puvis had established contacts with the dealer Durand-Ruel, and in 1887 he exhibited ten works in an Impressionist show held by the dealer in New York. Puvis shared responsibility with Rodin and Meissonier in 1890 in founding the Société Nationale des Beaux-Arts, which held salons to rival those of the Société des Artistes Français, and the following year he was elected chairman of the new organization. In 1895 Puvis served on the founding committee of the Venice Biennale and two years later he joined the editorial board of *Art et Décoration,* a monthly review of modern art published in Paris.

Despite his innovative role in the late nineteenth century, Puvis' reputation shortly after his death went into an eclipse from which it did not emerge until the 1970s.

160. Hope

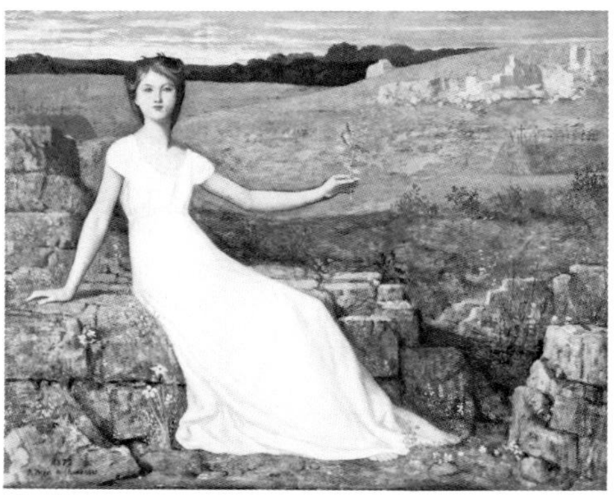

37.156 1871

Hope is personified by a young maiden holding a bough of laurel in her outstretched hand. She is seated on a rocky ledge amidst blossoming spring flowers. The landscape in the background is disfigured by shattered buildings and grave markers. The artist's symbolism, in this instance, can be traced to Ambrogio Lorenzetti's representation of Peace as a young woman holding a branch in his mural *Good Government* in the Palazzo Pubblico, Siena.

This painting marking the end of the upheavals of 1870–71 and expressing aspirations for the nation's regeneration is one of two variants. The Walters picture, the larger, was first exhibited at the Salon in 1872 (no. 1282), whereas the smaller (.707 x .82) , now in the Louvre (Inv. 20117), was not shown until 1887 when both works appeared together in an exhibition held by the dealer Durand-Ruel. The Louvre painting, which differs from the Walters in that Hope appears nude seated on a white drapery, as well as in a number of details in the background, is now thought to be contemporary with or to postdate the other.

When it was shown at the 1872 Salon, the Walters *Hope* inspired Armand Silvestre to write the following verses:

Blanc vêtue et si frêle, ainsi qu'une enfant née
Aux jours sombres, assise aux Champs où nos morts froids
Gisent sous le funèbre alignement des croix
L'Espérance! est-ce toi, douce vierge étonnée?
Dans nos champs ruinés où rôde la belette,
Si pâle qu'en tes yeux rêve l'étonnement
De vivre encore, oh! c'est bien toi, l'ange
Qui frissonnes au vent clément de l'aube violette! . . .

Otherwise, the painting was unfavorably received by most critics, including Bertall, who wrote of *Hope: "Elle est bien mince! . . . Le fait est qu'elle manque un peu trop de patriotisme?"* (*Le Grelot au Salon,* Paris, 1872); Claudius Stella, who described the maiden as a *"mannequin d'atelier"* dressed in a towel, seated on a chest with *"une feuille de papier peint à la main"* and Ernest Duvergier de Hauranne, who announced that Puvis was making himself out to be a Pre-Raphaelite—a *"genre commode pour qui ni sait ni dessiner ni peindre" (Revue des deux mondes).* These and other criticisms are discussed by Jacques Foucart in *Puvis de Chavannes,* catalogue, Paris, Ottawa, 1976–77, pp. 114–15).

Works related to the Baltimore painting include a drawing numbered 129 in Toulouse, Musée Paul Dupuy ("Rétrospective Puvis de Chavannes," Société Nationale des Beaux-Arts, Paris, 1924, no. 969) an oil sketch in a private collection, Paris (.23 x .25), caricatures by Bertall and Cham, and a drawing in a letter from Puvis to Paul de Saint-Victor, April 2, 1872, in the Institut Néerlandais, Paris. More closely related to the Louvre variant is a drawing numbered 128 in the Musée Dupuy, Toulouse, and a drawing in chalk dedicated to Léon Bouillon, purchased by Bryson Burroughs at the Field Sale, New York, December 10, 1918, no. 149, and presented to the Walters Art Gallery by Mrs. Burroughs.

Foucart in the 1976–77 catalogue cited a tradition that the model for *Hope* was the little Dobigny girl who also posed for Corot and Degas.

Alternative title: *L'Espérance.*

Support: Canvas, 1.025 x 1.295 (40⅜" x 50⅞")

Signed and dated at lower left: *1872 P. Puvis de Chavannes.*

Condition: Cleaned and lined in 1966.

Provenance: Artist to Durand-Ruel for 7,000 francs just prior to 1872 Salon; Durand-Ruel to Patou, Paris for 3,000 francs; Patou to Durand-Ruel for 2,000 francs; Durand-Ruel to Erwin Davis, New York in 1890 for 7,000 francs; E. F. Miliken Sale, New York, February 14, 1902, no. 25 to Henry Walters for $4,100.00.

Exhibitions: Paris, Salon, 1872, no. 1282; "Exposition de Tableaux, Pastels, Dessins par M. Puvis de Chavannes," Durand-Ruel, Paris, 1887, no. 19; "Exposition centennale de l'art français, 1789–1889," Paris, 1889, no. 5616; "Paintings, Pastels, Decorations by Puvis de Chavannes," Durand-Ruel, New York, 1894, no. 14; "Puvis de Chavannes and The Modern Tradition," Art Gallery of Ontario, Toronto, 1975, no. 15, illus.; "Puvis de Chavannes, 1824–1898," Grand Palais, Paris, and National Gallery of Canada, Ottawa, 1976–77, no. 90.

References: Claudius Stella, "Salon de 1872," *L'Opinion nationale,* June 7, 1872; Ernest Duvergier de Hauranne, "Le Salon de 1872," *Revue des deux mondes* (1872): 842–43; Bertall [Charles Albert d'Arnould], *Le Grelot au Salon;* 1ère livraison: *Le Salon de 1872 dépeint et dessiné par Bertall.* Paris, 1872. p. 8 (illus.); Cham [Amédée de Noé] *Le Salon pour rire.* Paris, Au Bureau du Charivari, 1872. illus.; Armand Silvestre, *Galerie Durand-Ruel, recueil d'estampes gravées à l'eau-forte.* Paris, Durand-Ruel, 1873. p. 27, illus. by Boilvin; Jules Clarétie, *Peintres et sculpteurs contemporains.* 2nd ed. Paris, Charpentier, 1874. pp. 190–91; Maurice Du Seigneur, *L'Art et les artistes au Salon de 1880.* Paris, P. Ollendorff, 1880. p. 97; Octave Mirbeau, "Puvis de Chavannes," *La France* (November 8, 1884): 3; Armand Silvestre, "Puvis de Chavannes, l'oeuvre et l'artiste," *La Grande revue, Paris et Saint-Petersbourg* 1, no. 3 (December 1887): 3–4; André Michel, "Exposition de M. Puvis de Chavannes," *GBA* 2nd pér. 37 (1888): 43; Gustave Khan, "Exposition Puvis de Chavannes," *La Revue indépendante* 6, no. 15 (June 1888): 145; Roger Riordan, "The atelier: Puvis de Chavannes," *The Art Amateur* 24, no. 1 (December 1890): 5–6, 34; Jules A. Castagnary, *Salons, 1857–1879.* 2 vols. Paris, Bibliothèque Charpentier, 1892. 2: 19; Lily Lewis Rood, *Pierre Puvis de Chavannes, a sketch.* Boston, L. Prang, 1895. p. 13; Léon Riotor, *L'Art et l'idée; essai sur Puvis de Chavannes.* Paris, Bureaux de *L'Artiste,* 1896. p. 40. (First published as a three-part article in *L'Artiste* 11, March–May 1896); Charles Florisoone, "Puvis de Chavannes," *Conference des Rosati Picards* 3 (October 29, 1898): 11; Robert de la Sizeranne, "Puvis de Chavannes," *Revue des deux mondes* (November 1898): 408; Marius Vachon, *Puvis de Chavannes, un maître de ce temps.* Art et les artistes. Paris, Société d'édition artistique, 1900. pp. 157–58; Léon Riotor, *Les arts et les lettres.* 3 vols. Paris, Lemerre, 1901–08. 1: 95–96; Arsène Alexandre, *Puvis de Chavannes.* Newnes' art library. London, G. Newnes, 1905: illus. no. 59 (as *Innocence*); Conrad de Mandach, "Lettres de Puvis de Chavannes, 1861–1876," *Revue de Paris* (December 15, 1910): 673–94; Jean Laran and André Michel, *Puvis de Chavannes.* L'art de notre temps. Paris, La Renaissance du Livre, 1911. pp. 53–54; Léonce Bénédite, "L'Espérance du Puvis de Chavannes au Musée du Luxembourg," *Les Musées de France* 1 (1913): 1–3; René Jean, *Puvis de Chavannes.* Art et esthétique. Paris, Alcan, 1914. pp. 160–61, plate XXIV; Lionello Venturi, *Les archives de l'impressionisme.* 2 vols. Paris, Durand-Ruel, 1939. 2: 192–93; William R. Johnston, "L'Espérance of Puvis de Chavannes," *WAGB* 21, no. 4 (January 1969): 2–4, illus.; Carl R. Baldwin, "The Salon of '72," *Art News* 71, no. 3 (May 1972): 23 (illus.), 62A; Aimée Brown Price, *Puvis de Chavannes: a study of the easel paintings and a catalogue of the painted works* (unpublished Ph.D. dissertation, Yale University, 1972), cat. no. 157; Aimée Brown Price, " 'L'Allegorie réelle' chez Pierre Puvis de Chavannes," *GBA* 6th pér. 89 (1977) : 31–32, 35 (illus.) ; Robert L. Delevoy, *Symbolists and symbolism.* New York, Skira/Rizzoli, 1978. pp. 36 (illus.) , 38.

161. Ludus Pro Patria

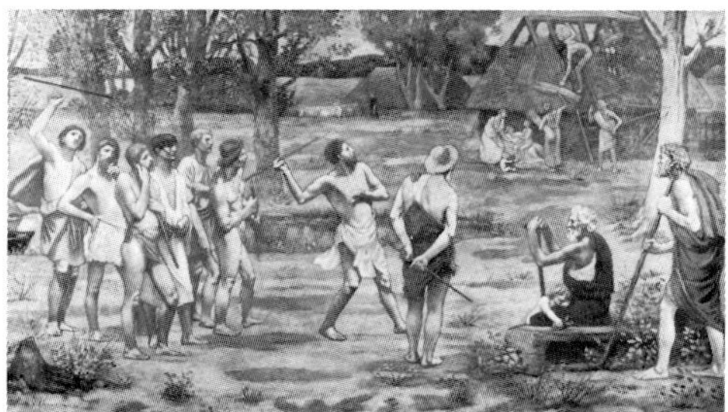

37.16 1883

In the "Art monumental et décoratif" section of the 1880 Salon, Puvis exhibited a carton (no. 7281), *Jeunes picards s'exercant à la lance* (3.57 x 15.82), for this mural destined for the north wall of the staircase of the Musée de Picardie, Amiens. The completed mural, *Pro Patria Ludus (Game for the Fatherland),* was shown in the 1882 Salon (no. 2223), again in 1887 at the Palace of Industry, and was finally installed in Amiens in 1888 following structural adaptations of the building.

The mural (4.5 x 17.5) treating the themes of Work, Family, and Fatherland, and bearing connotations of "Revanche" following the 1870–71 debacle, is rendered in terms of a "Golden Age" of ancient Picardy. Stretching across the shallow plain in the foreground are three clusters of inhabitants, varying in age from infancy to dotage, engaged in various tasks or in a state of repose. In the center, a group of young Gauls practice throwing the javelin or *pique,* an etymological reference to the province, Picardy, and its habitants who were noted for their use of this weapon.

In addition to the cartoon, now in Brussels, and the actual mural at Amiens, the artist produced several closely related paintings, including the small replica *Ludus Pro Patria* (.334 x 1.346) in the Metropolitan Museum of Art, New York, (58.15.1), and two enlarged details, the 1883 *Ludus Pro Patria* in Baltimore showing the central section of the original composition with some variations, and the *Fragment of a Replica of "Pro Patria Ludus"* (.94 x 1.25) in The Toledo Museum of Art (51.313), a portion of the right end of the composition. Other related works are a sketch for the project in pencil, chalk and oil on canvas (.62 x 2.51) of about 1879 in the Cabinet des Dessins, Musée du Louvre (R. F. 1742), another project sketch in sepia (.26 x 1.27) that was sold at the Hôtel Drouot, Paris, April 11, 1921, no. 83, as well as numerous drawings in Amiens, Paris, Marseilles, Algiers, and Princeton.

The Walters version with its Arcadian vista varying only slightly from that in the mural, is rendered in the same modulated colors. It exemplifies Puvis' practice, late in his career, of adapting his mural compositions as easel paintings. As a result of the reduced format, he has compressed the composition, eliminating some of the figures. A javelin-thrower with his back to the viewer, left of center in the mural and in the New York replica, and a cluster of individuals separating the elderly seated man and the figure leaning on his staff on the extreme right in the mural and other replicas do not appear in the Walters painting. Significantly, Puvis has extended the background, incorporating roof-thatching and cowherd scenes only partially portrayed in the other variants. Thus, he retains the mural's three themes of Work, Family and Fatherland.

Support: Canvas, 1.135 x 1.97 (44⅞" x 78")

Signed and dated lower left: *P. Puvis de Chavannes 83.*

References: Léon Riotor, *L'art et l'idée; essai sur Puvis de Chavannes.* Paris, Bureaux de *L'Artiste,* 1896. p. 37 (first published as a three-part article in *L'Artiste* 11 (March–May 1896) ; Walters cat., 1909, p. 6, no. 16; William Seitz, "Some studies by Puvis de Chavannes," *Record of the Art Museum, Princeton University* 10, no. 2 (1951): 19 (illus.), 21–22; Phoebe Pool, "The history pictures of Edgar Degas and their background," *Apollo* 80 (1964): 306 (illus.);Aimée Brown Price, *Puvis de Chavannes: a study of the easel paintings and a catalogue of the painted works* (unpublished Ph.D. dissertation, Yale University, 1972), cat. no. 237; Louise d'Argencourt, *Les peintures murales de Puvis de Chavannes au Musée de Picardie* (unpublished doctoral dissertation, University of Paris, 1973) ; Louise d'Argencourt, et al. *Puvis de Chavannes, 1824–1898* (exhibition catalogue, Paris and Ottawa, 1976–77) , pp. 167–68.

Théobold Chartran

French: Besançon, 1849 - Neuilly-sur-Seine, 1907

Chartran, a portraitist who specialized in celebrities and historical subjects, enjoyed a remarkable following in both France and America at the turn of the century. He entered the Ecole des Beaux-Arts as a pupil of Cabanel in 1867 and began to exhibit at the Paris salons in 1872. Five years later he won the Grand Prix de Rome, showing *The Taking of Rome by the Gauls.* At the beginning of the eighties Chartran began to exhibit abroad, showing portrait miniatures at the Royal Academy, London, in 1881 and 1883. Apart from painting such portraits as *Mounet-Sully as Hamlet,* 1887: *Calvé as Carmen, Leo XIII,* c. 1889, and *Sarah Bernhardt as Gismonda,* 1896, he executed a number of murals, including the decoration of the upper vestibule of the Sorbonne, rebuilt in 1884–89, with a series of scenes pertaining to the history of science in France, as well as similar work for the Salon des Arts of the Paris Hôtel de Ville, and for the marriage chambers of the mairie of Montrouge.

In 1893 Chartran received commissions from Perry Belmont for portraits of several family members, which resulted in his coming to America. His success on this occasion led to return visits which occurred annually, beginning in 1899. Among his American patrons was Henry Clay Frick, who commissioned a portrait of his friend Judge Thomas Mellon for the Pittsburgh Bar Association and a large *Signing of the Peace Protocol,* commemorating the end of the Spanish-American War, which was presented to the White House in 1900. Perhaps his most celebrated American works were portraits of Mrs. Theodore Roosevelt and her daughter Miss Alice Roosevelt painted in 1902. These were first exhibited in the residence of Ambassador Cambon and later presented by the French Government to the White House and President Roosevelt, respectively. In 1904 he came to Baltimore to work on a portrait of Cardinal Gibbons and allegedly nearly lost his life on this occasion while endeavoring to record from a tall building the fire that destroyed much of the downtown section of the city. Apart from his skill in presenting flattering images, executed with considerable bravura in a style in keeping with the eclectic interiors of the period, Chartran was admired for his "tact and bright sociability" that made him a "favorite among foreigners to visit New York."

162. Portrait of Jennie Walters (1853–1922)

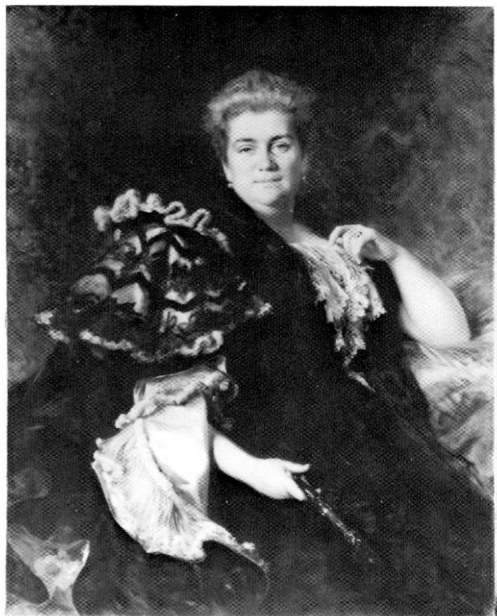

37.2490 c. 1900

Jennie Walters was the daughter of William Thompson Walters (1819–1894) and Ellen Harper Walters (1822–1862). She was raised by her father and in the course of her education attended school in Paris; St. Mary's Convent, Georgetown, and Harvard University. While in Cambridge she married Warren Delano. They lived in Orange, New Jersey, and later in New York. Mrs. Delano survived her husband by two years.

The subject was short in stature and full in figure. She is shown voluminously clad, seated in three-quarters length wearing a double layered dress, the outer being black tulle and lace and the inner white satin. Her sleeves are wide and ruffled and she wears a white lace "Bertha."

Support: Canvas, 1.36 x 1.08 (53⁹⁄₁₆" x 42⁹⁄₁₆")

Provenance: Gift of Mrs. Frederick B. Adams (daughter of the sitter), February 1973.

Belgian and Dutch Paintings

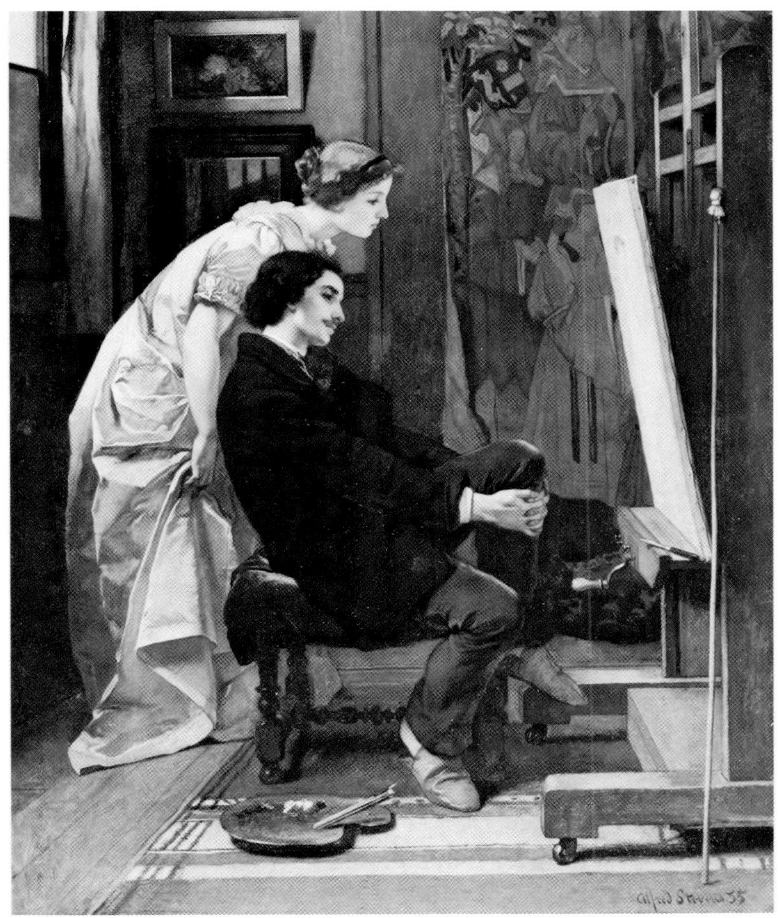

Stevens *The Painter and his Model,* no. 172

Ferdinand de Braekeleer

Belgian: Antwerp, 1792 - Antwerp, 1883

Ferdinand de Braekeleer enrolled in the Antwerp Academy in 1813 and trained under Mathieu van Brée. Winning Belgium's first *prix de Rome* in 1819, he accompanied his teacher to Italy, where he remained four years. Upon his return to Antwerp, De Braekeleer married Marie Thérèse Leys, sister of the artist H. J. A. Leys. He subsequently played an active role in his native city, serving as member of the town council from 1836–42 and holding the post of associate director of the museum. De Braekeleer instructed numerous pupils, including Henri Leys, Eugène de Block, Jacob Jacobs, A. P. P. Hunin, L. J. Somers, as well as his sons Ferdinand and Henri, and his nephew, Adrien.

The senior de Braekeleer began his career painting large pictures in a neoclassical vein. After his return from Rome, he chose subjects from the history of his homeland, such as *The Resistance of the Town of Tournai* (1833) and *The Spanish Fury in Antwerp* (1835), which were widely acclaimed at the salons. In the mid-thirties, he turned increasingly to small domestic genre pictures, carefully executed, that recalled the works of Adriaan van Ostade and David Teniers.

163. The Quarrel

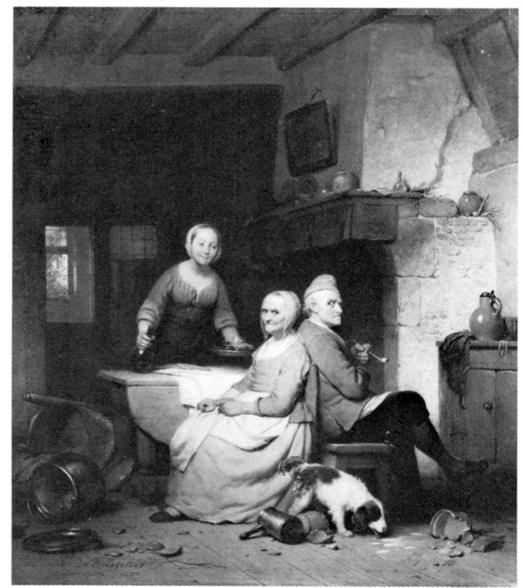

37.2372 1850

In a Flemish village interior an elderly couple are seated back-to-back, scowling. A pert maidservant, obviously amused by their recent spat, is about to pour them some wine. An overturned chair and broken pots and pans are evidence of the feud that has transpired. In the foreground, the couple's dog laps milk spilled on the floor.

This picture is characteristic of the stage-like interior scenes painted by de Braekeleer in the 1840s and 1850s. The elderly protagonists are identical to the figures that appear in many of his works such as *The Count of Mid-Lent in the Children's School* (1839) Musées royaux des beaux-arts de Belgique, Brussels, inv. 1186, *The Golden Wedding* (1839) Brussels, inv. 1186 and *The See-Saw*, 1852, (illustrated in *Art News*, Feb. 15–28, 1945, p. 37).

Support: Mahogany panel, beveled edges, .358 x .3 (14¼″ x 11$\frac{13}{16}$″)

Signed at lower left: *Ferdinand De Braekeleer ft/Antwerpen 1850*

Marks: Inscribed in pencil on reverse: *Colgate*

Provenance: Gift of Mrs. Margaret McCauley Turk, 1959.

164. Reconciliation

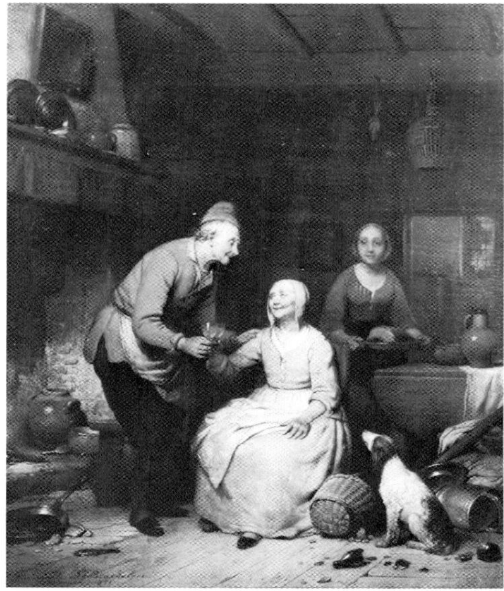

37.2373 1851

In this picture, which is apparently a pendant to *The Quarrel* despite the difference in dates, amends have been made and the man is about to drink a toast with his wife, who gazes benignly at him. The reconciliation is observed by the servant girl and the dog. The setting appears to be the same room as in *The Quarrel* although it is seen here from the opposite direction.

Support: Mahogany panel, beveled edges. .358 x .3 (14¼″ x 11$\frac{13}{16}$″)

Signed and dated at lower left: *Ferdinand De Braekeleer/Antwerp 1851*

Marks: Inscribed in pencil on reverse: *Colgate*

Provenance: Gift of Mrs. Margaret McCauley Turk, 1959.

Louis Gallait

Belgian: Tournai, 1810 - Schaarbeek, 1887

Gallait trained first under the classicist, P. A. Hennequin, at the academy in his native Tournai and later at the Antwerp Academy with Mathieu van Brée, a history painter who encouraged him to study seventeenth-century Flemish painting. A stipend from the State enabled Gallait to move to Paris in 1834 to work with Ary Scheffer and to study at The Louvre. There he befriended Paul Delaroche. Beginning in 1835, he exhibited historical and religious subjects at the Paris salons, and eventually received commissions for such works at Versailles. In 1841, his *Abdication of Charles V* received wide acclaim and brought him France's Legion of Honor and Belgium's Order of Léopold. He returned to Belgium in 1843 to serve as director of the Tournai Academy and in 1871 became President of the Royal Academy of Belgium. In 1870 he was elected a foreign associate of France's Académie des beaux-arts, replacing J. F. Overbeck.

Gallait was a highly eclectic artist who exerted considerable influence in the middle of the century in both Belgium and Germany. He is remembered for his large works depicting historical events drawn from Flanders' past as well as for his portraits of notable subjects, including Pius IX (1861), Leopold and Marie Henriette (1875), and fifteen historical personages for the Senate Chamber in Brussels. He also produced a number of genre scenes that were marked by sentimentality, and, occasionally, directness of approach bordering on brutality. Such works were widely admired and collected abroad.

165. Art and Liberty

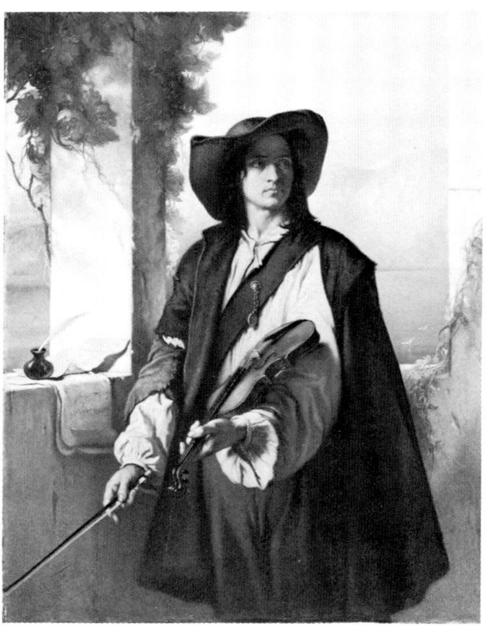

37.78 1859

A young political prisoner has sought solace in his violin. On the pier entwined with grape vines separating the windows of his prison are scratched the words *LIBERTA* and *AMALIA*. A plume with ink and several pages of music are visible on the window sill. Beyond are a lake and range of mountains.

This work is a reduced version of a painting dated 1849 in the Musées royaux des beaux-arts de Belgique, Brussels (inv. 2567, oil on canvas, 1.5 x 1.1). In the Brussels picture, however, the prisoner is posed against a cell wall and the window frame is inscribed *MARIA*.

This subject, presumably alluding to the North Italian-Austrian political struggles in Lombardy of 1848, was evidently one of the artist's most popular, since three other versions are listed by H. Mireur: San Donato Sale, Paris, 1870 no. 42 (perhaps the Brussels picture despite slight discrepancies in size and dating), Michel Yakountschikoff sale, 1870, .48 x .35, and Bolkow Sale, London, 1888.

Support: Mahogany panel with beveled edges, .86 x .65 (33⅞" x 25½")

Signed and dated lower left: *Louis Gallait / 1859*

Provenance: H. D. Hooft van Woudenberg van Geerestein Sale, 1880, 16,800 francs.

References: John R. Tait, "Art in Baltimore," *Lippincott's Magazine of Popular Literature and Science* 32 (November 1883): 533; Walters cat., 1884, and subsequent Walters catalogues; H. Mireur, *Dictionnaire des ventes d'art*. 7 vols. Paris, Ch. de Vincenti, 1911–12. 3: 247.

166. Power of Music

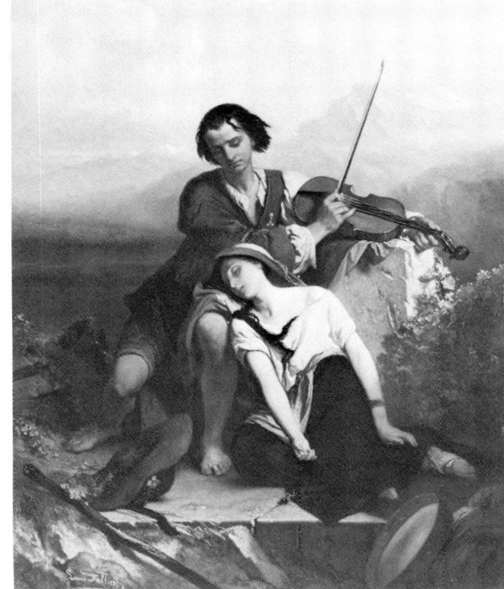

37.134

Transcribed in early Walters catalogues is a letter from the artist to the Baltimore collector dated July 20, 1860, explaining that this painting represents two destitute young musicians, a brother and a sister, who have stopped on the wayside to rest beside an old tomb. The brother is endeavoring to assuage the sorrow of his sister with violin music; she has dropped her tambourine and fallen into a state of sleep that brings with it "oblivion of all grief, mental and physical." A reduced version, *L'oubli des douleurs*, panel, .28 x .21, was presented to the Musées royaux des beaux-arts de Belgique, Brussels, by a descendant of the artist (inv. 4219). A variation on the theme of the same title, showing a young musician playing his violin for a mother and her two children, was among the works from the John W. Wilson collection exhibited at the Galerie du cercle artistique et littéraire de Bruxelles in 1873. A porcelain plaque manufactured by the Royal Porcelain Factory, Berlin, 1870–80, with this composition painted by E. Schade, was sold at Christies, New York, November 29, 1979, no. 56.

Alternative title: *Oblivion of Sorrows*

Support: Mahogany panel with beveled edges. .572 x .433 (22½" x 17$\frac{1}{16}$")

Signed at lower left: *Louis Gallait*

Provenance: Acquired by W. T. Walters before 1878.

References: James Dafforne, "Modern painters in Belgium," *The Art Journal* (London) 18 (1866): 103 as *Forgotten Sorrow;* Walters cat., 1878, p. 15 (Illus.), and subsequent Walters catalogues; Strahan, 1: 86 (illus.), 88, 94; Champlin and Perkins, 2: 107; Lamb, p. 250; Reizenstein, p. 250.

167. War

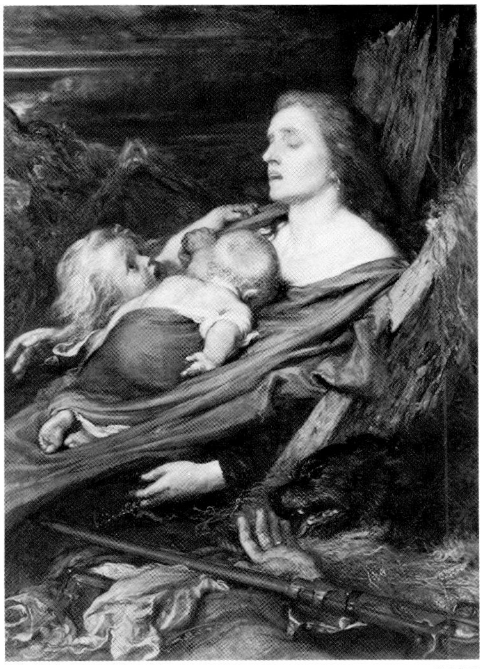

37.124 1872

In contrast to the bucolic *Peace, War* is a horrendous scene. Judging from their pallor, both the mother and suckling infant have perished. Visible in the immediate foreground is the outstretched arm of the husband whose hand has released its grip on the rifle. The dog lies dead beside its mistress. Only the daughter remains alive, wailing and grasping her mother's garments in terror. Seen against the darkened sky are burning haystacks. The artist probably intended *War* and *Peace* to be comments on the horrors of the recent Franco-Prussian War.

A preliminary sketch for *War* is also located in the Musées royaux des beaux-arts de Belgique, Brussels, (inv. 4216, oil on panel, .27 x .19).

Support: Canvas, 1.2 x .83 (47¼" x 32⅝")
Signed and dated on lower middle: *Louis Gallait RA / 1872*

Provenance: Acquired between 1878 and 1884.

Exhibitions: The Royal Academy, London, 1872, no. 1006; Vienna, International Exhibition, 1873.

References: René Ménard, "Exposition de Vienne," *GBA* 2nd pér. 7 (1873): 197; John R. Tait, "Art in Baltimore," *Lippincott's Magazine of Popular Literature and Science* 32 (November 1883): 533; Walters cat., 1884, and subsequent Walters catalogues; Champlin and Perkins, 2: 107; Algernon Graves, *The Royal Academy of Arts*. 8 vols. London, Henry Graves, 1905–06. 3: 195.

168. Peace

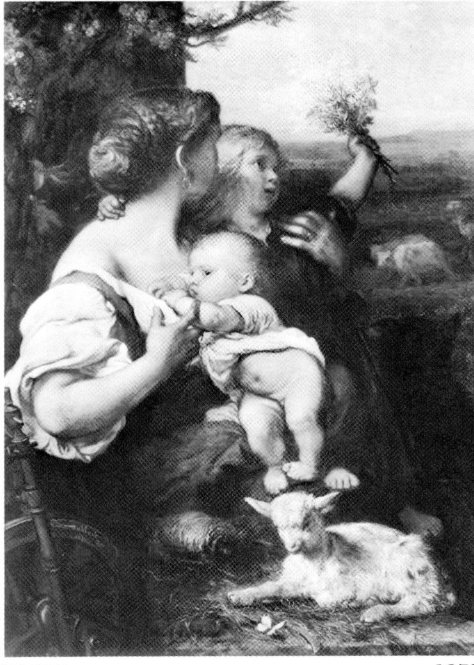

37.119 1872

Peace is personified by a mother nursing her infant son and embracing a young daughter who waves a bouquet of lilacs. At her side is a dog and in the foreground a spinning wheel, a bobbin of yarn, and a seated lamb. The father ploughs his field in the background.

A sketch for this painting is preserved in the Musées royaux des beaux-arts de Belgique, Brussels (inv. 4217, oil on panel, .27 x .19).

Support: Canvas, 1.18 x .823 (46½" x 32⅜")

Signed and dated on spinning wheel, lower left: *Louis Gallait RA / 1872* (Gallait was first listed as an honorary foreign member of the Royal Academy in 1870)

Provenance: Acquired between 1878 and 1884.

Exhibitions: The Royal Academy, London, 1872, no. 1005; Vienna, International Exhibition, 1873.

References: René Ménard, "Exposition de Vienne," *GBA* 2nd pér. 7 (1873): 197; John R. Tait, "Art in Baltimore," *Lippincott's Magazine of Popular Literature and Science* 32 (November 1883): 533; Walters cat., 1884, and subsequent Walters catalogues; Champlin and Perkins, 2: 107; Algernon Graves, *The Royal Academy of Arts*. 8 vols. London, Henry Graves, 1905–06. 3: 195.

Baron Hendrik Jan August Leys
Belgian: Antwerp, 1815 - Antwerp, 1869

Leys established a reputation as Antwerp's, if not Belgium's, principal artist in the mid-nineteenth century with his large historical paintings shown in exhibitions at Antwerp, Brussels, and Paris. Like a number of compatriots, he specialized in depicting episodes from the sixteenth century religious struggles of his native city.

The son of a vendor of religious prints, Leys studied with a furniture painter, briefly enrolled in the Antwerp Academy in 1829, and in 1830 entered the studio of his brother-in-law Ferdinand de Braekeleer, a genre and history painter.

As early as 1833, he began to exhibit his historical subjects and after the favorable reception of *The Massacre of the Magistrates of Louvain* at the Brussels Triennial Exhibition of 1836, he moved to Paris, studying briefly with Delacroix. His early paintings have been described as being in a romantic vein and resembling the battle pictures of his fellow Antwerp artist Gustaaf Wappers. However, Paul Mantz in "M. Henri Leys," *Gazette des Beaux-Arts* 20 (1866): 299, mentions early works apparently inspired by the domestic interiors of Gerard Dou and Gabriel Metsu. Leys' reputation in Belgium was assured by 1845, when he exhibited the *Revival of the Creed in Antwerp's Notre Dame Church* in Brussels; the following year he began to receive foreign recognition, winning a second-class medal at the Paris Salon with *A Peasants' Fete in the 17th century*.

About 1851, Leys' art began to undergo a transformation in which influences of sixteenth-century Flemish and German painting became dominant, a development reinforced by the artist's visit to Germany in 1852. His new, deliberately archaizing style was evident in his entries at the Brussels 1854 exposition; *Frans Floris Going to a Festival, New Year in Flanders, Promenade outside the Walls,* and *The Catholics.* The New Year's picture was acquired by Achille Fould and shown with two other works by Leys at the 1855 Exposition Universelle. He received a Grand Medal of Honor and was subsequently appointed Commander of the Order of Léopold. On this occasion, the critic Maxime Du Camp in "Exposition Universelle, Beaux-Arts," *Revue de Paris* 26, pt. 3 (1855): 426, acclaimed Leys as one of the greatest painters of all time and associated him with Holbein and Massys. The following year he visited Italy and Spain with another admirer, Théophile Gautier.

Leys continued to receive wide acclaim at the 1862 International Exhibition in London and at the 1867 Exposition Universelle in Paris. During his later years he was engrossed in a series of six murals for the Hôtel de Ville illustrating the history of Antwerp in the sixteenth century.

Apart from exhibiting regularly in Antwerp and Brussels, and in the Paris Salons, he sent paintings to the Royal Academy, London, in 1845 and 1868, and had works shown also in the fashionable French Gallery, Pall Mall, between 1863 and 1866. Principal pupils included Sir Lawrence Alma-Tadema and Joseph Lies.

169. Dutch Interior

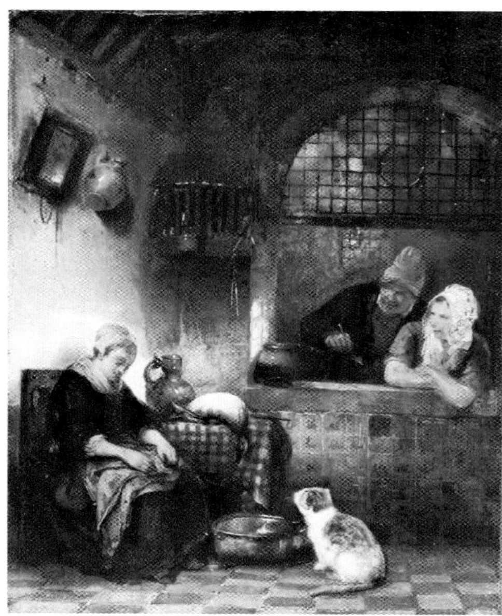

37.144 c. 1840

A servant girl has been found asleep by an older couple. Beside her, on a table covered with a checked cloth, is an unplucked dead goose and a large stoneware pitcher; at her feet waits a hungry cat beside a large copper basin. The artist has enriched the kitchen setting with such details as the broken mirror and the ceramic vase suspended from wall pegs, a large wooden-slatted bird-cage, and a wainscot of Delft tiles.

This painting illustrates the domestic genre practiced by Leys' master F. de Braekeleer and by Leys himself, early in his career. Paul Mantz cited a Flemish kitchen scene by Leys, dated 1841, "M. Henri Leys," *Gazette des Beaux-Arts* 20 (1866):249. Another *Intérieur flamand,* dated 1836, was sold at the John Wilson Sale, Paris, March 14–16, 1881, no. 168.

Alternative title: *Intérieur flamand*

Support: Mahogany panel, beveled edges. .375 x .29 (14¾" x 11⅜")

Signed lower left: *H* (conjoined) *Leys*

Marks: Paper sticker: *566;* inscribed in pencil: *560* and *5155;* black stencil: *429 V;* scratched: *332*

Condition: The picture has extensive traction crackle pattern in the upper right section of the painting. An old gouge in the panel's surface in the upper center has become visible.

Provenance: Acquired between 1878 and 1884.

References: Walters cat., 1888, p. 93, no. 152; William R. Johnston, "Salute to Belgium," *BWAG,* 32, no. 8 (May 1980) 1–2, fig. 2.

170. Edict (s) of Charles V

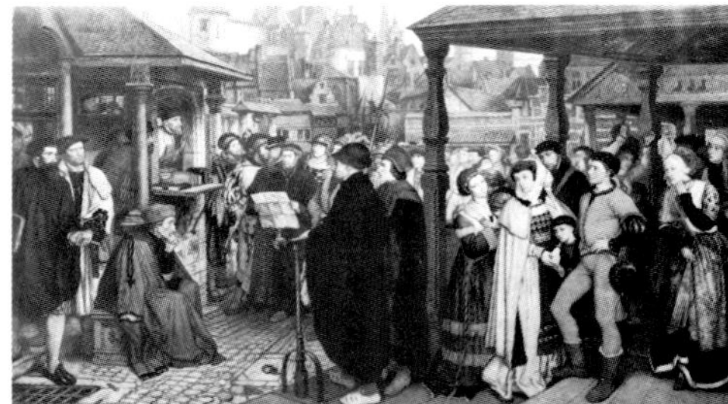

37.123 c. 1861

Between 1520 and 1550 Charles V issued eleven edicts that proscribed Protestantism in the Netherlands and resulted in fifty thousand deaths. Leys, as was his practice, depicted an indeterminate rather than specific historical episode. The setting is a square in a large town, presumably the artist's native Antwerp which, as a major humanistic and financial center, had attracted many foreigners, especially Protestants. A tall tower, visible in the center background, could be the famous spire of 1422–1518 of the Cathedral of Antwerp. In the left foreground is a book seller's shop and on the right, a couple of wooden covered porches. Painted on one of the gables is an unidentified coat-of-arms in gules and argent checky along with an incomplete inscription: *Hee . . . god/end . . . wynn laet de heeren de heeren syn.* The Emperor's herald is reading the decree to the populace, which reacts with varying degrees of consternation and grief. In the center, two gentlemen stand impassively, holding a Flemish leaning rail.

This picture exemplifies Leys' "archaic" style. The figures in their costume, stances, and physiognomies recall those found in sixteenth-century paintings, especially the works of the Flemish mannerists and of the German masters, Albrecht Dürer, Hans Holbein the Younger, and the Cranachs. Deliberate archaisms include the meticulous attention to detail, the subdued, uniform lighting and the avoidance of linear perspective.

Ironically, Paul Mantz in "M. Henri Leys," *Gazette des-Beaux-Arts* 20, (1866):310–11, interpreted these archaisms as faults and declined to illustrate this picture in his article.

In the Musées royaux des beaux-arts de Belgique is an unfinished study of the figures standing on the porch on the right side of the picture (inv. 3571, oil on panel, 1.04 x .76, bequest of P. J. Godefroy, 1901).

Leys initially treated the theme of the book-seller at the time of the Netherlandish religious wars in *Jacob van Liesvelt, Imprimeur à Anvers au 16 me Siècle,* a view of a book stall dated 1853, (Charles T. Yerkes Collection Sale, American Art Galleries, New York, April 5, 1910, no. 60).

Alternative titles: *Publication de l'édit de Charles Quint établissant l'inquisition dans les*

Pays-Bas; La proclamation des édits de Charles Quint à Anvers

Support: Panel, cradled before 1883, 1.38 x 2.45 (4' 6" x 8' ½")

Marks: Paper sticker on reverse: *Exhibition Historique de l'Art Belge./Nom de possesseur du tableau: Cte. W. de Bourgade/ Subjet de l'oeuvre: Publication des edits de Charles Quint/ Valeur/ Nom . . . de l'auteur: Bon Leys*

Provenance: Comte de Liedekerke-Beaufort of Dinant to Deschamps for 100,000 francs, October 24, 1883; Deschamps to Walters, for 110,000 francs, October 1883.

Exhibitions: Antwerp Exposition, 1861 (Paul Mantz, "L'exposition et les fêtes d'Anvers," *GBA* 11 (1861): 280–81); International Exhibition, London, 1862 (*Art Journal* (London) new series 1 (1862) : 167) ; Exposition Universelle, Paris, 1867.

References: Paul Mantz, "M. Henri Leys," *GBA* 20 (1866) : 310–11; James Dafforne, "Modern painters of Belgium, Baron Leys," *The Art Journal* (London) 21 (1869) ; Walters cat., 1884, p. 35, no. 48, and subsequent Walters catalogues; Champlin and Perkins, 3: 76; Cook, 3: 308; Mathews, p. 8; A. J. J. Delen, "Hendrik Leys," in U. Thieme and Felix Becker *Allgemeines Lexikon der bildenden Künstler*. 37 vols. Leipzig, E. A. Seemann, 1907–50. 23: 175; Eugène de Seyn, *Dictionnaire biographique des sciences, des lettres et des arts en Belgique*. 2 vols. Brussels, Editions l'Avenir, 1935–36. 2: 682; Gustave Vanzype, *Leys et son école*. Brussels, Renaissance du livre, 1949, p. 58; William R. Johnston, "Salute to Belgium," *BWAG* 32, no. 8 (May 1980) : 1–2, fig. 1.

PAUL-JEAN CLAYS
Belgian: Bruges, 1819 - Brussels, 1900

Paul Clays was regarded by contemporaries as Belgium's pre-eminent marine painter. He was raised in Westcapelle on the North Sea and was apparently attracted to the ocean from early youth. Escaping from school in Boulogne, he ran away to become a sailor, and eventually, with parental consent, served as a cabin boy aboard a channel boat.

Showing an inclination toward painting, Clays was sent to Paris where he enrolled in the studio of Horace Vernet and subsequently studied with the marine and history painter, Baron J.-A.-T. Gudin. He returned to Belgium, to Bruges; failed to earn a livelihood as an artist and returned to the sea as a sailor on a government schooner.

In the early fifties, Clays' fortunes improved. After marrying the daughter of the director of the Brussels Observatory, he removed to Antwerp, and began to make his reputation as a realist painter. In 1856 he established himself permanently in Brussels. His showing at the Exposition Universelle of 1867 greatly enhanced his international reputation. The following year he became a member of the Société libre des Beaux-Arts, which advocated a free and individual interpretation of Nature.

Described as "the painter of the Scheldt River," Clays did not seek recourse in the storms and tempests of the open seas, but chose his subjects along the coastal ways of Belgium and Holland. His forte was his skillful interpretation of the light and moisture-laden atmosphere of these regions.

171. Moonlight in Holland

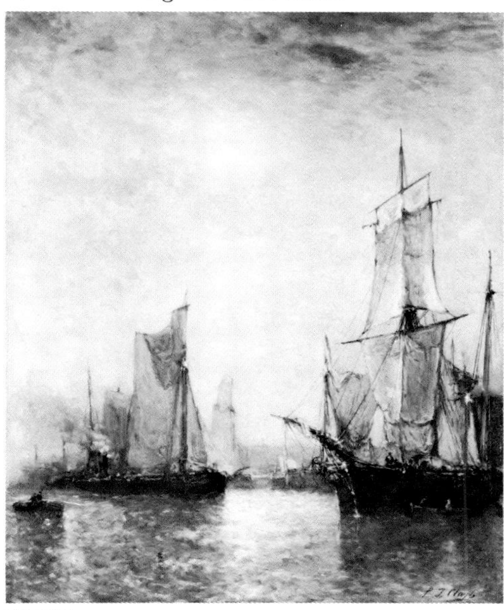

37.125

In this nocturnal view of an unidentified Dutch harbor ships with slackened sails rest at their moorings while sailors row their skiffs ashore.

Support: Mahogany panel, beveled edges, .734 x .59 (28⅞" x 23¼")

Signed lower right: *P.J. Clays*

Marks: Reverse: In ink on paper sticker: *176/ Clays;* printed on paper sticker: *319;* scratched in wood: *2;* in white chalk: *I*

Condition: Traction crackle in sky on left side at lower left and on the right near the tall foremast of the ship.

Provenance: This picture may be the "Clays Moonlight" that Lucas sent to S. P. Avery on March 20/21, 1880. Marked in a copy of the 1884 Walters catalogue in Henry Walters' handwriting is "Avery 1882."

References: Walters cat., 1884, p. 20, no. 23, and subsequent Walters catalogues.

ALFRED-EMILE-LÉOPOLD-VICTOR-GHISLAIN STEVENS
Belgian: Brussels, 1823 - Paris, 1906

Alfred Stevens came from a family prominent in Brussels art circles: his father, J.-F.-L. Stevens, a collector, owned several paintings by Delacroix, his elder brother, Joseph, was a successful painter of animals, and a younger brother, Arthur, became an influential critic for *Le Figaro* as well as artistic advisor to King Léopold. Stevens studied drawing in Brussels with F. J. Navez from 1840–1844 and then trained in Paris in the studio of Camille Roqueplan. He is also thought to have entered classes directed by Ingres at the Ecole des Beaux-Arts and to have worked in the studio of his compatriot, Florent Willems. He returned to Brussels in 1849, and submitted four historical subjects to the Brussels Salon of 1851.

By 1852, Stevens was back in Paris. The following year he made his debut at the Salon with three realist paintings, one of which was bought by the French State. He soon found his forte, the painting of beautiful, elegantly attired women, in fashionable interiors, engaged in reading, performing their toilette or other activities. Frequently his pictures contained artifacts from the Far East, an area of collecting in which he pioneered.

Having a convivial nature, Alfred Stevens was quickly accepted into avant-garde circles in Paris, meeting Rousseau, Couture and Isabey at the Restaurant du Havre in the fifties, and Manet, Degas, Berthe Morisot, and Baudelaire at Mme. Auguste Manet's weekly gatherings in the early sixties. The apogee of his career was undoubtedly the Exposition Universelle of 1867. On that occasion, he exhibited eighteen paintings, won a first-class medal, and was promoted to Officier of the Legion of Honor. Stevens continued to prosper in the 1870s, acquiring a large house at 65 rue des Martyrs in 1875, where he housed his growing collection of oriental bibelots and eighteenth-century furniture. In 1880 a bronchial infection aggravated by the inhalation of turpentine fumes necessitated a respite at the Normandy coast. At Sainte-Adresse, he began to paint plein-air marines and landscapes that were eagerly sought by the clients of his dealer, Georges Petit. He also accepted a number of students, many of them women, the most famous of whom was Sarah Bernhardt. Together with Henri Gervex and assistants, he executed the vast *Panorama du Siècle* (120 meters wide), which was shown in the Tuileries Gardens during the 1889 Exposition Universelle.

With the 1890 schism in the Paris Salon, Stevens allied himself with the Champ de Mars group, exhibiting thereafter at the salons of the Société Nationale des Beaux-Arts. He was given retrospective exhibitions at the Ecole des Beaux-Arts, in 1900, and posthumously, in Brussels and Antwerp in 1907.

At the height of his career, Alfred Stevens was admired as an important recorder of the bourgeois and aristocratic levels of *la vie moderne*. Late in the century, when his artistic prowess waned, he continued to be widely admired. His subtle color harmonies, and carefully contrived compositions were appreciated by the fin-du-siècle aesthetes.

172. The Painter and his Model

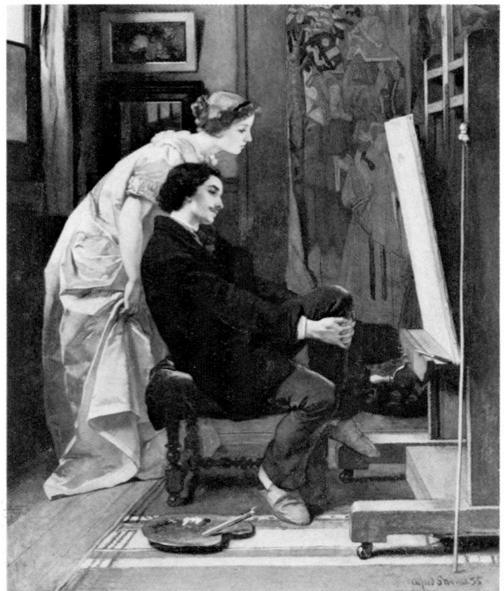

37.322 1855

A pretty model leans over the shoulder of the young artist, presumably Stevens, who is seated and regards his unfinished picture on an easel. Visible in the interior, lighted by a window at the extreme left, are a couple of framed pictures and a section of a Flemish tapestry showing an Adoration scene. This picture is the first of a number of studio scenes, the most famous of which is *L'Atelier* of 1869 in the Musées royaux des beaux-arts, Brussels. The relative simplicity of this interior has led William Coles to compare the painting to the seventeenth-century Dutch precedents and to cite the possible influence of the more eclectic painter, Florent Willems.

Alternative title: *The Painter in His Studio*

Support: Preprimed, finely woven fabric, .924 x .773 (36⅜" x 29")

Signed lower right: *Alfred Stevens 55*

Marks: Stretcher stamped: *Exposition de l'oeuvre d'Alfred Stevens, 1900; Palais des Beaux-Arts* in circular cartouche; stretcher stenciled: *Paris 876;* canvas stenciled: *Atelier . . . N/De FORGE / M . . . COULEURS/ Boulevard d . . . Martin . . .*

Condition: An old lining was removed and the picture relined in 1968.

Provenance: Polovtsoff Sale, Paris, 1908.

Exhibitions: *Exposition de l'oeuvre d'Alfred Stevens,* Ecole des Beaux-Arts, Paris, 1900. Possibly no. 16, *L'Atelier* owned by Abraham Andrews, Esq., London or no. 205 *Dans L'Atelier* owned by Thiébault-Sisson, Paris; "Alfred Stevens," exhibition catalogue by William Coles, The University of Michigan Museum of Art, Walters Art Gallery, and the Montreal Museum of Fine Arts, 1977–78, no. 3.

References: Peter Mitchell, *Alfred Emile Léopold Stevens.* London, John Mitchell and Sons, 1973, pp. 9 (illus. II), 10.

173. Palm Sunday

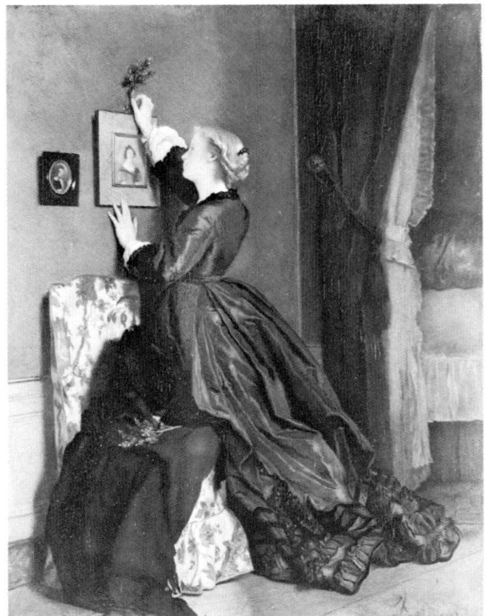

37.141 c. 1862

An elegantly dressed young lady is placing a sprig of box behind the frame of her mother's portrait hanging on the bedroom wall. Another bough, lying on her cloak, is intended for the adjacent miniature, presumably a portrait of her father.

This picture is a variant of the more elaborate *Les amours éternelles,* formerly in the collection of Robert Hoe, Sr., of New York. In the Hoe painting, a dark rather than fair haired model, still wearing her cloak, throws a kiss in the direction of her mother's portrait while placing the greenery above it. The Hoe picture also differs in the addition of a Persian cat arching its back in the foreground.

Other replicas discussed by Coles include *Im Boudoir,* in the Munich Museum (1936) and a picture that once belonged to Gabriel Astruc (illustrated in Madeleine Ochsé, "Alfred Stevens, peintre épris de modernité," *La Galerie* no. 126, April 1973, p. 44).

Robert de Montesquiou, (in "Alfred Stevens," *Gazette des Beaux-Arts,* 3rd pér. 23, 1900, p. 117), cited as a sequel to this composition a sketch of the young model seated in the interior that belonged to a baron B. . .

Alternative titles: *Les Rameaux; Les Amours éternelles*

Support: Panel, .342 x .26 (13½" x 10¼")

Signed at lower right: *A Stevens* (the A S conjoined)

Provenance: Acquired before 1878.

Exhibitions: "Alfred Stevens," exhibition catalogue by William Coles, The University of Michigan Museum of Art, Walters Art Gallery, and the Montreal Museum of Fine Arts, 1977–78, no. 9.

References: Walters cat., 1878, p. 18, and subsequent Walters catalogues; Strahan, 1:94.

174. News from Afar

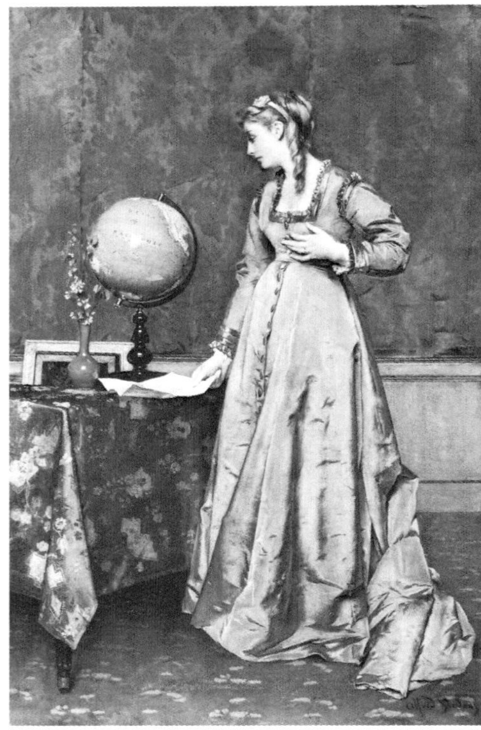

37.183 mid 1860s

A young lady in a mauve gown presses her left hand, on which she wears a wedding band, to her heart as she reads a letter. On a table, covered with a Chinese embroidered green silk cloth, rests a vase with a sprig of blossoms and a globe showing the South Seas. A flocked fabric covers the background wall and a gilt framed picture rests against the wainscot.

Coles regards this work, which he dates in the mid-sixties, as a forerunner of *Les Fleurs d'automne,* Musées royaux des beaux-arts, Brussels. The anecdotal convention is absent in the latter picture of about 1870, which shows the model holding a book in a state of contemplation.

Alternative title: *Sad News*

Support: Preprimed, finely woven fabric, .627 x .405 (24$\frac{11}{16}$" x 15$\frac{15}{16}$")

Signed lower right: *Alfred Stevens*: on the reverse of the canvas was painted in red letters the artist's monogram *A S* conjoined.

Condition: The canvas was lined with fiberglass in 1975.

Exhibitions: "Alfred Stevens," exhibition catalogue by William Coles, The University of Michigan Museum of Art, Walters Art Gallery, the Montreal Museum of Fine Arts, 1977–78, no. 11.

References: Walters cat., 1878, p. 38, and subsequent Walters catalogues; Strahan, 1: 94.

Florent Willems

Belgian: Liège, 1823 - Neuilly, 1905

Willems' training was confined to the study of drawing at the Malines Academy. He also benefited from his familiarity with earlier schools of Flemish painting acquired while working as a restorer for a Brussels picture dealer, M. Héris. His first patron, the British ambassador to Belgium, Sir Hamilton Seymour, gave him commissions about 1841 for portraits of his wife and children. The following year he exhibited two paintings in Brussels, one of which, *The Music Lesson,* was bought by the King. Thereafter, he exhibited from time to time in both Brussels and Paris. In 1844 he removed to the latter city. Willems was at the height of his career in 1855 when two of the three paintings he exhibited at the Paris Exposition, *The Interior of a Silk Mercer's Shop in 1660,* and *Coquetry* were purchased by Napoleon III and Eugénie respectively for the Palace of St. Cloud; the third, *The Hour of the Duel,* was acquired by Achille Fould. Among the honors he received were his appointments as Chevalier of the Order of Léopold in 1850, Commander of that order in 1860, Chevalier of France's Legion of Honor in 1853 and Commandeur in 1878.

Willems' talent fell within narrow bounds. He dealt almost solely with genre subjects set in sixteenth– and seventeenth–century Flanders or France. Portrayed were richly garbed cavaliers and ladies posed in stage-like settings. Willems' forte was the skillful rendering of the textures of various fabrics, brocades, satins, carpets and tapestries. His indebtedness to the Dutch seventeenth–century *petit maîtres* was readily apparent and earned him the sobriquet "the modern Terburg." Some of his paintings reflect the influence of his friend and compatriot Alfred Stevens who was also in Paris in 1844 and shared Willems' studio in 1849.

Charles Blanc (*Les artistes de mon temps,* Paris, 1876, pp. 493–94) while admiring Willems' technical skill, noted that his models served as mere pretexts for their costumes and he criticized the artificiality of his historical recreations.

175. The Health of the King

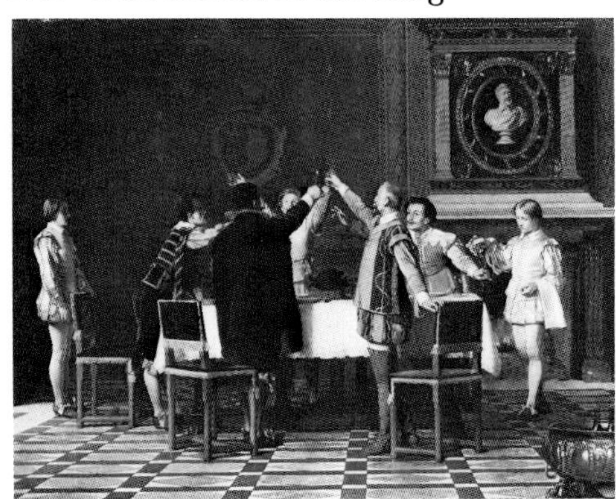

37.50 c. 1861

Five gentlemen, grouped around a table, toast the King. One page is replenishing a wineglass while another stands in attendance. Set in a Renaissance chimney piece in the right background is a marble bust of Henri IV of France. The wall at the left is covered with crimson fabric decorated with fleurs-de-lys and emblazoned with the arms of France and Navarre. Discernible on the lace-covered table is a Chinese pheasant that is being served in its skin. A large copper wine cooler dominates the right foreground.

Signatures: Obverse, lower right: *F. Willems;* Reverse, center: *F. Willems;* Paris stencil effaced, inscribed in pencil: *No. 12;* black crayon: *G 1677.*

Support: Mahogany panel, beveled edge, .318 x .41 (12½" x 16⅛")

Alternative title: *Au Roi*

Provenance: Duc de Morny Collection, sold Paris, May 31, 1865, no. 35, .32 x .43, 6,000 francs? (The description coincides with the Walters painting. However, a date of 1861 is given for the De Morny picture); Goupil et Cie; Knoedler and Co.

Exhibitions: "Free Exhibition of New Pictures," Knoedler and Co., New York, 1866.

References: "Art Matters," *New York Times,* January 22, 1866, p. 5; Walters cat., 1878, p. 23, and subsequent Walters catalogues; Strahan, 1: plate facing p. 86; pp. 92, 94; Clement and Hutton, 2: 352; Champlin and Perkins, 4: 434.

176. The Important Response

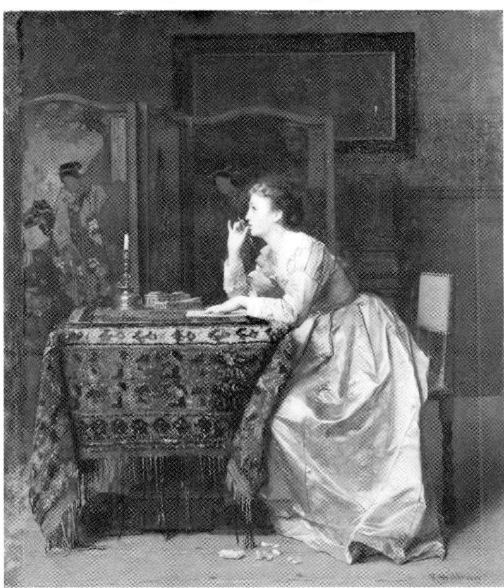

37.140

A lady in early seventeenth-century attire is seated at a table pondering a letter she is writing. In the background is a high Japanese screen. The artist has lavished great care in the rendering of the contrasting surfaces of his subject's satin dress and of the rug covering the table. In its intimacy and in its oriental note, this work approximates the painting of Alfred Stevens.

Support: Panel, cradled, .457 x .381 (18" x 15")

Signed lower right: *F. Willems*

Provenance: Acquired prior to 1878.

References: Walters cat., 1878, p. 24, and subsequent Walters catalogues; Strahan, 1: 92, 94; Champlin and Perkins, 4: 434.

Artist Unknown

177. Cattle by a Mountain Lake

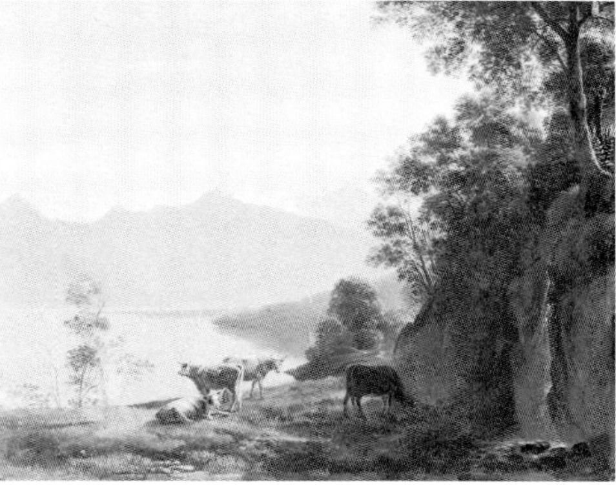

37.1785 1800–1830

Cattle graze on a slope overlooking a tranquil Alpine lake dotted with several sailing boats. The tranquility of the scene, the transparent atmosphere and the soft light suggest that the time of day is either dawn or dusk. When acquired, this painting was listed as the work of Adriaen van de Velde, (1636–1672). More likely it is by a northern European, perhaps Dutch artist, traveling in the Alps in the early nineteenth century.

Support: Cradled panel, .31 x .393 (12¼" x 15½")

Marks: Reverse: paper labels *740* and *127*

Provenance: Acquired by Henry Walters in 1902.

References: *Catalogue du Musée de peinture, sculpture et archéologie au palais Accoramboni,* 2 vols. Rome, Imprimerie du Vatican, 1897, 1: 128, no. 740 (Adrien Van der Velde, *Paysage*).

Artist Unknown

178. Mountain Landscape with Cattle

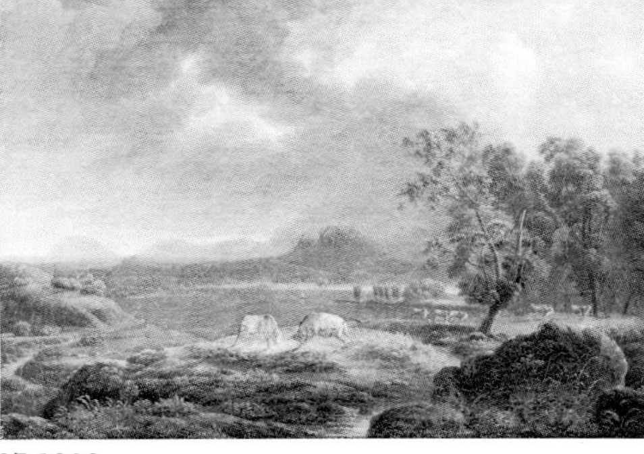

37.1806

The setting of this small painting is a brightly, though unevenly lighted landscape with a lake in the middle ground and high, rounded hills beyond. In the center foreground, two steers are locking horns in combat. Other cattle graze beneath trees at the right. The herbage in the foreground is rendered in meticulous detail.

When acquired, this picture was listed as the work of Karel Dujardin (1612–1678). It was subsequently attributed to Hendrik Voogd (1768–1839), a painter from Amsterdam who studied with Jurriaan Andriessen before establishing himself, in 1788, in Rome, where he received the epithet, the "Dutch Claude" for his Italianate landscapes portrayed at dawn or dusk. Evidence to confirm the attribution to Voogd remains insufficient, but the painting is probably the work of an early nineteenth-century Dutch artist.

Support: Canvas, .254 x .353 (10" x 13⅞")

Condition: Lined prior to 1902. Discolored varnishes removed in 1971, revealing minor losses along the edges. Some traction crackle throughout. Sprayed with synthetic resin.

Provenance: Acquired with the Massarenti Collection in 1902.

References: *Catalogue du musée de peinture, sculpture et archéologie au palais Accoramboni,* 2 vols. Rome, Imprimerie du Vatican, 1897, 1: 96, no. 536 (Jules de Jardin, *Scène de Campagne avec combat de taureaux*).

Joseph Israels

Dutch: Groningen, 1824 - Scheveningen, 1911

Among the members of The Hague School, Israels stands apart as a specialist in figurative and genre rather than landscape painting. He received lessons at the Minerva Academy in Groningen before moving, in 1842, to Amsterdam where he entered the studio of Jan Adam Kruseman and enrolled in the Royal Academy under Jan Willem Pieneman. Three years later, drawn by the success in France of his countryman, Ary Scheffer, Israels journeyed to Paris to study under Picot, to attend courses at the Ecole des Beaux-Arts, and to copy in the Louvre. Back in Amsterdam in 1847, he earned a livelihood as a portraitist. After distinguishing himself with his painting, *Ophelia,* in 1850, Israels returned to France and worked briefly at Barbizon. In 1855, at the fishing village of Zandvoort, he found his true forte, the recording of the lives of peasants. Israels married in 1863, and as a consequence family scenes became more common in his oeuvre. He settled in The Hague in 1871. Subsequently, he exhibited internationally, gaining a wide following of admirers. His paintings and watercolors of the tribulations in the lives of the peasants and fishermen as well as their simple, usually domestic pleasures, were avidly sought by Dutch and foreign collectors.

179. Old Man and Baby

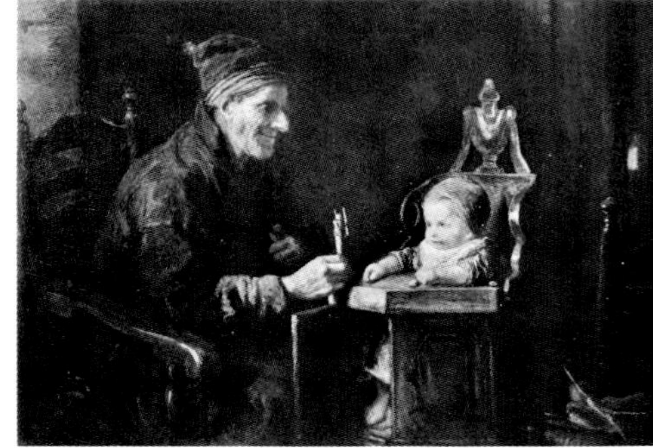

37.658 — 1880s–90s

In a dimly lighted interior a smiling elderly man, seated on a ladder-back chair, amuses an infant with a toy soldier. The child is seated in a *kakstoel,* or training chair. On a rush-covered seat at the right is a piece of knitting. This rustic interior is characteristic of the artist's depictions of peasant life in the eighties and nineties.

Support: Canvas, 1.1 x 1.48 (43¼" x 58¼")

Condition: This painting exhibits deterioration caused by the lavish use of bitumen, a defect encountered in many of Israels' full-scale works.

Provenance: Acquired by Henry Walters in 1926 according to early records of the Gallery.

Jacobus Hendricus Maris (Jacob Maris)

Dutch: The Hague, 1837 - Karlsbad, 1899

Jacob Maris was the eldest of three brothers associated with The Hague School of landscape painting in the second half of the nineteenth century. He was trained at The Hague Drawing Academy under J. A. B. Stroebel and Huib van Hove. From 1854 to 1856 Maris resided in Antwerp, sharing a studio with his brother, Matthys, and studying in the Academy. Royal grants in 1859–60 enabled both brothers to visit Oosterbeek and Wolheze in Brabant, and to go in 1861 to the Rhineland, Switzerland and France. In 1865, Jacob joined F. H. Kaemmerer and D. A. C. Artz in Paris and worked for several months with Ernest Hébert painting Italian peasant subjects. He also enrolled in the Ecole de Beaux-Arts and participated regularly in the Paris salons, showing mostly figure subjects that reflected the influence of Alfred Stevens. By 1870, under the possible influence of Corot and Veyrassat, Maris turned to landscape painting, his preferred genre in later years. His style gradually broadened and his use of colors simplified. River and coastal scenes with expansive skies and limpid atmospheres were his specialty.

180. Landscape with Canal

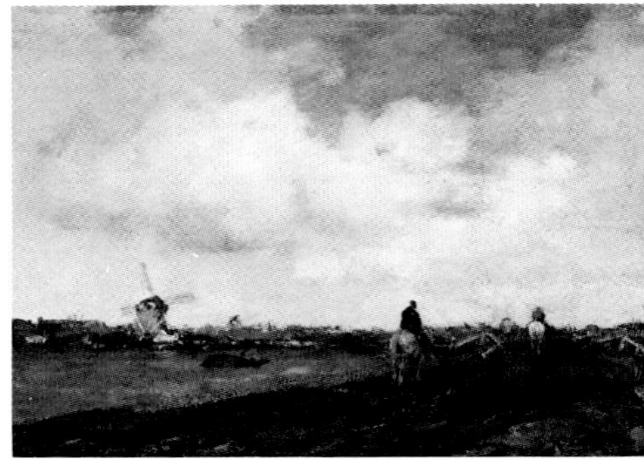

37.202 — c. 1885–90

A couple of men on horseback ride along the towpath of a waterway. Silhouetted against the horizon are two windmills, ubiquitous in Maris' landscapes. The expansive, overcast sky is characteristic of the artist's late works.

Support: Canvas, .323 x .453 (12¾" x 17⅞")

Signed at lower right: *J. Maris*

Provenance: M. Knoedler and Co., March 3, 1903 to Henry Walters for $4,250.00.

References: Walters cat., 1909, p. 67, no. 202.

Anton Mauve

Dutch: Zaandam, 1838 - Arnhem, 1888

Mauve, a major member of The Hague School, specialized in animal and figurative subjects. He received instruction, between 1854 and 1857, from the painter of cattle P. V. van Os, who encouraged him to draw from Nature; he was also taught by Wouterus Verschuur, an artist noted for landscapes and horse subjects. About 1858, Mauve began to visit Oosterbeek, befriending the painters Gerard Bilders and Willem Maris. Mauve established himself in Amsterdam in 1868. However, after his marriage in 1874, he settled with his wife in The Hague. There, he painted landscapes with animals, most often sheep. In many works, overcast skies predominate and the resulting low-keyed colors are rendered with remarkable subtlety. It was at The Hague, briefly in 1881–82, that he provided instruction to his wife's cousin, Vincent van Gogh. With the urban encroachment on the dunes in the mid-eighties, Mauve left The Hague for Laren in North Holland where he helped to establish another regional school of painting.

Mauve, together with Willem Maris and H. W. Mesdag, founded the Dutch Drawing Society in 1876 and he was for several years the Secretary of the Pulchri Studio.

181. Cattle

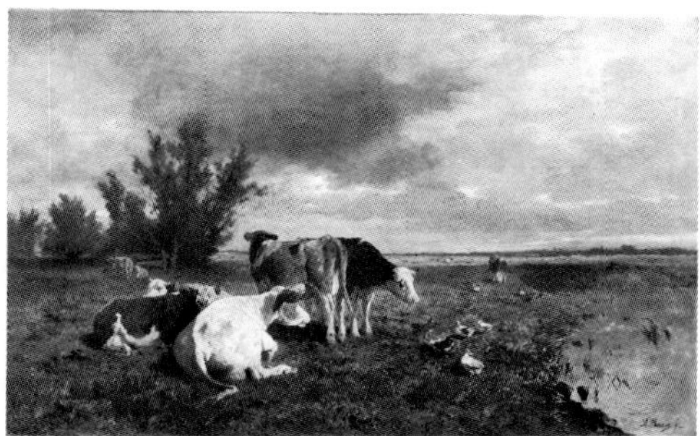

37.661 1870s–80s

In the foreground cattle graze or rest beside a marsh. Some ducks are waddling along the water's edge pecking for food. Across the background stretch flat plains interrupted at the left by several trees, beneath which graze sheep. The subdued lighting is characteristic of the artist's landscapes.

Alternative title: *Holland Meadows*

Support: Canvas, .874 x 1.375 (34½" x 54⅛")

Signed and dated lower right: *A. Mauve f.*

Marks: Stretcher marked in white chalk *60* and in black crayon *99*

Provenance: David H. King, Sale, American Art Association New York, March 25, 1905, no. 58 (illus.) $6,500.00 to W. G. Phillips; Phillips to Henry Walters.

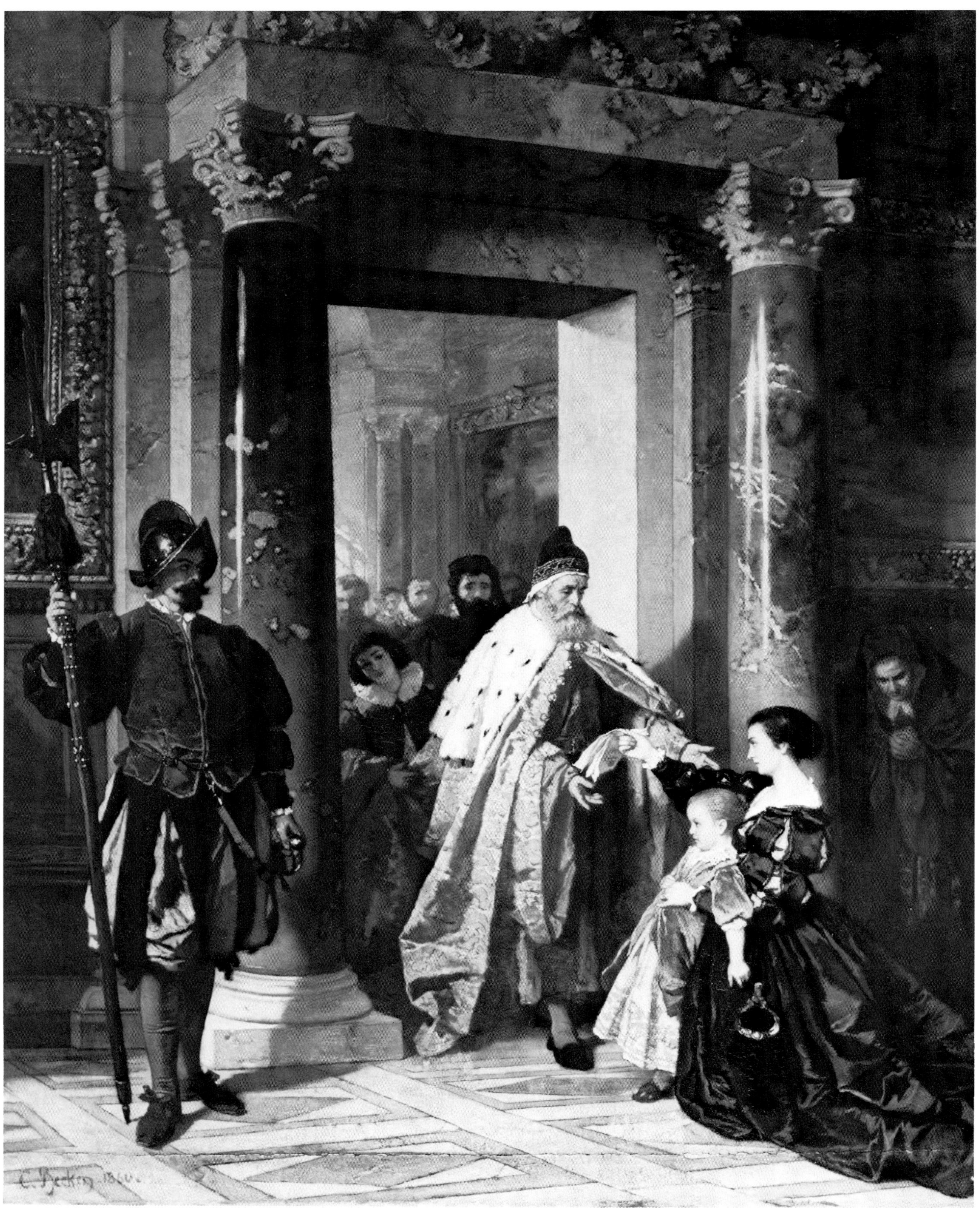

Becker *The Petition to the Doge,* no. 194

Scandinavian, Central and East European Paintings

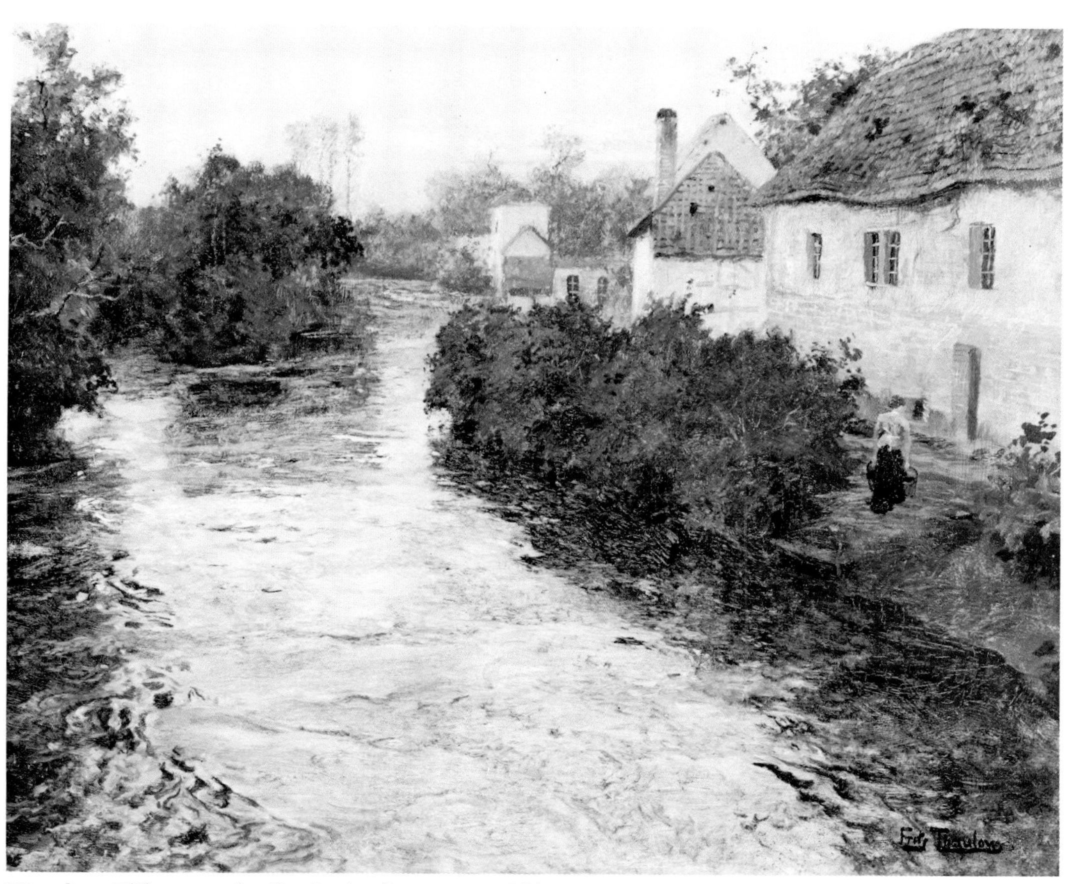

Thaulow *Village on the Bank of a Stream,* no. 184

Alexandre Calame
Swiss: Vevey, 1810 - Mentone, 1864

Alexandre Calame, the most noted Swiss Alpine artist of the mid nineteenth century, was born in Vevey, the son of a stone-cutter. At the age of fifteen, he was apprenticed to a banking firm and was compelled to raise extra support for his widowed mother by coloring prints of Swiss views. Subsequently he entered the studio of François Diday, the Geneva landscape painter. There Calame met his future father-in-law Jean Baptiste Muntz-Berger, a music professor and amateur artist who took him on sketching trips in the woods near Lausanne. Diday introduced him to the rougher terrain near the lakes of Thun and Brienz in the Bernese Oberland but it was a friend, Rodolphe Töpffer, who encouraged him to explore the higher Alps of Valais and central Switzerland. There he discovered his distinctive subject matter and felt the religious experience that he sought to express in his paintings of the summits, canyons, and glaciers.

In 1837 Calame visited Paris, where he quickly acquired a following of admirers and won a gold medal at the Salon of 1839 with his *The Handeck Falls in a Storm*. That year he departed for a tour of Germany and The Netherlands with the Geneva history painter Joseph Hornung. Upon his return to Geneva, he continued to serve a vast international clientele that included members of the reigning houses of Russia, The Netherlands and Württemberg. Later journeys included a visit to Italy in 1845, that was marred by ill health, and a tour up the Rhone Valley in 1860 with his son the artist Arthur Calame (1843–1919).

Although suffering from declining health for much of his career, Calame was not only a prolific painter but a successful graphic artist whose lithographs, numbering over eight hundred, and fifty-six etchings, were widely admired by his contemporaries. Apart from his spectacular subjects, it was Calame's dramatic handling of light and shadow rather than his rather subdued use of color that was usually praised. Calame's fame, however, proved ephemeral and by the end of the century his works had fallen into a period of neglect from which they are only now emerging.

182. The Jungfrau, Switzerland

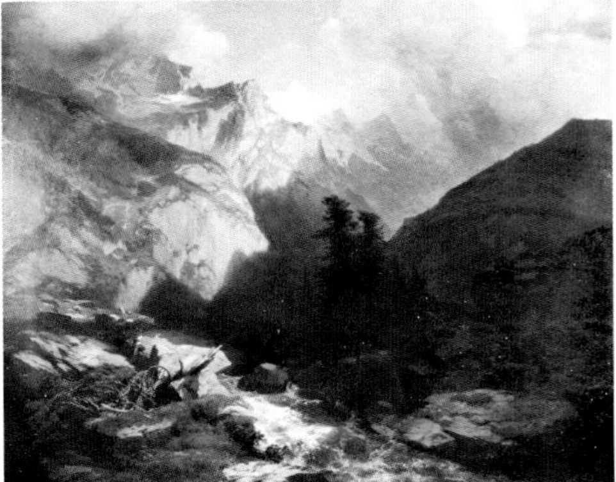

37.108 1853–1855

Towering above the valley of the Lauterbrunnen is the snow-capped peak of the Jungfrau. In the foreground a lone traveler maneuvers his way among boulders with a staff. A stream tumbles into a rocky gorge lost below in pine trees and shadows.

According to the artist's account-book, belonging to his heir, Christophe Van Loo of Ghent commissioned this "nature suisse, avec glaciers, sapins et arbres" for 3500 francs in 1853. In a letter of July 26, 1854, Calame wrote of the site: "Le coin perdu où je suis est vraiment admirable . . . comme si Dieu s'était complu à rassembler dans un coin de terre les plus grandes merveilles de la creation . . ." [Collection D. Buscarlet]

Support: Canvas, .853 x 1.055 (33⅝" x 41½")

Signed lower right: *A. Calame 1855*

Marks: Stretcher: A paper sticker on the reverse of the stretcher bears the following inscription: *Vue prise dans la valleé de Lauterbrunnen/ Canton de Berne/ des pins neige en fair/ partie O. la chaine de la Jungfrau./ Peint sur la commande & pour le cabinet de Monsieur Christophe Van-Loo- / Terminée en fevrier 1855- / Largeur 1 metre 05-cm/ Hauteur 0-85 cm/ Geneve 19 Mars 1855 / A Calame*

Provenance: Christophe Van Loo, Ghent; De Truenfels, Paris. Early Walters publications erroneously state that the painting had belonged to the Duc de Morny (1811–1865). George A. Lucas records paying 5512.50 francs for the painting at the Hôtel Drouot (De Truenfels Sale), Paris, April 9, 1867.

References: Walters cat., 1878, p. 36, and subsequent Walters catalogues; Strahan, 1: 94; Clement and Hutton, 1: 114; H. Mireur, *Dictionnaire des ventes d'art.* 7 vols. Paris, Ch. de Vincenti, 1911–12. 2: 9; Lucas, 2: 238.

Benjamin Vautier
Swiss: Morges (Vaud), 1829 - Düsseldorf, 1898

Vautier trained first in 1847 with Jules Hébert in Geneva, next in the drawing academy of the Musée Rath, and then in 1849 under the historical and genre painter, J. L. Lugardon. To support himself, he worked for the Swiss watchcase enameler, Claude Glardon, and executed the occasional portrait and landscape in watercolors.

Proceeding to Düsseldorf in 1850, he enrolled in the Academy for eight months and then entered the studio of Rudolf Jordan. In the summer of 1853 he traveled through the Bernese Alps observing the life and customs of the inhabitants as well as the scenery. Then, in 1856, inspired by the successes of Ludwig Knaus, he joined the ex-pupil of the Düsseldorf Academy in Paris where he stayed for six months before returning and settling in Düsseldorf. With Knaus he traveled through the Black Forest and the Rhenish Palatinate in 1858. In that year, his *In Church,* a rather droll scene of a choir singing in a Swabian church, drew considerable attention at the Munich Exhibition. Thereafter, Vautier rapidly acquired a reputation, international in scope, as a genre painter of German and Swiss rural life. He began to exhibit in Paris in 1865, winning a second-class medal at the 1867 Exposition Universelle. At the 1878 Exposition he received a first-class medal and was decorated a Chevalier of the Legion of Honor.

Vautier worked on a small scale, methodically producing precise drawings for his figurative compositions, which never numbered more than five or six a year. His works were admired for their draftsmanship and for their accuracy as records of the lighter aspects of village and country life. Vautier was also noted for his engravings, published in the *Munchhausen d'Immermann.*

183. Consulting His Lawyer

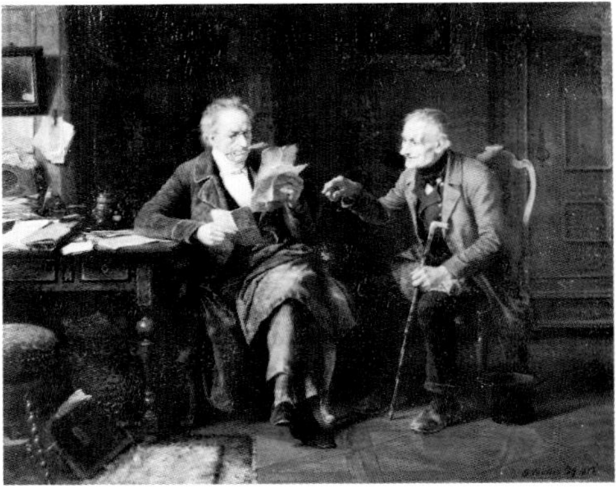

37.127 1872

A country lawyer in outmoded costume is seated beside a cluttered desk perusing some documents. He appears to ignore the gestures of his client, an elderly peasant whose gnarled hands, toothless grimace and soiled boots reflect the vicissitudes of life.

This low-keyed, carefully delineated interior typifies the work of Vautier, who was noted for interpretations of the lighter aspects of rural life.

Support: Panel, .54 x .705 (23¼" x 27¾")

Signed and dated at lower right: *B. Vautier del. 1872*

Alternative title: *Beim Advokaten*

Condition: The picture surface is discolored by yellowed varnish.

Provenance: Dr. Strauss, Vienna; purchased by W. T. Walters before 1878.

References: Walters cat., 1878, p. 83, and subsequent Walters catalogues; Strahan, 1: 91, 94; Clement and Hutton, 2: 313; Champlin and Perkins, 4: 327; Adolf Rosenberg, *Vautier.* Künstler-Monographien, 23; Bielefeld, Velhagen & Klasing, 1897, p. 39 (fig. 35), 45.

JOHAN FREDERICK (FRITZ OR FRITS) THAULOW

Norwegian: Christiania (Oslo), 1847–Volendam, The Netherlands, 1906.

Frits Thaulow was one of several artists in the 1870s and 1880s responsible for introducing the traditions of French naturalism to Norwegian art, hitherto dominated by the influences of the Düsseldorf and Munich schools of painting. In addition to being remembered for contributions to the art of his native land, Thaulow is frequently cited as one of the principal members of the international artistic milieu in France in the late nineteenth century.

Thaulow trained in Copenhagen under Carl F. Sørensen and in Karlsruhe in the studio of Hans Gude before journeying to Paris in 1874 where he was profoundly affected by the landscape paintings of Corot, Daubigny, and Cazin. Six years later he returned to Norway to found a plein-air school of painting in Modum, a village outside Christiania [Oslo].

Thaulow again left Norway in 1884 to visit Venice and Dieppe. Also working in the Normandy resort at this time were Gauguin, to whom Thaulow was briefly related through marriage (both painters being married to daughters of the Gad family of Copenhagen), as well as the artists Degas, Whistler, Sickert, Helleu, and Blanche. In Paris, Thaulow enjoyed considerable success exhibiting landscapes, particularly snow scenes recalling his Norwegian origin. In 1889, the year his *Ski-runners* was purchased by the State for the Luxembourg Museum, Thaulow served as a member of the jury for the Exposition Universelle. Even more cosmopolitan in his habits in the nineties, Thaulow worked at Montreuil in the first half of the decade, in Venice in 1894, and in his later years increasingly at Dieppe. Other travels included a visit to the United States in 1897–98, a stay in Spain in 1903–4, and his final trip to The Netherlands in 1906.

Despite these wanderings, Thaulow restricted his range of subjects. He was described by one critic as being "the painter of the snow, the night and the stream." Having mastered the principles of Impressionism, particularly as practiced by Monet, Thaulow continued to follow the precepts of the French movement long after they had been abandoned by their inventors.

Thaulow frequently exhibited in the salons of both the traditional and more liberal societies: the Société National des beaux-Arts in Paris, Les Vingt in Brussels, the Carnegie Institute's Annual in Pittsburgh and the Royal Academy in London. In 1898 he was invited to join the International Society of Painters, Sculptors and Gravers headed by Whistler, which included in its membership such diverse figures as Manet, Fantin-Latour, Rodin, Segantini, Zorn, and Maris. He also exhibited oils and pastels in Paris at the dealers Georges Petit and Montaignac.

Thaulow's awards included his election to the rank of Chevalier of the Legion of Honor in 1889 and to Officier in 1901. He won the Grand Prix at the Paris Exposition Universelle in 1900.

184. Village on the Bank of a Stream

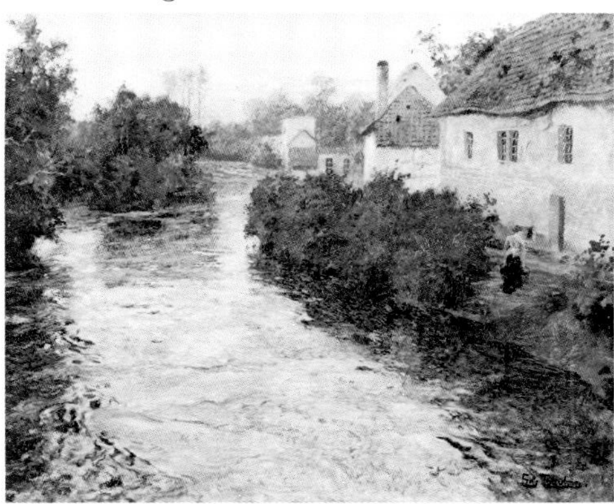

37.175 c.1890

An eddying stream rushes past several thatched farm buildings. The masterly rendering of water, the subdued coloring and lighting of the scene and the high horizon are idiomatic of this artist who retained a sensuous, impressionistic technique throughout the nineties.

A similar view, *Elv i Normandie,* is illustrated by Thaulow's biographer, Einar Østvedt, in *Frits Thaulow, Mannen og Verket,* Oslo, 1951, p. 133, and dated about 1890 when the artist was working in the Pas de Calais region of Normandy.

Support: Finely woven fabric, .649 x .809 (25⁹⁄₁₆" x 31¹³⁄₁₆")

Signed at lower right: *Frits Thaulow*

Marks: Paper label on stretcher inscribed in ink: *Lucas*

Condition: Discolored varnishes removed in March 1968, and in October 1978 picture was lined.

Provenance: Unknown.

References: W. R. Johnston, "Frits Thaulow, Norwegian Impressionist," *BWAG* 20, no. 8 (May 1968): 3–4, illus.

185. The Adige River at Verona

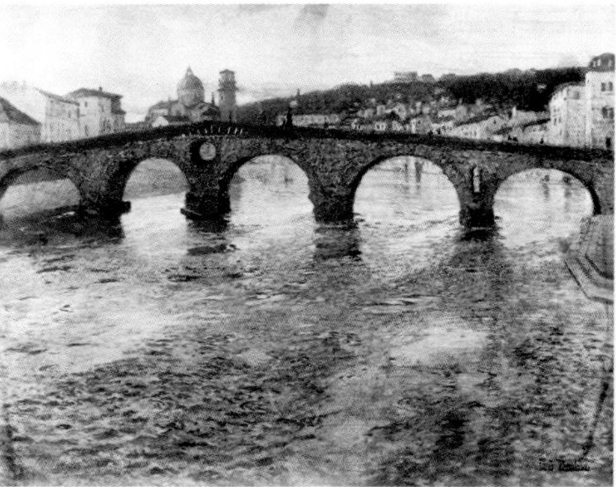

37.97 c.1894

Muted colors and subtle tonal harmonies characterize this view of the fast-flowing Adige River as it passes beneath the five arches of the Ponte della Pietra (two arches are Roman, the central two date from 1520 and the last was a reconstruction of about 1528). Discernible upstream at the left are several palazzi and the Duomo of S. Maria Matricolare, initially a Romanesque construction with later additions, including a campanile designed by Sanmichele, and at the right the region of S. Stefano and the bastion of S. Giorgio silhouetted against the horizon.

A related view entitled *Veronabroen,* showing the west end of the Ponte della Pietra, is illustrated in Einar Østvedt's biography, *Frits Thaulow, Mannen og Verket,* Oslo, 1951, p. 137. Both works are presumed to have been executed during Thaulow's trip across northern Italy to Venice in 1894.

Given the absence of references to other related subjects and judging from the large size of the Walters painting, both it and the work illustrated by Østvedt are probably the pictures exhibited at the Royal Academy, London, in 1900 as no. 365, *The old bridge in Verona* and no. 608, *View from the old bridge in Verona,* respectively.

Support: Canvas, .81 x 1 (31⅞" x 39⅜")

Signed at lower right: *Frits Thaulow*

Provenance: Possibly purchased by Henry Walters, either on April 2, 1902 from Georges Petit, for 8500 francs or on May 14, 1902, from the dealer Montaignac, together with a Marilhat for 22,000 francs. (Lucas, 2: 897, 899).

Exhibitions: The Royal Academy, London, 1900, no. 365; "A Baltimorean in Paris: George A. Lucas, Art Agent," Walters Art Gallery, 1978 (erroneously listed as "The Ponte Navi on the Adige, Verona").

References: W. R. Johnston, "Frits Thaulow, Norwegian Impressionist," *BWAG* 20, no. 8 (May 1968): 3–4.

Joseph Karl Stieler
German: Mainz, 1781—Munich, 1858

Stieler served as a major portraitist for the German monarchies. He trained initially as a miniature painter but turned to oil painting when he began to study with Christoph Fesel in Würzburg in 1789. By 1800, he was in Vienna working under Heinrich Füger. In 1805 he removed to Poland, to Warsaw and Cracow, and two years later he was in Paris where he studied with François Gérard. Stieler's travels took him to Frankfurt in 1808, to Milan and Rome in 1808–1810, and to Vienna in 1816, where he painted portraits of the Emperor and Empress. By 1820 he had established himself in Munich as the court painter. Apart from his royal portraits he is known for his likenesses of Goethe, Humboldt, and Beethoven.

Studio of Stieler
186. Portrait of Ludwig I, King of Bavaria

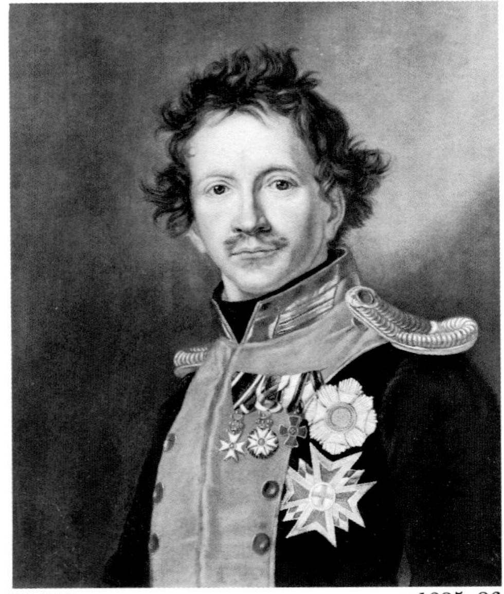

37.881 c.1825–26

Ludwig (1786–1868) succeeded his father, Maximilian Joseph, as King of Bavaria in 1825 and reigned until 1848 when popular opposition to the influence of his mistress, Lola Montez, compelled him to abdicate in favor of his son, Maximilian II. Initially, he reigned as a liberal but gradually he assumed a conservative stance. Through his building programs and patronage, Ludwig was to a large extent responsible for the emergence of Munich as a major centre for the arts in the nineteenth century.

The monarch is portrayed turned to the left and facing to the front. His general's uniform is dark green with red facing, gold collar, silver epaulettes and gilt buttons. He wears, from left to right, the Commander-Cross of the Military Order of Max-Joseph, the Cross of the Order of the Bavarian Crown, the Commemorative Military Medal for 1813–15 and, in addition, two stars, the Order of Saint Hubert above, and the Order of Saint George below. A zone of pale blue light isolates the King's head from the remainder of the background, which is grey. Walters Art Gallery records dating from 1934 incorrectly attributed this picture to François Gérard. It is, however, a painting from the studio of Gérard's pupil Joseph K. Stieler and resembles, in particular, two studies taken from life by Stieler in preparation for a coronation portrait. These studies are reproduced in Ulrike von Hase, *Joseph Stieler,* Munich, 1971, figs. 122a and b.

Support: Canvas, coarse uneven weave, .68 x .551 (26¾" x 21$\frac{11}{16}$")

Marks: Inscribed in pencil on the stretcher: *Ludwig I King of Bavaria*

Condition: The painting was lined and the top tacking edge of the canvas lost at an unknown date. Minor losses throughout were inpainted presumably at the same time. In 1972 the picture was treated by Walters conservators. Removal of old varnishes revealed a discolored area to the left of the figure's collar, indicating that the subject had been placed further to the left in the artist's initial design.

Provenance: Unknown.

Studio of Stieler
187. Portrait of Queen Therese of Bavaria

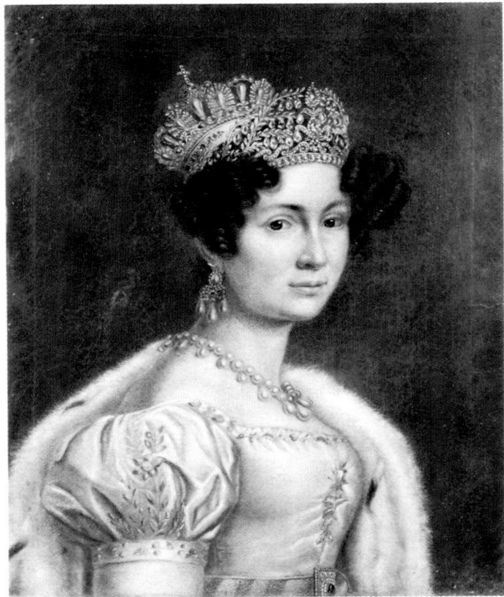

37.1833 c.1825–26

Princess Therese von Sachsen Hildburghausen (1792–1854) married Ludwig I Karl August in 1810 and subsequently bore four sons, including the heir to the throne of Bavaria, Maximilian, and the future King of Greece, Otto, as well as four daughters.

The subject is portrayed, turned to the right, facing front. She wears ermine, a white gown trimmed with gold foliate embroidery, and a gold mesh belt. Her jewelry includes a crown and diadem, pearl girandole earrings, a pearl necklace, and a belt buckle set with brilliants surrounding a central sapphire. The crown has been identified as that made by the firm of Biennais, Paris, in 1806 for the queens of Bavaria.

The painting replicates a detail from the Queen's Coronation portrait now known through a copy in Nymphenburg Castle, Munich (Ulrike von Hase, *Joseph Stieler,* Munich, 1971, fig. 128).

Support: Canvas, .675 x .547 (26⅝" x 21½")

Marks: Inscribed in pencil on the reverse of the stretcher: *Maria Theresa [Queen] of Bavaria Wife of Ludwig I*

Condition: At an unknown date, the canvas was lined and losses along the edges inpainted. Visible on the surface of the canvas, about .032 to .39 from the edges, are old stretcher marks indicating the portrait has been cropped along all sides.

Provenance: Unknown.

Artist Unknown
German School

188. Romantic Landscape

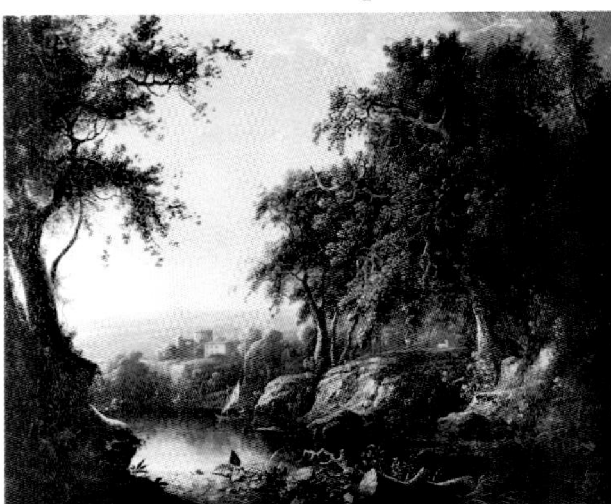

37.1217 c.1830

In this enigmatic landscape a man in a small sailboat glides across a still pond. Discernible on the far shore is a couple, the woman seated on the lawn and the man standing, and beyond, some buildings dominated by a round tower. Deer graze in the woods at the right. As the sun sets behind the trees at the left the scene is suffused with glowing warm light. The foliage is rendered in minute detail with distinctive swiggly strokes suggesting a German or Austrian hand.

Support: Canvas: .64 x .76 (25⅛" x 29⅞")

Marks: Paper label on reverse of stretcher: *X70 Landscape by John Martin;* Paper label: *814;* Canvas: *70* in ink

Condition: Covered by discolored varnish; small patch on reverse of canvas at bottom right.

Provenance: Purchased by Henry Walters in 1902 as part of the Massarenti Collection.

References: *Catalogue du musée de peinture, sculpture et archéologie au Palais Accoramboni,* 2 vols., Rome, Imprimerie du Vatican, 1897: 140, no. 814 (as Vue de Genève, XVII siècle).

Johann Wilhelm Preyer
German: Rheydt, 1803 - Düsseldorf, 1889

Preyer, once regarded as Germany's principal still life painter, was particularly admired at the middle of the last century in America, especially in New York, where his fruit and vegetable subjects were displayed in the "Dusseldorf Gallery" between 1849 and 1862.

Preyer entered the Düsseldorf Academy in 1822 and studied initially under Peter von Cornelius and later under Wilhelm von Shadow. In 1837 he moved to Munich and worked intermittently for a decade, returning occasionally to Düsseldorf. He visited The Netherlands in 1835, northern Italy and Switzerland in 1840, and the southern Tyrol and Venice in 1843. Thereupon, he returned to Düsseldorf where he remained active as a still life painter. Early critics often noted Preyer's indebtedness to the Dutch masters Jan van Huysum, Rachel Ruysch, Willem Kalf and others.

189. Still Life

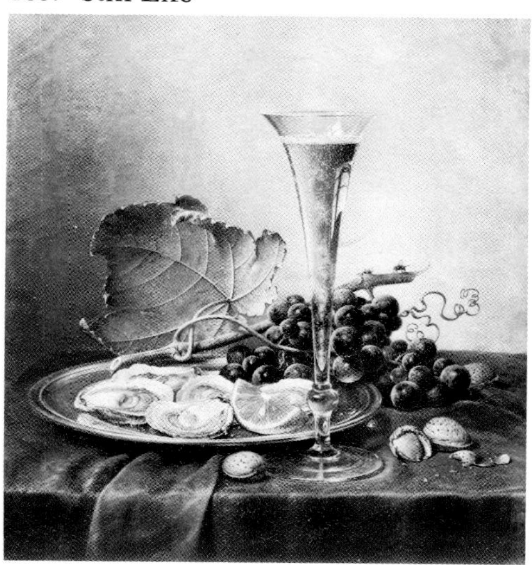

37.139 1859

On a table covered with a red cloth are a slender glass of sparkling wine, a silver salver bearing oysters, a slice of lemon, a bunch of purple grapes still attached to a sprig of vine with one large leaf, and several almonds. A housefly is perched on the stem of the vine.

Support: Canvas, .36 x .322 (14¼" x 12⅝")

Signed and dated in black at lower right: *J* (conjoined) *W* (conjoined) *Preyer 1859*

Provenance: Early Walters catalogues record that the picture was purchased directly from the artist before 1878.

References: Walters cat., 1878, p. 20, and subsequent Walters catalogues; Strahan, 1: 94.

Franz Xaver Winterhalter

German: Menzenschwand (Grand Duchy of Baden), 1805 - Frankfurt, 1873

Winterhalter, the celebrated portraitist of European nobility and royalty, was born of peasant stock in the Black Forest. He began training in the Herder Kunstinstitut in Freiburg in 1818 and six years later entered the Munich Academy under Robert von Langer. Though welcomed into the house of the court painter Joseph Karl Stieler he was at first obliged to support himself working for the lithography firm of Piloty and Selb. In 1828 Winterhalter returned to Karlsruhe as drawing master for the Margravine Sophie and painted members of the Grand Ducal house of Baden. Drawings and watercolors made during a journey to Italy in 1833–34 served as a basis for the paintings executed in Paris, where he settled in the mid-thirties. In 1836 he received a second-class medal, exhibiting a painting of a Neapolitan fisherman's family entitled *Il dolce far niente,* as well as representations of an Italian mother and child and of a dog. His most notable entry in the following Salon, *Boccaccio's Decameron,* a romantic view of some young men and women listening to a recitation of poetry in a garden, won him a first-class medal. After these successes he turned increasingly to portraiture, exhibiting elegant likenesses of members of the Orléans family in the late thirties. In 1839 he showed his first portrait of Louis Philippe, which was acquired for Versailles, and in 1842 he entered a portrait of the Queen painted for the royal household. In preparation for a painting representing Louis Philippe receiving the Order of the Garter, he visited London in 1845. Though this commission was never completed, Winterhalter did execute portraits of Queen Victoria and Prince Albert and, at the 1846 Salon, exhibited *The Salon of Windsor Castle: Queen Victoria presenting her children to Louis Philippe, October 8, 1844,* intended for the King's personal collection. In 1852 he journeyed to Spain to paint Queen Isabella, and by 1855, he had emerged as the foremost portraitist of France's Second Empire, exhibiting several portraits of the Imperial family at the Salon and painting for Versailles his remarkable *The Empress and her Ladies-in-waiting,* one of the principal records of the era. In the following years, he painted the members of most of the European ruling houses and their courts. Winterhalter's later portraits were marked by their elegance, and occasionally by their informal grace. The apparent facility of his works provoked their condemnation by some of the more progressive critics. Paul Mantz, for example, castigated the artist for the excessive coquetry displayed in his portraits of Russian princesses exhibited in the 1859 Salon. To maintain his formidable rate of production, Winterhalter developed the practice of quickly sketching his subjects' faces and leaving the painting of the costumes and accessories to his younger brother, Hermann. Winterhalter sojourned in Munich in 1868, went to Switzerland for a cure in 1870, returned to Karlsruhe in 1871, and died of typhus two years later in Frankfurt.

190. Princess Kotschoubey

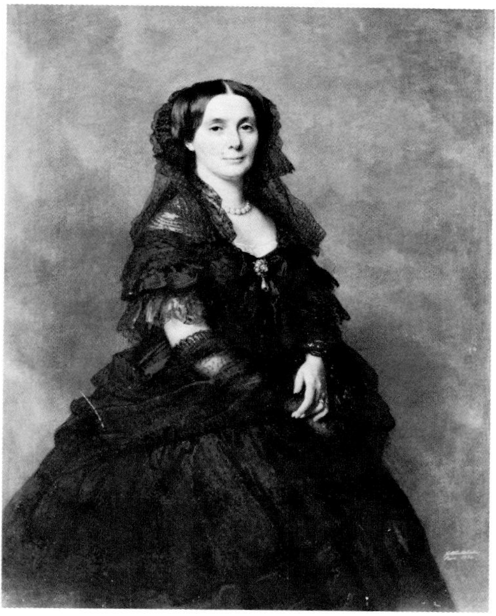

37.2396 1860

A woman of great wealth, even by the standards of her time, the Princess traveled extensively, mingling in the European courts, and entertaining lavishly. Her palace on the Nevsky Prospekt, St. Petersburg, was the setting for balls that rivaled those of the court in grandeur. She was born Hélène Bibikoff and had two marriages, the first to Prince Esper A. Belosselsky-Belozersky, great-grandfather of the portrait's donor, and the second to Prince Kotschoubey, son of Victor Pavlovich Kotschoubey, a Minister of the Interior and Chancellor of the Empire. Because of her cosmopolitan experience, Princess Kotschoubey was appointed *grande maîtresse de la maison* in the reign of Alexander III and in this office she maintained her role as social arbitress of the Imperial court, serving with particularly autocratic zeal, according to all accounts, until her death at an advanced age in 1888.

Winterhalter has depicted her in one of his customary formats, three-quarter length, nearly life-size, and painted against an overcast sky. She wears a black silk gown, black lace and jewelry including a necklace of large pearls, a pearl brooch with a large pendant pearl, a flexible, serpentine bracelet, and several rings. A portait of the Princess in her youth, by V. L. Borovikovski is preserved in the National Museum in Warsaw, inv. 127673.

Support: Canvas, 1.295 x .973 (51" x 38¼")

Signed and dated in red paint at lower right: *Fr Winterhalter/Paris, 1860*

Provenance: The descendants of Prince Esper A. Belosselsky-Belozersky; presented to the Gallery in January, 1964, by Prince Serge Belosselsky.

References: 'Recent Museum Acquisitions in Paintings," *Antiques* 87 (1965): 470, illus.

Andreas Johann Jacob Heinrich Müller

German: Kassel, 1811 - Düsseldorf, 1890

Andreas Müller first trained with his father, F. H. Müller, director of the Darmstadt Gallery. In 1832 he enrolled in the Munich Academy under Julius Schnorr von Carolsfeld and Peter Cornelius and in 1834 entered the Düsseldorf Academy as a pupil of Karl Sohn and Wilhelm von Schadow. From 1837 to 1842, he studied in Italy, working with several late Nazarene painters, including his brother Karl, Ernst Deger, and Franz Ittenbach, with whom he later executed a series of wall paintings for a church in Apollinarisberg, near Remagen, Germany. In 1853 Müller, working in a boiled oil medium that he devised, completed murals illustrating the life of St. Apollinaris. Subsequent works included twenty-six portraits of German artists painted for the picture gallery of the Hohenzollern castle at Sigmaringen, as well as a number of historical genre scenes and landscapes which were sold through lotteries of the Electorate of Hesse and the Art Union of the Rhineland and Westphalia. He also worked as an engraver, illustrating poety of R. Reinick. Müller served as a professor at the Düsseldorf Academy and as curator of its Gallery from 1856 until he became an invalid in 1882.

191. The Christ Child

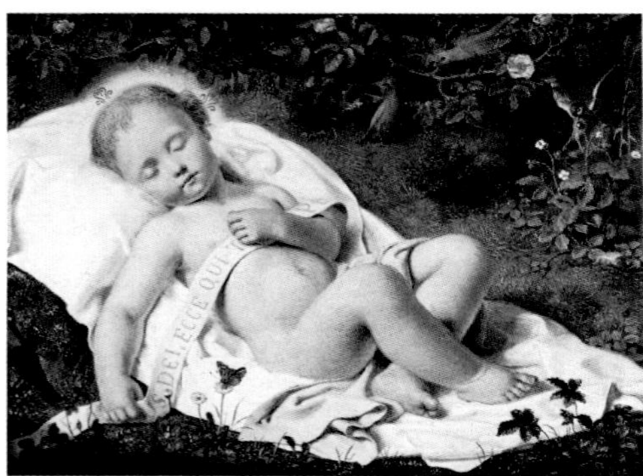

37.178 1849

The sleeping Child lies on a sheet of white cloth partially covered by a pink cloth. He is identified by the aureole of light and three stylized rays forming a halo and by the ribbon he holds which is inscribed [AGN] US DEI ECCE QUI T[OLLIS PECCATA MUNDI: MISERERE NOBIS] (Roman Missal, Communion: 3). He is surrounded by meticulously rendered flora and fauna, laden with Christian symbolism. The rose bushes allude to martyrdom, strawberry plants to perfect righteousness, violets to humility, several stalks of wheat to the human nature of Christ, some daisies to his innocence, the butterfly to the Resurrection, the goldfinch to the Passion, the pair of turtle doves to purity, and the swallow to the Incarnation.

This painting replicates a section of an unlocated picture of the Virgin and Saint John accompanied by three angels adoring the Christ Child, which was reproduced as a steel engraving by Wm. Ridgway in a Bible published by James S. Virtue, London, n.d.

Support: Panel, beveled, .116 x .155 (4⅞" x 6¼")

Marks: Inscribed on reverse in beige paint: *A* (conjoined) *Müller, pinx/1849/Düsseldorf.*

Provenance: Unknown.

Andreas Achenbach

German: Kassel, 1815 - Düsseldorf, 1910

Achenbach, one of Düsseldorf's early important landscape painters, departed from the historical landscape school of K. F. Lessing and J. W. Schirmer and moved in the direction of modern realism. This development is more clearly manifested in his studies from nature than in his finished canvases. In the latter, adhering to the Romantic tradition, he tended to dwell on the more ominous aspects of Nature.

A precocious youth, Achenbach was enrolled in the Düsseldorf Academy under W. von Schadow and W. Schirmer at the age of twelve and within two years he had sold a painting at the Art Union of the Rhineland and Westphalia.

As a young man Achenbach was an inveterate traveler. In 1832 he accompanied his father through The Netherlands, where he was particularly drawn to the works of Jacob van Ruisdael and Allart van Everdingen. Leaving Düsseldorf again, he toured through Munich, Frankfurt, and the Scandinavian countries in 1835, through the Bavarian Alps and the Tyrol in 1836, and returned to Norway in 1839. Commencing in the autumn of 1843, he traveled to Italy where he worked for two years in the Campagna and near Capri.

Though his range of subjects was confined for the most part to landscapes and marines, frequently scenes of coasts battered by storms, his technique did evolve from a minutely detailed, carefully finished facture to one of greater freedom of brush stroke. Apart from his paintings Achenbach also acquired a reputation as a gifted caricaturist and a graphic artist.

This artist was highly esteemed, especially in the northern European countries, and was awarded memberships in the academies of Berlin, Antwerp and Amsterdam. Though he won a first-class medal at the 1855 Exposition Universelle, the critic Maxime DuCamp, in *Les Beaux-Arts à l'Exposition Universelle de 1855,* commented adversely on the absence of movement in the artist's seascapes despite their apparent violence.

192. Clearing up—Coast of Sicily

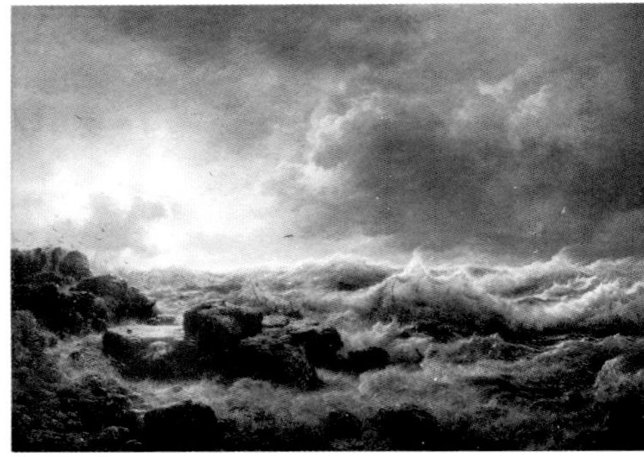

37.116 1847

At the left the evening sunlight breaks through the stormy sky to illuminate the turbulent sea breaking against the rocky coast. Seagulls struggle to fly in the violent wind. The only signs of human presence are a spar embedded in the rocks, a wooden keg adrift at the right, and a barely discernible, tattered American flag thrown against a cluster of rocks in the foreground, slightly left of center.

Storms on the Sicilian coast were recurrent themes in Achenbach's oeuvre. One such scene was exhibited at the Paris Exposition Universelle in 1855 and another was in the celebrated collection of John Wolfe (Sale, New York, 1863, $3,000.00). The presence of the American flag in this picture suggests that it may have been commissioned by John Godfrey Boker for the Dusseldorf Gallery, New York, where it was exhibited from 1849 to 1862. A drawing for the painting was also exhibited in the New York gallery (*Catalogue of Paintings and Original Drawings by Artists of the Düsseldorf Academy of Fine Arts,* New York, 1849, no. 8).

Alternative titles: *Sea Coast of Italy after a Storm; Küste Sizilien No. 4*

Support: Canvas, .825 x 1.161 (32½" x 45¾")

Signed and dated in black at lower left: *A Achenbach/ 1847*

Marks: Paper sticker on stretcher reads: *A Achenbach./ Küste Sizilien/ No. 4*

Condition: Cleaned and relined 1972.

Provenance: The Dusseldorf Gallery, New York (John Godfrey Boker, proprietor, 1849–1857; Cosmopolitan Art Association of Sandusky, Ohio, owners, 1857–1862). Perhaps John Wolfe Sale, December 22, 1863.

References: Dusseldorf Gallery, New York. *Catalogue of a private collection of paintings and original drawings by artists of the Düsseldorf Academy of Fine Arts.* New York, W. C. Bryant, 1849, no. 32, and subsequent catalogues of this institution; Walters cat., 1878, p. 18, and subsequent Walters catalogues; Strahan, 1: 94.

193. A Windy Day

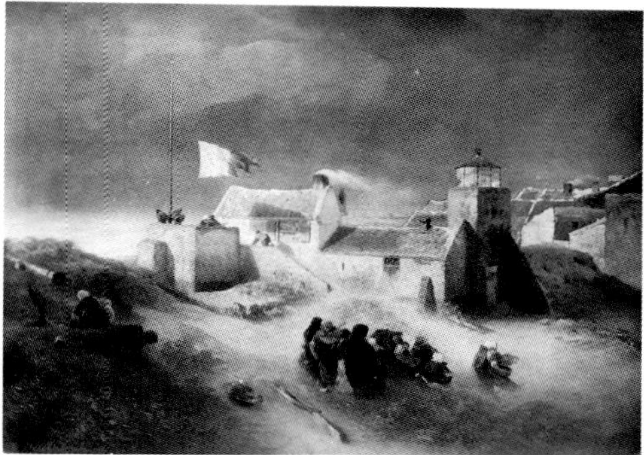

37.155 1870

A fishing village is being lashed by a violent gale. The fishermens' wives struggle across the dunes to mount an old fortification at the left. Beyond are an Argand lighthouse and the village houses with red tile roofs glistening in a shaft of light that has pierced the glowering sky. Several men struggle to raise a blue and white signal flag at a post near the sea's edge.

The former identification of the site as the coast at the village of Scheveningen, near The Hague, cannot be substantiated. The presence of a lighthouse in close proximity to houses did not occur at Scheveningen nor elsewhere, given the danger of fire.

Alternative title: *A Windy Day at Scheveningen*

Support: Panel, mahogany, beveled edges, .597 x .808 (23¾" x 31½")

Signed and dated in red at lower left: *A Achenbach 70*

Provenance: John Wolfe Sale, New York, 1882, no. 32, $1,600.00.

References: Walters cat., 1884, p. 46, no. 68, and subsequent Walters catalogues.

Karl Ludwig Friedrich Becker
German: Berlin 1820 - Berlin 1900

Becker studied with August von Kloeber at the Berlin Academy before going to Munich in 1843 where he trained under Heinrich von Hess in fresco painting. He then proceeded to Paris for a year, and from 1845 to 1847 he was in Rome. On several occasions Becker visited Venice, where he became enamored with the city's past and its artistic traditions. Back in Berlin, he exhibited paintings of historical and mythological scenes and undertook some murals (1854–55) for the Museum in Berlin. Beginning in the mid-fifties Becker specialized in Venetian subjects rendered in vibrant colors inspired by Venetian traditions in painting. This light palette proved revolutionary in Berlin. Works in this vein included *A Jeweler and a Venetian Senator* (1855), *Visit to a Venetian Noble,* and *Albrecht Dürer in Venice* (1872). He also drew subjects from German history of the sixteenth through the eighteenth centuries. Becker became a professor and eventually President of the Berlin Academy.

194. The Petition to the Doge

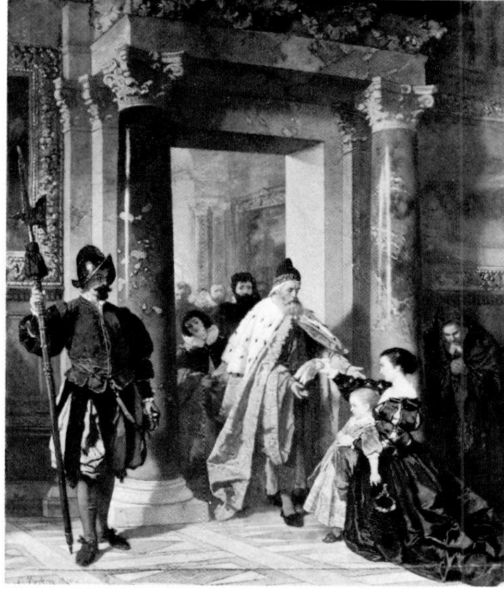

37.162 1860

A doge, standing in a palace doorway, is confronted by a petitioner; a lady in black, who, kneeling on the pavement, holds her young daughter before her. A halberdier, guarding the entrance, glances at the kneeling figure. Behind, in the shadows at the right, is an elderly woman with bowed head and clasped hands. The doge's retinue includes his page, who carries the trailing robe, and several attendants discernible in the sunlit interior beyond the portal. The artist's distinctively rich palette, said to have been inspired by the Venetian *Seicento,* is evinced in the sumptuous gold brocades, crimson velvet and white ermine of the doge's attire, the variegated marbles of the architecture, and the gilding of the picture frame at the left.

Another version of the subject, also entitled *Petition to a Doge,* dated 1862, is reproduced in Clarence Cook, *Art and Artists of Our Time,* New York, 1888, 2: 91. In this work the halberdier has been replaced by a large greyhound.

Support: Canvas, 1.321 x 1.06 (52" x 41¾")

Signed and dated in red at lower left: *C. Becker 1860*

Provenance: W. M. Webb, New York; 1876, bought through S. P. Avery.

References: Walters cat., 1878, p. 24, and subsequent Walters catalogues; Strahan, 1: 94; Champlin and Perkins, 1: 120.

Adolf Schreyer
German: Frankfurt, 1828 - Kronberg-im-Taunus, 1899

Schreyer, a secondary figure in the history of modern German painting, prospered from a remarkable international following, particularly in the United States. His often vividly-colored Arab subjects, somber, desolate, farm scenes of eastern Europe, and occasional battle paintings provided exotic notes in the collections of the Astors, Vanderbilts, Drexels, Walters and of other post-Civil War admirers.

Schreyer had studied at the Frankfurt Städel Institut and the academies of Düsseldorf and Munich before arriving in Vienna in 1848. The following year, according to early biographers, he traveled with Prince Thurn und Taxis, brother-in-law of the Emperor Franz Joseph, through Wallachia, Hungary, and southern Russia. During the Crimean War he again accompanied the Prince, not to the Crimea itself, as has been erroneously noted, but to the eastern reaches of the Danube, the Austrian army's field of action in the conflict. Schreyer made lengthy visits to Egypt and Syria in 1859, and to Algiers in 1861, mastering several Arab dialects and thoroughly immersing himself in Bedouin life. In 1862 he settled in Paris, and after exhibiting successfully at the 1864, 1865, and 1867 Salons, became assimilated into French cultural circles. Théophile Gautier compared him to Delacroix and Decamps, and, with considerably more justification, to Fromentin (*Moniteur Universal,* Paris, February 18, 1864). Paul Mantz observed that in *The Charge of the Artillery of the Imperial Guard,* shown in the 1865 Salon, he incorporated "toute la furie française" ("Salon de 1865," *Gazette des Beaux Arts* 18 (1865): 511). As a result of the Franco-Prussian War, Schreyer returned to Germany, settling in Kronberg. There he continued to produce for a growing clientele paintings of horse subjects set in eastern Europe or North Africa.

195. Arabs in Egypt, Sunrise

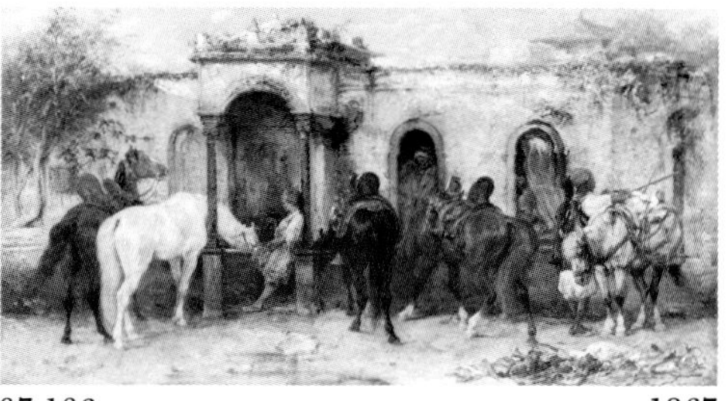

37.136 1867

Seen is a courtyard of an inn at dawn. The rising sun bathes the top walls with warm light, leaving the foreground in shadow; horses are being prepared for the day. One, already packed, is tended by an Arab, three others are saddled, and another, a handsome white steed, drinking water from a well, is watched by a young boy. Strewn across the ground at the right are various supplies.

Support: Canvas, .425 x .745 (16¾" x 29⅜")

Signed and dated lower left in brown: *Ad. Schreyer 1867/Paris*

Marks: Canvsa stenciled: *le Couleurs fine/. . . E OTTOZ/Rue de la Brière 22*

Condition: Cleaned and lined in 1966.

Provenance: Henry Probasco (Cincinnati), Sale, New York, April 18, 1887, no. 69, to S. P. Avery for W. T. Walters, $2,550.00.

References: Walters cat., 1888, p. 43, no. 61, and subsequent Walters catalogues; Clement and Hutton, 2: 245.

196. Embourbé (Mired), Plains of Hungary

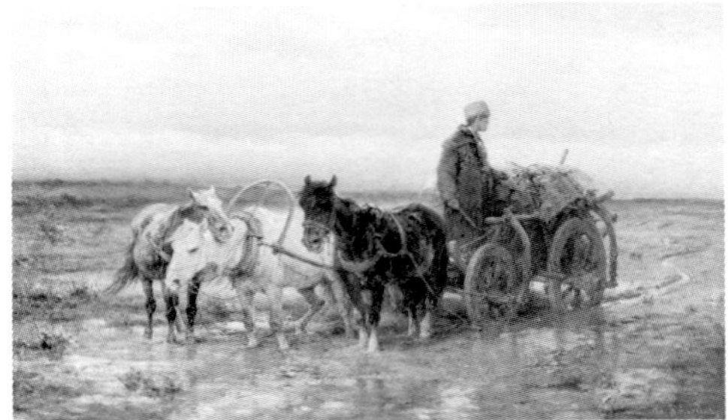

37.76 c.1873

A peasant standing on a heavily laden, four-wheeled cart, stares forlornly across the empty landscape. The cart, drawn by a troika of horses, appears to be thoroughly mired in mud. In this barren scene with its glowering sky and leaden atmosphere, the artist conveys a remarkable sense of desolation.

Alternative title: *A Wallachian Teamster tangled in the Marshes of the Danube*

Support: Canvas, 1.202 x 2.01 (47½" x 79⅛")

Signed lower right: *Ad. Schreyer*

Marks: Frame: Paper Sticker: *William Schaus/ Tableaux Modernes/479 Broadway/New York*

Condition: Painting suffered tear and abrasion in central area due to mechanical damage. Inpainted, cleaned and lined in 1958.

Provenance: William Schaus, New York (?); The John Wolfe sale, New York, April 6, 1882, $5,100.00.

Exhibitions: Vienna, International Exhibition, 1873.

References: Walters cat., 1884, p. 87, no. 143, and subsequent Walters catalogues; Champlin and Perkins, 4: 148; "Adolf Schreyer," exhibition catalogue, Paine Art Center and Arboretum, Oshkosh, Wis., 1972, p. 58, illus.

197. A Cold Day

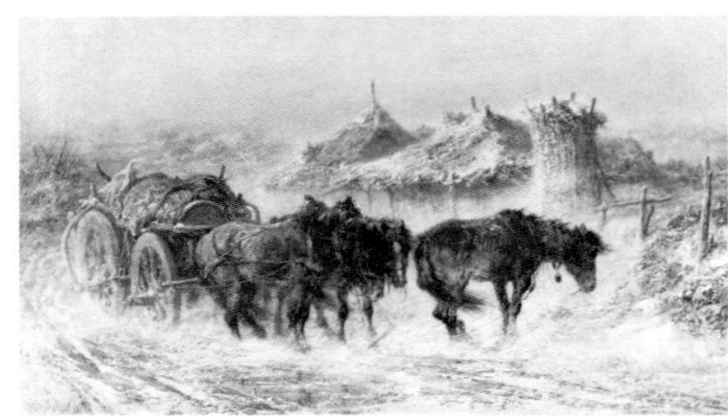

37.88

A team of horses, hitched to a cart outside several thatched farm buildings, is exposed to a driving wind and snow storm. Though a relatively small work, this painting exemplifies Schreyer's accomplishments as a painter of horses and as a portrayer of the more violent and dramatic aspects of nature.

Alternative titles: *Horses at Rest; Winter in Poland*

Support: Canvas, .44 x .643 (17¼" x 29¼")

Signed lower left in dark grey: *Ad. Schreyer*

Marks: Frame inscribed in black paint: *No. 119 Ad Schreyer,* stretcher stenciled *3448*

Provenance: E. Gambart & Co., 120 Pall Mall, London, April 5, 1867, £157.10, receipt in Gallery archives.

References: Walters cat., 1878, p. 26, and subsequent Walters catalogues; Strahan, 1: 94; Clement and Hutton, 2: 245; Champlin and Perkins, 4: 148; "Adolf Schreyer," exhibition catalogue, Paine Art Center and Arboretum, Oshkosh, Wis., 1972, p. 58, illus.

Ludwig Knaus

German: Wiesbaden (Nassau), 1829 - Berlin, 1910

The genre paintings of Ludwig Knaus have been described as having their literary parallels in the novels of Berthold Auerbach and Karl Immermann. More than most of his German colleagues, Knaus received international recognition, with many of his works being scattered in French, British, and American collections. In the United States, his paintings were initially distributed by the New York dealer William Schaus, and later by Samuel P. Avery.

Knaus first trained with O. R. Jacobi, court painter to the Duchy of Nassau and then, in 1846, entered the Düsseldorf Academy under Karl Sohn and Wilhem von Schadow. Rebelling against academicism, he joined the trend toward naturalism led by Lessing and Leutze. His most significant work at this point was *Hessian Peasant Dance under the Lindens* exhibited in Düsseldorf in 1849 and in Berlin in 1850. From late 1852 to 1860, Knaus was based in Paris though he undertook several excursions, the longest of which was to Italy in 1857–58. In Paris, where his scenes of village life met with considerable success, he received a second-class medal in 1853, and first-class medals in 1855 and 1857; in 1859 he was appointed a Chevalier of the Legion of Honor. Eight years later he was raised to Officier of the order. Following his marriage in 1859, Knaus returned to Wiesbaden, remaining until 1862, when he moved to Berlin for four years. Between 1867 and 1874, Knaus was chiefly active in Düsseldorf working together with the Swiss genre painter Benjamin Vautier and the Achenbach brothers. With the reorganization of the Berlin Academy under Adolf von Werner, Knaus was appointed head of one of the studios, a position he maintained from 1874 to 1882. Thereafter, he remained in Berlin working privately, with a certain elaboration of subject and a loosening of technique said to be a result of the study of Dutch seventeenth-century painting.

Knaus undoubtedly contributed to the trend toward naturalism that was international in scope. Though his direct influence in French painting may have been confined to the later works of Gustave Brion, as was noted by Alfred de Lostalot ("Louis Knaus," *Gazette des Beaux-Arts* 2nd pér. 25 (1882): 384), his followers among the German genre painters were legion.

198. The Truant

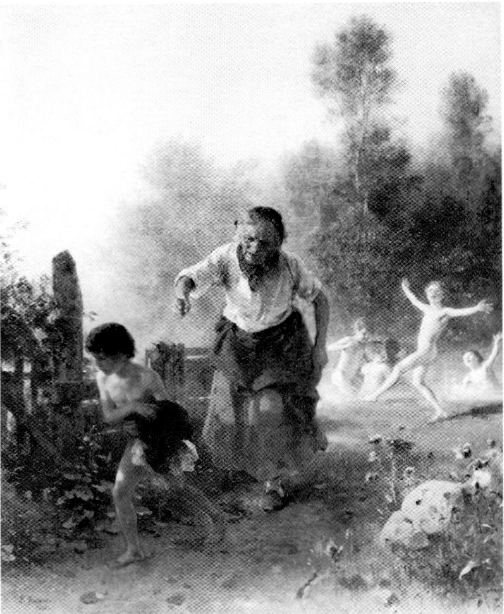

37.187 1861

An elderly teacher pursues a naked young boy who flees, carrying his clothes over his arm. Behind, in a shallow pond, several youths are cavorting, one of whom prances beside the water jeering at the departing figure. A warm evening light permeates the scene.

The model for the old teacher was used by Knaus in several works including *The Village Sorceress* (1885) and *The Potato Gathering* (1889).

Support: Canvas, .583 x .455 (23" x 18")

Signed and dated lower left: *L. Knaus/1861*

Condition: Cleaned and lined in 1975.

Provenance: Purchased by W. T. Walters between 1888 and 1892.

References: Lamb, p. 248; Walters cat., 1893, p. 6, no. 4, and subsequent Walters catalogues.

199. Mud Pies

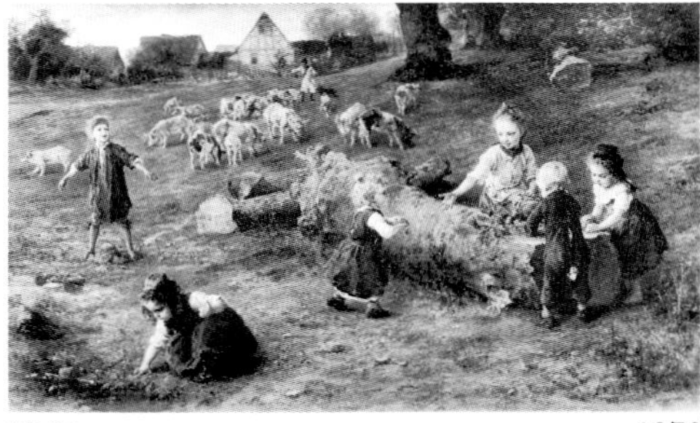

37.21 1873

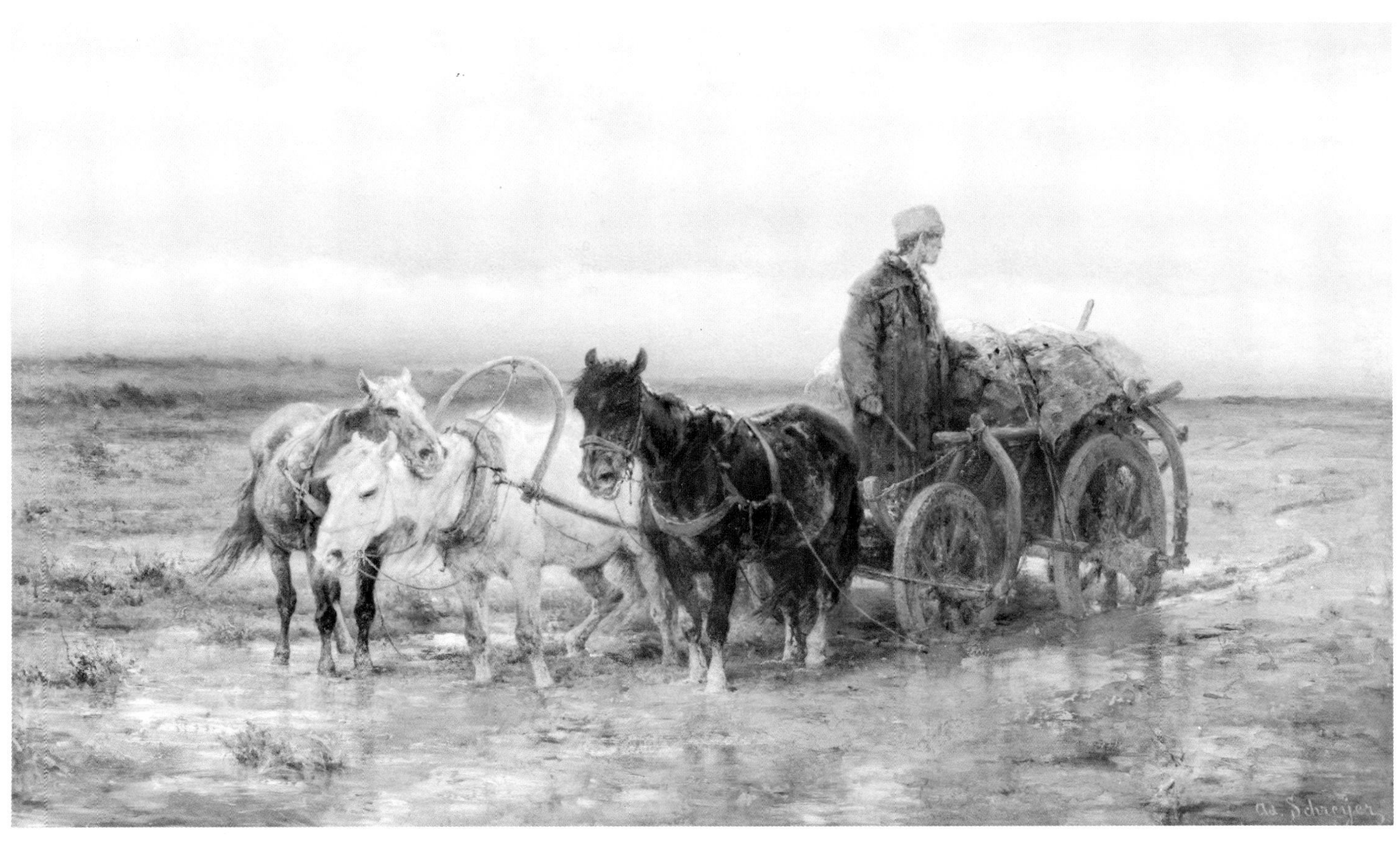

Schreyer *Embourbé (Mired), The Plains of Hungary,* no. 196

A girl seated on a log in the foreground supervises some children making mud pies. In the immediate left foreground a toddler kneels beside a puddle to gather a fresh supply of mud. Behind her a youth straddles a pile of dirt. In the middleground, a swineherd tends his pigs and at the horizon is a cluster of houses. As the daylight appears to be waning, colors throughout the work are uniformly low-keyed.

In the Staatsgalerie, Stuttgart, is a roughly sketched study for this picture in oils on paper, inv. 2143 (.18 x .29). A drawing for the little girl in the center of the composition was published in Ludwig Pietsch, *Knaus,* Leipzig, 1896, p. 29, fig. 20. The model for this girl also served as the principal figure in *A Critical Moment,* 1872, which shows her confronted by two angry geese.

Alternative titles: *Dirt Pies; Mudlarks; Spielende kinder; Kindervergnügen im Sand; Les petits cochons*

Support: Canvas, finely woven and preprimed, .644 x 1.094 (25⅜" x 43¼")

Condition: Cleaned and lined in 1975.

Signed and dated in black at lower right: *L. Knaus/1873*

Marks: Paper sticker on frame: *Th. Wilmurt and Son / New York;* Paper sticker on frame: *Spiegel - u. Bilder-Rahmen-Fabrik / C. Polster Hof-Vergolder / Behrens-Str. 12. Berlin / Rahmen in Holz geschnitzt und in Holzmass nach allen Arten / von Zeichnungen und Modellen*

Provenance: Anton Ritter von Oeltzelt, Vienna, 1878, no. 35, 17,000 gulden.

Exhibitions: "Ludwig Knaus," Museum Wiesbaden, Staatliche Kunstsammlungen Kassel, Kunstmuseum Düsseldorf, 1979–80, no. 91.

References: Walters cat., 1878, p. 37 and subsequent Walters catalogues; Strahan, I:94; Alfred de Lostalot, "Louis Knaus," *GBA* 2nd pér. 25 (1882): 381, engraving of painting by Th. Knesing reproduced p. 273; Helen Zimmern, "A painter of children," *The Magazine of Art* (London) 8 (1885): 332; Champlin and Perkins, 2: 393; Lamb, pp. 248, 249 (illus.); Ludwig Pietsch, *Knaus.* Bielefeld, Velhagen & Klasing, 1896. p. 29, illus. 20; Thomas B. Brumbaugh, "Lost in storage: Ludwig Knaus in American collections," *Art Journal* 27 (1968): 264, fig. 3.

Leopold Karl Müller
German-Austrian: Dresden, 1835 - Vienna, 1892

Leopold Karl Müller is noted for his realistic treatment of Near Eastern subjects. He studied at the Vienna Academy from 1852 to 1861 under Karl von Blaas and Christian Ruben. Following the death of his father Leopold M. Müller, the noted chromolithographer, he abandoned painting to support his mother and family, illustrating a newspaper. In 1867 Müller received a stipend from the Minister of Culture and Education in Vienna, enabling him to attend the Paris Exposition Universelle where he was drawn to the oriental subjects of the French painter, Eugène Fromentin. In 1871–72 he painted in Italy and in the winter of 1973–74 he first visited Egypt, where he met his fellow realists Hans Makart and Franz Lenbach. An outcome of this trip was the famed *Market in Cairo* completed in 1878. Müller subsequently divided his time between his studio in Vienna, and Cairo. He prospered from a large following, particularly in London where his works were sold in the French Gallery by H. Wallis, successor to Ernest Gambart. Müller was appointed a professor at the Vienna Academy in 1871 and became its director in 1890.

200. Profile Head of a Young Woman

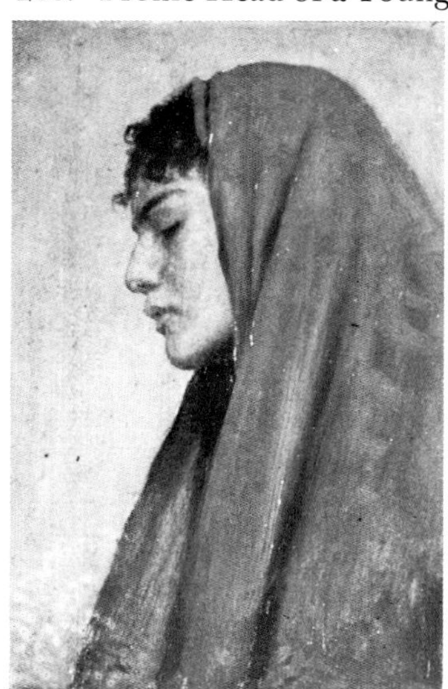

37.1012

The young Egyptian woman is shown facing left. She wears a bluish grey mantle over her head. The background has been lightly painted in a greyish tone. Early Walters catalogues list this work and the following picture as two of five studies painted from life in Egypt.

Support: Oil on panel, beveled sides, actual: .264 x .161 (10⅜" x 6⅜"); visible: .253 x .161 (9 15/16" x6⅜")

Marks: Panel impressed: *GIOSI/NAPOLI;* Frame stamped: *Cole Bros. London*

References: Walters cat., 1878, p. 40, and subsequent Walters catalogues; Strahan, 1: 94; Champlin and Perkins, 3: 312.

201. Profile Head of a Young Girl

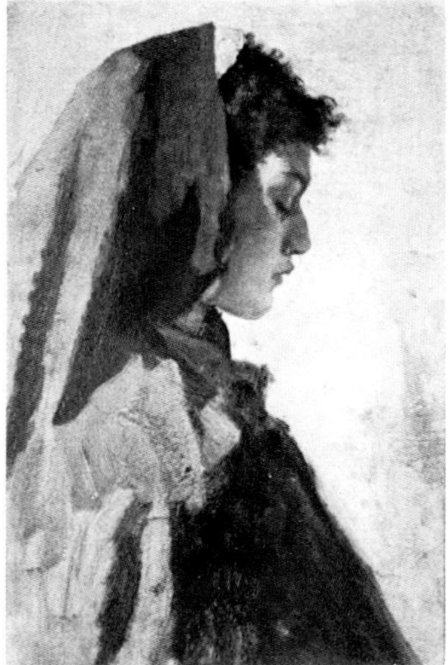

37.1013

The model for the previous painting is portrayed facing right. Her head is slightly bowed and eyes closed. Unlike the previous work, in which the illumination is low-keyed and even, in this rendering, the lighting is strong and directed from above and behind, creating shadows in the girl's face and in her garments. The background is light grey above and beige below.

Support: Panel, beveled sides, .263 x .164 (10 5/16" x 6⅜")

Marks: Reverse impressed: *GIOSI/NAPOLI*

References: Walters cat., 1878, p. 40, and subsequent Walters catalogues; Strahan, 1: 94; Champlin and Perkins, 3: 312.

Franz Seraph von Lenbach
German: Schrobenhausen (Munich), 1836 - Munich, 1904

Lenbach, the son of a village builder, received a rudimentary education from a trade school in Landshut and also studied at a polytechnical school in Augsburg. He painted initially with the animal specialist, J. B. Hofner, worked briefly in Munich with the sculptor Anselm Sickinger, and studied for less than two months in the studio of the Munich painter Albert Gräfle. Though essentially self-trained, he proved sufficiently competent to receive commissions for the occasional portrait and votive picture.

In 1857 he entered Karl Theodor von Piloty's atelier at the Munich Academy and after receiving a state stipend, he accompanied his teacher to Italy in the winter of 1858–59. The *Arch of Titus,* 1858, Munich, Städtische Galerie, painted at daybreak, illustrates Lenbach's early prowess as a colorist and naturalist. In 1860 he received a position at the Weimar Art School, where he taught with Arnold Böcklin and Reinhold Begas until 1862, when he returned to Munich. Thereupon Count Schack commissioned him to execute copies of Old Master paintings in Italy. From 1863 to 1866, Lenbach resided in Rome, sharing a studio with Böcklin and Ludwig von Hayn, and copying such works as Titian's *Sacred and Profane Love* in the Borghese Palace, Murillo's *Virgin and Child* in the Corsini, and further afield, in Florence, Giorgione's *Concert* and Andrea del Sarto's *Self-Portrait*. At the Paris Exposition Universelle of 1867, Lenbach exhibited portraits of his sister and himself, winning a third-class medal and establishing his reputation as a portraitist.

He continued to serve Schack as a copyist, going to Spain with a colleague, Ernst von Liphart, in the autumn and winter of 1867 and continuing with his patron to Tangier the following spring. This trip yielded copies of Titian's *Equestrian Portrait of Charles V*, Titian's *Herodias* and Velasquez' *Philip IV*, as well as several views of Granada and the Alhambra.

Thus, thoroughly steeped in sixteenth– and seventeenth–century painting, Lenbach began to devote his energies to portraiture, working in Munich, Vienna, and Berlin between 1871 and 1874. In 1875–76 he accompanied the painters Hans Makart and L. C. Müller to Egypt, a trip that proved to be of greater significance to his colleagues than to himself. At Bad Kissingen in 1878, he met Otto, Fürst von Bismarck. A result of the warm friendship that developed between the two men was a series of eighty portraits of the Chancellor that became national effigies.

In the eighties, Lenbach continued to produce portraits, dividing his time between Rome in the winter months, and Munich. In 1883 he commissioned the architect Gabriel von Seidl to design the Renaissance-style villa in Munich that now serves as the Städtische Galerie. Lenbach's later years were remarkably productive. Because of his formidable technical virtuosity and his energy, he was able to execute innumerable portraits, working at great speed and from only one or two brief sittings. As one of the most esteemed portraitists in the German-speaking countries, if not throughout Europe, he received commissions from royalty, heads of state, politicians, men of letters, musicians, artists, and numbers of beautiful women. Famous works include his portraits of Pope Leo XIII (1885), Kaiser Wilhelm I (1888), Albert of Saxony, Richard Wagner, Franz Liszt, among others.

202. Portrait of Otto Eduard Leopold von Bismarck, 1890

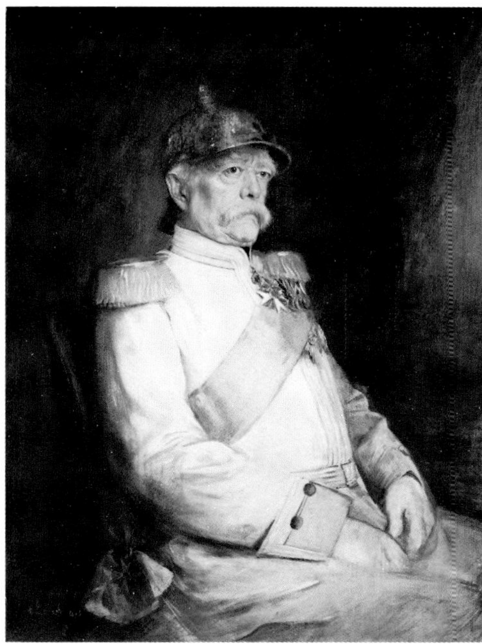

37.1007 1890

Bismarck, painted in his seventy-fifth year, is depicted seated, and turned slightly to his left. He wears the white uniform of the Magdeburg Cuirassiers' Regiment no. 7. Displayed across his breast is the yellow ribbon of the Order of the Black Eagle; the cross of that order is visible at his right hip. Pinned across his left side are a number of indecipherible medals. His gloved hands are held loosely in his lap. The cuirassier's helmet has been pushed upward to reveal the Chancellor's face with its distinctive bushy brows and mustache.

Early accounts (see below) indicate that this portrait was based on studies made from life in the winter of 1889–90. One of over eighty portraits of Bismarck, this picture is almost identical to a portrait in the Städtische Galerie im Lenbachhaus, Munich. The latter, measuring 1.19 x .96, is signed and dated *F. Lenbach/Friedrichruh 1890*.

Support: Panel, cradled, 1.21 x .875 (47⅝" x 34⁷⁄₁₆")

Signed and dated lower left: *F. Lenbach 1890*

Condition: An early photograph of this painting, preserved in the album, *German Painters of the Nineteenth Century*, Art Division, New York Public Library, indicated that in certain areas, particularly in the helmet, the pigment has lost some of its opacity.

Provenance: Purchased in New York by Henry Walters in the early twentieth century.

Exhibitions: This work was exhibited in Kunstvereins-Ausstellung, in Munich, March-April, 1890, and in the residence of the owner of Fleischmann's Hof-Kunsthandlung zu München on the Kaiserhof in Berlin in April and May, 1890, according to German newspaper clippings reproduced in an anonymous, undated pamphlet, *International Art Gallery*, 576 Fifth Avenue, New York, in the Art Division, New York Public Library; "War à la Mode," Walters Art Gallery, Baltimore, 1977, no. W.19.

Eduard Kurzbauer

Austrian-German: Vienna, 1840 - Munich, 1879

Before his untimely death at the age of thirty-nine, this artist achieved an international reputation, as a master of characterization and a recorder of Swabian and Tyrolean village life. In 1856 Kurzbauer began to attend the evening classes of Joseph von Führich at the Vienna Academy while working for a lithography firm. In 1867 a stipend from a family friend enabled him to enroll in Von Piloty's classes at the Munich Academy. In 1870 he exhibited *The Overtaken Fugitive* (Österreichische Galerie, Vienna) a painting which launched his career. Thereafter, he produced his distinctive genre scenes.

203. The Dispute

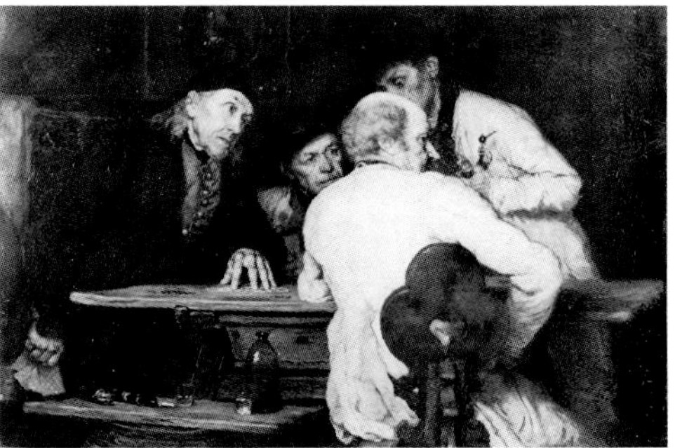

37.102 1877

Four elderly German men are playing cards. One, seated with his back to the viewer, turns his head away from his companions who, in annoyance, begin to rise to their feet. This painting exhibits Kurzbauer's adroitness at characterization.

Support: Canvas, .474 x .657 (18¾" x 25¾")

Signed and dated in black script at lower right: *E. Kurzbauer/München 1877*

Provenance: Acquired from S. P. Avery in 1878 according to a pencil notation by H. Walters in an early catalogue.

References: Walters cat., 1878, p. 36, and subsequent Walters catalogues; Strahan, 1: 94; Champlin and Perkins, 2: 47.

Gabriel Cornelius Ritter von Max

Austrian-German: Prague, 1840 - Munich, 1915

Max was associated with the Munich School as a painter of Biblical and historical themes marked by their sentimental, even lachrymose overtones. In Prague he trained with his father, the sculptor Joseph Franz Max, and in 1855, at the city's Academy under Eduard von Engerth. He was, from 1855 to 1859, at the Vienna Academy where he was reported to have been drawn more to the library than to the studio of his teacher, Carl von Blaas. Back in Prague in 1859–60, Max produced an album of highly personal and original illustrations to Beethoven's sonatas. In 1863, he entered the Munich Academy under Karl von Piloty. During his four years at the Academy, he shared studios first with Eduard Kurzbauer and later with Hans Makart. At the 1867 Munich Exhibition, he drew considerable attention with his painting, *Crucified St. Julia*. Thereafter, Max's reputation was established with such works as *Nydia, The Last Token* (1874), *Ahasuerus and the Body of a Child, The Child Murderess* (1878), and *Astarte* (1884). From 1879 to 1883, he served as professor at the Munich Academy. Late in his career, he executed a number of bizarre singeries, *Der Diplomat, Bücherfreunde* and the occasional ape-man subject such as the *Pithecanthropos alalos* (1894).

204. The Raising of the Daughter of Jairus

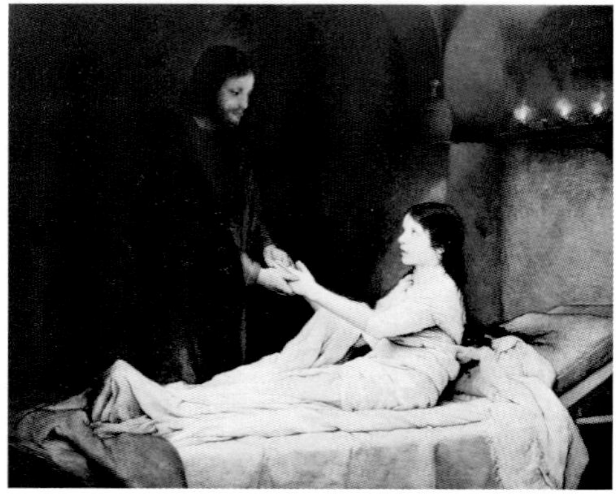

37.170 1881

Christ is depicted raising from the dead the twelve year old daughter of Jairus, a ruler of the Synagogue, as related in St. Mark 5: 22–43 and St. Luke 8: 41–56. Max shows Christ standing beside the bier taking the hands of the ashenfaced girl who stares at the Saviour and begins to rise. The setting is an interior, dimly illuminated by three oil lamps placed on a shelf behind the bier. In the right corner, a realistically painted beetle is crawling toward the child's pillow.

This painting is a sequel to the much larger *Talitha Cumi, The Raising of Jairus' Daughter* (1.232 x 1.801), exhibited at the 1878 Exposition Universelle and now in the Musée des Beaux-Arts, Montreal, no. 117. In the earlier picture, Christ is sitting on the bed contemplating the child, who lies unconscious before him. Visible on the girl's arm is a fly which achieves the same trompe l'oeil as the beetle in the Baltimore painting. The model for the figure of Christ, who appears identical in both works, has been identified by J. Beavington Atkinson, "'Gabriel Max," *The Art Journal*, London, (June 1881): 176, as Joseph Mair, who enacted the Lord in the Oberammergau Passion Play. The girl, however, in the two works differs. The model in the Walters picture is also shown in Max's *A Flower is Thrown to Her as the Last Token of Love*, a Colosseum subject, and in *Evangeline* and *Joan of Arc*. J. Beavington Atkinson (op. cit., p. 178) alluded to seeing a variation of the 1878 picture in Max's studio in Munich in 1880–81. This later work may be the Baltimore painting.

Support: Canvas, .719 x .879 (28 5/16" x 34 5/8")

Signed and dated lower right: *G. Max / 1881*

Marks: Stencils on canvas: *Wimmer & Co./Gallery of Fine Arts/Munich; Fritz Schachinger/ München;* Written in black chalk: *M 3900/Friedrich*

Condition: Cleaned and lined in 1967.

Provenance: Wimmer and Co., Munich, 1881; Heber R. Bishop Sale, New York, The American Art Association, 1906, no. 58, to Henry Walters for $1,850.00

References: J. Beavington Atkinson "Gabriel Max," *The Art Journal* (London) 33 (1881): 178; Walters cat., 1909, p. 58, no. 170, and subsequent Walters catalogues.

August Xaver Karl von Pettenkofen

Austrian: Vienna, 1822 - Vienna, 1889

The Austrian artist Pettenkofen evolved a luminist style of painting that paralleled French Impressionism.

He trained in the Vienna Academy from 1834 to 1841, when he undertook military obligations serving in swank mounted regiments until invalided by scrofula in 1843. Back at the Academy, he allegedly received guidance from the history and genre painter Josef Danhauser. Next he worked in Vienna as a portraitist and later entered the lithography studio of Franz Eybl. A gifted draftsman, Pettenkofen was soon widely admired for his lithographs illustrating the writings of Alois Leykum and Eduard Duller; he was also known for others recording the Hungarian military campaign of 1848–49, as well as for his illustrations used in the Viennese humorous journal, *Der Kobold*.

In 1851 Pettenkofen traveled to Paris and established contacts with J.-L.-E. Meissonier, the Belgians Alfred Stevens and Florent Willems, and several Barbizon masters. His painting quickly evolved from the dry, linear manner of his early Viennese works to a more expressive painterly style, a change which was first noted in *Transportation of the Wounded Hungarian Volunteers*, exhibited in 1852 at the Cercle de l'Union artistique in the Palais Bourbon. He soon became known as the "Austrian Meissonier," perhaps an allusion to similarities between his scenes of rural life in Hungary and Bohemia, his principal subjects after 1851, and the French artist's sunlit views of the countryside near Antibes. Regarded as somewhat idiosyncratic in his native city, Pettenkofen spent considerable time away in the sixties and seventies, traveling in central Europe and Italy. Nevertheless he received considerable official recognition: he was elected a member of the Vienna Academy in 1866 and of the Munich Academy the following year; in 1876 he was knighted a Chevalier of the Order of the Crown of Oak and was appointed a professor at the Vienna Academy in 1880. His career in the last decade of his life was hindered by deteriorating health.

205. The Market of Szolnok, Hungary

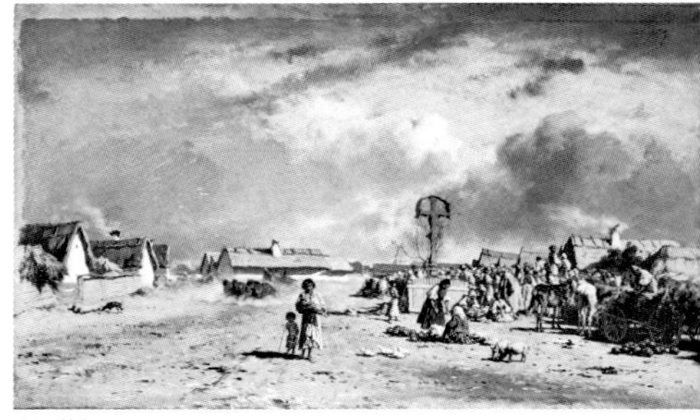

37.53

Szolnok, located on the Theiss River in central Hungary, was an important market centre of 11,000 inhabitants in the mid-nineteenth century. Pettenkofen first visited it in 1851, and returned repeatedly over the next thirty years.

In this work the sunlight has broken through the cloudy sky to illuminate a colorful marketplace surrounded by low houses with white walls and thatched roofs. On the right, near a wayside cross enclosed by a picket fence, peasants mill about the vegetable stands and wagons. Several piles of large green melons are visible. Livestock forage freely in the dusty terrain. Close to the foreground is a bedraggled gypsy nursing an infant followed by another child.

Alternative title: *Der grosse ungarische Markt*

Support: Panel of three-ply, laminated wood, beveled on three sides, .289 x .484 (11 3/8" x 19 1/16")

Marks: Signed in script, upper right: *Pettenkofen;* Stencil on reverse: *WIMMER & CO / GALLERY OF FINE ARTS/ MUNICH;* Impressed on reverse: *TACHET / BREVETTE / A PARIS*

Condition: Discolored varnish removed in 1972.

Provenance: F. J. Gsell, Sale, Vienna, March 14, 1872; Antoine W. Oelzelt, Sale, Vienna, November 18–19, 1878, no. 56, 8500 guldens.

References: Alfred de Lostalot, "Ventes à l'Hôtel Drouot," *GBA* 2nd pér. 15 (1877) : 415; Clement and Hutton, 2: 177; Walters cat., 1884, p. 70, no. 110; Champlin and Perkins, 3: 430.

Mihaly Munkacsy

Hungarian: Munkacs, 1844 - Endenich, 1909

Hungary's celebrated genre painter and early realist was born Mihaly Lieb in Munkacs, East Hungary (now the Ukrainian S.S.R.). After the death of his father during the 1848–49 national uprising and that of his mother two years later, he was adopted by an uncle who apprenticed him to a cabinet-maker in Arad. Overwork caused his health to deteriorate and while recuperating, he practised drawing by copying prints. A German-born provincial painter in Gyula, named Fischer, gave him his first instruction, but his principal early teacher was an itinerant artist, Elek Szamossy, who had been engaged to copy portraits in the Schloss Venkheim, Gyula. In 1863 Munkacsy arrived in Pesth (Budapest) where he befriended Pettenkofen and became a protegé of Antal Ligeti, the curator of the Bildergalerie. While there, Munkacsy also undertook illustrations for Budapest journals. In 1865 he proceeded to Vienna to become a pupil of Karl Rahl, but an eye affliction forced him to return to Budapest. Two years later, receiving a stipend from the local Art Society, he entered the Munich Academy under Franz Adam. Far more consequential for his development, however, was a journey to Paris that year to the Exposition Universelle. Admiring Courbet's exhibit, he sought out the French realist and met several Barbizon painters. Between 1867 and 1871, Munkacsy worked in Düsseldorf under the direction of Ludwig Knaus. It was there that he painted *The Last Day of a Condemned Man,* a picture showing the curious public visiting the cell of the condemned prisoner awaiting execution. This realistic depiction of a prevailing Hungarian practice was exhibited at the 1870 Paris Salon. It was enthusiastically praised by the critics Castagnary and Gautier and was later acquired by William P. Wilstach of Philadelphia, the first of Munkacsy's many American patrons. In 1872, the artist settled in Paris and worked for a while in the village of Barbizon with his compatriot Ladislas de Paal in 1873. The following decade proved an unqualified success both socially and professionally. He was married in 1874 to the wealthy widow of the Baron Demarches and within seven years was ensconced in a large hôtel on the Avenue Villiers. At the Salons, he exhibited stark, realistic views of contemporary life, set either in Hungary or in France, rendered in his distinctive, somber palette with brilliant, remarkably free brush strokes. The Medal of Honor was awarded to him at the 1878 Exposition Universelle, where he showed *Interior of a Studio* (1876), *The Conscript* (1877), and *Milton dictating "Paradise Lost" to his Daughters* (1878), his masterpiece now in the New York Public Library. About this time he produced a number of scenes of wealthy bourgeois interiors that recalled similar works by the Belgian Alfred Stevens and anticipated those of the American, William Merritt Chase. In the eighties, his energies were directed to a series of truly monumental historical and Biblical subjects which were featured in independent exhibits rather than at the Salons. His *Apothéose de la Renaissance,* painted as a ceiling decoration for the Kunsthistorisches Museum in Vienna, was shown in the 1890 Salon. Later travels included a triumphant return to Hungary in 1882 and a voyage to America in the winter of 1886–87 to promote the sale of his *Christ Before Pilate* (1881). There, he was fêted at dinners given by Secretary of the Navy Whitney and by the painter, Albert Bierstadt, and despite the brevity of his visit (six weeks), he painted portraits of Joseph Pulitzer, Henry C. Marquand, and Dr. McCosh, President of Princeton University. In 1895, while completing an *Ecce Homo,* he developed a nervous disorder which compelled him to leave Paris for Endenich near Bonn where he died in 1909.

206. The Story of a Battle

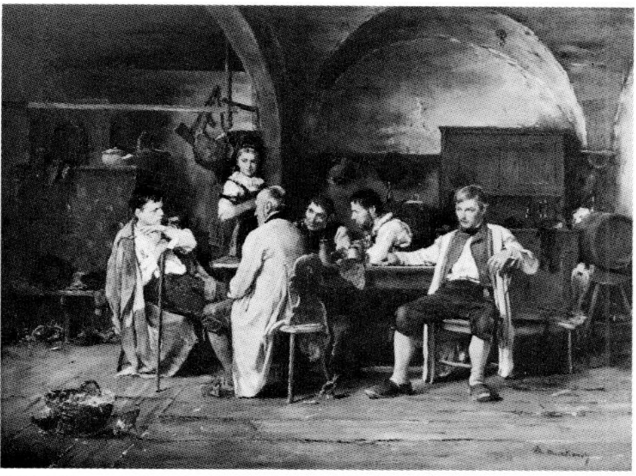

37.60 c. 1875

Four men are grouped around a table in an inn listening to a fifth who is describing a battle that occurred during the 1848–49 Hungarian uprising against Austrian Hapsburg domination. The narrator, a wan young man, distinguished by the great coat draped over his shoulders, and his military breeches with frogging, clutches a crutch as he talks. A young waitress in peasant costume stands behind the table. Discernible in the background are a green ceramic stove, a cupboard, a wine barrel, cooking utensils, and, suspended from pegs, a knapsack and musket, a pitcher and a hat. Poultry run loose across the floor.

Though undated, this painting can be associated with a couple of works pertaining to the 1848–49 uprising: *The Lint Makers* (1871), National Gallery, Budapest, in which figures are grouped around a table preparing bandages, and *The Recruits* (1877), showing a similar scene with a young man parting from a girl. It was the artist's practice to employ photographs in delineating his figures. A photograph of the model for the young soldier leaning on his crutch who is identical in pose and position to that of a similar figure in *The Lint Makers* is published by Bartha Attila in "A Munkácsy-hagvaték fotográfiáiról." *Müvészet* 78, no. 7 (July 1978): 8. fig. 5. Lajos Végvári in his *Katalog der Gemälde und Zeichnungen Mihály Munkacsys,* Budapest, 1959, lists, on p. 50, no. 219, another possibly related work, *Verwundeter Wanderer,* in the Municipal Museum, Szeged, as well as two preliminary charcoal studies, p. 108, nos. 108–109, one in the National Gallery, Budapest (N. G. 1935-2915), and the other unlocated. A study showing the servant girl posed in the right foreground rather than in the background is reproduced by René Delorme in *Chefs d'oeuvre d'art à l'Expositon universelle,* Paris, 1878, p. 68. Finally, a painting showing a servant, *Mädchen mit Tablett* (1876) very similar to the girl in the Baltimore picture is illustrated by Végvári in his 1959 catalogue, p. 50, no. 220.

Alternative titles: *Verwundeter Wanderer; Mese egy csatáröl*

Support: Fabric, 1.035 x 1.3993 (40¾" x 54⅞")

Signed lower right: *M Munkacsy*

Condition: Lined and cleaned in 1976.

Provenance: Acquired by W. T. Walters directly from Theodor Eggers of Vienna between 1878 and 1884.

References: Walters cat., 1884, p. 65, no. 106, and subsequent Walters catalogues; Champlin and Perkins, 3: 314; Lamb, p. 251; Dezsö Malonyay, *Munkácsy Mihály.* 2 vols. Budapest, Lampel R., 1907. 2:15; Lajos Végvári, *Katalog der Gemälde und Zeichnungen Mihály Munkácsys.* Budapest, Akadémiai Kiadó, 1959. pp. 50 (no. 218); 75 (no. 108).

Josef Brandt

Polish: Szczebrzeszyn, 1841 - Radom, 1915

Brandt, a painter of military campaigns and eastern European trail scenes in which horses serve as a recurring motif, distinguished himself as the leader of a coterie of Polish artists active in Munich in the 1870s.

Initially intending to become an engineer, Brandt left Poland in 1858 to study in Paris at the Ecole des Ponts et Chaussées. He was persuaded, however, by a Polish follower of Horace Vernet, Juliusz Kossak, to turn to painting, and enrolled in the atelier of Léon Cogniet. He also continued to receive the counsel of Kossak and Henryk Rodakowski. In 1862 Brandt transferred from Paris to Munich to train under Franz Adam, Theodor Horschelt and Karl Piloty. Four years later he opened his own studio in

Munich, which emerged as a focal point for the "Munich school of Polish painters," an informal band of realists of Polish origin that included Alfred Wierusz-Kowalski, Wojciech Kossak, Stanislaw Batowski and Maksymilian Gierymski. Each summer Brandt returned to his property at Oronsko near Radom, south of Warsaw. In search of exotic subjects he frequently traveled eastward, visiting the Volhynia and Podolia regions of the Ukraine and the then European portions of Turkey.

Brandt participated in various national and international exhibitions, winning a gold medal in Munich in 1869, and another in Berlin in 1876; in 1873, he received the order of Franz Joseph and was elected to the Berlin Academy in 1875 and the Munich Academy in 1878.

207. On Reconnaissance

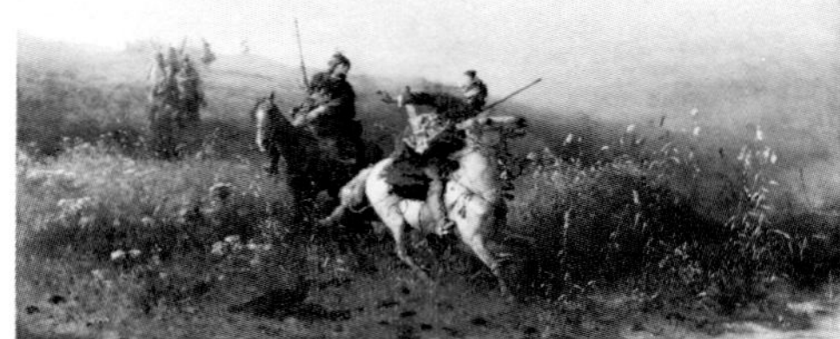

37.2569 1876

Brandt, a consummate painter of horses, shows in this relatively small painting, a procession of Tartar horsemen proceeding across a plain. The figure on a dapple horse in the central foreground, startled by something in the rushes at the right, halts and raises his hand to caution a companion.

Support: Preprimed fabric: .485 x 1.12 (19⅛" x 44⅛")

Signed at lower left: *Josef Brandt / 1876*

Condition: Prior to 1980 a small area in front of the foremost horse had been damaged and overpainted. Several small losses in the sky and the right foreground were inpainted in 1980; the fabric was lined, discolored varnishes removed and replaced with synthetic varnish.

Provenance: Gift of Mr. and Mrs. L. Whiting Farinholt, 1980.

Carl Pavlovich Brüloff
Russian: St. Petersburg, 1799 - Marciano (Italy), 1852

Brüloff, an early romantic painter in Russia, specialized in portraits and historical scenes. After studying at the Imperial Academy at St. Petersburg under A. A. Ivanoff, Brüloff left Russia in 1823 for Italy. In Rome, he executed a number of copies, including one of Raphael's *School of Athens,* commissioned by the Tsar. Other works from his Italian period included *The Last Day of Pompeii* and *The Death of Inès de Castro* (a Castillian girl killed in 1355). Returning to Russia, he was appointed an official court painter. Brüloff again departed from Russia in 1835 to travel in Asia Minor. Brüloff is represented in the Hermitage by a number of religious and early historical scenes as well as by portraits of such notable subjects as the Empress Alexandra-Fedorovna, A. P. Demidoff, Grand-duchess Marie Nicholaievna, and others.

Attributed to Brüloff
208. The Retreat from Russia

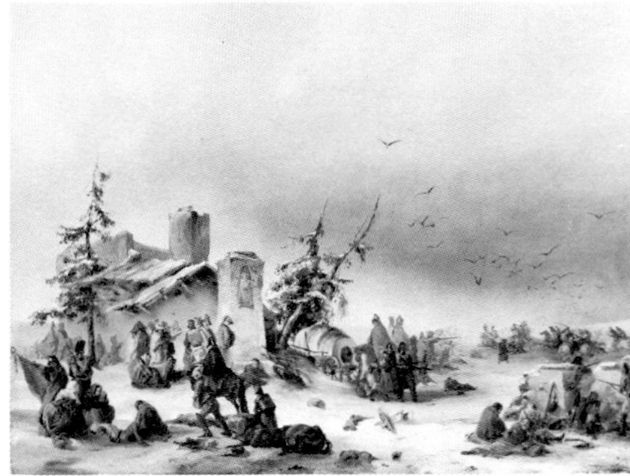

37.1742

Remnants of Napoleon's Grand Army retreating from Moscow in the winter of 1812–13 have bivouacked around a ruined church. The foreground is cluttered with debris and huddled figures. Discernible are grenadiers of the Garde Imperiale and members of the regular forces. A tonsured monk is praying at the base of a religious image exposed on the building's wall. In the background French soldiers ward off attacking Cossacks. Ominously hovering overhead in the leaden skies are flocks of vultures.

Support: Linen, .345 x .45 (13⅝" x 17¾")

Marks: Inscribed in ink on stretcher: *Roubles 160 Francs 700/ Le retour de la Russie Eboche* (sic) *Ch. Brueloff école russe*

Provenance: Marcello Massarenti Collection before 1897; purchased by Henry Walters in 1902 as part of the Massarenti Collection.

References: *Catalogue du musée de peinture, sculpture et archéologie au Palais Accoramboni,* 2 vols., Rome, Imprimerie du Vatican, 1897, 1: 146, no. 851.

Ivan Pavlovich Pochitonoff (Pokitonow)
Russian: Matrenowka, 1850 - Liège, 1923

Pochitonoff, a specialist in miniature landscapes and portraits, traveled extensively outside Russia beginning in 1878. He is represented in the Tretyakov Gallery, Moscow, by paintings executed at Pau (1885 and 1890) and Barbizon (1889) in France, Trou-Louette (1894–1895) and La Panne (1895) in Belgium and at Mount Vesuvius near Naples.

209. River Scene

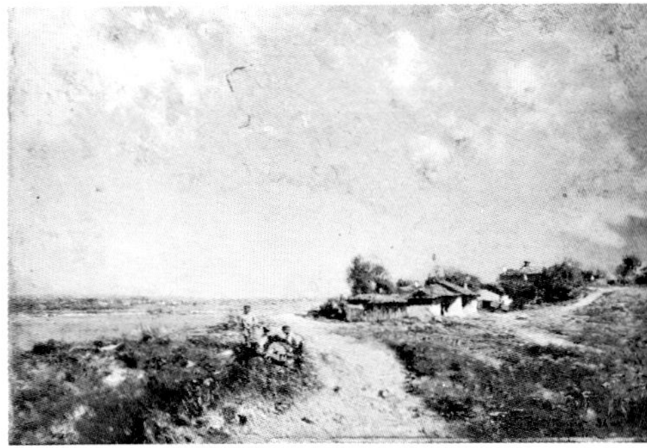

37.2432 1886

Several youths wearing grey caps are playing beside a dirt road that leads to a cluster of low, stuccoed houses beside a river. The flat terrain and the architecture of the houses suggest that the artist has represented a Russian scene.

A miniature pasture scene by Pochitonoff, also painted in 1886, was given to the Metropolitan Museum of Art, New York, in 1907, as part of the Thomas P. Salter Collection. It bears a similar signature to the Walters picture *"J Pokitonow 86"* and the number *N 26.*

Support: Panel, beveled edges, .108 x .155 (4¼" x 6⅛")

Signed and dated at lower right: *Pokitonow 86an/ N7*

Marks: Inscribed on reverse: *J Pokitonow 1886 Zoga;* Paper sticker numbered *5287*

Condition: In 1982, discolored varnishes were removed.

Provenance: Gift of Miss Laura Delano, 1965.

Spanish and Italian Paintings

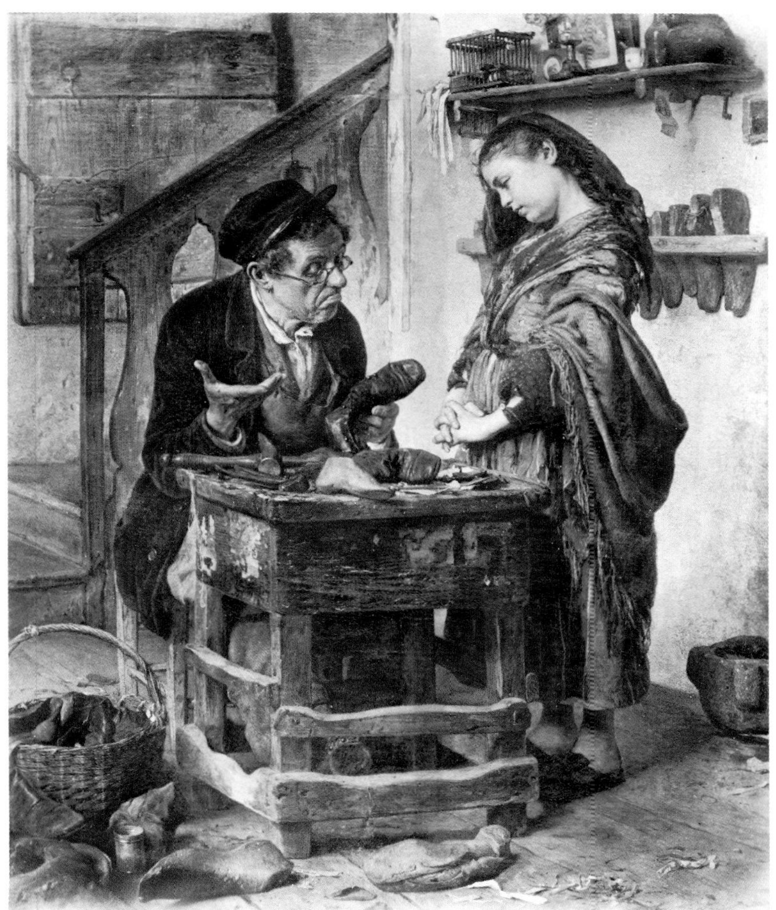

Rotta *The Hopeless Case,* no. 230

Eugenio Lucas y Padilla (the Elder)

Spanish: Alcalá de Henares, 1824 - Madrid, 1870

Little is known of this mid-century artist who worked in the manner of Goya in his late period. Jeannine Bactile in "Eugenio Lucas et les satellites de Goya," *La Revue du Louvre* 22, no. 3 (1972): 163–76, has ascertained that Lucas was in Paris in 1844 concurrently with Pérez Villaamil, another Spaniard who is credited with influencing his colleague's development. Among Lucas' earliest documented paintings were a portrait of the chaplain of Charles IV, *Excmo D. Leandro Alvarez* (1848) and the *Plaza partida* (1848) both of which were shown in the Exposition Universelle, Paris, 1855. Also exhibited on this occasion was *Révolution à Madrid,* recording an event of the previous year. Some inscribed drawings in the José Lázaro y Galdiano collection, Madrid, substantiate the report that Lucas was engaged in decorating the ceiling of the parterre of the Royal Theater in Madrid in 1850. Other inscribed drawings in the same collection confirm his presence in Venice in 1868. Finally, Bactile quotes the account-book of the Marcial Torres Adalid, which records commissions Lucas received for paintings executed in the manner of Goya and Teniers while visiting Orense, Galicia, between 1867 and 1870.

The paintings of Lucas' son, Eugenio Lucas y Villaamil (1861–1918) have often been confused with those of the father.

Circle of E. Lucas
210. The Procession

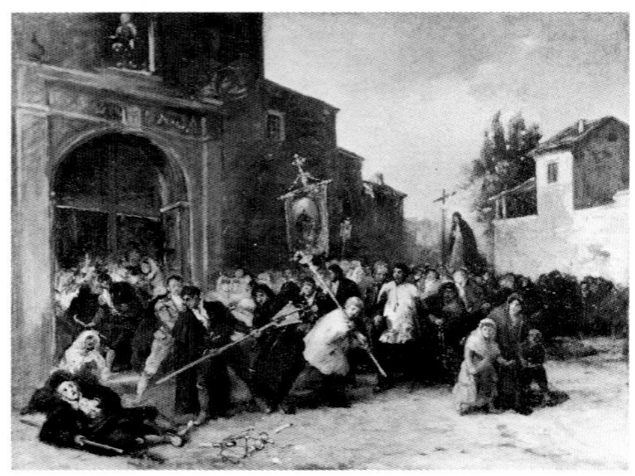

37.161

As a religious procession approaches a church, a scuffle between two lantern-bearers ensues in which the elder is left sprawled on the ground clutching the shattered shaft of his light. Varying degrees of consternation are expressed by the onlookers. An acolyte struggling with his heavy silver candlestick turns away, while a mother clutching her children scurries off to the right. Swaying over the throng are a banner, a lantern, and the *pasos* of the Via Crucis and the Mater Dolorosa.

Lucas frequently depicted processions associated with Holy Week. As Elizabeth Du Gué Trapier has observed in *Eugenio Lucas y Padilla,* New York, 1940, pp. 34–35, the artist preferred interrupted rather than dignified processions. Examples that could be cited include *A Procession,* The Hispanic Society of America, A 153, in which a storm threatens the proceedings, and *Procession attacked by a Bull,* also at the Society, A 216. In *Fight in a Procession,* Don José Graells collection, Barcelona, the broken lamp-shaft motif is encountered in the foreground and in *Procession, Holy Week,* formerly in the Señor Añes collection, Barcelona, a figure also lies sprawled in the foreground.

Recently, scholars have attributed the Baltimore painting to a follower of Lucas rather than to the artist himself, noting the picturesque quality of the scene and the lack of vigor in its execution.

Support: Coarsely woven fabric, .673 x .89 (26½" x 35")

Condition: In examining the picture under raking light, the contours of an earlier picture become visible. X-rays taken in 1972 reveal a provincial Spanish, late seventeenth- or early eighteenth-century religious subject painted vertically. Priscilla E. Muller of The Hispanic Society of America, has identified the subject as the Virgin of Mt. Carmel, intercessor for souls in Purgatory. At the left in the early painting there are several figures, perhaps those of souls in Purgatory. Barely discernible at the right is the Child depositing scapulars in a basket. The sky visible in the nineteenth-century picture has suffered some abrasion.

Provenance: Purchased by Henry Walters between 1903 and 1909.

References: Walters cat., 1909, p. 55, no. 161 (as by Goya).

Martín Rico y Ortega

Spanish: Madrid, 1833 - Venice, 1908

At the Exposition Universelle of 1878, Rico's rather small, luminous paintings depicting French, Spanish, and Italian views won for him the rank of Chevalier of the Legion of Honor and contributed substantially to Spain's strong showing at that event. The repetitive nature of his subsequent production has, however, detracted from his posthumous reputation.

After receiving early training from the classicist Vicente Camarón y Meliá, Rico enrolled in Madrid's Royal Academy of San Fernando as a pupil of the romantic landscape painter, Genaro Pérez Villaamil. Forbidden to draw directly from nature, he copied the landscape prints of Alexandre Calame and Hubert Robert. About 1859, Rico received a scholarship enabling him to study in France. There, after being rejected as a pupil by C.-F. Daubigny, he eventually turned to sketching out-of-doors, producing oils and watercolors of the rivers near Paris. He was encouraged in this direction by a visit to Switzerland in the summer of 1860 to work with Calame, a noted proponent of *plein air* painting. He also traveled to England two years later to study Turner's pictures.

When his scholarship expired in the mid-sixties, Rico supported himself by producing wood engravings and small oils of historical genre scenes in the manner of J.-L.-E. Meissonier. Although he had befriended Camille Pissarro, with whom he worked one summer at St. Maur, Rico remained unaffected by the Impressionist's theories and fell instead under the influence of Mariano Fortuny, who had arrived in Paris in 1866. The Barcelona genre painter's immediate impact on Rico was evident in the latter's *Leaving Mass* exhibited at the 1867 Exposicion Nacional de Bellas Artes in Madrid. Though this venture in contemporary genre painting proved short-lived, Rico continued to paint with his friend Fortuny in Paris in 1870 and in Rome in 1872. Both artists received the encouragement and patronage of the American champion of Spanish painting in Paris, William Hood Stewart.

Between 1874 and 1878, Rico divided his time between France, Italy, and Spain. Sixteen pictures produced during these travels were widely acclaimed at the Exposition Universelle of 1878. Thereafter, he continued to spend increasing amounts of time in Venice, producing rather small paintings of horizontal format. Rico preferred sunny weather and worked in a gondola sketching canal scenes. His pictures are characterized by sensitivity to atmospheric effects and distinctive luminosity.

211. Gathering Oranges, Granada

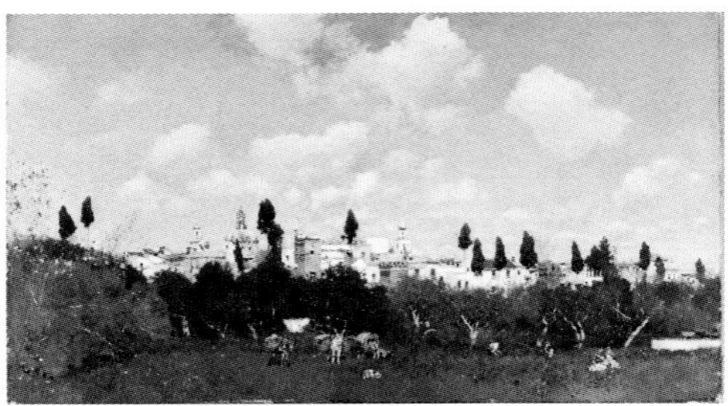

37.185

In an orange grove are three donkeys with panniers, a dog, a man and boy gathering fruit, and two seated women, all rendered in the small scale characteristic of Rico's figures. Behind is a town that was traditionally identified as Toledo, and above, a brilliant sky with scattered clouds. A sketch by the artist, from a slightly different viewpoint, showing the square tower and church dome on the left of the Walters picture, is correctly identified, however, as *Vue prise à Grenade,* in

Paul Lefort, "Les écoles étrangères de peintre," *Gazette des Beaux-Arts* 2nd pér. 18 (1878): 480. Approximately the same scene is the subject of an oil sketch on canvas (.25 x .41) belonging to the family of the artist, which is inscribed *Granada 1871.* Details of the architecture and the figures appear in a book of pencil sketches (.1 x .16), also in the family collection.

Alternative title: *Gathering Oranges, Toledo* (former erroneous title)

Support: Canvas, .42 x .75 (16½" x 29½")

Signed at lower left: *RICO;* Frame: Stamped *E. Carpentier Fils / Paris / 101 Faubourg St. Denis 101.*

Provenance: Acquired by W. T. Walters before 1878

Exhibitions: "Five Centuries of Spanish Art," The Milwaukee Art Institute, 1952, no. 40; "Fortuny and his Circle," Walters Art Gallery, 1970, no. 25.

References: Walters cat., 1878, p. 35, and subsequent Walters catalogues; Strahan, 1: 94; Champlin and Perkins, 4: 43; Lamb, p. 251; A. G. Temple, *Modern Spanish painting.* London, A. Fairbairns, 1908. p. 47; Elizabeth Du Gué Trapier, *Martin Rico y Ortega in the collection of the Hispanic Society of America.* Hispanic notes & monographs. Catalogue series. New York, Printed by order of the Trustees, 1937. pp. 24–25.

212. Venice

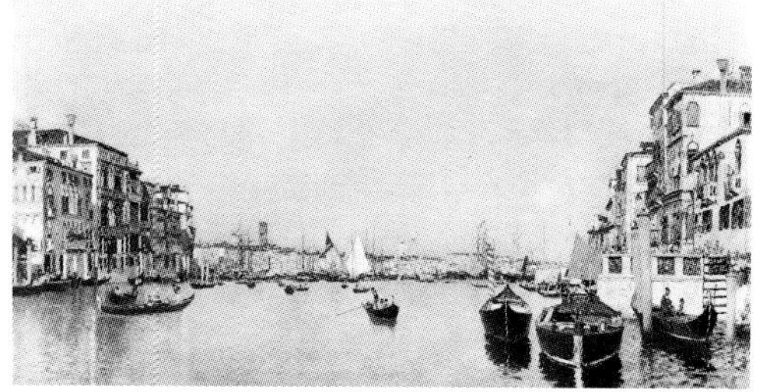

37.196 before 1875

The Grand Canal is shown in the evening, judging from the rose-tinted sky. Visible at the extreme left is the Gritti Palace and on the right, the Dario Palace. Though not mentioned in the William T. Blodgett estate sale (New York, April 27, 1876), this painting is listed in the early Walters catalogues as having belonged to the New York financier, who died November 4, 1875. Therefore this work may be one of Rico's earliest views of the city in which he worked more and more after 1874.

Support: Canvas, .424 x .717 (16$^{11}/_{16}$" x 28¼")

Signed at lower left: *RICO*

Stretcher: Stamped *G & C 8476;* Frame: Inscribed in pencil *No. 26*

Provenance: W. T. Blodgett, New York.

References: Strahan, 1: 94; Walters cat., 1884 and subsequent Walters catalogues; Champlin and Perkins, 4: 43; Lamb, p. 251; A. G. Temple, *Modern Spanish Painting.* London, A. Fairbairns, 1908, p. 45; Elizabeth Du Gué Trapier, *Martin Rico y Ortega in the Collection of the Hispanic Society of America.* Hispanic notes and monographs. Catalogue series. New York, printed by order of the Trustees, 1937. p. 24.

José Jiménez Aranda

Spanish: Seville, 1837 - Seville, 1903

Jiménez trained in Seville in the studio of Antonio Cabral Bejarano and at the Escuela de Bellas Artes under Eduardo Cano. He first exhibited at the Exposición Nacional de Bellas Artes in Madrid in 1864, showing three paintings, *The Traveling Musician, The Daughter of the Prisoner* and *The Orphan.* In the late sixties, Jiménez resided in Madrid, where he spent considerable time at the Prado. About 1871, he moved to Rome and fell into Fortuny's circle of friends although he could not have met the Catalan at this time, as is generally reported, because the latter was then in Spain. In 1874 Jiménez returned to Spain, spending a year in Valencia before settling in Seville, where he remained until the eighties, when he moved to Paris. Jiménez exhibited in various salons and expositions, winning third-class medals in Madrid (1881), and in Paris (1882), first-class medals in Munich (1883), Paris (1889) and Madrid (1890) and special awards in Berlin and Chicago in 1893. During the nineties, his style underwent a transformation as he espoused a naturalism resembling that of Bastien-Lepage. In 1893, the artist returned to Seville, and during his last years served as professor at the Escuela de Bellas Artes.

213. Figaro's Shop

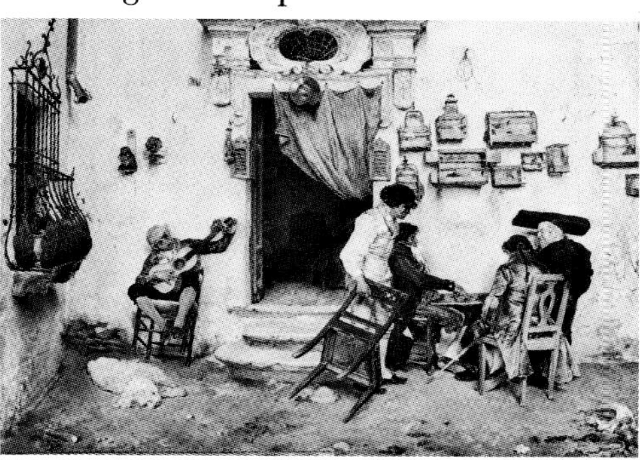

37.4 1875

The artist's genial humor is exemplified by this courtyard scene. At the right, a group of individuals, including a cleric and two gentlemen in colorful frockcoats, is seated playing checkers. The barber joins them, drawing up his chair. At the left, a young man, tilting back in his seat, strums a guitar while a dog dozes at his feet. The interior of the shop is partially obscured by a curtain draped across the doorway, though the occupation of its proprietor is indicated by the polished brass barber's bowl suspended above the entrance.

Jiménez apparently took delight in dazzling the viewer with his attention to picturesque detail. The elaborate wrought iron of the window-grill at the right is faithfully rendered; mounted on the background wall are perches for chained owls, cages for finches, and, incised in the plaster, are children's graffiti; even the lettering of a crumpled newspaper in the debris at the lower right corner is decipherable.

Vibrant colors, cheerful, anecdotal subjects and technical virtuosity are associated with the most "fortunyesque" phase of Jiménez Aranda's career. He did not, however, share his mentor's concern for the recording of the subtle, transitory effects of changing light.

Alternative title: *Boutique de Figaro*

Support: Canvas, .456 x .575 (17$^{15}/_{16}$" x 22⅝")

Signed and dated in brown at lower left: *J. Jimenez Aranda / Roma / 1875*

Condition: The painting was cleaned and varnished in 1941.

Provenance: Acquired by W. T. Walters before 1878.

References: Walters cat., 1878, p. 27; Champlin and Perkins, 2: 343; *Bryan's Dictionary of Painters and Engravers.* New ed., revised and enlarged under the supervision of George C. Williamson. 5 vols. New York, Macmillan, 1903–05. 3: 112; A. G. Temple, *Modern Spanish painting.* London, A. Fairbairns, 1908. p. 89.

Mariano José-Maria-Bernardo Fortuny y Marsal

Spanish: Reus, 1838 - Rome, 1874

In his brief career this Catalan painter acquired an extensive following internationally as well as among his countrymen. A brilliant technician, Fortuny assimilated with remarkable facility the progressive trends of his time, producing oils and watercolors much in demand in European and American art markets.

Fortuny was raised by his paternal grandfather, who encouraged him in his career, taking him to Barcelona in 1852 to enroll in the Academia de Bellas Artes under Claudio Lorenzale, a disciple of Overbeck. Though he was drawn to the lithographs of Gavarni, Fortuny's early oils were of religious and historical subjects. He won a *bourse* from the municipality of Barcelona in 1857 with his painting, *Raymond III nailing the arms of Barcelona on the tower of the Castle of Foix,* (Barcelona, Museo de Arte Moderno, no. 1.740). These funds enabled him to travel to Rome. There, he painted copies of seventeenth-century masters as well as *The Statue of Dionysius,* (J. G. Johnson Collection, Philadelphia Museum of Art), still in the tradition of Overbeck.

In 1860 Fortuny accompanied the Spanish military expedition to Morocco, led by General Prim. Returning to Barcelona, he exhibited campaign sketches and was commissioned to execute a monumental *Battle of Tetuan.* In preparation for the project, he made his first visit to Paris, to study Horace Vernet's celebrated battle painting *La Smalah* in Versailles and in 1862 he returned briefly to Morocco for further studies. Completion of the panoramic battle painting proved an uncongenial undertaking for Fortuny and he was eventually relieved of the commission. The vast canvas (3 x 9.72), still unfinished at his death, was given to Barcelona (Museo de Arte Moderno, no. 1.773). He did, however, complete a ceiling decoration, *Queen Christine passing in review her Troops,* for the monarch's hôtel on the Champs-Elysées. Working in Rome in the sixties, Fortuny attracted to his studio a number of colleagues, including Agrasot, Tapiro, Vallès and an Italian, Attilio Simonetti, who became a veritable disciple.

In 1866 Fortuny was in Paris, where he encountered the dealer Goupil, as well as the artists Meissonier and Gérôme, and in Madrid, where he met the director of the Prado, Federico de Madrazo, whose daughter Cecilia he married the following year. In December 1868 Fortuny signed a contract with Goupil authorizing the French dealer to be his agent.

By 1869 Fortuny had established close ties with a number of French artists—most notably Regnault, Clairin and the sculptor D'Epinay. He was visited in Rome that year by an American expatriate from Philadelphia, William Hood Stewart, who brought for the artist's examination a small Meissonier painting, *End of a Game of Cards* (Walters Art Gallery, 37.149). Stewart emerged as Fortuny's principal patron, buying works not only for himself but encouraging a number of Philadelphian collectors to follow his precedent. That year, the artist again went to Paris, spending a summer in Gérôme's studio and moving in the autumn to the Maison Vallin on the Champs-Elysées. In 1870 Goupil purchased and exhibited *La Vicaria* (Private collection, Paris) which drew considerable attention, as well as the praise of Théophile Gautier. During the remainder of the year, Fortuny traveled to Madrid, Seville, and Granada. In 1871 he returned to Rome and then went (with his followers Tapiro and Ferrandiz) to Tangier where he was joined by Clarin.

During 1872 Fortuny was active in Granada and Seville, painting brilliant sun-drenched scenes such as the *Gypsy Caves, Granada* (Corcoran Gallery of Art, no. 26.89) and *Farmhouse Courtyard in Alhambra* (Fogg Art Museum, no. 1942.192) in which the shadows are rendered transparent by flecks of reflected color. Returning to Italy, he worked in Rome and Naples, beginning *The Choice of a Model* and *The Garden of the Arcadians.* In the last year of his life he once more visited Paris and accompanied Baron Davillier, the noted collector, to London, where he met Millais. That summer he was back in Italy working at Portici near Naples on a series of pictures including *The Beach at Portici* and *Two Children in a Japanese Salon,* which revealed his interest in the wave of Japanese influence then sweeping the West. His sudden death from malaria in November 1874 was mourned by colleagues throughout Europe.

214. Hindoo Snake Charmers

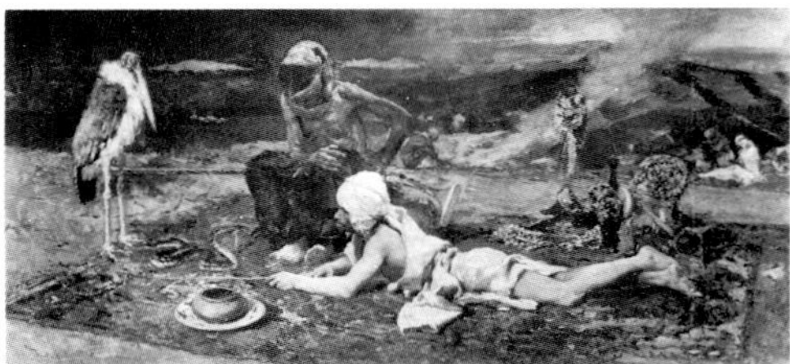

37.117 1869

A turbaned Indian, sprawled across a carpet, mesmerizes a cobra with a reed. Behind him squats an Arab observer wearing a burnoose with a Kabyle musket resting across his knees. Standing at the left, is a marabou. The artist, an inveterate collector of Islamic decorative arts, has included such accessories as a copper bowl, a luster plate, and a saddle. The scene is set outdoors at twilight, and discernible in the background are Arabs seated around their campfire.

This painting is one of two versions; the other, painted for Ed. André in Paris in 1869, was offered in the spring of 1887 to W. T. Walters, who refused it (Lucas 2:647).

In the André painting, now in the Hermitage, Leningrad, the Arab holds a musical instrument rather than a musket, the Indian wears an armlet on his left shoulder, and the snake is devouring a rabbit.

A drawing of the model for the Indian, posing nude, belongs to the Museum of Castres, no. 73, EN 6791.

Alternative title: *The Serpent Charmer*

Support: Coarsely woven, seamed canvas, .585 x 1.245 (23" x 49")

Signed and dated at lower left: *Fortuny/R 1869*

Condition: Dammar varnish applied in 1951.

Provenance: D. H. Foll, Geneva; A. T. Stewart, New York, Sale March 23-30, 1887, no. 128, to S. P. Avery, Jr., for $13,100.00; Avery to W. T. Walters before 1889.

References: J. C. Davillier, *Fortuny, sa vie, son oeuvre, sa correspondance.* Paris, A. Aubry, 1875. pp. 55–56; W. Fol, "Fortuny," *GBA* 2nd pér. 11 (1875): 275–76; "In the footsteps of Fortuny and Regnault," *Century Magazine* 23, no. 1 (November 1881): 29; R. Hitchcock, "The Stewart paintings," *The Art Review* 1 (November 1886): 7–8; Walters cat., 1888, p. 35, no. 46 and subsequent Walters catalogues A. G. Temple, *Modern Spanish painting.* London, A. Fairbairns, 1908. p. 82; *Fortuny.* Masters in art. Boston, 1909. p. 29, 38; M. Fortuny y Madrazo, *Fortuny, 1838–1874,* Milan, Alfieri, 1931; plate 25.

215. Arab Fantasia

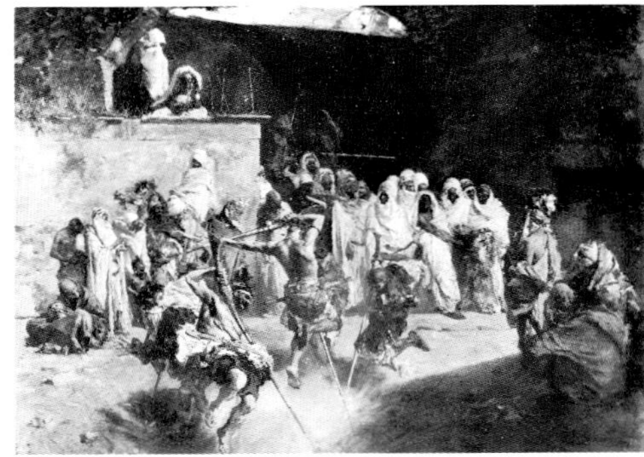

37.191 1867

In 1862 the municipal government of Barcelona authorized Fortuny to return to North Africa to refresh his memory for painting the *Battle of Wad-Ras.* He left Rome in September and spent two months making drawings and studies in oils and watercolors near Tangier, Tetuan, Fondach, and Wad-Ras. On his return to Europe in December he spent several months in Barcelona at the home of his early benefactor, Beunaventura Palau, to whom he presented the first version of this subject. Subsequently, he painted a variant which entered the collection of M. Foll of Geneva and eventually that of William H. Vanderbilt of New York (Sale, April 18–19, 1945, no. 43, *Arab Fantasia,* .508 x .622).

The Walters version, dated 1867, was sent by Fortuny to Goupil et Cie, in Paris, where it was purchased by William H. Stewart, January 1868, at the instigation of the painter Zamacoïs. Other versions include the *Arab Fantasia,* canvas, .369 x .47, sold at the E. Secrétan Sale, Paris, July 1, 1890, no. 28, and also, perhaps, a large unlocated work listed as *Fantasia Arabe à Grenade,* 1. x 1.8, at the Fortuny Sale, Paris 1875, no. 65, and as *Fantasia arabe à la porte de Tanger* at the Sedelmeyer Sale, Paris, April 30, May 2, 1877, no. 119. In addition, a *Fantasia arabe à Tanger* (.32 x .58), was listed at the Fortuny Sale, Paris, 1875, no. 85, as a preliminary study for the Stewart-Walters picture. A drawing of the principal figures is in the Hípola Collection, Madrid.

Fortuny's composition is a departure from the usual representation of the subject as seen in paintings by Delacroix and Fromentin, in that the Arab warriors are performing their wild, ritualistic exercise on foot rather than on horseback. In the Walters picture the scene transpires before an indistinct cavernous background, whereas in the Foll and Secrétan variants an architectural backdrop is clearly defined. With its overhead lighting and sharp contrast between the brilliant colors of the costumes of the performers and spectators and the darkness of the background, the Walters painting is perhaps the most dramatic variant.

The cavernous background in the Walters picture also is seen in *Arabs outside a Grotto,* canvas, .312 x .445, Sotheby Parke Bernet, New York, December 15, 1978, Sale 4197, no. 360.

Alternative titles: *Fantasia de la poudre, Arabes jouant la poudre, Convulsionnaires kabyles, Danza Marroqui*

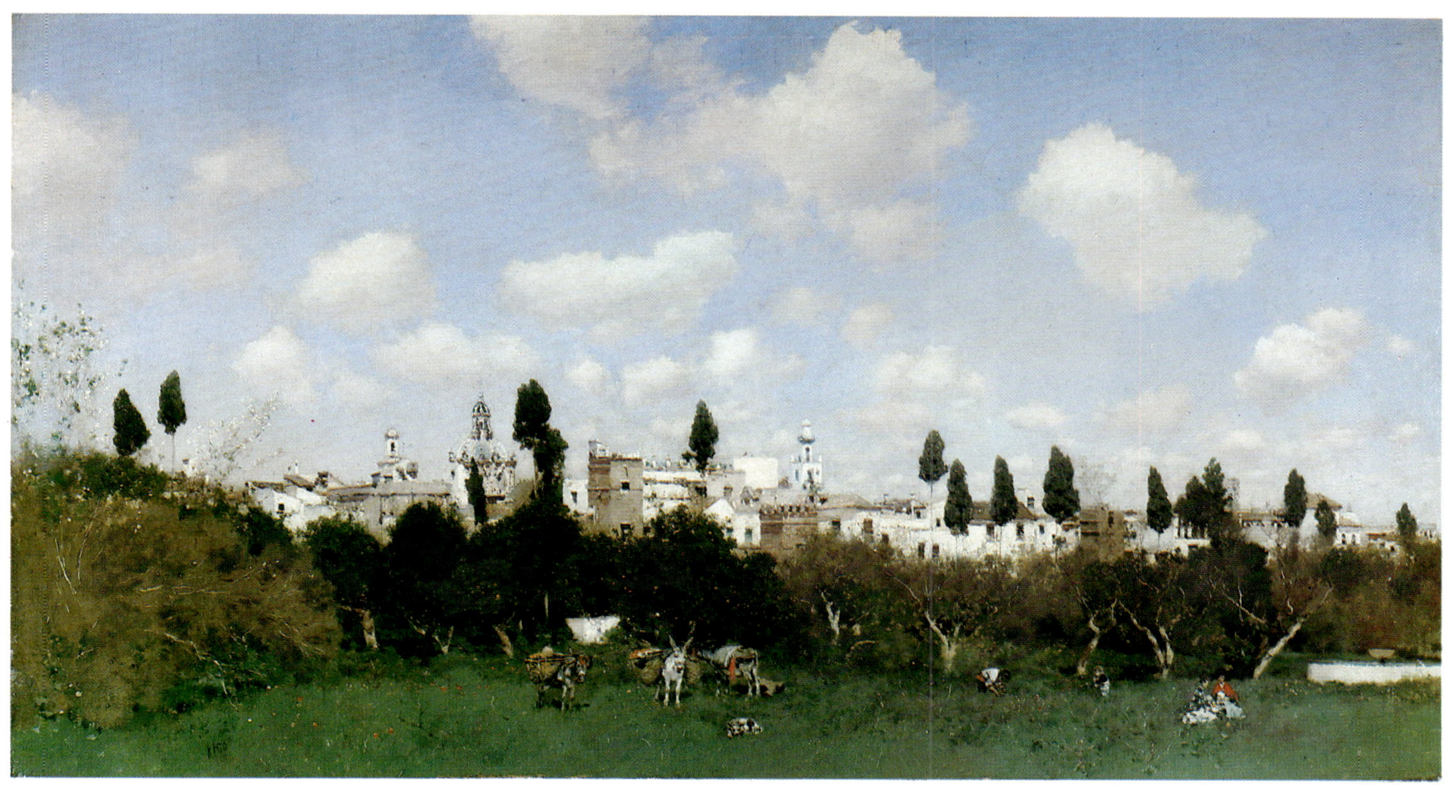

Rico *Gathering Oranges, Granada,* no. 211

Support: Canvas, .52 x .67 (20½" x 26⅜")

Signed and dated, lower right: *Fortuny Roma 1867*

Condition: Discolored varnish removed in 1951; revarnished with mastic resin. Mastic varnish replaced with synthetic varnish in 1969.

Provenance: William H. Stewart Sale, New York, February 3–4, 1898, no. 27, $12,000.00.

Exhibitions: "Cent Chefs d'Oeuvres," Galerie Georges Petit, Paris, 1885; Exposition Universelle, Paris, 1878; "Fortuny and his Circle," Walters Art Gallery, 1970, no. 1.

References: Charles Yriarte, "Fortuny," *L'Art* 1 (1875): 371 (illus.) W. Fol, "Fortuny," *GBA* 2nd pér. 11 (1875): 275–76. Edward Strahan, ed., *The chefs-d'oeuvre d'art of the International Exhibition, 1878.* Philadelphia, Gebbie & Barrie, 1878–80. p. 83; Strahan, 1: 36; S. Sanpere y Miquel, *Mariano Fortuny; album.* Barcelona, Imprenta Religiosa y Científica, 1880, plate 59; J. Yxart, *Fortuny.* 2nd ed. Barcelona, Doménech, 1882. plate 125; W. H. Stewart, "Reminiscences and notes," in J. C. Davillier, *Life of Fortuny.* Philadelphia, Porter & Coates, 1885. p. 198; F. Miquel y Badía, *Fortuny, su vida y obras.* Barcelona, Torres y Seguí, 1887. plate 47; J. C. Van Dyke, "Two private collections in Paris," *The Art Review* 2, no. 4 (December 1887): 63. Walters cat., 1899, p. 103, no. 171; J. Ciervo, *El arte y el vivir de Fortuny.* Barcelona, M. Bayés, n.d. p. 149; M. Fortuny y Madrazo, *Fortuny, 1838–1874.* Milan, Alfieri, 1931. plate 14; Joseph Butler, "The American way with art," *Connoisseur* 175 (1970): 61 (illus.); W. R. Johnston, "W. H. Stewart, the American patron of Mariano Fortuny," *GBA* 6th pér. 77 (1971): 184 (illus.), 186, 187.

216. An Ecclesiastic

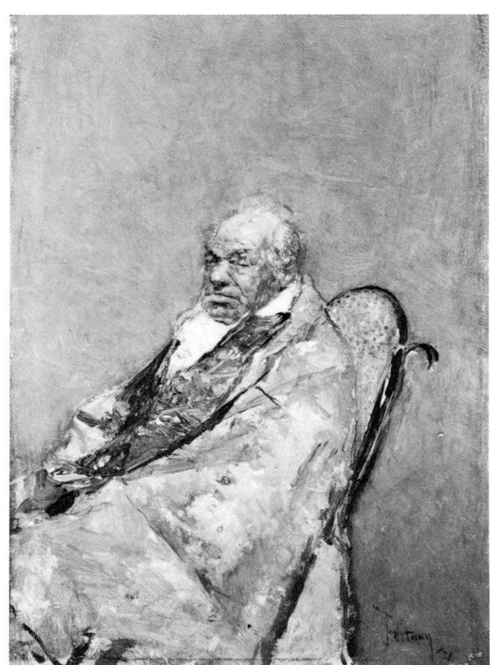

37.150 c 1874

An elderly model, clad in rose-colored robes, is seated in a bent-wood chair. He is posed against a brilliant vermilion background.

Such works exemplify Fortuny's daringly innovative experiments with colors. A photograph taken in the artist's studio in the Villa Martinori, Rome, where he had moved in the autumn of 1873, shows Fortuny seated before an easel bearing this picture already framed (Foto MAS, Barcelona, reproduced in W. R. Johnston, "Fortuny and his Circle," *BWAG* 22, no. 7 (April 1970) : 2).

Support: Panel, .19 x .13 (7½" x 5⅛")

Signed: *Fortuny/74* (?)

Condition: Discolored varnishes removed in 1951; mastic varnish applied.

Provenance: Acquired by W. T. Walters between 1878 and 1884.

References: Walters cat., 1884, p. 47, no. 79, and subsequent Walters catalogues; R. B. Gruelle, "Mariano Fortuny and Léon Bonnat: notes on their pictures in the Walters collection, Baltimore," *Modern Art* 1 (1893); *Fortuny,* Masters in art. Boston, 1909. p. 28; Gerald M. Ackerman, "Crónica: Una exposición de Fortuny en Baltimore," *Archivo español de arte* 42 (1969): 214; W. R. Johnston, "Fortuny and his circle," *BWAG* 22, no. 7 (April 1970): 4 (illus.).

Raimundo de Madrazo y Garreta
Spanish: Rome, 1841 - Versailles, 1920

Raimundo de Madrazo attained the pinnacle of success at the Paris 1878 Exposition Universelle at which he was represented by fourteen pictures, including portraits, landscapes, a decorative panel and his now unlocated chef-d'oeuvre, the contemporary genre painting, *Departure from the Masked Ball.* On this occasion, he was acclaimed successor to his brother-in-law, Mariano Fortuny, as the leader of contemporary Spanish painting and he was appointed Chevalier of the Legion of Honor.

Madrazo represented the third generation of Spain's most enduring dynasty of artists, founded by José de Madrazo y Agudo (1781–1859), court painter to Carlos IV. Born in Rome where his father, Federico Madrazo y Kuntz (1815–1894), resided for two years, Raimundo spent most of his youth in Madrid and trained with his father at the Academia de San Fernando. His first visit to Paris took place in 1855 when he accompanied his father to the Exposition Universelle. In 1858, he showed in Seville *The Carrying to Spain of the Body of the Apostle of Santiago* and in 1861 he returned to Paris to enter the Ecole des Beaux-Arts as a pupil of Léon Cogniet.

Madrazo's early years in Paris are sparsely documented. A colleague, Martín Rico, recalled accompanying him to various museums and galleries in the early sixties. About 1863–64 the artist received a commission for a ceiling decoration for the hôtel of María Cristina of Bourbon on the Champs-Elysées. During the Franco-Prussian War he remained in France, serving in the American Ambulance Corps, and in the spring of 1872 he joined his brother-in-law Fortuny in Seville. He was also briefly absent from Paris in 1874 when he accompanied Rico to Venice. Though Madrazo did not participate in the Paris Salons, his early years in France must have been highly productive inasmuch as he had acquired a considerable following among Parisian and American collectors prior to 1878. In his survey of American collections, *The Art Treasures of America,* published in Philadelphia in 1879, Strahan listed over thirty-five paintings by the artist, including Spanish and gypsy subjects, rococo themes, and a few contemporary genre paintings. Presumably Madrazo was selling his pictures through Goupil et Cie, a dealer specializing in the works of Spanish expatriates in Paris.

After 1878 Madrazo continued to attract an international clientele. He exhibited at the Munich Exhibition in 1883; at the French Gallery in London in 1884, and at the Salon in Paris the same year. At the Exposition Universelle of 1889 he received a gold medal and was elevated from the rank of Chevalier to that of Officier of the Legion of Honor.

Toward the end of the century Madrazo turned increasingly to the North and South American art markets, acquiring a reputation as a fashionable portraitist. In 1897 he visited New York, exhibiting at Oehme Gallery. The following year he returned, occupying Charles Dana Gibson's studio in the Life Building. Among his American sitters were Mrs. H. M. Flagler, Mrs. Harry Payne Whitney, Mrs. Cornelius Vanderbilt, Mrs. O. H. P. Belmont and Robert L. Stuart. In 1902 he stopped briefly in Baltimore to receive commissions through Bendann's Gallery in the city.

Madrazo died at his residence in Versailles in 1920 after about a decade of retirement.

217. Coming out of Church

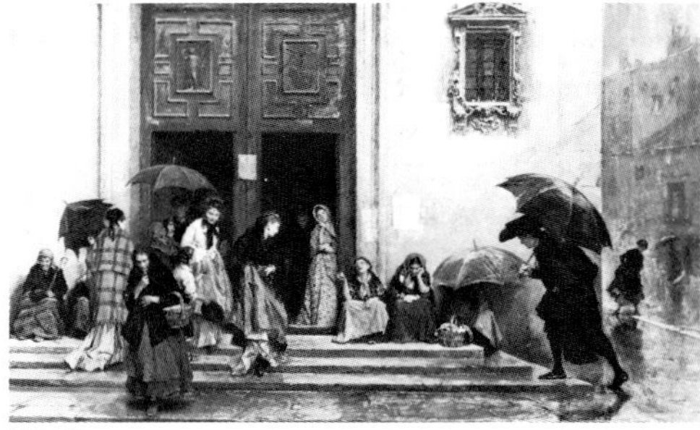

37.48 before 1875

Madrazo displays his dramatic sense of color and technical virtuosity in this genre scene of parishioners leaving a Spanish church after vespers. As was often his practice, the artist imparts variety to the scene by contrasting the two fashionably attired ladies descending the steps with the other participants—beggars, elderly women, a street urchin and a priest protecting himself from a downpour with an umbrella. In the right background, figures disappear down a rain-slicked street.

Early in his career Madrazo painted several contemporary scenes involving churches. Among them were *Santa Maria della Pace, Roma,* once belonging to Alexander Brown of Philadelphia, *Selling Rosaries in Front of a Spanish Church,* formerly in the possession of T. R. Butler of New York, and an *Interior of a Church* dedicated to M. De Goyena of Seville and last recorded in the collection of Sr. Abelardo Linares of Madrid. In these works, Madrazo repeated the device of contrasting the social and economic classes of the figures represented.

Within Madrazo's immediate circle the artist most generally associated with such themes was his brother-in-law, Fortuny. The two painters could have met as early as 1860 when both were in Madrid and they undoubtedly were acquainted with one another by 1867 when the Catalan married Madrazo's youngest sister Cecilia. In preparation for his celebrated *La Vicaria,* illustrating Molière's theme "Le mariage inégal," first shown in 1870, Fortuny executed a number of studies involving church scenes in Madrid and Rome. Nearest in composition to Madrazo's *Coming out of Church* was Fortuny's *Procesión interrumpida por la lluvia,* Museo Nacional de Bellas Artes, Buenos Aires, in which a procession of clerics bearing a crucifix enters a church on a rainy day. Fortuny, however, presents a sensuous impression of climatic effects whereas Madrazo dwells more on such descriptive details as the dress, social strata and ages of his subjects. Other related works by Fortuny include an ink sketch of figures huddled beneath umbrellas outside a church on a rainy day, in the British Museum, no. 1950-5-20-9, and an unlocated drawing of himself and Raimundo Madrazo's brother, Ricardo, crossing the Champs-Elysées in the rain as they proceeded to Martín Rico's wedding (Charles Davillier, *Fortuny, sa vie, son oeuvre, sa correspondance,* Paris, 1875, p. 53).

Alternative titles: *Une sortie de vêpres; Vespers; Nach dem Gottesdienst*

Support: Canvas, .64 x 1 (25¼" x 39⅜")

Signed at lower left: *R. de Madrazo*

Provenance: William H. Stewart, Paris, before 1875; Robert L. Cutting Sale, New York, March 22, 1892, no. 85 for $5,500.00 (purchased by S. P. Avery on behalf of W. T. Walters).

Exhibitions: This painting was accessible to the public in William H. Stewart's private gallery in Paris about 1875. "Five Centuries of Spanish Art," The Milwaukee Art Institute, 1952, no. 43; "Fortuny and his Circle," Walters Art Gallery, 1970, no. 16.

References: Lucy H. Hooper, "Private American art galleries in Paris," *The Art Journal* (London) (1875): 284; Strahan, 2: 34–35; David Hannay, "Madrazo the Spanish painter," *The Magazine of art* (1884): 12; Walters cat., 1893, p. 98, no. 160, and subsequent Walters catalogues; L. Scheewe, "Madrazo," in U. Thieme and F. Becker, *Allgemeines Lexikon der bildenden Künstler.* 37 vols. Leipzig, E. A. Seemann, 1907–50. 23: 536; William R. Johnston, "A contemporary genre painting by Raimundo de Madrazo y Garreta," *JWAG* 33–34 (1970–1971): 34–41, illus. p. 34.

Eduardo Zamacoïs y Zabala
Spanish: Bilbao, 1842 - Madrid, 1871

This short-lived genre artist is remembered both as the gifted Spanish pupil of J.-L.-E. Meissonier and as the influential friend of Mariano Fortuny y Marsal. Before pursuing his career in Paris, Zamacoïs studied with an artist named Balaco, in Bilbao and at the Escuela Superior de Pintura, Escultura y Grabado in Madrid. In Paris, he entered Meissonier's atelier, adopting the master's meticulously detailed, smoothly surfaced technique. A precocious student, he made his first appearance at the Salon in 1863 with two paintings, one showing the conscription of Cervantes into the army and the other, a meeting of Diderot and d'Alembert. The following year Zamacoïs exhibited *The Conscripts in Spain* and in 1866 he entered as a joint endeavor with Vibert *The Toreadors before entering the Arena,* now in the Walters Art Gallery (37.197). That year, he served as intermediary between the Catalan painter Mariano Fortuny and the influential dealer, Goupil. In 1868, Zamacoïs traveled to Rome, where he stayed in the studio of Fortuny, who was absent in Madrid. Accompanying him on this trip was William H. Stewart, the expatriate American collector of contemporary Spanish painting. Zamacoïs' major work was probably *The Education of a Prince* which he showed at the Munich Exhibition in 1870, winning a gold medal, and at the Paris Salon the same year. During the Franco-Prussian War he was in Madrid, where he died of angina pectoris in January 1871.

218. Spain, 1812—French Occupation

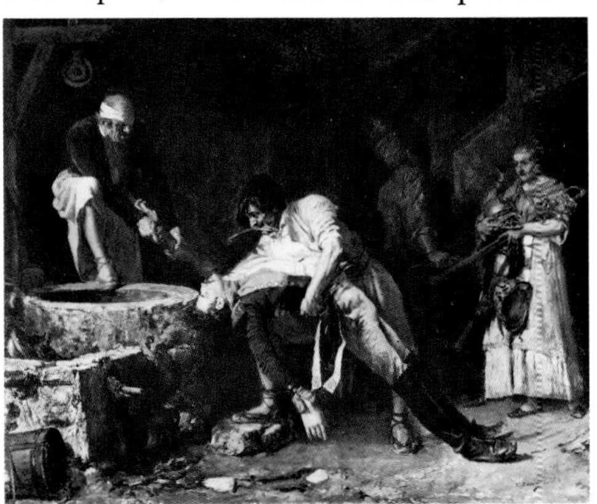

37.39 1866

In a darkened chamber, two Spaniards, an elderly man with a bandaged head and a younger accomplice clenching a stiletto in his teeth, struggle to dispose of the corpse of a French Cuirassier by dropping it down a well. An old woman passes through the entrance at the right carrying the helmets and swords of the victim and of another who has presumably met the same fate. A Spaniard, clutching a knife, keeps watch. The Spaniards' dress, particularly the aprons of the figures carrying the corpse, suggest that the setting is a cabaret.

Zamacoïs shared with Meissonier an interest in the Napoleonic era as well as preoccupation with historical veracity in the rendering of detail. However, he portrays the incident from his own country's point of view, avoids any direct borrowing of composition from his mentor and employs a slightly more spontaneous brushstroke, thus asserting his individuality in a manner unlike many of Meissonier's other pupils.

Alternative title: *Episode of the French Invasion of Spain*

Support: Panel, .443 x .52 (17½" x 20½")

Signed and dated, lower right: *Ed Zamacois 66*

Condition: Discolored varnish removed in 1951.

Provenance: R. B. Gruelle in *Notes/Critical and Biographical, Collection of W. T. Walters,* 1894, pp. 88–89, related that W. T. Walters had failed to persuade Zamacoïs to part with this painting and that four years after the artist's death, the widow sold the painting to the Baltimore collector.

Exhibition: "Fortuny and his Circle," Walters Art Gallery, 1970, no. 14.

References: Walters cat., 1878, pp. 44–45, and subsequent Walters catalogues; George William Sheldon, *Hours with art and artists.* New York, D. Appleton, 1882. p. 118; Champlin and Perkins, 4: 460; A. G. Temple, *Modern Spanish painting.* London, A. Fairbairns, 1908. p. 87.

José Villegas Cordero
Spanish: Seville, 1848 - Madrid, 1921

Villegas initially trained in his native Seville under José Romero and Eduardo Cano. The latter provided him with prints by leading contemporary French artists to copy. His early paintings include a scene of two young girls begging for alms and an historical subject, *Columbus seeking refuge in the Convent of Rábida,* which was purchased by the Duc de Montpensier. Continuing his studies in Madrid, Villegas was particularly drawn to the works of Velázquez in the Prado.

Late in 1868, Villegas accompanied Luís Jiménez Aranda to Rome, where during the days he drew from a model which he shared with several fellow students and in the evenings he joined his colleagues at the Accademia Chigi. From 1870 to 1886 he painted numerous watercolors which lacked the degree of finish to satisfy the clients of Goupil and Agnew. Initially, in Rome, he adopted the brilliant technique and bold colors associated with Fortuny and his followers, though the influence of the celebrated history painter, Eduardo Rosales, grew increasingly important for him. Villegas' first major client in Rome, a Swiss col-

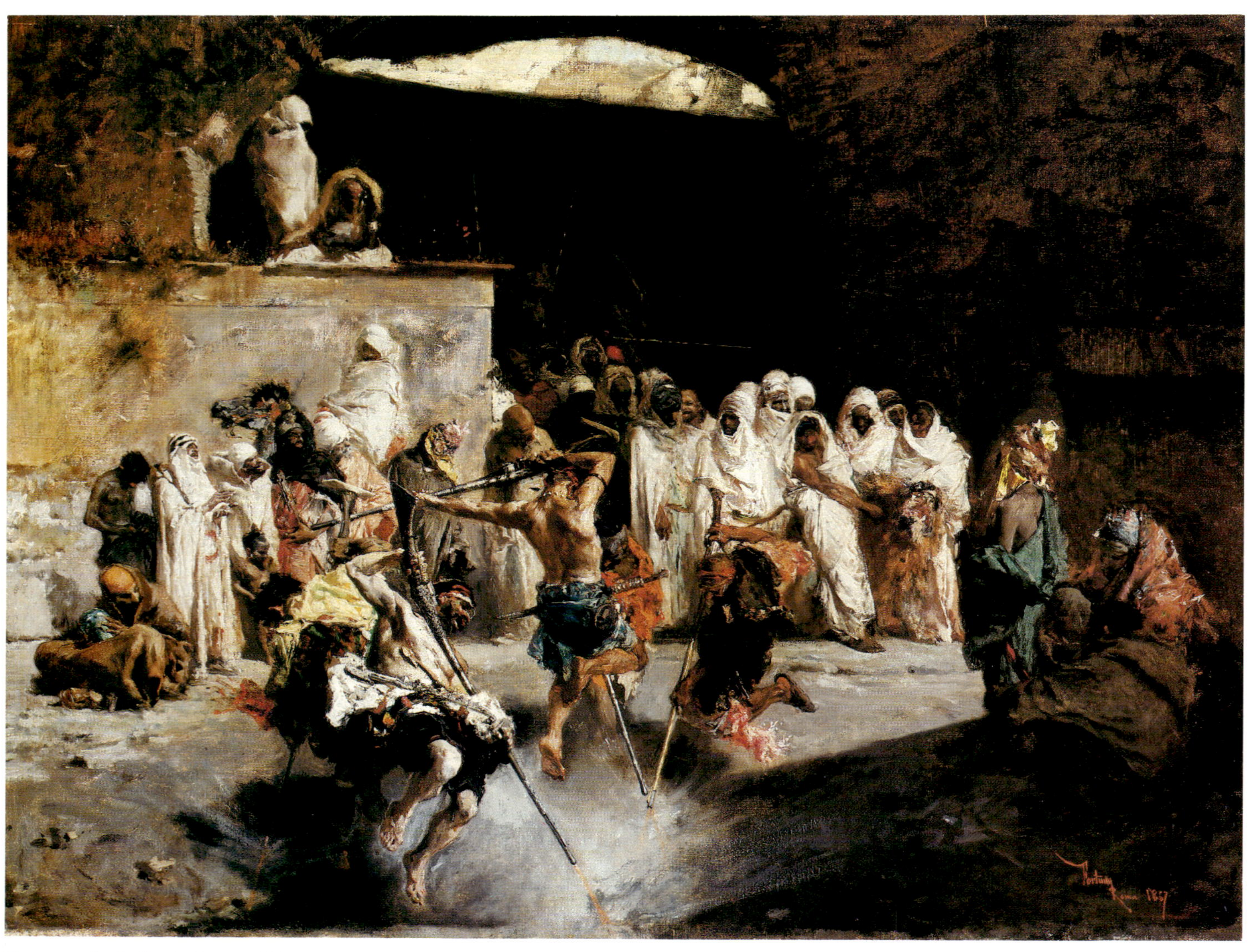

Fortuny *Arab Fantasia,* no. 215

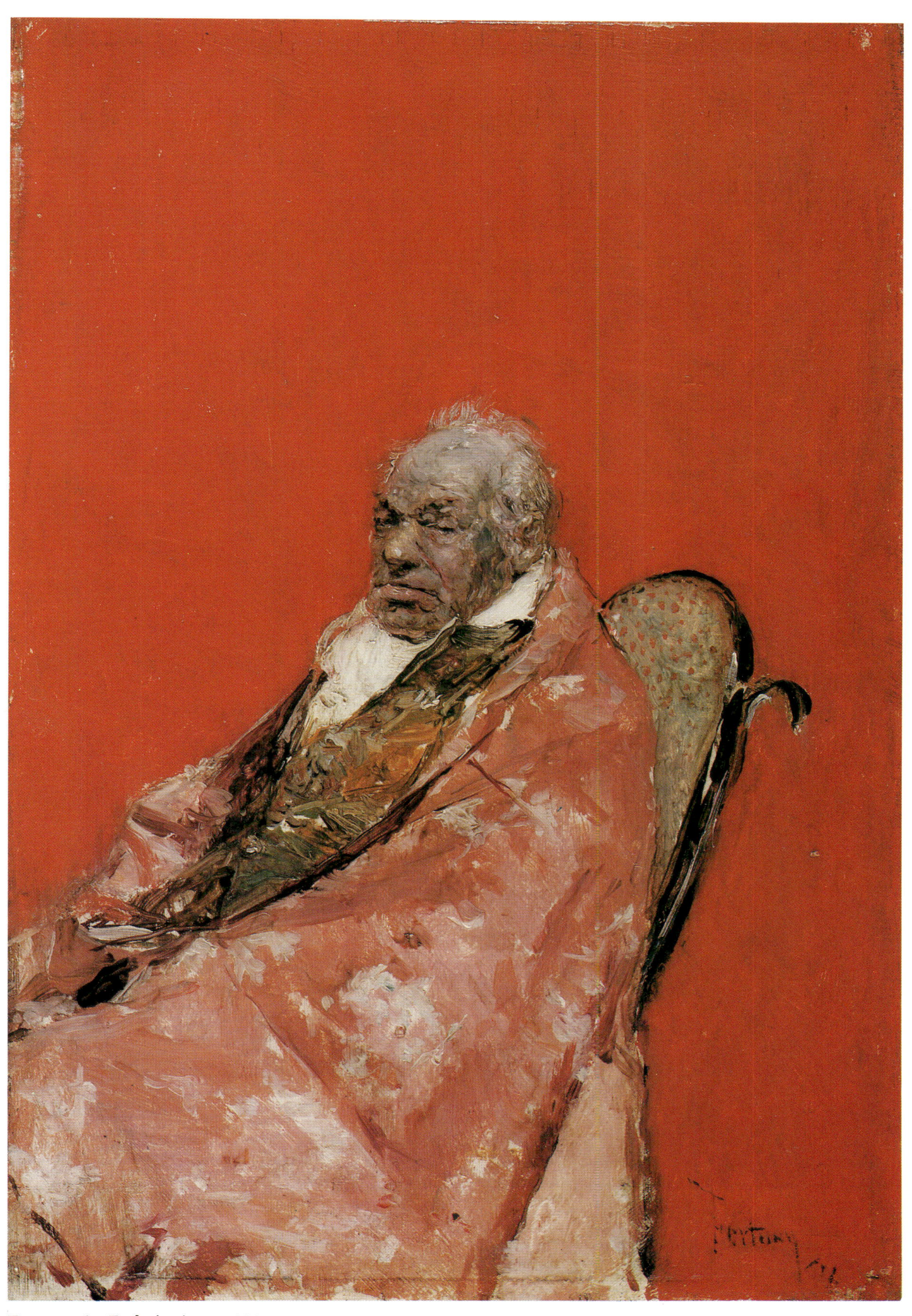

Fortuny *An Ecclesiastic,* no. 216

lector, Foll, purchased the *Improvised Retreat* and subsequently sold it to the collector Michael Botkin, physician to the Tsar. Subsequently, Villegas developed an extensive American clientele which included J. P. Morgan, W. T. Blodgett, and William H. Stewart, the influential patron of many Spanish artists. The Count d'Epinay bought a number of his oils and watercolors and resold them to the Vanderbilts and other Americans. Villegas was a prolific painter, producing over two hundred portraits, one thousand "finished" paintings, thirty thousand sketches and innumerable watercolors.

In 1898 Villegas was appointed director of the Academia Española de Bellas Artes in Rome and three years later was named director of the Prado, a post which he held until 1918.

219. The Slipper Merchant

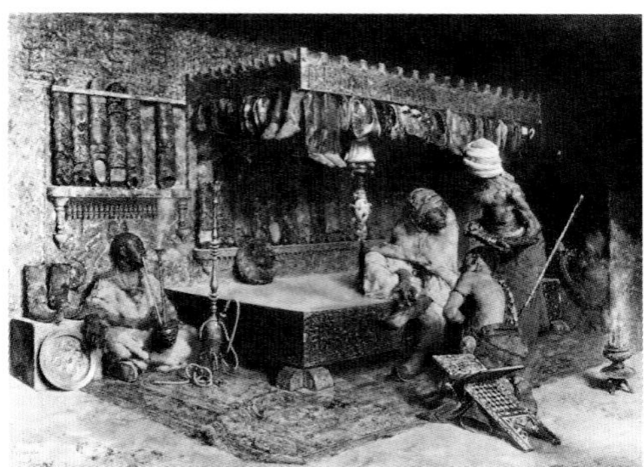

37.105 1872

Villegas has developed a subject popularized by his mentor Fortuny in the *Carpet Merchant,* a watercolor of 1870 now in a private collection in Barcelona. Unlike Fortuny, who showed the transactions being negotiated in the brilliant sunlight outside the shop, Villegas brings the viewer within a dimly lit, though richly colored, interior. A turbaned merchant holding a slipper is serving a customer seated on an elaborate divan. Kneeling in front of him is an attendant and almost lost in the darkened right corner is a craftsman at work. To the left, a black African smokes a hookah.

The shop abounds with Islamic bric-a-brac, hookahs, an inlaid Koran-stand, a burning brazier and a copper dish that would have been encountered in the studio of any artist pursuing the themes of Orientalism at this time.

Related works by Villegas include *The Cobblers,* H. L. Satterlee sale, New York, 1948, no. 87, *Moorish Faience Vendor,* O. L. Mills sale, New York, 1938, no. 426, and *Bazaar in Tunis,* formerly in the Montreal Museum of Fine Arts.

Alternative title: *El zapatillero árabe*

Support: Canvas, .482 x .651 (19" x 25⅝")

Signed and dated lower left: *Villegas/1872*

Condition: Discolored varnishes removed in 1951; revarnished in 1970.

Provenance: William T. Blodgett sale, New York, 1876, no. 60, $4,100.00; J. Pierpont Morgan, c. 1879 (Strahan, 3:10 as in the Morgan Collection).

Exhibitions: "Five Centuries of Spanish Painting," The Milwaukee Art Institute, 1952, no. 44; "Fortuny and his Circle," Walters Art Gallery, 1970, no. 18.

References: Strahan, 3: 10; Champlin and Perkins, 4: 370, as *Cairo slipper merchant;* Walters cat., 1884, p. 43, no. 67 and subsequent Walters catalogues; *Enciclopedia universal illustrada europeo-americana.* 80 vols. Barcelona, Espasa, 1907–33. 68: 1562, 1569; A. G. Temple, *Modern Spanish painting.* London, A. Fairbairns, 1908. p. 94.

220. Poultry Market, Tangiers

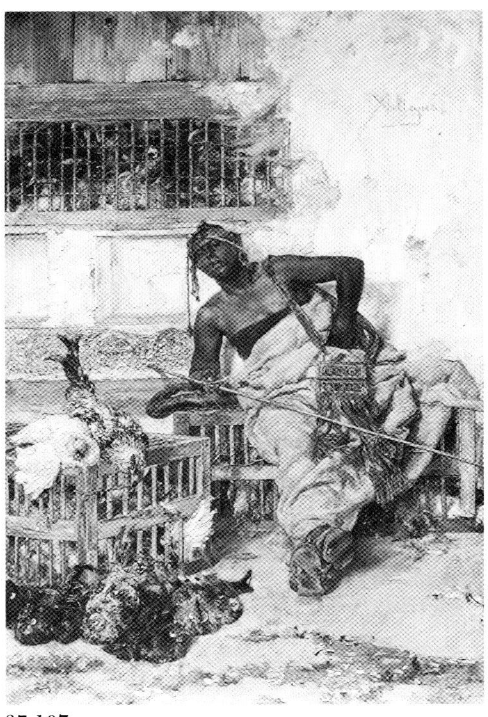

37.107

A black poultry merchant is lolling on a chicken coop against a partially stuccoed building. Beside him is another coop on which some colorful birds roost. The model appears to be the same figure as that seen at the left of *The Slipper Merchant.* (37.105)

Alternative title: *Marchand de Volailles au Maroc*

Support: Mahogany panel, .532 x .352 (21" x 13⅞"

Signed upper right: *Villegas*

Condition: Discolored varnish removed in 1951; revarnished.

Provenance: Everard Sale, 1881, as *Marchand de Volailles au Maroc,* 9,000 francs; acquired by W. T. Walters between 1881 and 1884.

Exhibitions: "Fortuny and his Circle," Walters Art Gallery, 1970, no. 19.

References: Walters cat., 1884, p. 35, no. 53; Champlin and Perkins, 4: 370; A. G. Temple, *Modern Spanish Painting,* London, A. Fairbairns, 1908, p. 94.

221. The Baptism of Christ
Italian School, Early 19th Century

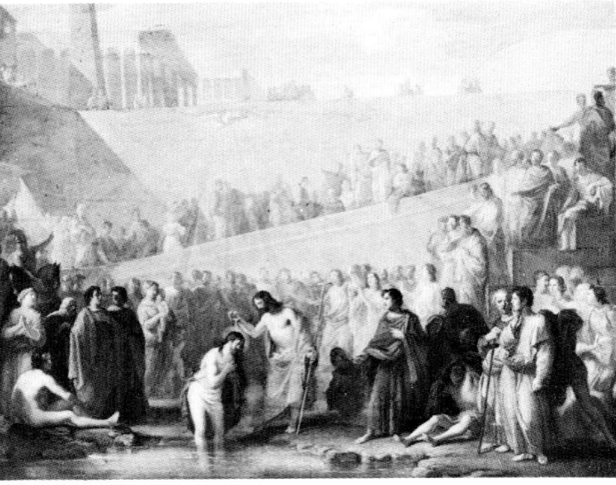

37.1017 c. 1800

"And Jesus being baptized, forthwith came out of the water: and lo, the heavens were opened to him: and he saw the Spirit of God descending as a dove and coming upon him."—*St. Matthew 3:15*

The artist has compressed the incident as narrated in the Bible, combining a view of a throng of spectators on the walls of Jerusalem with the baptismal scene at the Jordan River. High in the background are discernible a number of vast, classical buildings including, at the right, a rotunda, presumably the Temple of Jerusalem.

In the Massarenti collection this panel was attributed to Andrea Appiani (1754–1817) of Milan, Napoleon's court painter in Italy. Though no exact parallels for this picture are recorded in this artist's oeuvre, its monumental architecture with the distinctive severity and volumetric clarity is in keeping with an artist of Appiani's generation.

Support: Panel, cradled, .277 x .349 (10$^{15}/_{16}$" x 13¾")

Condition: Paint losses have occurred along several horizontal cracks extending the width of the panel. The reverse of the panel is extensively worm-eaten. Surface grime and darkened overpainting were removed in 1963, blisters laid down with wax, and losses inpainted. Minor losses were inpainted in 1969.

Provenance: Acquired by Henry Walters as part of the Don Marcello Massarenti Collection in 1902.

Exhibitions: "Maryland Heritage, Five Baltimore Institutions Celebrate the American Bicentennial," Walters Art Gallery, 1976, p. 50, no. 89.

References: *Supplément au catalogue du musée de peinture, sculpture et archéologie au Palais Accoramboni.* Rome, Impr. de Cajetan Pistolesi, 1900, p. 9, no. 58.

Francesco Hayez
Italian: Venice, 1791 - Milan, 1882

Hayez was born in Venice to parents from Valenciennes, France. Initially, he studied with an artist named Zanotti and with Francesco Maggiotto. Beginning in 1804, he entered the life classes at the Venetian Academy and four years later he attended courses in history painting given by Teodoro Matteini. At the age of eighteen, Hayez received a scholarship to Rome. There he was profoundly affected by the neoclassicism emanating from the studio of Canova. Other contacts that determined the course of his later development were with Pelagio Palagi, V. Camuccini, T. Minardi, J.-A.-D. Ingres, and various members of the Nazarene Movement. In 1817, Hayez returned to Venice for three years before settling in Milan. He taught at the Brera Academy beginning in 1822 and eventually, in 1850, succeeded G. Sabatelli to the chair of painting. In Milan, Hayez responded to the conflict between neoclassicism and romanticism, developing a personal style that was in technique more closely allied to the former though his subjects were decidedly romantic.

Hayez also worked as a graphic artist, producing in 1821 lithographs illustrating Walter Scott's *Ivanhoe*.

222. Christ and the Woman Taken in Adultery

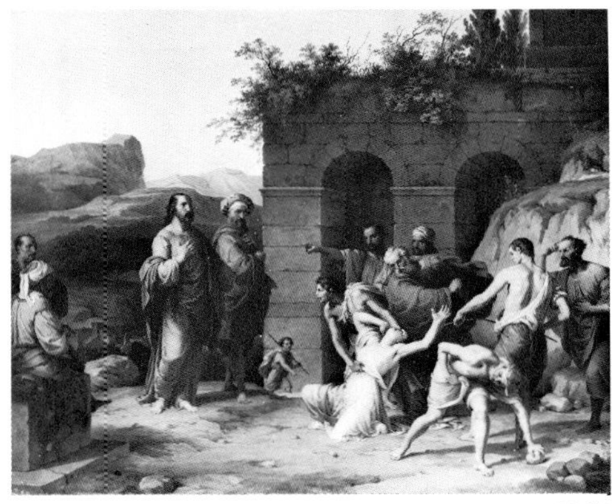

37.1825 1841

Shown is the incident from St. John 8:3–11. The adulteress, forced into a kneeling position, flails her arms as her executioners prepare to act. To the left stands the serene, imposing figure of Christ. Spectators include Pharisees and scribes.

The exterior setting in front of arches overgrown with shrubbery, rather than the more traditional location within the temple, has resulted in misinterpretation of the subject: the early Massarenti cataloguers identifying the scene as the miracle of Christ casting out unclean spirits (St. Mark 5:3–13).

This small painting with its carefully delineated idealized figures and its remarkably lucid atmosphere is reminiscent of the Nazarenes, a school of German painters active in Rome in the early nineteenth century.

Support: Canvas, .432 x .539 (17" x 21¼")

Signed and dated at lower left: *F Ayez 1841* (the last two digits of the date are no longer legible).

Condition: Cleaned and lined in 1950, when the overpainting masking the figure with the stone climbing the slope in the central middle-ground was removed.

Provenance: Marcello Massarenti Collection before 1881; purchased by Henry Walters in 1902 as part of the Massarenti collection.

Exhibitions: "The Life of Christ," Washington County Museum of Fine Arts, Hagerstown, Md., 1951, no. 27.

References: *Catalogue d'une collection de tableaux de diverses écoles.* Rome, 1881. p. 82, no. 313, as *Le Sauveur guérissant une possédée; Catalogue du musée de peinture, sculpture et archéologie au Palais Accoramboni.* 2 vols. Rome, Imprimerie du Vatican, 1897. 1: 145, no. 842, as *Le Christ guérissant un possédé.*

Alfonso Chierici
Italian: Reggio Emilia, 1816 - Rome, 1873

Chierici began his career at the Academy of Reggio as a pupil of Prospero Minghetti. Subsequently he studied at Modena and in Rome, where he worked in the circle of the classical artist Tommaso Minardi. He is chiefly remembered for large conventional religious subjects such as *Christ expelling the Moneylenders from the Temple,* shown in Rome in 1844, and *Christ giving the keys to St. Peter,* both of which are preserved in the Galleria Civica in Reggio Emilia. He also executed a stage curtain for the theater in the town of his birth.

More lively are some small genre sketches such as the work in Baltimore. At the Royal Academy in London in 1856, Chierici exhibited two "costume-pieces," one showing an Albanian woman reading a love-letter, and the other a sailor being greeted by his wife and child at Moda di Gaeta.

223. A Storm in the Roman Campagna

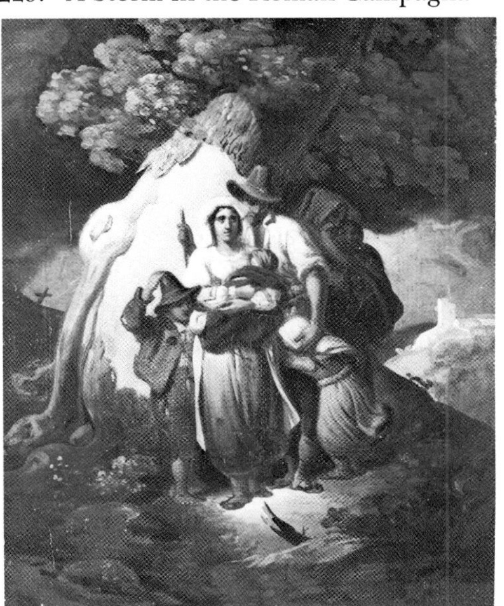

37.1150 1850s

A violent thunderstorm has arisen in the Roman Campagna, causing a peasant family wearing the distinctive *Ciociara* costume of the region to seek refuge beneath a tree. Also sheltering are a couple of monks lost in the shadows. Flashes of lightening momentarily illuminate the scene, revealing a cross silhouetted against the sky at the left and a gleaming tower at the right.

Support: Canvas, .29 x .225 (10⅞" x 8⅜")

Signed at lower right: *A.C.*

Condition: Lined prior to 1902.

Provenance: Acquired by Henry Walters in 1902 as part of the Massarenti Collection.

References: *Catalogue du musée de peinture, sculpture et archéologie au Palais Accorambani.* 2 vols. Rome, Imprimerie du Vatican, 1897, 1: 146, no. 849.

Giulio Cesare Ferrari
Italian, Bologna: 1818–?

Ferrari is listed as a history painter who worked on a large scale and in cool colors. He is also recorded to have been a professor at the Academy of Bologna. In the pinacoteca of that city there are preserved several of his pictures including an *Esmeralda,* illustrating a scene from Victor Hugo's *Nôtre Dame de Paris.*

224. Linda di Chamounix

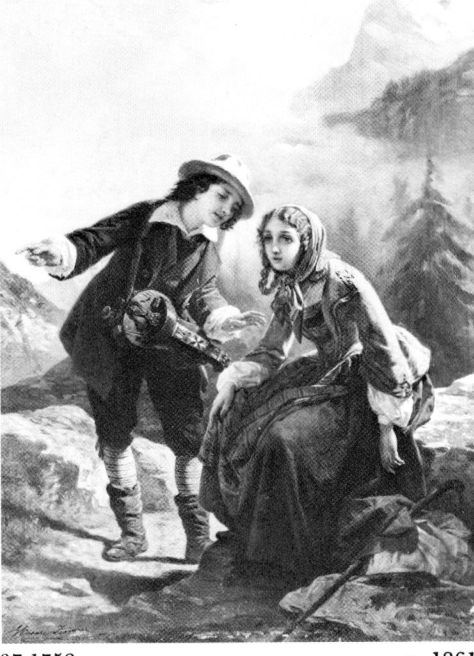

37.1758 c. 1861

In this scene from "Linda di Chamounix," an opera by Gaetano Donizetti with libretto by Gaetano Rossi, Carlo, the nobleman, disguised as a painter, has returned to the village of Chamonix to find Linda crazed with grief at the thought of being abandoned by him. Here, in Act II, he restores her sanity by singing "Hear the voice that softly singing . . ."

Carlo, suitably attired in Bohemian garb, carries a hurdy-gurdy strapped over his shoulder. His love, seated on a rock, is in the process of emerging from her madness.

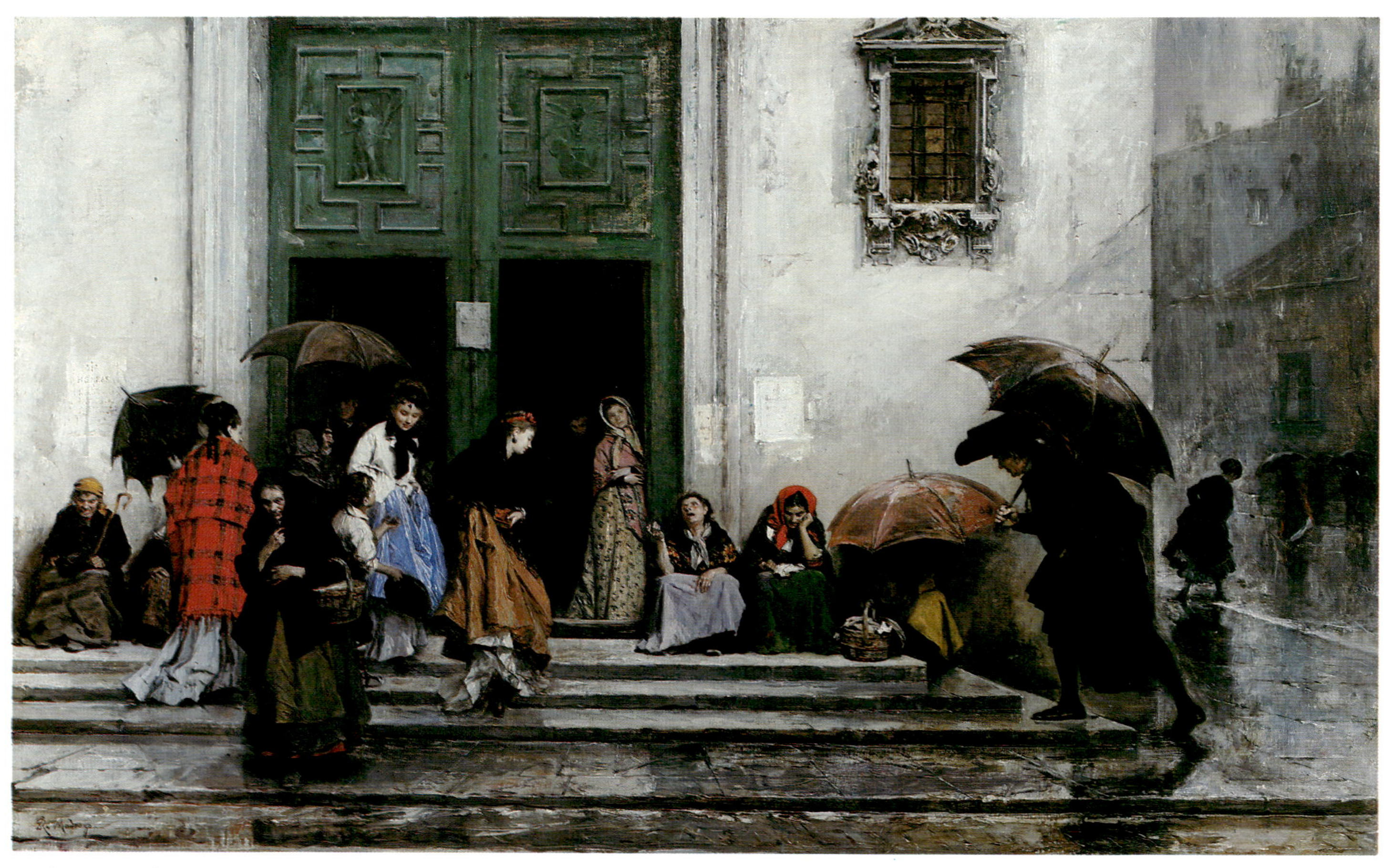

Madrazo *Coming Out of Church,* no. 217

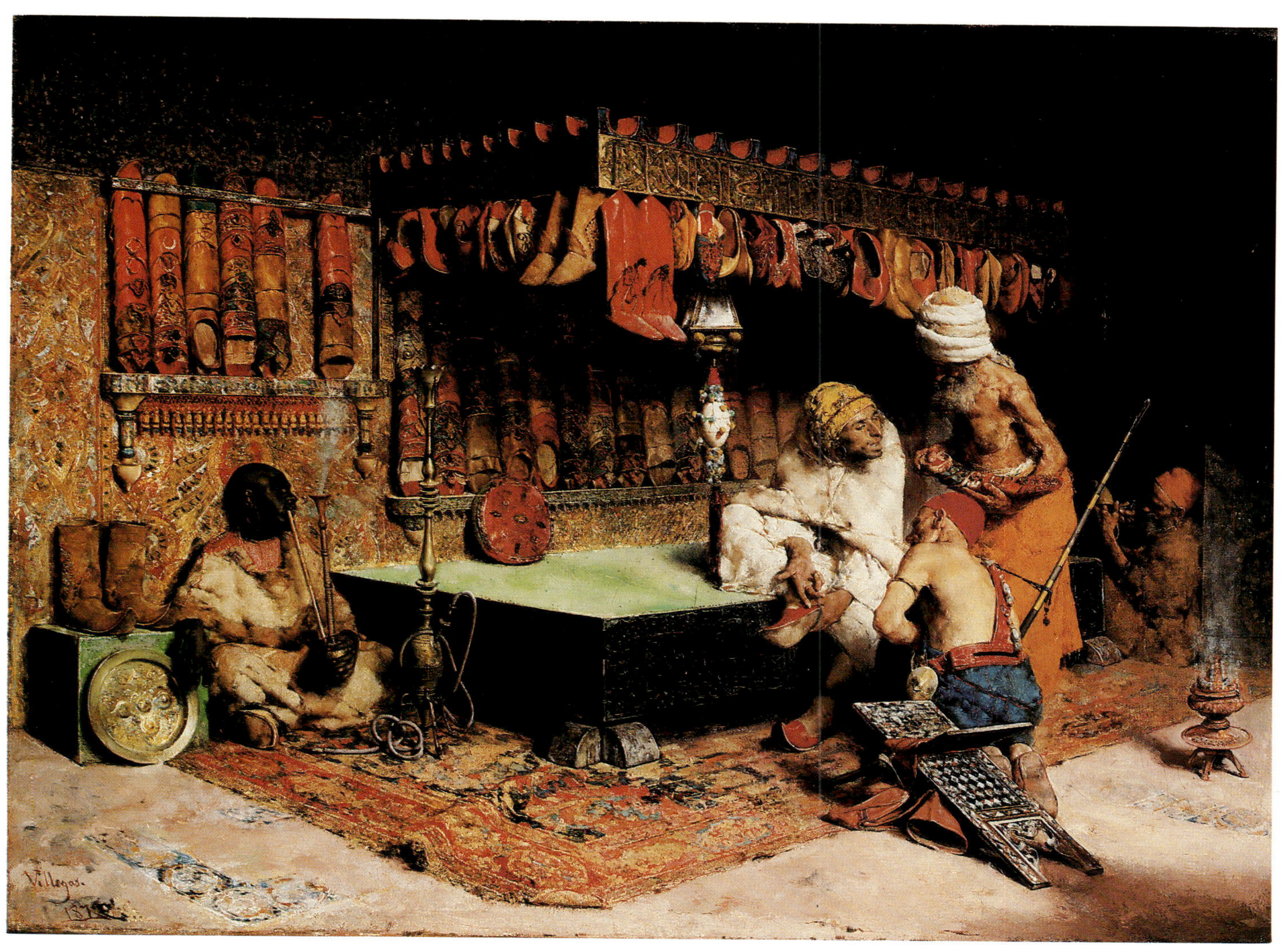

Villegas *The Slipper Merchant,* no. 219

In the background is an Alpine peak, perhaps Mont Blanc.

The opera, set in Paris and in Chamonix, a village in Upper Savoy, was first performed in Vienna on May 19, 1842.

The small size of this painting suggests that it is a replica of the *Linda di Chamounix* that was listed by Thieme-Becker in *Allegemeines Lexikon der bildenden Künstler,* 11: 455, as having been exhibited in Florence in 1861.

Support: Panel, beveled edges, .340 x .249 (13⅜" x 9⅞")

Signed at lower left: *G Cesare Ferrari*

Condition: Some abrasion along top and bottom edges caused by the frame.

Provenance: Acquired by Henry Walters in 1902 as part of the Massarenti Collection.

References: *Catalogue du musée de peinture, sculpture et archéologie au Palais Accoramboni,* 2 vols. Rome, Imprimerie du Vatican, 1897, 1: 38, no. 203 as César Ferrari, (vers 1818) *Linda de Chamounix.*

Alberto Pasini
Italian, Busseto, 1826 - Cavoretto, 1899

Pasini studied painting at the Accademia of Parma under G. Boccaccio and G. Magnani before turning to lithography. After having served in the 1848 War of Independence he moved briefly to Turin and then to Geneva, eventually settling in Paris, where he enrolled in the studio of the engraver Henriquel Dupont. There Pasini established a close rapport with the engraver and watercolorist Eugenio Cicéri. His earliest entry in the Salon was a lithograph, *Le Soir,* shown in 1853. Befriending Eugene Isabey and Théodore Rousseau, he also began to paint along the Seine and in the Forest of Fontainebleau. Soon, however, attracted by Eugène Fromentin's North African subjects, Pasini turned to Orientalism, and, through the intervention of Théodore Chassériau, he was invited in 1855 to accompany the French diplomatic expedition of Prosper Bourée to Persia, stopping in Turkey and Egypt on his return. Back in Paris, Pasini exhibited three oil paintings and three drawings recording the expedition. Subsequently he continued, with considerable success, to submit Near Eastern subjects to the Salons, winning a third-class medal in 1857, and a second-class medal in 1863 and again in 1864. He was appointed Chevalier of the Legion of Honor in 1868 and was elevated to Officier in 1878. Later travels included an extended visit to Constantinople and Athens in 1867–68 and a tour of Spain and Belgium accompanied by J.-L. Gérôme in 1869. After the 1870–71 turmoil in France, Pasini settled in the hamlet of Cavoretto near Turin, though he continued to visit Paris frequently. Among his later subjects were views of Venice.

In discussing Pasini's works at the time of the 1878 Exposition Universelle, the critics, though conceding the artist's Italian origin, associated him with the French school. Charles Tardieu in "La peinture à l'Exposition Universelle de 1878: l'école italienne (fin)," *L'Art* 14 (1878): 246 distinguished Pasini among Orientalists as a specialist in subjects pertaining to Turkey and its possessions. This critic also observed that Pasini's orientalism was that of a landscape rather than of a genre or figure painter.

225. Damascus

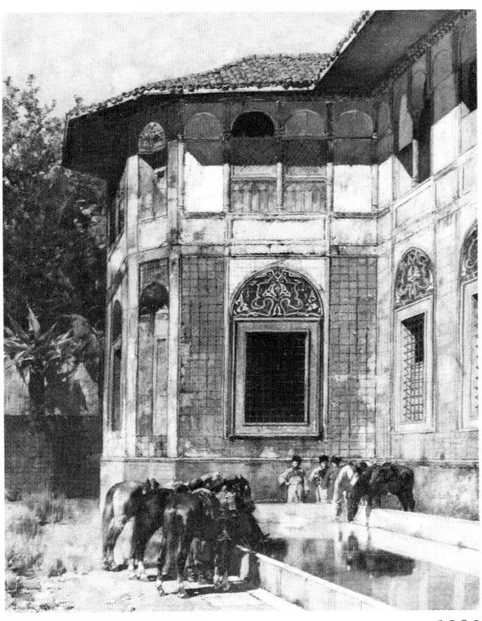

37.193 1880

In this small painting Pasini records a courtyard scene. Several Turkish soldiers appear engrossed in conversation as their horses are being watered at a well.

With characteristic subtlety, Pasini portrays the play of subdued daylight on the crumbling stucco surfaces, the tiles and the lattice windows of the background building.

Though the site of this scene is questionable it should be noted that the artist exhibited a *Cavalli al pascolo in Siria* at the Promotrice Torinese in 1880, the year of the Walters picture. Horses at a well were recurrent in Pasini's oeuvre. Other examples include *The Old Armory,* Cincinnati Art Museum, *Entrance to a Mosque,* formerly in the Metropolitan Museum of Art, New York, and *Cavaliers gardant des chevaux,* C. S. Smith Sale, New York, April 24–25, 1919, no. 104.

Support: Finely woven fabric, .426 x .32 (16 9/16" x 12 11/16")

Signed and dated lower left: *A Pasini 1880*

Marks: Reverse: paper label *2782*

Provenance: Acquired by W. T. Walters before 1884.

References: Walters cat., 1880, p. 16, no. 20; Champlin and Perkins, 3: 400, as *Damascus.*

E. Pastina
Italian, active in the second half of the nineteenth century.

No biographical information is available pertaining to this view painter active in the vicinities of Rome and Naples in the 1860s.

226. Lago di Nemi

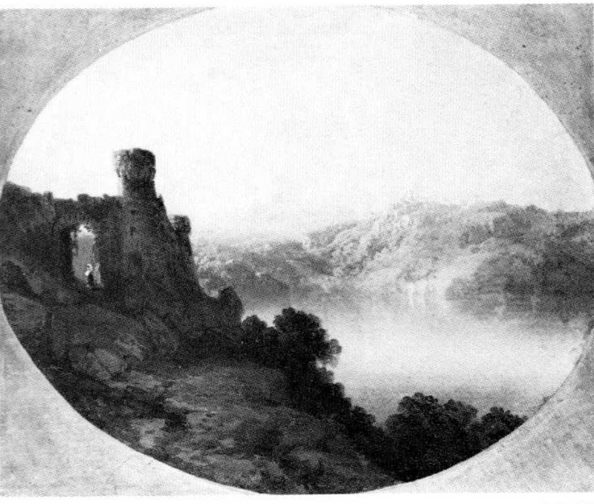

37.1810 1860

Looking across Lake Nemi in the Alban Hills southeast of Rome, one sees the medieval village of Nemi. The lake, nestled in the crater of a volcano, is seldom ruffled by the wind, and has received the epithet, "The Mirror of Diana." The painting appears to be a companion to the *View of Castel Gondolfo,* no. 227.

Canvas: .38 x .463 (15" x 18½")

Signed and dated lower left: *Pastina/Roma 1860*
Reverse: Inscribed in ink: *Lago di Nemi Pastina*

Condition: Lined before 1902.

Provenance: Purchased by Henry Walters as part of the Massarenti collection in 1902.

References: *Catalogue d'une collection de tableaux de diverses écoles.* Rome, 1881. p. 81, no. 306, as *Vue de Némi; Catalogue du musée de peinture, sculpture at archéologie au Palais Accoramboni.* 2 vols. Rome, Imprimerie du Vatican,, 1897. 1: 144, no. 837.

227. View of Castel Gandolfo

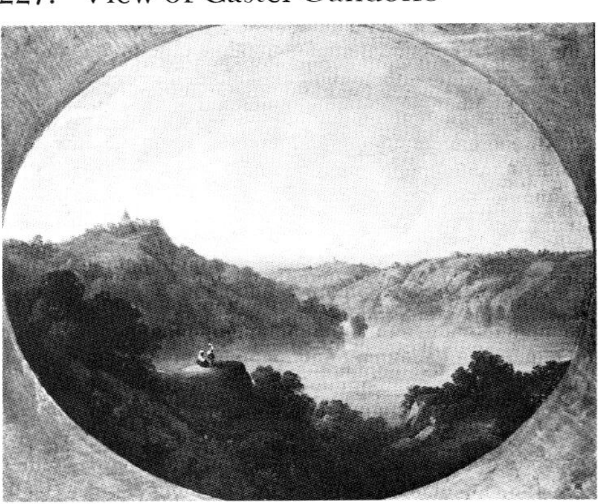

37.1752 c. 1860

George Stillman Hillard wrote of Lake Albano in *Six Months in Italy,* Boston, 1856, p. 403:

> This lake is one of the most beautiful sheets of water in Italy or anywhere else. It is about six miles in circumference and fills up the crater of an extinguished volcano. Its form is nearly circular and its outline as symmetrical as if shaped by the hand of art. . . . A landscape-painter might study here to great advantage two important elements of his art—the character of foliage, and the effects of shadows upon water.

Pastina has observed these features in this small, oval painting of the scenic view.

The spandrels created by the oval format on the rectangular canvas have been painted gold.

Support: Canvas, .393 x .46 (15½" x 18⅛")

Marks: Inscribed in ink on reverse: *Lago di Castelgandolfi Pastina;* Paper sticker: *838*

Provenance: Purchased by Henry Walters as part of the Massarenti Collection in 1902.

References: *Catalogue d'une collection de tableaux de diverses écoles.* Rome, 1881, p. 81, no. 305; *Catalogue du musée de peinture, sculpture et archéologie au Palais Accoramboni.* 2 vols. Rome, Imprimerie du Vatican, 1897. 1: 144, no. 838, as *Vue de Castel Gandolfo,* .25 x .32 (?).

228. View of the Coast at Amalfi

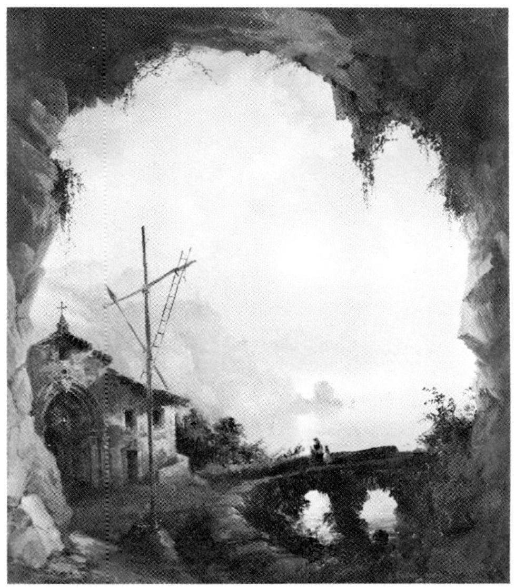

37.1882 1867

During the nineteenth century tourists provided a ready market for paintings of scenic views. Here, the Amalfi coast is shown from a grotto west of the town. In the foreground is a wayside cross and the remains of the Capuchin monastery closed in 1815. The town, perched on the bluffs beyond, is scarcely discernible in the morning mists, though the contours of the *torre dello zirro* standing high on a cliff, and *torre di Amalfi* at the water's edge, are readily recognizable. The sun is rising, casting a reflection across the sea.

This painting is one of four purchased in the Massarenti collection and listed simply as the works of "Pastina." Subsequently, the signature "E. Pastina" and dates on two of the four paintings were overlooked and the pictures were catalogued as being by Giuseppe Pastini (Bari, 1863–?) a South Italian artist who trained in Naples under Domenico Morelli and Giovanni del Re before pursuing a career in Rome as a landscape and portrait painter. No documentation has been discovered for E. Pastina who signed the Massarenti pictures. He apparently specialized in conventional scenic views which he painted with particular sensitivity for the effects of sunlight at dawn or twilight.

An almost identical view, differing principally in the addition of figures on the bridge and the presence of several Capuchins outside the monastery, was presented to the Corcoran Gallery of Art by W. W. Corcoran in 1869 and subsequently listed as a *Scene on the Coast of Calabria* by "Amati," the artist's inscription *Amalfi 1851* being misconstrued. It was sold at Parke Bernet, New York, Sale no. 4240, lot 31, *On the Coast,* canvas, .725 x .61.

Records of this particular scene were evidently much in demand, judging by the number of views in oils and gouaches of varying quality that have survived.

Support: Canvas, .665 x .586 (26¼" x 23")

Signed at lower right: *E. Pastina 1867*

Condition: The varnish was reformed with solvents in 1944.

Provenance: Purchased by Henry Walters as part of the Massarenti collection in 1902.

References: *Catalogue d'une collection de tableaux de diverses écoles.* Rome, 1881. p. 81, no. 308, as *Vue de Pausilippe; Catalogue du musée de peinture, sculpture et archéologie au Palais Accoramboni.* 2. vols. Rome, Imprimerie du Vatican, 1897. 1: 144, no. 839, as *Vue de Posilipo.*

229. View of Castel Gandolfo

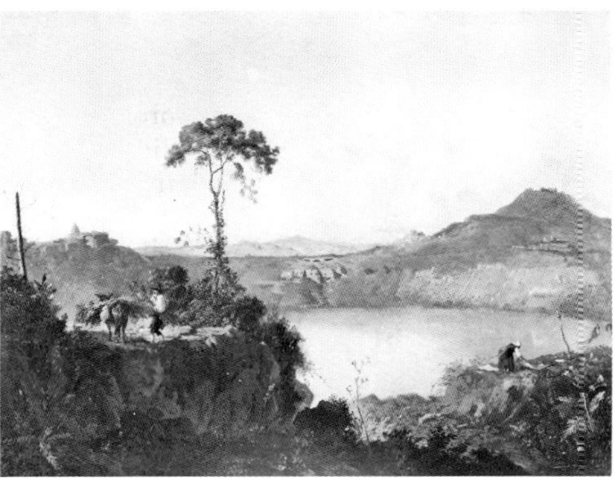

37.1935 1860s

Looking across Lake Albano one sees, at the left, Castel Gandolfo, the summer residence of the popes. Standing against the horizon is Bernini's dome for the Castel Gandolfo church. At the right, towers Monte Cavo and slightly beyond, perched on the spur of the mountain, is Rocca di Papa. In the foreground, a peasant is packing rushes on the back of a mule and a *contadina* prepares her laundry. The scene appears to be in the morning, and mists are still rising from the water.

Support: Canvas, .746 x .985 (29½" x 36¾")

Signed at lower left: *E Pastina*

Condition: Discolored varnishes were removed in 1967; the fabric was lined; a synthetic resin was applied.

Provenance: Purchased by Henry Walters as part of the Massarenti collection in 1902.

References: *Catalogue d'une collection de tableaux de diverses écoles,* Rome, 1881, p. 81, no. 305; *Catalogue du musée de peinture, sculpture et archéologie au Palais Accoramboni,* 2 vols. Rome, Imprimerie du Vatican, 1897, 1: 144, no. 836, *Vue du château de Castel Gandolfo,* .25 x .32 (?).

Antonio Rotta

Italian: Gorizia (Friuli), 1828 - Venice, 1903

Beginning in 1841, Rotta trained at the Accademia di Belle Arti in Venice under Ludovico Lipparini. Though he painted a number of religious and historical subjects said to have been rather stiff in execution, his reputation was based on the extensive production of sentimental genre subjects directed principally towards a bourgeois clientele in Venice, Austria, and Germany. Following a tradition initiated in Venice by Eugenio Bosa, Rotta specialized in paintings representing scenes from the childhood of the more impoverished levels of Venetian society. He worked in painstakingly meticulous detail in a technique that lent itself to being reproduced by lithography or photography, media through which his works were distributed. Though the exact circumstances are unknown, Rotta was in Paris in 1873 selling pictures through S. P. Avery of New York with G. A. Lucas serving as intermediary.

230. The Hopeless Case

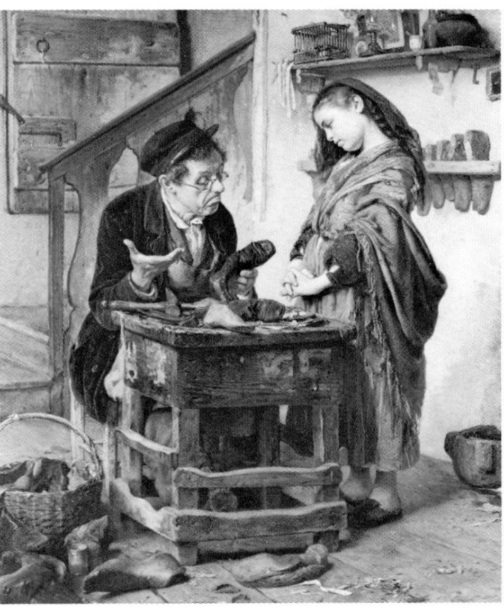

37.182 1871

A young girl wearing a typical Venetian shawl listens stoically as the shoemaker reports upon the hopeless condition of her boot. The artist has depicted this cluttered interior with characteristic detail.

The painting was evidently widely known in the nineteenth century. Charles Tardieu in discussing the Italian Section of the 1878 Exposition Universelle, did not cite Rotta's entry on that occasion, "The Young Brood," a poultry scene, but recalled instead the comic gravity of *Ciabattino,* the Gallery's picture, which had been popularized through photography.

Rotta returned to the theme of the shoemaker on several occasions. Advertised by M. Newman in the May 1976 issue of *The Connoisseur* was *At the Shoemakers,* panel, .52 x .635, in which an elderly shoemaker measures the calf of a young customer as an assistant looks over his shoulder. The interiors of the shops in the Newman and Walters picture are similar and the model for the assistant in the Newman picture appears to be identical to that of the shoemaker in the latter. The London picture may have been painted in preparation for a larger, more detailed work, the *Pleasant Occupation* recorded in the Witt Library, London, though now unlocated.

Alternative title: *Niente da fare; Ciabattino*

Support: Thinly primed fabric, .635 x .520 (25" x 20½") (wooden strips were added to the tacking edge on both sides.)

Signed and dated, lower right: *Antonio Rotta/ Venezia 1871*

Condition: Wooden strips removed in 1978. Discolored varnishes removed, and surface coated with synthetic resins.

Provenance: Anton Ritter von Oelzelt Sale, Vienna, November 18, 1878, no. 64, *Niente da Fare,* 3000 gulden; purchased by G. A. Lucas on behalf of W. T. Walters for 6100 florins.

Exhibitions: "A Baltimorean in Paris, George A. Lucas, Art Agent, 1860–1909," Walters Art Gallery, 1979.

References: Walters cat., 1878, p. 38; Strahan, 1: 92, 94, illus. facing p. 88; Charles Tardieu, "La peinture à l'Exposition Universelle de 1878: l'école italienne (fin)," *L'Art* 14 (1878): 222–23; Lamb, p. 248.

G. Mazzolini

No records have been found pertaining to the mid nineteenth-century artist who signed the following work.

231. The Letter

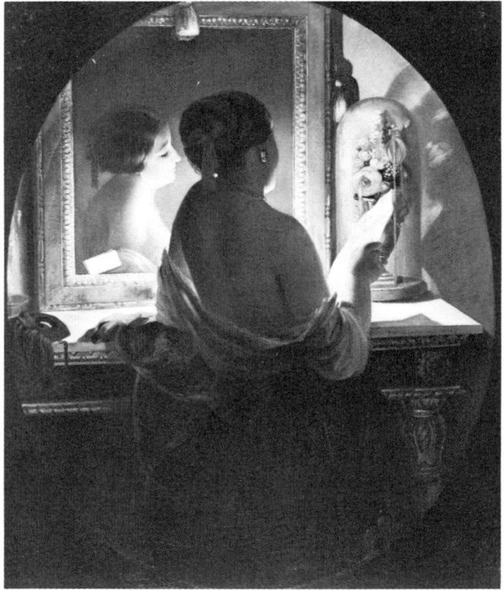

37.2565 c. 1855

In this intimate boudoir scene a young woman is strategically positioned in front of a mirror so that the light source, blocked from view, reveals the reflection of her face and shoulder while silhouetting her actual form. Her chemise falls from one shoulder to reveal her back. Around her neck is a strand of coral beads, gleaming in the light, and in her hair is tied a green ribbon. She leans against a pier table reading a letter in which only the greeting *May dear* is legible. On the table at the left is a discarded mask and on the right a bouquet of dried flowers beneath a glass dome.

Inserted beneath the rabbet of the mirror frame is a card inscribed *W.H.D.C. Wright/ Rome.* William Henry De Courcy Wright (1795–1864) of "Blakeford," Queen Anne's County, Maryland, traveled in both South America and Italy. The painting passed through five generations of descendants to its donor to the Gallery. Unaware of the artist's signatures, the family traditionally attributed this picture to Hans Heinrich Bebie (c. 1800–1888) a specialist in portraits and enigmatic domestic genre scenes. Bebie was a native of Zurich who emigrated to Baltimore.

Support: Canvas (oval image), .67 x .537 (26⅜" x 21⅛")

Signed on edge of marble table-top: *G. Mazzolini*

Signed along bottom, left edge: *G. Mazzolini*

Marks: Paper label on stretcher inscribed: *BACK DRAWING P*

Condition: Discolored varnishes removed in 1980; painting lined; synthetic varnishes applied.

Provenance: Descendants of William Henry De Courcy Wright through five generations to Anne Gordon Boyce Baldwin. Gift of Anne Gordon Boyce Baldwin (Mrs. Ludlow Baldwin) in memory of Mrs. Anne Gordon Johnston and Miss Mary Gordon Thom.

Tommaso de Simone

Italian: active in Naples in the second half of the nineteenth-century

The De Simones were a Neapolitan family of ship-portrait specialists who worked in oil and gouache in the second half of the nineteenth century. The most illustrious member of the family, Antonio, is represented in the Maritime Museum, Greenwich, by fourteen ship-portraits in oil, eight in watercolor, and a painting of the bombardment of Alexandria; and a portrait of the American barque *Wabash* in the Mariners Museum, Newport News. Tommaso is represented in Greenwich by a representation of H.M.S. *Liffey* dated 1858. A later De Simone was responsible for a gouache of Henry Walters' yacht *Narada* painted in Naples in 1905.

232. The Frigate Congress Outside Naples

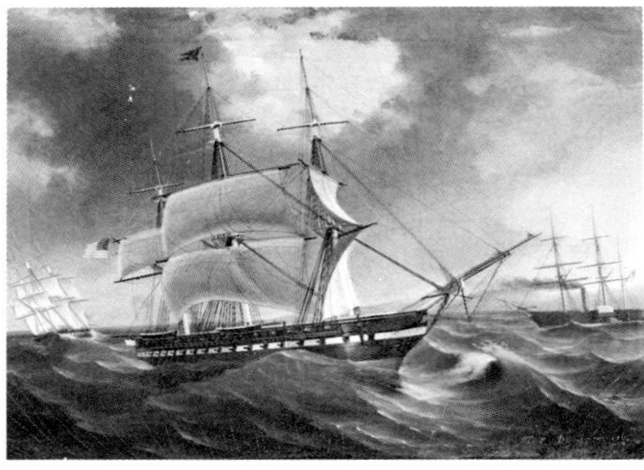

37.2566 1857

The United States frigate is sailing through high seas toward port. At the right, a paddle-wheel ship flying the American ensign is under steam and at the left is another American naval ship under sail. The waning sun breaks through the cloud cover near the horizon, casting a warm light across the scene.

Records belonging to the donor's family include a letter dated 1855 which is addressed to Lieutenant William May who served on the Frigate *Congress,* presumably the ship portrayed in this painting.

Support: Fabric, .451 x .659 (17¾" x 25$\frac{5}{16}$")

Signed and dated at lower right: *Tom. so De Simone 1857*

Marks: Stretcher inscribed: *Tomaso De Simone*

Condition: Discolored varnishes were removed in 1980 and the painting was lined with a fiberglass interleaf.

Provenance: The ship-portrait passed through the descendants of Clintonia Wright, wife of Lieutenant May, for four generations to Anne Gordon Boyce Baldwin. Gift of Anne Gordon Boyce Baldwin (Mrs. Ludlow Baldwin) in memory of Mrs. Anne Gordon Johnston and Miss Mary Gordon Thom.

233. The Frigate Congress in the Bay of Naples

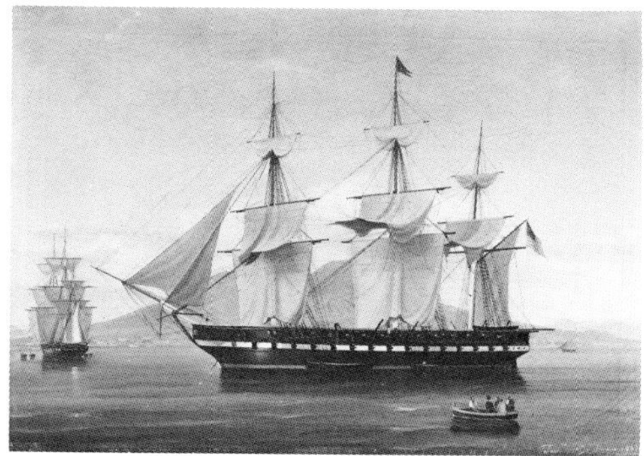

37.2567

Two American frigates are shown becalmed in the Bay of Naples. In the background rises Mount Vesuvius.

In its direct approach this ship-portrait, presumably of the U.S. frigate *Congress,* is characteristic of works executed in both oil and gouache by numerous Neapolitan artists for foreign visitors in the nineteenth century.

Support: Fabric, .464 x .654 (18¼″ x 25¾″)

Signed and dated at lower right: *Tom. so De Simone 1857*

Marks: Inscribed on stretcher: *Lieut May*

Condition: Discolored varnishes were removed in 1980; picture was lined and treated with synthetic varnish; minor losses were inpainted.

Provenance: The ship-portrait passed through the descendants of Clintonia Wright, wife of Lieutenant May, for four generations to Anne Gordon Boyce Baldwin. Gift of Anne Gordon Boyce Baldwin (Mrs. Ludlow Baldwin) in memory of Mrs. Anne Gordon Johnston and Miss Mary Gordon Thom.

Domenico Torti

Italian, active in Rome in the 1880's

Torti's name does not appear in any anthology of Italian art. He did, however, execute a ceiling decoration for the Sala dei Candelabri in the Vatican during Ludovico Seitz's renovations in the early 1880s.

234. The Virgin of the Immaculate Conception

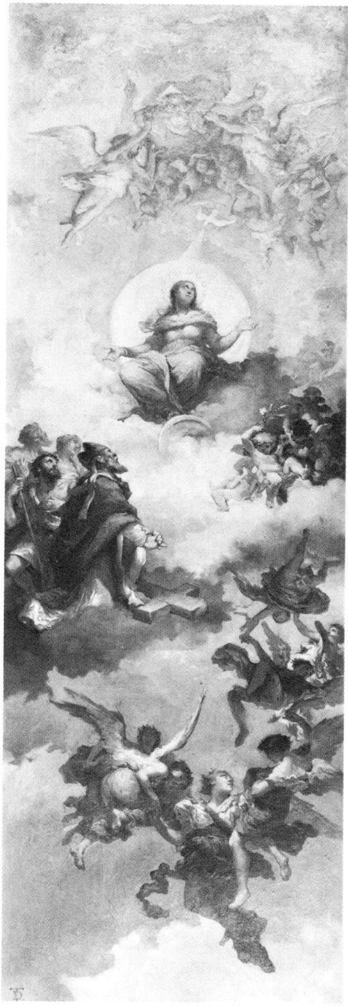

37.1693 1880's

The *Virgin of the Immaculate Conception* is posed against an aureole of light. Emanating from her head is a nimbus of stars, and at her feet is the half-moon. Above, is God the Father, the heavenly host, and the dove of the Holy Spirit. Below her are several saints, including a bishop kneeling in adoration. Angels hover in the clouds surrounding her.

In pose and physiognomy, the Virgin resembles a comparable figure occurring in Carlo Maratta's *Saint John and the Doctors meditating on the Immaculate Conception* (1686) in Santa Maria del Popolo, Rome. Its narrow format suggests that the Walters painting was intended to serve as a study for a ceiling decoration.

In listing the picture as *The Fine Arts Blessed by Religion,* painted as a study for the ceiling of the Sala dei Candelabri in the Vatican, the early cataloguers of the Massarenti collection were undoubtedly alluding to Torti's only other recorded work, a ceiling decoration executed about 1884 during the alterations by Ludovico Seitz (1844–1908) to the Sala dei Candelabri. *The Fine Arts Blessed by Religion,* however, was completed by Seitz, who was both an artist and keeper of the Pontifical collections.

Support: Canvas, 1.651 x .556 (65″ x 21⅞″)

Signed at lower left: *TD* (conjoined)

Provenance: Purchased by Henry Walters in 1902 as part of the Massarenti Collection.

References: *Catalogue du musée de peinture, sculpture et archéologie au Palais Accoramboni.* 2 vols. Rome, Imprimerie du Vatican, 1897. 1: 148, no. 858, as *La Religion, entourée des anges, bénissant les Beaux-Arts* (Etude du plafond de la Salle des Candélabres au Vatican).

British Paintings

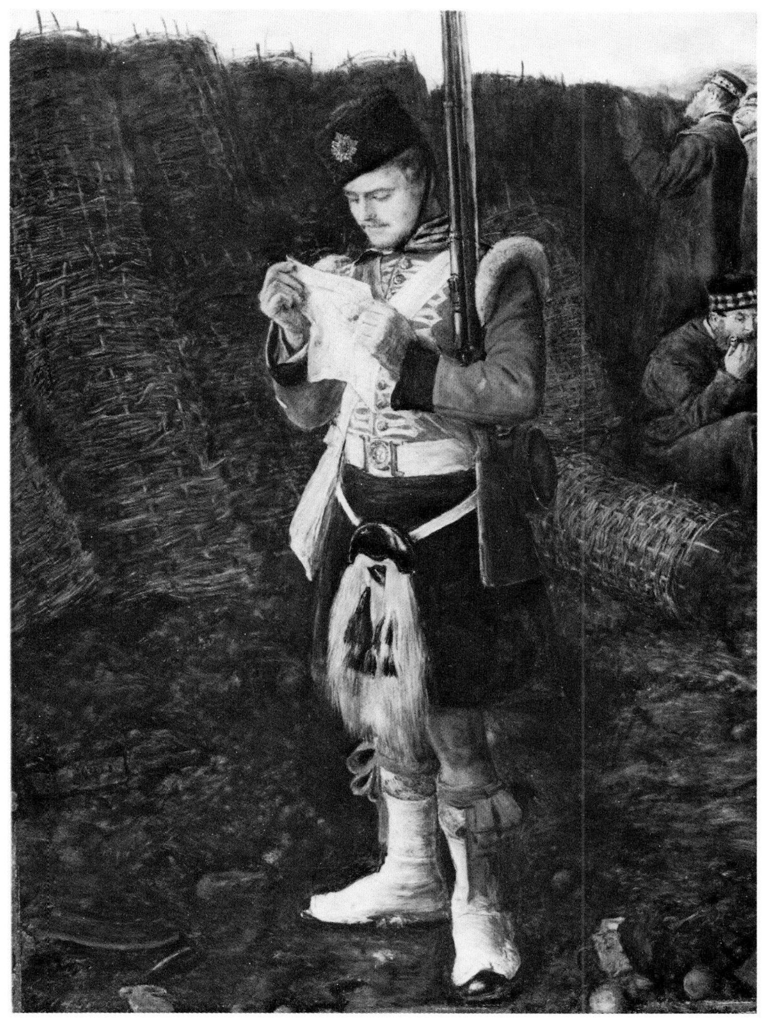

Millais *News from Home,* no. 261

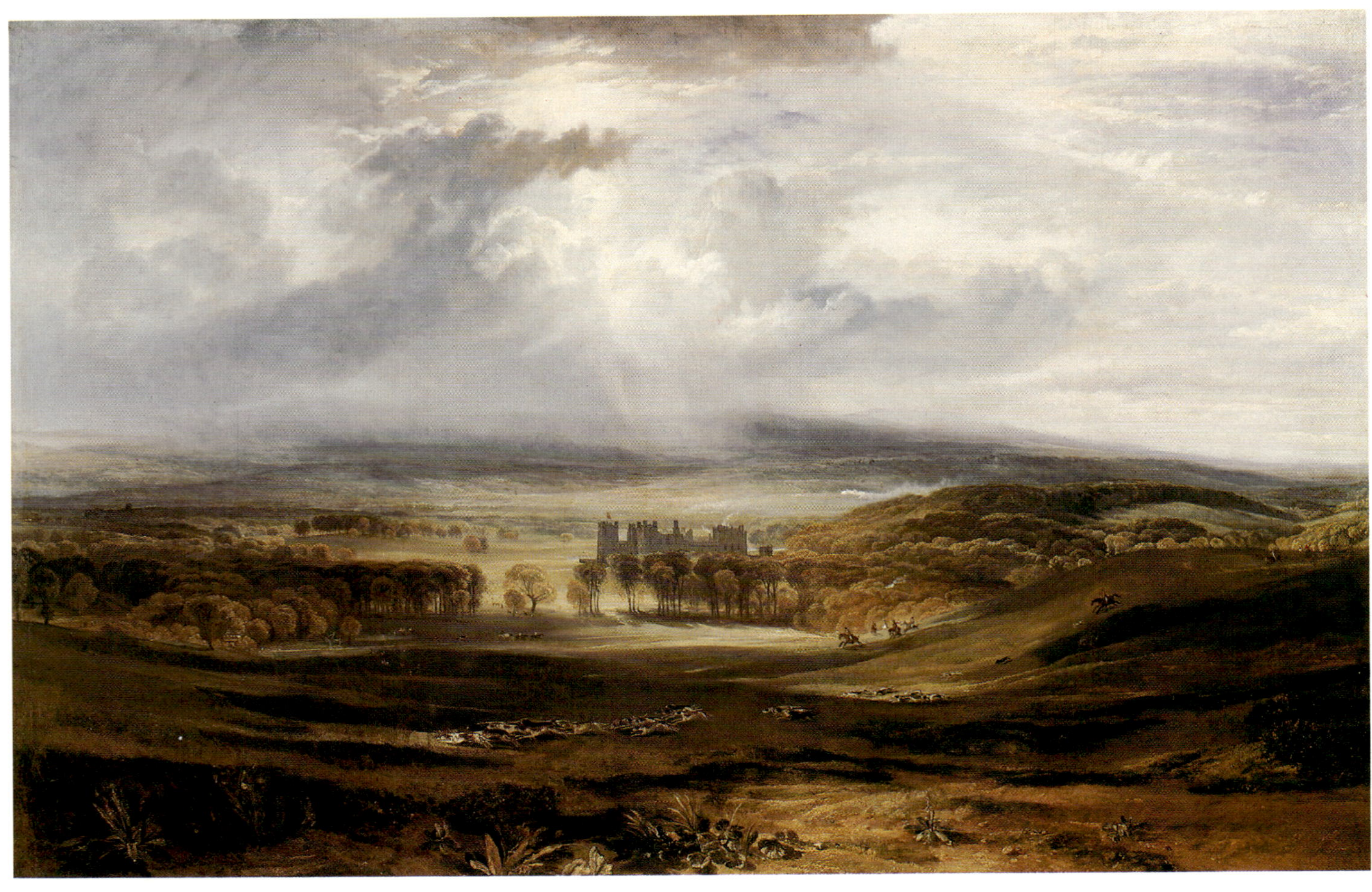

Turner *View of Raby Castle,* no. 243

Sir William Beechey, R.A.
English: Burford, 1753 - Hampstead, 1839

Between 1776 and 1839 Beechey exhibited three hundred and sixty-two portraits at the Royal Academy. Prior to enrolling in the Royal Academy schools in 1772, he had worked in a solicitor's office in Stowe. In 1793 he drew royal recognition at the Academy and was appointed "Portrait Painter to the Queen." The success of his large equestrian portrait, *George III at a Review,* (Windsor Castle, inv. 3013), exhibited in 1798, resulted in his being knighted and elected an academician, but by 1804 he had fallen from favor at Court.

Attributed to Beechey
235. Lady Clinton?

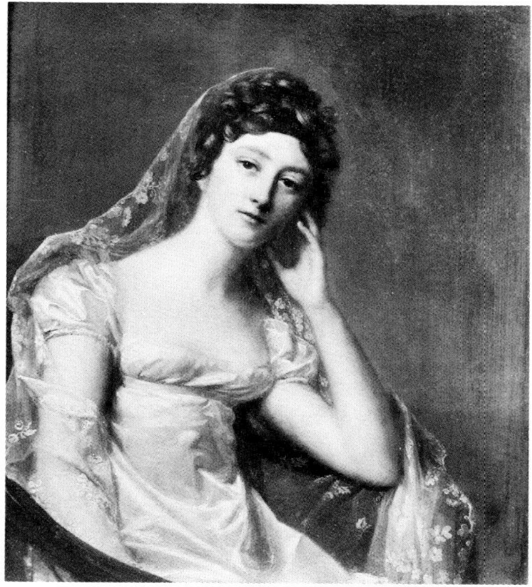

37.176 1807–10

A young lady wearing an embroidered mantle and a white satin dress with square decolletage is portrayed seated.

Should the traditional identification of the subject as Lady Clinton (1795–1875) be correct, she would have been about fourteen years old when this style of dress was in fashion. The identification is based on a newspaper clipping, attached to the reverse of the panel bearing the obituary of the Dowager Lady Clinton, second wife of Sir Horace Seymour, who served as "lady of the bed-chamber" to Queen Adelaide for several years prior to 1837.

Support: Panel, .3 x .242 (11¾" x 9½")

Condition: Removal of discolored varnishes in 1945 revealed traces of overcleaning in the background; these were inpainted and the surface coated with mastic varnish and wax.

Provenance: Purchased by Henry Walters between 1893 and 1909.

References: Walters cat., 1909, p. 59, no. 176, and subsequent Walters catalogues.

William Owen, R.A.
English: Ludlow, 1769 - London, 1825

Owen trained under Charles Catton and at the Royal Academy schools. He began to exhibit at the Academy in 1792 and continued to participate in exhibitions, acquiring an extensive clientele that included William Pitt, Lord Grenville, John Soane and the Earl of Bridgewater. In 1810 he succeeded John Hoppner as "Portrait-Painter to the Prince of Wales." He was elected Associate of the Academy in 1804 and became a full member in 1806. Owen was active until about 1821 when ill health forced him to abandon his profession.

Attributed to William Owen
236. Portrait of the Countess of Wilton?

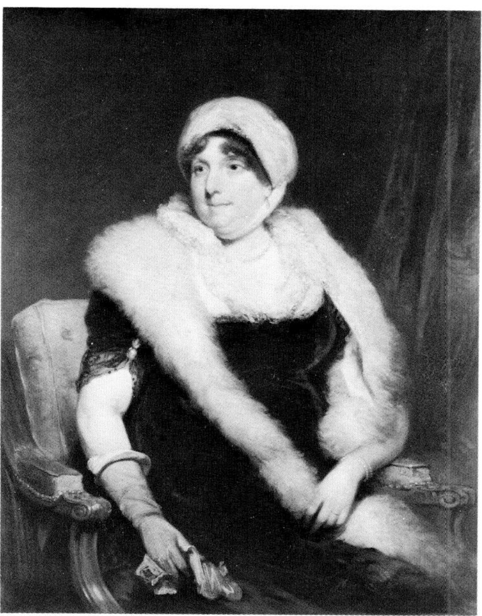

37.236 c. 1810

A middle-aged woman wears a high-waisted black dress, an ermine stole, a turban, long tan gloves, and pearl jewelry. The style of her costume suggests a date for the portrait of about 1810.

Early Walters catalogues, citing a label on the reverse of the stretcher, identify this painting as Sir Thomas Lawrence's portrait of the Countess of Wilton. As noted by Kenneth Garlick in a letter written to the Gallery, November 30, 1971, the portrait is stylistically closer to the work of Owen than to that of Lawrence. A portrait of Mary Margaret Stanley (died 1858), wife of Thomas Grosvenor, Second Earl of Wilton, painted by Lawrence (illustrated in *Les Arts,* April 1912, no. 124, p. 1), shows a much younger woman than the individual portrayed in the Baltimore picture. More likely, the Walters portrait shows Eleanor, daughter of Sir Ralph Assheton, Third Baronet of Middleton, who married Viscount Grey de Wilton, Earl of Wilton and Wilton Castle. This first Countess Wilton, who died in 1816 at the age of sixty-six, was the subject of a portrait in charcoal, wash and sanguine by H. Edridge, that was sold in the Doistau Sale, Paris, June 1909, no. 106, illustrated.

Support: Canvas, 1.13 x .873 (44½" x 34⅜")

Marks: Labels on reverse: *Alfred Morrison Esq No 115* [Alfred Morrison (1821–1897), Fonthill House, Hendon, Wiltshire] *Portrait of The Countess Wilton / by Sir Thomas Lawrence / 28/12/84 p. 67; on Hall / 7.* Frame bears label of American Art Association inscribed: *Countess of Wilton;* Owner: *S . . .* (obliterated). Frame stenciled: *211*

Condition: Lined before 1934.

Provenance: Purchased by Henry Walters at the Frederic Bonner Sale, New York, April 10, 1900.

References: Walters cat., 1901, p. 106, no. 184.

Sir Thomas Lawrence, P.R.A.
English: Bristol, 1769 - London, 1830

Lawrence, a pre-eminent portrait painter, was essentially self-taught. As a youth, he derived income by drawing profiles at his father's inn at Devizes and, from 1780 to 1786, by sketching portraits in pastel at Bath. Lawrence moved to London in 1786, began to exhibit at the Royal Academy the following year, and in 1791 was elected Associate of the Academy. George III, admiring his work, appointed him in 1792 "Principal Painter in ordinary." After the death of John Hoppner in 1810, Lawrence was acknowledged as the principal portraitist of his generation, much as Sir Joshua Reynolds had been in his time.

In 1818 Lawrence was dispatched to Aix-la-Chapelle by the Prince Regent to record the likenesses of the various dignitaries present at the signing of the treaty between the major powers at the end of the Napoleonic Wars. He toured the Continent, visiting Vienna and Rome. After his return to London in 1820, Lawrence succeeded Benjamin West as President of the Royal Academy.

237. The Marchioness of Sutherland

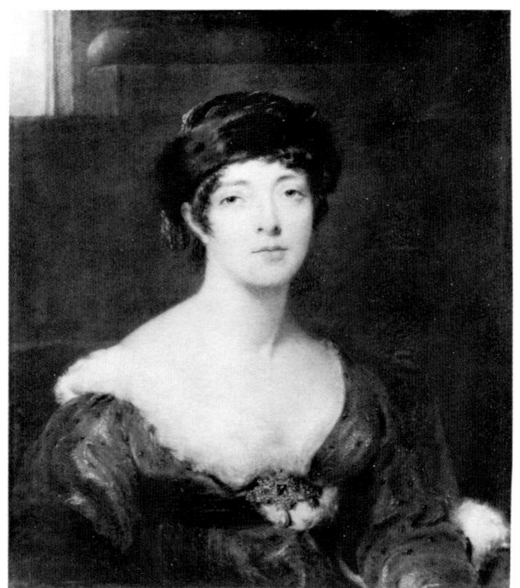

37.227 after 1816

The Countess is portrayed wearing a fur-trimmed turban and an ermine-lined, golden-yellow gown. Attached to her bodice is a large jeweled brooch from which is suspended a baroque pearl.

In a 1971 letter to the Gallery, Kenneth Garlick described the Walters picture as a "nice early, and perhaps studio version" of the portrait by Sir Thomas Lawrence that belongs to the Duke of Sutherland, Dunrobin Castle.

Lawrence exhibited the original portrait at the Royal Academy in 1816 (no. 48). The composition in the Walters painting has been cropped slightly along the lower edge, perhaps as a result of a lining process.

Elizabeth, Marchioness of Stafford, was born in 1765, married in 1785, and died in 1839. She was Countess of Sutherland in her own right, and after 1833, first Duchess of Sutherland.

Support: Canvas, .763 x .634 (30″ x 25″)

Condition: Lined before 1933.

Provenance: Reputed in 1898 to have belonged to the grandson of the Steward of the Dunrobin Estates; purchased by Henry Walters from T. J. Blakeslee, New York, in December 1898.

References: Walters cat., 1903, p. 102, no. 168, and subsequent Walters catalogues.

Formerly attributed to Lawrence
238. Mrs. Foote

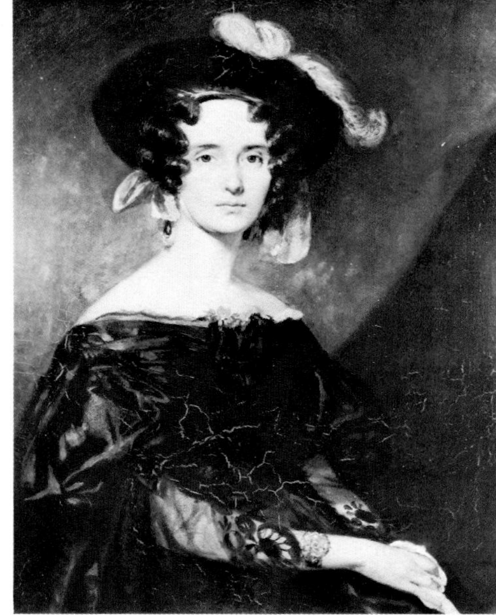

37.237 c. 1829

An attractive woman is portrayed seated, clad in a black silk dress, and wearing a wide-brimmed hat adorned with a white plume. Her hair falls in close curls over her temples. The traditional attribution of this painting to Sir Thomas Lawrence is no longer accepted, although the original identification of the subject as Miss Foote appears in keeping with other representations of the actress. In 1831 Maria Foote (1797(?)–1867) married Charles Stanhope, Fourth Earl of Harrington, after pursuing a successful career on the stage.

Among the painters to whom this portrait has most recently been attributed is William Etty (1787–1849).

Support: Canvas, .894 x .693 (35$\frac{3}{16}$″ x 27¼″)

Condition: Lined before 1934; darkened varnish removed in 1948, revealing extensive crackle losses in the grey-black areas of the garment; losses inpainted, surface treated with mastic varnish; surface cleaned and varnished in 1951.

Provenance: Acquired by Henry Walters between 1903 and 1909.

References: Walters cat., 1909, p. 74, no. 237, and subsequent Walters catalogues.

Sir Martin Archer Shee, P.R.A.
Irish: Dublin, 1769 - Brighton, 1850

Shee was a proficient and fashionable portrait painter who succeeded Lawrence as President of the Royal Academy.

After studying at the Dublin Society's Schools, Shee left his native city for London at the suggestion of Gilbert Stuart and there, following the advice of Sir Joshua Reynolds, enrolled in the Schools of the Royal Academy. In 1789 he exhibited two "heads" at the Academy and two years later he submitted a more ambitious, full-length figure. In addition to being an able painter Shee was a convivial well-connected individual who quickly achieved the trappings of success. He was elected an associate member of the Academy in 1798, full member in 1800, and in 1830 he succeeded Lawrence as President. Early portraits tended to be of actors and actresses, though subsequently he turned to leaders of Society, painting the Duke of Clarence (1800); Lieutenant General Sir Eyre Coote (1810); the Bishop of Norwich (1818); the Bishop of Winchester (1833); the King (1835); the Queen (1843). In Bryan's *Dictionary of Painters and Engravers,* London, 1905, 5: 74, Shee's art was described as "solid and commonplace but not without dignity."

In addition to being a painter, Shee was a writer, publishing *Rhymes on Art* in 1805, *Elements of Art* in 1809, as well as a play *Alasco, a Tragedy* that was banished from the stage by the Lord Chamberlain.

239. Portrait of Miss Moffat

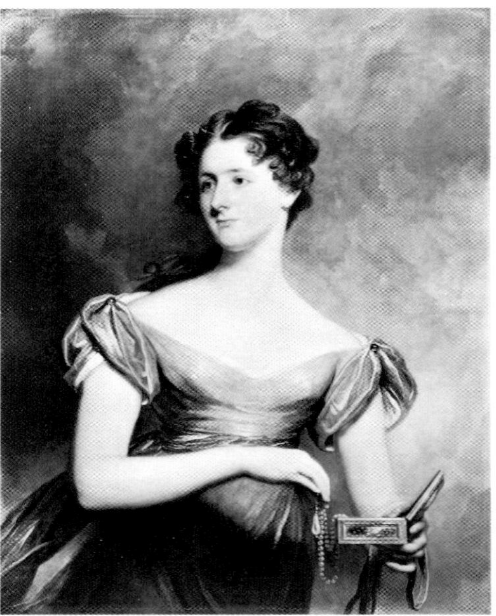

37.72 1826

A young woman of high complexion and light brown hair, identified only as Miss Moffat, is removing a strand of pearls from a gold jewel box. She wears a henna-colored dress and is posed against a dramatic, partially overcast sky.

Support: Canvas, .918 x .715 (36¼″ x 28$\frac{1}{16}$″)

Condition: The picture was partially cleaned in 1948.

Provenance: Sold at Christie's, London, June 10, 1899; acquired by Henry Walters before 1901.

Exhibitions: The Royal Academy, London, 1826, no. 74.

References: Walters cat., 1901, p. 105, no. 178, and subsequent Walters catalogues; W. G. Strickland, *A Dictionary of Irish artists.* 2 vols. Dublin, Maunsel, 1913. 2:342.

George Sanders
Scottish: Kinghorn, Fifeshire, 1774 - London, 1846

Sanders received his training in Edinburgh under the coach-painter Smeaton, and worked there as a miniature painter, drawing-instructor and illustrator. In 1807, when he departed for London, he continued miniature painting, receiving encouragement from his patron Lord Byron. Eventually he turned to portraiture in oils. His works were regarded as fashionable even though he participated only once, in 1834, in a Royal Academy exhibition.

240. Portrait of George Gordon Byron (6th Baron) 1788–1824

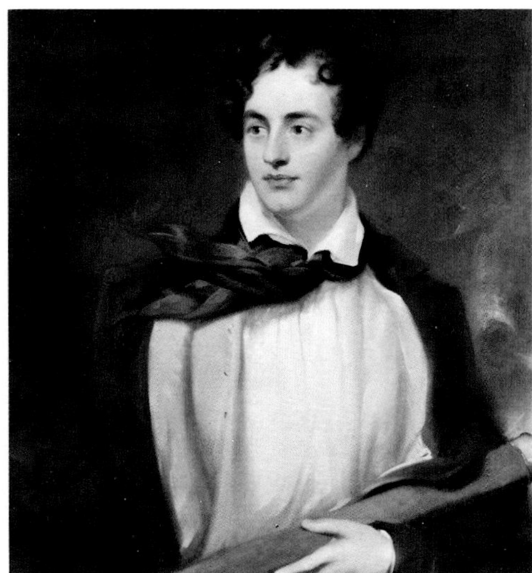

37.217

This picture replicates the head and torso of the principal figure in Sanders' *Portrait of Lord Byron and a Companion* (canvas, 1.08 x .89), in the Royal Collection, Windsor Castle. In the full composition, Byron stands on the seashore with his right hand resting on a large rock. He wears a navy-blue suit with open jacket and a blue cravat waving in the breeze. Behind him, a companion steadies a dinghy and visible further back in the cove is a yacht flying the red ensign. The background is comprised of a mountainous landscape. This painting is reputed to commemorate a visit undertaken by the poet in the summer of 1807 to the Western Isles of Scotland. That Byron was not fully satisfied with the likeness is indicated in a letter to his mother of July 1, 1810, quoted in Lionel Cust, "Notes on Pictures in the Royal Collections," *The Burlington Magazine,* 27 (1915): 4:

> I am glad you have received my portrait from Sanders. It does not *flatter* me I think, but the subject is a bad one and I must even do as Fletcher does over his Greek wines make a face and hope for the better.

The painting was eventually presented to the poet's Cambridge companion, John Cam Hobhouse, whose daughter bequeathed it to George V in 1914.

The Baltimore replica differs from the Windsor painting in several respects. The poet is shown with his left arm holding a telescope rather than hanging freely, and he is posed against a stormy sky instead of a mountain. More significantly, the subject wears an unbuttoned cream-colored waistcoat, rather than the blue, partially buttoned, garment shown in the original painting. This discrepancy is not found in Edward F. Finden's engraving of the poet published by John Murray in 1834 but it does occur in several other replicas, including William Finden's engraving of the complete composition published by John Murray in 1830, a well-known Rockingham biscuit porcelain statuette of the poet based on the picture, and an unattributed miniature showing the poet waist-length, sold at Sotheby's, London, December 14, 1976, lot 181. The prevalence of this variation in dress leads one to conjecture that it represented an alternative composition which the artist first expressed in a painted replica such as the Walters picture.

Sanders' miniature portraits of the poet, dating from 1808 to 1810, differ in both pose and costume.

Support: Canvas, moderately fine weave, .916 x .714 (36⅛" x 28⅛")

Marks: Reverse: A paper label on the stretcher is inscribed: *AMELIA MARIANNE LEIGH*

Condition: The picture was cleaned and lined in 1962–64. The use of highly soluble varnish glazes in the darker areas of the picture complicated the cleaning process.

Provenance: Amelia Marianne Leigh(?).

References: Walters cat., 1909, p. 71 no. 217, and subsequent Walters catalogues.

John (Jock) Wilson, R.S.A.
Scottish: Ayr, Scotland, 1774 - Folkestone, England, 1855

After having been apprenticed to the Edinburgh house-painter Norie, Wilson trained briefly with Patrick Nasmyth. For several years he taught at Montrose on the North Sea, and about 1798 he moved to London where he worked initially as a scene-painter. Beginning in 1807, he began to exhibit regularly in London at the exhibitions of the Royal Academy, the British Institution, and the Society of British Artists. He also retained a connection with Scotland, entering works in the Royal Scottish Academy exhibitions. His principal patron was Lord Northwick, who acquired *The Battle of Trafalgar* at the British Institution exhibition of 1825 (Spencer Churchill Sale, Christie's, London, June 25, 1965). Wilson was an exceedingly prolific artist, who is remembered primarily for his dramatic coastal views of England, Holland, and France rather than for his more restrained inland scenes. He was a vigorous rather than a sophisticated painter. His son, John James Wilson (1818–1875) worked in his father's tradition.

241. English Barnyard

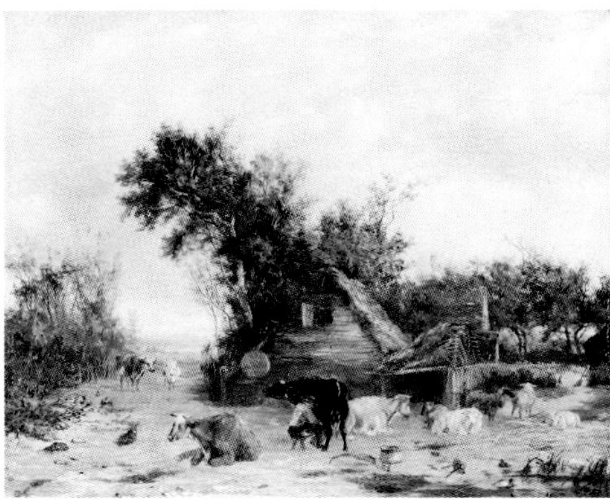

37.211 1839

The scene portrayed is a barnyard containing cattle and sheep. One cow is being milked by a farmer seated on a stool. Behind him are various farm structures, a cow barn, a dilapidated shed, and a house with a smoking chimney nestled amidst trees. In the immediate right foreground is a duck pond.

Wilson depicted the same buildings in his *A Farmyard, Surrey* illustrated in the advertisement of Vicars Brothers, *Apollo 19* (1934): 114.

Support: Fabric, preprimed, .381 x .457 (15" x 18")

Marks: Signed and dated lower left: *J.W., 39*

Condition: Discolored varnishes were removed in 1978, revealing some overpainting along picture edges

Provenance: Acquired by Henry Walters before 1909.

References: Walters cat., 1909, p. 70, no. 211, and subsequent Walters catalogues.

242. Seascape

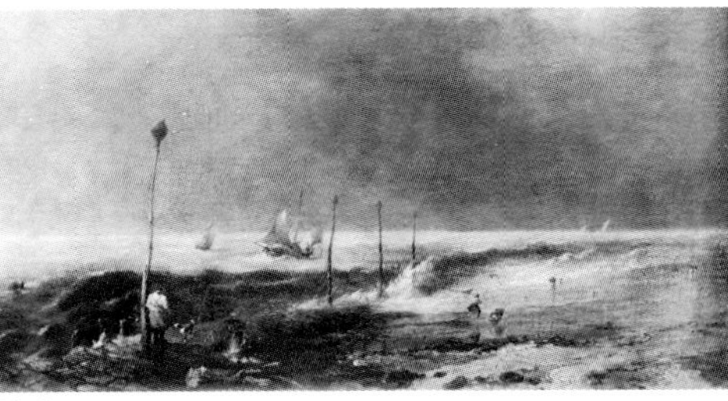

37.79

This coastal scene exhibits a strong contrast in light and dark areas, characteristic of Wilson's marine subjects. Beneath a glowering sky, several ships are sailing in high seas that do not appear to discourage the woman gathering clams or the bathers shown on the beach at the right. On a jetty in the left foreground, a fisherman is leaning against a post beside his traps.

Support: Fabric, .42 x .63 (16⅝" x 24¾")

Condition: In 1939 discolored varnish and overpaint were removed, revealing extensive abrasion in much of the sky.

Provenance: Acquired by Henry Walters between 1903 and 1909.

References: Walters cat., 1909, p. 26, no. 79, and subsequent Walters catalogues.

Joseph Mallord William Turner, R.A.

English: London, 1775 - Chelsea, 1851

Turner emerged from the late 18th-century English topographical tradition of landscape painting as the country's most profoundly imaginative, romantic painter. Basing his historical landscapes on French seventeenth-century precedents, he revitalized this tradition by subordinating narrative content to the rendition of the elemental forces of nature. Because of the highly personal treatment of his "impressions," the preoccupation with light, and the exploitation of the textural qualities of his pigments, Turner was frequently acclaimed a harbinger of Impressionism, though he did not, in fact, share the French artists' commitment to *plein-air* painting and their preoccupation with the transitory effects of light.

Turner received scanty formal training until about 1789, the year in which he was admitted to the Royal Academy Schools, and began his studies with Thomas Malton, the Younger, a watercolor painter of architectural subjects. Also influential in his early development was three years of experience, beginning in 1794, in copying the drawings of J. R. Cozens for a Dr. Thomas Munro. Turner first exhibited a watercolor at the Academy in 1790, and an oil six years later. Throughout his career he pursued success within the context of the Academy, becoming an Associate in 1799, a full Member in 1802, and holding the position of Professor of Perspective from 1807 to 1837. In 1802 he visited the Continent, admiring in particular the landscapes of Claude in the Louvre. He did not go abroad again until 1817. Thereafter he traveled most years, frequently visiting France, the Low Countries, the German States, Switzerland, and Italy.

Turner's highly varied production ranged from his early topographical house-portraits, a genre which ended with *Raby Castle,* 1818, in the Walters Art Gallery, through historical landscapes with subjects drawn from classical, Biblical, literary and contemporary sources, dramatic seascapes and coastal scenes, Alpine scenery and Venetian views. An important aspect of his oeuvre included pictures intended for reproduction. Among these were his scenic views which appeared in such works as Cooke's *Southern Coast* (1814–1826), *The Rivers of England* (1824), *The Rivers of France* (1833–1835), Scott's *Works* (1834), and Rogers' *Italy* as well as his own *Liber Studiorum,* begun in 1807, a publication illustrating different facets of landscape painting produced in emulation of and in competition with Claude's *Liber Veritatis.*

A prodigious worker, Turner left to the Nation over 20,000 drawings and watercolors (British Museum) and three hundred and eighteen oils (The National Gallery and the Tate Gallery).

243. Raby Castle, the Seat of the Earl of Darlington

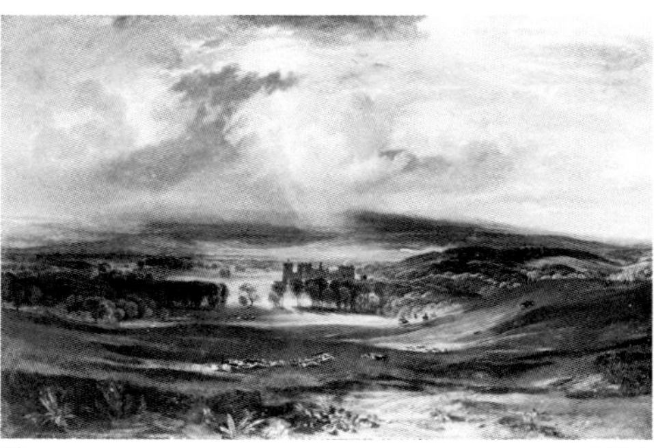

37.41 1817

Raby Castle, a fourteenth-century structure with some possibly eleventh-century foundations as well as eighteenth and nineteenth-century alterations, is located in County Durham near the town of Darlington. It has been portrayed by Turner at a distance, from a rise of land to the north. A fox hunt is in progress: the prey, at the left, is being pursued by a pack of hounds in the center followed by huntsmen who converge from the crest and base of a hillock at the right. Close examination reveals deer grazing in the park, a four-in-hand carriage followed by horsemen proceeding along a road leading from a gate-house westward in the middle ground, some cursorily rendered hunters to the east of the castle, a spire in the village of Staindrop at the extreme left, and smoke rising from several cottages hidden in the woods at the right. It is an autumnal scene of sombre hues with the trees, mainly beeches, touched with yellows and browns. Growing in the immediate foreground, cropped by the bottom edge of the painting, is a variety of broad-leafed vegetation. The hills intercepting the horizon-line appear somewhat exaggerated in their height and proximity according to modern viewers. The most dramatic feature of the painting is the shaft of light breaking through the cloud-laden sky to illuminate the castle and its park.

The painting, executed for the third Earl of Darlington, later first Duke of Cleveland, was based on sketches drawn by Turner in the autumn of 1817, after his return from the Rhine in mid September and prior to his arrival in Farnley in November. Most closely related is a panoramic view of the castle and its park, drawn in pencil from a view-point closer to the building, in the "Raby" sketchbook, British Museum, Turner Bequest, CLVI f.f. 11a, 21a, and 23. The book contains numerous related sketches as well as some drawings that served as a basis for a now lost watercolor, showing a hunt at Raby Castle, engraved by S. Rawle for Robert Surtees' *The History and Antiquities of the County Palatine of Durham, 1816–1840.* In the "Hints River" sketchbook, British Museum, Turner Bequest, CXLI, there is a reference to the oil painting in a list of pictures in hand, and in the "Liber Notes (2)" sketchbook, British Museum, Turner Bequest, CLIV(a), its price is given as 200 guineas. A draft of a letter inviting the Earl of Darlington to examine the picture prior to its removal to the Academy on May 1, 1818, is found in the "Guards'" sketchbook, British Museum, Turner Bequest, CLXIV, p. 14.

The significance of this painting within Turner's oeuvre is two-fold; it was his last and perhaps most successful "house portrait," a genre that the young artist had found highly remunerative, and secondly, it exemplified his interest in exploiting the dramatic potential of cloudy skies, an interest concurrently manifested in the "Skies" sketchbook, c. 1818, British Museum, Turner Bequest, CLVIII.

Raby Castle, however, met with a less than favorable reception when first shown at the Royal Academy in 1818. Finberg cites, in particular, the critics' lack of enthusiasm for the "huntsmen and pack of hounds in the foreground," now no longer visible.

Support: Canvas, 1.186 x 1.806 (46⅞" x 71⅛")

Condition: Prior to its acquisition by Henry Walters, the painting was relined and overpainted in certain areas, particularly in the foreground. In 1957–58, the picture was treated in the Conservation Laboratory of the Gallery under the direction of Elisabeth C. G. Packard. She removed the discolored varnish and overpainting of the turn of the century, to reveal such details as the fox, the carriage and accompanying horsemen, and the huntsmen descending the hill at the right, which had been masked. She also exposed a deep crackle pattern in the foreground. Discernible within its fissures were sections of red paint. X-rays and infra-red photography showed the presence of three huntsmen riding from right to left across the foreground toward the kill, in which a standing huntsman holds aloft the fox surrounded by the hounds. This last figure is about five and a half inches (.14) high and is placed seven and a half inches (.19) from the bottom of the picture and twenty inches (.514) from the left side. Finding the overpainting quite impervious to organic solvents, Miss Packard concluded that these larger figures, presumably those that offended the critics in 1818, had been covered at a very early date, probably by Turner himself, prior to the delivery of the picture to the Earl of Darlington.

Provenance: Painted for the third Earl of Darlington, 1817–18; listed as hanging on the staircase of the Castle in "The Private collections of England, No. XXIII, Raby Castle," *The Athenaeum,* London, (August 26, 1876): 275; sold by the widow of the fourth Duke of Cleveland prior to May 27, 1899, to Messers. Wallis of the French Gallery, London: exhibited at W. Scott and Sons, Montreal, November, 1899: purchased subsequently by Henry Walters.

Exhibitions: The Royal Academy, London, 1818, no. 129; The French Gallery, London, May–June, 1899; W. Scott and Sons, Montreal, November, 1899.

References: John Burnet, *Turner and his Works*, London, D. Bogue, 1852, p. 114, no. 125; George Walter Thornbury, *The life of J. M. W. Turner*. London, Chatto & Windus, 1877. p. 574, no. 131; C. F. Bell, *A list of the works contributed to public exhibitions by J. M. W. Turner*. London, G. Bell, 1901, p. 101, no. 139; Sir Walter Armstrong, *Turner*. London, T. Agnew, 1902. pp. 60, 227; Walters cat., 1909, p. 14, no. 41, and subsequent Walters catalogues; William T. Whitley, *Art in England, 1800–1820*. New York, Macmillan, 1928. p. 285; A. J. Finberg, *The life of J. M. W. Turner, R.A.* Oxford, Clarendon Press, 1961. pp. 251, 479, no. 198; John Rothenstein and Martin Butlin, *Turner*. New York, G. Braziller, 1964. p. 27, plate 58; John Gage, *Colour in Turner: poetry and truth*. New York, Praeger, 1969. pp. 111, 250, n. 189; Graham Reynolds, *Turner*. New York, Abrams, 1969. p. 106, fig. 87; Gerald Wilkinson, *Turner sketches, 1802–1820*. New York, Watson-Guptill, 1974. pp. 168–69; *Turner, 1775–1851*. London, Royal Academy of Arts, 1974. pp. 84–85, nos. 195, 202; Martin Butlin and Evelyn Joll, *The paintings of J. M. W. Turner*. 2 vols. New Haven, Yale University Press, 1977. 1: 90–91; 2: plate 121.

Artist Unknown, English

244. The Burning of the Houses of Parliament

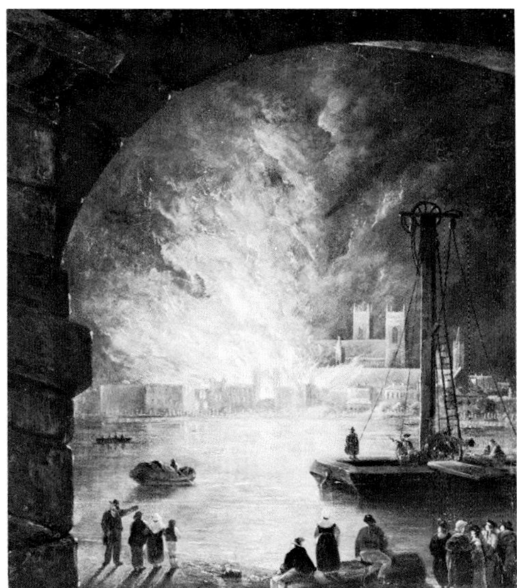

37.772 c. 1834

In the early evening of October 16, 1834, a fire, caused by the overheating of a stove burning used tally sticks, erupted in the old Palace of Westminster, the Houses of Parliament, and burned throughout the night consuming many of the principal structures including The House of Lords, the Painted Chamber, the Royal Gallery, the library of the House of Commons; only Westminster Hall was spared. The flames rose to great heights, drawing swarms of spectators, including the architect Pugin who wrote: "Oh it was a glorious sight to see his [Wyatt's] composition mullions and cement pinnacles and battlements flying and cracking while his 2[S] and 6[d] turrets were smoking like so many manufacturing chimnies till the heat shivered them into a thousand pieces" (M. S. letter, Pugin to E. J. Willson, 6 November 1834, Fowler Collection, The Johns Hopkins University). Among the painters present were Callcott, Constable, Cotman, and Turner. The most celebrated depictions of the fire are two paintings by Turner, based on impressions that he recorded in his sketchbooks CCLXXIII and CCCLXXXIV. One, in the Philadelphia Museum of Art, shows the conflagration from the opposite shoreline near Westminster Bridge whereas the other in the Cleveland Museum of Art was painted from Waterloo Bridge.

The vantage point for the Walters picture is on the opposite shore underneath an arch of the old masonry Westminster Bridge. Spectators are clustered along the shore. In the river is a barge carrying a wooden derrick that can also be seen in Turner's painting in Philadelphia, as well as a couple of boats.

This rather naive work bore the label "Turner," presumably because of its subject, when it was acquired by Henry Walters. More recently, it has been suggested that the picture was executed by a follower of Henry Pether (1828–1865) who was noted for his moonlit views of the Thames.

Support: Panel, cradled, .356 x .304 (14" x 12")

Condition: Blisters that occurred along the edges have been laid down with glue. Discolored varnish was removed by the reforming method in 1957.

Provenance: Acquired by Henry Walters, source unknown.

James Lonsdale

English: Lancashire, 1777 - London, 1839

Lonsdale studied under George Romney and at the Royal Academy. A noted portraitist, he was one of the founders of the Society of British Artists. He exhibited regularly at this society, at the British Institution and at the Royal Academy.

After James Lonsdale

245. Portrait of H. R. H. Charlotte Caroline Augusta (1796–1817)

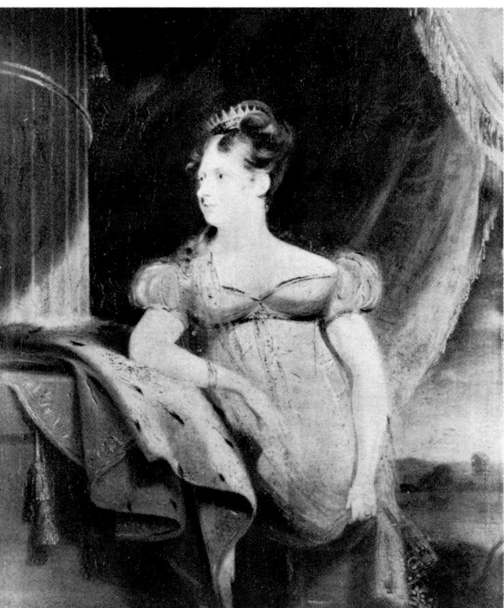

37.766

Princess Charlotte Augusta, the only child of George IV by Queen Caroline, was married in 1816 to Leopold of Saxe-Coburg, later King of the Belgians. The demise in childbirth of this popular princess in the following year resulted in public mourning said to have been unequaled since the death of Admiral Nelson twelve years earlier.

She is portrayed three-quarters length, standing frontally with her head turned to the left and her left arm resting on a parapet covered by an ermine-lined robe. She wears a high-waisted, white gown and a tiara. Behind her are heavy red draperies with gold embroidered borders, and beyond, a view of the landscape. A fluted column rises from the parapet on the left.

This picture, acquired as the work of Sir Thomas Lawrence (1769–1830) and later attributed to George Dawe (1781–1829), is now known to be a copy of James Lonsdale's portrait of Princess Charlotte Augusta, canvas, 1.423 x 1.09, in the Guildhall, London.

Support: Panel, .457 x .345 (18" x 13⅝")

Marks: Reverse: Paper label reads: *Princess Charlotte of Wales Daughter of Queen Caroline Married Prince Leopold who afterwards became King of the Belgians — Presented by Lady Anne Hamilton* (perhaps Anne, the daughter of Archibald, 9th Duke of Hamilton who died in 1846).

Provenance: Unknown.

Sir Augustus Wall Callcott, R.A.

English: Kensington (London) 1779 - Kensington, 1844

Callcott was a popular landscape painter who worked in both oil and watercolor. He studied at the Royal Academy schools under John Hoppner, making his first appearance at the Academy's exhibitions with a portrait in 1799. After 1803 he specialized in landscapes, though he also produced several literary subjects. Initially he painted English views, and then Dutch and French scenes. In 1827 Callcott married and traveled through Italy. Thereafter, classical and Italianate landscapes reflecting the influence of Claude Lorrain dominated his oeuvre.

Callcott became an Associate of the Royal Academy in 1806 and a full member four years later. In 1837 he was knighted, and in 1844 he became Keeper of the Royal Collection.

246. Landscape

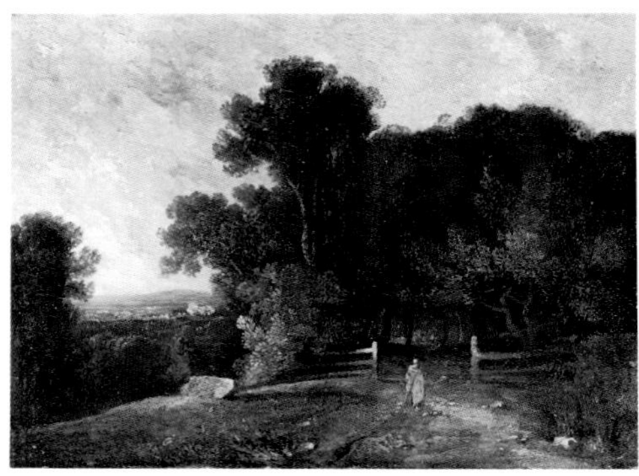

37.760 1820s

In the foreground, a figure, walking along a pathway leading into woods, approaches a gateway. To the left, an opening in the trees reveals a vista of the English countryside.

This small, rather insignificant view is characteristic of Callcott's work of the 1820s.

Support: Canvas, .303 x .355 (12″ x 14″)

Provenance: Unknown.

Patrick Nasmyth

British: Edinburgh, Scotland, 1786 - Lambeth, England, 1831

Patrick Nasmyth was the eldest of the eight children of Alexander Nasmyth (1758–1840), all of whom became proficient painters. He trained with his father and, in 1810, exhibited some landscapes in Edinburgh which echoed the senior Nasmyth's Italianate style. That year he removed to London and turned to depicting more subdued environs. His English views are marked by their fine draftsmanship and their restrained brushwork. The influence of Dutch seventeenth-century landscape painting became increasingly apparent in these canvases. Patrick Nasmyth began to exhibit both at the Royal Academy and the British Institution in 1811, and in 1824 he became a member of the Society of British Artists. His works were widely admired and frequently forged.

Attributed to Patrick Nasmyth

247. Landscape, View near Dorking

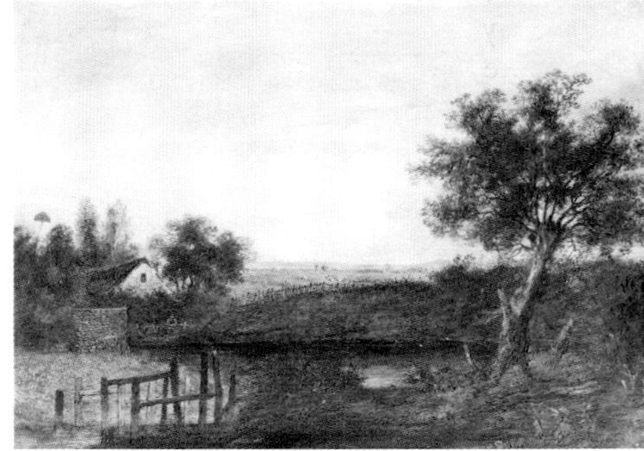

37.768

Shown is a rather placid view of a stream flowing through the Surrey countryside. On the bank in the right foreground is a gnarled tree. Across the river in a cluster of trees at the left one sees a cottage. A man leans against a fence in front of the cottage. An old label on the reverse of the painting ascribes it to the artist.

Support: Panel, .293 x .408 ($11\frac{1}{2}$″ x 16″)

Provenance: Unknown.

Alfred Vickers

English: St. Mary, Newington, Surrey, 1786 - London, 1868

Alfred Vickers, a self-taught landscape painter, worked in a sketchy, loose technique using distinctively bright, fresh colors. Though known primarily for his coastal marines painted on the Isle of Wight and his views of Wales, Vickers traveled through much of England recording the countryside. He exhibited regularly at the British Institution beginning in 1828, the Royal Academy after 1831, and the Society of British Artists.

His son Alfred Gomersal Vickers (1810–1837) worked in a similar manner during his brief career.

248. Landscape with Windmill

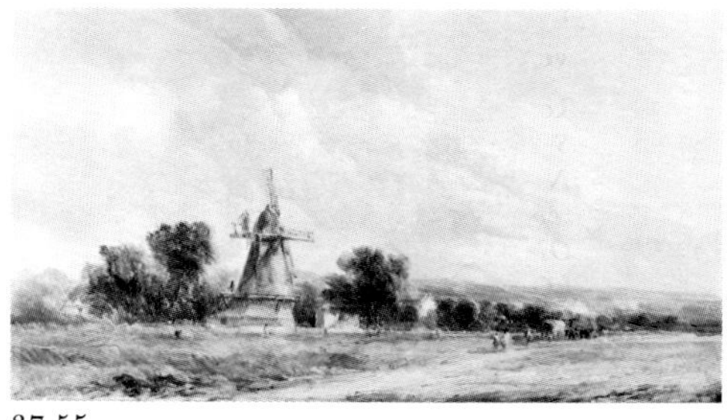

37.55

The rolling countryside is dominated by a tower windmill. On a route leading diagonally across the meadow is a caravan and several figures.

Support: Panel, .126 x .225 (5″ x $8\frac{7}{8}$″)

Condition: Discolored varnishes were removed in 1963.

Provenance: Unknown.

References: Walters cat., 1909, p. 19, no. 55, and subsequent Walters catalogues.

249. On the Derwent, Derbyshire

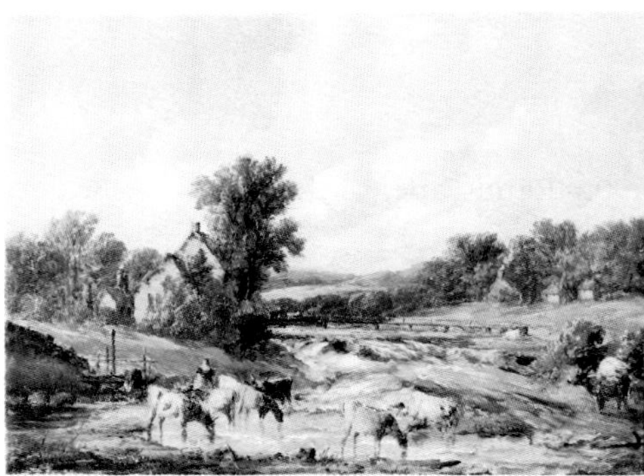

37.2406 1861

A river falls rapidly through hilly countryside, passing beneath a bridge. At a pool in the left foreground, cattle are being watered. There are several buildings with smoking chimneys on both banks of the river.

The same scene appears in Vickers's *A River Landscape with Cattle Watering,* canvas, .349 x .52, Sotheby's, Belgravia, Sale, July 30, 1974, no. 103 and in his *The Old Mill,* canvas, .356 x .508, advertisement for Richard Green, London, *Country Life,* December 1, 1966.

Support: Canvas, .285 x .383 ($11\frac{1}{4}$″ x $15\frac{1}{8}$″)

Marks: Signed and dated lower left: *Vickers/ 1861*(?)

Condition: In 1965, slight flakes of paint were infused with wax and pressed flat.

Provenance: Gift of Mrs. Helen R. Cleland, 1964.

James Arthur O'Connor

Irish: Dublin, 1793 - London, 1841

James trained with his father William O'Connor, an engraver and print seller. However, apart from lessons in painting received from William Sadler, the young O'Connor was otherwise self-taught. In 1809 he began to exhibit at Dublin's Society House, Hawkins Street. Four years later he accompanied George Petrie and Francis Danby on an unsuccessful journey to London. Petrie was the first to abandon the trip, followed shortly thereafter by O'Connor who returned to Ireland to paint landscapes in the vicinity of Dublin and in County Wicklow. Toward the end of the decade, he was also active in the west of Ireland. Although benefiting from the patronage of Lords Sligo and Clanricarde, O'Connor scarcely eked out a livelihood and in 1822 he returned to London. There he participated in exhibitions of the Royal

Academy, the British Institution and the Society of British Artists. He also retained ties with Dublin, submitting works to the Royal Hibernian Academy in 1836 and 1840. Visits to the Continent included a year-long sojourn in Brussels in 1826 and an eight-month stay in Paris followed by a tour of the Rhine in 1833. By November that year he had returned to London, where he died in straitened circumstances in 1841.

250. Landscape, the Forest Road

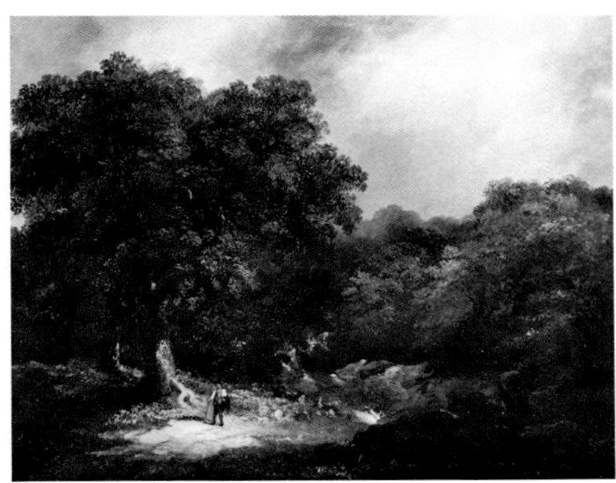

37.221 1839

A solitary figure trudges along a dirt road leading through rocky, wooded terrain. The wild scenery and luxuriant foliage rendered in bright tones are characteristic of O'Connor's landscapes painted from memory in London in the 1830s. A similar view, *A Wooded Landscape* (.241 x .343) also dated 1839, was sold at Sotheby's London, March 31, 1976, no. 87.

Support: Canvas, .46 x .608 (18⅛" x 24")

Marks: Signed and dated in right center: *J. A. O'Connor 1839*

Condition: Discolored varnishes were removed in 1946; a coating of mastic varnish and wax was applied.

Provenance: Acquired by Henry Walters between 1903 and 1909.

Reference: Walters cat., 1909, p. 71, no. 221.

John Frederick Herring, Sr.

English: Blackfriars, Surrey, 1795 - Tunbridge Wells, Kent, 1865

Herring is remembered for his paintings, prints and illustrations recording the principal horses of the English Turf. He was born in Surrey, but raised in London. In 1814 he left home for Doncaster, where he began to paint coaches as well as to drive them, traveling on the London-York, Wakefield-Lincoln and Doncaster-Halifax routes. In his spare time, Herring began to paint, establishing a local reputation as an artist-coachman. His first exhibition entry was a *Portrait of a dog* shown at the Royal Academy in 1818. Though seldom exhibiting them at the Academy, he became renowned for portraits of the winners of the various races, the St. Leger Stakes, the Epsom Derby and the Oak Stakes at Epsom. In 1831 he moved to Fulbourne-Six-Mile-Bottom near Newmarket and two years later went to London where he studied briefly with Abraham Cooper, R.A. As his fame grew, he traveled extensively, going to France in 1841 to paint the race horses of the Duke of Orléans. He was also patronized by British royalty and was appointed in 1845, "Animal Painter to H. R. H. the Duchess of Kent," the Queen's Mother. In the later forties, Herring turned from horse portraits to specialize in rural, barnyard scenes. Because of declining health, he settled in 1853 in the countryside at Meopham Park, Tunbridge Wells in Kent.

During his career, Herring exhibited primarily at the Society of British Artists from 1841 to 1852, at the British Institution from 1830 to 1865, and intermittently at the Royal Academy from 1818 to 1846.

John Frederick Herring, Jr., (died in 1907) worked in the manner of his father.

251. Mare with Foal

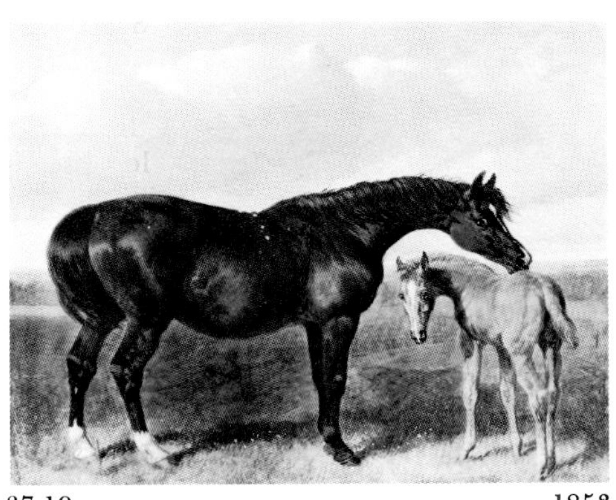

37.19 1853

A black mare is shown in profile, facing right, with a chestnut foal. The background is a pasture.

Support: Panel, mahogany, bevelled edges, .248 x .305 (9¾" x 12")

Signed lower right: *J.F. Herring Senr. 1853*

Marks: Reverse: Stencil: *144*. Paper label: *CHARLES ROBERSON & CO., Artists' Colourmen, MANUFACTURERS OF WATER* [*AND OIL*], *Materials for Drawing, Painting, 51 LONG ACRE LONDON*. Impressed: *ROBERSON & CO. / 51 LONG ACRE LONDON*

Provenance: Acquired by W. T. Walters before 1878.

References: Walters cat., 1878, p. 20 and subsequent Walters catalogues.

252. Barnyard Scene

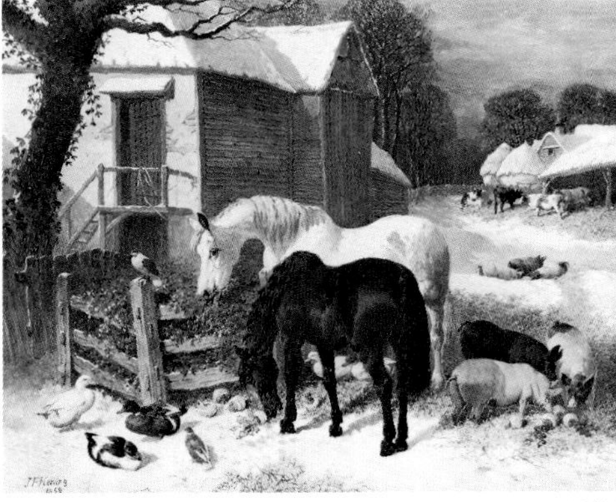

37.2568 1858

The artist shows a barnyard scene in winter. In the foreground are ducks, a couple of horses, and pigs feeding on swedes. Discernible in the distance at the right are the farmhouse with its smoking chimney, several haystacks and feeding cattle. This painting may be the work of J. F. Herring, Jr.

Support: Canvas, .61 x .508 (20" x 24¼")

Signed and dated at lower left: *J. F. Herring/ 1858*

Condition: Prior to 1979 losses in the sky had been inpainted and the signature reinforced.

Provenance: Gift of Mrs. R. Denison Frick, 1979.

ARTIST UNKNOWN, PROBABLY NORWICH SCHOOL

253. A Country Lane

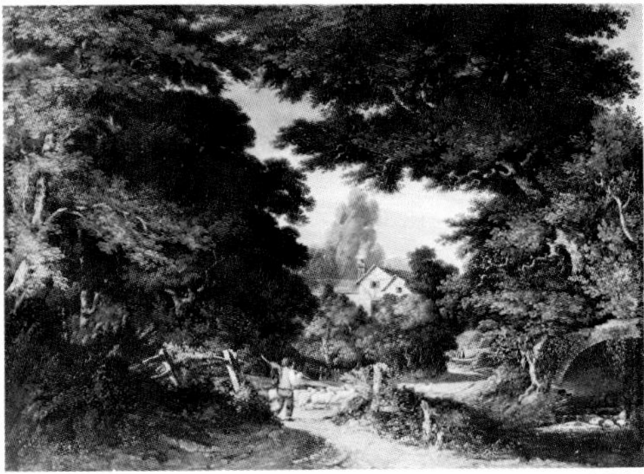

37.229 c. 1830

A lad with a pole over his shoulder conducts his sheep along a winding country lane. Through a break in the trees in the center background one sees a half-timber house with a smoking chimney. In the right corner, a masonry bridge spans a creek. The traditional attribution of this attractive landscape to George Vincent, the Norwich School master, is no longer accepted.

Support: Canvas, .935 x 1.22 (36⅞" x 48")

Provenance: J. D. Ichenhauser Sale, American Art Association, New York, 1903, no. 137 illus.

References: Walters cat., 1909, p. 72, no. 229.

William Collins, R.A.
English: London, 1788 - London, 1847

Collins was noted in the second quarter of the century for his rustic genre scenes. Influences in his youth included his father, an art dealer and biographer of George Morland, Morland himself, and a T. Smith who taught Collins the technical rudiments of painting. From 1807 to 1814 Collins was enrolled in the Royal Academy schools. As early as 1807 he exhibited at the Academy, and in 1808 he began to enter pictures in the exhibits of the British Institution. In 1814 he was elected an Associate and in 1820 he became a full member of the Academy.

As was observed in "British Artists: Their Style and Character," *The Art Journal,* (London), 1855, p. 144, "The bright side of English peasant-life has never had so able an exponent through the medium of pencil, nor so willing an illustrator." Agreeable scenes of cottagers' children at play were among his preferred subjects, though after the patronage of Sir Thomas Heathcote had enabled him to visit Hastings in 1815, his coastal scenes proved equally popular. Among his other influential early patrons were Sir Robert Peel, Lord Liverpool, Sir George Beaumont and George IV. Friends of long standing who may have influenced his development included Sir David Wilkie and Charles Robert Leslie. In 1817 he accompanied the latter and the American painter Washington Allston on a trip to Paris. Wilkie's urgings that he broaden his range of interests by traveling abroad resulted in a tour of Holland and Belgium in 1828 and in an extended sojourn in Italy in 1836/38. From 1840 to 1842 he held the position of librarian of the Royal Academy.

Although Collins was widely popular in his life-time, modern criticism has tended to dismiss his works as attractive though rather facile. His two sons achieved equal fame, Charles Allston as a Pre-Raphaelite painter and writer and Wilkie as a novelist and "inventor of the mystery story."

254. A Harvest Shower, Landscape with figures

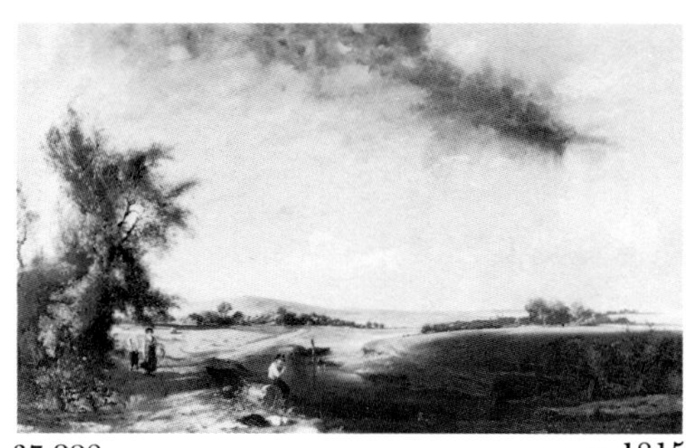

37.228 c. 1815

Wilkie Collins, in *Memoirs of the Life of William Collins, Esq., R.A.,* London, 1848, vol. 1, p. 70, relates the following genesis of this picture:

> "The 'Harvest Shower' was suggested on a visit to Windsor, by a beautiful effect, produced during a shower, by the appearance of bright clouds behind falling rain. As soon as he perceived it, although reminded by his companion, Mr. Stark, of an engagement they had the moment before been hastened to fulfill, Mr. Collins produced his sketchbook; and careless alike of rain and punctuality, made a study of the scene, which he afterwards transferred to canvass, and exhibited as above related."

The rolling expanse of landscape is bisected by a stream. At the left, in the immediate foreground, a young man seated on a log is baiting his fishing line. His jacket lies on the ground beside a hamper. Further left, are several gnarled trees and some vegetation including poppies and burdock. A girl and a young boy carrying bundles of wheat make their way towards the viewer along a path that extends back into a distant field in which grain is being harvested. Beyond is a wood in which there are a number of houses and in the remote background hills rise. The bank of the stream in the right foreground is lost in shadow. Cattle graze in the fields further back, and a couple of spires are visible through the woods in the background on the right side. The most startling feature of this composition is the juxtaposition of the dark rain cloud against the sunlit sky.

A replica of this painting, measuring 1.015 x 1.575, from the collection of John Rhodes, Esq., was first shown in the Royal Academy exhibition "Works of Old Masters," 1894, no. 37 (0.978 x 1.549).

Support: Twill canvas, 1.027 x 1.643 (40 7/16" x 64 5/8")

Condition: The painting was cleaned and lined in 1960. The dark areas in browns and greens were painted in glazes containing varnish, making cleaning difficult.

Provenance: Isaac Currie (1819); J. D. Ichenhauser sale, New York, 1903, no. 73, illus.

Exhibitions: The Royal Academy, London, 1815, no. 246.

References: Wilkie Collins, *Memoirs of the life of William Collins, Esq., R.A.* 2 vols. London, Longman, Brown, Green and Longmans, 1848. 1: 69–70, 155; Algernon Graves, *The Royal Academy of Arts.* 8 vols. London, Henry Graves, 1905–06. 2: 112; Walters cat., 1909, p. 72, no. 228, and subsequent Walters catalogues; John Hayes, "British patrons and landscape painting, 5: the encouragement of British art," *Apollo* 86, (1967): 361–62, illus.

255. Landscape with Children at Play

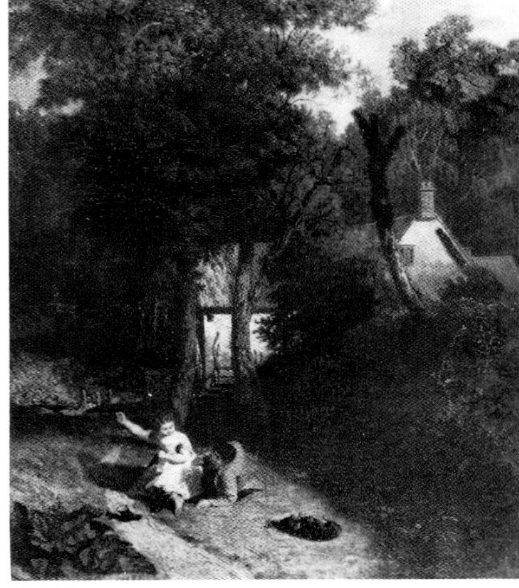

37.222

A young boy and girl are romping together in the foreground. A dog rolls on his back beside them. Beneath the trees in the middle ground a thatched cottage is visible. Such scenes of cavorting cottagers's children are prevalent in the artist's early career.

Support: Canvas, .615 x .512 (24 1/4" x 20 1/8")

Provenance: Unknown.

References: Walters cat., 1909, p. 71, no. 222, and subsequent Walters catalogues.

Frederick Richard Lee, R.A.
English: Barnstaple, 1798 - Cape Colony, 1879

Because of failing health, Lee, in his youth, abandoned a career in the British infantry to enter the schools of the Royal Academy. He first exhibited at The British Institution in 1822 and at The Royal Academy two years later. Beginning in 1827, Lee participated annually in Academy exhibitions, rising from the rank of associate in 1834 to full member four years later. Many of his entries in the 1830s and 1840s were landscapes of his native Devonshire. From 1848 to 1856 Lee submitted a number of works executed in collaboration with the noted "cow-painter" Thomas Sydney Cooper. Titles of later entries suggest that he traveled extensively in the Mediterranean in the 1860s. He ceased to exhibit after 1870.

256. Landscape

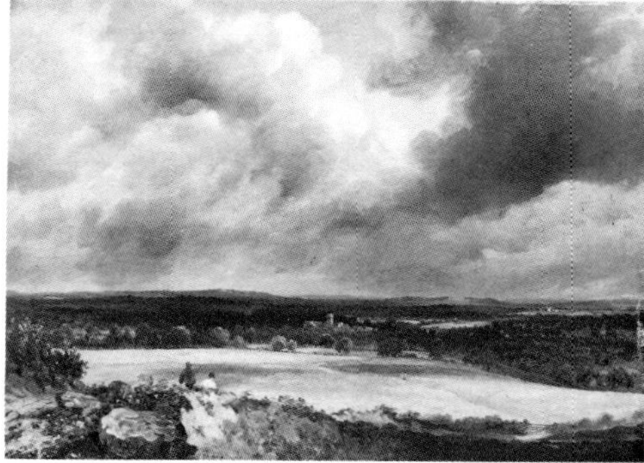

37.174 1840s

From a rise of land a couple of figures overlook a landscape marked by rolling hills partially covered with woods. In the center middleground is a church and beyond a windmill. This view is similar to that found in Lee's landscapes painted near Crediton in Devon in the 1840s.

Support: Canvas, .45 x .615 (17¾" x 24³⁄₁₆")

Condition: Discolored varnishes removed in 1939.

Provenance: Purchased by Henry Walters between 1899 and 1901.

References: Walters cat, 1901, p 104, no 175, and subsequent Walters catalogues.

John Scarlett Davis

English: Hereford, 1804 - London (?) 1845–46

Davis was known for his paintings of the interiors of picture galleries and libraries. The son of a Hereford shoemaker, he studied at the Royal Academy. As early as 1822 he exhibited a landscape at the Academy's exhibition and by 1830 he had discovered his forte, the painting of interior views. In 1831, he traveled to the Continent with a commission from Lord Farnborough to paint views of the Vatican and the Escorial. His subsequent travels took him to Florence, Rome, Ghent and Amsterdam. Davis's last work to be exhibited was a vast, (2.18 x 3.00) *Interior of St. Peters, Rome,* shown at the British Institution in 1844. He died in England, about 1846, after a short career, reputed to have been marred by alcoholism.

257. Interior of the Painted Hall, Greenwich Hospital

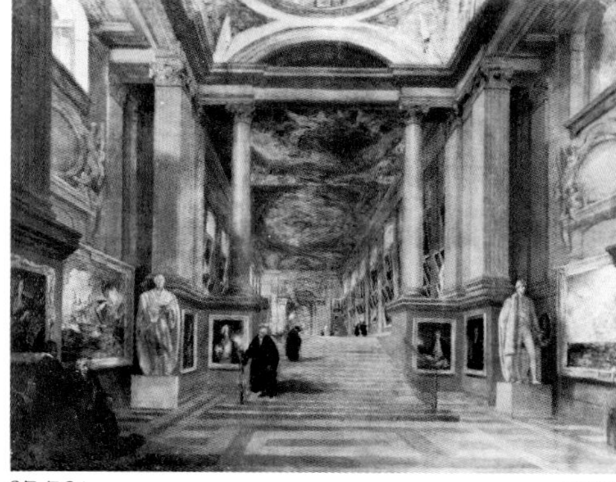

37.761 c. 1831

Though in unfortunate condition, this painting is of interest as a record of the Painted Hall during the first half of the last century. The structure, designed by Sir Christopher Wren between 1696 and 1704 and painted by Sir James Thornhill between 1708 and 1727, served as a refectory until 1824. Then it was transformed into a Naval Picture Gallery, with all its lower windows blocked to accommodate the paintings. Not until 1926 was the collection transferred to the National Maritime Museum.

Davis shows the interior looking from the vestibule, through the 106 foot long Great Hall, toward the Upper Hall. A couple of elderly naval pensioners are seated at the left while others are shown on the flight of stairs and in the Hall. In the foreground, are two of four large plaster casts taken from the statues of British admirals by Flaxman, Westmacott and Baily in St. Paul's Cathedral. Also displayed in the vestibule are a number of paintings, which were later moved to the Great Hall. Recognizable among them are Turner's *Battle of Trafalgar* and Nathaniel Dance's *Portrait of Captain Cook* on the right, and possibly Kneller's *Portrait of Sir George Byng* and De Loutherburg's *The Battle of the Glorious First of June, 1794* on the left.

In 1831 Davis exhibited at the British Institution, no. 153, *Interior of the Painted Hall, Greenwich Hospital* (1.626 x 1.879), which was acquired by his patron, Lord Farnborough. This work could, in fact, be the Walters painting, the discrepancy in size being explained by the Institution's practice of listing, for the convenience of the purchaser, the dimensions of the frame rather than of the canvas, as noted by M. H. Spielmann F.S.A., "Pictures of Picture Galleries, I, John Scarlett Davis," *The Connoisseur* 33 (1912): 215–22. Spielmann (*op. cit.*, p. 218) also transcribed the comments on the painting by a critic for the *Library of the Fine Arts,* London, 1831, vol. 1, who wrote:

> Mr. Davis also has but one, The Interior of the Picture Gallery Greenwich Hospital; a picture of beautiful effect most skillfully and delicately touched. The subject is one difficult to be well executed; but Mr. Davis has performed it so as to demand our unequal approbation.

Preserved at the National Maritime Museum is a drawing *Chapel, Greenwich Hospital* by Davis which is dated 1830, and presently unlocated is another painting of a related subject, *Jack, after a successful Cruise, visiting his old comrades at Greenwich,* sent by the artist to the Royal Academy exhibition in 1841.

Support: Canvas, 1.127 x 1.435 (44⅜" x 56½")

Condition: No attempt has been made to remove the discolored varnish because the picture has already suffered from overcleaning and abrasion.

Provenance: Lord Farnborough (?) Acquired by Henry Walters, source unknown.

Exhibitions: The British Institution, London, 1831, no. 153 (?).

George Wilfrid Anthony

English; Manchester, 1810 - Manchester, 1859

Anthony received his training from John Ralston of Manchester and J. V. Barber of Birmingham. In 1831 he submitted *Richmond Market* to the Royal Academy and for the next several years he exhibited both oils and watercolors at the British Institution and the Royal Society of British Artists, as well as at the Acaemy. In 1835 he married and abandoned painting to become a bookseller, stationer and professor of drawing. From 1851 to 1856, Anthony served as art critic for the *Manchester Guardian,* writing under the name of Gabriel Tinto. His drawings and sketches, which included views of Switzerland and the English countryside, were dispersed by his daughter at a sale in 1905.

258. Market Scene

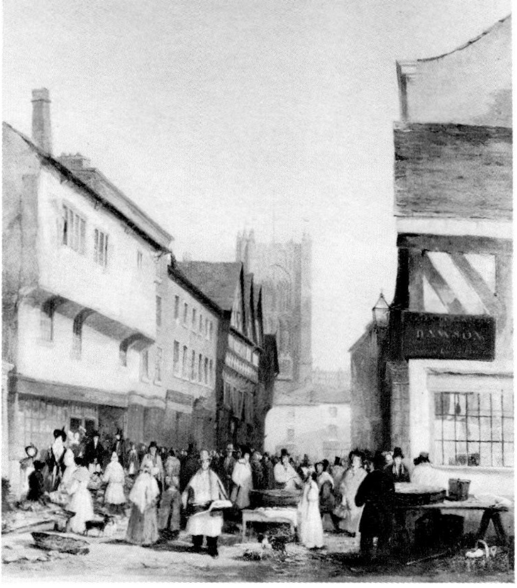

37.755 1832

Shown is a market area of Manchester known as "Smithy Door." Throngs of shoppers and hawkers mill about food stands. The surrounding buildings are primarily of halftimber construction. On one shop at the right is a sign: *PETER ECKERSLEY/Late/ DAWSON/Importers of Linens* . . . At the left, is a store displaying dishes in its window and next to it is a shop identified as: *CRASTON SHOE MAKER*. Seen in the background is the early fifteenth-century tower of the collegiate church of Manchester, which was elevated to the rank of cathedral in 1847. In the City Art Gallery, Manchester, is an undated lithograph of "Smithy Door" by H. G. James (inv. 1947.340).

Support: Preprimed fabric, .76 x .628 (29$\frac{15}{16}$" x 24¾")

Marks: Signed and dated at lower left: *GWA 1832.* Paper label on stretcher: *Smithy/Manchester/The late G. W. Anthony*

Condition: Discolored varnish was removed in 1978 revealing some overpainting in the sky and along the left and right edges of the painting.

Provenance: Unknown.

John Rogers Herbert, R.A.

English: Malden, 1810 - London, 1890

Herbert trained at the Royal Academy schools between 1826 and 1828 and first participated in an exhibition in 1830 with a *Portrait of a Country Boy*. In the thirties he turned to romantic genre, exhibiting a number of Italian subjects. About 1840, Herbert converted to Roman Catholicism, fell under the influence of the architect Pugin, and began to specialize in the Biblical subjects that were to dominate the remainder of his production. Though he never visited the East, his scenes set in the Holy Land were admired for their authenticity. In 1846 he received, along with William Dyce, E. M. Ward and Daniel Maclise, commissions for frescoes for the new Houses of Parliament. Herbert exhibited regularly at the Royal Academy from 1830 to 1889, becoming an Associate in 1841 and a full member in 1846. In addition, he entered works in the exhibitions of the Royal Society of British Artists between 1832 and 1835 and of the British Institution between 1832 and 1844.

259. Portrait of the Rt. Hon. W. E. Gladstone (1809–1898)

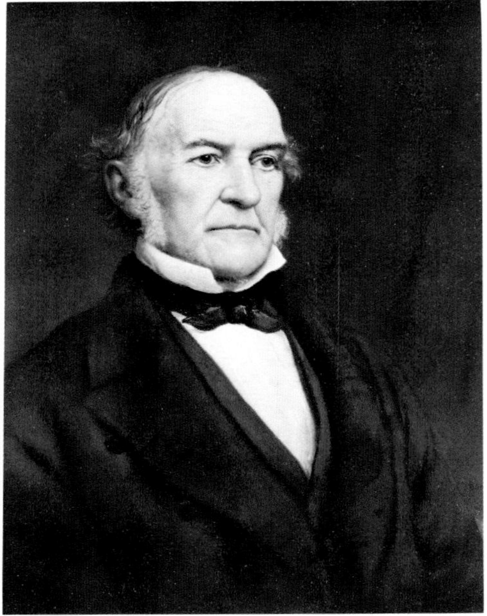

37.67

In his advanced years, William Ewart Gladstone, the great British statesman who served four times as Prime Minister, frequently sat for portraits and for photographs, many of which are discussed by T. Wemyss Reid in "Mr. Gladstone and his Portraits," *The Magazine of Art,* (London) September 23, 1890.

Herbert shows him bust-length, turned slightly to the right, wearing a black frock coat and waistcoat, white shirt with raised collar and black knotted stock. He is seated in a red chair against a dark green ground. The artist's inscription notes that the picture was executed at the subject's residence, Hawarden Castle, near Chester.

Support: Canvas, gesso ground, .675 x .515 (26⅝" x 20¼")

Marks: Inscribed lower right: *J.R. HERBERT/ R.A./ Sittings at Hawarden.* Frame bears sticker reading *830*

Condition: Discolored varnish removed in 1944.

Provenance: Acquired by Henry Walters before 1909.

Exhibitions: The Royal Academy, London, 1883, no. 299.

References: Algernon Graves, *The Royal Academy of Arts*. 8 vols. London, Henry Graves, 1905–06, 4:78; Walters cat., 1909, p. 27, no. 67 and subsequent Walters catalogues.

Henry Wyndham Phillips

English: London, 1820 - London, 1868

Phillips, the son and pupil of Thomas Phillips, R.A. (1770–1845), first exhibited at the Royal Academy in 1838. He continued to participate in the Academy exhibitions and, from 1848 to 1868, was also active at the British Institution. Though portraiture was his principal genre, the younger Phillips painted the occasional Biblical subject. His major work, however, was a group-portrait of *The Royal Commissioners for the Exhibition of 1851,* which showed assembled the Prince Consort, Richard Cobden, Joseph Paxton, Lord John Russell, Sir Robert Peel and Lord Derby.

Phillips served for several years as secretary of the Artists' General Benevolent Institution.

260. His Excellency The Prince Metternich

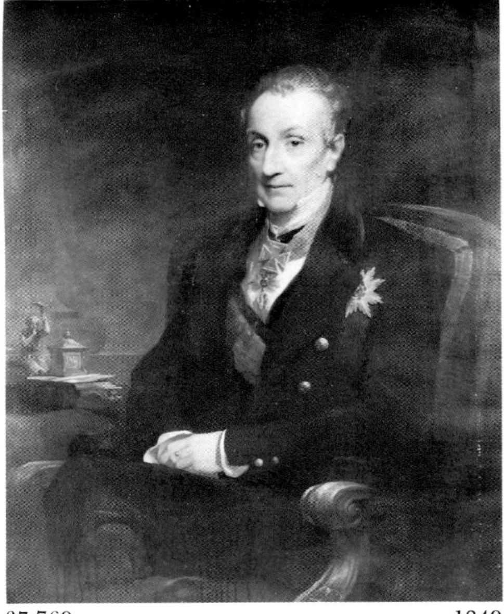

37.769 1849

On March 22, 1848, Prince Clemens Wenzel Lothar Metternich, after having directed his efforts to maintaining stability in Europe and to preserving the power of the Hapsburg dynasty during much of the first half of the century, was ordered to leave his homeland. From April 20, 1848, to October 10, 1849, the controversial Austrian ex-diplomat and statesman sought asylum in Great Britain, resting initially in London and then continuing to Brighton and Richmond.

Phillips portrays the exiled prince seated, wearing his regalia, in much the same pose as in Sir Thomas Lawrence's celebrated portrait executed thirty-one years earlier at the Congress of Aix-la-Chapelle. Though the subject's aquiline features had altered only slightly in the course of time the later portrait differs dramatically in its somber mood. Phillips shows the prince in a darkened interior, his frailty is readily apparent in his wan complexion and stilted pose. In contrast to the colorful dress in Lawrence's portrait, Metternich is now garbed in black. He still wears the Great Gold Civil-Honor Cross for 1813–14, the badge of the Order of the Golden Fleece suspended from his neck, and the star of the Royal Hungarian Order of Saint Stephen pinned to his breast.

Reinforcing the cryptic character of his subject, Phillips includes, on the desk in the background, an inkstand with a finial in the form of a kneeling figure holding its finger to its lips.

Support: Canvas, 1.175 v .895 (46¼″ x 35¼″)

Provenance: Purchased by Henry Walters after 1929 (unlisted in Walters catalogues).

Exhibitions: The Royal Academy, London, 1849, no. 22.

John Everett Millais, Bart., P.R.A., D.C.L.

English: Southampton, 1829 - London, 1896

Millais, an exceptionally precocious youth, was taken by his family to London at the age of nine, to pursue his career as an artist. With the encouragement of Sir Martin Archer Shee, the boy was permitted to draw at the British Museum and to enroll in a private academy maintained by the portrait painter, Henry Sass. In 1839 he received a silver medal from the Society of Arts for a drawing, *The Battle of Bannockburn,* and the following year, when still only eleven years of age, he was admitted to the schools of The Royal Academy. His first exhibition entry at the Academy, *Pizarro seizing the Inca of Peru,* was shown in 1846, and the following year he was awarded a gold medal for *Elgiva,* an eleventh century Norman subject. In 1848 an exchange of views between Millais and his close friend, William Holman Hunt, led to the establishment of the Pre-Raphaelite Brotherhood. Other artists to join the movement that stressed the faithful delineation of Nature included Dante Gabriel Rossetti and his brother William M. Rossetti, F. G. Stephens, Thomas Woolner and James Collinson. At the initial meeting at Millais' residence, they examined engravings after the frescoes in the Campo Santo at Pisa by Benozzo Gozzoli and Orcagna. The first picture exhibited bearing the Brotherhood's initials "PRB" was *The Girlhood of Mary Virgin* shown by D. G. Rossetti at the Free Exhibition, Hyde Park, in the spring of 1849. Later that year, both Millais and Hunt submitted works to the Royal Academy in the new manner. From 1849 until 1853, the year he was elected an Associate of the Royal Academy, Millais employed the "minute detail and bright color with a minimum of shadow" associated with the Brotherhood. Among his masterpieces in this vein were *Christ in the House of his Parents* (1849), *Mariana in the Moated Grange* (1851), *Ophelia* (1853) and *The Huguenot* (1852).

In the summer of 1853, Millais traveled to Scotland with John Ruskin, whose favorable reviews had greatly advanced the cause of the Pre-Raphaelites. In the course of the tour and during the following winter, Millais executed his celebrated portrait of Ruskin. In 1855, Millais married Ruskin's former wife, Euphemia Chalmers Gray of Perth, who undoubtedly helped to sustain his interest in Scottish themes. The artist's style soon began to broaden as the emphasis on detail, so distinctive of Pre-Raphaelite painting, diminished. The new manner was manifested in *Sir Isumbras,* exhibited in 1857. In the sixties and later, Millais flourished as one of the most popular artists of the era, producing narrative, often sentimental paintings that were widely admired. Most frequently cited are *The Black Brunswicker* (1860); *My First Sermon* (1863); *The Parable of the Tares* (1865); *Waking* (1867) and *The Boyhood of Raleigh* (1870). In addition, Millais turned increasingly to portraiture, working in an increasingly broader technique that was inspired by such artists as Velásquez, Van Dyck, Titian and Reynolds. Many prominent individuals sat for him, including Gladstone, Tennyson, Carlyle, Lord Rothschild, and even John Garrett of Baltimore. His portrait of Mrs. Bischoffsheim (1873) shown at the 1878 Exposition Universelle drew wide acclaim and contributed to the artist's receiving the Medal of Honor and being created officier of the Legion of Honor. For the remainder of his career, Millais continued to receive international acclaim; in 1896, shortly before his death, he succeeded Lord Leighton as President of the Royal Academy.

In addition to working in oils, Millais was an able watercolorist and gifted illustrator.

261. News from Home

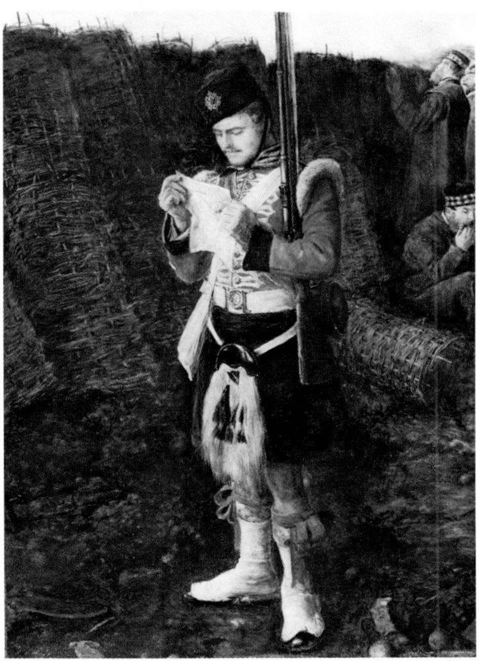

37.85 1856–57

A Highland soldier, standing in a trench with an Enfield musket over his shoulder, is engrossed in reading a letter. Behind him, a couple of officers in grey overcoats peer over the fortifications while another soldier is seated, smoking a pipe.

Early exhibition records identify the foreground figure as a member of the 42nd Royal Highland Regiment, the famed Black Watch. This regiment, together with the 79th and 93rd Highlanders, formed the Highland Brigade led by Sir Colin Campbell that distinguished itself at the battle of Kourganè Hill in the Crimean War. The wet weather and the heavy artillery of the opposing Russian forces necessitated the reinforcement of the trenches with panniers as shown here.

Millais, an opponent of the War, followed the campaign with concern. In May 1856 he attended a public lecture on the War given by William Howard Russell, a correspondent of *The Times* (J. G. Millais, p. 157) and later that year at the Academy he exhibited two works alluding to the conflict, the Walters picture and the larger now lost *Peace Concluded, 1856.*

The artist's biographer, Spielmann (p. 156), recorded that objection was raised to *News from Home* on the grounds that the soldier was "altogether too clean and too well-groomed in his newest uniform for such a position." Ruskin, in this vein, sarcastically commented: "We will pass this [News from Home] for the present; merely asking, as we pass, whether Millais supposes this to be the generally bright aspect of a Highlander on a campaign ? or whether he imagines that Highlanders at the Crimea had dress portmanteaus as well as knapsacks, and always put on new uniforms to read letters from home in ?" (John Ruskin, *Notes on Some of The Principal Pictures exhibited in the rooms of the Royal Academy,* 5 vols. London, Smith Elder & Co., 1857, 3:95).

Support: Panel, .355 x .25 (14″ x 9⅞″)

Marks: Labels on reverse of panel: *No 3/ News from Home/ John Everett Millias,* inscribed in ink on paper; *Charles Roberson & Co./Artists' Colourmen, Manufactureers of Water and Oil Colours/ Materials for Drawing and Painting,/ 51, Long Acre, London* (printed on paper)

Condition: Discolored varnishes removed in 1942; picture treated with mastic varnish and wax. Small losses along bottom edge inpainted in 1964.

Provenance: Arthur J. Lewis, London; purchased by W. T. Walters from Charles W. Deschamps in 1880 (See letter from G. H. Boughton to Deschamps dated April 24, 1880).

Exhibitions: The Royal Academy, London, 1856, no. 50; "The Pre-Raphaelites" Herron Museum of Art, Indianapolis; Gallery of Modern Art, New York, 1964, no. 50.

References: Walters cat., 1884, p. 58, no. 94; Marion Henry Spielmann, *Millais and his works, with special reference to the exhibition at the Royal Academy,* 1898. Edinburgh, Wm. Blackwood, 1898. p. 30, 156, 169; John Guille Millais, *The life and letters of Sir John Everett Millais.* 3rd ed. London, Methuen, 1905. pp. 149, 376; A. Lys Baldry, *Millais.* Masterpieces in colour. London, T. C. & E. C. Jack, 1908. p. 38; J. Eadie Ried, *Sir J. E. Millais, P.R.A.,* London, The Walter Scott Publishing Co., 1909. p. 47; Barbara C. Banks, "A Pre-Raphaelite painting," *WAGB* 24, no. 8 (May 1972): 3, illus.

George Henry Boughton, R.A.

English, near Norwich, 1833 - London, 1905

George Henry Boughton was the son of a Norwich farmer who emigrated to America with his family in 1834 to settle in Albany, New York. By copying engravings, Boughton taught himself to draw, and in 1852 he exhibited *The Wayfarer* at the American Art Union. That year he opened a studio in Albany, listing himself as a landscape painter. In 1856 he traveled to Great Britain, visiting the Lake district for several months and touring Scotland and Ireland. Returning to Albany, Boughton continued to submit paintings to the National Academy until 1860.

Boughton left America in 1860 to train for a couple of years in Paris. There, he sought the advice of Edouard Frère and of Edouard May, a pupil of Couture. Though intending to return to America in 1862, he stopped in London en route and settled there. That year Boughton entered two pictures in the British Institution and the following year he drew considerable attention, showing pictures at both the Institution and the Royal Academy. Thereafter, he exhibited regularly at the Academy, receiving praise for his pictures which were said to be marked by "freshness of imagination and daintiness of thought." In 1867 Boughton turned from the Breton themes to submit *Early Puritans of New England Going to Worship,* a picture signalling a departure from his early work in which the influence of Frère had been pre-eminent. In the new vein were such paintings as *The March of Miles Standish, Pilgrims' Sunday Morning, Return of the Mayflower* and *The Testy Governor*. These literary and historical genre subjects gave way in the early eighties to scenes set in the Netherlands, based on travels which he recorded in *Sketching Rambles in Holland,* New York, 1885. He continued to receive recognition from his contemporaries for his genre subjects with their sentimental overtones. Boughton rose from the level of Associate of the Royal Academy in 1879 to full membership in 1896. In addition to working in oils and watercolors, he was an able illustrator.

262. The Waning Honeymoon

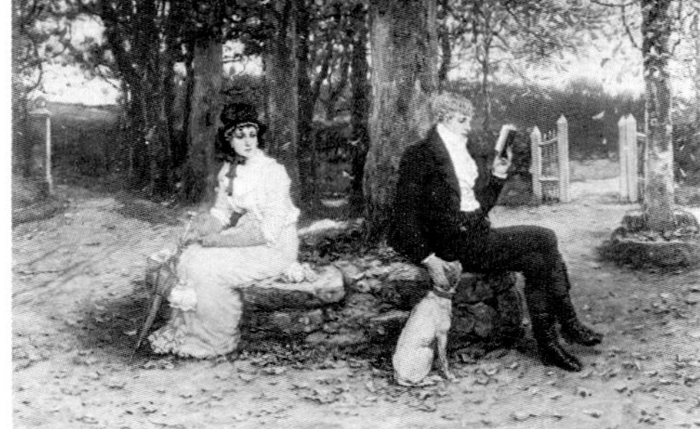

37.129 — 1878

Readily apparent are the implications of this scene set in the Regency period. As noted by the artist:

> A young pair are seated under a tree—late autumn, the big leaves all about—he is reading a book and carelessly caressing his dog; and she is pouting prettily, but thinking no pretty thoughts of him. *(Excerpt from a now unlocated letter from Boughton to W. T. Walters reproduced in the early Walters catalogues).*

Foreboding ill for the couple's future is their position at the fork of diverging paths.

Small narrative paintings rendered in detail with rich coloring and subdued even lighting, are characteristic of Boughton's later production in England.

Support: Canvas, .508 x .762 (20" x 30")

Signed and dated, lower left: *G.H. Boughton 18 78*

Marks: Paper label, inscribed in ink on reverse: *The waning of The Honeymoon/ G. H. Boughton West House/ Campden Hill Road.* Canvas stenciled: *W. BENHAM / ARTISTS' COLOURMEN. . . , PREPARED BY/ WINSOR & NEWTON / 38, Rathbone Place/ LONDON*

Condition: 1972: discolored varnish removed, surface treated with synthetic varnish; 1976: Fiberglass lining applied; 1977: picture treated for water damage.

Provenance: Purchased by W. T. Walters from the artist, about 1878.

Exhibitions: The Royal Academy, London, 1878, no. 5; "American Expatriate painters of the Late Nineteenth Century," The Dayton Art Institute, 1976, no. 5.

References: Walters cat., 1878, p. 10, and subsequent Walters catalogues; Strahan, 1: 91 (illus.), 94; Clement and Hutton, 1: 78; Champlin and Perkins, 1: 189.

263. Venus and Neptune

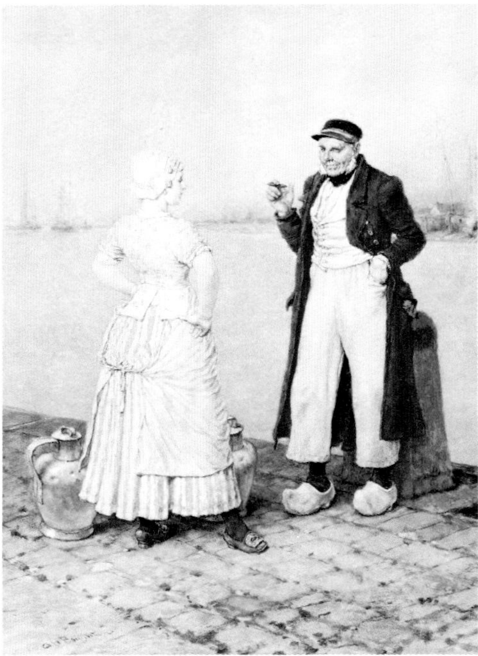

37.198 — c. 1882

Boughton visited the Dutch coastal towns in the early eighties searching for picturesque subjects. In this costume-piece, he has added a touch of humor by contrasting the appearances of the two participants, a pretty milkmaid and a wizened seaman.

A date of about 1882 is proposed on the basis of similarities between this work and *The Weeders of Pavement, North Holland,* which was formerly in the Tate Gallery, London. In the latter, dated 1882, the same two models appear in different roles, the seaman leaning against a pier in the background and the girl sweeping the pavement in the foreground.

Boughton's title for the Baltimore picture may have been derived from L. Alma-Tadema's *'Twixt Venus and Bacchus,* a watercolor purchased by Walters from Deschamps with Boughton's encouragement in 1882.

Support: Panel, .535 x .355 (21$\frac{1}{16}$" x 14")

Signed at lower left: *G. H. Boughton*

Marks: Reverse inscribed: *Venus and Neptune G.H. Boughton A R A*

Condition: Discolored varnishes removed in 1977; surface treated with synthetic varnish.

Provenance: Purchased by W. T. Walters from Deschamps, London in 1882 (see letter from Walters to M. Deschamps, November 29, 1882 in which reference is made to the purchase).

References: Walters cat., 1884, p. 75, no. 43; Champlin and Perkins, 1: 189.

Sir Lawrence Alma-Tadema, R.A.

Dutch-British: Dronrijp, 1836 - Wiesbaden, 1912

Alma-Tadema's reputation was based on his genre scenes, which, though set in Antiquity, were strongly permeated with the sentiments of his own era. Oil was his principal medium, although he also worked extensively in watercolor and produced the occasional print. Late in his career he turned, successfully, to portraiture and designed some stage scenery.

He was born Laurens Tadema in Dronrijp, Friesland, and raised in nearby Leeuwarden. Ill health served as an excuse to abandon the study of law for painting, an abiding interest since early childhood. Enrolling in the Antwerp Academy in 1852, he worked initially for Gustave Wappers and then for Nicaise de Keyser. While in Antwerp he became acquainted with the German Egyptologist Georg Ebers and the Belgian historian Louise de Taye. The former's influence was reflected in such Egyptian subjects as *Death of the First Born,* 1859, Johannesburg Art Gallery, and that of the latter in the medieval themes that dominated Alma-Tadema's early oeuvre. In 1859, he entered the studio of Baron Henri Leys and assisted the master in painting historical panels for the Antwerp Town Hall. During the 1860s Alma-Tadema traveled extensively, going to Cologne in 1861 and visiting London in 1862 to see the British Museum and the International Exhibition. In 1862 he won a gold medal in Amsterdam with *Venantius Fortunatus reading poems to Radagonda,* (Dordrecht Museum) and when he married the following year he traveled to Italy on his honeymoon. As a result of this Italian sojourn, he was increasingly drawn to Greek and Roman subjects, although he still worked in the sombre palette associated with Leys and his school.

Alma-Tadema settled in Brussels in 1864 but sold his works abroad chiefly through his London dealer, Ernest Gambart. In 1870, following the death of his first wife, he removed to London, married again in 1871, this time to his English pupil Laura Epps, and became a British subject in 1873. His assimilation into British life was facilitated by the prevailing classicizing taste apparent in the works of Lord Leighton, A. J. Moore, Edward Armitage, and Sir Edward J. Poynter. Alma-Tadema's British career was highly productive, particularly in his historical reconstructions, which were based on his knowledge of classical literature, his travels abroad and his extensive library of archeological photographs, now preserved in the Birmingham University Library. In England his colors grew brighter, especially in the outdoor scenes, in which marble structures were frequently juxtaposed against brilliant azure skies.

A cosmopolitan artist, Alma-Tadema continued to travel and exhibit abroad, spending the winter of 1876–77 in Rome. High points in his career included the 1878 Exposition Universelle, Paris, where ten of his paintings were shown in the British Section. As a result he received a first-class medal and was appointed an Officier of the Legion of Honor. In 1882 he was the subject of a major retrospective exhibition, comprised of two hundred and eighty-seven pictures, at the Grosvenor Gallery, London. As late as 1902, he was invited to attend the opening of the Assiut and Aswan dams, after which he painted *The Finding of Moses* for Sir John Aird. Edward VII was so moved by this work that he conferred the Order of Merit on the artist. In the course of his career, Alma-Tadema had been appointed to the academies of almost every nation and had received almost every award offered to artists. He outlived his success, however, and shortly after his death his reputation suffered a drastic decline, from which it is only now emerging.

264. A Roman Emperor

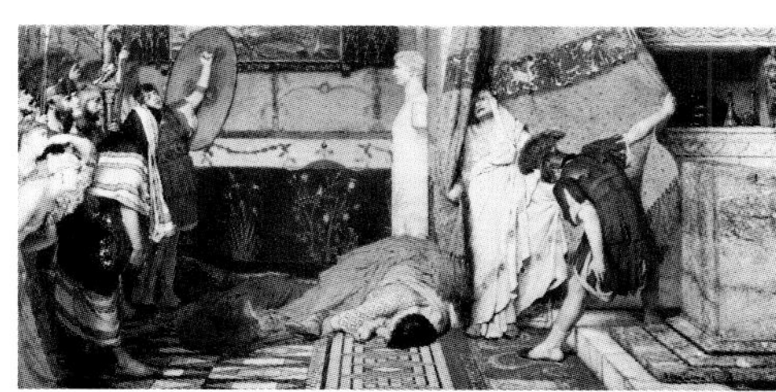

37.165 1871

Portrayed is the acclamation of Claudius as Emperor following the assassination of Caligula on January 24, 41 A.D. In illustrating this episode in the history of the Julio-Claudian dynasty Alma-Tadema has drawn from, and condensed, three early sources: Dio's *Roman History,* LIX, 29-30, LX, 1; Suetonius, *De Vita Caesarum,* Book IV, LVIII-LX, Book V, X, and Josephus, *Jewish Antiquities,* XIX, 103-200, 216-220.

At the right, a palace guard, identified as Gratus by Josephus, has recognized the feet of Claudius and pulled aside the curtain to reveal the cowering, fifty-year old nephew of the fallen emperor. A number of guards and two women stand at the extreme left. One of the soldiers raises his shield to hail Claudius as the new Emperor. Beneath a marble herm in the center of the picture lie the bodies of Caligula, his wife Caesonia, their young daughter, and to the left an unidentified male, perhaps one of the bystanders recorded by Josephus as having been slain by Caligula's bodyguard. The blood-stained herm serves not only as a narrative device suggesting the struggle involved in the assassination, but also denotes the setting, the Hermaeum, an apartment in the Palace in which Claudius according to Suetonius, had sought refuge. The artist successfully imparts a sense of verisimilitude to the setting. At the left hangs a painting, in polyptych form, showing the naval battle of Actium, at which Octavius, the founder of the Julio-Claudian line, defeated Anthony in 31 B.C. The wall itself is decorated in the Second Pompeian manner. On the right is a rose marble altar, and in the white marble wall there is a niche containing a basalt figure of a coiled rattlesnake, inexplicably of Aztec origin, three Roman green glass flasks, and a lamp in the form of a male caryatid. The floor at the left is a pavement of colorful stone and at the right a mosaic in which is depicted a serpent before an altar, representing the *Genius loci.* The phrase *GENIUS HUIUS LOC[I],* visible in the mosaic before the altar suggests that the artist intended to represent the room at the right as a lararium. On the curtain, which is apparently of Oriental origin, is an embroidered band of galloping horses. This picture is one of three devoted to this subject. The others are *Proclaiming Claudius Emperor,* opus XLVIII, .467 x .606, collection of Charles F. Stein, Baltimore, in which the dead Caligula does not appear and Claudius is shown groveling on his knees before the Roman guard who, in turn, bows to him, and *Ave Caesar! Io Saturnalia!* opus CCXVII, .212 x .457, Akron Art Institute, Akron, Ohio. In this last version the composition is reversed, with the soldiers and women spectators on the right and the guard revealing Claudius on the left. As in the Baltimore picture, the setting is clearly subdivided, with an open area on the left. It also differs in that there are three herms in the background and live serpents crawl across the floor near the altar.

Alternative titles: *Claudius, Ave Caesar!, Io Saturnalia!*

Support: Canvas, .86 x 1.743 (33⅞" x 68⅝")

Signed on altar socle: *L Alma Tadema 71*

Provenance: Purchased in 1882 by W. T. Walters from the artist with Charles W. Deschamps acting as agent.

Condition: In 1966, the picture was lined and discolored varnishes were removed.

Exhibitions: Exposition Universelle, Paris, 1878; Grosvenor Gallery Exhibition, London 1882 (lent anonymously by W. T. Walters).

References: James Dafforne, "The works of Laurence Alma-Tadema, R.A.," *Art Journal* (London) 27 (1875):11; P. G. Hamerton, "M. Rajon's new etching after Mr. Alma-Tadema," *The Portfolio* (London) 8 (1877): 125–26; Edward Strahan, ed. *The chefs-d'oeuvre d'art of the International Exhibition, 1878.* Philadelphia, Gebbie & Barrie, 1878–80. pp. 115 (illus.), 116; Clement and Hutton, 1: 11; F. G. Dumas, *Illustrated biographies of modern artists.* Paris, L. Baschet, 1882. p. 90; "The works of Laurence Alma-Tadema, R.A.," *Art Journal* (London) 35 (February 1883): 67; (March 1883): 67; "Art chronicle," *The Portfolio* (London) 14 (1883): 23; *The Illustrated London News,* November 27, 1886, p. 591, as *Ave Caesar! Io Saturnalia!* In this wood engraving the altar is shown with pietra dura panels inserted in the sides; Georg Ebers, *Lorenz Alma-Tadema; his life and works,* from the German by Mary J. Safford. New York, W. S. Gottsberger, 1886, p. 61; Helen Zimmern, *L. Alma Tadema, royal academician; his life and work.* The art manual, 1886. London, H. Virtue, 1886. pp. 11–12; Champlin and Perkins, 1: 30; Lamb, p. 244; Ellen Gosse, "Laurens Alma-Tadema," *Century Magazine* 47 (1894): 486; Cosmo Monkhouse, "Laurens Alma-Tadema,

R.A.," *Scribner's Magazine* 18 (1895): 668, 675; Frederick Dolman, "Sir Lawrence Alma-Tadema, R.A.," *The Strand Magazine* 18 (1899): 609; Cosmo Monkhouse, *British contemporary artists.* New York, Charles Scribner's Sons, 1899. pp. 205, 207; Percy Cross Standing. *Sir Lawrence Alma-Tadema, O.M., R.A.* London, Cassell, 1905. pp. 50–51; Algernon Graves, *The Royal Academy of Arts.* 8 vols. London, Henry Graves, 1905–06. 1: 28; F. Becker, "Sir Lawrence Alma-Tadema," in Ulrich Thieme and Felix Becker, *Allgemeines Lexikon der bildenden Künstler.* 37 vols. Leipzig, E. A. Seemann, 1907–50. 1: 326; Vern G. Swanson, *Alma-Tadema, the painter of the Victorian vision of the ancient world.* New York, Charles Scribner's Sons, 1977. pp. 40 (illus.), 41, 47, 136.

265. My Sister is not at Home

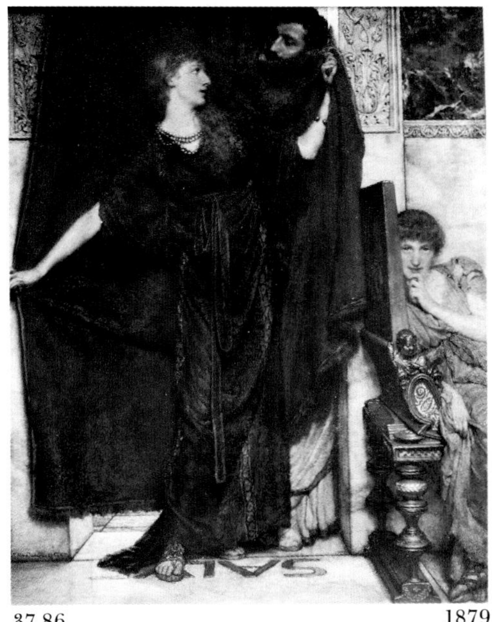

37.86 1879

A Roman maiden draws a curtain across the doorway to conceal her sister crouching behind the headboard of a couch. Her male admirer peers through a gap in the curtain. Visible in the threshold is the word, *SALVE,* the greeting that also appeared over the door to Alma-Tadema's residence on Townshend Road, London. The artist has displayed his archeological knowledge in the depiction of the Roman couch with its finial in the form of the infant Hercules strangling two serpents.

Alma-Tadema may have drawn inspiration for this subject from J. L. Hamon's well-known *néo-grec* painting of the same title which appeared at the 1853 Paris Salon.

Support: Panel, .405 x .312 (16" x 12⅜")

Signed on door jamb at lower left: *L Alma Tadema op. CCX*

Exhibitions: The Royal Academy, London, 1880, no. 195.

Provenance: Henry Walters inscribed in an 1884 catalogue of the collection that this work was bought through S. P. Avery.

References: Strahan, 1: 94; Walters cat., 1884, p. 13, no. 14, and subsequent Walters catalogues; Georg Ebers, *Lorenz Alma-Tadema; his life and works,* from the German by Mary J. Safford. New York, W. S. Gottsberger, 1886. p. 88; Helen Zimmern, *L. Alma Tadema, royal academician; his life and work.* The art annual, 1886. London, H. Virtue, 1886. p. 21; Reizenstein, p. 554; Percy Cross Standing, *Sir Lawrence Alma-Tadema, O.M., R.A.* London, Cassell, 1905. p. 29; Algernon Graves, *The Royal Academy of Arts.* 8 vols. London, Henry Graves, 1905–06. 1: 29; Rudolf Dircks, "The later works of Sir Lawrence Alma-Tadema, O.M., R.A.," *Art Journal* (London), Christmas issue 1910, p. 30; Mario Amaya, "The painter who inspired Hollywood," *Sunday Times magazine* (London) February 18, 1968, p. 34; Vern G. Swanson, *Alma-Tadema, the painter of the Victorian vision of the ancient world.* New York, Charles Scribner's Sons, 1977. p. 138.

266. Sappho

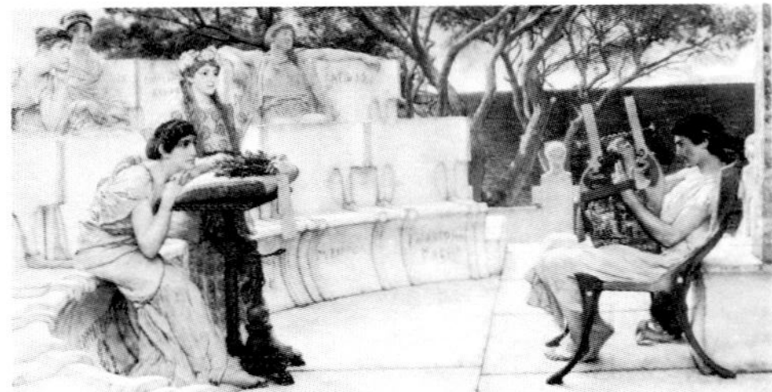

37.159 1880

The setting is a marble exedra on Lesbos (Mytilene) in the late seventh century B.C., when the island was the centre of Aeolian culture. The renowned poetess Sappho is seated, leaning forward with her arms and chin resting on a cushion-covered lectern. She appears to be listening intently to her famous contemporary, the poet Alcaeus, who, seated on a klismos, plays a kithara, the instrument of Apollo. At his feet is a silver rhyton. Standing beside Sappho is a young girl, perhaps her daughter Kleis, wearing a patterned dress and wreath of flowers and holding a scroll. Three of Sappho's followers are seated on the upper tier of the exedra. Visible in the background are olive trees and beyond, the sea.

Alma-Tadema imparts a note of veracity to his painting with such archeological details as the seating of the exedra which approximates in appearance the marble chairs of the Theater of Dionysius, Athens, even to the inclusion of the inscribed names. In the painting the inscriptions refer to members of the Thiasos or sacred sorority, who left Lesbos and were subsequently mentioned in Sappho's poetry. They can be identified as (Mnasi) dika, Gongyla of Colophon, and Atthis on the upper tier and Erinna of Telos, . . ., Gyriano, and Anactoria of Miletus on the bottom. The head of Sappho conforms to ancient portraits such as the Villa Albani and Oxford busts.

Interpretations of the subject vary as to whether Alcaeus is declaring his love for the poetess as recorded in Aristotle, *Rhetoric,* I, 9 or merely attempting to enlist her support in a political scheme (David M. Robinson, *Sappho and her Influences,* Boston, 1924, pp. 31-33).

In this picture two of Alma-Tadema's principal motifs are illustrated: the exedra in an exterior setting, and the poet or musician performing for an audience. *Anacreon reading his poems at Lesbia's house,* opus LXXX, 1870, unlocated, may be regarded as a precursor of this work and *A Reading from Homer,* opus CCLXVII, 1885, 0.914 x 1.828, Philadelphia Museum of Art, as the culmination of the theme. The revival of interest in the poetess in the second half of the nineteenth century was sparked by two publications in Germany, Theodor Kock's *Alkaös und Sappho,* Berlin, 1862, and Theodor Bergk's *Poetae Lyrici Graeci,* Leipzig, 1867.

Support: Panel, .66 x 1.22 (26" x 48")

Signed at lower right: *L Alma Tadema Op CCXXIII* (painted in 1880)

Provenance: Henry Walters, in the company of Charles W. Deschamps and George H. Boughton, saw this work at the 1881 Royal Academy exhibition. It was then acquired by W. T. Walters through Charles W. Deschamps for £2500.

Exhibitions: The Royal Academy, London, 1881, no. 269; "The Greek Tradition in painting and the minor arts," Baltimore Museum of Art and Walters Art Gallery, Baltimore, 1939.

Reproductions: Etching by Charles Oliver Murray; etching by J. Cather Webb, 1881, photograph by W. K. Vickery.

References: Strahan, 1: 94; "The works of Lawrence Alma-Tadema, R.A.," *Art Journal* (London) 35 (March 1883): 66–68; Walters cat., 1884, pp. 20–24, no. 32, and subsequent Walters catalogues; J. Eugene Reed, ed., *The Gallery of contemporary art, an illustrated review of the recent art productions of all nations by A. Silvestre and other writers.* 2 vols. Philadelphia, Gebbie, 1884–85. 2: 7; Henry T. Wharton, *Sappho,* London, D. Scott, 1885. Frontispiece (detail of Sappho's head, etched by J. Cather Webb); Champlin and Perkins, 1: 30; Georg Ebers, *Lorenz Alma-Tadema; his life and works,* from the German by Mary J. Safford, New York, W. S. Gottsberger, 1886. pp. 88–89; Helen Zimmern, *L. Alma Tadema, royal academician; his life and work.* The art annual, 1886, London, H. Virtue, 1886, illus. facing p. 1, p. 22; Lamb, pp. 244–45; Cosmo Monkhouse, "Laurens Alma-Tadema, R.A.," *Scribner's Magazine* 18 (1895): 670, 677; F. G. Stephens, *Laurence Alma-Tadema, R.A.* London, Berlin Photographic Co., 1895. plate VIII; Reizenstein, pp. 547, 554; Mrs. Arthur Bell, *Representative painters of the XIXth century.* London, Sampson, Low, Marston, 1899. p. 184; Frederick Dolman, "Sir Lawrence Alma-Tadema, R.A.," *The Strand Magazine* 18 (1899): 604; Cosmo Monkhouse, *British contemporary artists.* New York, Charles Scribner's Sons, 1899. pp. 209, 218; Percy Cross Standing, *Sir Lawrence Alma-Tadema, O.M., R.A.* London, Cassell, 1905. p. 70; Algernon Graves, *The Royal Academy of Arts.* 8 vols. London, Henry Graves, 1905–06. 1: 29; Richard Muther, *The history of modern painting.* 4 vols. London, J. M. Dent, 1907. 3: 354 (illus.); Rudolf Dircks, "The later works of Sir Lawrence Alma-Tadema, O.M., R.A.," *Art Journal* (London), Christmas issue 1910, p. 31; Esther Singleton, ed. *Modern paintings as seen and described by great writers.* New York, Dodd, Mead, 1911. pp. 232–37; "Alma-Tadema," *The Literary Digest* 45 (July 20, 1912): 105; Basil L. Gildersleeve, "Brief mention," *American Journal of philology* 34 (1913): 106; David M. Robinson, *Sappho and her influences.* Boston, Marshall, Jones, 1924. pp. 31–33; George Boas, "The Greek tradition in painting," in *The Greek tradition in painting and the minor arts* (exhibition catalogue), Baltimore, 1939. pp. 32–36, illus. p. 33; Mario Amaya, "The Roman world of Alma-Tadema," *Apollo* 76 (1962): 773; Vern G. Swanson, *Alma-Tadema, the painter of the Victorian vision of the ancient world.* New York, Charles Scribner's Sons, 1977. pp. 49 (illus.), 138.

267. The Triumph of Titus

37.31 1885

After being proclaimed Emperor in 69 A.D. Vespasian hurried back to Rome, leaving the campaign against the Jews to his son Titus. The following year Titus conquered Jerusalem and returned to Rome to celebrate an elaborate triumph with his father and his brother, Domitian.

In the center foreground of this picture the Imperial family, headed by Vespasian, shown in a white toga and carrying a patera and ewer, is descending a flight of marble stairs. Titus in a gold thorax holds the hand of his daughter Julia who turns her head to address her uncle Domitian, also in toga. Preceding the party, though cropped by the picture frame, are lictors carrying fasces. Five Roman officers follow the Imperial family. Discernible in the brightly sunlit background are a temple facade, an altar, rows of priests with palm leaves officiating at the altar, and musicians playing double flutes. The spoils from Jerusalem, the menorah, a golden table and a copy of the Jewish Law can be seen near the altar.

In a transcription of a letter presumably from the artist to W. T. Walters, published in the early Walters catalogues, the subject is identified as the "offering after the 'Triumph of Titus' of a part of the spoil brought from the Temple of Jerusalem to the Temple of Jupiter Victor, at the Palatine." According to Josephus, *Jewish War,* VI, 132-157, the triumphal possession was actually to the Temple of Jupiter Capitolinus rather than to a temple on the Palatine. The images of the individual Flavians all correspond closely with standard, ancient sculptural representations.

A possible precedent in Alma-Tadema's oeuvre for this composition was *An Audience at Agrippa's,* opus CLXI (.883 x .628), of 1875, in which M. Vipsanius Agrippa is shown descending a staircase, passing the Vatican statue of Augustus Imperator.

Support: Panel, .443 x .29 (17½" x 11½")

Signed on steps at right: *L Alma Tadema Op CCLXIX (1885)*

Provenance: The painting was commissioned by W. T. Walters in 1881 with Charles W. Deschamps, London, acting as agent. It was not delivered until after the 1884 opening of Mr. Walters' new picture gallery. In a letter to Deschamps dated November 29, 1882, Walters mentioned that Alma Tadema had changed "the scene of *Titus* from Jerusalem to Rome." The artist received £20,000 for *Titus* according to a letter of January 8, 1883 from Walters to Deschamps.

References: Walters cat., 1887, pp. 10–11, no. 12, and subsequent Walters catalogues; Lamb, p. 245; Reizenstein, p. 554; Vern G. Swnason, *Alma-Tadema, the painter of the Victorian vision of the ancient world.* New York, Charles Scribner's Sons, 1977. p. 139.

Briton Riviere, R.A.

English: London, 1840 - London, 1920

Briton Riviere was the most prominent member of a Huguenot family that produced a number of painters over several generations. He received his formal education at Cheltenham College, where his father (1806–1876) served as master of drawing, and at Oxford where the elder Riviere had been appointed Teacher of Painting in 1859. Briton trained with his father and with William Q. Orchardson and John Pettie. A precocious student, he was only eleven when he submitted two pictures to the British Institution, and at eighteen he participated in his first Royal Academy exhibition. He was elected an Associate of the Academy in 1878 and two years later a full member.

Briton Riviere's early works have been described as Pre-Raphaelite in manner. *The Sleeping Deerhound* of 1865 marked the emergence of his mature style. Thereafter, he came to be regarded as Sir Edwin Landseer's successor as an animal painter. In this aspect, his popularity may have been enhanced by his illustrations produced for *Punch* between 1868 and 1871. Riviere's historical and literary pictures, usually incorporating animals, were highly esteemed by both his fellow academicians and the public. His numerous anecdotal and sentimental paintings of dogs established his later reputation.

268. Syria, The Night Watch

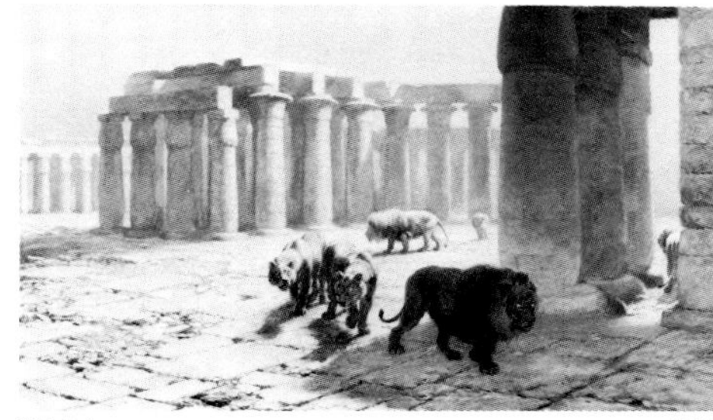

37.84 1880

In 1880 the Walters picture, a moonlit scene in which ferocious looking lions stalk among some ancient ruins, met with a favorable reception at the Royal Academy, where it was listed simply as *The Night Watch.* The reviewer for *The Art Journal* identified the setting as a temple at Luxor. The rows of columns with bud and papyriform capitals approximate in appearance those at the mortuary temple of Ramses II at that site. By 1884 the picture had received its present title. Extracts from a letter presumably from the artist to W. T. Walters, published in the early catalogues, associated the painting with Syria and its desolated ancient cities. In 1889 the critic Alfred Mathews observed that the picture was "a sermon—an intense symbolism—of the seeming slow but always swift mutations of time in the affairs of men and nations."

This work represented a variation on the theme of *Persepolis* exhibited by Riviere in 1878, (The Royal Academy, No. 201). Also a moonlit scene with animals prowling through ruins, the earlier picture illustrated the lines from Edward FitzGerald's *Rubiyat of Omar Khayyam:* "They say the lion and lizard keep, The courts where Jamshyd gloried and drank deep." A third variation, *The King's Gateway* (unlocated) of 1881 was listed by Walter Armstrong.

Support: Canvas (lined), .965 x 1.678 (38" x 66")

Signed at lower left: *B Riviere/1880.* Frame: paper label, *Thos. A. Wilmurt/54 East 13th Street N.Y.*

Condition: Lined and treated for discolored varnish in 1976.

Exhibitions: The Royal Academy, London 1880, no. 298.

Reproductions: Engraved by Frederick Stacpoole, 1882.

References: *Art Journal* (London) 32 (1880): 187–88, 252; Walters cat., 1884, and subsequent Walters catalogues; Mathews, p. 6; Walter Armstrong, *Briton Rivière, royal academician; his life and work.* The art annual, 1891. London, Art Journal, 1891. p. 18; Lamb, pp. 247–48; Reizenstein, pp. 549 (illus.), 554.

Abbreviations of Bibliographic References

Barye Monument Association

Catalogue of the works of Antoine-Louis Barye exhibited at the American Art Galleries under the auspices of the Barye Monument Association . . . Nov. 15, 1889 to Jan. 15, 1890. New York, 1889.

Champlin and Perkins

John D. Champlin and Charles C. Perkins. *Cyclopedia of painters and paintings.* 4 vols. New York, Charles Scribner's Sons, 1886–87.

Clement and Hutton

Clara Erskine Clement and Laurence Hutton. *Artists of the Nineteenth Century and their Works.* Boston, Osgood, 1879.

Cook

Clarence C. Cook. *Art and Artists of our Time.* 3 vols. New York, Selmar Hess, 1888.

GBA

Gazette des Beaux-Arts

JWAG

Journal of the Walters Art Gallery

Lamb

M. J. R. N. Lamb, "The Walters collection of art treasures: its history and educational importance," *Magazine of American history* 27, no. 4 (April 1892) : 241–64.

Lucas

George A. Lucas. *The Diary of George A. Lucas, an American Art Agent in Paris, 1857–1909.* Transcribed and with introduction by Lilian M. C. Randall. 2 vols. Princeton, N.J., Princeton University Press, 1979.

Mathews

Alfred Mathews, "The Walters Art Collection at Baltimore," *Magazine of Western History* 10, no. 1 (May 1889) : 1–16.

Reizenstein

Milton Reizenstein, "The Walters Art Gallery," *New England Magazine* new series 12 (July 1895) : 545–60.

Strahan

Edward Strahan (Earl Shinn), ed. *The Art Treasures of America, being the choicest works of art in the public and private collections of North America.* Philadelphia, Gebbie and Barrie, c. 1878.

Stranahan

C. H. Stranahan. *A history of French Painting from its Earliest to its latest Practice.* New York, Charles Scribner's Sons, 1893.

WAGB

Walters Art Gallery Bulletin

Walters cat.

W. T. Walters Collection. A descriptive catalogue prepared for the "Poor Association" by a well known critic connected with the press and sold for their exclusive benefit. Baltimore, Md. From the Press of Daughterty and Wright, n.d. (1878).

Collection of W. T. Walters, 65 Mt. Vernon Place, Baltimore. Baltimore, 1884.

The Art Collections of Mr. William T. Walters, 65 Mt. Vernon Place, Baltimore. Catalogue and descriptive and critical articles, published by permission of Mr. Walters. Baltimore, Published by the Baltimore American, n.d. (1884).

Collection of W. T. Walters, 65 Mt. Vernon Place, Baltimore. Baltimore, Press of L. Friedenwald, 1887.

Collection of W. T. Walters, 65 Mt. Vernon Place, Baltimore. Baltimore, Press of L. Friedenwald, 1888.

Collection of W. T. Walters, 65 Mt. Vernon Place, Baltimore. Baltimore, Press of L. Friedenwald, 1893.

Richard B. Gruelle, *Notes: Critical & Biographical; collection of W. T. Walters,* Indianapolis, J. M. Bowles, 1895.

The Walters Collection, 5 Mt. Vernon Place, Baltimore. Baltimore, Press of the Friedenwald Co., 1897.

The Walters Collection, 5 Mt. Vernon Place, Baltimore. Baltimore, Press of the Friedenwald Co., 1899.

The Walters Collection, 5 Mt. Vernon Place, Baltimore. Baltimore, Press of the Friedenwald Co., 1901.

The Walters Collection, 5 Mt. Vernon Place, Baltimore. Baltimore, Press of the Friedenwald Co., 1903.

The Walters Collection, Baltimore. Baltimore, Md., The Lord Baltimore Press, n.d. (1909).

The Walters Collection, Baltimore. Baltimore, Md., The Lord Baltimore Press, n.d. (1929).

Handbook of the Collection, Walters Art Gallery, Baltimore, 1936.

A Selection of Nineteenth-Century Paintings, Baltimore, 1965